INDEX AND COMPLETE CONTENTS LISTS

Vision and Visual Dysfunction

General Editor Professor John Cronly-Dillon
Dept of Optometry and Vision Sciences, UMIST, Manchester, UK

Volume 1. Visual optics and instrumentation
Edited by W. N. Charman

Volume 2. Evolution of the eye and visual system
Edited by J. R. Cronly-Dillon and R. L. Gregory

Volume 3. Neuroanatomy of the visual pathways and their development
Edited by B. Dreher and S. R. Robinson

Volume 4. The neural basis of visual function
Edited by A. G. Leventhal

Volume 5. Limits of vision
Edited by J. J. Kulikowski, V. Walsh and I. J. Murray

Volume 6. The perception of colour
Edited by P. Gouras

Volume 7. Inherited and acquired colour vision deficiencies
Edited by D. H. Foster

Volume 8. Eye movements
Edited by R. H. S. Carpenter

Volume 9. Binocular vision
Edited by D. Regan

Volume 10. Spatial vision
Edited by D. Regan

Volume 11. Development and plasticity of the visual system
Edited by J. R. Cronly-Dillon

Volume 12. Visual agnosias
By O-J. Grüsser and T. Landis

Volume 13. Vision and visual dyslexia
Edited by J. F. Stein

Volume 14. Pattern recognition by man and machine
Edited by R. J. Watt

Volume 15. The man–machine interface
Edited by J. A. J. Roufs

Volume 16. The susceptible visual apparatus
Edited by J. Marshall

Volume 17. Index

VISION AND VISUAL DYSFUNCTION
VOLUME 17

Index
and Complete Contents Lists

CRC Press, Inc.
Boca Raton   Ann Arbor   Boston

Published in the USA, its dependencies, and Canada by
CRC Press, Inc.
2000 Corporate Blvd., N.W.
Boca Raton, FL 33431, USA

Typeset in Monophoto Ehrhardt by August Filmsetting, Haydock, St Helens, UK
Printed and bound in Great Britain

Library of Congress Cataloging-in-Publication Data
Vision and visual dysfunction/edited by John Cronly-Dillon.
    p.   cm.
  Includes index.
  ISBN 0–8493–7500–2 (set)
  1. Vision. 2. Vision disorders. I. Cronly-Dillon, J.
  [DNLM: 1. Vision. 2. Vision Disorders. WW 100 V831]
QP474.V44
612.8′4—dc20
DNLM/DLC
for Library of Congress   90–1881
                                          CIP

Vision and visual dysfunction: (comprehensive index covering all 16
  volumes)/edited by John Cronly-Dillon.
      p.   cm.—(Vision and visual dysfunction: v.17)
  ISBN 0–8493–7517–7
  1. Vision–Indexes. 2. Vision disorders—Indexes. I. Cronly
-Dillon. J. II. Series.
  [DNLM: 1. Vision—indexes. 2. Vision Disorders—indexes. WW 100
V831 v.17]
WP474.V44 vol.17
612.8′4 s—dc20
[612.8′4]
DNLM/DLC
for Library of Congress   90–1894
                                          CIP

Contents

PART I

CONTENTS LISTS OF VOLUMES 1–16

1 Visual Optics and Instrumentation

Edited by W. N. Charman

Foreword to Vision and Visual Dysfunction, by John Cronly-Dillon   iii
Preface   xiii
The contributors   xv

1. **Optics of the human eye**   1
   W. N. Charman
   Introduction   1
   Optical components of the eye   1
   Eye models and refractive error   5
   Transmittance of light by the eye media   8
   Ocular radiometry and retinal illumination   9
   Retinal image quality   10
   Ocular depth-of-focus   19
   Matching between optical and neural quality   20

PART I. OCULAR AMETROPIA AND ITS CORRECTION

2. **Refractive error in relation to the development of the eye**   29
   F. A. Young and G. A. Leary
   Introduction   29
   Ocular components and refractive error   29
   Changes in refraction with age   30
   Possible causative factors   31
   Some further studies of refractive change   33
   The role of accommodation in myopia   37
   Emmetropization   39
   Clinical implications   41
   Conclusions   42

3. **Possible causes of abrupt changes in refraction**   45
   J. W. Howe and A. M. Glenn
   Introduction   45
   Lid and orbital diseases   45
   The cornea   45
   Accommodation   46
   The lens   47
   Retinal diseases   48
   Systemic disease   49
   Surgery   49
   Drugs   51

4. **Paraxial optics of visual correction**   53
    W. F. Long
    Introduction   53
    Effectivity   53
    Prismatic effects   56
    Magnification   58
    Notation summary   62

5. **Correction by spectacle lenses**   64
    C. Fowler
    History of spectacle correction   64
    Lens materials   64
    Lens design   66
    Other varifocal lenses and systems   74

6. **Contact lens correction**   80
    N. Efron
    Introduction   80
    Historical development   82
    Contact lens materials   84
    Material properties   85
    Contact lens manufacture   88
    Physiological basis of lens wear   89
    Clinical application of contact lenses   94
    Contact lens maintenance systems   101
    Ocular response to contact lens wear   104
    Special contact lenses   111
    Future trends   115

7. **Intraocular lens implants**   120
    A. E. A. Ridgway
    Cataract   120
    History of lens implantation   121
    Surgical methods, results and complications   123
    Correction of aphakia   126
    Rigid IOL materials   127
    Lens design   129
    Sterilization   132
    Selection of implant power   132
    Conclusion   134

8. **Surgical techniques for refractive correction**   138
    B. L. Halliday
    Introduction   138
    Corneal relaxing and tensioning   138
    Lamellar procedures   147

9. **Binocular vision through correcting lenses: aniseikonia**   163
    J. A. M. Jennings
    Introduction   163
    Magnifying devices   163
    Aniseikonia and spatial perception   164
    Adaptation to aniseikonia   169
    Anisophoria/dynamic aniseikonia   170

Eikonometry   171
Effects of aniseikonia on binocular vision   176
Clinical management   176
Unresolved aspects   179

10. Optical aids for low vision   183
C. M. Dickinson
Definition of low vision   183
The size of the problem   183
Implications of low vision   185
Low-vision aids   185
Magnification   186
Prescribing magnification   214
Optical aids for peripheral field loss   218
Lighting control for low-vision patients   221

PART II. OTHER ASPECTS OF VISUAL OPTICS

11. Accommodation and its anomalies   231
K. J. Ciuffreda
Overview of accommodation   231
Basic steady-state aspects of accommodation   236
Basic dynamic aspects of accommodation   240
Accommodation: Its stimulus, cues and influences   245
Factors affecting accommodation   250
Modelling of the accommodation system   266
Anomalies of accommodation   267
Conclusion   272

12. Retinal fibre optics   280
J. M. Enoch and V. Lakshminarayanan
Introduction   280
Waveguides and photoreceptors   281
Psychophysical measures   287
Retinal receptor orientation, directionality and alignment   295
Theories of SCE   303

13. Polarized light and the eye   310
L. J. Bour
Introduction   310
Cornea   313
Lens   318
Macula and Haidinger's brushes   319
Clinical applications   323

14. Binocular vision in relation to stereoscopic instruments and three-dimensional displays   326
W. N. Charman and J. A. M. Jennings
Introduction   326
Geometry of stereoscopic vision through binocular visual instruments   326
Stereoscopic recording   330
Television methods   333
Holography   335
Miscellaneous methods for producing 3-D images   340
Clinical tests for stereovision   341

15. **Entoptic phenomena**   345
     D. A. Palmer
     Introduction   345
     Types of entoptic phenomena   346
     Effects from a point object focussed on the retina   350
     Retinal effects   352

**PART III. INSTRUMENTATION FOR DETERMINING THE OPTICAL PARAMETERS
AND REFRACTION OF THE EYE AND CORRECTING LENSES**

16. **Non-optical techniques for visualizing the eye**   359
     W. N. Charman
     Introduction   359
     Ultrasonography   359
     X-ray methods   362
     MRI   365
     ECT   366
     The future   368

17. **Optical methods for measurement of ocular parameters**   371
     D. B. Henson
     Introduction   371
     Ophthalmoscopes   371
     Keratometers   378
     Ophthalmophakometry   381
     Slit lamps   384
     Pachometry   388
     Specular microscope   390
     Pupillometry   392
     Refractometry   393
     Scattering of light   394

18. **Determination of ocular refraction**   399
     H. C. Howland
     Introduction and definitions   399
     Methods of refraction   401
     Comparison of methods   413

19. **Instrumentation for the verification of spectacle and contact lens parameters**   415
     D. F. C. Loran and C. Fowler
     Introduction   415
     Spectacles   415
     Contact lenses   424
     Conclusion   433

Index   437

2 Evolution of the Visual System

Edited by J. R. Cronly-Dillon and R. L. Gregory

Preface   ix
The contributors   xi

PART I: GENERAL CHARACTERISTICS

1. **Evolution of visual behaviour**   3
   J. N. Lythgoe
   Introduction   3
   Evolution of eye structure   3
   Physical and physiological constraints   5
   Co-evolution   12

2. **Origin of invertebrate and vertebrate eyes**   15
   J. R. Cronly-Dillon
   Introduction   15
   Morphological characteristics of animal photoreceptor organs   19
   Vertebrates evolved from a nemertine-like ancestor   29
   Origin of pineal and parietal eyes   31
   Cephalic organ   35
   Origin of the vertebrate lens   44
   Evolution of decussation of the vertebrate visual pathway   46
   Concluding remarks   48

3. **Origins of eyes – with speculations on scanning eyes**   52
   R. L. Gregory
   Introduction   52
   Eye and brain: a hen-and-egg problem   53
   Simple and compound eyes   55
   Scanning eyes   55

PART II: EVOLUTIONARY DEVELOPMENTS

4. **The evolution of vertebrate visual pigments and photoreceptors**   63
   J. K. Bowmaker
   Introduction   63
   Visual pigments   64
   Photoreceptors   65
   Evolution of photoreceptors and visual pigments   66
   Conclusions   78

5. **The vertebrate dioptric apparatus**   82
   W. N. Charman
   Introduction   82
   Basic optics   82
   Physical constraints on optical design   86
   Limits on optical image quality at the retina   92
   Overall retinal image quality   99
   Retinal aspects   100
   Depth-of-focus, ametropia and accommodation   104
   Conclusion   112

6. **Optics of the eyes of the animal kingdom**   118
   M. F. Land
   Introduction   118
   Camera eyes with corneal lenses   119
   Aquatic lens eyes   121
   Multi-element lenses   122
   Concave mirror lenses   123
   Biological mirrors   126
   Compound eyes   127
   Apposition optics   127
   Superposition optics   128
   Conclusion   133

7. **Considering the evolution of vertebrate neural retina**   136
   I. T. Thompson
   Introduction   136
   Photoreceptors   137
   Between the plexiform layers   139
   Retinal ganglion cells   141
   General observations   147

8. **Functions of subcortical visual systems in vertebrates and the evolution of
   higher visual mechanisms**   152
   D. J. Ingle
   Introduction   152
   Visuomotor systems in amphibia   153
   Modulation of tectal functions by satellite visual structures   157
   Comparisons of motion sensitivity between fish and mammals   160
   Shape recognition in vertebrates: advantages of a visual cortex   162

9. **Neural control of pursuit eye movements**   165
   R. Eckmiller
   Introduction   165
   Sensory inputs for smooth pursuit system   167
   Possible role of cerebral cortex in smooth pursuit control   174
   Neural activity in cerebellum and brain stem   180
   Missing links and model considerations   189
   Conclusions   191

10. **Patterns of function and evolution in the arthropod optic lobe**   203
    D. Osorio
    Introduction   203
    Organization of visual processing   204
    Evolution   212

11. **Evolution of visual processing**   229
    G. A. Horridge
    Introduction   229
    The laws of optics govern eye evolution   230
    The evolution of vision   237
    Insect vision   240
    The evolutionary approach   241
    The template model   243
    Other models   251
    Two-dimensional vision   253
    Semivision performance   254
    Larger templates   260
    Whole-eye templates   263
    Beyond semivision   267
    Conclusion   268

12. **Evolution of binocular vision**   271
    J. D. Pettigrew
    Introduction   271
    Hallmarks of binocular vision   271
    Cats, owls, monkeys and machines   276
    Evolution of avian stereopsis   280
    Stereopsis in other vertebrate groups?   281

13. **Evolution of colour vision**   284
    C. Neumeyer
    Introduction   284
    Ability to discriminate wavelengths   285
    Dimensionality of colour vision   289
    Phylogeny of colour vision   293
    Comparative colour perception   297
    The question 'Why?'   298

14. **Uses and evolutionary origins of primate colour vision**   306
    J. D. Mollon
    Introduction   306
    Advantages of colour vision   306
    Trichromacy and its evolution   310
    Polymorphism of colour vision in platyrrhine primates   314

PART III: PHYLOGENETIC EVOLUTION OF THE EYE AND VISUAL SYSTEM

15. **Photosensory systems in eukaryotic algae**   323
    J. D. Dodge
    Introduction   323
    Description of the eyespots and associated structures   323
    Function of the photosensory apparatus   334
    Evolution of the photosensory apparatus   336

16. **Evolution of the cellular organization of the arthropod compound eye and optic lobe**   341
    I. A. Meinertzhagen
    Introduction   341
    The compound eye   342
    Evolution of the ommatidium   344
    The optic lobe   353
    Conclusions   360

17. **Photoreception and vision in molluscs**   **364**
    J. B. Messenger
    Introduction   364
    Classification   364
    Extra-ocular photoreception   364
    Non-cephalic eyes   368
    Cephalic eyes   371
    Visual processing   383
    Summary   391

18. **Evolution of vision in fishes**   **398**
    S. M. Bunt
    Introduction   398
    Constraints on evolution   398
    Deuterostomes   399
    Agnatha   401
    Transition from the agnathan to the gnathostome   405
    The aquatic visual environment   407
    Conclusions   417

19. **Central visual pathways in reptiles and birds: evolution of the visual system**   **421**
    T. Shimizu and H. J. Karten
    Introduction   421
    Phylogeny: reptiles, birds and mammals   421
    Basic Sauropsida plan   423
    Reptilian plan   426
    Avian plan   429
    Evolution of the visual system   435
    Conclusion   436

20. **Evolution of mammalian visual pathways**   **442**
    G. H. Henry and T. R. Vidyasagar
    Introduction   442
    Mammalian characteristics in the primary visual pathway   442
    Comparative view of features of the visual pathway   442
    Conclusions   459

Appendix. Mammals   **467**
    G. L. Walls
    Introduction   467
    Monotremes and marsupials   467
    Placentals   472
    Tentative schema of the evolution of the visual cells in vertebrates   480

Index   483

3 Neuroanatomy of the Visual Pathways and their Development

Edited by B. Dreher and S. R. Robinson

Preface   viii
The contributors   x

1. **Functional organization of the retina**   1
   M. H. Rowe
   Introduction and overview   1
   Retinal image quality   4
   Retinal sampling   6
   Photoreceptors   9
   Postreceptoral mechanisms   30
   Summary and conclusions   58

2. **Development of the mammalian retina**   69
   S. R. Robinson
   Introduction   69
   Embryonic development of the retina   71
   Cytogenesis in the ventricular zone   78
   Subventricular cytogenesis   82
   Genesis of non-neural cells in the retina   84
   Development of the plexiform layers   90
   Neuronal death   94
   Neuronal differentiation   98
   Non-uniform retinal expansion   105
   Ipsilateral projection and the nasotemporal division   110
   The fovea   113
   Focus of retinal maturation   117
   Summary and conclusions   118

3. **Development of mammalian retinofugal pathways**   129
   C. A. White and L. M. Chalupa
   Introduction   129
   The mature retina   129
   Development of retinofugal pathways   132
   Concluding remarks   143

4 **Retinotopic and visuotopic representations in the mammalian superior colliculus** 150
   R. W. Rhoades, R. D. Mooney and S. E. Fish
   Introduction   150
   Laminar organization of the superior colliculus   150
   Multiple retinal projections to the mammalian superior colliculus may result in more than one retinotopic
      representation   152

Laminar organization of the superior colliculus and changes in visuotopy with depth   157
Dendritic arbours, receptive fields and the relationship between afferent pathways and collicular
  'output channels'   160
Role of non-retinal inputs in shaping the receptive fields of collicular neurones   166
Organization of the visual representation in the intermediate and deep collicular laminae   169
Summary and conclusions   170

5. **The organization of the visual thalamus**   **176**
    L. J. Garey, B. Dreher and S. R. Robinson
    Retinofugal projection   176
    Lamination and retinotopic organization of the LGNd complex   177
    Retinal projections to the LGNd   183
    Medial interlaminar nucleus   186
    Relay cells and interneurones in the LGNd   187
    Cortical afferents to the LGNd   192
    Subcortical projections to the LGNd   193
    Ultrastructure of the LGNd complex   195
    Projections from the LGNd   198
    Perigeniculate/thalamic reticular nuclei   200
    Ventral lateral geniculate nucleus   202
    Intralaminar thalamic nuclei   204
    Lateral posterior and pulvinar nuclei   207
    Summary and conclusions   215

6. **The organization of the striate cortex**   **235**
    F. Valverde
    Introduction   235
    Basic aspects of organization   236
    Three-dimensional architecture of the visual cortex   252
    Intrinsic organization   257
    Extrastriate connections and final synthesis   267

7. **The localization of neurotransmitters in the geniculostriate pathway**   **278**
    D. Fitzpatrick and D. Raczkowski
    The geniculostriate system: an overview   278
    The dorsal lateral geniculate nucleus   279
    Cortical area 17   288
    Summary and conclusions   296

8. **The organization of extrastriate visual cortex**   **302**
    J. H. Kaas and L. A. Krubitzer
    Introduction   302
    Simple brains: visual cortex in mice and rats   303
    Moderately expanded visual cortex: squirrels and tree shrews   305
    Expanded visual cortex in non-primates: domestic cats   309
    Visual areas in owl monkeys   311
    Visual cortex in other primates   313
    Processing hierarchies   316
    Modular organization of visual areas in primates   317
    Conclusions   318

9. **Callosal pathways in primates and their compliancy to general rules governing the organization of corticocortical connectivity** 324
H. Kennedy, C. Meissirel and C. Dehay
Introduction 324
Callosal connections of sensory and motor maps 326
Heterotopic callosal connectivity 335
Visuotopic organization of callosal connections 340
Convergence and divergence: the functional geometry of cortical connections 342
Conclusions 347

10. **The ontogenesis of the subcortical and cortical visual centres** 360
K. Sanderson
Neurogenesis of visual cortex, dorsal lateral geniculate nucleus and superior colliculus 360
Synaptic differentiation 364
Dendritic differentiation 366
Developmental expression of neurotransmitters 368
Development of cortical connections 370

Index 377

4 The Neural Basis of Visual Function

Edited by A. G. Leventhal

Preface   ix
The contributors   x

1. **Detection of movement by neural interactions at the inner plexiform layer of the vertebrate**   1
   retina
   F. S. Werblin, G. Maguire, P. Lukasiewicz and S. Eliasof
   Introduction   1
   Separate on and off pathways to the inner plexiform layer (IPL)   2
   Presynaptic $GABA_B$ inhibition at bipolar cell terminals   3
   Synaptic inputs and outputs at the bipolar terminal   4
   Components of a neural subunit   6

2. **The receptive field structure of retinal ganglion cells in cat and monkey**   10
   E. Kaplan
   Introduction   10
   Receptive fields of ganglion cells in the cat retina, cell types and properties   11
   Pharmacological aspects of X and Y receptive fields in cat retina   24
   Effects of adaptation on the receptive field organization in cat   26
   Receptive fields of ganglion cells in the monkey retina, cell types and properties   27
   Effects of adaptation in monkeys   34
   Function of M and P cells in monkey vision   35
   Conclusions   36

3. **Lateral geniculate nucleus: a review of its physiology and function**   41
   V. A. Casagrande and T. T. Norton
   Introduction   41
   Overview   42
   Structural organization   45
   Signal transmission   52
   Parallel pathways   62
   Changes in magnification   71
   Visual information processing   73

4. **Functional organization of the superior colliculus**   85
   B. E. Stein and M. A. Meredith
   Introduction   85
   Two visual systems   86
   Laminar organization   86
   Sensory organization   87

Motor representation 92
Motor activity 96
Receptive field properties 97
The concept of two corticotectal systems 101
Conclusions 104

5. **The accessory optic system in frontal-eyed animals** 111
   K. L. Grasse and M. Cynader
   Introduction 111
   Anatomical organization of the cat and primate AOS 111
   Physiological response properties in cats and primates 113
   The abnormal AOS: experimental studies 120
   General significance of cortical-subcortical interactions 127
   Functional considerations 127
   Conclusion 136

6. **Visual function of the pulvinar** 140
   L. M. Chalupa
   Introduction 140
   The modern era of pulvinar research 141
   What does the pulvinar do? 149
   Conclusion 155

7. **Cortical visual areas in mammals** 160
   M. I. Sereno and J. M. Allman
   Introduction 160
   Definition 160
   Visual cortical areas of different mammal groups 161
   Evolution of visual cortical areas 167

8. **Quantitative electrophysiology of visual cortical neurones** 173
   G. A. Orban
   Introduction 173
   Different techniques 173
   Choices for the establishment of parameter response curves 174
   Spatial parameters in cat visual cortex 174
   Spatiotemporal analysis of retinal images by cat cortical cells 180
   Disparity selectivity of cat cortical cells 192
   Coding of spatial parameters by monkey cortical neurones 201
   Spatiotemporal analysis of retinal images by monkey visual cortical neurones 205
   Stereoscopic mechanisms in monkey visual cortex 211
   Conclusion 217

9. **Afferent inputs, receptive field properties and morphological cell types in different laminae** 223
   of the striate cortex
   G. H. Henry
   The story of lamination since 1900 223
   Primary pathways to the striate cortex 224
   Receptive field changes in the progression to the striate cortex 226
   Current views on the laminar pattern 228
   Laminar variation in cellular morphology 231
   Laminar variation in the response properties of spinous cells 234
   Lamination of smooth stellate cells 237

Efferent paths   239
Summary   240

10. **Striate receptive fields as linear filters: characterization in two dimensions of space**   246
L. A. Palmer, J. P. Jones and R. A. Stepnoski
Introduction   246
Linear systems and filters   247
Estimation of striate receptive field structure   250
Hidden mechanisms   257
Models of receptive field organization   260

11. **Columnar organization of the visual cortex**   266
S. LeVay and S. B. Nelson
Introduction   266
Ocular dominance columns   267
Contrast (on/off) columns   275
Orientation columns   278
Directionality columns   283
Colour columns: cytochrome oxidase blobs   284
Spatial frequency   291
'Retinotopic columns'   293
Is all cortex columnar?   294
Columns and tangential connections   294
Dissection of cortical columns   296
Large-scale processing units   299

12. **Colour vision**   316
B. M. Dow
Introduction   316
Photoreceptors   316
Psychophysics and photoreceptors   318
Subcortical processing   318
Cortical processing   322
Colour wiring   330
Colour and cognition   331
Neurophysiology and colour theory   332
Conclusions   334

13. **Functions of extrastriate visual cortex in non-primate species**   339
P. D. Spear
Introduction   339
Overview   339
Cat extrastriate cortex   342
Rodent extrastriate cortex   362
Rabbit extrastriate cortex   363
Sheep extrastriate cortex   364
Tree shrew extrastriate cortex   364
Conclusions   365

14. **Beyond extrastriate cortex: the parietal visual system**   371
B. C. Motter
Introduction   371
Streams of visual information   371
Visual cortical pathways to parietal lobe   372

Visual response properties of parietal cortical neurones   374
Functions of the parietal visual system   383

15. **Neural basis of saccadic eye movements in primates**   388
    J. D. Schall
    Introduction   388
    Brainstem   389
    Cerebellum   394
    Superior colliculus   396
    Basal ganglia   401
    Thalamus   405
    Cortex   409
    Discussion   422
    Conclusion   425

Glossary   443
Index   453

5 Limits of Vision

Edited by J. J. Kulikowski, V. Walsh and I. J. Murray

Foreword, by Gerald Westheimer   ix
The contributors   xi

1. Introduction: physiological and perceptual limits of vision   1
I. J. Murray

2. On the limits of visual detection   6
D. Laming
Introduction   6
The absolute limit to vision   6
Four configurations of luminance differences   9
Threshold characteristics   12
Experimental methods for determining thresholds   13

3. Signal detection theory   15
D. Laming
Introduction   15
Signal detection theory   17
The confidence-rating procedure   18
Increment detection   19
Two-alternative forced-choice procedures   21

4. Theoretical basis of the processing of simple visual stimuli   23
D. Laming
Introduction   23
The square-law transform   24
Fourth power transform   28
Negative masking   29
Summary   32

5. Contrast sensitivity   35
D. Laming
Introduction   35
Contrast sensitivity as a function of spatial frequency   35
Weber's law   38
The square root law   41
The transition illuminance   41

6. **Some limitations to human peripheral vision**   **44**
   P. E. Hallett
   A model of the peripheral visual pathways   44
   The intensity range of vision   48
   Sensitivity to light   54
   Sensitivity to pattern   65

7. **Limits on visual performance set by the eye's optics and the retinal cone mosaic**   **81**
   W. N. Charman
   Introduction   81
   Optical aberrations of the eye   81
   Intraocular scatter and related effects   86
   Directional characteristics of the retinal receptors   86
   Transmittance of the ocular media   87
   Overall optical performance of the human eye   88
   Interaction with the receptor mosaic of the retina   91
   Conclusion   92

8. **Spatial frequency channels**   **97**
   D. Laming
   Introduction   97
   Detection of simple gratings   97
   Visual channels   99
   Detection of edges   102

9. **Over the limit: encoding contrast above threshold in human vision**   **106**
   M. A. Georgeson
   Contrast encoding   106
   Contrast matching and contrast constancy   106
   Magnitude estimation of contrast   110
   Perceived contrast and adaptation   111
   Temporal factors in contrast perception   114
   Contrast discrimination   115
   Models of contrast encoding and constancy   116

10. **Limiting factors of texture and stereoscopic depth perception in humans**   **120**
    M. Fahle and T. Troscianko
    Introduction   120
    Resolution limits of the optics and photoreceptor lattice of the eye   120
    The perception of texture   120
    The perception of stereoscopic depth and hyperacuity   123
    The role of image parameters   124
    Pathology of stereo vision and texture discrimination   128
    Development of stereo and texture discrimination and their disturbances   129

11. **Neural model of stereoacuity based on a distributed representation of binocular disparity**   **133**
    S. R. Lehky and T. J. Sejnowski
    Introduction   133
    Alternative encodings of disparity   133
    Neurophysiological and psychophysical data   134
    Modelling depth discrimination   137
    Calculations of disparity threshold curves   140
    Discussion   144

12. **Human sensitivity to flicker and motion**   147
    D. C. Burr
    Introduction   147
    Sensitivity to flicker   147
    Modulation in space and time   149
    Movement sensitivity   149
    Mechanisms of motion perception   153

13. **Limits of velocity perception**   160
    A. T. Smith
    Introduction   160
    Contrast sensitivity   160
    Motion thresholds   161
    Velocity perception in the periphery   163
    Velocity discrimination   163
    Computational models   164
    Implementation in the brain   166
    Conclusion   169

14. **Flicker as a function of wavelength and heterochromatic flicker photometry**   171
    P. K. Kaiser
    Introduction   171
    Defining flicker   171
    Linear systems analysis   172
    Basic and applied flicker   172
    Heterochromatic flicker photometry   172
    Temporal deLange functions for red, green and blue lights   174
    Physiological evidence regarding flicker   179

15. **Spectral sensitivity in primate vision**   191
    B. B. Lee
    Introduction   191
    Receptors and the visual pathway   191
    Behavioural measurements of spectral sensitivity   195
    Some ancillary issues   199
    Conclusions   199

16. **On the limits of colour detection and discrimination**   202
    J. J. Kulikowski and V. Walsh
    Introduction   202
    Colour as a stimulus   202
    Methodological aspects of psychophysical studies   203
    Spectral sensitivity functions   205
    Colour discrimination and categories of colours at threshold   211
    Chromatic contrast sensitivity as a function of spatial frequency   214
    Conclusions   217

17. **The physical constraints on visual hyperacuity**   221
    S. P. McKee
    Introduction   221
    Luminance   222
    Contrast   223
    Wavelength   227
    Exposure duration   227

Eccentricity   229
Blur   230
Target length   230
Concluding comments   231

18. **Vision at equiluminance**   **234**
    P. Cavanagh
    Introduction   234
    Colour: what is it good for?   234
    Pathways and equiluminance   235
    Capacities   236
    Equiluminance: what is really lost?   247
    Equiluminance: what is it good for?   248

19. **Neural substrates and threshold gradients of peripheral vision**   **251**
    N. Drasdo
    Threshold gradients and neural substrates: methods of comparison   251
    Cortical magnification and ganglion cell density   252
    Psychophysical correlates   256
    Overview   261
    Conclusions and proposals for future theories and experiments   261

20. **Limits in pattern discrimination: central and peripheral factors**   **266**
    A. Fiorentini and N. Berardi
    Introduction   266
    Effects of practice and its limits in pattern discrimination   266
    Pattern discrimination in peripheral viewing   268
    Orientational anisotropies in peripheral vision   270
    Visual field asymmetries in pattern discrimination   271
    Limits in the interhemispheric transfer of visual information   272
    Conclusion   274

21. **Effects of senescence**   **277**
    R. A. Weale
    Introduction   277
    Thresholds   277
    Visual resolving power   279
    Colour vision   281
    Conclusion   282

22. **What really limits vision? Conceptual limitations to the assessment of visual function
    and the role of interacting channels**   **286**
    J. J. Kulikowski
    Introduction   286
    Complexities of visual limits   286
    Functions describing the visual system: sensitivity to sinusoidal modulations   288
    Summary of spatiotemporal limits   300
    Constituent channels and units processing visual signals   300
    Interactions between channels   314
    Perceptual significances of channels and their interactions   318
    Fundamentals of visual processing: a summary   323

Index   331

6 The Perception of Colour

Edited by P. Gouras

Preface   ix
The contributors   xi

1. The history of colour vision   1
P. Gouras
Introduction   1
Physics of colour   2
Psychology of colour   5
Biology of colour vision   7

2. The measurement of colour   10
W. D. Wright
From Newton to Maxwell   10
Spectral composition   12
Measuring colour   12
Colour-measuring instruments   19
The future   19

3. Chromatic and achromatic visual systems   22
P. E. King-Smith
General considerations   22
Monochromatic vision   24
Dichromatic vision—colour matching   27
Dichromatic vision—chromatic and achromatic signals   31
Trichromatic vision   40

4. Colour appearance and colour constancy   43
J. Pokorny, S. K. Shevell and V. C. Smith
What is colour appearance?   43
Some basic terms   43
Unrelated colours   44
Related colours   45
Problems of brightness and luminance, lightness and the luminance factor   48
Psychophysical techniques   49
What is colour constancy?   53
How is colour constancy possible?   54
Principle issues in theories of colour constancy   55
Computational theories of colour constancy   56

5. **The evolution of visual pigments and colour vision**   62
    T. H. Goldsmith
    Introduction   62
    Visual pigments of vertebrates and invertebrates are similar and ancient   62
    Phylogeny and chromophores   67
    Phylogeny and photoreceptor organelles   68
    Evolutionary causes of λ_{max} are hard to identify   68
    Transmutation revisited, or when is a rod a rod?   71
    The universal basis for colour vision is the presence of more than one visual pigment   72
    What do we mean by 'colour vision'?   73
    A great variety of animals have multiple visual pigments   75
    Gordon Walls and the evolution of vertebrate colour vision   76
    Molecular clues to the evolution of primate colour vision   78
    Why primates and other mammals do not have UV receptors   80
    An evolutionary look at pigment triangles   81
    Graphical representation of tetrachromatic pigment space   83
    Effects of cone oil droplets on colour vision   84
    Why many vertebrates have more than three cone pigments   84

6. **Molecular biology of colour vision**   90
    T. P. Piantanida
    Background   90
    Photoreception   93
    Transduction   101

7. **Visual pigments, oil droplets and photoreceptors**   108
    J. K. Bowmaker
    Introduction   108
    Receptor types   110
    Visual pigments and colour vision   111
    Fish   112
    Amphibians   118
    Reptiles and birds   119
    Mammals   122

8. **The anatomical basis for colour vision in the vertebrate retina**   128
    H. Kolb and L. E. Lipetz
    Introduction   128
    Chromatic organization of photoreceptor mosaics   128
    Connections between photoreceptors   133
    Connections between cones and horizontal cells   134
    Cone connectivity of bipolars   137
    Colour-coded neural circuitry in primates   139

9. **Cone photoreceptor physiology and cone contributions to colour vision**   146
    R. A. Normann, I. Perlman and P. E. Hallett
    Physiology of the cone receptor   146
    Cone physiology and visual perception   154

10. **Precortical physiology of colour vision**   163
    P. Gouras
    Introduction   163
    On- and off-channels   163

Spatial and spectral antagonism   165
Chromatic and achromatic contrast   169
Retinal output (ganglion cells)   170
Lateral geniculate nucleus   174
Physiological principles of colour vision   176

11. **Cortical mechanisms of colour vision**   179
    P. Gouras
    Introduction   179
    Visual area 1, orientation, ocularity and hypercolumns   179
    Chromatic and achromatic contrast columns   180
    Magnocellular system   186
    Parvocellular system   187
    Colour vision and the remapping of visual space   189
    Physiological measurement of colour   191
    Parallel organization of vision modules   193

12. **Colour contrast in form perception**   198
    K. T. Mullen and F. A. A. Kingdom
    Introduction   198
    Role of colour in spatial vision   198
    Chromatic coding of two-dimensional form   201
    Colour vision beyond the primal sketch   212

13. **Colour appearance systems**   218
    G. Derefeldt
    Introduction   218
    Historical background of colour ordering   219
    Modern colour appearance systems   224
    Comparisons between colour appearance systems   246
    Concluding remarks   256

14. **Colour vision in insects**   262
    R. Menzel and W. Backhaus
    Introduction   262
    The input system: spectral receptor types   263
    Receptor models   269
    Poly-dimensional colour vision systems   274
    Spectral opponency   276
    Colour constancy   282
    Colour vision and wavelength-selective behaviour   282
    Ecology and evolution of photopigments and colour vision   285
    Conclusion   288

15. **Colour television**   294
    W. Cowan
    Introduction   294
    Description of the shadow mask CRT   294
    Colorimetric properties of the shadow mask CRT   297
    Colour CRTs as an image display medium   300
    Colour television as an information display medium   302
    Novel display technologies   305
    Conclusions   306

Index   309

7 Inherited and Acquired Colour Vision Deficiencies

Edited by D. H. Foster

The contributors — vii

1. **Introduction** — 1
   D. H. Foster

2. **Psychophysics of inherited colour vision deficiencies** — 4
   K. H. Ruddock
   Introduction — 4
   Normal colour vision: basic features — 4
   Red-green deficiencies — 9
   Blue-green deficiencies — 21
   Monochromacy — 24
   Other congenital colour vision deficiencies — 28
   Conclusions — 30
   Appendix: Colour matching — 31

3. **Psychophysical methods for the investigation of acquired colour vision deficiencies** — 38
   P. E. King-Smith
   Introduction — 38
   Review of relevant neurophysiology — 38
   General principles: threshold methods — 40
   Chromatic thresholds — 42
   Detection thresholds: effect of test target colour — 43
   Detection thresholds: effects of adaptation and of spatial and temporal factors — 48
   Relation to other threshold tests — 50
   Complicating factors in threshold measurements — 52
   Conclusion — 54

4. **Electroretinographic aspects of colour vision deficiencies** — 56
   D. van Norren
   Introduction — 56
   Recording the ERG — 56
   Red-green deficiencies — 57
   Early receptor potential — 60
   Blue cones — 60
   Achromats — 61

5. **Electrophysiological aspects of colour vision deficiencies** — 64
   P. Gouras
   Introduction — 64

Chromatic and achromatic systems 64
Scotopization 68
The parvo- and magnocellular systems 69
Visual cortex 70

6. **Vulnerability of the blue-sensitive mechanism** 72
   H. G. Sperling
   Introduction 72
   Photopigments and photoreceptors 72
   Anatomy and physiology 73
   Psychophysics 77

7. **Genetics of inherited colour vision deficiencies** 88
   T. Piantanida
   Background 88
   Types of inherited colour vision deficiencies 88
   Molecular biology of the human colour vision genes 101

8. **Colour vision deficiencies in ophthalmic diseases** 115
   H. Krastel and J. D. Moreland
   Introduction 115
   General characteristics of colour vision deficiencies as symptoms of ophthalmic diseases ... 115
   Tests for evaluating colour vision in ophthalmic diseases 118
   Acquired deficiencies of colour vision in ophthalmic disease diagnosis: affected structures and
        corresponding colour vision decay patterns 123
   Rules correlating affected structures and type of colour vision deficiency ... 162

9. **Disorders of colour vision in diseases of the nervous system** 173
   G. T. Plant
   Introduction 173
   Disorders of the optic nerve 173
   Disorders due to central lesions 183

10. **Variations in colour vision in non-human primates** 199
    G. H. Jacobs
    Introduction 199
    Old World primates 199
    New World primates 204
    Genetics 211

11. **Colour vision tests: general classification** 215
    J. Birch
    Introduction 215
    Clinical test design 217
    Anomaloscopes 218
    Pseudoisochromatic tests 220
    Hue discrimination (arrangement) tests 223
    Adaptation tests for tritan deficiencies 228
    Colour vision lanterns 229
    Tests for achromatopsia 229
    Tests for colour vision deficiencies in children 230
    Colour perimetry 230
    Test batteries 231

Index 235

8

Eye Movements

Edited by R. H. S. Carpenter

The contributors   viii
Glossary of symbols and abbreviations   x

1. **The visual origins of ocular motility**   1
   R. H. S. Carpenter
   Introduction   1
   Gaze-holding   3
   Gaze-shifting   5
   An oculomotor job description   9

PART I. OCULOMOTOR FUNCTIONS – GAZE-HOLDING

2. **The vestibular contribution**   13
   G. Melvill Jones
   Introduction   13
   Structure of mammalian vestibular receptors   14
   Biophysics of the mechanical response   17
   Mechano-electrical transduction of receptor cells   22
   The afferent neural signal   26
   Central 'management' of vestibular information in the organization of oculomotor control   31

3. **The optokinetic contribution**   45
   H. Collewijn
   Introduction   45
   The nature of optokinetic eye movements   46
   Steady-state horizontal OKN   48
   OKN as a function of time   52
   OKN elicited by open-loop stimulation   58
   The role of the central and peripheral retina   60
   Non-horizontal OKR   64

4. **The stability of gaze and its implications for vision**   71
   E. Kowler
   Introduction   71
   Initial accurate measurements of maintained fixation   71
   The role of saccadic and slow eye movements in the maintenance of stable gaze   74
   How is stable gaze maintained?   75
   The stability of gaze in freely moving subjects   79
   Overview of gaze stability   84

Vision with a moving retinal image   84
Discussion   89

PART II. OCULOMOTOR FUNCTIONS – GAZE-SHIFTING

5. **Saccades**   95
    W. Becker
    Introduction   95
    Dynamics   99
    Reaction time   112
    Amplitude, accuracy and error correction   117

6. **Smooth pursuit: response characteristics, stimuli and mechanisms**   138
    J. Pola and H. J. Wyatt
    Introduction   138
    Basic aspects   138
    Response characteristics of the pursuit system   139
    Stimulus processing in the pursuit system   146
    Internal mechanisms   151

7. **Vergence**   157
    S. J. Judge
    Introduction   157
    Components of vergence   158
    Interaction with accommodation, and models of interaction   163
    Other sensory cues   165
    Mixed version and vergence movements   166
    Vertical and cyclofusional responses   167
    Development and its disorders   168
    Comparative aspects   169

PART III. OCULOMOTOR MECHANISMS

8. **The periphery: extraocular muscles and motor neurones**   175
    R. F. Spencer and K. W. McNeer
    Introduction   175
    Gross anatomy   175
    Embryological origin   177
    Microscopic anatomy   178
    Motor innervation   183
    Sensory innervation   187
    Pre- and postnatal development   189
    Denervation   190
    Conclusion   191

9. **The brainstem**   200
    E. L. Keller
    Introduction   200
    Anatomical organization   200
    Neurophysiological organization   200
    Brainstem generation of motor neurone signals   206
    Neuronal organization for vestibulo–ocular movements   215

10. **The cerebellum**   224
    F. A. Miles
    Introduction   224
    The vestibulo–ocular reflex   226
    Smooth pursuit   232
    Optokinetic responses   234
    Saccadic eye movements   236
    Vergence eye movements   238

11. **Control of saccadic eye and gaze movements by the superior colliculus and basal ganglia**   244
    D. Guitton
    Introduction   244
    General anatomical organization of the superior colliculus   245
    Properties of superior colliculus cell discharges that control orienting gaze shifts   248
    Saccades evoked by electrical stimulation of the superior colliculus   255
    Effects of superior colliculus lesions   255
    Relationship between superior colliculus motor discharges and brainstem oculomotor circuits   256
    Super colliculus control of gaze shifts when the head is unrestrained   265
    Control of saccadic eye movements by the basal ganglia   267

12. **Cerebral cortex**   277
    B. Fischer and R. Boch
    Introduction   277
    Cortical areas involved in eye movements   277
    Striate cortex   278
    Prestriate cortex   281
    Middle temporal and medial superior temporal areas   282
    Parietal cortex   283
    Inferotemporal cortex   285
    Frontal eye fields   286
    Prefrontal cortex   288
    Supplementary eye fields   289
    Conclusion   290

13. **Oculomotor disorders**   297
    R. J. Leigh and D. S. Zee
    Introduction   297
    Disorders of gaze-holding   297
    Disorders of gaze-shifting   304
    Adaptive responses to disorders of the oculomotor periphery   00
    Review of some effects of focal neurological lesions in humans   312
    Visual consequences of abnormal eye movements   314

14. **Overview**   320
    D. A. Robinson
    Introduction   320
    Simplifications and advantages   320
    Moving down to neural networks   322
    Moving up to more complex problems – the saccadic system   325
    Motor plasticity   327
    Functions of eye movements   328

Index   333

9 Binocular Vision

Edited by D. Regan

Preface   viii
The contributors   xi

1 Binocular visual directions of an object when seen as single or double   1
H. Ono
Introduction   1
Binocular eye movements   2
Visual direction   3
The cyclopean eye: centre for visual direction   9
Perception arising from stimulation of noncorresponding points   12
Perception arising from stimulation of corresponding points   15

2. The horopter and binocular fusion   19
C. W. Tyler
Introduction   19
Definitions   19
Binocular visual direction and the horopter   19
The point horopter   24
Empirical deviations from the geometric horopter   28
Characteristics of fusion   30
The spatial limits of fusion   33

3. Cyclopean vision   38
C. W. Tyler
One world through two eyes   38
Cyclopean stereopsis   40
The Keplerian projection and pre-cyclopean aspects of the correspondence problem   43
Cyclopean solutions to the correspondence problem   45
Inverse cyclopean effects and psychoanatomy   49
Non-random cyclopean stereopsis   52
Temporal aspects of cyclopean vision   54
Smooth surfaces and the cyclopean disparity gradient limit   56
Inhibition in the cyclopean domain   58
Fine and coarse disparity processing   60
Hysteresis in cyclopean perception   65
Neurontropy and the effects of binocular correlation   66
Hypercyclopean perception   67
Conclusion   71

4. **Binocular space perception**   75
   J. M. Foley
   Introduction   75
   Direction   76
   Distance   77
   Geometry of binocular visual space   81
   A model of binocular visual space   83
   Models of the computation of effective disparity   83
   Phenomena occurring with closely spaced stimulus elements   87
   Processes underlying distortions in binocular space perception   90

5. **Binocular rivalry**   93
   R. Fox
   Introduction   93
   Stimulus determinants of rivalry alternation   97
   Response variables   101
   The suppression state   102
   Theoretical issues   104

6. **Cyclofusion**   111
   A. E. Kertesz
   Introduction   111
   The effect of stimulus size   113
   Symmetric disparity presentation   115
   Asymmetric disparity presentation   115
   Strictly peripheral stimulation   117
   Cyclofusional stimulations that contain depth cues   118
   Discussion   119

7. **Binocular fusion, stereopsis and stereoacuity with a moving head**   121
   H. Collewijn, R. M. Steinman, C. J. Erkelens and D. Regan
   Constraints in traditional analyses of stereopsis   121
   Absolute and relative disparities   122
   Stereopsis and disparity   123
   Effects of oculomotor imperfection on stereopsis   124
   Effects of head movements   126
   Effects of various kinds of target motion   129

8. **Depth from motion and motion-in-depth**   137
   D. Regan
   Introduction   137
   Role of motion in the perception of relative and absolute depth   137
   Dynamics of disparity-driven position-in-depth perception   141
   The Pulfrich effect   143
   Disparity coding of motion sensitivity   144
   Stereo motion-in-depth   144
   Changing size and motion-in-depth   151
   Comparison of changing-disparity and changing-size as stimuli for motion-in-depth sensation   161
   Self motion and the retinal flow pattern   162

9. **Development of binocular vision and stereopsis**   170
   R. Held
   Introduction   170
   The 1980 watershed   170

10 Spatial Vision

Edited by D. Regan

Preface   viii
The contributors   xii

1. **A brief review of some of the stimuli and analysis methods used in spatiotemporal vision research**   1
   D. Regan
   Systems analysis in vision research   1
   Signal analysis in vision research   13
   Methods for generating spatial patterns   25

2. **Temporal properties of normal and abnormal spatial vision**   43
   G. T. Plant
   The spatiotemporal contrast sensitivity function (CSF)   43
   Can the characteristics of the centre-surround organization of receptive fields be used to explain spatiotemporal interactions?   45
   Is the spatiotemporal CSF an 'envelope function'?   46
   The development of ideas relating to the sustained/transient dichotomy and its neural basis   51
   The relationship of temporal properties of human vision to motion perception   53
   The temporal response function in neurological disease   54
   Conclusion   60

3. **Psychophysical models of spatial vision and hyperacuity**   64
   H. R. Wilson
   Introduction   64
   Spatial filters   65
   Spatial pattern discrimination   68
   Foveal hyperacuity   74
   Peripheral pattern discrimination   76
   Discrimination at large separations   78
   Comparison with other models   79
   Discussion   81

4. **Hyperacuity**   87
   M. J. Morgan
   Introduction   87
   Factors limiting hyperacuity   93
   Spatial primitives in hyperacuity   96
   An inventory of spatial hyperacuities   100
   A rational classification of hyperacuities   109
   Theories of hyperacuity: a summary   110

5. **Theories of visual texture perception**   **114**
J. R. Bergen
Introduction   114
Development of theories of texture perception   117
Computational models of human texture segregation   122
Where are we now?   130
Conclusions   132

6. **Spatial vision for objects defined by colour contrast, binocular disparity and motion parallax**   **135**
D. Regan
Introduction   135
Spatial form vision for objects defined by colour   137
Spatial form vision for objects defined by binocular disparity   160
Spatial form vision for objects defined by relative motion   163

7. **Development of spatial vision**   **179**
G. Mohn and J. Van Hof-van Duin
Introduction   179
Spatial form vision for objects defined by colour   180
Assessing infants' visual functions: methods of study   183
Basic visual functions   186
Spatial vision   188
Conclusions   203

8. **Spatial vision in amblyopia**   **212**
D. M. Levi
Introduction   212
Visual acuity   212
Spatial contrast sensitivity   213
Suprathreshold contrast perception   221
The 'spatial sense'   222
Intrinsic positional uncertainty and intrinsic blur   229
Amblyopia and peripheral vision   231
Modelling abnormal position acuity   232

9. **Spatiotemporal abnormalities of vision in patients with multiple sclerosis**   **239**
D. Regan
Introduction   239
Contrast threshold abnormalities in patients with multiple sclerosis   239
Abnormalities of suprathreshold contrast perception   245
A possible physiological basis for spatial frequency and orientation selectivity of contrast sensitivity loss   246
Visual evoked potential delay   247

10. **Spatiotemporal contrast vision in Parkinson's disease and MPTP-treated monkeys: the role of dopamine**   **250**
I. Bodis-Wollner and D. Regan
Introduction   250
Electrophysiological studies of vision in Parkinson's disease   251
Contrast sensitivity in Parkinson's disease   252
Studies suggesting additional non-retinal dopamine-dependent visual dysfunction in Parkinson's disease   257

11. **Spatial vision after cortical lesions**   **261**
K. H. Ruddock
Introduction   261

The visual pathways in non-human primates   261
Human visual function within perimetrically blind areas of the visual field   265
Disturbances of spatial vision in perimetrically normal areas of the visual field   274
Conclusions   282

12. **Neural mechanisms of contrast sensitivity**   **290**
R. Shapley
The roles of contrast and assimilation in brightness perception   290
Contrast, contrast sensitivity and contrast gain   290
Contrast versus reflectance: simultaneous contrast   292
Contrast sensitivity, adaptation and protection from saturation   294
Contrast sensitivity as a function of illumination level: psychophysical evidence   296
Gain control in retinal ganglion cells of the cat   300
Contrast gain in primate retinal ganglion cells   303

Index   307

11 Development and Plasticity of the Visual System

Edited by J. R. Cronly-Dillon

Preface   ix
The contributors   xi

PART I. PATTERN FORMATION IN DEVELOPMENT

1. **Homeobox genes and vertebrate embryonic development**   3
   P. T. Sharpe
   Introduction   3
   Drosophila homeoboxes   3
   Vertebrate homeoboxes   6
   From *Drosophila* to mammals—conservation at all levels?   7
   Expression in limb buds   19
   Homeoproteins as transcription factors   20
   Direct injection of homeobox gene RNA into embryos: phenotypic effects   21
   Disruption of homeobox gene expression using transgenic mice   22
   Future prospects   23

2. **Cell lineage and compartments in vertebrate neurogenesis**   28
   J. Price
   Introduction   28
   Neural histogenesis   28
   Cell lineage   30
   Compartments   37
   A comparison of cell lineages   43

3. **Theories of morphogenetic fields**   47
   H. Meinhardt
   Introduction   47
   Pattern formation by short-range autocatalysis and long-range inhibition   48
   Interpretation of positional information   55
   Segments as morphogenetic fields   57
   Borders and intersection of borders as organizing regions for morphogenetic subfields   60
   Formation of net-like structures   62
   Summary and conclusion   64

4. **Cell recognition molecules and pattern formation in the developing visual system**   68
   D. Trisler
   Introduction   68
   Molecules that regulate cell migration and axonal growth   70
   Topographically graded molecules in retina and optic tectum   74

Cell lineage and regulation of TOP expression 77
Function of TOP $_{DV}$ in retinal development 79
Molecules that identify cell type and cell stratum in retina 81
Conclusions 83

5. **The formation of topographically ordered connections during development and regeneration of the vertebrate visual system** 88
   C. A. O. Stuermer
   Introduction 88
   Theories on the establishment of topographically organized projections 89
   Analysis of the pathways of regenerating and embryonic retinal axons 91
   Axonal growth *in vitro* 99
   Organization of the retinotectal pathway in adult goldfish 102
   Open questions and perspectives 108

6. **Proto-oncogenes and development** 112
   D. G. Wilkinson
   Introduction 112
   Proto-oncogenes encoding secreted factors 114
   Proto-oncogenes encoding membrane receptors and tyrosine kinases 116
   Proto-oncogenes encoding cytoplasmic serine kinases 118
   Proto-oncogenes encoding GTP-binding proteins 119
   Nuclear proto-oncogene products 119
   Overview 122
   Future prospects 123

PART II. CELL AND MOLECULAR FACTORS AFFECTING CELL SHAPE AND POSITIONING IN DEVELOPING NERVOUS TISSUE

7. **The neuronal cytoskeleton and its possible role in synaptic plasticity** 133
   E. Fifková and M. Morales
   Introduction 133
   Microtubules 133
   Microfilaments 137
   Neurofilaments 143
   Conclusion 144

8. **Dendritic morphology and the factors affecting the pattern of dendritic growth** 148
   M. Berry
   Introduction 148
   Morphology and function 148
   Development 149
   Remodelling of an established dendritic tree 151
   Methods of analysis 152
   Morphology and synaptology of retinal cell dendritic fields 154
   Development of dendritic trees in the retina 160
   Definition of size and shape of dendritic fields in the retina 162
   Functional correlates of dendritic fields in the retina 163

9. **Cell surface interactions and cell locomotion** 171
   G. W. Ireland
   Introduction 171
   Crawling mechanism of locomotion 171

Role of extrinsic factors in the control of cell locomotion   177
Future work   182

10. **The goldfish visual system as a model for the study of regeneration
     in the central nervous system**   190
     B. Grafstein
     Introduction   190
     The role of axonal transport in regeneration   191
     Characteristics of regeneration of the goldfish optic axons   192
     Regulation and regeneration   195
     Summary and conclusions   201

11. **Glial cell response to axonal injury in fish and rat optic nerves: implications for nerve
     regeneration**   206
     M. Schwartz, T. Sivron and E. Blaugrund
     Introduction   206
     The cellular composition of the axonal environment   207
     Glial response to axonal injury   209
     Environmentally derived soluble substances and regeneration   211
     Cell surface and extracellular matrix elements and regeneration   211
     Involvement of the target in the process of regeneration   212

PART III. REGULATORY FACTORS IN THE FORMATION OF NERVE CONNECTIONS

12. **The role of GAP-43 in axon growth and synaptic plasticity in the visual system:
     Evolutionary implications**   219
     J. J. Norden, B. Wouters, J. Knapp, S. Bock and J. A. Freeman
     Introduction   219
     GAP-43 and axon growth in the visual system   220
     GAP-43 and synaptic plasticity   221
     The 'GAP hypothesis' and the influence of environmental factors   223
     The role of GAP-43 in nerve growth and synaptic plasticity   225
     Conclusions   227

13. **Axonal plasticity in the context of development**   232
     S. Jhaveri, G. E. Schneider and R. S. Erzurumlu
     Introduction   232
     How do axons grow? Observations on the optic tract   232
     Competitive interactions in determining normal and altered axonal projections   239
     Brain damage and development: plasticity and how to control it   241
     Axon growth after brain injury: what blocks it after critical ages in development   247
     Conclusion: a picture of multiple factors which can vary across axon systems   251

14. **Synaptic rearrangements in the developing and regenerating visual system**   257
     H. T. Cline and M. Constantine-Paton
     Introduction   257
     Synaptic rearrangements in the mammalian visual system   257
     The Hebbian synapse hypothesis   258
     Cellular mechanisms underlying synaptic rearrangements   259
     Synaptic rearrangements in the cortical subplate   262
     Synaptic rearrangements in lower vertebrates   263

15. **The cytoskeleton as a regulator of cell shape, nerve growth and nervous plasticity** 275
    J. R. Cronly-Dillon
    Introduction 275
    The neuronal cytoskeleton 275
    Properties of neuritic growth cones 280
    Cytoskeletal changes during postnatal brain development 282
    The cytoskeleton and functionally driven plasticity 287
    The regulation of nerve growth 292
    Competition: the selection and elimination of nerve contacts 299
    Growth and form 302

16. **Intracerebral transplantation of mammalian retina** 314
    R. D. Lund, J. D. Radel and G. M. Horsburgh
    Introduction 314
    Technical considerations 315
    Factors influencing transplant survival 316
    Immunological implications 319
    Vascular supply 320
    Connectivity of transplanted retinas 320
    Development of the transplant projection 323
    Functional integration of transplanted retinas 326
    Discussion 332

PART IV. MORPHOLOGICAL AND FUNCTIONAL DEVELOPMENT OF THE VERTEBRATE VISUAL SYSTEM

17. **The development of visual cortical afferents** 337
    D. J. Price
    Introduction 337
    Organization of the visual cortex 337
    Normal formation of the cortical plate 338
    Normal development of thalamocortical afferents 339
    Normal development of callosal and corticocortical afferents 340
    Functional development 344
    Control of afferent development 345

18. **Development of neurotransmitters in the mammalian visual system** 353
    M. E. Cavanagh, A. Dinopoulos and J. G. Parnavelas
    Introduction 353
    Subcortical visual areas 353
    The intrinsic neurones of the visual cortex 357
    Conclusions 364

19. **Interactions between visual and other sensory modalities and their development** 369
    T. R. Vidyasagar
    Introduction 369
    Multimodal convergence and its significance 369
    Development of cross-modal functions 374
    Induction of cross-modal connections 379
    Limits of intermodal interactions 380
    Conclusions 381

12 Visual Agnosias and Other Disturbances of Visual Perception and Cognition

O.-J. Grüsser and T. Landis

Preface   x

1. **Introduction**   1
   Definition and types of visual agnosias   1
   Physical and cognitive 'descriptors' of 'natural' and 'artificial' visual stimuli   3
   Historical observations: the discovery of the principles of visual data processing   3
   Eye movements and visual perception   6
   The modern search for descriptor functions of the optic image   7
   Behavioural dimensions in visual object classification   14
   Searching for the neuronal mechanisms of visual cognitive function: the primate model and
       man-specific visual abilities   15
   Developmental aspects of visual perception and cognition   17
   Correlations between brain activity and perceptual phenomena   22

2. **Early concepts of visual perception and cognition**   25
   Introduction   25
   Ancient Greek thought on visual perception   25
   Church fathers, Arabian scientists and theologians discuss vision and brain function   28
   Representation of the visual world by brain functions: a Renaissance approach   32
   From Johannes Kepler to René Descartes: the creation of modern physiological optics   36
   Progress in neuroanatomy: new models of visual perception and cognition   40
   A physicist and a mathematician contribute to the physiology of vision: Newton and Mayer   42
   Paths and wrong tracks leading towards localization of higher brain functions   46
   The discovery of the visual cortex: early concepts of optic agnosia   47

3. **The functional organization of the human eye and the lateral geniculate nucleus**   52
   Introduction   52
   The spatial frequency modulation transfer function of the eye optical apparatus and its importance
       for form vision   53
   Classes of photoreceptors: spectral, spatial and temporal response properties   54
   The generation of task-specific neuronal channels by signal processing within the retina   59
   Projection sites of retinal ganglion cell axons   61
   Signal processing in the LGN   61

4. **The primary visual cortex, signal processing for visual perception of shapes, space, colour
   and visual movement**   65
   The representation of the visual field in brain structures   65

Elementary rules of signal processing within the primary visual cortex   67
Non-visual and 'efferent' visual signals reaching area V1   75

5. **Extrastriate visual areas: examples of higher-order visual data processing**   **77**
    Introduction   77
    Criteria for cortical 'visual association areas' or 'visual integration areas'   77
    Projections from area V1 to 'higher' cerebral visual centres   78
    Elaboration of contour perception in area V2   81
    Cerebral neuronal mechanisms of colour perception   83
    Neuronal networks for visual motion perception   85

6. **The posterior parietal lobe and the cerebral representation of the extra-personal visual space**   **92**
    Introduction   92
    The anatomical subdivision and the connections of the primate area 7   92
    Functional deficits after inferior parietal lobe lesions in primates   94
    Visuo-spatial and visuo-motor neuronal data processing in area 7   96
    Quantitative evaluations of area 7 neuronal responses: gaze fields, visual receptive fields and first steps
    towards a model of cerebral space representation   103

7. **Visual object recognition and temporal lobe functions: the evidence from experiments in primates**   **107**
    Introduction   107
    Historical review   107
    The inferior temporal cortex: structure and neuronal connections   109
    Neuronal signal processing in the inferior temporal cortex   109
    Face-responsive neuronal activity in the temporal cortex of primates   117
    Visual signal recognition and the temporal lobe   125

8. **Brain lesions: grey or white matter – it matters**   **127**
    The telephone network – an early but misleading brain function model   127
    Anterograde and retrograde degeneration after axotomy   129
    Brain lesions of the cortical grey matter and plasticity of cortical neuronal circuits   132

9. **The visual world shrinks: visual field defects, hemianopias and cortical blindness**   **136**
    Introduction   136
    Historical background   136
    Principles of perimetry   138
    Functional differences in the different parts of the visual field   142
    On visual field defects and their topical diagnostic values   144
    Variability of homonymous field defects in cortical lesions   145
    Cortical blindness   147
    Blindsight   148
    Spontaneous visual sensations in cortical blindness or in the hemianopic visual field   155

10. **Light not illuminating the world: phosphenes and related phenomena**   **158**
    Introduction   158
    Retinal phosphenes   158
    Phosphenes and inhibitory effects evoked by electrical stimulation of the afferent visual system
        during neurosurgery   166
    Light sensations evoked by electrical stimulation of the primary visual cortex   170
    Migraine phosphenes   172

11. **Agnosias of visual form, object and scene recognition**   **179**
    Historical introduction   179

Development of concepts on visual agnosia   187
Visual form and object agnosia: clinical examination strategies   190
Five dimensions applied in agnosia classification   198
Apperceptive visual agnosia (form agnosia)   200
Visual associative agnosia (visual object agnosia)   207
Visual agnosia in slowly progressive dementia   212
Defective perceptual categorization: a focal disturbance of apperception?   212
Optic aphasia   215
Simultanagnosia   215

12. **Man as a social partner in the visual world: perception and recognition of faces and**
    facial expression   **218**
    Introduction   218
    Is face recognition distinct from that of other complex visual patterns?   219
    Hominid phylogenesis and face recognition   220
    Faces, masks and portraits   221
    Faces as visual stimuli   224
    Symmetry and left–right laterality in human face recognition   226
    Hemispheric specialization in human face perception as revealed by tachistoscopic tests 230
    A special memory for faces?   235
    Development of face recognition   237
    Recognizing one's own face   239

13. **The search for face-responsive components in the visual evoked potentials of the human**
    electroencephalogram   **240**
    Introduction   240
    Methodological approaches to stimulation, EEG recordings and computerized data evaluation 241
    EEG responses to highly schematic faces   242
    EEG responses to 'realistic' drawings of a face, a tree and a chair   243
    EEG responses evoked by black and white photographs of faces and non-faces   244
    Category-related components in the evoked potentials recorded during a recognition task 247
    EP response to known and unknown faces   247
    EEG responses to known and unknown flowers   248
    Extending face stimuli to person stimuli: the category-responsive components in the evoked potential differ 248
    Different gestures used as stimulus patterns do not lead to different EPs   253
    Wavelet analysis of the EPs further corroborates face-responsive components   255
    Conclusions   257

14. **Faces lost: prosopagnosia**   **259**
    Historical introduction and elementary clinical signs of prosopagnosia   259
    Questions in prosopagnosia research   260
    Clinical examination   261
    Frequency and aetiology of prosopagnosia   262
    Subdivision of symptoms and formal testing of prosopagnosic patients   262
    Different approaches to cerebral localization of the lesions crucial for prosopagnosia   263
    Brain neuropathology   264
    Neuroimaging and neurosurgical reports   266
    A possible contribution of left-hemisphere lesions to prosopagnosia   267
    Conclusions on specificity in prosopagnosia and correlated cerebral lesions   268
    Associated memory disturbances in prosopagnosia   268
    Primary visual disturbances frequently associated with prosopagnosia   270
    Complex visual disturbances associated with prosopagnosia   271
    Prosopagnosia and the 'specificity of faces'   271
    Prosopo-metamorphopsia   274

'Covert knowledge' in prosopagnosia   277
Childhood prosopagnosia   280
Impairment of face and person recognition in non-prosopagnosic patients suffering from brain lesions
    outside of the medial occipito-temporal region   280

15. **Impairment of perception and recognition of faces, facial expression and gestures in**
    schizophrenic patients   287
    Schizophrenia and the phylogenetic development of the human brain   287
    Paraprosopia in schizophrenic patients   289
    Neuropsychological investigations of the recognition of faces, facial expression and gestures in
        schizophrenic patients   290
    Problems and conclusions   295

16. **The splitting of 'I' and 'me': heautoscopy and related phenomena**   297
    Introduction   297
    Seeing a '*Doppelgänger*'   297
    Neuropathology and pathophysiology of heautoscopy   300
    Negative heautoscopy   302
    Alienation with faces   302

17. **Reading and script: historical, statistical and neuropsychological observations** 304
    Introduction   304
    The history of script   304
    Precursors of script and some phylogenetic considerations   308
    A flow diagram of reading   309
    Statistics of script   310
    Handwriting and printed words   315
    Reading competence and eye movements during reading   316
    Reading without eye movement: tachistoscopic projection of letters or words   320
    'Reading' and 'writing' in apes   330

18. **Lost letters: pure alexia**   333
    Definition   333
    Historical review and clinical signs of pure alexia   333
    Symptoms frequently associated with pure alexia   336
    Alexia and neurolinguistic models   338
    Clinical examination of alexic patients   339
    Cerebral lesion localization and aetiologies in alexia   342
    Left posterior cerebral artery strokes, neuroimaging of the lesion and correlations with the different
        syndromes associated with pure alexia   343
    Visual naming in pure alexia   346
    Pure alexia and hemialexia subsequent to splenial lesions   347
    Kanji and kana alexia in patients with lesions of the posterior corpus callosum   348
    Tachistoscopic studies in hemialexia   349
    Preserved access to written information in pure alexia   350
    Alexia and shorthand   355
    Neuronal circuits for reading: a proposed model   356

19. **Visual movement agnosia, or motion blindness: a rare clinical symptom**   359
    Introduction   359
    Different types of movement perception and their biological relevance   359
    Apparent visual movement   362
    Visual movement perception and efference copy mechanisms   371
    Cerebral impairment of complex movement perception: a case report   372

Neuronal circuits for local and global movement perception   382

20. **Achromatopsia, colour agnosia and impairments of colour vision by cerebral lesions**   385
Introduction   385
The history of achromatopsia up to the end of the nineteenth century   388
A case report introducing the main symptoms of cortical colour blindness   392
Testing for colour vision, and typical responses of patients suffering from achromatopsia   393
Residual colour vision in achromatopsia   400
Symptoms associated with achromatopsia   400
Pure homonymous hemiachromatopsia   401
Colour agnosia   402
Colour anomia and colour aphasia   406
Neuronal circuits involved in cerebral colour deficiencies   408

21. **Getting lost: topographical disorientation and topographical agnosia**   411
Introduction: perception and orientation in the extra-personal space   411
Different types of topographical disorientation   417
Six early cases of topographical disorientation   419
Clinical examination of patients suffering from topographical disorientation   421
Are unilateral occipital lesions sufficient cause for topographical agnosia?   422
Further considerations on cerebral localization and aetiology of topographagnosia (types C and D)   424
Neuroimaging and neurosurgical findings in patients suffering from a loss of topographical familiarity   425
Topographical orientation disorders and parietal lobe lesions   427
Other cognitive disabilities frequently associated with topographagnosia   428
Compensatory strategies in topographical disorientation   429

22. **Only half the world: visual hemineglect and related disorders**   431
Introduction   431
Coordinates, perceived constancy and multimodal aspects of the extra-personal space   431
A short history of the discovery of spatial neglect and other visuo-spatial disorders   434
Symptoms of visual hemineglect and other visuo-spatial disorders   439
Visuo-spatial difficulties after unilateral impairment of the left or right parietal lobes   447
Tests used to evaluate symptoms of spatial hemineglect or hemi-inattention   452
Spatial hemineglect and inattention in patients suffering from brain lesions located outside the parietal lobe   460
Alterations in hemineglect and hemi-inattention caused by vestibular and optokinetic stimulation   461
Multi-level space representation: a neuronal hypothesis   462
Bilateral lesions of the inferior parietal lobule   462

23. **Non-existent visual worlds: afterimages, illusions, hallucinations and related phenomena**   467
Introduction   467
The *Eigengrau*   467
Afterimages   469
Silent films without a cinema: scenic visual illusions   470
To be or not to be: visual patterns and scenes generated from meaningless random stimuli   471
Light sensations produced by inadequate stimulation of the retina and the central visual system:
    phosphenes and photisms   473
Deep shadows   473
Visual perseveration: palinopsia   475
Multiplication of visual objects: polyopia   475
Objects in the wrong place: visual allaesthesia   476
Visual hallucinations and pseudohallucinations   476

References   483
Index   584

13 Vision and Visual Dyslexia

Edited by J. F. Stein

Preface   ix
The contributors   xii

1. **Cortical visual areas and the visual guidance of movement**   1
   M. Glickstein
   Introduction   1
   Image formation and the problem of who looks at the picture   1
   Efferent connections of the parietal lobe   7
   Functional properties of the cortico–ponto–cerebellar pathway   8
   Cerebellum and motor learning   8
   Vestibulo–ocular reflex and its modifiability   9
   Conclusion   9

2. **Visuospatial and visuomotor functions of the posterior parietal lobe**   12
   M. Husain
   Introduction   12
   Anatomy   12
   Physiology   15
   Lesions   22
   Functions of the PPC   29

3. **Review of human visual development: crowding and dyslexia**   44
   J. Atkinson
   Introduction   44
   Normal development of sensory, perceptual and cognitive vision   44
   Vision in pre-school children   48
   Visual crowding   51

4. **Visual search in dyslexia**   58
   K. H. Ruddock
   Introduction   58
   Background to visual psychophysics   58
   Psychophysics of reading   65
   Reading in patients with low vision   68
   Dyslexia   69
   Conclusions   75

5. **Right hemisphere costs of right handedness**   84
   M. Annett
   Introduction   84

Genotype distribution of the rs^+ locus   84
Bias to right handedness causes left hand and right hemisphere weakness   86
Evidence for differences in abilities   88
Implications for reading   91

6. **The genetics of dyslexia**   **94**
   I. C. McManus
   Introduction   94
   Biological correlates of dyslexia   95
   Phenotypes of dyslexia   97
   Evidence for genetic effects in dyslexia   99
   Specific genetic models of dyslexia   101
   Evidence for environmental effects in reading ability   107

7. **Dyslexia and visual dyslexia**   **113**
   A. L. Benton
   Historical background   113
   Concept of DD   115
   Problems of measurement   115
   Types of dyslexia   115
   Discussion   118

8. **Clinical and electrophysiological correlates of dysphonetic and dyseidetic dyslexia**   **121**
   J. M. Flynn and E. Boder
   Introduction   121
   Dyslexic sub-types: the Boder system   122
   The Boder Test of Reading-Spelling Patterns   124
   Validity of the dysphonetic and dyseidetic subtypes   125
   Conclusions   128

9. **Visual processing and dyslexia**   **132**
   D. J. Johnson and S. G. Zecker
   Historical perspectives   132
   Methodology   135
   Clinical studies and observations   137

10. **Binocular control in dyslexics**   **141**
    M. S. Fowler
    Introduction   141
    Dunlop test   141
    Visual localization   142
    Treatment of unstable binocular control   143
    Investigation of visual problems of dyslexics   144
    Vergence eye movements   146
    Recent studies   146

11. **Spatial frequency processing in dyslexic and normal readers**   **148**
    W. Lovegrove
    Introduction   148
    Spatial frequency analysis   148
    Sustained and transient channels   149
    Transient/sustained interactions in SRD   150
    Conclusions   153

12. **Visual discomfort and reading**   **155**
     A. Wilkins
     Introduction   155
     Stripes can be harmful   155
     Visual and clinical effects of the 'stripes' in text   162
     Preventing eye-strain, headaches and seizures   164
     Improving text without increasing costs   167
     Overload of the visual system   168
     Temporal factors   168
     Dyslexia and visual discomfort   169
     Conclusion   169

13. **Glare, scotopic sensitivity and colour therapy**   **171**
     G. V. Stanley
     Introduction   171
     Glare effects   171
     Colour defects   171
     Syntonics   172
     Scotopic sensitivity syndrome   172
     Colour, mood and performance   178
     Conclusion   179

14. **Visuospatial sense, hemispheric asymmetry and dyslexia**   **181**
     J. F. Stein
     Introduction   181
     Visuospatial functions of the right hemisphere   181
     Dyslexics' visuospatial problems   182
     Treatment of binocular instability   183
     Dyslexics' right hemispheres   184
     Relation to other reported visual deficits in dyslexics   185
     Hemispheric specialization   187

15. **Dyslexia: defects in the development of grapheme-phoneme correspondence?**   **189**
     M. Snowling and J. Rack
     Introduction   189
     The two-route model of reading   189
     Dyslexics' difficulty in phonological reading   190
     Conflicting results on the nonword reading deficit   192
     Individual differences amongst dyslexic readers   193
     Dyslexia in the context of reading development   194
     Conclusions   194

16. **Teaching the dyslexic child reading and spelling**   **196**
     M. E. Thomson
     Introduction   196
     Evaluation studies   196
     Discussion   201
     Conclusions   202

17. **Specific dyslexia and eye movements**   **203**
     L. W. Stark, S. C. Giveen and J. F. Terdiman
     Introduction   203
     The multilevel control of eye movements   203

Normal reading eye movements   217
Abnormal reading eye movements   221
Specific dyslexia   225

18. **Eye movements in skilled reading: implications for developmental dyslexia**   233
    R. K. Morris and K. Rayner
    Introduction   233
    Basic characteristics of eye movements during reading   233
    Perceptual span   234
    Control of eye movements in reading   236
    Eye movements and dyslexia   238

19. **Eye movements in dyslexic and normal readers**   243
    R. K. Olson, F. A. Conners and J. P. Rack
    Introduction   243
    Background   243
    Is Pavlidis correct?   244
    Dyslexic and normal readers' eye movements in target search   244
    Dyslexic and normal readers' eye movements in text   246
    Individual differences in eye movements   247
    Conclusions   249

20. **Children's eye movements during reading**   251
    G. W. McConkie, D. Zola, J. Grimes, P. W. Kerr, N. R. Bryant and P. M. Wolff
    Introduction   251
    Developmental changes in eye movements   251
    Eye behaviour of a group of developing readers   252
    Concerning eye movement data and diagnosis of reading problems   261

21. **Diagnostic significance and relationship between dyslexia and erratic eye movements** 263
    G. T. Pavlidis
    Why are eye movements so important?   263
    What is dyslexia?   264
    Dyslexia and erratic eye movements during reading   264
    Dyslexics' erratic eye movements in non-reading studies   265
    A recent study   266
    Summary and conclusions   268

22. **Interhemispheric interactions and dyslexia**   271
    H. T. Hermann and Y. Y. Zeevi
    Problems inherent in clinical categorization of developmental dyslexia   271
    Anatomical studies   271
    Physiological studies   272
    Experiments with multiple targets   274
    Responses of development dyslexics to bihemifield stimuli   276
    Future directions   278

Index   281

14 Pattern Recognition by Man and Machine

Edited by R. J. Watt

The contributors   vii

1. Pattern recognition and visual perception   1
R. J. Watt
Motivation   1
Patterns in images   2
Pattern processing   3
Scene understanding   4
Objecting understanding   5
Concluding remarks   7

2. Encoding spatial relations   8
C. A. Burbeck
Introduction   8
Relative location as a basic visual function   8
Independence of target identity and separation encoding   12
Linking experimental tasks and visual mechanisms   12
Spatial and temporal integration in localization judgments   13
Modelling the mechanisms of localization   15

3. Transformations after Gibson: biological and ecological constraints on vision 19
P. C. Dodwell
Introduction   19
Visual transformations and vectorfields   20
Consequences of LTG/NP for visual pattern recognition   21
Theoretical considerations   25
Conclusion   26

4. Computational vision: a critical review   30
S. Edelman and D. Weinshall
Vision as an information-processing task   30
The components of vision   32
Case studies   40
Discussion and prognosis   45

5. Operating on spatial relations   50
D. H. Foster
Introduction   50
Localization and reference frames   52
Classification of spatial relations   53

Image rotations and invariances   55
Matching relations, sense-reversal and pattern rotation   56
Global-position relations and continuous-shift operations   58
Implications of a horizontal-vertical reference system   59
Spatially selective internal operations   61
Symmetry   63
Operations independent of spatial relations   64
Operations that precede spatial relations: indexing   65
Conclusion   66

6. **Pattern properties, invariances and classification**   69
   H. Glünder
   Introduction   69
   Signal representations and signal similarity   70
   Template matching and deterministic linear classification   72
   Geometrically invariant classification   73
   Direct translation invariant classification   74
   Polynomial approach to pattern decomposition   75
   Multilinear approach to pattern decomposition   78
   Discussion and assessment   79
   Extraction of invariant feature by 'neural networks'   81

7. **Ideal perceptual observers for computation, psychophysics and neural networks**   83
   D. C. Knill and D. Kersten
   Introduction   83
   A probabilistic approach to perception   83
   Ideal observers and psychophysical investigations of human visual perception   86
   Comparison with other approaches   89
   Application of ideal observer analysis to neural networks and natural computation   92

8. **Regularities and singularities in line images**   98
   J. C. Simon
   Introduction   98
   First-level features and operators   100
   Line images   102
   Conclusion   106

9. **Representation and process in face recognition**   107
   T. Valentine
   Introduction   107
   Information available in faces   107
   Recognition of objects and faces: implications of a computational level theory   111
   Models of concept learning and the relationship between recognition, identification and categorization   118

10. **The perception of visual numerosity**   125
    J. Allik and T. Tuulmets
    Introduction   125
    Terminology   125
    Estimation   128
    Discrimination   132
    Non-standard observers   136
    Ecologically meaningful situations   137
    What is numerosity?   137

Index   143

15 The Man-Machine Interface

Edited by J. A. J. Roufs

Preface   vii
The contributors   x

1. **Health-related aspects of VDT use**   1
   U. Bergqvist
   Introduction   1
   Potential and possible health complaints   1
   Conclusions   5

2. **Fitting physical screen parameters to the human eye**   7
   J. E. Farrell
   Introduction   7
   Time   7
   Space   11
   Space and time   20
   Conclusions   20

3. **Visual comfort and performance**   24
   J. A. J. Roufs and M. C. Boschman
   Introduction   24
   Search for suitable quality measures   24
   Comparison of quality measures   28
   Intersubject comparison and the effect of font   32
   The role of sharpness in comfort judgment and performance   34
   Considerations on scaled visual comfort   36
   Summarizing the conclusions   37

4. **Lighting and lighting conditions**   41
   P. R. Boyce
   Introduction   41
   Lighting in context   41
   Lighting problems   41
   Lighting criteria: the facts   43
   Lighting criteria: the recommendations   50
   Solutions in principle   50
   Solutions in practice   51
   Conclusion   53

5. **Visual function and monitor use**   **55**
   H. Krueger
   Introduction   55
   Ergonomic objectives   55
   Displays   56
   Requirements on vision   56
   Results of epidemiological studies   57
   Quality of the display and visual functions   58
   Work design and visual comfort   63
   Personal aspects   66

6. **Visual ergonomics of displays**   **70**
   F. L. van Nes
   The visual work environment   70
   Legibility of texts on visual displays   70
   Graphs and graphics   75
   Windowing systems   77
   Future developments   80

7. **Vigilance: sustained visual monitoring and attention**   **83**
   A. Craig and D. R. Davies
   Introduction   83
   Origins of vigilance research   84
   Signal detection theory   86
   Criterion shifts   87
   The sensitivity decrement   90
   Conclusions   95

8. **Models of user information requirements and user support**   **99**
   T. Bösser
   Information requirements for computer-aided work   99
   Models of human cognition for human-computer interaction   100
   Technology for information presentation and user support   108
   Concluding remarks   111

9. **The interaction of sensory modalities in the man-machine interface**   **114**
   K. D. Eason, C. Johnson and S. Fairclough
   Introduction   114
   Controls   115
   Sound as a display medium in the man-machine interface   118
   Speech in the man-machine interface   120
   Conclusions: towards the qualities of man-man interaction?   124

Index   127

16 The Susceptible Visual Apparatus

Edited by J. Marshall

Preface   ix
The Contributors   x

1. **Characteristics of optical radiation sources and their potential to cause ocular injury**   1
   A. F. McKinlay
   Introduction   1
   Relevant quantities and units   1
   Biological effects relevant to the assessment of ocular hazards   3
   Recommended maximum exposure levels and protection standards   4
   Production of optical radiation   6
   Lamps and lighting systems   8
   Gas and arc welding   17
   Solar radiation   17
   Lasers   19
   Other sources   20

2. **Measurement of light and the geometry of exposure of the human eye**   23
   D.H. Sliney
   Introduction   23
   Quantities and units   23
   Radiometric and photometric measurements   24
   Retinal irradiance calculations   24
   Published studies of retinal injury thresholds   26
   Spectral weighting and accumulated retinal exposure   26
   Outdoor environmental exposure of the eye   27
   Conclusions   29

3. **The interaction of light with biological tissues and the potential for damage**   30
   J. Mellerio
   Introduction   30
   Atomic structure   30
   Atomic energy states   32
   Molecular structure   32
   Molecular energy states   35
   Light interaction with specific molecular types   37
   Interactions mechanisms   39

4. **The effects of ultraviolet radiation and blue light on the eye**   54
    J. Marshall
    Introduction   54
    Transmission and absorption of optical radiation in the eye   55
    Target tissues   55
    Tissue ageing and repair mechanisms   57
    UVR damage thresholds for ocular tissues   58
    Eye conditions related to exposure to optical radiation   59
    Photochemical damage   60
    Free radicals   60
    The role of light in relation to retinal ageing   61
    Light in ophthalmic practice   65

5. **Phototoxicity: the problem of drug and chemical enhancement**   67
    P. Dayhaw-Barker and F. M. Barker II
    Introduction   67
    Endogeneous and exogenous photosensitization   68
    Mechanisms and clinical evidence of damage   70
    Conclusions   73

6. **The macula, ageing and age-related macular degeneration**   76
    J. Marshall
    Introduction   76
    Ageing populations   77
    Cellular ageing   78
    Molecular ageing   78
    Embryology   79
    The adult macula   79
    The ageing macula   80
    The role of light in relation to retinal ageing   87
    Conclusion   90

7. **Light hazards and clinical practice**   93
    J. A. Khan and M. A. Mainster
    Introduction   93
    Environmental/recreational hazards   93
    Occupational hazards   95
    Clinical hazards   97

8. **Light and the developing visual system**   104
    I. Abramov and L. Hainline
    Introduction   104
    Light damage   104
    Affected visual functions   109
    Infant populations and light environments   113
    The infant visual apparatus   116
    Light-induced visual dysfunction in infants and children?   124
    Conclusions   128

9. **Epidemiology of the ageing retina**   134
    L. Hyman
    Introduction   134
    Classification of AMD-associated changes   134
    Occurrence of AMD   135

PART II

CUMULATIVE INDEX VOLUMES 1–16

Index

A

Abbe number 1.421
Abbe refractometer 1.393, 1.421
Abducens internuclear neurones 8.184, 8.205, 8.216, 8.219
Abducens muscle 8.175, 8.178–9, 8.182, 8.185
Abducens nerve 8.183
Abducens nucleus 8.183, 8.185, 8.201, 8.248
  accessory 8.185
Abduction nystagmus 8.310
Aberration-free eye, *see* Diffraction-limited eye
Aberrations 2.85, 14.84
  axial monochromatic 5.81–2
  chromatic 1.14–5, 1.68–9, 2.6, 2.94–5, 2.312, 3.22, 5.84–6, 5.215–7, 16.110
    and equiluminance 5.236, 5.239, 5.244–7
    in evolution of retina 2.139
    and evolution of vision 2.410, 2.412
    in eye evolution 2.417
    and eye optics 2.120
  coma-like 1.12–3
  control of 1.66–8
  degrading effects of 5.90
  in dioptrics 2.86, 2.89, 2.92–9, 2.105, 2.109
  lateral chromatic 1.15, 2.94–5
  longitudinal chromatic 10.137–8
  longitudinal chromatic (LCA) 2.84, 2.94–5, 5.81, 5.84–6, 5.88, 5.92
  monochromatic 5.86
  off-axis 2.94, 2.119–20, 5.81–4
  optical 5.81–6, 5.280
  overall monochromatic wavefront 1.13–4
  and Rayleigh's quarter-wave criterion 1.11
  regular monochromatic 1.11–3
    distortion 1.11
    and the homocentric approximation 1.11
    oblique astigmatism 1.11–3
    and ocular coma 1.12–3
  Seidel 1.10–1, 1.13, 10.137
  in spatial perception 10.227–8
  spherical 1.11–2, 2.84, 2.94–7, 2.119–21, 5.81–2
  transverse 1.15
  transverse chromatic 1.66, 10.137–8

transverse chromatic (TCA) 5.81, 5.84–6, 5.88
wavefront 1.10, 5.82, 5.88–9
Aberroscope 1.16
Aberroscope technique 1.13
Ablation 12.179
  and prosopagnosia 12.269
Ablation studies 10.261, 10.264–5
Abney shift 6.281
Abney's law 6.25–6, 6.29
  and tritanopes and normals 6.38–9
Abscess, left parietal intracerebral 12.351
Absolute depth
  and motion parallax 9.140–1
  role of motion in the perception of 9.137–41
Absolute disparities 9.122, 9.145
  differences between 9.135
  dynamic changes in 9.132–5
Absolute distance, and motion parallax 9.140–1
Absorption
  and ageing 16.155
  in ageing lens 16.76
  and ageing macula 16.81, 16.88–9
  blue, across retina 5.244
  breakdown due to 5.7
  and dichroism 1.312
  lens 5.87–8, 5.277–88
  light 2.407–8, 7.4–5, 7.12
  and light damage 16.63
  and light hazards 16.96
  and light interactions 16.37–9, 16.43–5, 16.50, 16.52
  maxima 2.295
  nuclear 5.278
  and optical radiation 16.3
  photon 5.52, 5.57
  pigment 5.192
    densitometric determinations 7.11
  pre-retinal 5.278, 5.282–3
  quantal 5.24, 5.26
  selective 2.8
  spectral 2.9, 3.9, 5.191
  spectrally selective 7.4
Absorption spectra 2.229–30, 2.284, 2.290, 2.292, 2.294, 2.299, 2.301, 7.5–6, 7.18, 7.31

AC/A ratio 8.158, 8.162, 8.164–5, 8.169, 8.239
Acalculia 12.201–2, **12.**271, **12.**406
Acanthodii 2.406
Acceleration
 circular **12.**432
 linear **12.**432
 of optokinetic response 8.56–7
 of smooth pursuit 8.139–41, 8.212, 8.215
Accessory extraocular muscles 8.177
Accessory oculomotor nuclei 8.2, 8.200
Accessory optic system 8.48, 8.201, 8.213, 8.234
 abnormal
  experimental studies on 4.120–6
   effects of dark-rearing 4.122–3
   effects of decortication 4.120–1
   effects of monocular deprivation 4.122–6
   effects of visual deprivation 4.120–1
 analysis of visual motion by 4.128–30
  direction and velocity selectivity 4.128–30
 anatomical organization of, in cat and primate 4.111–3
 direction selectivity in, of cat and primate 4.115–7
 efferent connections to, in cat and primate 4.113
 in frontal-eyed animals 4.111–39
 functional considerations of 4.127–36
 general receptive-field properties of, in cat and
   primate 4.113–5
 Glossary explanation of 4.443
 ocular dominance in, of cat and primate 4.118–9
 and optokinetic asymmetries 4.133
 and optokinetic nystagmus 4.133
 other potential roles of 4.134–6
 physiological response properties of, in cat and
   primate 4.113–20
 receptive-field properties in, of cat and primate 4.113–5
 retinal and cortical input to, in cat and primate 4.112–3
 size of receptive field of 4.128
 terminal nuclei of, in cat and primate 4.111–2
 velocity selectivity in, of cat and primate 4.115–7
 and vestibular nucleus neurones 4.130
Accessory optic tract 4.112
Accommodation 2.104–12, 8.158, 8.163–5, 10.186–7, **12.**191,
   13.216, **14.**89
 active 2.109–10, 2.112
 adaptation 8.165
 and ageing **16.**150, **16.**158
 amplitude of 1.263, 2.107–11
 anatomical aspects of 1.233
 anomalies of 1.231–79
  botulism type B 1.272
  in cerebral palsy 1.271
  in ciliary muscle damage 1.272
  in diabetes mellitus 1.272
  disease-related causes of 1.270–2
   congenital nystagmus 1.270–1
  following brain damage 1.271
  following inferior oblique myectomy 1.272
  in myasthenia gravis 1.271
  non-disease-related causes of 1.267–70
   fatigue 1.267–8

   ill-sustained 1.267–8
   inertia 1.268
   insufficiency 1.267–8
   spasm 1.268–70
  in peripheral nerve damage 1.272
  in trauma-induced partial lens subluxation 1.272
  in Wilson's disease 1.272
 basic dynamic aspects of 1.240–5
  steady-state inputs 1.240–5
   and accommodative oscillations 1.240
   and blur detectability 1.241
   and continuous feedback control 1.243
   and depth-of-field 1.241
   and open-loop gain 1.241
   and perceptual blur threshold 1.241
   ramp 1.243–4
    dual mode 1.245
    pre-programming in 1.243–4
   sinusoidal 1.243
    Bode plots in 1.243
    diurnal variation in 1.243
   and small-amplitude oscillations 1.240
   step and pulse 1.241–3
 basic steady-state aspects of 1.236–40
  accommodative stimulus/response function 1.236
 biochemical aspects of 1.233
 brainstem responses 8.219
 and chromatic contrast 5.215–6
 closed loop 1.239
 components of 1.236
  convergence 1.236
  proximal or psychic 1.236
  reflex 1.236
  tonic 1.236
 cues to 1.245–9
  to direction of the blur 1.247–9
  non-optical 1.248
   disparity vergence 1.249
   other monoculars to depth 1.249
   size and proximity 1.248–9
  optical 1.247–8
   astigmatism 1.247
   chromatic aberration 1.247
   fixational eye movements 1.248
   microfluctuations of 1.247–8
   spherical aberration 1.247
 and cycloplegia 1.399
 and dark focus **15.**61
 and developing visual system **16.**123
 development of 1.236
 in dioptrics 2.85, 2.100
 and distance, in visual-display terminals **15.**61–3
 dynamic response 2.107
 and dyslexia **13.**145
 effect of contrast on 1.254
 and equiluminance 5.236, 5.244
 error 5.90
 in evolution of eye 2.21
 and evolution of vision 2.404, 2.411–2

factors affecting 1.250–66
  depth-of-focus/field 1.261
  higher levels of 1.261–3
    the instruction set 1.261–3
  retinal eccentricity 1.258–9
  retinal image 1.250–66
    contrast 1.254–8
    spatial frequency 1.250–4
      complex gratings 1.252–4
      simple sinusoidal and square-wave gratings 1.250–4
  retinal-image motion eccentricity 1.259–60
  target luminance 1.260
fatigue of 8.162
free 5.84
illusion and hallucination 12.467–8
impairments of 15.65–6
influences on 1.245, 1.249–50
  cognitive level/task 1.250
  disparity vergence 1.249
  mood 1.250
  prediction 1.250
  training 1.249
  vestibular stimulation 1.249
  visual imagery 1.250
  voluntary effort 1.250
and light hazards 16.97
in mammals 2.469, 2.471, 2.474–5, 2.477–8
mechanisms 2.107–12, 2.119
methods for measuring 1.233–6
  electrical activity 1.236
  lens geometry 1.233–4
  retinal image 1.234–6
microfluctuations of 1.247–8
neurophysiology of 1.233
ocular 1.55–6
optical methods for relaxation of, 'fogging' the
    subject 1.399–400
over-accommodation 2.108
overview of 1.231–6
peripheral apparatus/mechanical aspects of 1.263–6
  age 1.263–4
  disease/trauma 1.266
  and topically applied diagnostic ophthalmic
      drugs 1.264–6
    parasympatholytic 1.265
    parasympathomimetic 1.265
    sympatholytic 1.266
    sympathomimetic 1.265–6
in peripheral vision 5.46, 5.55
phosphenes 12.467
and pretectum 2.157
principal plane 1.56
and reading competence 12.317
and reflected images associated with visual-display
    terminals 15.42
role of, in myopia 1.38–9
size change and 8.165
spectacle plane 1.55
static response 2.107

stimuli to 1.245–7
  'defocus blur' 1.245–6
  and even-error responses 1.246
  retinal defocus 1.245
in strabismics 13.49
tonic 1.400, 8.164
  level of 1.39
  see also under Tonic accommodation
under-accommodation 2.108
and vergence 8.158, 8.160–5
and visual movement agnosia 12.372
and visual performance 5.81, 5.83
and visuo-spatial disorders 12.436
Accommodation reflex 7.27
Accommodation stimulation 9.188
Accommodation systems
  modelling of 1.266
    and computer simulations 1.266
    and experimental measurements for
      ABIAS 1.266
      ACG 1.266
      closed-loop gain 1.266
      depth-of-focus 1.266
    Hung and Semmlow model of 1.266
Accommodation vergence 9.188
Accommodative stimulus/response function 1.236
  initial non-linear portion 1.237
  linear 'manifest zone' 1.237
  non-linear transitional region of 'soft saturation' 1.237
Accommodative velocity 1.241
Accommodative vergence 8.160–2, 8.168
Accuracy
  of saccades 8.96, 8.117–22
  of vergence 8.160
A-cells 4.92
  Glossary explanation of 4.450
N-Acetylaspartyl glutamate 4.46
Acetylcholine 3.279, 3.284–5, 3.296, 11.200–1
  in amacrine cells 3.43, 3.47
  in dendrites 11.163
  Glossary explanation of 4.443
  in LGNd 3.194
  in neuronal cytoskeleton 11.281, 11.287, 11.298
  and neurotransmitters 11.355, 11.363–4
  in non-retinal inputs to the lateral geniculate
      nucleus 4.59–60
  receptors 11.198, 11.200, 11.298
  in synaptic rearrangements 11.260
  in visual cortex neurogenesis 3.368
Acetylcholinesterase, Glossary explanation of 4.443
ACh, *see* Acetylcholine
AChE, *see* Acetylcholinesterase
Achromatic contrast 6.169–70, 6.180–6, 7.64, 7.68–70
Achromatic detection 5.217
Achromatic fibres 7.39
Achromatic mechanisms 5.193, 5.204, 5.208–10,
    5.215–6
Achromatic sensitivity 5.288
  threshold methods 7.44

Achromatic space **6**.169, **7**.65
    unit area of **6**.176, **6**.182
Achromatic system **7**.64–8
    vulnerability **12**.409
Achromatic thresholds **7**.46–8, **7**.51, **7**.54
Achromatic vision **7**.178–81, **7**.185
Achromaticity
    and cone contrast **6**.37
    and sensitivity loss **6**.37–8
Achromatizing lens **5**.84, **5**.86, **5**.215–6, **5**.246
Achromatopsia **2**.306, **7**.30, **7**.88, **7**.95, **7**.117, **10**.282
    acquired **7**.116, **7**.136, **7**.139–40, **12**.390
        symptoms of **12**.392
    atypical complete **7**.100
    caused by cerebral lesions **12**.385–410
        associated symptoms **12**.400–1
        colour agnosia **12**.402–6
        colour anomia and colour aphasia **12**.406–8
        cortical colour blindness **12**.392–3
        history of **12**.388–92
        neuronal circuits in cerebral colour deficiencies **12**.408–10
        pure homonymous hemiachromatopsia **12**.401–2
        residual colour vision **12**.400
        testing for colour vision and patient responses **12**.393–400
    central **12**.400, **12**.402–3
        and loss of topographical familiarity **12**.426
    cerebral **7**.185–91, **7**.193, **12**.390, **12**.393, **12**.395, **12**.398–400, **12**.403, **12**.409
        acquired **12**.388
        and colour agnosia **12**.405
        complete **12**.388
    and cerebral achromatopsia **7**.188
    complete **7**.88, **7**.98–9, **7**.185, **7**.188, **12**.209, **12**.390, **12**.402, **12**.406
        without reduced visual acuity **7**.99–101
    congenital, in cone dystrophy **7**.136–7, **7**.139–40
    cortical **6**.188–9, **12**.140, **12**.395, **12**.397–8, **12**.400
    emotional responses **12**.392–3, **12**.400, **12**.402
    genetics **7**.101, **7**.110
    and hemiachromatopsia **7**.183–4
    incomplete **7**.88, **7**.99, **7**.101, **7**.192
    and loss of topographical familiarity **12**.425
    in ophthalmic disease **7**.118
    patient responses **12**.393–400
    peripheral **12**.403
    and photophobia **13**.171
    primate physiology and **7**.189–90
    and prosopagnosia **12**.266, **12**.271
    psychophysics **7**.100–1
    pure **12**.389
    and pure alexia **12**.344
    tachistoscopic testing **12**.401–2
    thresholds **12**.398
    types **7**.98–9
    X-linked incomplete, in cone dystrophy **7**.137
Achromats **7**.25, **7**.61
Acoustic impedance **1**.360

Acoustic radiation **15**.1
Acridine orange **16**.40
Across-fibre processing **2**.249, **2**.251
Acrylamide **10**.52
Acrylamide damage, to P-beta cells **5**.274
ACT*, *see under* Architecture of cognition
Actin
    associated proteins **11**.137–9, **11**.143–4
    binding proteins **11**.174
    in cell locomotion **11**.174–5
    cortical **11**.174, **11**.177
    in critical period plasticity **11**.289–90
    and cytoskeleton **11**.276
    depolymerization **11**.138
    development changes **11**.284–6
    distribution **11**.139
    modulators **11**.138
    in neuronal cytoskeleton **11**.277, **11**.279, **11**.284
    polymerization **11**.137–8, **11**.174, **11**.176, **11**.226
    in regeneration **11**.193–4
    in SCb **11**.191
Actin filaments **11**.42–4, **11**.133, **11**.137–40
    in cell locomotion **11**.172, **11**.174, **11**.176, **11**.182
    dendrite **11**.148–51
    in neuronal cytoskeleton **11**.277–82, **11**.297
α-Actinin **11**.172–3
Actinopterygii **2**.400–1, **2**.407, **2**.412, **2**.415
Action
    and pattern **14**.3
    visually controlled **14**.1
Activating system, ascending reticular **12**.478
Activity, spontaneous **12**.466–7, **12**.470
Activity profile, Glossary explanation of **4**.443
Acuity
    abnormal position **10**.232–5
    bisection **5**.221, **5**.223, **5**.230–1, **14**.9, **14**.11–4, **14**.16
    bumps and raggedness **10**.102
    chevron **10**.107–8
    chromatic grating **10**.142
    curvature **5**.221, **5**.225, **5**.228, **5**.231, **5**.270, **10**.110
    cyclopean grating **10**.163
    detection **10**.188
    dynamic visual (DVA) **16**.154
    extrapolation **10**.91, **10**.101–2
    at fovea **5**.92
    and functional organization of retina **3**.13
    and ganglion cells **3**.56, **4**.32–3
    grating **5**.90, **5**.258, **10**.224–9
    grating resolution **10**.93
    Landolt C **5**.258, **14**.14
    length **10**.105–7
    limits **5**.60, **5**.67–8, **5**.71, **5**.122, **5**.168
    longitudinal studies **5**.279
    low contrast, and contact lenses **1**.90
    measurements **5**.82
        with Keystone instrument **5**.279
    motion **5**.221–2, **5**.225–6, **5**.229–30
    orientation **5**.221–2, **5**.226–7, **10**.94, **10**.103–5, **10**.110
    Ortho Rater **16**.154

of P-and M-ganglion cells **4**.32–3
periodic vernier **10**.102–3
peripheral **5**.90
photopic **16**.153
positional **10**.223
prediction **5**.92
recognition **10**.191–2
resolution **5**.222, **5**.228–9, **10**.188–90
rod, in man **5**.71
see also Hyperacuity; Stereoacuity; Vernier acuity
Snellen **5**.279, **10**.169–70, **10**.224–9
spatial **5**.24, **5**.47, **5**.50, **5**.149, **5**.236
spatial discrimination **10**.192–3
spatial frequency **10**.105–7
and spatial frequency filtering **10**.141–2
spatial interval **5**.221–2, **5**.226–30, **10**.105–7, **10**.110
static **5**.83
static visual (SVA) **16**.153–4
step vernier **10**.93–4
    in hyperacuity **10**.95, **10**.101, **10**.110
stereoscopic **1**.327–9
temporal **5**.24, **5**.147
velocity **5**.152
vernier **5**.120, **5**.221–2, **5**.225–31, **10**.101, **10**.150, **10**.163,
        12.195, **14**.8–10, **14**.12–5
    cyclopean **10**.107, **10**.163
    dichoptic **5**.128
    and equiluminance **5**.236
    in hyperacuity **10**.87, **10**.89–91
    for motion-defined bar **10**.167
    in pattern discrimination **5**.266, **5**.269
    in peripheral vision **5**.257–8, **5**.261
    in psychophysical models **10**.74–6, **10**.82
    and senescence **5**.280–1
    texture and stereo depth **5**.124–8
visual **8**.3–8, **10**.155, **10**.188–93, **12**.19–20, **12**.37, **12**.43–4
    and ageing **16**.152
    and ageing retina **16**.136–8
    age-related degradations in **16**.76
    and agnosia **12**.180–1, **12**.184, **12**.195, **12**.197, **12**.199,
        12.202, **12**.209, **12**.212, **12**.215
    in amblyopia **10**.212–3
    and blindsight **12**.152
    cell death **5**.280–1
    decay **5**.274
    and developing visual system **16**.110, **16**.112, **16**.125,
        16.128–9
    illusion and hallucination **12**.478–9
    and image motion **5**.151
    impairment by acrylamide **5**.274
    and light hazards **16**.94
    mesopic level **5**.279
    motivation **10**.190–1
    and MTF **12**.53–4
    neural basis **10**.191
    in pattern discrimination **5**.268–9
    in peripheral vision **5**.270–1
    photopic level **5**.279
    and photoreceptors **12**.57–8

and pure alexia **12**.339, **12**.354
in reading and script **12**.317, **12**.319
reduced **12**.478
retinal area **10**.190
and retinal eccentricity **8**.6–9
and retinal image velocity **8**.3–5, **8**.86–9, **8**.314
and senescence **5**.279–90
and senile miosis **5**.278
and single letter recognition **12**.322
and spontaneous nystagmus **8**.315
stimulus differences **10**.190
texture and stereo depth **5**.129–30
threshold criteria **10**.190
and topographagnosia **12**.419–21, **12**.423
and tremor **8**.71–2
and visual object recognition **12**.121
width **10**.105–7
Acuity-luminance function in cone–rod dystrophy **7**.141
Acute zones **2**.266
Adaptation **5**.304, **10**.142–8, **10**.291–2
    accommodation **8**.165
    bandwidth **5**.102, **5**.314–5
    biphasic dark **7**.99
    Blakemore and Campbell's tuning curve **5**.102
    characteristics of cones **5**.192
    chromatic **5**.174–6, **5**.184, **5**.191–5, **5**.204–5, **5**.210, **5**.214,
        5.245, **7**.58, **10**.152
    colour temperature backgrounds **5**.214
    complete **5**.320–1
    contrast (CA) **5**.111–3, **5**.116
    and contrast encoding **5**.109
    and contrast sensitivity **5**.40
    cortical **5**.113
    dark **2**.168–70, **2**.374, **2**.378, **2**.382, **3**.41, **5**.41, **5**.58, **5**.224,
        5.278–9, **5**.283, **7**.58, **7**.100, **7**.184, **7**.229, **10**.187–8,
        11.258, **12**.271, **12**.466–7
        and ageing **16**.150–2
        and developing visual system **16**.110–1, **16**.118, **16**.124
        in monochromacy **7**.25–7
        and phototoxicity **16**.70
        rod-'red-cone' monochromats **7**.28
    and equiluminance **5**.238–9
    and flicker detection **5**.11
    lateral **7**.11
    light **2**.168, **2**.170, **2**.356, **2**.374, **2**.376, **2**.378, **3**.9, **3**.11,
        3.40–1, **5**.60, **5**.113, **5**.179, **5**.192, **10**.187–8, **12**.271
    light–dark **12**.468
    local luminance **5**.111–2
    luminance **2**.168, **2**.171, **5**.187
    to maximum acuity **5**.72
    mechanisms **3**.30
    model **10**.147–8
    in monkeys, effects of **4**.34–5
    motion **5**.163, **5**.239
    and motion detection **5**.167–8
    neutral **5**.193, **5**.196
    neutral background **5**.211
    in peripheral vision **5**.45–6, **5**.50, **5**.59, **5**.61, **5**.66, **5**.69,
        5.72

Adaptation (*continued*)
  phoria 8.162
  photoreceptor 6.150–2
  prism 12.416–7
  pseudo- 5.321
  reference signal determining 5.66
  rod 5.60
  and senescence 5.281
  spatial frequency 10.65, 10.73–4
  to spatially structured stimuli 7.20
  specific properties of 5.305–6
  and velocity perception 5.160–1
  visual 6.54
  to weightlessness 12.411
  to white or coloured backgrounds 5.204–5
Adaptation level theory 14.130
Adaptationist programme 2.136, 2.144–7
Adaptive plasticity
  of natural drift velocity 8.81
  in peripheral disorders 8.308–12
  of post-saccadic drift 8.125–7
  of saccades 8.123–7
  of vestibulo-ocular reflex 8.35–40, 8.81
    cerebellar 8.37, 8.226–32, 8.238, 8.312, 8.327
      single-unit recordings 8.228–32
    cognitive and perceptual correlates 8.38–40
    site of 8.229
    volitional control of 8.39
Adaptive post-saccadic drift 8.125
Adaptive procedures (staircase methods) 5.13–4
ADB, *see* Apparent distance bisection
Additivity 5.174, 5.185, 10.141
Adenine 7.102–3
Adenoma, pituitary 12.144–5, 12.162, 12.166
Adenosine triphosphatase (ATPase) 7.132
ADHD, *see* Attentional deficit hyperactivity disorder
Adhesion
  in cell locomotion 11.175–81
  in crawling 11.171–4
  differential 11.180
  as guidance mechanism 11.178
  in neuronal cytoskeleton 11.293, 11.297
  pathways 11.178
Adhesion molecule on glia (AMOG) 11.71–2
Adjustment method 10.36
Adnexal tumours
  dacryoceles 1.45
  haemangiomas 1.45
Adolescents
  and emotional responses to colour 12.387
  and visual hallucinations 12.477
Adults, and visual hallucinations 12.477
AEDC, *see* Apparent equidistant circle
Aesthetes 2.368
Affective and cognitive stimuli 9.99
Afferent motion perception, Glossary explanation of 4.443
Afferent saccadic delay 8.117
Afferents
  in albinos 11.348–9

callosal 11.340–2, 11.344, 11.346–7, 11.349–50
control of maturation of pathways 11.337–8, 11.344
cortical 11.337–50
corticocortical 11.340, 11.342–7
dendrites as 11.148
development control 11.345–50
effects of mutations on 11.348–50
electrical stimulation of 11.149
geniculo-cortical 4.298, 11.339–40, 11.343–7, 11.349–50
LGNd 3.198
retinal, of LGNv 3.202
retinocollicular 11.235
subcortical 3.210
thalamocortical 11.339–40, 11.345, 11.350
type I 3.195
type II 3.195
type III 3.195
to visual cortex 11.338
of visual thalamus 3.215, 3.217
volleys 11.148
AFPP, *see* Apparent fronto-parallel plane
After-effects
  complementary (CAE) 14.22
  pattern contingent 14.21–3, 14.25
  in pattern processing 14.4
After-image 2.165–7, 2.169, 5.60–1, 8.77, 8.84, 8.87, 8.146,
      8.149, 8.315, 10.267, 12.386
  displacement 12.432
  illusion and hallucination 12.466–8, 12.475
  and light hazards 16.96, 16.99
  and light measurement 16.23
  movement 12.364–5, 12.371
  negative 12.468
  oscillatory 12.468
  perceived velocity 12.365
  perception 12.432
  and phosphenes 12.158
  retinal 12.174, 12.473
  and visual hemineglect 12.431–2
  and visual movement agnosia 12.361, 12.363–4, 12.366
After-image contrast 5.111–3
After-image localization techniques 9.129
After-nystagmus, optokinetic 8.33, 8.51, 8.53–60, 8.65,
      8.214, 8.225, 8.234–5
Age
  and face recognition 12.236
  and light absorption 7.4–5
  and threshold measurements 7.54
Ageing
  biological 12.133
  and photopic sensitivity 5.282
  visual 5.277–83
    and daily tasks 16.156, 16.158
    and driving 16.157–8
    and highway signs 16.157
    self-reports 16.156
    and work 16.156–8
Agenesis 3.348
Age-related macular degeneration 16.42–3, 16.76–90, 16.134

atrophic/non-exudative **16**.135, **16**.137, **16**.141
blindness from **16**.138–9
case-control studies **16**.141
and chemical work exposure **16**.145–6
and cigarette smoking **16**.145
classification **16**.134–5
diagnosis **16**.135, **16**.144, **16**.146
and eye colour **16**.146–7
genetic/familial factors **16**.146–7
increase in prevalence with increasing age **16**.137
and light exposure **16**.144–5, **16**.147
medical conditions/physiologic measurements **16**.141–2
multifactorial aetiology **16**.146–7
natural history **16**.139, **16**.147
neovascular/exudative (N/E) **16**.135, **16**.137, **16**.144,
    16.147
    high risk characteristics **16**.139, **16**.141
nutritional factors **16**.144–5
occurrence **16**.135–8
prevalence **16**.135–41, **16**.146
prevalence studies **16**.139–41
and race **16**.141, **16**.143, **16**.145–6
risk factors **16**.139–47
and sex **16**.141
standardized, reproducible classification system **16**.146
trace elements and **16**.144
uniform reporting procedures **16**.146
visual acuity criteria for diagnosis **16**.136
Agnatha **2**.398–405, **2**.414, **2**.416–7
Agnosia **7**.117, **7**.173, **7**.187, **7**.191, **12**.179–217
anti-localizationist arguments **12**.187–90
apperceptive **12**.2, **12**.183–4, **12**.198, **12**.200–8,
    12.212
    focal disturbance **12**.212–5
    Gestalt aspect **12**.204–6
    visuo-motor abilities **12**.206–7
apperceptive (form) **12**.200–7
    concepts **12**.200–4
associative **12**.2, **12**.183–4, **12**.198, **12**.200, **12**.207–12,
    12.215, **12**.271
    case description **12**.180–4
    varieties **12**.211–2
bedside clinical examinations **12**.191–4
classification **12**.198–200
cognitive **12**.198
colour **12**.266, **12**.337, **12**.392, **12**.399
    and achromatopsia **12**.400
    caused by cerebral lesions **12**.402–6
    and colour anomia **12**.408
    and colour deficiencies **12**.410
    pure **12**.403
    and pure alexia **12**.342, **12**.345–6
cortical visuo-motor defects **12**.2–3
defective perceptual categorization **12**.212–5
definition and types **12**.1–3
development of concepts **12**.187–90
disjunctive (ideational) **12**.180
dissociated awareness **12**.197
early concepts **12**.47–51

early studies **12**.179–87
elementary perceptual **12**.198
face **12**.2, **12**.260, **12**.271
finger **12**.436
form and object **12**.190–8
general **12**.2
hemispatial **12**.463
hierarchical models **12**.187
for highly stylized drawings **12**.336
and human visual system **12**.15, **12**.17
left tactile **12**.348
and MTF **12**.53–4
for non-canonical views **12**.194
object **12**.18, **12**.277, **12**.390–1
    and achromatopsia **12**.401
    and colour agnosia **12**.406
    space-related **12**.425
    and spatial hemineglect **12**.457
    and topographical disorientation **12**.414
    and visual hemineglect **12**.450
    and visuo-spatial disorders **12**.436
    without alexia **12**.346
and object classification **12**.14
optic **12**.337
optic aphasia **12**.179, **12**.215
optic spatial **12**.437
optic–agnosic varieties **12**.337
partial **12**.190
partial unawareness **12**.200
patient interview **12**.197–8
patients **12**.14
perceptive **12**.2
productive symptoms **12**.3
and prosopagnosia **12**.274
psychological theory **12**.187
self-awareness **12**.197
shape **12**.18
and signal transfer **12**.58–9
similarity relationships **12**.210
simultanagnosia **12**.215–7
simultaneous **12**.436–7
and slowly progressive dementia **12**.212
spatial **12**.196–7, **12**.271, **12**.446
syndrome, general visual **12**.337
topographic **12**.465
topographical, *see* Topographagnosia
visual **10**.261, **10**.274–6, **12**.260, **12**.336, **12**.338, **12**.390–1
    and alexia **12**.333
    associative **12**.337
    general **12**.358
    object **12**.108, **12**.407
        associative **12**.337
        and topographagnosia **12**.420
    and prosopagnosia **12**.266
    and pure alexia **12**.344–5
    symptoms **12**.337
    and topographagnosia **12**.420–1
    and topographical disorientation **12**.414
    and visual movement agnosia **12**.380

Agnosia (*continued*)
  visual field **12.198–9**
  visual movement **12.333, 12.359–84**
    related disorders **12.379**
    twelve years of **12.378–9**
  visual spatial **12.437**
Agraphia **12.201, 12.209**
  alexia without **12.260, 12.264, 12.274**
  reading and script **12.304**
  and visuo-spatial disorders **12.436**
Aguilonius, Franciscus **12.36–8, 12.43, 12.371**
AI, *see* Artificial intelligence
AIDS, toxoplasma encephalitis associated with **12.343**
Airy diffraction pattern **1.11, 2.92, 5.82**
Al Kindi **12.28**
Alarms **15.119**
Albertus Magnus **12.29–31, 12.33–4, 12.40, 12.127, 12.388**
Albinism **3.180**
Albinos **3.85, 3.107, 3.110–1, 3.113, 3.116**
  afferents in **11.348–9**
Alcmaeon of Croton **12.25, 12.158**
Alcohol consumption **12.133**
Alexander's Law **8.302**
Alexia **7.187, 7.192–3, 10.274, 12.198, 12.266, 12.391–2, 12.462**
  agnosic **12.215, 12.333**
  with agraphia **12.335, 12.355, 12.358, 12.406**
  asthenopic **12.337**
  case reports **12.336**
  cognitive defect **12.320**
  and colour anomia **12.408**
  cortical **12.335**
  covert knowledge in **12.334, 12.352**
  defined **12.333**
  in Far-East languages **12.338**
  global **12.209**
  and hemiachromatopsia **12.402**
  for Kanji **12.339**
  left tactile **12.348**
  for letters **12.335, 12.345**
  literal **12.333, 12.394**
  for musical notes **12.345**
  in nineteeth century **12.333**
  for numbers **12.345**
  occipital **12.333**
  optic **12.333**
  origin of **12.336**
  posterior **12.333**
  primary **12.333**
  and prosopagnosia **12.275, 12.277–8**
  pure **12.2, 12.179, 12.182, 12.189, 12.208–9, 12.211–2, 12.271, 12.333–58, 12.387**
    and achromatopsia **12.394, 12.401**
    anatomical considerations **12.344**
    associated symptoms **12.338**
    associated syndromes **12.343–6**
      type I **12.344**
      type II **12.344**
      type III **12.344–6**
    atypical neuropathological findings **12.342**
    awareness, conscious **12.341**
    awareness in **12.339**
    cerebral dominance **12.342**
    cerebral lesion localization and aetiologies **12.342–3**
    clinical examinations **12.339–42**
    clinical investigations **12.338**
    clinical signs **12.333–6**
      motor efference copy **12.334**
      proprioceptive input **12.334**
      tracing with finger **12.334**
    clinical syndromes **12.343**
    clinico-pathological correlation **12.343–4**
    and colour agnosia **12.406**
    and colour anomia **12.406–8**
    and colour deficiencies **12.410**
    complex graphical analysis **12.356**
    and complex scenes **12.340**
    conscious visual input **12.344**
    and correct detection **12.334**
    covert knowledge in **12.334, 12.354–5, 12.357**
    denial in **12.352**
    frequency distribution **12.338**
    handwriting recognition without reading **12.336**
    Kanji and Kana **12.348–9, 12.355**
    large series of patients **12.338**
    lexical decisions **12.347, 12.355**
    mental status examination **12.354**
    mesial occipital cortical involvement **12.344**
    mesial occipito-temporal involvement **12.344**
    for musical scores **12.336**
    neo-disconnectionistic approach to higher cortical focal disturbances **12.337**
    neurolinguistic models **12.338–9**
    neurological examination **12.342**
    neuronal circuits for reading **12.356–8**
    ophthalmological examination **12.342**
    preserved access to written information **12.350–5**
    reading
      mathematical symbols **12.336**
      by motor tracing **12.336**
      numbers **12.336**
      preserved **12.345, 12.347**
        abilities **12.351**
        letter **12.336**
        of numbers **12.342**
      single-letter **12.336**
    right hemifield **12.345**
    and shorthand (stenography) **12.330, 12.343, 12.355–6**
    single cases **12.338**
      Chinese patients **12.339**
      Japanese patients **12.339**
    symptoms **12.336–8, 12.345**
    tachistoscopic presentation
      exposure duration **12.341, 12.351**
      short exposure **12.340**
      of stimuli **12.340**
    tachistoscopic testing **12.352**
      exposure duration **12.354**

therapeutic approach 12.351
unawareness 12.339
verbal awareness 12.352, 12.354
verbal unawareness 12.351–2
visual naming 12.346–7
anatomo–clinical correlation 12.347
double dissociation of function 12.347
reading and script 12.304, 12.308, 12.314–6, 12.319–21
receptive 12.333
sensory 12.333
subcortical 12.335
varieties 12.335
verbal 12.216, 12.333, 12.351–2
visual 12.333
and visual movement agnosia 12.373
and visuo–spatial disorders 12.436
without agraphia 12.260, 12.264, 12.274, 12.333–7, 12.354
for words 12.335, 12.407
Alezzandrini's syndrome 7.146–8
Algorithms
colour 14.36
complexity 14.98–9
computer vision 14.30, 14.32–4, 14.39–42, 14.44–5
constraints 14.89
feature operator 14.101
line-finding 14.105
machine stereopsis 2.276–7
motion 14.34
motion detection 2.252
recognition 14.26, 14.43
shape from shadows 14.36
thinning 14.105
Alhazen 12.26, 12.28–31, 12.33, 12.35
Aliases
in foveal sampling 3.19–20
spatial 3.20, 3.24
two-dimensional 3.20, 3.22
Aliasing 1.20, 2.102–3, 3.7–8, 5.72, 5.91–2, 5.124, 5.268,
10.64, 10.76, 10.78
blue cone 3.22
in hyperacuity 10.88–9
retinal 1.355
Alignment
in binocular vision 2.272–3
and segmentation 14.6
vertical 2.448
Allaesthesia 12.449, 12.451
visual 12.426, 12.476
Allen separator 1.377
α-Actinin 11.172–3
α-Tubulin 11.135, 11.194–5
Alphabet
Cyrillic 12.308
Greek 12.308
Latin 12.308
Alter ego 12.299, 12.301
Alternation, increase of 9.97
Alzheimer's disease 4.418, 8.304, 11.288, 12.212
abnormal eye movements in 13.263

Amacrine cells 4.3, 5.252–5, 6.143, 6.165–7, 6.171
different time courses of synaptic input to 4.5
GABAergic narrow field 4.4–5
glycinergic wide field 4.5
local signal receiving of 4.5–6
narrow field 4.4–6
on-and off-centre 6.139–43, 6.166–7
on–off 4.5
sustained 4.6
transient 4.6
wide field 4.6
Ambidexterity 12.342, 12.444
Ambient vision 3.204, 3.217
Ambiguity and shape perception 14.35
Ambiocular vision 9.180–1, 9.184–7
Amblyopes, accommodation responses to sinusoids in 1.251
Amblyopia 1.269, 5.116, 5.283, 7.155, 9.198, 10.212–35,
12.150, 12.188, 12.392, 13.54
anisometric 13.48
anisometropic 5.130
constant errors in 10.227
contrast sensitivity 10.213–6, 10.218–9
cortical 10.269, 12.390
deprivation 12.20, 13.48
and the exit-pupil of the eye 1.301
general cortical 12.200
hyperacuity, Snellen and grating acuities 10.224–9
intrinsic positional uncertainty and intrinsic blur 10.229–
31
luminance dependence 10.219–21
meridional 5.130, 13.49, 13.52
modelling abnormal position acuity 10.232–5
patients 12.199
and polarized light 1.323
prediction of 13.51
spatial vision channels 10.216–7
strabismic 5.130, 12.386
suprathreshold contrast perception 10.221–2
tobacco–alcohol 7.175–7
visual acuity 10.212–3
AMD, *see* Age-related macular degeneration
American Conference of Governmental Industrial Hygienists
(ACGIH) 16.2, 16.4–5, 16.11–4, 16.16–7, 16.99–100
American National Standards Institute (ANSI) 16.6
American Optical Company (Hardy, Rand and Rittler)
plates, *see* AO HRR plates
Ametropia 1.29, 1.53, 2.82–3, 2.104–12
component 1.31
correlation 1.31
explanation of 1.400
ocular 1.6–7
spherical, compensation for, in telescopes 1.215
Amino acids 11.359
348 7.107
364 7.107
excitatory
in visual cortex 3.311
in visual cortex neurogenesis 3.369
in visual thalamus 3.183, 3.185, 3.192

radioactive 3.182
see also EAA
Amino phosphonoheptanoic acid (APH) 11.269
Amino-acid protein, 348 7.106
γ-Aminobutyric acid, *see* GABA
γτ-Aminobutyric acid, *see* GABA
Aminoglycerides, ototoxic 8.23–4
2-Amino-4-phosphonobutyrate 3.34
2-Amino-4-phosphonobutyric acid 4.275, 4.331
AMLS, *see* Anterior medial lateral suprasylvian visual area
Ammann, Johann Konrad 12.331
Ammocoetes 2.402–5
Amnesia 12.201
    anterograde 12.392
        complete 12.269
    for biographical information 12.269
    and cerebral achromatopsia 7.187
    for colours 12.405
    for contextual (episodic, autobiographical)
        information 12.269
    for general events 12.269
    for generic (semantic) information 12.269
    for physiognomies 12.260
    and prosopagnosia 12.268–9
    retrograde 11.291, 12.269
    syndrome 12.268
    topographical 7.189, 7.191, 12.423, 12.427
        anterograde/retrograde 12.422
Amphibians 2.71–2
    colour vision 2.285–7, 2.290, 2.299
    dioptrics 2.89, 2.110
    eye embryology 11.394
    feeding selectivity 2.157
    photoreceptor system 2.68–9
    and visual cortex 2.152
    visuomotor systems 2.153–7, 2.159–62
Amphioxus 2.15, 2.17–8, 2.24, 2.31, 2.48, 2.399, 2.403,
    2.405
Amplitude
    in hyperacuity 10.91
    saccadic 8.119–21, 8.127–32, 8.238
        bistable pattern 8.120–1
        computation 8.95–6, 8.127–9
        and diazepam 8.119
        global effect 8.119–21
        transition function 8.128–9
Amplitude frequency curves 5.172
Amplitude spectra
    and linear filters 4.249
    of motion detectors 5.155
Ampulla 8.14
Amsler grid 8.315
Amsler grid scotomas 1.350
Amusia 12.450
Amygdala 11.373–4, 11.381, 12.269, 12.347
    and visual object recognition 12.109, 12.119
Anableps 2.405, 2.412, 2.417
Anaesthesia, pentobarbital 12.472–3
Anaglyphic glasses 9.202

Anaglyphs 1.331
    red–green random-dot 7.30
Anaspids 2.402
Anatomical tracing studies, in relation to saccadic eye
    movements 4.388
Anaxagoras of Klazomenai 12.26
Angiography 12.349, 12.475
    fluorescein 16.134
Angioma, splenial 12.349
Angle α 1.11–2, 1.15, 2.272–3, 5.81, 5.83, 5.85
Angle of anomaly 9.180, 9.188–9
    direct measurement of 9.193–4
        Douse test 9.193
        Hering–Bielchowsky after-image test 9.193
        maculo-macular test 9.193–4
Angle of strabismus 9.194
Angle-of-gaze effect 4.382
Anguilla (eel) 2.69
Angular discrimination 9.149
Angular sensitivity 2.232, 2.235
Animal-House Test 13.137
Animals, in illusion and hallucination 12.471, 12.480
Aniridia, and the Stiles–Crawford effect of the first
    kind 1.301–2
Aniseikonia 1.163–82
    adaptation to 1.169–70
        and asthenopia 1.170
        and cyclophoria 1.169
        and the Nonius horopter 1.169
        ortho-eikonization 1.170
        and pseudoscopic vision 1.170
    after radial keratotomy 1.143
    anisophoria (dynamic) 1.170–1
    axial 9.215–6
    clinical management of 1.176–8
        contact lenses 1.178
            and validity of Knapp's Law 1.178
        contact/spectacle lens telescope 1.178
        diagnosis, signs and symptoms 1.176–7
            heterophoria 1.177
        eikonometry 1.178
        intraocular implant lenses 1.178
        isogonal lenses 1.177–8
        position and form of lenses 1.177
        reducing of prescription and modification of
            cylinders 1.177
        of regular and irregular 1.176
    dynamic (anisophoria) 1.170–1
    effects on binocular vision 1.176
    and eikonometry 1.171–5
    and the 'geometrical effect' 1.165
    and horizontal magnification 1.165
    and intraocular lens correction 1.127
    lateral 9.216
    magnifying devices in 1.163–4
        size-lenses 1.163–4
        variable magnification units 1.164
    and oblique magnification 1.165–6
        and the declination 1.165–6

Aniseikonia (*continued*)
  and prism adaptation 1.171
  role of vertical disparity in 1.167–9
    and absolute distance 1.167
    and angle of gaze 1.167
  and spatial perception 1.164–5
  unresolved aspects of 1.179
    anisophoria and 1.179
    credibility of clinical eikonometry 1.179
    stereoscopic precision 1.179
    strabismus and 1.179
  and vertical magnification (the 'induced effect')
    1.166–7
  and the apparent fronto-parallel plane horopter 1.166
  and assymetrical convergence 1.167
Anisometria 9.216–7
Anisometropia 8.310, 9.215
Anisophoria 9.216–7
  and aniseikonia 1.179
Anisotropic mapping, Glossary explanation of 4.443
Anisotropy 2.276–7
  of cortical maps, in area V2 of the cat 4.300
  foveal 5.258
  functional 5.271
  local 5.266
  optical 1.311–2
    and extraordinary rays 1.311
    and ordinary rays 1.311
    and uniaxial crystals 1.312
  orientational 5.270–2, 5.274
  in peripheral vision 5.253–6, 5.258
Annelid worms 2.122
Annett's right-shift model 13.106
Annulus of Zinn 8.178
Anomaloscope 7.91, 7.228–9
  in achromatopsia 7.100
  Besançon 7.121, 7.160, 7.216, 7.218, 7.220, 7.232
  and cerebral achromatopsia 7.187
  in cone–rod dystrophy 7.140
  Engelking–Trendelenberg 7.23, 7.218, 7.220
  in evaluating ophthalmic diseases 7.121
  Moreland 7.121
  Nagel 7.53, 12.393–5, 12.399, 12.405
    in colour vision tests 7.216, 7.218–9, 7.231
    and genetics 7.89–90
    in ophthalmic disease 7.121, 7.137, 7.148, 7.153
    in optic-nerve disease 7.174, 7.179, 7.191–2
    in Stargardt's disease 7.142, 7.144
  Neitz 7.121, 7.216, 7.219
  neutral adaptation 7.158
  Oculus 7.121
  in ophthalmic disease 7.119, 7.128
  Pickford–Nicolson 7.43, 7.121, 7.179, 7.216, 7.220
  projection 12.394
  in toxic optic neuropathy 7.161
  tuned 7.158
Anomaloscope matching ranges 7.43
Anomaloscopy 7.109, 7.149
Anomalous fusion 9.195–6

Anomalous movements 9.189
Anomalous pigment 2.78
Anomalous retinal correspondence 9.180–1
  clinical characteristics of 9.187–93
  clinical diagnosis of 9.193–6
  depth and breadth of 9.196
  implications of horopter results in 9.191–3
  multiple processes underlying 9.187
  spatial variability of retinal correspondence in 9.190–3
  temporal instability of 9.187–90
    and covariation 9.187–9
  theoretical basis of 9.180–1
Anomaly
  congenital 12.350
  colour 12.393
Anomia 12.274
  colour 12.215, 12.334, 12.336–7, 12.390–2, 12.398–9,
    12.406–8
    and achromatopsia 12.400
    and colour agnosia 12.403, 12.405
    and colour deficiencies 12.409–10
    disconnection hypothesis 12.408
    and pure alexia 12.343–6, 12.352, 12.354
    spatial orientation problems 12.407
  dissociated visual 12.347
  modality-specific 12.215
  object 12.336, 12.339, 12.407
    without alexia 12.346
  for photographed objects 12.336
  photographic 12.339
  and prosopagnosia 12.275
  and pure alexia 12.336
Anosodiaphoria 12.197
Anosognosia 12.148, 12.197, 12.441, 12.449–50
Anoxia 16.150
Anschauungsbilder, subjective optische (eidetic images) 12.470,
  12.475
Antagonism
  centre-surround 5.62
  cone 7.65–8
  lateral 5.45–6, 5.58, 5.60–1
  surround 5.60, 5.63, 5.71
Antennapedia complex 11.12, 11.14, 11.18, 11.40
Anterior lateral gyrus 4.362
  in visual cortex 3.309–10
Anterior medial lateral suprasylvian cortex 4.356–7
Anterior medial lateral suprasylvian visual area, Glossary
  explanation of 4.443
Anterograde tracing techniques 3.151
Anterolateral suprasylvian cortex 4.359–62
  area 20 4.359–60
  area 21 4.360
Anteromedian complex 8.184
Anti-aliasing 3.8–9, 3.27, 3.57
Antibodies
  E21 11.109
  e567 11.109
  monoclonal 11.74
Anti-caricature 14.114, 14.116

Anticipatory saccades **8.112, 8.114**
Anticonvulsants **7.152**
Antigens **3.85**
Antioncogenes **11.123**
Antioxidants **16.68**
Antiquity, alexia in **12.333**
Anti-saccades **8.102–3, 8.113, 8.244, 8.270, 8.304–5**
Anton's syndrome **12.197**
'Anwesenheit' phenomenon **12.299**
AO HRR plates **7.119, 7.179, 7.216, 7.221–2, 7.230–1**
AO HRR test **7.192–3, 7.232**
AOS, *see* Accessory optic system
Aotes trivirgatus (owl monkey) **3.15–6, 7.209**
APB, *see* 2-Amino-4-phophonobutyrate; 2-Amino-4-phosphonobutyric acid
Aperture
  aphakic **2.97**
  numerical **2.91–2, 2.96–7, 2.100, 2.102, 2.104, 2.110**
Aperture colours **4.332**
Aperture problem **14.40–1**
Apes **7.199**
  great **12.220, 12.330–1**
    language abilities **12.331**
    'reading' and 'writing' in **12.330–2**
APH (amino phosphonoheptanoic acid) **11.269**
Aphakes **16.2, 16.5, 16.29, 16.59**
  and ageing **16.151–2**
  and ageing retina **16.143**
  and light damage **16.65**
Aphakia **9.216, 16.94, 16.147**
  colorimetric procedure **5.283**
  correction of **1.126–7**
    contact lens **1.127**
    intraocular lens **1.127**
    spectacle, and the 'Jack-in-the-box' phenomenon **1.126**
  and intra-ocular lenses **1.114–5**
Aphakic eyes **5.282–3**
Aphakic space **2.414**
Aphasia **7.187, 12.179, 12.271, 12.274, 12.283**
  and alexia **12.333–4**
  amnesic **12.282, 12.284, 12.336–7**
    and colour anomia **12.406, 12.408**
    general **12.408**
  anomic **12.342**
    amnesic **12.334**
  Broca's **13.222**
  colour **12.398–9, 12.406–8**
    and achromatopsia **12.400**
    and colour agnosia **12.403, 12.405**
    and colour deficiencies **12.409**
    naming of 10 different colour tokens **12.408**
  common **12.406**
  comprehension deficits **12.282**
  conduction **12.128**
  fluent sensory (Wernicke) **12.282, 12.450**
  global **12.448**
  non-fluent **12.316, 12.333**
    Broca **12.282**
  optic **12.179, 12.208, 12.215, 12.336–7, 12.408**

  and pure alexia **12.345**
  and prosopagnosia **12.264, 12.275, 12.280–1**
  and semantic paralexia **12.328**
  sensory **12.336, 12.408**
  statistical analysis **12.338**
  transcortical **12.128**
  and word recognition **12.326–8**
  workup **12.339**
Apical dendrites, Glossary explanation of **4.443**
Aplysia **2.365–7, 2.372–3**
Apodization, Stiles–Crawford **1.16, 5.87–8**
Apogon brachygrammus (cardinal fish) **2.69**
Apolipoprotein-A-1 **11.197–8, 11.201, 11.211**
Apolipoprotein-E **11.211**
Apoplexy, cerebral **12.389–90**
Apparent distance bisection **9.78**
Apparent equidistant circle **9.78**
Apparent fronto-parallel plane **9.78**
Apparent motion **5.291, 5.298, 10.270, 10.272**
  on visual displays **15.20**
Apparent phase reversal (APR) **5.112**
Apperception **12.182–4, 12.187, 12.198, 12.211**
  of colour **12.405**
  focal disturbance **12.212–5**
  mechanisms **12.321**
Apraxia **12.274**
  constructional **12.373, 12.381, 12.414, 12.419, 12.425–6**
    and spatial hemineglect **12.457**
    and visual hemineglect **12.449**
    and visuo-spatial disorders **12.436, 12.440–4**
  dressing **12.271, 12.419, 12.425–7**
    and visual hemineglect **12.449**
    and visuo-spatial disorders **12.436**
  gaze **12.95, 12.435**
    optical **12.436**
  ideational **12.414, 12.450**
  ocular **12.216–7, 13.27–8**
  and prosopagnosia **12.275**
  and pure alexia **12.347**
  of the right hand **12.462**
  syndrome (Liepmann) **12.337**
APV (2-amino-5-phosphonovaleric acid) **11.260–1, 11.265–70**
Aquapendente, Fabricius ab **12.136**
Aqueous, and radiation **16.56, 16.58**
Aqueous humour, anterior chamber of **1.3**
Arachnata **2.341**
Arborization
  axonal **3.34–5, 3.38, 3.46, 3.211, 3.343–4, 11.236–9, 11.241–2, 11.246–51, 11.268**
  terminal **11.325**
Arbours
  terminal **11.91–2, 11.94–6, 11.99, 11.103–4**
    shifting of **11.105–8**
ARC, *see* Anomalous retinal correspondence
Archistriatum **2.426**
Architectonics, Glossary explanation of **4.443**
Architecture of cognition **15.104–6**
Architeuthis (giant squid) **2.376**

Arcus senilis **16**.143
Area 7a **4**.412
Area 17 **4**.101–2, **4**.410, **4**.443
  Glossary explanation of **4**.444
Area 17 cells **4**.191, **4**.194–8
Area 17 complex cells **4**.198–9
Area 17 simple cells **4**.198
Area 18 **4**.101–2
  Glossary explanation of **4**.443–4
  see also V2
Area 18 cells **4**.191, **4**.199
  dynamic depth sensitivity of **4**.199–201
  position disparity of **4**.199
Area 19, Glossary explanation of **4**.444
Area 19 cells **4**.199
  position disparity of **4**.199
Area 20a, Glossary explanation of **4**.444
Area 21a, Glossary explanation of **4**.444
Area calcarina **12**.342, **12**.391
Area centralis **8**.7
  amacrine cells **3**.42, **3**.44, **3**.48
  and binocular vision **2**.271–2, **2**.278
  bipolar cells **3**.36, **3**.38
  dendritic fields at **3**.103
  in evolution of retina **2**.143–4
  in evolution of vision **2**.411
  fovea homologue **3**.115–6
  and functional organization of retina **3**.6, **3**.11
  ganglion cells **3**.50, **3**.56
  Glossary explanation of **4**.443
  horizontal cells **3**.39
  and ipsilateral projection **3**.110, **3**.112
  in mammals **2**.476
  primate **3**.15
  and retinal development **3**.78, **3**.118
  and retinal expansion **3**.105, **3**.107–8
  and retinofugal pathways **3**.130
  in visual cortex **3**.310
  and visual pathways **2**.428, **2**.443, **2**.455
  and visual thalamus **3**.182
Area MT **4**.374
Area PG, visual properties of neurones in **4**.378
Area striata **12**.48–50, **12**.75, **12**.345, **12**.391
  geometrical organization **12**.178
  partial lesion of **12**.405
  and pure alexia **12**.356
Argon **16**.12–3, **16**.19, **16**.21
Aristostomias scintillans (deep-sea fish) **2**.88
Aristotle **12**.25–9, **12**.218, **12**.289, **12**.298, **12**.386, **12**.468–9
Arithmetic, operations **12**.335
AR-L 115 BS **7**.134–5
Arrangement tests **7**.118–9, **7**.176
  in cerebral hemisphere lesions **7**.192
  in cone–rod dystrophy **7**.140
  desaturated **7**.160
  in diabetes **7**.151
  in DIOA **7**.155, **7**.157
  in glaucoma **7**.152
  in hemiachromatopsia **7**.185

  and Köllner's rule **7**.174–5
  in ophthalmic disease **7**.124–8, **7**.135
  in retinitis pigmentosa **7**.144
  in Stargardt's disease **7**.143
Arrays
  axon **11**.148
  bipolar
    spatial sampling characteristics **3**.36
    two-dimensional **3**.38
  cone **3**.38
    regularity of **3**.21
  dendritic **11**.148, **11**.150
  detector **5**.66, **5**.68
  disorder **5**.54
  extrafoveal cone **3**.22
  foveal cone **3**.20
  ganglion cell **3**.30, **3**.57
  of hypercolumns **5**.73
  neural sampling **5**.72
  orthogonal **2**.249, **2**.254, **11**.210
  peripheral cone **5**.54
  photoreceptor **3**.4, **3**.19, **3**.57–8, **5**.72
    as postreceptoral mechanism **3**.30
    spatial sampling by **3**.16–24
  pixel **5**.72
  postreceptoral neuronal **3**.30
  receptor **5**.91–2
  rod **3**.38
  rod bipolar **3**.38
  sampling **2**.263, **2**.266–7, **3**.31, **5**.71
    cone **3**.16–7
    in fovea **3**.18–9
    photoreceptor **3**.16, **3**.25
  short-wave cone **5**.91
  spectral sampling **3**.29
Arrestin **6**.103
Arrhenius equation **16**.47
Art, styles **12**.356
Artery
  cerebral, calcarine, splenial and mesial temporal
      branches **12**.344
  posterior cerebral **12**.390, **12**.394
    and colour agnosia **12**.404
    and hemiachromatopsia **12**.401–2
    illusion and hallucination **12**.473
    lesions **12**.342, **12**.354
    and loss of topographical familiarity **12**.427
    right **12**.260
    and topographagnosia **12**.422–4
  vertebral–basilar **12**.473
Arthropodization **2**.213
Arthropods
  compound eye and optic lobe **2**.341–60
  history of vision **2**.220–2
  optic lobe **2**.203–24
  origins **2**.213–4
Artificial intelligence **4**.246
  computational approach to **4**.246
Artificial retinal image stabilization **8**.316

Arts, visual **12**.16
Ascending tract of Deiters **8**.216
Aspartate
  in visual cortex **3**.311
  in visual cortex neurogenesis **3**.369
  in visual thalamus **3**.183–5, **3**.192
L-Aspartate, Glossary explanation of **4**.443
Aspheric lenses **1**.69–71
  'blended lenticular' type **1**.70
  and conic surfaces **1**.69
  polynomial front surfaces of **1**.70
Aspheric surface **2**.96
Asphericity **2**.109
  of spectacles **1**.422–3
Asphericity parameter (*Q*), and relationship with shape factor
    and eccentricity **1**.3
Assay
  Bonhoeffer choice **11**.99, **11**.102
  enzymatic, and neurotransmitters **11**.354
  in vitro **11**.89, **11**.96, **11**.99–101
Assimilation **10**.290, **10**.293–4
  see also Colour assimilation
Association, multimodal visuo-tactile **12**.337
Association pathways **3**.326, **3**.335–6, **3**.340, **3**.342, **3**.344,
    3.346, **3**.348, **3**.350–1
Astereognosia **12**.449
Asthenia, gaze **12**.452
Asthenopia
  in aniseikonia **1**.170–1
  anisometropic **1**.179
  cerebral **12**.148, **12**.271
  functional **15**.55
  ocular **15**.55
Astigmatism **1**.53, **1**.56, **1**.247, **2**.98, **2**.111, **5**.128, **5**.130,
    10.180, **13**.49, **16**.123
  against-the-rule **1**.31, **1**.45–6
    explanation of **1**.400–1
  changes in, with advancing age **1**.45
  correction of **1**.61
    by toric contact lenses **1**.111–2
  explanation of **1**.400
  following surgery **1**.49–50
  inherent
    incisions for **1**.143–7
      circumferential relaxing **1**.145–6
      combined radial and circumferential relaxing **1**.146–7
      other **1**.147
      wedge **1**.147
    sutures for **1**.143–7
      removal of **1**.144–5
  irregular, correction of, using a hard contact lens **1**.138
  and the keratometer **1**.379–80
  oblique **1**.11–3, **1**.18, **1**.376, **2**.94, **2**.97, **5**.81–3, **5**.90
    lens design for the control of **1**.66–8
  post-keratoplasty **1**.144
  and refractive error **1**.31
  regular, correction of, using asymmetrical incisions
      combined with sutures **1**.138
  with-the-rule **1**.31

explanation of **1**.400
Astrocytes **11**.30–1, **11**.34–5
  and axon growth **11**.244
  cell lineage **11**.43
  and compartments **11**.42
  in fovea **3**.114, **3**.117
  in neuronal cytoskeleton **11**.277, **11**.297
  in optic nerve regeneration **11**.206–9
  and proto-oncogenes **11**.114
  in regeneration **11**.198
  in retinal development **3**.81, **3**.84, **3**.86, **3**.90
Astronauts, flash perception **12**.411
Astronomical telescopes **1**.330
Astronomy and hyperacuity **10**.87–8
Asymbolia **12**.187
Asymmetric disparity, presentation of **9**.115–7
Asymmetric matching **6**.50
Asymmetric motion-in-depth after-effects **9**.152
Asymmetrical fixation, effect of, within the visual
    plane **9**.25–6
Asymmetry **5**.274
  dynamic **12**.229
  functional cerebral **12**.232
  hemispheric **5**.266, **12**.232
  of human face **12**.226
  left–right **12**.229, **12**.238–9, **12**.437
  nasotemporal **3**.5–6, **3**.14, **3**.16, **5**.128–9, **10**.197
  of optokinesis **8**.51–2, **8**.64
  of smooth pursuit **8**.213, **8**.306
  of vestibulo-ocular reflex **8**.299
  visual field **5**.271–2
    in face processing **12**.231
Ataxia
  and hemiachromatopsia **12**.402
  optic **12**.206, **12**.217, **12**.336, **12**.451–2, **13**.28–9
    and pure alexia **12**.344
  visuomotor **12**.451, **13**.28–9
Ateles (spider monkey) **7**.208–9
Atrophy
  gyrate **7**.131
    and the Stiles–Crawford effect of the first kind **1**.297,
      1.302
Atropine
  in accommodation elimination **1**.41
  and cycloplegia **1**.399
Attention
  control of spatially directed **12**.464
  deficit **12**.189, **12**.191
  fluctuating **12**.215
  focal **12**.463
  and gaze control **8**.73, **8**.277
  in infants **10**.198
  mechanisms **12**.115–6, **12**.371
  motor **12**.463
  object-directed **12**.80
  and saccade dynamics **8**.102–3
  and saccadic initiation **8**.114, **8**.282, **8**.284, **8**.289, **8**.304
  shifts in **12**.464
  and smooth pursuit **8**.79, **8**.86, **8**.147–9

Attention (*continued*)
 spatial disturbance of **12**.217
 spatially directed **12**.80, **12**.435
 visual **10**.117, **10**.132, **12**.437
 and visual evoked potentials **12**.240–1, **12**.247
 and visual movement agnosia **12**.365, **12**.377
 visual spatial **12**.462
 and voluntary control **9**.100
Attentional deficit hyperactivity disorder **13**.266
Attentional disorders **13**.271
Attentional mechanisms, development of **13**.50
Attentional shifts **10**.196–8
Attentive fixation **4**.378, **4**.380–1, **4**.384
 Glossary explanation of **4**.443
 modulation of excitability by **4**.380–1
Attenuation
 characteristic functions **5**.172
 and contrast **5**.106–7, **5**.109, **5**.115
 and deLange functions **5**.178
 multiplicative **5**.116
 optical **5**.116
 in silent substitution **5**.176
 in visual processing **5**.25
Attractor states **11**.303
Audible sound emissions, from visual-display terminals **15**.5
Auditory biofeedback, in reduction of myopia **1**.270
Auditory cortex **4**.301
Auditory displays **15**.119–20
Auditory responses, from the superior colliculus **8**.251
Auditory stimuli, for saccades **8**.102, **8**.250
Auditory tones **15**.120
Augustinus, Aurelius **12**.28
Aura
 visual
  epileptic **12**.479
  phenomena **12**.479
Australopithecines **12**.16, **12**.52, **12**.332
Australopithecus **12**.220
Autism **12**.2
Autocatalysis **11**.48–55, **11**.58, **11**.62–5
 oscillating reactions **11**.303
Autocorrelation functions, of visual evoked
  potentials **12**.242–4
Autocorrelation theory **2**.251
Autokinesis **12**.369
Autopsy **12**.180
 and agnosia **12**.207
 and alexia **12**.334, **12**.344
 findings of alexia patient **12**.335
 and hemialexia **12**.350
 and prosopagnosia **12**.260, **12**.264, **12**.277
 and pure alexia **12**.342–4, **12**.354
Autoradiography **3**.182, **3**.330, **5**.254, **7**.105, **11**.89
 [³H]-thymidine **3**.78, **3**.80, **11**.262, **11**.357–8, **11**.361
  in visual cortex neurogenesis **3**.360, **3**.363–5
 tritiated thymidine **2**.432
Autoscopy, *see* Heautoscopy
Autostereograms **1**.333, **9**.40
Autostereoscopy, raster **1**.332

Autotopagnosia **12**.440
Average evoked potentials **12**.125
Averaging saccadic responses **8**.121
Averroes **12**.28
Avicenna **12**.26, **12**.28–9
Axes
 horizontal and vertical **14**.52–3, **14**.59, **14**.61, **14**.64, **14**.66
 optic **3**.5–6, **3**.14, **3**.20, **3**.56, **10**.173
 systems of **8**.20–1, **8**.66, **8**.216, **8**.320
 visual **3**.2, **3**.5–6, **3**.56
Axial aniseikonia **9**.215–6
Axial length, measurement of, by x-ray methods **1**.362–3
Axo-axonal contacts, Glossary explanation of **4**.443
Axon
 collaterals **12**.129
 conduction **12**.127–8
 degeneration **12**.129, **12**.275
  and metamorphopsia **12**.275
 development of terminals **12**.19
 local sprouting of terminals **12**.133
 myelinization **12**.19
 projection sites
  of afferent optic tract **12**.60
  of retinal ganglion cell **12**.61
 sprouting **12**.19
Axon terminals, modulation of $GABA_B$ release from bipolar
  cells **4**.3–4
Axonal collaterals, Glossary explanation of **4**.443
Axonal transport techniques
 and tracer injection **4**.267–9
  with [³H]-proline **4**.268–9
  with horseradish peroxidase **4**.268
  with rhodamine **4**.268
Axons **7**.158, **7**.163
 active **11**.94–5
 activity **11**.90, **11**.96
  effects of **11**.242
 activity-deprived **11**.94, **11**.99
 arborization **11**.236–9, **11**.241–2, **11**.246–51, **11**.268
 arbour remodelling **3**.129
 behaviour in *in vitro* assays **11**.96
 cellular composition of environment **11**.207–9
 chronotopic order **11**.102–3
 collateralizing **11**.236
 collaterals **11**.237
 competition **11**.239–41, **11**.250–1
 correct targeting **11**.95
 corticofugal **11**.237
 course correction **11**.92, **11**.97
 in critical period plasticity **11**.290
 and dendrites **11**.156, **11**.158–61
 development in embryos **11**.97–9
 electrical activity **11**.248, **11**.251
 extrafascicular **11**.105–8
 'follower' **11**.233–4
 ganglion cell **11**.68, **11**.70
 geniculo-cortical **4**.267–8
 glial environment of **11**.243–7
 growth **11**.70–4

Axons (*continued*)
  after brain damage 11.247–51
  blocking 11.247–51
  in vitro 11.99–102
  in vitro assays 11.89
  modes 11.232–9, 11.242–3, 11.247–9, 11.251
  in neuronal cytoskeleton 11.293, 11.295, 11.297, 11.303
  role of GAP-43 11.219–21, 11.223, 11.225–9
  and synaptic rearrangements 11.257
 guidance 3.134–6, 11.70, 11.108
 high degree of target selectivity of embryonic 11.98
 injured spinal and brain 11.207
 injury 11.207, 11.209–12, 11.241
 injury response 11.232
 LGN 11.287
 mammalian optic 11.197, 11.200
 matrix 11.191
 in mature retina 3.130–1
 microtubules 11.133–7
 misrouted 11.91–5
 myelinated 3.187, 3.197, 11.209, 11.246
 nasal, in fish and chick 11.100–1
 neurofilaments 11.144
 neuronal cytoskeleton 11.276–9, 11.284, 11.293
 new 11.103, 11.108–9
 new ganglion cell 11.103
 optic
   and GAP-43 11.223–4
   goldfish 11.194–5, 11.198, 11.200–1, 11.221
   in neuronal cytoskeleton 11.295–6, 11.298
 in optic nerve regeneration 11.206–7
 order 11.103–5
 outgrowth 3.129, 3.132, 3.134–7, 11.191–6, 11.198,
   11.200–1
 pathfinding 11.108–9
 pathways 11.90, 11.92, 11.95, 11.97
 phase of exploratory growth 11.91
 pioneer 3.134, 11.180, 11.233–4, 11.325

 plasticity 11.232–51
   after brain injury 11.247–51
   brain damage and development 11.241–7
   competitive interactions in projections 11.239–41
   optic tract 11.232–9
 preferential selection of target oriented branches 11.92
 pruning 11.250
 regeneration 11.90, 11.108–9, 11.210–3
   extending critical age for 11.248–50
   in goldfish 11.190–9, 11.297
   intratectal path 11.91–4
   responses 11.100
   retinal 11.91–7
   and synaptic rearrangements 11.257
 remodelling 11.237
 remyelination 11.211
 retinal ganglion cell, and GAP-43 11.220, 11.224
 in retinal transplantation 11.314, 11.316, 11.320–1,
   11.323–5
 retinofugal 3.132–4, 3.136, 3.138–9, 3.141, 11.232, 11.236,
   11.240–1, 11.243, 11.250
 retinogeniculate 11.238
 retinotectal 11.245
 see also Collaterals
 stabilization 11.289
 in synaptic rearrangement 11.265, 11.269, 11.271
 systems 11.251
 target selection 11.108
 target-directed 11.92, 11.97
 trajectories 3.343–4, 3.346
 in visual thalamus 3.177, 3.180–1, 3.183–9, 3.191–7,
   3.199–202, 3.206–7
Axoplasma flow 11.191, 12.130–1
Axotomy 11.193, 11.196–7, 11.200, 12.128–32
 in neuronal cytoskeleton 11.293
 and retinal transplantation 11.316, 11.323

B

Babies, and face recognition **12**.237
Background activity
  intrinsic **5**.30
  random neural **5**.30
Background illuminance **5**.63–4
Background level, continuous **5**.23
Background luminance, continuous **5**.23–4, **5**.32
Background noise **2**.410, **2**.413–4
Background retinal illuminance **5**.61
Backgrounds **2**.261, **12**.466
  and colour vision **2**.300
  dappled **2**.306–8, **2**.316
  flickering **5**.56
  and saccade dynamics **8**.102–3
  and smooth pursuit **8**.148–9, **8**.233
  visual **12**.411, **12**.415
  in visual processing **2**.239, **2**.254–5, **2**.257
Backlight irradiance **2**.409
Back-propagation **14**.93
Backscattering **1**.395, **2**.407–9
Baclofen **4**.4
Bacteriorhodopsin **2**.39, **2**.44, **6**.65
Badal optometer **1**.235
Badal principle **1**.236
Baglioni striated glass test **9**.195
Bailey-Lovie charts, logMAR scale of **1**.215
Bailey's method **1**.199
Balfour's theory **2**.31, **2**.35
Balfour's theory of eye embryology **11**.396–400
Bálint–Holmes syndrome **12**.217, **12**.359, **12**.462
Bálint's syndrome **10**.279, **12**.212, **12**.418, **12**.427, **13**.23
Band magnifiers **1**.427
  see also Magnifiers, measuring
Band-pass filtering **6**.201, **6**.204–7
Bandwidth **10**.35
  disparity-tuning **5**.143
  in edge detection **5**.103
  Gaussian noise **5**.25
  Glossary explanation of **4**.443–4
  masked contrast sensitivity function **5**.102
  in motion perception **5**.154–5
  sampling array **3**.29
  spatial **3**.16–8, **3**.20, **3**.24, **3**.30–1, **3**.57, **5**.46
  spatial frequency **10**.67, **10**.145, **10**.174
  spectral **2**.6, **2**.11, **3**.29, **5**.50
Bandwidth estimation **5**.101–2, **5**.314–5
  compound grating **5**.101
  fourth power transform **5**.102
  power law transform **5**.102
  simple grating **5**.101
  square law stages **5**.102
  square of signal grating's contrast **5**.102
  threshold ratio **5**.101–2
Bandwidth orientation **10**.68
  and size tuning **5**.122
Bandwidth-proportional-to-peak rule **5**.141–2
Bar, motion-defined **10**.167

Bar and flat-field magnifiers **1**.202
  solid hemicylindrical **1**.202
  solid hemispherical **1**.202
Bárány test **8**.19–20
Barrier avoidance **2**.153–6, **2**.158–60, **2**.162–3
'Barrier' hypothesis **3**.90
Basal dendrites, Glossary explanation of **4**.444
Basal ganglia
  and control of reflexes **8**.39
  effects of lesions **8**.314
  and saccades **8**.267–76
  in visual function, and effects of lesions in **4**.401–5
Base out prism distortion **9**.213
Basic reflex neurological control **1**.251
Basilar pontine nucleus **8**.211
Basket cell neurones, Glossary explanation of **4**.448
Basket cells **3**.258, **3**.260, **3**.262, **3**.265, **3**.289–90
  see also Cortical cells
Bates's system of relaxation, in refractive error **1**.42
Bats **2**.145, **2**.451, **2**.458
Battle's Culture-free Self-esteem Inventory **13**.201
Bayesian classifier **14**.85
Bayesian estimator **14**.92
Bayesian framework in computer vision **14**.86
Bayes's rule **14**.84–5, **14**.94
BBZ, *see* 'Blob-bounded zones'
B-cells, Glossary explanation of **4**.450
Beads, rosary **12**.306
Beans, marked **12**.306
Beats, visual **12**.164–5
Bee
  celestial compass **2**.265
  colour vision **2**.285, **2**.287–8, **2**.294, **2**.297–9, **2**.301–2
  eidetic image **2**.262
  visual discrimination **2**.261
  visual illusion **2**.263
  visual processing **2**.255, **2**.261
Behaviour **2**.260
  detour **2**.158–60, **2**.163
  graphomotor **12**.315
  visually directed **2**.390–1
Behavioural studies **10**.183–5
Behavioural tests, for non-human primates **7**.205–7, **7**.209–12
Bell, Charles **12**.218, **12**.364, **12**.371
Berengario da Carpi, Jacopo **12**.34
Berkeley, George **12**.17, **12**.43
Berkeley Colour Threshold test **7**.229
Bernhard, Thomas **12**.318
Besançon anomalometer, *see* Anomaloscope
Best's disease, and the Stiles–Crawford effect of the first kind **1**.297
β-Galactosidase **11**.32
β-Tubulin **11**.135–6, **11**.194
β-Wave **12**.166
Bezold–Brücke shift **6**.281
Bias **5**.9, **5**.13
  focusing **5**.84
  intrinsic **5**.16

Bias (*continued*)
   judgmental 5.21
   orientational 5.266, 5.270–1
   in pattern processing 14.4
   and senescence 5.280
   space-order 5.21
   time-order 5.21
Bicuculline, Glossary explanation of 4.444
Bifocal lenses 1.71–2
   fused 1.71
   solid 1.71
Bifoveal fixation 9.193
Bilateral labyrinthectomy, effect on optokinesis 8.56
Bilirubin 16.114, 16.116, 16.128
Binary hue, CIE definition of 6.225
Binary relations 14.53
Binocular competition 10.218
Binocular control, unstable, in dyslexia 13.141–7
Binocular co-ordination 9.126
Binocular correlation, and neurontropy 9.66–7
Binocular correspondence
   Glossary explanation of 4.444
   least course 6.213–4
Binocular cortical cells 9.180–1
Binocular depth-sensitive cells 4.198
Binocular disparities 6.193, 8.9, 8.158–60, 9.76, 9.139, 9.203,
      10.135, 10.160
   effective 9.76
   functions of ocular dominance columns in 4.273–4
   Glossary explanation of 4.450
Binocular eye movements 8.9, 8.75, 8.157–72, 9.2–3
Binocular facilitation 9.182
Binocular fixation 9.125
Binocular function
   development of 13.49–50
   and plasticity 13.48–9
Binocular fusion 6.213–4, 8.9, 8.158, 8.168, 8.330, 9.19–37,
      9.93, 9.211–8, 9.224
   clinical tests of 9.217–8
      correlogram 9.217–8
      cyclofusion 9.217
      red glass 9.217
      space eikonometer 9.217
      stimulus for 9.211–7
   functions of ocular dominance columns in 4.273
   and the horopter 9.19–37
   with a moving head 9.121–36
   suppression theory of 9.93
Binocular fusion theories 2.446
Binocular instability 13.183–5
   use of monocular occlusion in 13.183
Binocular instruments 1.330
   astronomical telescope 1.330
   hand-held binoculars 1.330
      astronomical 1.330
      Galilean 1.330
   low-power stereo microscopes 1.330
   stereoscopic rangefinders 1.330
Binocular matching, *see* Haploscopic matching

Binocular motion suppression 5.240
Binocular only cells, Glossary explanation of 4.444
Binocular optokinesis 8.52
Binocular organization 5.33–4
Binocular overlap 2.271, 2.275, 2.436, 2.442–3
   and visual pathways 2.448, 2.455
Binocular parallax 9.76
   effective 9.76
Binocular perimetry 9.202
Binocular processing, cyclopean level of 9.40–1
Binocular retinal correspondence 9.179–96
Binocular rivalry 6.213–4, 9.93–110, 9.197
   attributed to attention 9.93
   definition of 9.95–6
   functions of ocular dominance columns in 4.273
   induction of 9.94–5
   ocular dominance during 9.198
Binocular sensory disorders 9.179–223
Binocular space perception 9.75–92
   processes underlying distortions 9.90
Binocular stereodepth perception 12.465
Binocular summation 9.176, 9.181–2
Binocular suppression 10.219
Binocular vision 2.435–6, 2.443, 2.446
   correcting lenses for 1.163–82
   disorders of 9.151
   evolution of 2.271–81
   functional 2.271–5
   and infants 9.170
   mammals 2.274–6
   organization 2.280–1
   in relation to stereoscopic instruments and three-
         dimensional displays and images 1.326–44
   spatial relationships in 1.329
   and stereopsis, development of 9.170–8
   and visual pathways 2.455
Binocular visual direction
   definition of 9.19
   and the horopter 9.19–24
   laws of 9.7
Binocular visual space
   geometry of 9.81–2
   models of 9.83
Binocularity, primitive 9.175
Binocularly perceived motion 9.133
Binocularly rivalling stimuli 9.172
Binoculars, hand held 1.330
Biofeedback, in refractive error 1.41–2
Bio-illuminescence
   in fish 6.112
      blue emitting 6.113
      red emitting 6.113
   see also Bioluminescence
Biological clock 2.18, 2.33, 2.35
Biology
   developmental 2.136–7
   evolutionary 2.137
   global behaviour in 11.304
Bioluminescence 2.12, 2.68, 2.414

and dioptrics 2.86–7
in evolution of vision 2.409–10
in photoreception 2.374, 2.381
see also Bio-illuminescence
Biometry
 ocular 1.133
 ultrasonic 1.133
Biomicroscopy 7.116
 and polarized light 1.323
 slit-lamp 1.330, 16.99
Biophysics of computation 14.39–40
Bipartite field 5.37–8, 5.42, 10.173
Bipedal position 12.124
Bipolar cells 4.318–9, 4.330–1
 broad band 6.173–4
 cone connectivity of 6.137–9
 Glossary explanation of 4.444
 midgets 6.170
 narrow band 6.173
 off- 6.164, 6.166
 off-centre 6.166, 6.170
 on- 6.164, 6.166
 on-centre 6.166, 6.170
 presynaptic GABA$_B$ inhibition at 4.3–4
 in the primate fovea 6.170
 see also Bipolars
 segregation of on-and off-responses in separate populations
  of 4.2–3
 and spatial antagonism 6.165
Bipolar neurones, Glossary explanation of 4.448
Bipolar terminals, synaptic inputs and outputs at 4.4
Bipolars 7.65–9, 7.77
 see also Bipolar cells
Biquantization of faces 14.108, 14.110
Birds 2.72–3
 binocular vision 2.271–3, 2.276–7, 2.280
 colour vision 2.286–9, 2.291–2, 2.295–6, 2.298–9,
  2.302
 dioptrics 2.86–7, 2.89, 2.94, 2.98, 2.110
 diurnal 2.77–8, 2.287, 2.292
 diving 2.85
 in evolution of retina 2.142–3, 2.146–7
 eye embryology of 11.394
 nocturnal 2.470
 recognition of silhouettes 12.274
 visual pathways 2.421–36, 2.442
Birefringence 1.310–25
 of the cornea 1.313, 1.317–8
 and dichroism 1.319–22
 due to the crystalline structure of the lens 1.318–9
 form 1.312
 lenticular 1.4
 macular 1.9, 1.320
 of the ocular media 1.312–3
 in relation to optical elements of the human eye 1.310
Bisection acuity 5.221, 5.223, 5.230–1, 9.203
 in localization modelling 14.16
 and location 14.9, 14.11
 and separation 14.12

in temporal integration 14.14
and visual mechanisms 14.13
Bistable saccadic responses 8.121
Bithorax complex 11.8, 11.12, 11.14, 11.57
Bivariate contour ellipse area 8.77
Black body 16.17, 16.21
 emitters 16.1, 16.6–7, 16.18, 16.20
Blank (catch) trials 5.16–7, 5.203–4
Bleaching 5.56, 5.67, 5.196
 in diabetes 7.149–50
 effects on foveal colour matches 7.14
 in monochromacy 7.24–5
 retinal 7.21
Blicklähmung, seelische (gaze apraxia) 12.435
Blickschwäche (gaze asthenia) 12.452
Blind spot 1.349, 12.137–8, 12.146, 12.152–3
 filling-in 12.142
 and migraine 12.176
 and phosphenes 12.162
Blindness 2.456–7, 12.31, 12.47
 and ageing macula 16.76–7, 16.86–7
 and agnosia 12.188, 12.202, 12.209, 12.212
 from AMD 16.145–7
  prevalence of 16.138–9
 auditory signals for 12.433
 cerebral 7.193–4
 colour 7.88–9, 7.91–2, 7.95–6, 12.184
  acquired 12.388
  amnesic 12.179, 12.406, 12.408
  congenital total 12.386, 12.388
  cortical 5.238, 12.392–3
  partial 12.389
  peripheral 12.391
  total 12.390, 12.392
   acquired 12.391
 complete 12.149–50
  and topographagnosia 12.421, 12.423
 cortical 7.190–1, 12.48–9, 12.136–57
  and agnosia 12.179
  and heautoscopy 12.303
  and hemiachromatopsia 12.402
  illusion and hallucination 12.479–80
  negation or unawareness of 12.148
  post-trauma 12.390
  and pure alexia 12.337
  recovery from 12.409
  spontaneous visual sensations 12.155–7
  and visual movement agnosia 12.379
 day 7.24
 denial of 12.197
 and developing visual system 16.114
 early human 11.376
 effect on eye movements 8.299, 8.302–3
 and heautoscopy 12.301
 letter 12.333, 12.336
 and light damage 16.66
 mind, *see* Agnosia, visual
 motion, *see* Agnosia, visual movement
 night 7.125–6, 7.144, 7.148, 16.157

Blindness (*continued*)
  from outer retinal degeneration 11.332
  and prosopagnosia 12.259
  psychic, *see Seelenblindheit*
  pure word 12.333
  registry data (US) 16.138, 16.146
  snow 16.29
  statutory definition of 1.184
  word 12.336
Blindsight 10.272–3, 12.148–54, 12.380
  oculomotor effects 12.153
  semantic 12.355
Blinks, eyelid 12.370
Blinks and saccades 8.304
'Blob-bounded zones' 4.304–5
  Glossary explanation of 4.444
Blobs 3.349, 6.187–8, 7.69–70, 12.12
  and colour deficiencies 12.409
  and colour perception 12.83–4
  and contour perception 12.81
  cytochrome oxidase 2.313, 2.453, 2.458, 3.308, 3.317–8
  elongated 5.121
  regions 12.68–9
  see also Cytochrome oxidase blobs
Bloch's law 5.56, 6.152, 10.44
Blood flow, in extraocular muscle 8.182
Blood vessels 3.86
'Blue light hazard' 1.9
Blue-sensitive mechanism
  anatomy and physiology 7.73–7
  photopigments and photoreceptors 7.72–3
  psychophysics 7.77–85
  vulnerability of 7.72–87
Blur 2.94–5, 2.166, 2.231, 5.120
  in accommodation and vergence 10.187
  in amblyopia 10.229–31
  circles 2.105, 2.232
  and equiluminance 5.236
  and equiluminous image 5.244
  Gaussian 5.230
  ground-glass 5.230
  and hyperacuity 5.227, 5.230, 10.88, 10.90, 10.93
  and illusions 5.242
  intrinsic 5.230
  motion 5.153
  optical 5.88, 7.53, 10.203
    in hyperacuity 10.91, 10.95–6, 10.98, 10.101, 10.109
    in infants 10.203
  and prosopagnosia 12.270
  retinal 5.83
  selective 5.92
  spectacle 5.230
  texture and stereo depth 5.124–5, 5.128
Blur detectability 1.241
Blur and face recognition 14.108
Blur signals, generation of 1.256
Bode plots 1.243
Boder Test of Reading–Spelling Patterns 13.121, 13.123–6, 13.128–9

  reliability studies of 13.125–6
  validity studies of 13.126–8
    auditory event-related potentials 13.126
    dichotic listening task 13.126
    EEG 13.127–9
    electrophysiological 13.126–7
    hemispheric time sharing 13.126, 13.128
    Stanford Achievement Test and 13.126
    time to speech compression task 13.126
Bodian Silver stain 11.89–90
Body
  concept of our own 12.411
  doubled 12.449
  ritualized movements of 12.307
Body gestures, socially relevant 12.125
Body image 12.416
  somatosensory 12.297–8
Body language 12.16, 12.219–20, 12.294, 12.296
Body movements, whole 12.341
Body parts 12.341, 12.467
Body position 12.124
Body shapes 12.389
Boerhaave, Hermann 12.46, 12.434
Bond
  covalent 16.33–4, 16.38, 16.40
  ionic 16.33
'Bootstrapping' 14.64
Border contrast 12.398–9
  Mach's 12.397
Border contrast enhancement 12.397
Borders
  achromatic 5.209
  chromatic 5.236–7, 5.245, 5.247–8
  and equiluminance 5.236, 5.239
  illumination 5.234
  luminance 5.236–7
  material 5.234
  perception 5.197
  in peripheral vision 5.50
  shadow 5.234, 5.248
  tritanopic 5.242
  and wavelengths 5.213–4
Borelli, Gian Alfonzo (Giovanni Alphonso) 12.40
Bottleneck theory 2.435
Botulinum toxin 8.191
Botulism type B, and accommodation anomalies 1.272
Bouillaud, J.B. 12.47
Boundary detection 5.38
Boveri's theory of eye embryology 11.399–400
Bowman's layer 16.59
Bowman's membrane 2.470, 2.473, 16.55
Boyle, Robert 2.306–8
Bradycardia 12.201
Braille alphabet 1.185
Brain
  activity and perception 12.21–4
  area entorhinalis 12.287–8
  axonal myelinization during postnatal development 12.288
  connectionist ideas 12.336

Brain (*continued*)
  damage and development 11.241–51
  and developing visual system 16.118–20
  and eye 2.237
  focal damage 12.186
  hominid
    phylogenesis 12.287
    size of 12.287
  human, phylogenetic development 12.287
  imaging 12.345
    techniques 12.260
  lesioned patients and visual object recognition 12.107
  lesions 3.330, 12.127–35
    axon arborization after 11.250–1
    of cortical grey matter 12.132–5
    filling-in effects 12.134–5
    plasticity of cortical neuronal circuits 12.132–5
    retrograde degeneration after axotomy 12.129–32
    see also Lesions, brain
    telephone network 12.127–9
  localization theories 12.29, 12.46–7
  maturation 11.288
  medial temporo-occipital infarction 12.425
  neocortical structures developed during hominid
      phylogenesis 12.287
  neuropathology 12.264–5
  occipito-temporal areas 12.467
  organization and development 11.304–6
  and origins of eye 2.53–5
  plasticity 11.288, 11.306–7
  postnatal development 11.282
  postnatal maturation 12.288
  primate 12.359
  simple 3.304–5, 3.319
  slices, standardized anatomical 12.344
  split- 12.352, 12.357, 12.410
  surgery, open 12.168
  tumour 12.199
  visual 12.356
  and visual pathways 2.442–3
Brain and computational vision 14.40
Brain and visual perception 14.19–20
Brainstem 3.200–1, 3.205, 8.200–23, 12.52, 12.63, 12.478
  anatomical organization 8.200–2
  and blindsight 12.154
  burst neurones 8.97, 8.206, 8.208–11, 8.258, 8.325–6
  electrical stimulation of human 12.167
  injury 12.281
  motor neurones 8.175–99, 8.202–5
    behaviour during saccades 8.205
    hysteresis 8.203
    position and velocity sensitivity 8.203
  and optokinesis 8.214
  in pursuit system 2.172–3, 2.176, 2.179–89, 2.191
  saccade generator 8.96–7, 8.206–11
    models 8.209–11
  see also under individual nuclei
  and smooth pursuit 8.153–4, 8.211–5
  and vergence 8.218–9

  and vestibulo-ocular reflex 8.216–8
  and visual data processing 12.78
  and visual pathways 2.423, 2.425, 2.429–30, 2.455, 2.459
Brainstem nuclei 3.194–5
Branchiopoda 2.222
Brightness 5.199, 5.202, 6.43–5
  and achromatopsia 12.394–5, 12.400
  CIE definition of 6.225
  discrimination 12.203
  enhancement effect, Brücke–Bartley 12.397–8
  and equiluminance 5.246
  and flicker 5.171, 5.173
  and illusions 5.242
  and luminance 6.48–9
  matching 5.173–4
  perceived 5.108
  in peripheral vision 5.47, 5.49–50
  and stimulus intensity 12.8
Brightness contrast, in character identification 15.28–9
Brightness discrimination 3.204
Brilliance 6.47
British Ability Scales, Matrices and Similarities
      sub-tests 13.182, 13.197–8
Broad fields 5.290
Broadband stimuli 1.252
Broca, Paul 12.333
Broca–Sulzer effect 5.115
Broca's aphasia 13.222
Broca's speech area 12.287–8, 12.356
Brodmann, Korbinian 12.50
Brodmann areas 12.462
Brodmann areas 39 and 40 12.463
Brodmann areas
  5 8.284, 22 8.284
  6 (including supplementary eye fields) 8.289–90, 8.305
  7 (parietal association cortex) 8.40, 8.153–4, 8.283–5
  8 (frontal eye fields) 8.67, 8.115, 8.244–6, 8.255, 8.270,
      8.283, 8.286–8
  17 (striate cortex) 8.278–81, 8.306
  18 and 19 (extrastriate cortex) 8.281–2, 8.284–5, 8.306,
      10.262
  20 and 21 (inferotemporal cortex) 8.277, 8.285–6
  22 8.284
  37 and 39 8.306
  46 (prefrontal cortex) 8.284, 8.288–9
Brodmann's 'organs of the brain' 3.302
Bromide 12.477
Bronze Age 12.221, 12.239
Bruch's membrane
  and ageing macula 16.82–7
  and ageing retina 16.134, 16.137
  and phototoxicity 16.70
Brücke–Bartley brightness enhancement effect 12.397–8
Brunswick's representative functionalism 14.91
BS 5043 (1973), and calculation of magnification 1.190
BTRSP, *see* Boder Test of Reading–Spelling Patterns
Bubble 16.49, 16.51
  cavitation 16.51
  jet 16.51

C

C complex 3.177–8, 3.198
Ca^{2+}
  in cell locomotion 11.176, 11.179, 11.182
  cytoplasmic 11.133–4, 11.137, 11.143–4
  in dendrites 11.152
  and GAP-43 11.219, 11.225, 11.227
  in growth cones 11.226
  in neuronal cytoskeleton 11.279–81, 11.283, 11.287–8,
    11.297, 11.299
  in phospholipid metabolism 11.226
  in synaptic rearrangement 11.271
Ca^{2+}/calmodulin activated protein kinase II
  (CAMKII) 11.143
CA/C ratio 1.236, 8.163–5
Cable properties, of ganglion cell dendrites 3.48
Cadherins 11.179–80
Caecal period 3.69, 3.74–5, 3.118
  and differentiation 3.100
  and fovea 3.115
  and neurone death 3.98
  and retinal development 3.79
  and retinal expansion 3.105
  and retinofugal pathways 3.134, 3.137
  in visual cortex neurogenesis 3.360–1
Caenorrhabditis 11.33, 11.43
Café Wall illusion 5.242
Cajal
  interstitial nucleus of 8.200–1, 8.216, 8.248, 8.314
  Ramon y 3.324–5, 3.339
Cajal–Retzius cells
  Glossary explanation of 4.448
  see also Cortical cells
Calcarina, area 12.342, 12.391
Calcium
  in cell locomotion 11.174, 11.182
  in cells 11.226
  channels and GAP-43 11.227
  intracellular 3.11
  in neuronal cytoskeleton 11.278, 11.285, 11.287
  regulation of growth cones 11.280–1
Calculating ability 12.185
Calculation, and pure alexia 12.346
Callicebus 7.209, 7.212
Callicebus moloch (dusky/Titi monkey) 2.76, 7.208
Calliphora 2.207, 2.215
Callithrichidae 2.76, 3.314, 7.207
Callithricid monkey 7.207, 7.209–11
Callithrix 7.209, 7.212
Callithrix jacchus (common marmoset) 2.76–7, 2.316, 5.191,
  7.209–10
Callosal connectivity, heterotopic 3.335–40
Callosal pathways 3.324–51, 4.274
Calmodulin 11.182, 11.192
  in dendrites 11.149, 11.152
  and GAP-43 11.219, 11.226
  in neuronal cytoskeleton 11.281
Cambrian explosion 2.220

Cambridge Crowding Cards 13.50–5
Cambridge Easy Reader 13.164–6
Camera 2.127
  and eye optics 2.118
  fundus 16.99
  ultra low-light CCD 2.413
  and visual processing 2.229, 2.232, 2.236–7, 2.245
cAMP
  in critical period plasticity 11.290
  in neuronal cytoskeleton 11.288, 11.305
Campbell, Walter 12.50
Campimetry, noise-field 12.141–2, 12.173
Canal of Schlemm 2.469, 2.471, 2.474
Canal–canal convergence 8.323
Cancellation
  of optokinetic response 8.61–3, 8.148–9, 8.218
  of vestibulo-ocular reflex 8.108–10, 8.217–8, 8.308
Cancer
  bladder 16.72
  lung 16.72
Canis familiaris (domestic dog) 2.74
Cannabis 12.471
Canny algorithm 14.35, 14.42
Canthaxanthine retinopathy 7.126–7
Capgras's syndrome 12.279
Capsulotomy 16.49, 16.51
Car simulators 12.463
Carassius auratus (goldfish) 2.69–70
Carcinogenicity 16.68
Cardano, Geronimo 12.469
Cardiac arrest 12.199, 12.261
Cardiovascular disease 16.141–2
Carets 15.79–80
Caricature 12.221–4, 12.233
  computer generated 14.111, 14.114, 14.116
Caricature generator 14.118
Carotenoid 2.72
Cartesian co-ordinate system 11.77, 11.84
Cartoons 12.307
Cartridges 2.344, 2.348, 2.353, 2.355–8
Cat
  binocular vision 2.276–7, 2.279
  callosal pathways 3.343–5, 3.347–8, 3.351
  colour vision 2.293, 2.300
  dioptrics 2.85, 2.95, 2.98–100
  expanded visual area 3.309–11
  LGNd projections 3.198–9
  photoreceptor system 2.74
  retina 3.16
  Siamese
    callosal projections in 11.349
    retinogeniculocortical pathways of 11.348–9
    split-chiasm 3.340–2
    visual cortex neurogenesis 3.366, 3.368, 3.370–1
Cataplexy 12.302
Cataract surgery, astigmatism following 1.144
Cataractogenesis 16.24, 16.43, 16.96
Cataracts 2.88, 5.128, 5.283, 7.118, 7.123–4, 7.128, 7.162,
  7.177, 7.193

Cataracts (*continued*)
  and ageing macula **16.**76–7, **16.**89–90
  and ageing retina **16.**143
  bilateral **12.**18
  brunescent **16.**68
  degenerative **1.**120
    aetiology and treatment of **1.**120
    cortical 'cupuliform' opacity **1.**120
    cortical striae and wedges **1.**120
    nuclear sclerosis **1.**120
  and developing visual system **16.**105
  effects on focusing of **1.**351
  and extracapsular cataract extraction **1.**121–3
  extraction of
    early surgical complications of **1.**124
    extracapsular **1.**122–3
    intracapsular, complications of **1.**124
    late surgical complications of **1.**124–5
  formation of **12.**199
  and glaucoma **7.**154
  infantile **1.**120
  and intracapsular extraction **1.**121
  light damage and **16.**63–4
  and light hazards **16.**94–8
  and light interactions **16.**42–4, **16.**51
  and phototoxicity **16.**70–1
  and radiation **16.**55, **16.**58–60
  risk factors for formation **16.**94
  secondary **1.**120
  traumatic **12.**20
  unilateral **12.**20
  and visual-display terminals **15.**2
Catarrhine monkeys **2.**73, **2.**76–7, **7.**199–203
Catch trial (null trial) **5.**16–7, **5.**203–4
Catch-up saccade **8.**140, **8.**329
Catecholamines **11.**353–4
  in vertebrate retina **3.**44, **3.**46–7
Categories of vision **2.**263, **2.**268
Categorization **2.**254, **2.**268, **14.**107, **14.**118, **14.**127
  object **2.**260
Cathedral, Gothic **12.**417
Cathode-ray tubes **15.**1–2, **15.**7–23, **15.**28–31, **15.**56,
    15.58–60
  decay times of **15.**8
  display design of **15.**9–11, **15.**13–20
    retinal eccentricity **15.**17–8
  see also Shadow-mask cathode-ray tube
  space modulation of display luminance of
    display characterization **15.**11–3
      linearity **15.**12–3
      resolution **15.**11
    human spatial sensitivity
      characterization of **15.**13–20
      contrast sensitivity **15.**13
  in visual displays **15.**56, **15.**58–9
Cauchy functions **10.**21–2
Caudate nucleus **8.**267, **8.**269–70, **8.**287, **8.**291, **8.**314
  involvement in visual function **4.**403
C-cells **4.**226–8, **4.**234–7, **4.**240

Glossary explanation of **4.**450
CCK, *see* Cholecystokinin
CCT, *see* Cognitive complexity theory
Cebidae **2.**76, **7.**207–9, **7.**212
Cebus apella (tufted capuchin) **2.**76, **7.**208
Cebus monkey **7.**204–9, **7.**212
Cécité verbale, see Alexia, pure
CED metric, *see* Contrast energy difference metric
Celestial compass of bee **2.**265
Celestial orientation **2.**390
Cell adhesion molecule (CAM) **11.**177, **11.**179–81
  L1 **11.**210, **11.**212, **11.**235, **11.**293–4
  neural (N-CAM) **11.**108–9, **11.**180, **11.**212
    in axon growth **11.**234–5, **11.**243
    in retinal transplantation **11.**323–4
  neural-glia (Ng-CAM) **11.**282, **11.**294
  in neuronal cytoskeleton **11.**281–2, **11.**300
  in optic nerve regeneration **11.**211–2
Cell cycles **3.**90, **3.**97, **3.**101
  in retinal development **3.**78–83
Cell responses **4.**160–72, **4.**223–45, **4.**266–315, **4.**339–70
  bipolar cells **4.**318–9
  ganglion cells **4.**320–1
  horizontal cells **4.**319–20
  lateral geniculate nucleus **4.**321–2
Cells
  0-2A **11.**30–1, **11.**34, **11.**37, **11.**43, **11.**208
  adhesion **11.**279–80
  ageing **16.**78
  alpha **2.**278–9, **2.**445
  amacrine **2.**136, **2.**140–1, **2.**143, **11.**32, **11.**37, **11.**68–9,
      11.83, **11.**388, **12.**59
    AII **3.**3, **3.**35–6, **3.**42–3, **3.**46
    axon-bearing **3.**46
    birth of **3.**82
    cholinergic (starburst) **3.**43–4
    class specification **3.**101–2
    and dendrites **11.**154–6, **11.**160, **11.**163–4
    differentiation **3.**98, **3.**100
    displaced **3.**94, **3.**96–7, **3.**129–30, **3.**134
    dopaminergic **3.**44–7
    GABAergic **3.**47–8
    and horizontal cells **3.**41
    in plexiform layer **3.**32
    and postreceptoral mechanisms **3.**32
    processes **3.**41
    and retina **3.**1–2, **3.**4, **3.**80, **3.**91–2, **3.**117
  in area MT and computer vision **14.**41
  atrophy of **12.**264
  autocatalytic oscillating reactions **11.**303
  basophilic **3.**177–8
  beta **2.**278, **2.**445
  binocular **2.**443
  bipolar **2.**208, **2.**313, **5.**51–2, **5.**56, **5.**75, **5.**192, **11.**32,
      11.68–9, **11.**388, **12.**59
    bistratified **3.**33, **3.**35
    blue-cone **3.**3, **3.**55
    class specification **3.**101–2
    cone **3.**32, **3.**35–6, **3.**42–4

density 3.35
depolarizing 3.35, 3.55
differentiation 3.100–1
diffuse 3.32–3
distribution and sampling 3.35–8
in evolution of retina 2.136, 2.140–1
flat 3.32–5
flat cone 3.33
flat midget 3.113
and ganglion cells 3.48
giant 3.33
and horizontal cells 3.40
hyperpolarizing 3.35, 3.55
and interplexiform cells 3.47
invaginating 3.32–5
invaginating midget 3.113
midget 3.32–3
and neurone death 3.96
OFF-centre 2.140, 3.33–4, 3.113
ON-centre 2.140, 3.33–4, 3.113
and photoreceptor coupling 3.26
physiology 3.33–5
in plexiform layer 3.32–6, 3.38, 3.41
and postreceptoral mechanisms 3.30
processes 3.32–3, 3.41–2
recognition 11.81, 11.83
and retina 3.1–2, 3.4, 3.80–1, 3.83–4
rod 3.3, 3.32–4, 3.36, 3.40, 3.42–3, 3.47
structure 3.32–3
broad-band 2.170
C-type 2.140–1
calcium in 11.226
cholinergic amacrine 11.157–8, 11.162, 11.164–5
class specific molecules 11.81, 11.83
class specification 3.101–2
coding analysis by metabolic imaging 14.19
colour coding 3.39
colour-opponent 2.170, 2.298
complex, of striate cortex 5.34
cone 2.351
contact 11.279
contact guidance 11.181
conventional (starburst) amacrine 11.157, 11.161–2, 11.164
corneagenous 2.350
in cortical area VI and computer vision 14.41
crawling 11.174
cycle control 11.119
cytoskeleton 11.275
death 3.81, 11.163, 12.132–4, 16.40, 16.44, 16.47, 16.51
    and axon growth 11.239
    and axotomy, retrograde 12.129
    and brain damage 11.241
    and developing visual system 16.119
    in synaptic rearrangement 11.262
debris 3.85
differential addition 3.106–7
diffuse bipolar 2.140
disparity-sensitive 5.135
displaced amacrine 11.157–8, 11.161–2, 11.164

divisions 11.52–3, 11.58
DNA 12.128
doctrines 12.28, 12.30–2
dopamine, transplant 11.314
duplication of types 2.360
ependymal 11.208
face 12.119–21
fate 2.346, 2.355, 3.101–2, 11.29, 11.34–7, 11.39
FS9 11.180
functional reorganization 12.134
gamma 2.445
ganglion
    β- 12.63
    fast α- 12.63
geometry 11.278
glial 3.114, 3.117
gliosis 12.264
growth and proto-oncogenes 11.112–4, 11.117, 11.119–20
HI 3.38–40, 11.159–60, 11.165
HII 3.38–40, 11.159–60, 11.165
histogenesis of retinal 11.316
horizontal 2.136, 2.140, 3.37–41, 5.192, 5.195, 11.388,
        12.56–7, 12.59, 12.63, 12.159–60, 12.163
    and amacrine cells 3.44
    birth of 3.82
    colour coding 3.39
    in dendrites 11.158–60, 11.165
    dendritic processes 3.39
    differentiation 3.100–1
    H1 3.38–40, 11.159–60, 11.165
    H2 3.38–40, 11.159–60, 11.165
    and interplexiform cells 3.47
    local contrast 3.40
    in mammals 3.38–9
    membrane potential 3.39
    and neuronal death 3.96
    and postreceptoral mechanisms 3.32
    processes 3.32, 3.40–2
    and retina 3.1–2, 3.4, 3.80
    type A 3.38–9
    type B 3.38
interplexiform 2.136, 2.141, 3.1–3, 3.41, 3.47, 11.157
isomorphic 2.360
isomorphy 2.357
IT 12.112
large monopolar (LMC) 2.204, 2.206–8, 2.210, 2.213,
        2.218–9, 2.224
layer II 11.261
layer III 11.261
layer IV 11.260, 11.262, 11.271
layer V 11.260
layer VI 11.260, 11.262
LGN 12.58, 12.134
    and axotomy 12.130–2
    relay 12.63
        number of 12.64
light-sensitive 2.19–21, 2.23
lineage 3.101, 11.30–7, 11.43
    and TOP expression 11.77–9

Cells (*continued*)
  locomotion **11.171–83**
  luminosity-type **2.140–1**
  M **2.171, 2.444, 2.450, 5.192–9**
  magnocellular, *see* Cells M
  midget **3.3**
  midget bipolar **2.140, 5.192**
  migration **11.70–4**
  mosaic **11.156, 11.162–5**
  mRNA **12.128**
  Müller **11.68–9, 12.56**
    birth of **3.80–1**
    and brain damage **11.241**
    density **3.117**
    at fovea **3.117**
    in fovea **3.113–4**
    in optic nerve regeneration **11.209**
    recognition **11.81, 11.83**
    in retinal development **3.73, 3.76–9, 3.83–4**
  Müller glial **11.43, 11.81**
  nerve
    colour-specific **12.356**
    differentiation of dendrites **12.19**
    movement-sensitive **12.72**
    MT **12.86–91**
    orientation-selective **12.69–70**
  neural crest **11.72, 11.171, 11.182**
  neuroblast **11.54, 11.63**
  new ganglion, in fish retina **11.103, 11.105**
  non-concentric **2.170**
  as non-linear dynamical system **11.303–4**
  non-neural **3.84–90**
  non-neuronal
    and axon regeneration **11.206–7**
    in optic nerve regeneration **11.197–8, 11.200–1, 11.209, 11.211, 11.213**
  off-bipolar **12.56–7, 12.160**
  off-centre ganglion **12.56, 12.159, 12.161, 12.164–5, 12.472–3**
    illusion and hallucination **12.467–8**
    retinal **12.165**
  off-ganglion **12.160, 12.163**
  on-bipolar **12.56–7, 12.159–60**
  on-centre ganglion **12.56, 12.159, 12.161, 12.164–5, 12.472–3**
    illusion and hallucination **12.466**
    latency class II (X-) **12.468**
  on-ganglion **12.160, 12.162–3**
    retinal **12.163**
  on-off-amacrine **12.56**
  opponent-colour **5.167**
  orientationally selective **5.34, 11.345–6**
  P-beta, damage by acrylamide **5.274**
  parvocellular (P) **2.171, 2.444–5, 2.450, 5.192–9**
  phagocytic **11.213**
  pigment **2.350**
  pigment epithelial **3.9**
  polarity **11.175**
  precursor

    multipotential **11.32–7, 11.43**
    in neurogenesis **11.29–35**
    pluripotential **11.33–5, 11.43**
  primary pigment **2.351**
  Purkinje **2.180–3, 2.188, 11.82, 11.150–2**
  radial glial **11.34, 11.42–3**
  rarely-encountered **2.170, 2.172**
  recognition molecules **11.68–84**
  regeneration control **11.195–200**
  relay **3.187–92**
  responding to individual faces **12.121–2**
  responses of, *see* Cell responses
  retinal ganglion **12.59, 12.62–3**
    activity **12.472–3**
    atrophy of **12.154**
    and axotomy **12.129, 12.132**
    and brain lesions **12.133–5**
    classes of **12.61**
    goldfish **11.194, 11.196, 11.198–201**
    illusion and hallucination **12.466**
    spatial density of **12.64**
  retrovirally marked **11.42**
  rod (AII) amacrine **11.156–7**
  rod–cone bipolar **2.140, 2.147**
  Schwann
    and axon growth **11.244**
    and cellular organization **11.72–3**
    in neuronal cytoskeleton **11.298**
    in optic nerve regeneration **11.207, 11.210–2**
  screening pigment **2.351**
  see also Ganglion cells; Glia; Glial cells; Neurones
  shape **11.133, 11.275–6, 11.280, 11.288–9**
  simple, of layer IVb of striate cortex **5.39**
  simple, of striate cortex **5.34**
  single, and prosopagnosia **12.276**
  spindle **3.86–7**
  states **11.57–62**
  surface, and optic nerve regeneration **11.211–2**
  surface interactions **11.171–83**
  surface proteins **11.75, 11.84**
  surface shape **11.176**
  sustained (X) **5.161**
  symbiosis **11.304–6**
  synaptic reorganization **12.129, 12.132–5**
  transient (Y) **5.161**
  V4 **12.111**
  W **2.278, 2.444, 2.450–3, 2.455, 2.459**
  W neurones **11.345**
  X **2.444–5, 2.450, 2.452–3, 2.459**
    in pursuit system **2.170–2, 2.175, 2.191**
  X neurones **11.345**
  Y **2.278, 2.444–5, 2.450, 2.452–3, 2.455–6, 2.459, 5.161**
    in pursuit system **2.170–2, 2.175–6, 2.191**
  Y neurones **11.345**
Cells of Meynert, *see* Meynert cells
Cellular morphology
  laminar variation in **4.231–4**
    in cells of the striate cortex **4.231–2**
Central caudal nucleus **8.184**

Central lateral nuclei 4.407
Central mesencephalic reticular formation 8.201, 8.208–9
Central nervous system (CNS)
  injury 11.210, 11.213, 11.220, 11.223, 11.227–9, 11.242
  lower vertebrate, neurone regeneration 11.209, 11.212–3
  mammal 11.278
    and axon growth 11.248–50
    neurone regeneration 11.206–13
  pathways 11.220
    of adult mammals 11.221, 11.223
    mammalian/non–mammalian vertebrates 11.227
  regeneration 11.190–201, 11.219, 11.228, 11.248–50
  vertebrate 11.72–3
    neurogenesis 11.28–32, 11.34–5, 11.37, 11.39, 11.41–3
Central scotomata and optokinesis 8.60–4
Central serous retinopathy (CSR) 7.125
Centre-of-gravity (COG) operations 5.45–7
Centre-surround cells, Glossary explanation of 4.444
Centre-surround interaction 4.15, 4.26–7
Centre-surround organization, in signal transmission 4.54–6
Centre-surround phase lag 4.22–3
Centre-surround receptive-field organization 4.375
Centre-surround sensitivity 4.55–6
Centrifugal pathway 2.425, 2.427, 2.429, 2.432–3
Centrifugal saccades 8.101, 8.117
Centring tendencies 8.78
Centripetal saccades 8.101, 8.118
Centroid analysis 10.89–91, 10.110
Centroid and location 14.9–10, 14.12
Centroid in pattern recognition 14.72–4
Cephalaspidomorphs 2.402–3
Cephalic organ 2.15, 2.17–8, 2.21, 2.25, 2.30–1, 2.35,
    2.37–40, 2.42, 2.48
  and origin of lens 2.44–5
Cephalopods 2.3–4, 2.13
  in evolution of eye 2.29–31, 2.39–40, 2.46–7
  eyes 2.21, 2.23
  origin of lens 2.45
  origins of eye 2.54
  photoreception 2.364–5, 2.367, 2.371–2, 2.374–8, 2.380–2,
    2.384–5, 2.388, 2.390–1
Cercopithecus 2.77, 2.310, 12.95
Cercopithecus aethiops (African green monkey) 7.203
Cercopithecus cephus 2.314
Cerebellar peduncle, superior 8.216
Cerebellum 8.224–43
  climbing fibres 8.37, 8.224–6, 8.234–5, 8.328
  deep nuclei 8.244, 8.328
  lesions 8.227–8, 8.232, 8.234, 8.236, 8.301, 8.312–3
  mossy fibres 8.153, 8.224–5, 8.230
  motor learning 8.327–8
  optokinesis 8.214, 8.234–6
  periodic alternating nystagmus 8.234, 8.299–301, 8.312–3,
    8.322
  proprioceptive afferents 8.189, 8.238
  in pursuit system 2.174, 2.179–89, 2.191
  saccades 8.236–8
  see also under Spatial frequency analysis; Visual channels
  smooth pursuit 8.153–4, 8.232–4

vergence 8.238–9
vestibulo-ocular reflex 8.37, 8.216, 8.226–32, 8.238, 8.327
in visual function 4.394–6
  and connectivity 4.395
  effects of electrical stimulation on 4.394
  effects of lesions on 4.394
  physiological properties of 4.394–5
    flocculus 4.395
    vermis 4.394–5
  and visual pathways 2.424, 2.427, 2.429, 2.449
  and visuo-spatial disorders 12.435
Cerebral blindness 7.193–4
Cerebral cortex 6.179–89, 8.277–96
  extrastriate 8.281–2, 8.284–5, 8.306
  frontal eye fields 8.67, 8.115, 8.213, 8.244–6, 8.255, 8.270,
    8.277, 8.283, 8.286–8
  inferotemporal 8.277, 8.285–6
  middle and middle superior temporal 8.153, 8.211, 8.213,
    8.215, 8.282–3
  parietal 8.40, 8.153–4, 8.283–5
  prefrontal 8.284, 8.288–9
  prestriate 8.281–2
  in pursuit system 2.174–80, 2.183
  striate 8.245, 8.247, 8.278–81, 8.306
  supplementary eye fields 8.289–90, 8.305
Cerebral damage
  posterior
    bilateral 12.262
    right 12.263, 12.272
    unilateral 12.262
Cerebral hemispheres, unilateral lesions of 7.192–3
Cerebral palsy, accommodation anomalies in 1.271
Cervico-ocular reflex 8.312
Cetaceae 2.274
CFF, *see* Critical flicker fusion; Critical flicker frequency;
    Critical fusion frequency
CFFF, *see* Critical flicker fusion frequency
cGMP phosphodiesterase 6.102, 6.104–5
Chandeliere cells 3.258, 3.261–2, 3.265, 3.290
  Glossary explanation of 4.448
Changing size
  and motion-in-depth 9.151–2
  selective adaptation to 9.154–6
Changing-size after-effects, and motion-in-depth after-
    effects 9.153
Changing-size channels 9.156–7
  non-linear analysis of 9.157–8
Changing-size system 9.148
Channel theory 10.110
Channels
  achromatic 3.49, 12.386
  bandwidth estimation 5.101–2
  chromatic 12.386
  cone 12.395
  cyclopean spatial frequency 10.162
  detection 10.135–6
  discrimination 10.135–7
  dynamic range of off-peak 5.102
  generation of neuronal 12.59–61

hypothesis 10.298
multiple parallel 10.143, **10.157**
parallel 5.99
psychophysical 10.136
quality-specific 12.54
R + G 10.159
red–green and blue–yellow 7.38–40, 7.68
separate 5.101
sets of 10.136, 10.150–1
spatial 10.47, 10.173
   in amblyopia 10.216–7
spatial frequency 10.136, 10.199
   in texture perception 10.121–2
sustained 10.49–51, 13.61, 13.149–51
temporal 10.48
temporal frequency, in MS 10.241
transient 10.49–51, 13.61, 13.149–51
Chaos 11.275
   deterministic 11.303–4
Character recognition 14.69, 14.81
Characteristic feature, *see* Feature
Characters
   Chinese 12.329–30
   ideographic 12.307
   Kanji 12.308
   prelinguistic perception of 12.309
   printed 12.315
   and reading competence 12.316–7
   in reading and script 12.319–20
   for script 12.305
   set of 12.315
   typewriter 12.317
Charcot, Jean-Martin 12.49
Charybdea 2.238
ChAT, *see* Choline acetyltransferase
Chelicerata 2.213, 2.217
Chelonia 2.426–7
Chemical affinities 11.90
Chemoaffinity hypothesis 11.323
Chemoreception 2.249
Chemospecificity theory 11.88–9
Chemotactic system 11.62
Chemotaxis 11.62, 11.181
Chequerboard model 4.325
Cheselden, William R. 12.17–8
Chevreul's chromatic circle 6.220–1
Chevron acuity 10.107–8
Chiasm in eye evolution 2.415
Chiasm syndrome 12.186
Chiasma 2.354–5, 2.357
Chiasmal compression 7.161–2
   chronic 7.177
Chiasmal infiltration 7.161–2
Children
   blind 12.309
   colour naming abilities of normal kindergarten 12.387–8
   development of face recognition 12.238
   and emotional responses to colour 12.387
   schizophrenic 12.288–9, 12.477

Chimpanzees 7.199, 12.220
   and face recognition 12.239
   and human language 12.331
   pygmy 12.331–2
Chitons 2.364–5, 2.368, 2.371, 2.383, 2.390
Chloramphenicol acetyl-transferase (CAT) 11.20
Chlorophyll 2.8, 2.11
Chloroquine 16.70
Chloroquine toxic retinopathy 7.126–8
Choice preference, colour and 12.385
Cholecystokinin 3.279, 3.294–5, 11.363
   in visual cortex neurogenesis 3.363
Choline acetyltransferase 3.284, 3.286–8, 3.295–6
   in dendrites 11.161, 11.355
Cholinergic system 11.355
Chorioretinal diseases 7.175
   and the Stiles–Crawford effect of the first kind 1.297
Chorioretinitis, luetic 7.146–7
Chorioretinopathy 7.118
   central serous, and the Stiles–Crawford effect of the first kind 1.297
Choroid, and ageing macula 16.82–5
Choroid damage 7.126–8
Choroidal atrophy, central areolar 7.131
Choroideal body 2.414
Choroideremia 7.130–1, 7.135
Choroidosis, degenerative myopic 7.131
Chroma, CIE definition of 6.226
Chromascope, Lehmann 5.242
Chromatic aberration 1.68–9, 1.247, 1.352, 7.53
   in foveal vision 4.326
   longitudinal 1.9, 1.340
   see also Aberration
Chromatic acuity 7.118–9, 7.134
   in diabetes 7.149–50
   in glaucoma 7.154
   in toxic optic neuropathy 7.161
Chromatic channels 2.312–3
   to bipolar cells 6.137–9
      in cats 6.138
      in fish 6.137–9
      in humans 6.139
      in primates 6.138–9
      in turtles 6.139
      in *Xenopus* toad 6.139
   to horizontal cells 6.134–7
      in birds 6.134
      in fish 6.134–5, 6.137
      in humans 6.134, 6.136–7
      in primates 6.134
      in reptiles 6.137
      in teleost 6.137
      in turtles 6.134–7
Chromatic circles, Chevreul's 6.220–1
Chromatic coding
   of two-dimensional form 6.201–12
      and colour-contrast sensitivity and colour resolution 6.201–4
Chromatic contrast 6.169–70, **6.180–6**, 7.68–70, **15.19–20**

Chromatic contrast sensitivity function, *see* Contrast
  sensitivity function
Chromatic detection 5.215–7
Chromatic dispersion, and the constringence (*V*) of the
  material 1.421
Chromatic fibres 7.39
Chromatic flicker 7.50, 7.181–2
Chromatic increment functions 5.195
Chromatic mechanisms 5.196–8, 5.204, 5.207–9, 5.234–6,
  5.246–7
Chromatic patches 5.215
Chromatic pathway 5.204, 5.234–6, 5.246–7
Chromatic properties, of cells of lateral geniculate
  nucleus 4.68–9
Chromatic response functions 5.199
Chromatic sensitivity 5.288
  threshold methods 7.43–6
Chromatic space 7.64–8
  unit area of 6.176, 6.182
Chromatic spatial localization 6.210–1
Chromatic spectral sensitivity
  derived from cone absorption space 6.34–5
  determination of, by hue cancellation 6.34
Chromatic system 7.64–8
  vulnerability 12.409
Chromatic temporal response function 7.181–2
Chromatic thresholds 7.46, 7.48, 7.51, 7.74
Chromatic vision 7.180–1
  in hemiachromatopsia 7.185
  selective disturbance 7.178–9
Chromaticity 5.85, 5.188
  CIE definition of 6.226
  CIE diagram 5.203
  and cone contrast 6.37
  and flicker 5.171
  matches 5.214
  and the ratio of cone absorption rates 6.31–2
  sinusoidal modulation 5.193
Chromaticity co-ordinates 7.31
  CIE definition of 6.226
Chromaticity diagram 5.282, 7.31–2
  CIE definition of 6.226
Chromaticness
  CIE definition of 6.225
  hue 6.272
  saturation 6.272
Chromatic-opponency 5.180, 5.210, 5.213
Chromatin 2.472, 2.476
Chromatolysis 11.193
Chromatopsia 7.116–7
  after cataract extraction 7.123–4
  complementary 16.97
  in ophthalmic disease 7.125, 7.130, 7.132, 7.134
Chrome-orthoptics 13.172
Chromophores 16.38, 16.40–2, 16.45–8
  3,4-dehydroretinal 6.67
  3-dehydroretinal 6.70–1, 6.108–9
  3-dehydroxyretinal 6.62, 6.70
  and phototoxicity 16.67–9

of visual pigments 6.62
  3-dehydroxyretinal 6.67, 6.70, 6.108
  3-hydroxyretinal 6.70–1, 6.108–9
  4-hydroxyretinal 6.62, 6.67
  11-*cis* retinal 6.108
Chromosome 3, human 7.105
Chromosome 7, human 7.106
Chromostereopsis 1.340–1, 5.86
Chronotopy in optic nerve 3.135
Chrysopa 2.234
α-Chymotrypsin, in intracapsular cataract extraction 1.124
CIE (Commission International de l'Eclairage) 5.171,
  5.183–4, 5.186, 5.196, 5.207, 6.43–4
  co-ordinate system 5.202–3, 5.211, 5.214
CIE photopic *V*$_\lambda$ curve 10.139
CIE system of calorimetry (1931) 6.14–20, 6.221–2
CIELAB colour space 6.240–1, 6.246–53, 6.300
  specifications of hue angle, chroma and lightness 6.241
CIELUV colour space 6.238–40, 6.246–52, 6.254, 6.304
  and the CIE 1976 UCS diagram 6.238–9
  and colour-vision deficiencies 6.239
  specifications of hue angle, chroma, saturation and
    lightness 6.239–40
Cilia
  connecting 3.9
  in evolution of eye 2.26–9, 2.40–3
  photoreceptors 2.27–8, 2.365–6, 2.368–72, 2.375–6
  vestibular 8.22–4
Ciliary body 2.469, 2.471, 2.473, 2.475, 2.477, 11.393–4
  muscle 2.469, 2.471, 2.475
  web 2.469, 2.471, 2.474
Ciliary corona 1.351
Ciliary epithelium 11.393
Ciliary ganglion 1.233
Ciliary muscles 1.233
  and reduction of zonular tension 1.231
  relative changes in 1.236
Ciliary nerves, short 1.233
Ciliary neurotrophic factor (CNTF) 11.30
Cinema and apparent motion 5.152
Cingulectomy, unilateral 12.463–4
Cingulotomy
  bilateral 12.455
  unilateral 12.455
Circadian oscillator 2.372
Circadian rhythm 2.367, 2.373, 2.425
Circadian system 2.368
Circular acceleration 12.432
Circular vection, horizontal 12.462–3
Circularvection 8.32, 8.40
Circumlocutions 12.347
Circumventing strategies 12.208
City University test 7.216, 7.224, 7.230
Clammys caspica (turtle) 2.287
Clare–Bishop area 9.161, 13.4
Classification
  deterministic linear 14.72–3
  of faces 14.114–7, 14.120–1
  false 14.69, 14.72

Classification (*continued*)
  geometrically invariant **14**.70, **14**.73–4
  invariant list **14**.79–80
  laminar **2**.424
  linear **14**.72, **14**.74, **14**.78
  list **14**.75, **14**.77, **14**.79–80
  of noisy signals **14**.72
  and pattern invariance **14**.69–81
  polynomial **14**.74
  shape **14**.37
  translation invariant **14**.70, **14**.74–5, **14**.77–9
Classifier
  Bayesian **14**.85
  linear **14**.74, **14**.76, **14**.78–9, **14**.101
  list **14**.74, **14**.76
  normalized linear **14**.81
  parabolic **14**.81
  polynomial **14**.79
  template matching **14**.72
Claustram **4**.298
Clay tablet **12**.306
Clay tokens **12**.305
Clewed cells **3**.251–2, **3**.258, **3**.262, **3**.292–3
Climbing fibres **8**.37, **8**.224–6, **8**.234–5, **8**.328
Clinical reflectors **1**.234
Clock face **12**.455
Closed-circuit television
  advantages of, over optical aids **1**.204
  and contrast reversal **1**.204
  disadvantages of, over optical aids **1**.205
  and the 'steady eye strategy' **1**.204
  and transverse magnification **1**.185–6, **1**.192, **1**.203–5
    and field-of-view **1**.203
    types available **1**.203–4
      'portable' **1**.203–4
      'versatile' **1**.203
Clutch cells
  Glossary explanation of **4**.448
  see also Clewed cells; Cortical cells
CMF, *see* Cortical magnification factor
CO, *see* Cytochrome oxidase
CO blobs, *see* Cytochrome oxidase blobs
Coarse stereopsis **9**.207
Cod dioptrics **2**.83
Coding
  of brainstem signals **8**.209, **8**.244
  of collicular signals **8**.256–66
Coelacanths **2**.71–2
Coelenterata, statocysts **8**.13
Co-evolution **2**.12–3, **2**.302, **2**.313–4
Cognition
  and agnosia **12**.191, **12**.198
  and brain activity **12**.21–4
  development of **12**.17–21
  historical observations **12**.25–51
    Ancient Greek thought on perception **12**.25–32
    creation of modern physiological optics **12**.36–40
    localization theories **12**.46–7
    Newton and Mayer **12**.42–5

    progress in neuroanatomy **12**.40–2
    Renaissance approach **12**.32–5
    visual cortex and agnosia **12**.47–51
  man-specific abilities **12**.15–7
  operations in visual–verbal domain **12**.326
  and perception **12**.209
  primate model **12**.15–7
  visual **12**.321
  and reading **12**.309
Cognitive complexity theory **15**.103
Cognitive correlates of vestibular adaptation **8**.38–40
Cognitive demand **15**.83
Cognitive penetrability **14**.137
Cognitive science **14**.45
Cognitive vigilance increment **15**.83
Cognitive vigilance tasks **15**.91
Cognitively driven saccades **8**.250
Coincidence detection **14**.73, **14**.78, **14**.80–1
Coincidence detectors **14**.81
Colchicine **11**.175
Cold spot **3**.80, **3**.106, **3**.117
Coleoptera optics **2**.130
Colinearity
  in hyperacuity **10**.99, **10**.101, **10**.110
  in texture perception **10**.131
Collateral formation in axon growth **11**.235
Collateral invasion in axon growth **11**.235
Collaterals
  axon **11**.237, **11**.241, **11**.247
  axonal **3**.371
    elimination of **3**.370
    and retinofugal pathways **3**.129, **3**.134, **3**.139, **3**.141
  bifurcating **3**.338
  optic tract **11**.250
Collicular magnification factor **3**.151
Collicular neurones, receptive fields of **3**.166–9
Colliculus
  inferior **3**.136, **3**.364
    in retinal transplantation **11**.319–20, **11**.324
  superior **8**.244–76, **10**.263–5, **10**.271, **10**.273, **11**.223–5,
    11.369–71, **11**.381
    anatomy **8**.201, **8**.245–8
    auditory receptive fields **8**.251
    and axon competition **11**.241
    and axon growth **11**.232, **11**.237, **11**.243, **11**.245–6,
      11.249–50
    burst neurones **8**.249–54, **8**.257–65
    cell discharges **8**.248–54, **8**.256–7, **8**.326
    coding of signals **8**.256–66
    commissural fibres **8**.253
    cortical connections **3**.370
    and cross-modal connections **11**.379–80
    and cross-modal functions **11**.378
    cross-modal interactions in **11**.369, **11**.374–7
    electrically evoked saccades **8**.255
    enhancement of responses **8**.248
    and express saccades **8**.252–3
    and eye-head co-ordination **8**.34, **8**.262–7
    foveal representation **8**.251

Colliculus (*continued*)
foveation hypothesis 8.252
and frontal eye fields 8.244, 8.286–7
functional topography 8.252, 8.256, 8.263
and ganglion cells 3.56
and GAP-43 11.228
and gaze control 8.34, 8.262–7
laminated structure 8.245
lesions 3.213, 8.255–6, 8.314
and LGNv 3.202–4
in mature retina 3.131–2
models of function 8.257–65, 8.326
modular organization 8.247
neurogenesis 3.360, 3.364–6, 3.368
and neuronal cytoskeleton 11.300
omnipause neurones 8.53–4
and optic nerve regeneration 11.206
population coding of saccade vectors 8.256–7
quasi-visual neurones 8.249–53, 8.266
in retinal transplantation 11.319–20, 11.322–6
in retinofugal pathways 3.136–8, 3.140–1
and spatio-temporal transformation 8.244
and substantia nigra 8.254
synaptic differentiation 3.366
T-neurones 8.247–9, 8.251, 8.253
TR(S)N neurones 8.248, 8.250–3, 8.255–6, 8.263, 8.266–8
and visual thalamus 3.183, 3.185, 3.193–5, 3.205, 3.209–14, 3.216–7
visually triggered movement neurones 8.249
visual-motor neurones 8.249
X-neurones 8.247–9, 8.251, 8.254, 8.265
Collinearity 14.38, 14.64, 14.93
Coloboma, congenital 3.76
Coloration 2.301–2
body 2.302
cryptic 2.302
Colorimetry 5.48
and appearance 6.20, 6.22
CIE-style 6.19–20
and colour discrimination 6.22
and colour matching 6.22
colour-appearance 6.20
display-based 6.20
Colour 5.274
absurd 12.398–9
of objects 12.405, 12.408
achromatic 12.397
achromatic system 5.204, 5.215–6
additive mixture 12.395
and agnosia 12.181, 12.184, 12.194, 12.203, 12.215
analysis 5.241, 5.248
apperception of 12.405
balance 12.385
biology of 6.7–8
blindness, see Blindness, colour
categories 5.202, 5.211–4, 5.217, 12.404, 12.407
abstract 12.407
concrete object-related 12.407

categorization 12.181, 12.386–7, 12.404
and colour deficiencies 12.410
category processor 12.356–7
centre 12.391, 12.402, 12.406, 12.408
parieto-temporal 12.410
and chromatic aberration 15.63
and chromatic contrast 15.19–20
chromatic system 5.204
circle 2.301, 12.398
class concept of 12.331
code 12.307
coding, opponent 2.298
complementary 2.297, 2.301
of afterimage 12.398
in computer vision 14.41–2
concept, abstract handling of 12.407
cone response 5.204
constancy 2.153, 2.267, 2.300–1, 2.310, 2.458, 5.59, 5.204, 5.214, 5.287, 12.13–4, 12.386, 12.393, 14.36
mechanism 12.385
and perception 12.84–5
and visual object recognition 12.111
and contour information correlation 12.404
contrast 5.85, 5.227, 12.85, 12.396
spatial 12.400
and visual object recognition 12.111
contrast phenomena 2.301
correct association to objects 12.407
defective observers 5.283
defects, acquired 12.388
deficiencies 12.58
neuronal circuits in cerebral 12.408–10
'derived' 2.297
detection and discrimination limits 5.202–17
detection mechanisms 5.212
discrimination 2.230, 2.249, 2.254, 2.258, 2.300, 2.302, 2.456, 12.144, 12.184, 12.203, 12.216, 12.387, 12.390–1, 12.394, 12.396
and colour agnosia 12.404
and colour anomia 12.407
drawings appropriately 12.399
of drawn object 12.398
in dreams 12.393, 12.399
effects of
on mood and performance 13.178–9
on reducing reading difficulties 13.178
eidetic 12.399
emotional aspects 12.356
emotional responses 12.407
equations of 6.13–4
and equiluminance 5.234–5, 5.238, 5.245
and equiluminant mixtures 15.63
and flicker fusion 5.179
and hyperacuity 5.227
hypoemotionality 12.403, 12.406, 12.409
identification by 2.310
illuminant sources of 5.203
and illusions 5.244
incorrect 12.398

Colour (*continued*)
  information
    emotional **12**.357
    interhemispheric visual transfer of **12**.344
  irradiation **12**.404
  and its effects on legibility **15**.73
  in 'landmarks' **12**.405
  loss of emotional quality **12**.405
  matching **5**.191, **5**.203, **5**.282, **12**.184, **12**.215, **12**.345,
    12.398–9
  and colour agnosia **12**.404
  measurement of **6**.10–21
    and the 1964 CIE system of colorimetry for 10° field
      sizes **6**.16
    foundations of **6**.10
    in the future **6**.19–20
    and Helmholtz's theory of colour perception **6**.11–12
    instruments for **6**.19
      tristimulus colorimeters **6**.19
    and Maxwell's colour box **6**.10
    and Maxwell's spinning top **6**.10–1
    and metamerism **6**.16
    and spectral composition **6**.12
    and the standard observer for colorimetry (1931
      CIE) **6**.13–14
    and the transformation of the RGB colour-mixture
      curves to the XYZ colour-matching
      functions **6**.14–6
    and variables of brightness and colour appearance **6**.13
    and visual research **6**.16–19
    and the V_λ curve **6**.12–13
    and Young **6**.11
    see also Colorimetry
  memory **5**.204, **5**.214
  mixtures **5**.203
  monitor **5**.246–7
  and object recognition **14**.36
  opponency, double **2**.453
  pairs **5**.236, **5**.242
  patches **5**.202, **5**.204, **5**.217
  perception **2**.297–8, **5**.214
  photopic conditions **5**.204
  physics of **6**.1–4
    and Fresnel **6**.3
    and Helmholtz **6**.4
    and Newton's experiments **6**.2–4
    and Young's proposal **6**.2
  post-receptoral cone opponent response **5**.204
  psychology of **6**.5–7
    and Chevreul **6**.6, **6**.220–1
    and Hering's theory **6**.5–6, **6**.222–4
  psychophysical studies **5**.202–5
  'pure' **2**.297–8
  and pure alexia **12**.353
  recognition **12**.259, **12**.271
    by matching **12**.337
  red–green mixture **12**.394–5, **12**.398
  rod contribution **5**.204
  saturated **12**.400

  selection of correct **12**.404
  sematic cues **12**.355
  sensation, elementary **12**.405
  and shape perception **14**.35–6
  signal transfer of **12**.54–5
  sorting
    and colour anomia **12**.407
    and matching of yarn **12**.393, **12**.395, **12**.400, **12**.406–7
  space **12**.31, **12**.37, **12**.44–5
  spreading **5**.237
  standards **5**.203
  as stimulus **5**.202–5
  surface **12**.403–7, **12**.410
  temperature **5**.203, **5**.210, **5**.214
  terms **5**.214
  and texture information correlation **12**.404
  theories **12**.386, **12**.389
  triangle **12**.44–5
  tritanopic **5**.237
  'unique' **2**.297–8
  and visual channels **5**.97
  as a visual cue **5**.286
  words, basic **12**.387
  Young–Helmholtz trichromatic theory **12**.386
Colour appearance **6**.43–54, **6**.189, **6**.193
  and achromatic colours **6**.43–4
  brightness **6**.43
  categorizing systems for **6**.218–61
    basic attributes of **6**.229–330
      chromaticness **6**.229
      clearness **6**.229
      hue **6**.229
      lightness **6**.229
      saturation **6**.229
    comparisons of **6**.246–55
      between the NCS, Munsell, DIN, CIELAB and
        CIELUV **6**.248–54
        in relation to hue and chroma
          (chromaticness) **6**.248–50
        in relation to lightness (value) and
          blackness **6**.250–3
        in relation to NCS nuances and Munsell value/
          chroma **6**.253–4
      between the NCS, Ostwald and DIN **6**.248
      between the OSA/UCS and the CIE, CIELUV and
        Munsell **6**.254–5
    historical background of **6**.219–22
      early theories and early ordering systems **6**.219–20
      the nineteenth century and early twentieth
        century **6**.220–4
    models of **6**.229
    modern **6**.224–46
      CIELAB colour space **6**.238, **6**.240–1
      CIELUV colour space **6**.238–41
      Deutsches Institut für Normung (DIN) **6**.235–8
      NCS (natural colour system) **6**.233–5
      Optical Society of America uniform colour
        scales **6**.241–6
      terminology used in **6**.224–8

the Munsell colour system **6.231–3**
  basic concepts and principles for scaling and notation
     of variables of **6.231–3**
    chroma **6.231–2**
    hue **6.231–2**
    value **6.231–2**
the nineteenth century and early twentieth century
  based on the mixture of light
    CIE 1931 colorimetric **6.221–2**
    Grassmann **6.221**
    Helmholtz **6.221**
    Newton **6.221**
  based on pigments and on visual attributes
     6.220–1
    Chevreul **6.6, 6.220–1**
    Goethe **6.5, 6.220**
  psychology and colour perception **6.222–4**
    Ebbinghaus **6.222**
    Hering **6.5–7, 6.222–4**
    Wundt **6.222**
the Ostwald colour system **6.230**
restrictions on **6.228–9**
  influence of surrounding factors and illumination
    on **6.228**
  standard viewing conditions **6.228–9**
and chromatic colours **6.43–4**
definition of **6.43**
and equilibrium colours **6.45**
hue **6.43**
mode of **6.43**
  illuminant **6.43**
  object **6.43**
  surface **6.43**
psychophysical techniques in relation to **6.49–53**
  colour categories **6.52–3**
  estimation **6.51–2**
    hue **6.51–2**
    magnitude **6.52**
  matching **6.49–51**
    asymmetric **6.50**
    haploscopic **6.50**
    hue cancellation **6.50–1**
    memory **6.50**
and related colours **6.43, 6.45–8**
  brilliance and fluorescence **6.47**
  chroma **6.46**
  colourfulness **6.47–8**
  dark **6.48**
  interactions between lightness and chroma **6.46–7**
  lightness **6.46**
  systems for specification of **6.46**
    Munsell Color System **6.46–7**
    OSA Uniform Color Space **6.46–7**
saturation **6.43**
and surface reflection **6.23**
and unrelated colours **6.43–5**
  hue, saturation and brightness **6.44–5**
  interaction of **6.45**
Colour assimilation **6.183**

Colour atlases
  Hesselgren's **6.233**
  NCS **6.233**
Colour bleeding, see Colour assimilation
Colour blindness **2.74, 2.242, 2.308, 2.314, 2.390, 7.88–9,**
    7.91–2, 7.95–6
  congenital **16.111**
  see also Monochromacy, typical
Colour categories **6.52–3**
Colour cells
  complex **6.188**
  orientation selective **6.183–4, 6.208–9**
Colour charts, DIN **6.235**
Colour circles **4.333**
  Forsius's **6.219**
  Goethe's **6.220**
  Hering's **6.222–4**
  Newton's **6.219**
  Ostwald's **6.230**
Colour coding, grouping and conspicuity of **15.73**
Colour coding cells **3.39**
Colour and cognition **4.331–2**
Colour columns **4.323**
  anatomy of **4.285–7**
  comparative aspects of **4.291**
    in baboon **4.291**
    in bushbaby **4.291**
    in cat **4.291**
    in ground squirrel **4.291**
    in macaques **4.291**
    in man **4.291**
    in mouse **4.291**
    in owl monkey **4.291**
    in rabbit **4.291**
    in rat **4.291**
    in rhesus monkey **4.291**
    in squirrel monkey **4.291**
    in tree shrew **4.291**
  and the cytochrome oxidase blobs **4.284–91**
  physiology of **4.287–9**
    spatial frequencies **4.287**
  in V4 **4.289–91**
Colour constancy **4.290, 6.53–61, 6.157–8, 6.175–6**
  computational approaches to **6.55–6**
  computational theories of **6.56–9**
    Land's retinex model **6.57, 6.192–3**
    von Kries Coefficient Law **6.56**
  definition of **6.176**
  explanation of **6.53–4, 6.157–8**
  Glossary explanation of **4.444**
  in insects **6.282**
  principal issues in theories of **6.55–6**
  relative **6.198–9**
  and relative quantum absorption rates **6.38**
  and the 'white' or neutral point of a scene **6.55**
Colour contrast **3.40, 10.135**
  in form perception **6.198–217**
  in insects **6.280**
  simultaneous **6.184**

Colour contrast sensitivity
  and colour resolution 6.201–4
    isoluminance tests for 6.202–4
Colour defects
  absorption 7.173
  alteration 7.173–4
  reduction 7.173–4
  SWS cone system 7.151–2
Colour deficiencies
  acquired 7.40, 7.215, 7.219
    and anomaloscopes 7.220–1
    bilateral 7.163
    classification 7.117–8
    and FM 100-Hue test 7.225–8
    neurophysiological review 7.38–9
    psychophysical investigation 7.38–55
      general principles of 7.40–1
  blue 7.88, 7.110
  blue–green 7.117–8
  blue–yellow, and ERG 7.60
  carriers 7.59–60
  of central origin 7.30
  congenital 7.40, 7.176
    and FM 100-Hue test 7.225–7
    human 7.211
    and non-human primates 7.202
    and tests 7.215
    threshold measurements of 7.53
  electrophysiological aspects of 7.64–71
  in females 7.117
  filter-induced tritan 7.123
  inherited
    blue 7.95–6, 7.98
    blue–green 7.5, 7.21–4
    human genetics 7.88–114
    molecular biology 7.101–11
    psychophysics of 7.4–37
    red–green 7.5–6, 7.9–21, 7.29, 7.88, 7.119
      discrimination of spectral differences 7.9–11
      genetics 7.91–5
      post-receptoral responses 7.18–20
      psychophysics of 7.90–1
      small field conditions 7.11
      spectral sensitivity functions 7.11–2
      types of 7.88–90
      without LWS loss 7.117–8
      in women heterozygotes 7.20–1
    types of 7.88–101
  in neurological disease 7.173–98
    optic-nerve disorders 7.173–83
    owing to central lesions 7.183–94
  in optic-nerve and -tract conduction 7.163
  progression and remission 7.116
  red–green
    genes 7.101
    in glaucoma 7.152
    impaired optic-nerve conduction 7.160
    Leber's hereditary optic atrophy 7.159
    in ophthalmic disease 7.124
    in optic neuritis 7.158
    with and without LWS loss 7.117–8
    rules correlating affected structures and types 7.162–3
    see also Colour vision tests; Deutan; Protan; Tritan; Tritan-like defect
  as symptoms of ophthalmic disease 7.115–8
  temporal changes in 7.116
  tests for 6.200
  unilateral 7.28–30, 7.116
Colour discrimination 10.265, **10.272**, **10.275**
  achromatic 7.38–9
  atypical monochromacy 7.26
  blue–green 7.21–2, 7.39
    in diabetes 7.149
    in ophthalmic disease 7.127, 7.130
  blue-sensitive mechanism 7.73
  blue–yellow 7.40, 7.42, 7.53
  and disease 7.64, 7.119
  perimetry 7.122
  purity 7.9–10, 7.21–2, 7.42–3
  red–green 7.18, 7.38, 7.40, 7.42, 7.117
    loss in visual field disturbances 7.163
    in ophthalmic disease 7.130, 7.140
  red–green heterozygotes 7.20–1
  rod-'green-cone' monochromats 7.27
  rod-'red-cone' monochromats 7.28
  of spectral differences 7.9–10
  unilateral deficiencies 7.29
Colour discrimination tasks 4.331
Colour discrimination threshold 7.43
Colour mapping, central 7.30
Colour matching 7.8, 7.174, **16.152**
  alteration by scotopization 7.68
  blue blindness 7.96
  blue system 7.78
  blue–green 7.22–3, 7.125
  dichromatic, variability of 7.15
  and dichromatic vision 6.27–31
  in macaque monkeys 7.200–1
  metameric 7.119
  in monochromats 7.26–7
  in optic neuritis 7.178
  parametric variations 7.6–7, 7.31–2
  red–green 7.9–10, 7.12–7
  in red–green heterozygotes 7.20–1
  and reflected light 6.22
  unilateral deficiencies 7.29
Colour measurement, physiological 6.191–3
Colour Mondrian **6.53**, **6.55**, **6.57**
  and the standard reference patch **6.57**
Colour naming 7.117
Colour opponency 4.285, 5.209–10, 5.236, 6.167–9
  Glossary explanation of **4.444**
  perceptual model of, in insects 6.280–1
Colour opponency responses 5.235
Colour opponency spectral sensitivity functions 5.202
Colour opponency systems 5.214–5
Colour opponent neurones, see Cone opponent neurones
Colour perception, CIE's proposed basic definitions of terms

of 6.43–4
Colour perimetry 7.49–52, 7.117–8, 7.128, 7.156, 7.174
 blue preferential 7.123, 7.126, 7.150, 7.153
  in DIOA 7.155, 7.157
  in drusen 7.158
  in ophthalmic disease 7.127, 7.130–1, 7.162
  in retinitis pigmentosa 7.146–8
 blue selective 7.123, 7.145, 7.153
 computerized red 7.129
 computerized static increment 7.147
 cone 7.123
 in deficiency evaluation 7.122
 discrimination 7.122
 in hemiachromatopsia 7.184–5
 kinetic 7.176
 red increment 7.135
  in cone disease 7.136–7, 7.140, 7.142
  in retinitis pigmentosa 7.146
 red-light 7.116
 saturation 7.122
 in Stargardt's disease 7.142–3
 static 7.49–50, 7.145, 7.155
 white increment, in ophthalmic disease 7.142–3, 7.145,
  7.148, 7.153–5, 7.158
Colour photography 7.73–4
Colour pyramids
 Ebbinghaus's 6.222
 Runge's 6.220
Colour resolution 6.201–4
Colour sensation, theories of 6.55
Colour signals 3.28–30
 natural 3.28–9
 predictive coding effects 3.30
Colour solids 4.333
 NCS 6.235
Colour space, Ostwald's 6.230
Colour spheres
 Forsius's 6.219
 Munsell's 6.254
 Wundt's 6.222
Colour stimulus, CIE definition of 6.226
Colour systems
 Munsell's 6.231–3
 Ostwald's 6.230
Colour television 6.294–307
 as an information-display medium 6.302–5
  set-up and calibration of the cathode-ray tube 6.304
  and stimulus generation using CRTs 6.304–5
  and symbolic colour use 6.304
 and novel display technologies 6.305–6
  colour liquid crystal 6.306
 and the shadow-mask cathode-ray tube 6.294–302
Colour therapy, for reading difficulties 13.171–2,
  13.176–9
Colour triangles
 Hering's 6.222–4
 Maxwell's 6.221
 NCS 6.235, 6.254
 Ostwald's 6.230

Colour vision 2.6–11, 3.49, 4.316–38, 5.46–7, 8.8, 9.149,
  12.12–4, 12.44–5, 12.357, 16.96–7
 absence of 2.388, 2.390
 additive and subtractive processes 5.203
 advantages of 2.306–10
 and ageing 16.151–2
 anomalies 12.58
 arthropod 2.204, 2.223–4
 biology of
  and Golgi 6.7
  and Polyak 6.7
 cone contributions to 6.146–62
 in cone dystrophy 7.136
 cortical mechanisms of 6.179–97
 decachromatic 2.295
 and developing visual system 16.111–2, 16.126
 dichromatic 2.73, 2.75–6, 2.78, 2.284, 2.289, 2.292–3,
  2.296, 2.299–300
 dimensionality 2.299
 effects of cone oil droplets on 6.84
 and evolution of eye 2.43
 evolution of 2.284–302, 6.62–89
  dimensionality 2.289–95
  phylogeny 2.284, 2.295–7
  wavelength discrimination 2.285–8
 and evolution of retina 2.142
 and evolution of vision 2.410
 genes 7.101–5
  LP, MP and SP 7.105–11
 genotypes in 6.97
 green system 7.72, 7.78
 history of 6.1–9
 and hue 6.23
 human 2.297, 2.299–301, 5.191
 impairments of, caused by cerebral lesions 12.385–410
 infant 16.112
 in insects 2.254, 2.257, 6.262–93
  in Apis mellifera 6.262–3
  in Collembola 6.262
  colour constancy in 6.282
  and ecology and evolution of photopigments 6.285–8
   in Diptera 6.287–8
   in hawkmoths 6.288
   in Musca 6.285–6
  in Hymenoptera 6.262
  input systems of 6.263–9
   comparison of photoreceptor action spectra 6.264–7
    in Blattoptera 6.265
    in Caelifera 6.266
    in Coleoptera 6.265–6
    in Diptera 6.265, 6.267
    in Hemiptera 6.265
    in Heteroptera 6.266
    in Hymenoptera 6.265–6
    in Lepidoptera 6.265–6
    in Odonata 6.265
    in Orthoptera 6.265
    in Plannipennia 6.265
   constraints of spectral sensitivities 6.263–4

Colour vision (*continued*)

determination of the spectral sensitivity of single
photoreceptors 6.264–9
in Calliphora 6.267
in Hymenoptera 6.268
in Orthoptera 6.268
in Papilio 6.268
in Hymenoptera 6.263
in Lepidoptera 6.263
number of spectral inputs 6.269
in Aeschnia 6.269
in ants 6.269
in Ascalaphus 6.269
in Callonychium 6.269
in cockroach 6.269
in Gryllus 6.269
in Hymenoptera 6.269
in Lepidoptera 6.269
in Musca 6.269
in Notonecta gluaca 6.269
in Papilionaceae 6.269
in Sympetrum 6.269
in Orthoptera 6.263
in Notonecta 6.262
pentachromatic 6.269, 6.275
polydimensional systems of 6.274–6
in Callonychium petuniae 6.274–5
in Cataglyphus bicolour 6.275–6
in Papilio 6.275
receptor models of 6.269–73
in Apis mellifera 6.270
in Hymenoptera 6.273
in Osmia rufa 6.273
see also Insects, colour vision in
spectral opponency in 6.276–82
from colour contrast phenomena 6.280
from neurophysiology of visual neurones 6.276–9
in Apis mellifera 6.276–8
in butterflies 6.276
in the cockroach 6.279
from a perceptual model in Apis mellifera 6.280–1
tetrachromatic 6.269, 6.274–5
trichromatic 6.269
and wavelength-selective behaviour 6.282–4
in ants 6.283
in butterflies 6.283–4
in crickets 6.283
in the fly 6.283
in the honey bee 6.282–4
in Melipona quadrifasciata 6.283
in the water bug 6.283
level of 6.112
and lightness 6.23, 6.26–7
loss of 2.306
M scaling 5.257
in mammals 2.478
genetic models in 6.123
meaning of 6.73–5
mechanisms 2.13, 16.113

molecular biology of 6.90–107
basic genetic concepts of 6.90–2
DNA 6.90–1
genes 6.90
rhodopsin 6.92
RNA 6.91
X chromosomes 6.90
Y chromosomes 6.90
and biochemical analysis 6.92–3
probes in 6.92
photoreception 6.93–100
motion blind 2.259
neurophysiology of 4.332–4
non-foveal dichromatic 7.14
normal 5.244, 7.4–9
and optics 5.87
pentachromatic 2.71–3, 2.289, 2.291
and peripheral vision 5.48
and photoreceptors 6.23–4
phylogenetic tree 2.295–6
physiological principles of 6.176–7
polychromatic 2.73
population coding 5.134
post-receptoral organization 7.8–9
precortical physiology of 6.163–78
chromatic and achromatic contrast 6.169–70
and the lateral geniculate nucleus 6.174–6
on-and off-channels 6.163–5
and retinal output/ganglion cells 6.170–4
spatial and spectral antagonism 6.165–9
primate 2.306–17, 2.444, 12.52
evolution of 6.78–80
primordial subsystem 2.312–3
progressive concomitant impairment 7.115–6
protan, in New World monkeys 7.208
psychophysics of 13.63
red system 7.72, 7.78
red–green 7.77
and the remapping of visual space 6.189–90
residual, in achromatopsia 12.400
and saturation 6.23
scheme of cerebral functions 12.403
second subsystem 2.313–4
see also Achromatopsia; Anomia, colour; Aphasia, colour-
chromatic mechanisms
and senescence 5.281–3
signal transfer of 12.55
and stereoacuity 5.137, 5.144–5
testing for 12.393–400
tetrachromatic 2.69, 2.289–92, 2.299
theory of 2.248, 4.332–4
and Retinex theory 4.332
trichromatic 2.72–3, 2.75–7, 2.284, 2.289, 2.292–4, 2.296,
2.314, 3.54
uses of
detection 6.22
recogition 6.23
vertebrate, evolution of 6.76–8
and visual movement agnosia 12.372

and visual pigments **6.**111–2
Colour vision genetics, see Genetics of inherited colour
    deficiencies
Colour vision locus, X-linked **7.**91–3
Colour vision replacement model **7.**93–4
Colour vision tests
    for achromatopsia **7.**229–30
    adaptation, for tritan deficiencies **7.**228–9
    anomaloscope **7.**216–20
    for children **7.**230
    for classification **7.**215–32
    design **7.**217–8
    diagnostic **7.**216, **7.**224, **7.**232
    for grading **7.**215–7, **7.**219, **7.**222, **7.**224, **7.**230–1
    hue discrimination (arrangement) **7.**215–8, **7.**223–8
    lantern **7.**216–7, **7.**229
    on non-human primates **7.**200–2, **7.**204, **7.**209
    perimetry **7.**230–1
    pseudoisochromatic **7.**220–2
    for screening **7.**215–8, **7.**221–2, **7.**224, **7.**228–32
    test battery **7.**215, **7.**218, **7.**231–2
    vocational **7.**215–6, **7.**223, **7.**229
Colour wiring **4.**330–1
Colour–object correlations **12.**392, **12.**407
Colour-coded neural circuitry, in primate retinas **6.**139–43
Colour-defective vision, genes and pigments in **6.**98–100
Coloured lenses
    Irlen **13.**173–6
    non-Irlen, studies of patients with reading disabilities
        using **13.**176
Coloured overlays, studies of patients with reading disabilities
    using **13.**176–8
Colourfulness **6.**47–8
    CIE definition of **6.**225
Colour-mixture thresholds **7.**46–8
Colour-opponent notch **7.**122
Colour-opponent pathways **7.**94
Colour-opponent system **7.**78
Colour-vision genotypes **6.**97
Colour-vision phenotypes **6.**98
Columba livia (pigeon) **2.**70, **2.**286, **2.**288
Columnar organization **6.**180
    of the visual cortex **4.**266–315
Columns **3.**333
    of cerebral cortex **11.**42
    dominance **3.**142, **3.**199, **3.**318, **11.**199
    Glossary explanation of **4.**444
    monocular **5.**253–4, **5.**261
    ocular dominance **5.**271, **11.**345–7, **12.**72
        and synaptic rearrangement **11.**258–9, **11.**264–5, **11.**271
        in visual cortex **11.**338, **11.**340, **11.**344
    organization of **5.**48, **5.**271
    orientation **3.**142, **3.**318, **11.**345–6
Coma **2.**94, **2.**97, **12.**281
Combinatorial explosion **2.**262
Comfort judgement, of visual displays **15.**25
Comfort and performance
    in relation to visual displays **15.**24–40
        intersubject comparisons and the effect of font

on **15.**32–4
    methods of measuring **15.**24–8
        category scaling by users **15.**25
        comparisons of **15.**26–8
        eye-movement characteristics **15.**25–6
        metric scaling by users **15.**25, **15.**27
        non-metric scaling by users **15.**25
        paper reference **15.**28
        reaction-time measurement **15.**28
        registration of judgement **15.**27
        response time **15.**26–8
        search velocity **15.**25–7
Comics **12.**307
Commissural connections **5.**272
Commissural pathways **3.**326, **3.**339
Commissurectomy **3.**348
Commissures **2.**444
    anterior **3.**339–40, **12.**112
    forebrain **3.**324–6
Commissurotomy **3.**325, **3.**330, **5.**273–4
Commitment **11.**34, **11.**39
Common axis **9.**3–4
Common-source hypothesis of oblique saccades **8.**106
Communication
    between apes and humans **12.**331
    emotional components of **12.**306
    by script **12.**306
    verbal **12.**304, **12.**306
    verbal–visual **12.**305, **12.**308
    visual **12.**332
    by visual signals **12.**306–7
Communication theory **2.**73, **10.**34
Comparator, explanation of **9.**105
Compartmentalization **11.**137–8, **11.**144, **11.**275–7, **11.**279
Compartments
    in *Drosophila* **11.**37–41, **11.**59, **11.**61
    histochemical **11.**42
    morphogenetic subfields **11.**60–1
    neuronal **11.**42, **11.**133, **11.**144
    somatodendritic **11.**279
    in vertebrate neurogenesis **11.**29–30, **11.**37–43
    in *Xenopus* **11.**38–9
Compartment-specific molecules **11.**81
Compensation, auditory **12.**260
Compensation method **5.**176
Compensation strategies **12.**208, **12.**261, **12.**268, **12.**272
    topographical disorientation **12.**418, **12.**420, **12.**425,
        12.429–30
Compensatory eye movement **8.**107–8
Competence theory of vision **14.**45
Competition, axon **11.**239–41, **11.**250–1
Complaints, psychological **16.**97
Complementary after-effect (CAE) **14.**22
Completion effects, scotoma **12.**146, **12.**151
Complex cells **4.**296
    anisotropy in **4.**281
    Glossary explanation of **4.**444
    optimal spatial frequency of **4.**292
Complex colour cells **6.**188

Complex spikes 8.224–5
Complexion 2.310
Complexity 14.98–9
 computing 14.106
 of feature operator 14.101
Component hypothesis of oblique saccades 8.103–6
Comprehension
 auditory 12.347
 of complex visual information 12.352
 hidden 12.341
 reading 12.340–1, 12.354
 of single letters 12.340
 speed 12.340
 unaware 12.355
 of written or spelled information 12.340
Compression 5.60
 and additivity 5.174
 chiasmal 7.161–2, 7.177, 10.60
 in contrast encoding 5.111, 5.116
 non-linear 5.23, 5.62, 5.154
 optic-nerve 7.116, 7.161–2
 signal 5.50, 5.59, 5.61, 5.69–71
Compressive non-linearity in visual processing 5.23
Compressive/expanding (P) motion 10.172
Computation and 3D representation 14.44
Computation, biophysics of 14.39–40
Computation and decision element 8.98
Computation, natural 14.91–6
Computation time, for saccades 8.117
Computational models 4.383, 10.122–30
Computational paradigm 14.32–3, 14.45
Computational theories 10.34, 10.107, 14.31–2
Computational vision 14.30–46
 algorithm 14.30, 14.32–4, 14.39–42, 14.44–5
 case studies 14.40–5
 components 14.32–40
 Marr's approach 14.30–2, 14.41, 14.43, 14.45
 vision as information processing 14.30–2
Computed tomography, *see* Computer tomography (CT)
Computer graphics 14.88
 in relation to receptive-field properties of visual
  cortex 4.217
Computer quantization 12.224
Computer simulations, of colour organization 4.326
Computer tomography (CT) 1.363, 12.129, 12.207, 12.209,
  12.260, 12.264
 and achromatopsia 12.393
 and colour agnosia 12.403
 and hemiachromatopsia 12.401–2
 and hemialexia 12.347
 illusion and hallucination 12.475
 and loss of topographical familiarity 12.425, 12.427
 positron emission 2.453, 5.255
 and prosopagnosia 12.266, 12.269–70, 12.275–8, 12.283,
  12.285
 and pure alexia 12.342, 12.347, 12.354
 single photon emission (SPECT) 12.207
 and topographical disorientation 12.429
 x-ray, in visualizing the eye 1.363–5

Computer vision 12.5, 12.7, 12.11, 12.14, 12.17
Computer-aided work
 information requirements for 15.99–113
  the function of information presentation 15.99–100
  the role of the human in computer-based man–machine
   systems 15.100
  tasks 15.100
 models of user requirements and user support for 15.99–
  113
  cognitive, for the design of interactive computer
   systems 15.106
   SANE 15.106–7
  computational, of cognition and skilled
   behaviour 15.103–6
   ACT* 15.104–6
   SOAR 15.104–6
  display rate and system response times 15.101–2
  GOMS 15.103–4, 15.106
   cognitive complexity theory 15.103
  human action 15.102–3
  human cognition for human–computer
   interaction 15.100–1
  human perception and motor control 15.101
   model human processor 15.101
  skills, learning and information requirements 15.106,
   15.108
 technology for information presentation and user
  support 15.108–11
  documentation 15.109–10
  error messages 15.110
  help 15.109–10
  hypermedia 15.110
  intelligent interfaces 15.110–1
  tutorials 15.110
  visual metaphors for user interfaces 15.108–9
   direct manipulation 15.109
   graphical displays 15.108–9
   Hyper-Card 15.109–10
   Rank-Xerox STAR 15.109
   ROOMS 15.109
Computer-assisted tomography, *see* Computed tomography
Concatenated speech 15.120–1
Concept exemplars 14.118
Concept learning 14.107, 14.118–22
Concept of number 14.126–7
Concepts, verbal 12.233
Condition-and-test paradigms 4.260
Conditioning stimuli 4.258
Conduction velocity 4.32
Conductivity, dielectric 1.312
Cone antagonism 6.165–9, 7.65–8
Cone contribution in monochromacy 7.24
Cone dysfunction syndrome 7.137
Cone dystrophy 7.116, 7.135–9
 progressive 7.219
Cone embryology 11.394–6, 11.398–400
Cone fundamentals 2.289, 2.291
Cone mosaics, in vertebrate retina 6.128–33
Cone opponency 6.165–9

Cone opponent neurones **6**.171–6
Cone opsins **7**.93 **7**.95
  LWS, MWS, SWS and genes **7**.105–11
Cone outer segment misalignment **7**.125
Cone pathway **10**.302–3
Cone perimetry **7**.123
Cone photopigment genes **7**.18, **7**.72–4
Cone photoreceptors
  physiology of **6**.146–62
    in amphibians **6**.146
    and encoding of light intensity **6**.146–8
    in fish **6**.146, **6**.148
    in higher vertebrates **6**.146
    in humans **6**.146, **6**.148
    in lower vertebrates **6**.146–61
    in primates **6**.146, **6**.153–4
    and the principle of univariances **6**.148–9, **6**.169–70
    in salamander **6**.146
    in turtles **6**.146–61
      and dependence on coloured stimuli **6**.148–9
    and visual perception research experiments **6**.154–61
  sensitivity control and light adaptation **6**.150–2
    in humans **6**.152
    in mudpuppies **6**.150–2
    in turtles **6**.150–2
    and the Weber fraction **6**.151
    and the Weber–Fechner Law **6**.151–2
  spatial properties of **6**.149–50
    in turtles **6**.149–50
  temporal properties of **6**.152–3
    and Bloch's Law **6**.152
Cone pigment absorbance, low foveal **7**.145
Cone pigment complement in non-human primates **7**.207, **7**.210, **7**.212
Cone pigment variation in Callicebus monkey **7**.208
Cone spacing **10**.204
Cone vision **5**.49
Cone of vision **12**.26, **12**.34, **12**.136
Cone vision
  absolute threshold **5**.278
  adapting field **5**.278
  dark-adapted **5**.58
  in peripheral vision **5**.55–7, **5**.71
Cone–rod dystrophy (CRD)
  early-onset **7**.139–40
  late-onset **7**.140, **7**.142
Cone–rod inhibition **7**.137
Cone-blindness **7**.24
Cone-opsin genes **6**.95–6
  blue, *see* S-cones
  green, *see* M-cones
  and probes **6**.95–6
  red, *see* L-cones
Cones **1**.233, **4**.317–20, **5**.210, **12**.56
  adaptation characteristics **5**.192
  ageing **16**.62
  and ageing macula **16**.81–2, **16**.89
  blue **3**.11, **3**.15–6, **7**.60–1, **7**.77–8, **7**.80–1, **7**.83–5
    and colour signals **3**.29

and dark light **3**.25
  in foveal sampling **3**.20–1
  and ganglion cells **3**.55
blue-sensitive **5**.47
colour deficiency neurophysiology **7**.38–9
in colour discriminability **5**.213
in colour perimetry **7**.49
in colour vision **2**.296, **2**.316–7
dark light **3**.25
density
  in cat retina **3**.16
  in fovea **3**.17
  in foveal sampling **3**.20–1, **3**.24
  in primates **3**.14–5
and developing visual system **16**.107, **16**.110, **16**.113, **16**.118–9, **16**.125–6
double **2**.66, **2**.68, **2**.70–2, **2**.296, **2**.470, **2**.472, **2**.477
and equiluminance **5**.235
and ERG **7**.57
in evolution of eye **2**.5, **2**.8, **2**.10, **2**.12–6
  vertebrate and invertebrate **2**.35, **2**.37, **2**.39–44
evolution of red **3**.54
in evolution of retina **2**.136–40, **2**.143
in evolution of vision **2**.404, **2**.412–3
excitation **5**.180
in fish colour vision **2**.290
forbidden **7**.94
foveal **3**.113, **3**.115–6, **5**.222
fundamentals of **5**.191–2, **5**.196, **5**.198, **5**.210
generalized **14**.112–3
Glossary explanation of **4**.444
green **7**.76, **7**.81, **7**.85
green-sensitive **5**.47
and horizontal cells **3**.38–9
irregular spacing **3**.21
L- **12**.55, **12**.57, **12**.61, **16**.109, **16**.112, **16**.126–8
and light damage **16**.66
long-to middle-wavelength (L/M) **5**.192
long-wavelength (L) **5**.174–6, **5**.179–81, **5**.185, **5**.193–4, **5**.199
M- **12**.55, **12**.57, **12**.61, **16**.109, **16**.112
in mammals **2**.476–8
mechanisms **5**.167, **5**.178, **5**.193, **5**.196
medium-wavelength (M) **5**.174–6, **5**.179–81, **5**.185, **5**.193–4, **5**.199
mosaics **2**.139
non-foveal **5**.277
normally functioning **5**.210
opponency **5**.192, **5**.195
opponent mechanisms **5**.199
output synapse **3**.26
in peripheral vision **5**.44–5, **5**.47, **5**.49–50, **5**.56, **5**.58, **5**.61, **5**.66
photoreceptors **3**.9–13
pigment **2**.410, **5**.56, **5**.191, **5**.210
primate **7**.72–5
in pursuit system **2**.168–70
and radiation **16**.57, **16**.61
red **7**.76, **7**.80

red-sensitive 5.47
reduced optical density of 7.163
responses of, pooling 1.259
and retinal organization 5.41
S- 12.55, 12.57, 12.61, **16.106, 16.109, 16.111–2,
    16.126–9**
see also under L-, M-or S-cones
sensitivity 5.210
short-wavelength (S) 2.309, 2.311–3, 5.174–5, 5.179–80,
    5.192–4, 5.199, 5.207
and signal transfer 12.59
signals 5.191, 5.194–5, 5.244, 5.268
single 2.470, 2.472, 2.476–7
spacing 3.29
    extrafoveal 3.22, 3.24
    in fovea 3.20, 3.24
    and photoreceptor coupling 3.27
spectral absorption curves of 12.55
spectral sensitivity 5.188, 5.191–3, 5.210
summation, linear model 5.195
telodendria 3.26
threshold methods 7.40, 7.45–6
in trichromacy 2.310–3
ultraviolet-sensitive 2.290, 2.292
weightings 5.193–5
Cones and dendrites 11.159–60, 11.164
Confabulation 12.182, 12.197
Confidence-rating procedure 5.15, 5.18–21
Confocal laser scanning ophthalmoscope 1.378
Confrontation tests 9.202
Confusion colours 7.32
Confusion line 7.22, 7.177
dichromatic 7.119
in optic-nerve disease 7.179
in red–green defects 7.9–10
tritanopic 7.120
Confusion loci 7.96
Confusion point, tritanopic 7.22
Confusions, tritan 7.134–7, 7.148, 7.150
Congenital nystagmus 8.299, 8.302–3, 8.315–6, 8.323
Congruent borders, of cortical areas 4.170
Conic surfaces 1.69
Conicoid, contact-lens surface as 1.3
Conjugacy principle of ghost images 9.46–7
Conjugate eye movements, Glossary explanation of 4.444
Conjunctiva, hyperaemia of 1.109–10
Conjunctivitis, papillary 1.110
Connections
associational 3.350, 3.371
callosal 3.371, 12.476
    columnar organization 3.349
    excitatory and inhibitory influences 3.349
    heterotopic 3.348, 3.351
    homotopic 3.348–9, 3.351, 12.357
    sensory and motor maps 3.326–35
    visuotopic organization 3.340–2, 3.344–6, 3.348
commissural 3.371
cortical 3.342–7
    extrinsic 3.348

intrinsic 3.348–9
    in visual cortex 3.370–1
dominant inhibitory, in alexia 12.356
eye-specific 11.269
feedback 3.336, 3.351
feedforward 3.351
geniculocortical 11.258
growth of new neuronal 12.19
heterotopic 3.335, 3.340
homotopic 3.335, 3.340
inferotemporal cortex 12.109
interhemispheric 12.350
intrinsic 3.350–1, 3.371
limbic 12.326
neuronal, for reading 12.356
of primate area 7 12.92–4
principle of 12.128
refinement 3.132
splenial 12.406
synaptic 11.257
transcortical 12.19
Connectivity
corticocortical 3.324–51
graph 3.344
heterotopic callosal 3.335–40
Consciousness 12.259
delirant changes in 12.477
loss of 12.349
Consonants 12.355
Constancy
contrast 10.200
object 10.163
shape 10.202
size 10.202
Constant stimuli method 10.36
Constraints
biological and ecological 14.19–28, 14.83–9, 14.91
in computational vision 14.33–4, 14.40–1, 14.44
hardware 14.40
implementational 14.44
learned 14.89
physical, and computational vision 14.43
rigidity 14.34
smoothness 14.41, 14.92
Constrast, Glossary explanation of 4.444
Constringence 2.95
Construction plans 12.307
Constructional apraxia 13.24
Contact lens optical lever technique 8.71–5, 8.80
Contact lens systems, search coil-based 9.112
Contact lenses
and the aftercare examination 1.100–1
    and corneal staining with fluorescein 1.101
    and discomfort 1.101
    and dryness 1.101
    and lens soiling 1.101
    and reduced vision 1.101
back vertex power of 1.428
    measurement with a focimeter 1.428

Contact lenses (*continued*)
  corneal, *see under* Contact lenses, hard
  correction using 1.80–119, 9.216
  definitions of thicknesses of 1.429
    axial 1.429
    axial edge lift 1.429
    centre thickness 1.429
    radial 1.429
    radial edge lift 1.429
    radial edge thickness 1.429
  diameter tolerances on 1.429
  fitting and assessment of 1.96–9
    hard 1.96–7
      assessment of lens performance 1.97
      assessment of lens-cornea bearing 1.97
      'edge lift' 1.96
      initial choice of 1.97
      and over-refraction 1.97
    scleral 1.96
    soft 1.97–9
      assessment of lens performance 1.98
      assessment of lens-cornea bearing 1.98
      flexure effects of 1.99
      initial choice of 1.98
      over-refraction 1.98–9
  'fitting philosophies' of 1.96
  hard 1.80–1
  historical development of 1.82–4
    early theories of 1.82
    glass scleral 1.82–3
    hard 1.83
    hard gas permeable 1.84
    plastic scleral 1.83
    silicone elastomer 1.84
    soft 1.83–4
  insertion and removal of various types of 1.99–100
  inspection of 1.95–6
  maintenance systems for 1.101–4
    in-eye lubrication and rewetting 1.104
    protein removal 1.103–4
    rinsing 1.101–2
      with normal saline 1.101–2
      with preservatives 1.102
    storage and disinfection 1.102–3
      by heat 1.103
      by hydrogen peroxide 1.103
      and infections 1.103
        Pseudomonas aeruginosa 1.103
      by microwave irradiation 1.103
      by ultrasonics 1.103
    surface cleaning 1.102
    wetting solutions 1.103
  manufacture of 1.88–9
    cast moulding 1.89
    glass blowing and grinding 1.88
    impression 1.88
    lathing 1.88–9
    spin casting 1.89
  materials used in the manufacture of

    glass 1.84–5
    hard plastics 1.85
    hydrogels 1.85
    polymethyl methacrylate 1.84–5
    silicone rubber 1.85
  measurement of light transmission of 1.431
  measurement of permeability and transmissibility
    of 1.431–2
    and the diffusion coefficient 1.432
    by a dual-chamber technique 1.432
    by polarography 1.432
    and the solubility coefficient 1.432
  measurement of quality of surface and materials of 1.431
  measurement of specific gravity of 1.431
  measurement of water content of 1.431
  measurement of wettability of 1.432–3
    by the captive-bubble method 1.433
    and the contact angle 1.432
    of hydrophylic 1.432
    by the sessile-drop method 1.433
    and the wetting angle 1.433
  methods for the determination of surface curvatures
    of 1.426–8
    comparison of 1.428
    keratometry 1.427
    miscellaneous 1.428
      interferometric techniques 1.428
      Moiré fringes 1.428
    projection methods 1.427
    radiuscopes 1.426
    sag measurements 1.426–7
  methods for the measurement of diameter of 1.428–9
    measuring magnifiers 1.429
    projection 1.429
    V-gauge 1.428–9
  methods for the measurement of power of 1.428
  ocular responses to
    conjunctiva 1.109–11
      hyperaemia 1.109–10
      papillary conjunctivitis 1.110
      superior limbic keratoconjunctivitis 1.110–1
    corneal epithelium 1.108–9
      bedewing 1.109
      impaired hydration control 1.109
      pleomorphism 1.109
      polymegethism 1.109
    the wearing of 1.104–11
      corneal epithelium 1.104–6
        compromised junctional integrity 1.106
        hypoaesthesia 1.106
        infectious keratitis 1.106
        microcysts 1.105
        oedema 1.104–5
        reduced mitosis 1.105
        reduced oxygen flow 1.106
        staining 1.104
          fluorescence 1.104
          'three o'clock' and 'nine o'clock' positions 1.104
        thinning 1.105

Contact lenses (*continued*)
  ulcerative keratitis 1.106
  corneal stroma 1.106–8
    acidosis 1.107
    folds 1.107
    infiltrates 1.107–8
    keracyte death 1.107
    oedema 1.106–8
    shape change 1.108
    striae 1.106–7
    thinning 1.107
    vascular response 1.108
  and patient instructions 1.100
  physiological bases of wearing 1.89–94
    and the closed-eye environment 1.93–4
    corneal physiology 1.90–1, 1.93
      and hypercapnia 1.92
      and hypoxia 1.91
      and temperature 1.92–3
    corneal topography 1.90
    tear physiology 1.93
    visual performance 1.89
      and the contrast-sensitivity function 1.90
      and the use of low-contrast acuity 1.90
  properties of materials used in the manufacture of 1.85–8
    density 1.87
    flexure 1.87
    hydration 1.88
    mechanical strength 1.87
    optical and refractive indexes 1.88
    permeability to oxygen and carbon dioxide 1.86–7
    specific gravity 1.87
    wettability and 'contact angle' 1.87–8
  refractive index of 1.429
  scleral 1.80–1
  soft 1.80–1
  special types of 1.111–5
    for the correction of astigmatism 1.111–2
      toric 1.111–2
        manufactured by crimping 1.111
        prism ballasting of 1.111
        reversed prism 1.111–2
        stabilization position in 1.112
        truncation in 1.111
        use of thin zones in 1.111
    for the correction of presbyopia
      alternating vision bifocal 1.112–3
      diffractive bifocal 1.113
      monovision 1.112
      pinhole 1.112
      simultaneous vision bifocal 1.113
      spectacle over-correction 1.112
    future trends in 1.115–6
    therapeutic 1.113–5
      aphakia 1.114–5
      collagen bandage 1.114
      keratoconus 1.114
        hybrid 1.114
        'piggy-back' system 1.114

    orthokeratology 1.115
    post-radial keratotamy 1.115
    tinted 1.113
      artificial iris 1.113
      iris print 1.113
      transparent 1.113
      ultraviolet-blocking 1.113
  specifications and tolerances for 1.424–6
  surface approximation as a conicoid 1.3
  thicknesses of 1.429
    methods for the measurement of 1.429–31
      gravimetric 1.430
      pachometry 1.430
      projectors 1.430
      radioscope 1.430
      thickness gauge 1.429–30
      ultrasonography 1.430
  wear modalities of 1.94–101
    continuous 1.94
    daily 1.94–5
    disposability of 1.95
    extended 1.94
    flexible 1.94
    planned replacement of 1.95
Context, facilitation, visual pattern 12.339
Continuity 5.286
Continuous error processing, in saccadic control 8.131–2
Continuous-shift operations 14.55, **14.58–60**, 14.62, 14.66
Contour density 10.202
Contour perception 4.282
Contours 5.286
  and agnosia 12.198, 12.205
  articulation of 2.309
  contrast 12.70
  and equiluminance 5.245
  explicit 5.241, 5.248
  illusionary 12.81–3, 12.151, 12.154, 12.191–2
  and illusions 5.242–4
  implicit 5.241, 5.248
  object 12.5
  occluding 12.12, 14.5, 14.37
  orientation 12.188
  perception in area V2 12.81–3
  subjective 5.241, 5.246, 5.248, 12.81–3
  as visual cues 5.286
  in visual data processing 12.80
Contraceptives, oral 7.152
Contraction, in cell locomotion 11.176–7
Contralateral neglect, as a result of parietal lesions 4.413
Contrast 2.168–9, 2.300, 5.120, 10.290–4
  achromatic 5.50
  adaptation (CA) 5.111–3, 5.116
  after-image 5.111–3
  chromatic 5.50, 5.214, 5.216
  colour 5.85, 5.227, 10.135
  cone 5.199
  constancy 5.106–8, 5.110–1, 5.113–4, 5.116–7, 10.200
  definitions 5.106
  detection thresholds 5.167

discrimination 5.320–2, **10**.201, **10**.221–2
effects of, in hyperacuity **10**.94–5
encoding 5.106
  left–right asymmetry 5.109
and equiluminance 5.240, 5.245
gain 5.108–9, 5.113, 5.154
in hyperacuity 5.223–8, 5.230–1
magnitude estimation 5.106, 5.109–12, 5.116
matching 5.106–12, 5.114, 5.117, **10**.221
Michaelson **10**.19–20, **10**.290
in modulation detection 5.11
'over-constancy' 5.117
perceived 5.111–5
perception 5.107–9, 5.112, 5.114–5, 5.117
  in amblyopia **10**.221–2
in peripheral vision 5.49–50
range of chromatic image 5.237
Rayleigh **10**.290–1
reversed 2.276
signal transfer of **12**.54–5, **12**.58
suprathreshold 5.110, 5.112, 5.114–5, 5.161, 5.322,
  10.221–2
temporal 2.243, 2.245, 2.252
texture and stereo depth 5.124–5
Weber **10**.290–1
Contrast amplitude 1.254
Contrast chart, Regan High and Intermediate **16**.154
Contrast columns 4.275–8
Contrast energy difference metric **15**.16–7
Contrast gain **10**.290–1, **10**.303–4
Contrast gain control 4.16, **10**.145
  and signal transmission 4.54
Contrast gradient 1.254
Contrast increment detection **10**.98–100
Contrast rendering factor **15**.64
'Contrast sensation', *see* Contrast, perceived
Contrast sensitivity 8, 84, 2.445, 2.454, 5.35–42, 8.3, 9.209,
  10.193–5, **10**.290–302, **16**.154–5, **16**.158
achromatic 5.214–6
age-related degradations in **16**.76
age-related loss 5.92
and agnosia **12**.195
in amblyopia **10**.213–6, **10**.218–9
and apparent motion 5.153
'blue-cone' monochromats 7.27
chromatic 5.214–7
in contrast encoding 5.109, 5.111
and contrast perception 5.114
in early life 5.282
and edge detection 5.103
and flicker 5.149, 5.180
letter chart, Pelli–Robson **16**.154
luminance 5.214
masking 5.102
and motion sensitivity 5.150–1
and nervous system 5.279
in Parkinson's disease **10**.252–4
in pattern discrimination 5.266–8, 5.270–1, 5.274
in peripheral vision 5.54–5, 5.67–71, 5.73, 5.256–8,

5.261–2
photon-based theory 5.71
photopic **10**.299–300
and retinal image movement 8.3–5, 8.86–9
and senescence 5.279–81
and sine-wave gratings 5.103
spatiotemporal, in Parkinson's disease **10**.253
static 5.295
suprathreshold 5.106–7, **10**.245–6
temporal 5.147, **16**.156
temporal and spatial factors 5.281
texture and stereo depth 5.125
and velocity perception 5.160–1
and visibility 5.236
and visual channels 5.98, 5.100
in visual processing 5.29
Contrast sensitivity function 2.106–7, 4.42, 4.56–7, 5.291–5,
  10.65, **10**.91
and the absence of low-frequency decline 6.201
achromatic 6.201
chromatic 6.201
  low-pass characteristics of 6.201
and colour resolution 6.203–4
and contact lenses 1.90
and detection thresholds 7.52, 7.54
and developing visual system **16**.111, **16**.120, **16**.125–8
Glossary explanation of 4.444
luminance 6.201, 6.206
and optimum colour and luminance contrast 6.201–3
spatial 4.67–8, **10**.44–5
spatiotemporal **10**.43–5
in specifically disabled readers and controls **13**.151
temporal 4.68
Contrast sensitivity response 7.7
Contrast threshold elevation 9.182–3
Contrast thresholds 5.102, 5.106, 5.108, 5.152–3, 5.280,
  5.321, 5.323, **10**.193
abnormalities in **10**.239–45
Contrast-control hypothesis 1.251
Control theory 8.71
Controls, *see* Sensory modalities
Convergence 1.58, 2.118, 5.228, 8.157, 8.205, **11**.257, **12**.191,
  14.89
amacrine cell 3.43
in arthropods 2.203–4, 2.206, 2.212–4, 2.217, 2.219–21,
  2.223
binocular 5.33
and binocular vision 2.273–5, 2.277
and callosal pathways 3.340–1, 3.350–1
in commissural pathways 3.326
and developing visual system **16**.123
in dyslexia **13**.145, **13**.182
evoked by crossed disparities 9.122
in evolution of retina 2.139, 2.143
feedforward connections 3.338, 3.342
and ganglion cells 3.48, 3.58
multimodal **11**.369–74, **11**.376, **11**.380–1
and origins of eye 2.57
in peripheral vision 5.45, 5.51, 5.60, 5.72, 5.75

Convergence (*continued*)
  and postreceptoral mechanisms 3.30
  receptor-bipolar 3.25
  rod-bipolar 3.26, 3.35–6
  and synaptic rearrangement 11.259
  and torsion 8.168
  and visuo-spatial disorders 12.436
  zone 3.345–6
Convergence points in colour confusions 7.32
Convergence-to-accommodation ratio 1.236
Conversion, internal 16.35
Convolution 2.93, 3.8, 3.18–9, 3.23, 14.4
Co-operative processes 9.135
Co-ordinate systems
  horizontal-vertical 14.58
  object-centred 14.53–4, 14.59
  viewer-centred 14.53–4, 14.59
Co-ordinate transformation 8.244, 8.323, 8.326–7
Co-ordinates
  allocentric 12.411, 12.416
  craniotopic 8.327
  egocentric 12.411, 12.414–6, 12.431–4
    and posterior parietal lobe 12.92, 12.105
  internal (retinal) 8.98, 8.132, 8.210, 8.327
  motor error 8.251
  optokinetic 8.66
  of perceived extrapersonal space, stabilization of 12.98
  retinal 12.431
  retinotopic 12.431, 12.433
    illusion and hallucination 12.468, 12.470
    and posterior parietal lobe 12.92, 12.105–6
  space
    extrapersonal 12.435
    transformation of 12.434
  spatial 8.98, 8.132, 8.210
  spatiocentric 12.411
  spatiotopic 12.431, 12.433
    global 12.434
    illusion and hallucination 12.468, 12.470
    local 12.434
    and posterior parietal lobe 12.92, 12.105–6
  system, allocentric 12.433
  vestibular 8.20–2, 8.216, 8.323
Copepods optics 2.121–2, 2.125
Copilia quadrata 2.55–9
Copy
  efference 12.4, 12.6–7
    see also Signal, efference copy
Copy mechanisms, efference 12.364
Copy signals 12.463
  efference 12.465
  kinaesthetic 12.465
  somatosensory 12.465
Copying
  and alexia 12.335
  and pure alexia 12.340, 12.342
  and spatial hemineglect 12.455
  and visual movement agnosia 12.373–4
  written material 12.336

Corinth, Lovis 12.445–6
Cornea 11.393–4
  ageing processes in 5.277
  aspheric 2.99
  birefringence of 1.313, 1.317–8
  curvature 2.109
  decompensation of 1.124–5
  in dioptrics 2.82, 2.84–5, 2.88–9, 2.91, 2.95–6, 2.99, 2.103, 2.107–8, 2.110
  and evolution of vision 2.399, 2.404, 2.409–12
  experimental data on 1.314–7
  in eye evolution 2.17, 2.414
  and eye optics 2.120–1
  human 1.2–3
    contour of 1.2
  iridescence 2.89
  in mammals 2.468, 2.470, 2.473, 2.475
  optical properties of 1.313–4
    refractive index 1.313
  and oxygen uptake via the tear pump 1.91
  physiology of 1.93
    and contact lenses 1.90
  polarization cross of 1.314
  and radiation 16.55–7, 16.59–60
  response to stress of 1.317
  and strain distortion 1.317
  structure of 1.313
  topography of, and contact lenses 1.90
Corneal ectasia
  keratoconus 1.45–6
  pellucid marginal degeneration 1.46
Corneal endothelium 1.108–9
  bedewing of 1.109
  blebbing of, due to the wearing of contact lenses 1.108
  impaired hydration control of 1.109
  and Maurice's specular microscope 1.390
  oedema of, due to the wearing of contact lenses 1.108
  pleomorphism in 1.109
  polymegethism in 1.109
  specular microscopy of 1.125
Corneal flattening 1.3
Corneal inlays
  keratophakia 1.154–5
  polysulphone 1.154–5
  synthetic
    hydrogel lenses 1.155–6
    polysulphone lenses 1.155–6
Corneal stroma
  acidosis of 1.107
  oedema of 1.106
  and striae 1.106–7
Corneal 'warpage', and the long-term wearing of contact lenses 1.108
Corner reflectors 2.130
Cornsweet's model of fixational control 8.74–5
Corollary discharge 8.189, 8.212
Corona ciliaris 11.392–3
Corpus callosum 2.444, 2.456, 3.324–5, 3.332, 5.272–4, 10.262, 10.282

anterior **12**.349
and callosal pathways **3**.335, **3**.340–2, **3**.346, **3**.348
and face recognition **12**.230
posterior **12**.348–9
and prosopagnosia **12**.274
sections of **12**.347
and spatial hemineglect **12**.463
splenium of **12**.335, **12**.343, **12**.345–7
  and colour anomia **12**.408
  and hemiachromatopsia **12**.402
  inferior third of **12**.349
  posterior, arteriovenous malformations (AVM) **12**.349–50
  surgical splitting **12**.347
  transection **12**.348
surgery **12**.350
surgical section **12**.348
Corpus geniculatum laterale, *see* Lateral geniculate body
Corrective saccades **8**.9, **8**.122–3
Correlated states **9**.170
Correlates, anatomical **12**.336
Correlation and motion perception **5**.156
Correlation quadrangles **14**.64
Correlation theory **2**.252
Correlations
  anatomo-clinical **12**.334
  clinico-pathological **12**.263–4
  pattern property **14**.2–3
  simultaneous **2**.254
  and spatial relations **14**.52
Correlogram **9**.217–8
Correspondence problem **9**.84
  computational constraints in **9**.43–4
  cyclopean solutions to **9**.45–9
  and Keplerian projection **9**.43–5
  orientation specificity in **9**.44–5
  size specificity in **9**.44
Correspondence shift **9**.184–5
Corresponding points **9**.8, **9**.20
Cortex
  acquired colour deficiencies **7**.38–9
  agranular retrosplenial **12**.94
  angular gyrus **12**.264
  areas 1, 2, 4 and 5 **7**.70–1
  auditory **3**.304–5, **3**.311, **3**.336
  calcarine **3**.331
  caudal inferotemporal **3**.314, **3**.316
  cerebral **3**.311, **5**.161, **7**.184, **8**.277–96
    cell lineage in **11**.42–3
    columnar organization **11**.42
    and compartments **11**.41
    critical period plasticity **11**.288
    histogenesis **11**.43
    malformations **3**.363
    multipotential precursor cells in **11**.32, **11**.34–6
    neurogenesis **11**.28–9
    rat **11**.282
  development of **10**.182–3
  expanded **3**.319

extrastriate **3**.371, **7**.39, **8**.245, **8**.281–2, **8**.284–5, **8**.306, **11**.337, **12**.148
  and callosal pathways **3**.331–2, **3**.334–5, **3**.337–8, **3**.346
  in visual cortex **11**.342, **11**.344
and flicker **5**.179, **5**.187
flicker responses **5**.183–8
frontal **3**.305, **3**.313
frontal eye fields **8**.67, **8**.115, **8**.213, **8**.244–6, **8**.255, **8**.270, **8**.277, **8**.283, **8**.286–8
fusiform **12**.264
inferotemporal **7**.70–1, **8**.277, **8**.285–6, **12**.108, **12**.386
  input signals to **12**.111–2
  signal processing in **12**.109–17
  structure and connections **12**.109
left calcarine **12**.342
limbic **3**.302–3, **3**.305, **3**.308, **3**.310
mammalian striate **10**.122
medio-basal occipito-temporal **12**.480
mesial occipital **12**.344
mesial occipito-temporal **12**.344
  inferior **12**.401
mesial temporal **12**.344
middle and middle superior temporal **8**.153, **8**.211, **8**.213, **8**.215, **8**.282–3
moderately expanded **3**.319
motor **3**.311, **3**.330–1, **3**.335, **11**.283, **11**.286, **11**.290
occipital **3**.371, **11**.42–3, **11**.235, **12**.148
occipital–temporal **3**.302, **3**.304–6, **3**.308, **5**.258
parietal **2**.173–4, **8**.40, **8**.153–4, **8**.283–5
parieto-insular vestibular (PIVC) **12**.154, **12**.300, **12**.434, **12**.464
peristriate **12**.467
prefrontal **8**.284, **8**.288–9
prestrate **7**.188–9, **8**.281–2, **10**.264
primary motor **12**.463
primary sensory **12**.269
primary visual **12**.50, **12**.144–5, **12**.467
  and blindness **12**.147–8
  and blindsight **12**.148–9, **12**.154
  and colour agnosia **12**.403
  and colour deficiencies **12**.409
  and computational vision **14**.32
  direct stimulation **12**.168–71
  electrical or magnetic stimulation through skull **12**.171
  electrical stimulation of **12**.168–72
  and migraine phosphenes **12**.176–7
  and phosphenes **12**.167
  and reading **12**.323
  signal processing in **12**.65–76
    elementary rules **12**.67–75
    non-visual and efferent signals **12**.75–6
    retino-cortical magnification **12**.65–7
processing chain **12**.346
retroinsular **12**.300
secondary visual **12**.467
see also Visual cortex
sensory **3**.330
somatosensory **3**.304, **3**.311, **3**.326–30
  area S1 **3**.327–8

Cortex (*continued*)
   area S2 3.327–30, 3.335–7
   callosal pathways 3.335
   lesions 3.327
   vestibular area 3aN ('neck' region) 12.434
   striate 3.302, 3.314, 7.39, 7.70, 7.184, 7.189, 7.193, 8.245,
      8.247, 8.278–81, 8.306, 10.266, 11.337, 11.342–4,
      12.467
   and callosal pathways 3.331, 3.334, 3.336, 3.346
   neurogenesis 3.360
   in pursuit system 2.170, 2.172
   structures, mesial occipito-temporal 12.345
   supergranular layers of monkey VI 5.271
   supplementary eye fields 8.289–90, 8.305
   temporal 3.319
   vestibular 12.480
   visual 10.110, 10.147
      areas of
         of cat and monkey 5.135, 5.137–8
         in pattern discrimination 5.268, 5.270–1
         and stereoacuity 5.133
         V1 (striate) 5.133–5, 5.166, 5.208, 5.224, 5.230,
            5.251–6, 5.260–1
            cat and monkey neurones of 5.165
            direction-sensitive neurones of 5.169
            hypercolumns of 5.65
            of macaque 5.133
            neural substrate of 5.251–3
            orientation columns of 5.48
            in peripheral vision 5.44–5, 5.75, 5.255
            retinotopic mapping of 5.271
            simple cells of layer IVb 5.39
            spatial sampling in 5.73
         V2 5.134–5
         V3, of monkey 5.271
         V4 5.287
         V5 (MT) 5.135, 5.287
         VP 5.271
         of monkey 5.271
      association (integration) 12.133, 12.345, 12.393
         illusion and hallucination 12.474–5, 12.478
         temporal 12.80
      and colour anomia 12.407
      connections 12.79–80
      discovery of 12.47–51
      electrical stimulation of surface 12.170
      epileptogenic activity 12.132
      extrastriate 12.77–91
         association (integration) areas 12.77–81, 12.84, 12.89
         colour perception 12.83–5
         contour perception 12.81–3
         motion perception 12.85–91
         projections from area V1 to higher visual
            centres 12.78–81
      feedback mechanism 12.475
      focal atrophy 12.180
      focal degeneration 12.180
      grey matter lesions 12.132–5
      mesencephalic region 12.478

   plasticity of neuronal circuits 12.132–5
   and prosopagnosia 12.267
   and pure alexia 12.343
Cortical achromatopsia 6.188–9
Cortical area 17 1.233
Cortical area MT (i.e. V5) 10.147
Cortical area VI 10.147
Cortical areas
   and callosal pathways 3.331, 3.337, 3.341, 3.343, 3.348
   definition 3.327
   evolution of 4.167
   Glossary explanation of 4.444
   and LGNv 3.203
   polysensory 3.310–1
   in pulvinar complex 3.212–4
   see also under the appropriate area
   striate/extrastriate 11.338
   visual 11.337–8
   in visual cortex 3.302–3, 3.305, 3.308, 3.310, 3.316–7,
      3.319
   and visual thalamus 3.183, 3.186–7, 3.192, 3.198–200,
      3.204–7, 3.209–10, 3.216–7
Cortical blindness 7.190–1
Cortical cells, Glossary explanation of 4.448
Cortical channels 5.58–9, 5.63–4
Cortical circuitry 3.350–1
Cortical coding 5.56
Cortical columns, dissection of 4.296–9
Cortical flow of actin 11.174, 11.177
Cortical hypercolumns 5.66, 5.69
Cortical lesions 9.151
Cortical magnification 2.453–5, 5.74
   areal 2.454
Cortical magnification factor 2.453–5, 7.6, 9.215, 14.129
Cortical neurones 9.150–1, 9.160–1, 9.227
Cortical visual areas
   localization of, and the visual guidance of
      movement 13.1–11
   in mammals 4.160–72
   in turtles 4.169
Cortical–subcortical interactions, general significance
   of 4.127
Corticocortical connectivity, *see* Connectivity
Corticocortical projections 4.160
Corticogenesis and neurotransmitters 11.361
Corticonuclearmicrocomplexes (CNMC) 2.180–1
Corticotectal pathways 2.455–6
   to deep-layer cells 4.101–2
      behavioural consequences of disruption 4.103–4
   to superficial layer cells 4.101–2
Corticotectal projections 3.167–8
Cosine phase of compound grating 5.97
Cosmic rays 1.354
Costa ben Luca 12.28
Cotton wool spots 16.45–6
Counting 8.85, 14.125–30, 14.133–4, 14.137
Counting statistics 2.89–90
Coupling
   between photoreceptors 3.11

cone–cone 3.11
electrical 3.9, 3.11, 3.26, 3.35, 3.40–1, 3.43, 3.58
horizontal cell 3.41, 3.47
photoreceptor 3.20, 3.24–7
  effects of 3.25–7
resistance 3.41
rod–cone 3.11, 3.26
rod–rod 3.11, 3.26
Coverage, horizontal cell 3.40
Coverage factors 3.30–1
amacrine cell 3.44, 3.46
ganglion cell 3.51–2, 3.57–8
horizontal cells 3.39–40
cpd, *see* Cycles per degree
Craik–Cornsweet illusion 5.25, 5.38, 12.5, 12.398–9
Craik–O'Brian–Cornsweet illusions 9.140
Craniopharyngeoma 12.144
Craniotopic co-ordinates 8.327
Crawling 11.171–7
Creativity, poetic 12.442, 12.444
CRF, *see* Contrast rendering factor
Criterion of accuracy 5.39
Criterion in signal detection 5.16–9
Criterion-free procedures 5.266–7
Critical angle 3.12
Critical flicker frequency (CFF) 10.45, 16.111, 16.126, 16.128–9
  and ageing 16.155–6
  see also Critical flicker fusion; Critical flicker fusion frequency; Critical fusion frequency
Critical flicker fusion 5.56, 5.84, 5.171, 5.216, 5.258
  limits of 5.147–9
Critical flicker fusion frequency 7.5, 7.7, 7.18, 7.181–2, 7.184, 15.58–61
Critical fusion frequency 10.272, 13.58, 13.149, 13.151
Crocodilia 2.429
Cross-adaptation effects 10.144
Cross-callosal pathway, alternative 12.348
Cross-correlation
  Glossary explanation of 4.444
  of pattern signals 14.75
Cross-correlation detectors 5.101
Cross-correlation functions, of visual evoked potentials 12.242–4, 12.253
Cross-correlation techniques 4.174, 4.287
  for investigating neuronal connections 4.174
Crossed disparities 9.144
Cross-hatching 12.184, 12.205–6, 12.209, 12.340–1
Crossing, intersystem 16.35, 16.40, 16.67
Cross-modal connections, induction of 11.379–80
Cross-modal functions
  compensation hypothesis 11.376
  critical periods 11.376, 11.378, 11.381
  development of 11.374–9
  interdependence theory 11.376
Cross-modal interactions 11.369, 11.380–1
Cross-modulation terms 10.7
Cross-orientation inhibition 4.262, 4.295
Cross-species tests 11.100–1

Crotalus viridis (rattlesnake) 2.428
Crowding 10.225
  see also Visual crowding
CRTs, *see* Cathode-ray tubes
Crustacea
  ancestral 2.348
  colour vision 2.295
  eye evolution 2.341–3, 2.345–6, 2.348, 2.350–1, 2.353–5
  eye optics 2.118–9
  macruran decapod 2.130
  optics 2.121–2, 2.125–7, 2.129
  and origins of eye 2.54
  visual processing 2.203–4, 2.208, 2.213–4, 2.217–8, 2.220–4, 2.238, 2.241
Cryoprobes, in intracapsular cataract extraction 1.124
Cryotherapy 16.114
Crystalline lens 5.50, 5.55–6, 5.88, 5.92, 5.277–80
CSF, *see* Contrast sensitivity function
CT, *see* Computed tomography
Cubomedusa 2.238
Cue saliency 14.107–8, 14.111
Cues
  in computational vision 14.32, 14.37, 14.41–2
  and ideal observer 14.89–91
  spatial layout of scene 14.4–5
Culture, Neolithic 12.221
Culture-free Self-esteem Inventory 13.201
Cummings 12.478
Cuneate nucleus 8.189
Cuneus 12.342, 12.345
Cupula 8.1–6
  mechanical properties 8.17–20
Cursors and cursor controls 15.79–80, 15.116–8
Curvature 10.82, 10.102–3, 10.110
Curvature acuity 5.221, 5.225, 5.228, 5.231, 5.270
Curvature sensitivity, of cells of cat visual cortex 4.179
Cusanus, Nicolaus 12.33–4, 12.371
Cut-off frequency, *see* Nyquist encoding limit
Cuttlefish optics 2.122
Cyanopsia 7.132, 7.159, 7.163
Cyclegram, Glossary explanation of 4.444
Cycles per degree, Glossary explanation of 4.444
cyclic AMP (cAMP) 3.41
cyclic guanosine monophosphate (cGMP) 3.34, 7.135, 7.144
Cyclofusion 8.330, 9.31–3, 9.111–20, 9.217
  and vergence 8.167–8, 8.330
Cyclofusional response 9.111–2
  motor component of 9.111, 9.114
  sensory or non-motor component of 9.111, 9.114
Cyclography, impedance 1.236
Cycloheximide 11.120
Cyclopean bandwidth limitation 9.57
Cyclopean depth motion 9.56
Cyclopean disparity gradient limit 9.41, 9.57–8
  and smooth surfaces 9.56–8
Cyclopean domain, inhibition of 9.58–60
Cyclopean eye 9.8–12
  centre for visual direction 9.8–12
Cyclopean learning, effects of texture in 9.51–2

Cyclopean lustre 9.66–7
Cyclopean matching algorithms 9.45–6
Cyclopean perception 6.213
Cyclopean portrayal of illusions 9.70–1
Cyclopean response time, physiological data on 9.55
Cyclopean retinotopic visual space 12.464
Cyclopean stereoanomalies 9.207–8
Cyclopean stereopsis 9.40–3
    global cooperative phenomena in 9.48–9
    hysteresis in 9.65–6
    non-random 9.52–4
Cyclopean texture processing 9.50–1
Cyclopean vision 9.38–74
    evoked potential studies in 9.64
    neurophysiological studies in 9.63–4
    psychophysical evidence for 9.54–5
    temporal aspects of 9.54–6
Cyclophoria, in aniseikonia 1.169
Cycloplegia 5.82, 5.90
    and accommodation 1.399–400
    and atropine 1.399
Cycloplegic refraction 1.399
Cyclorotatory optokinesis 8.65–6
Cyclostomes 2.66–7
    dioptrics 2.85, 2.109–10
    in evolution of retina 2.137, 2.140
Cyclotorsional movements 9.113
Cyprinids 2.69–70, 2.290
Cyst, colloid, of third ventricle 12.347
Cystoid macular oedema 1.125
Cytoarchitectonics 2.432, 2.451, 12.50–1
    of border between V1 and V2 3.331
    of macaque area S1 3.327
Cytoarchitecture 3.316, 3.342
Cytoblast layer 3.78, 3.90–1, 3.97, 3.100
Cytochalasin B 11.176
Cytochrome C 2.66, 2.73
Cytochrome oxidase 4.271–2, 4.285–6, 9.230
    discovery of, in monkey visual cortex 4.278
    Glossary explanation of 4.444–5
Cytochrome oxidase activity 3.349
Cytochrome oxidase blobs 2.313, 2.453, 2.458, 3.292,
    4.303–4, 4.325, 4.327, 10.147
    and the colour columns 4.284–91

fracture lines in 4.304
Glossary explanation of 4.445
in squirrel monkey area V1 4.295–6
of the striate cortex 6.181, 6.187, 6.207
Cytochrome oxidase interblobs, Glossary explanation
    of 4.445
Cytochrome oxidase pale stripes, Glossary explanation
    of 4.445
Cytochrome oxidase staining 4.324, 4.328–9, 12.69
    in area V2 12.81
Cytochrome oxidase stripes 4.284, 4.301
Cytochrome oxidase thick and thin stripes, Glossary
    explanation of 4.445
Cytogenesis
    cessation of 3.74–5, 3.115, 3.117–8
    and class specification 3.102
    in differentiation 3.100
    and neurone death 3.96–7
    in pigment epithelium 3.85
    in plexiform layer 3.90
    and retina 3.74–5, 3.81–2
    and retinal expansion 3.106–7
    in retinofugal pathways 3.132
    subventricular 3.82–4
    ventricular 3.80, 3.82–3
Cytokines 11.213
Cytoplasmic Ca^{2+} 11.133–4, 11.137, 11.143–4
Cytoplasmic fins 3.14
Cytosine (C) 7.102
Cytoskeleton
    cell 11.275, 11.299
    competitive interaction 11.299
    microtubular, of dendrites 11.150
    neuronal 11.133–45, 11.275–80
        neurotrophic effects 11.297–8
        regional differences 11.276
        transneuronal effects 11.293
        trophic factors 11.293
    plasticity 11.200
    polarity of components 11.276
    polymerized 11.191, 11.196
    in regeneration 11.196–7, 11.201
    slow transport in 11.191
Cytostatic factor (CSF) 11.119

D

2-D gel electrophoresis and GAP-43 11.221
2-D gel fluorography and GAP-43 11.220–1
3-D vection, *see* Three-dimensional vection
3-D visual stimulation, *see* Three-dimensional visual stimulation
da Vinci, Leonardo, and the development of the contact lens 1.82
Dacryoceles 1.45
Dalton, John 12.389
Dancing, expressive 12.307
Dark
    adaptation 12.271, 12.466–7
    enhancement 12.23
    interval 12.370
Dark adaptation 3.41, 11.258
    see also Adaptation, dark
Dark colours 6.48
Dark light 3.25–6, 5.48–9, 5.51, 5.55, 5.61
    in peripheral vision 5.64–5, 5.67, 5.69–70, 5.73–4
    time-integrated 5.69
    X 5.57–8
Dark rearing 11.258–60, 11.346–7, 11.374–6, 11.380
    studies of the effects of, in the abnormal accessory optic system 4.122–3
Dark vergence 9.90
Dark-adapted vision 5.48
Darkschewitch, nucleus of 8.200–1, 8.248
Dartnall's nomogram 6.110
Darwin, Charles 2.52–3, 12.16, 12.218, 12.220
Darwin, Erasmus 12.46, 12.371
Data processing
    face-related 12.257
    visual
        discovery of principles 12.3–6
        higher-order 12.77–91, 12.141, 12.144
Day blindness 7.24
Daylight, retinal mechanisms for 5.51–2
'Daylight rods' 7.99
de Vries–Rose law 5.12–3, 5.27, 5.30, 5.37–8, 10.44–5, 10.90
Deafferentation 11.152, 12.132
    acute 12.130–1
Deaf-mute 12.331
Decay system 7.115–6, 7.119
Decision processes 15.86
    in saccadic initiation 8.116–7
Decoding, grapho-phonemic 12.328
Decomposition of faces 14.113–4
Decomposition of objects 14.39, 14.112
Decrement, logarithmic 10.36
Decussation 3.131, 3.176
    double 2.280
    in evolution of eye 2.16, 2.46–8
    naso-temporal 2.279
    of optic fibres, imperfect 3.341
    partial 2.273, 2.280, 2.443, 2.446–8, 2.459, 2.468
    patterns 2.278–80
    in retinofugal pathways 3.135–6, 3.138

total 2.273, 2.446
    in visual pathways 2.430, 2.443
Deep cerebellar nuclei 8.244, 8.328
Deep collicular laminae, organization of visual representations in 3.169
Defasciculation 11.232
'Defect' defined 7.1
'Deficiency' defined 7.1
Defocus 2.104–6, 5.90, 5.280
    dioptric 5.230
Degeneracy 2.142–3, 5.134
Degeneration 3.330
    anteretrograde 3.182
    anterograde 12.129–33, 12.198, 12.201
    axonal 12.129
    Bietti's corneal 16.59
    post-traumatic delay of 11.211
    retinal 12.199
    retrograde 3.198–9, 12.129–35, 12.198, 12.201
        transsynaptic 12.129, 12.132, 12.135
    synaptic 12.133
    and visual cortex 3.331–4
Degrees of freedom of signal 14.70
Dehydroretinal 2.9
3-Dehydroretinal 2.64–5, 2.69, 3.29
Deiters' tract 8.216
deLange functions 5.147, 5.172
    and flicker 5.179–80, 5.186
    ganglion cells of macaque 5.181–3
    luminance 5.177
    psychophysical 5.178–9, 5.184–5
    temporal 5.174–9
Delirium tremens, alcoholic 12.300, 12.477
Della Porta, Giambattista 12.218
Della Torre, Giovanni Maria 12.41–2
Della Torre, Marcantonio 12.32–3
Delta function 3.7
Dementia
    senile 11.288
    slowly progressive 12.212
Democritus 12.27
Demodulation
    and bipolar cells 3.38
    colour signal 3.28
    in foveal sampling 3.21
    and postreceptoral mechanisms 3.31
    and retina 3.5, 3.8
Demons 12.221
Demultiplexing, of colour and luminance signals 6.182, 6.206–10, 6.214
Demyelinating disease 10.54
Demyelination 10.239
Demyelinization 12.199
    in splenium of corpus callosum 12.343
Dendrites
    collapse 11.152
    development 11.149–51
    differentiation in visual cortex 3.366–8
    excitatory and inhibitory postsynaptic potentials 11.148–9

Dendrites (*continued*)
  functional correlates 11.163–5
  mammalian retinal cell 11.148, 11.154–60
  microtubules 11.133–6, 11.148–52
  morphology 11.157–8, 11.160, 11.163
    and growth 11.148–65
  neurofilaments 11.144, 11.148–9, 11.152
  neuronal cytoskeleton 11.276–9, 11.284, 11.292
  of pyramidal cells 3.244–52
  remodelling 11.150–2, 11.161–2
  see also Spines
  smooth 3.289
  sprouting 11.149, 11.283
  stratification in IPL 3.55–6
Dendritic arbours 3.160–6
Dendritic architecture 3.51, 3.55
Dendritic displacement 3.109–10
Dendritic fields 2.385, 2.387, 11.153–4
  differentiation 3.98, 3.100
  fractal analysis 11.154
  of neurones 11.148
  retinal cell 11.154–60
  and retinal development 3.118
  and retinal expansion 3.107
  size and shape 3.102–4, 3.109–10, 11.162–3
Dendritic regression 11.281
Dendritic shaft 11.149–51, 11.157
Dendritic territories, of horizontal cells 3.39
Dendritic trees 11.151–2, 11.158, 11.162–3
  development in retina 11.160–1
  ganglion cell 3.49–55
  of relay neurones 3.187–90
  structure 11.152–4
Denervation of extraocular muscles 8.190–1
Densitometry
  reflection 7.91, 7.99–100
  retinal 7.57
Densitometry on human colour vision genes 7.108
Dentate–interpositus complex 3.203
Dentistry 16.93
2-Deoxyglucose 4.300, 4.304
  in study of cortical columns 4.271–2
2-Deoxyglucose autoradiography 4.278–80, 4.289, 4.292–4
  in the cat 4.280
  in the monkey 4.279–80, 4.293
2-Deoxyglucose labelling 4.324
[^{14}C]-2-Deoxyglucose, Glossary explanation of 4.445
Depolarization 1.310, 2.28, 2.42–3
  in colour vision 2.298
  in photoreception 2.366–8, 2.370, 2.380, 2.383
  in visual processing 2.218, 2.230
Depolymerization, actin 11.138
Depression 12.392
  bipolar 12.301
  endogenous 12.302
  spreading 12.177–8
Deprivation
  amblyopia 12.20
  auditory 11.376, 11.378

  binocular 12.18, 12.20–1
  monocular 12.20–1
  see also Visual deprivation
  sensory 12.480, 16.113
  visual 12.20–1
Depth
  cues, pictorial 5.240–1
  and equiluminance 5.236–9
  estimation 12.374, 12.378
    and visuo-spatial disorders 12.441
  motion 5.240
  and prosopagnosia 12.270
  in random-dot stereogram 5.247
  stereoscopic 5.123–8
  visual, and visuo-spatial disorders 12.437
  as a visual cue 5.286
Depth after-effects 9.140
Depth corrugation frequency 9.68
Depth discrimination 9.172
Depth of focus
  ocular 1.19–20
    and low-vision patients 1.19
Depth mixture 9.89
Depth perception 12.12, 12.184, 12.191, 12.360, 12.378, 12.381, 13.25–6, 13.145, 13.182
  and agnosia 12.203
  and the coloured Mondrian 6.200
  dynamics of 9.137
  stereoscopic 5.274
  and visuo-spatial disorders 12.438
Depth-from-motion 9.137–69
Depth-of-focus, *see* Eye
Depth-of-focus/field
  and blur thresholds 1.261
  and detection of just-detectable blur 1.261
  and ocular focal length 1.261
  and pupil size 1.261
  and reduction of visual acuity and contrast 1.261
  and retinal blur circle 1.261
  simple geometrical optics model of 1.261
Depth-sensitive cells, binocular 4.198
De-repression 11.196
Dermal sensitivity in molluscs 2.364–6
Descartes, René 1.231, 12.36–40
  and the development of the contact lens 1.82
Descemet's membrane 2.470–1, 2.473–4, 16.55
Describing functions 5.172, 10.8, 10.34
Descriptors
  cognitive 12.3, 12.14
  Fourier 12.113
  functions 12.7–14, 12.17
Desegregation, of eye-specific segregation zones 11.266–7
Desktop metaphor 15.79
Destriate monkeys 10.264–5, 10.270
Detection 5.11–2, 5.323
  acuity 10.188
  channels 10.135–6
  chromatic 5.203–4, 5.215–7
  of compound gratings 5.99

by confidence-rating experimental paradigm 5.15
contrast increment 10.98–100
correct 5.17
discrete motion-defined area 10.165–7
of increments 5.24
mechanisms for colour analysis 5.212
motion 10.53
motion-defined grating 10.165–6
in negative masking 5.31
and negative masking 5.31
normal integral 5.27
and perception limits 5.6, 5.8–9, 5.11–2
shape, in contrast sensitivity 5.38
signal 10.36
for sinusoidal grating 5.97
of sinusoidal modulation 5.28
in spectral sensitivity 5.191
suprathreshold levels 5.212–3
texture 10.116
in visual processing 5.27, 5.33
Detection threshold 5.160, 5.195, 5.211–3, 10.184
see also Threshold methods
Determinate transfer, equal 5.25
Detour behaviour 2.158–60, 2.163
Deutan deficiency 7.215, 7.217, 7.220–1
Deuteranomaly 7.9, 7.15–8, 7.20–1, 7.23, 7.88, 7.94
alleles 7.95
congenital, in glaucoma 7.153–4
extreme 7.88
unilateral 7.28–9
Deuteranopes 2.310, 6.95, 6.98, 7.9–15, 7.18–20, 7.89, 7.91,
7.94, 7.97
and achromatopsia 7.99
hybrid genes in 6.98
Deuteranopia 2.311, 7.9, 7.21, 7.26, 7.28, 7.83, 7.88, 7.92,
7.191, 12.386
alleles 7.95, 7.101, 7.111
carriers 7.93, 7.97
and ERG 7.57
and non-human primates 7.207
and tritanopia 6.39–41
unilateral 7.28–9
Deuterostomes 2.399–401
Deutsches Institut für Normung (DIN) colour system
basic concepts and principles for scaling and specification
of the variables of 6.236–8
hue 6.236–8
scaling of darkness degree 6.236–8
scaling of saturation 6.236–8
Deutsches Institut für Normung (DIN) colour-appearance
system 6.246–9
Development
extraocular muscle 8.177–8, 8.189–90
vergence 8.168–9
vestibulo-ocular reflex 8.299
Developmental dyslexia, *see* Dyslexia, developmental
Developmental studies, into binocular vision and
stereopsis 9.170–8
Developmentally advanced region (DAR) 3.88–91, 3.94,

3.107, 3.115
Dextrans, fluorescent 11.173
2-DG, *see* [^{14}C]-2-Deoxyglucose
Diabetes 7.120, 7.229, 7.232
as a possible cause of abrupt change in refraction 1.47–8
Diabetes mellitus 7.149–50
accommodation anomalies in 1.272
Diabetic retinopathy 1.297, 7.148–51, 7.228
Diagnostic ophthalmic drugs, for presbyopia 1.264–6
Diaschisis 12.180
Diastereopsis, in cyclopean perception 9.61–2
Diastereotest 9.210
Diazepam, and saccades 8.119
Dichoptic masking 9.96
Dichoptic matching, *see* Haploscopic matching
Dichoptic stimulation 9.104
Dichoptic summation 9.181
Dichroic ratio 1.312
Dichroic semi-reflecting mirrors 1.220
Dichroism
and absorption 1.312
and birefringence 1.319–22
and the 'Maltese' cross 1.319
form 1.312
intrinsic 1.312
macular 1.321
Dichromacy 12.386, 12.388–9
anomalous 12.403
congenital 7.42
incomplete 7.96
induced by intense spectral light 7.79–83
in non-human primates 7.206, 7.208–12
red–green 7.17–8
Dichromatic vision
and chromatic and achromatic signals 6.29
and colour matching 6.27–31
and cone-absorption space 6.27–8
in primates 5.191
'push–pull' or opponent nature of 6.33–4
and vector addition representation 6.28–9
Dichromats 2.290, 2.293, 2.295, 2.315–7, 7.9, 7.26
congenital 7.45
flicker measurements 7.18
red–green 7.11–5, 7.18, 7.20, 7.31, 7.89, 7.91
Dictation 12.333–5, 12.340, 12.342
writing on 12.335
Dictyostelium discoideum ('social amoeba') embryonic
development 11.62, 11.305–6
Didelphis virginiana (common opossum) 2.467, 2.471
Dielectric conductivity 1.312
Dielectric waveguides 5.87
'Difference' detection 12.322–4
Difference of Gaussians 5.60, 10.22, 10.93, 10.96–7
Difference of Gaussians continuous spectra stimuli 1.254
Difference of Gaussians function 4.56
Difference of Gaussians model 4.21–4, 4.56–7
revised 4.23–4
Differential coupling 5.24–5, 5.38–9, 5.41, 5.99
Differentiation

Differentiation (*continued*)
  in contrast sensitivity 5.39, 5.42
  dendritic, in plexiform layer 3.90
  and edge detection 5.104
  exact 5.39, 5.41
  of extraocular muscle 8.178, 8.189–90
  figure-ground 3.28
  increment detection 5.100, 5.104
  mathematical 5.99
  in negative masking 5.30
  neuronal 3.98–104
  same channel 5.100
  of stimulus input 5.24
Diffraction 2.92–4, 2.231–2, 2.408, 5.72, 5.81–2
  X-ray 2.377
Diffraction limited 3.5
Diffraction limits 2.5
  in dioptrics 2.86, 2.103
  and eye optics 2.120, 2.127
  in visual processing 2.235–7
Diffraction patterns, Airy 1.11
Diffraction-limited eye 1.11
Diffrequency tilt perception 9.53–4
Digit span 12.458–62
Digital imaging 11.174, 11.177, 11.182
Digitalis, in photoreceptor impairment 7.132–4
Digitoxin 7.132, 7.134
Digoxin 7.132, 7.134
DIJOA, *see* Dominantly inherited juvenile optic atrophy
Dilation 14.20–1, 14.25, 14.51, 14.53, 14.55
Dimness 12.270
Dinopsis (net-casting spider) 2.120
DIOA, *see* Dominant infantile optic atrophy
Diogenes of Apollonia 12.26
Dioptrics
  basic optics 2.82–6
  depth-of-focus, ametropia and accommodation 2.104–12
  of the eye 5.92
  optical image quality limits 2.92–9
  physical constraints on design 2.86–92
  retinal aspects 2.100–4
  vertebrate 2.82–112
Diorama 14.84–5, 14.88, 14.94
Diplopia 9.1, 9.147, 9.197, 10.24, 10.243–4
  definition of 9.19
  Glossary explanation of 4.445
  pathological 9.179
  physiological 9.196
    basis of 9.30–1
Diplopia perimetry 9.202
Diplopic images 9.8
Dipoles 10.118–9
Diptera
  eye evolution in 2.346–9, 2.355–9
  visual processing in 2.204–12
Dirac delta function 5.143, 14.84, 14.91, 14.95–6
Direct manipulation 15.116
Direct vision, theory of 14.19
Directed attention 4.380

Direction
  ability to recognize 12.437
  Glossary explanation of 4.450
  selectivity 12.86, 12.88–91
Direction constancy 13.30–1, 13.142, 13.182
Direction discrimination 10.47–8
Direction index, Glossary explanation of 4.445
Direction of motion in depth 9.145–6
Direction selectivity 4.327
  in accessory optic system of cat and primate 4.115–7
  and analysis by visual motion 4.128–30
  and correlation between velocity selectivity in the LTN 4.117–8
  in cortical cells 4.188–92
    modulation of 4.191–2
  in depth 4.200
  and direction tuning 4.208–10
  monocular deprivation in 4.125–6
Direction transition function 8.130
Direction tuning
  in cortical cells 4.188–91
  and direction selectivity 4.208–10
Directional motion 2.210, 2.212–3
Directional selectivity 2.210–3, 2.219, 2.426, 2.431–2
  of otolith receptors 8.23–6, 8.29–30
Directional sensitivity 2.213, 4.378
Directional tuning
  Glossary explanation of 4.445
  see also Direction tuning
Directionality columns 4.283–4
  in monkey 4.284
  in rabbit 4.283
Directionally selective movement detection, Glossary explanation of 4.445
Disability glare
  effects on focusing of 1.351
  and equivalent veiling luminance 1.351
  and the Stiles–Halladay formula 1.351
Discharge, electrical (gaseous) 16.7, 16.9–10
Discomfort, musculoskeletal 16.97
Disconjugate errors 8.126–7, 8.167, 8.310
Disconnection
  anatomical 12.352
  complete functional 12.354
  functional 12.351–2
  hypothesis for colour anomia 12.408
  intrahemispheric 12.336
  partial anatomical 12.351
  visual 12.346
Disconnection syndrome 12.335
  incomplete posterior anatomical 12.354
  visual–limbic 12.276
  visual–speech 12.215
Discontinuities
  cortical projections from 4.161
  depth 14.33
Discrimination
  channels 10.135–7
  colour 5.75, 5.179, 5.203, 10.265, 10.272, 10.275

and colour categories 5.211–4
by confidence-rating experimental paradigm 5.15
contrast 5.115–6, 5.224–6, **10**.201, **10**.221–2
and contrast sensitivity 5.36–7
curvature **10**.82, **10**.102
and decision-making ability 5.281
difference 5.9, 5.12, 5.18–9, 5.32, 5.38, 5.102
  in visual processing 5.25, 5.28
direction **10**.47–8
disparity 5.133, 5.135–6, 5.142, 5.144
Glossary explanation of 4.445
in hyperacuity **10**.89
hypercyclopean **10**.161
image 5.54
limits in pattern 5.266–74
line-orientation **10**.92
magnification **10**.270
in motion detection 5.167
motion direction 5.267
orientation 5.74, **10**.148–9, **10**.162–3, **10**.270
  in amblyopia **10**.228–9
  of cyclopean form **10**.162
  forced-choice paradigm **10**.50
  in hyperacuity **10**.102
  for motion-defined bar **10**.167
  in MS **10**.246
  and specificity **10**.200
  theories **10**.170
pattern **10**.265, **10**.269–71
and perception limits 5.6, 5.8
peripheral pattern **10**.76
in peripheral vision 5.44, 5.51
phase **10**.201
saturation 5.198
see Colour discrimination; Wavelength discrimination
sensitivity 5.33, 5.282
shape **10**.129–30, **10**.167–9
and signal detection 5.18, 5.21
size **10**.270
sound-direction **10**.89
spatial **10**.33
spatial frequency **10**.72–3, **10**.149–50
  in hyperacuity **10**.94, **10**.106
  in MS **10**.246
spatial interval 5.230
spatial and temporal 5.158, 5.281
spatiochromatic 5.75
temporal frequency **10**.47–9
texture 5.121–3, 5.128–30, **10**.115–8
threshold for disparity 5.136–9
thresholds 5.195, 5.211
velocity 5.163–4, 5.168–9
vernier acuity **10**.192
in visual processing 5.25
wavelength 5.211–3, **10**.68–9
Discrimination index *d′* **14**.58, **14**.62, **14**.64–5
Disease
brain **12**.302–3
  diffuse **12**.300

cerebro-vascular **12**.263
chorioretinal 7.175
choroidal 7.118
cone, of retina 7.162
degenerative dementing **12**.212
demyelinating 7.158–9, 7.177
and heautoscopy **12**.298, **12**.301
heredo-degenerative **12**.199
neurological 7.173–98
  classification of colour disorders 7.173–7
  due to central lesions 7.183–94
  optic-nerve 7.39, 7.118, 7.173–83, 7.231
occipito-parietal **12**.216
parietal **12**.212
Parkinson's **12**.463
retinal 7.21, 7.118, 7.230
rod 7.162
schizophrenic **12**.296
see also Ophthalmic disease
vascular **12**.350
viral **12**.199
X-linked eye 7.117
Disinhibition, afferent **12**.478
Disinhibition phenomena **12**.481
Disjunctive eye movements 9.236
Disjunctive vergence acuity 9.183
Disorder
anatomical **12**.334
functional **12**.334
language **12**.338
metabolic **12**.268
naming **12**.334
'spatial thought' **12**.444, **12**.449
tactile functions **12**.449
toxic **12**.268
visual **12**.333
visual–verbal integration **12**.333
visuo-spatial **12**.434–8
  after unilateral impairment of left or right parietal
    lobes **12**.447–52
  patients **12**.436
  from right parietal lobe lesions **12**.438–47
Disorientation **12**.179
right–left **12**.436
topographical **12**.183, **12**.209, **12**.337, **12**.411–30
  associated cognitive disabilities **12**.428
  clinical examination **12**.421–2
  compensation strategies **12**.429–30
  early cases of **12**.418–21
  episodes of **12**.429
  loss of familiarity **12**.425–7
  neuropsychological tests **12**.430
  orientation disorders and parietal lobe lesions **12**.427–8
  perception and orientation in extrapersonal
    space **12**.411–7
  and pure alexia **12**.342
  symptoms **12**.420
  topographical agnosia **12**.422–5
  types of **12**.417–8

Disorientation (*continued*)
 visual **12**.430
  and visual hemineglect **12**.445, **12**.450
  and visuo-spatial disorders **12**.436–8
 visual **12**.217
Disparity **2**.275, **5**.229–30
 absolute **9**.122–3, **9**.145
  discrimations of **9**.123
 artificial **1**.340–1
 binocular **2**.448, **5**.133–45, **5**.244, **5**.248
  physiological data **5**.134–5, **5**.140–1
  psychophysical data **5**.134–6, **5**.139–40
 computing **14**.33
 convergent **2**.279
 crossed **9**.144
  and evocation of convergence **9**.122
 detection **2**.273–4, **2**.436
 discrimination **5**.133, **5**.135–6, **5**.142, **5**.144
 distributed representations **5**.133–4, **5**.145
 divergent **2**.278
 encoding **5**.142–3
 fine and coarse **9**.60–4
 fixational **8**.162
 Glossary explanation of **4**.445
 horizontal **2**.277
 interocular **2**.454
 interval coding **5**.134, **5**.143–5
 local representations **5**.133–4
 map **14**.32, **14**.34
 orientation **9**.232–3
 pedestal **5**.135–6, **5**.141
 population encoding **5**.134
 rate encoding **5**.134, **5**.143–5
 relative **9**.122–3, **9**.145
 retinal **2**.277–8
 see also Stereopsis
 selectivity **2**.277–8
 stereo **14**.42
 and stereopsis **9**.123–4
 stereoscopic **5**.257
 temporal **9**.233
 threshold **5**.140–4
 uncrossed **9**.144
  and evocation of divergence **9**.122
 vergence **8**.158–60
 vertical **2**.276–7
Disparity averaging **9**.47–8, **9**.89
Disparity coding, motion sensitivity of **9**.144
Disparity contrast **9**.89
Disparity curves **4**.197
Disparity discrimination function **9**.41–2
Disparity gradients **9**.86, **9**.213–7
Disparity pulse **9**.141
Disparity response curves, Glossary explanation of **4**.445
Disparity selectivity
 of cat cortical cells **4**.192–201
 horizontal **4**.193
Disparity vergence **1**.249
 influence on accommodation **1**.249

Disparity-selective neurones **9**.224
Disparity-tuning curves **5**.137–43
Displacement **12**.355, **12**.360–1
 step **5**.50
Displacement detection **10**.109
Display addressability **15**.14–5
Display modulation transfer functions **15**.14
Display polarity **15**.18–9, **15**.46
Display resolution **15**.14–5
Displays
 equiluminous **5**.245–7
 see also Sensory modalities; Vision; Visual displays
 tritanopic **5**.246–7
Disproportion **7**.230
'Dissection', functional **10**.34
Dissociating red-glass test **9**.195
Dissociation
 of anosognosia **12**.450
 double **12**.183, **12**.214
  and prosopagnosia **12**.260, **12**.269, **12**.272, **12**.274
 of optic ataxia **12**.452
 of spatial hemineglect **12**.448–9
Dissolved organic matter (DOM) **2**.8
Distance, estimation of **12**.203, **12**.441
Distance perception, and visuo-spatial disorders **12**.437
Distinctiveness of faces **14**.110–1, **14**.114–5, **14**.117–23
Distorted horopter **9**.193
Distortion
 of background non-facial features **12**.274
 calculation of **1**.68
 hemifacial **12**.274, **12**.276
 and prosopagnosia **12**.274–5
 simple perceptual facial (metamorphopsia) **12**.274
 of vision **12**.473
 in visual coordinates **12**.271
Distractibility **15**.95
Disturbance
 higher cortical focal **12**.337
 peripheral 'perceptual' form of written language **12**.337
 pseudo-agnosic **12**.148
Diurnal/nocturnal/crepuscular habits, Glossary explanation of **4**.445
Divergence **8**.157, **8**.205
 and callosal pathways **3**.350–1
 in commissural pathways **3**.326
 evoked by uncrossed disparities **9**.122
 extrinsic **3**.348
 heterotopic projections **3**.335
 intrinsic **3**.348
 post-ganglionic **5**.253
Divergence nystagmus **8**.302
Dix, Otto **12**.446
dLGN, *see* Dorsal lateral geniculate nucleus
DNA (deoxyribonucleic acid) **7**.101–9
DOG
 Glossary explanation of **4**.445
 see also Difference of Gaussian continuous spectra stimuli
Dog colour vision **2**.293
DOG model, *see* Difference of Gaussians model

Dog photoreceptor system 2.74
DOGs, *see* Difference of Gaussians
Dolphin dioptrics 2.83
Dominance
  ocular 11.260, 11.288
  see also Columns
  visual 11.377–8, 11.381
Dominance and suppression shifts 9.107
Dominance and suppression states, alternating cycles of
  9.93
Dominant infantile optic atrophy (DIOA) 7.118, 7.155–7,
  7.159–61, 7.163
Dominant wavelength (of a constant stimulus), CIE
  definition of 6.227
Dominantly inherited juvenile optic atrophy (DIOJA) 7.61,
  7.98, 7.116
Donaldson colorimeter 5.47
Donders, F. C. 2.311, 2.313
Donder's law 8.168, 8.260
Dopamine 3.41, 3.194, 10.250–7, 11.287, 11.353
  in amacrine cells 3.44–7
  in dendrites 11.158, 11.161, 11.163
Doppelgänger 12.297–301
  somaesthetic 12.298–9
Doppler methods 1.361–2
Dorsal cortex 2.426
Dorsal lateral geniculate nucleus 3.161–2, 3.164, 3.176,
  3.235, 3.239, 3.241, 3.248, 3.253, 3.255, 3.267, 4.339,
  4.342–3, 10.46, 10.262
  complex 3.177–82, 3.192, 3.210, 3.215–6
  cortical afferents 3.192–3
  cortical connections 3.370
  GABAergic interneurone morphology of 3.279–82
    axons 3.282
  ganglion cells in 3.52–3
  in humans 3.177–80, 3.182, 3.191, 3.195
  lamination 3.186
  location of neurotransmitters in 3.278–88
  magnocellular 3.49
  in mature retina 3.131–2
  monoaminergic and cholinergic circuitry in 3.284–8
  neurogenesis 3.360–1, 3.363–6, 3.368
  parvocellular 3.49
  projections from 3.198–200
  relay cells and interneurones 3.187–92
  retinal projections to 3.183–6
  in retinofugal pathways 3.136–8, 3.140–3
  subcortical projections 3.193–4
  synaptic differentiation 3.366
  ultrastructure of complex 3.195–8
  in visual cortex 3.309–10, 3.317
  in visual function 4.405
Dorsal lateral geniculate nucleus cells 4.352, 4.357
Dorsal lateral suprasylvian cortex 4.359–62
  area 20 4.359–60
  area 21 4.360
Dorsal pathway 10.246
Dorsal terminal nucleus
  Glossary explanation of 4.443

of the optic tract 8.201, 8.214
  relationship with cat nucleus of the optic tract 4.119–20
  see also Accessory optic tract
Dorsal ventricular ridge (DVR) 2.423–6, 2.432–4
Dorsolateral pontine nucleus 8.153, 8.202, 8.211–4
  speed tuning 8.212
Dosimetry 16.26, 16.54
Dot clusters 14.62, 14.65
Dot number 14.52, 14.56, 14.64–5
Dot patterns, *see* Pattern
Dots, localization of small 12.144
'Double', *see* Doppelgänger
Double bouquet cells 3.258, 3.262–3
  Glossary explanation of 4.448
  see also Cortical cells
Double dissociation 2.456
Double imaging, *see* Diplopia
Double opponency 6.176, 6.185
Double target saccades 8.119–21, 8.127–32, 8.252
Double vision 9.1
Double-opponent cells 4.288–9, 4.330
Douse test 9.193
Downbeat nystagmus 8.301
Dragonfly
  eye evolution 2.354, 2.357–9
  ommatidium 2.347
  visual processing 2.233, 2.255
Drawings
  apraxic 12.441
  line 12.341
  meaningless 12.345
  random 12.455
Dream(s) 12.469
  colour in 12.393, 12.399
  epileptic states 12.480
  and heautoscopy 12.301–2
  states 12.259, 12.298, 12.300, 12.302, 12.480–1
Drift
  optokinetic influence 8.56
  postsaccadic 8.123, 8.125–7, 8.236, 8.320, 8.322
  velocity, natural value 8.4, 8.86
Driving 16.152, 16.154, 16.157–8
Drosophila
  compartments 11.37–41, 11.59, 11.61
  gene activation in 11.55, 11.57
  and homeoboxes 11.3–23
  leg disc 11.61
  mutations 11.348
  pattern formation 11.54–5
  positional information 11.48
  and proto-oncogenes 11.114–9, 11.121–3
  segmentation in 11.57, 11.59
  wing disc 11.61
Drug abuse 12.133, 12.300
Drugs 12.300
  diagnostic ophthalmic, for presbyopia 1.264–6
  distribution of 16.72
  effects of, on visual sensations 12.476
  hallucinogenic 12.481

Drugs (*continued*)
  and heautoscopy **12**.303
  use of, illusion and hallucination **12**.471–2
Drusen **7**.125
  and ageing macula **16**.85–6, **16**.90
  and ageing retina **16**.134–9, **16**.141–2, **16**.145–6
  and light damage **16**.63–4
  optic-nerve head **7**.157–8, **7**.163
Drusen of Bruch's membrane **7**.130–1
Drysdale's radioscope **1**.380
DTN, *see* Dorsal terminal nucleus
Dualism **12**.22
Duane–Fincham theory **1**.264
Duane's Syndrome **13**.222
Dunlop Test **13**.141–6, **13**.182–3
Duplicity theory of vision **2**.137, **12**.55
Dürer, Albrecht **12**.11, **12**.225, **12**.228
Dyads **2**.358
Dye
  fluorescent **11**.90, **11**.97–8
  fluorescent 'fast blue' **3**.138
Dye injection
  in cell lineage **11**.30–2
  in vertebrate neurogenesis **11**.33, **11**.38–9, **11**.41
Dynamic depth sensitivity
  of Area 18 cells **4**.199–201
  Glossary explanation of **4**.445
Dynamic field of view **8**.6
Dynamic luminance imbalance **15**.44–5
  and eye discomfort **15**.44–5
  and task performance **15**.44
  and transient adaptation **15**.44
  and visual-display terminals **15**.41–2
Dynamic motor error **8**.97, **8**.211
Dynamic occlusion **9**.140
Dynamic random-dot displays **9**.170
Dynamic retinoscopy **1**.236
Dynamic stereopsis
  and invariance **4**.216
  motion-in-depth **9**.204–7
  and selectivity for direction in depth **4**.216–7
Dynein **11**.136
Dysaesthesia **12**.275
Dyscalculia, spatial **12**.271
Dyschromatopsia **7**.128, **7**.160, **7**.163, **7**.190–1, **12**.388,
  12.396
  cerebral **12**.397
Dysgraphia, spatial **12**.440
Dyslexia **7**.185, **11**.381, **12**.2, **13**.69–75, **13**.113–20
  acquired **13**.26
    after right hemisphere damage **13**.184
    and link with developmental dyslexia **13**.181
    and alexia **12**.333
    attentional **12**.338
  binocular control in **13**.141–7, **13**.182–3
    and crossed laterality **13**.141
    and the Dunlop test **13**.141–6
    and monocular occlusion **13**.142, **13**.183
    and ocular dominance **13**.141

    unstable, occlusion treatment of **13**.143–4, **13**.183
    vergence eye movements **13**.146, **13**.184
    and visual localization **13**.142–3
  biological correlates of **13**.94–7
    left-handedness and atypical cerebral lateralization **13**.96
    sex differences in **13**.95
  central **12**.338
  chromosomal abnormalities in **13**.104
  'colour' **12**.388
  colour effects on **13**.173
  colour vision disorders in **13**.186
    and chromatic aberration **13**.186
    and spatial frequency analysis **13**.185
    and wearing of tinted spectacles **13**.186
  contrast sensitivity of **13**.185–6
  crowding effects in **13**.54, **13**.169
  'deep' **12**.328, **12**.338
  defects in development of grapheme–phoneme
    correspondence **13**.189–95
  developmental **12**.387, **13**.113–9, **13**.238–41
    anatomical studies of **13**.271
      microdysgenesis of the planum temporale **13**.271
      bilateral symmetry in **13**.271
      clinical categorization of **13**.271
      eye movements in **13**.71, **13**.238–41
        in dyslexics **13**.238–41
        in skilled readers **13**.233–42
      and link with acquired dyslexia **13**.181
      physiological studies of **13**.272–4
        abnormalities in the EEG power spectra **13**.272
        bihemifield stimulation **13**.273, **13**.276–8
        bihemispheric decision paradigm **13**.273
        reduced lateralized specialization **13**.272
        unstable eye dominance **13**.272
      responses of, to bihemifield stimuli **13**.276–8
      and vergence eye movements **13**.146
  diagnosis of **13**.269
  disordered hemispheric specialization, genetics of **13**.187
  dyseidetic **13**.122–4
    clinical and electrical correlates of **13**.121–31
  dysphonetic **13**.122–3
    clinical and electrical correlates of **13**.121–31
  erratic eye-movement studies in **13**.264–9
  explanation of **13**.264
  eye movements in **13**.238–41
    during reading **13**.264–5
  general reading backwardness **13**.97–8
  genetic effects **13**.94–112
    adoption studies **13**.99–100
    aetiology **13**.248–9
    familial studies **13**.99
    monozygotic and dizygotic twins **13**.278
    twin studies **13**.100–1
  glare symptoms in **13**.171
  historical descriptions and background of **13**.94, **13**.99,
    13.113–4
  indirect genetic theories of **13**.105–7
    Annett's Right-shift Model **13**.84, **13**.106
    Geschwind's Theory of Cerebral

Lateralization 13.106–7
McManus's Genetic Model 13.106
individual differences in 13.193–4
inheritability of 13.266
and interhemispheric interactions 13.271–80
investigations of visual problems of 13.144–6
  accommodation 13.145
  convergence using the 'RAF' rule 13.145
  Cover Test 13.145
  Dunlop Test using a synaptophore 13.145–6
  ocular movements 13.145, 13.183, 13.186, 13.239
  stereoacuity using the Randot Test 13.145
  visual acuity 13.145
involving neglect 12.338
as a linguistic problem 13.278
and the National Child Development Study 13.96
neurobiological correlates of 13.95–6
  abnormalities of EEGs in 13.95
  structural and functional abnormalities in 13.96
and 'no visual deficit' position 13.148
and non-dextrality 13.86
non-visual factors in 13.69–71
oculomotor control disorders in 13.186, 13.239
peripheral 12.338
phenotypes of 13.97–9
phonological 12.338
phonological awareness in 13.148
phonological reading difficulties in 13.190–2
population distribution of reading skills in 13.229
problems of measurement of 13.115
reading development models of 13.194
reading and script 12.308, 12.319
and right-handedness 13.91–2
Rutter and Yule's definition of 13.97–8
saccadic eye movements in, and microsequencing 13.266
severe 12.388
similarity of, to other developmental syndromes 13.96–7
spatial 12.271, 12.440
spatial frequency processing in 13.148–54
spatial vision in 13.71–2
specific
  definitions of 13.225
  genetics of 13.228–9
  neurology of 13.227–8
  psychology of 13.228
  subtypes of 13.115–8, 13.219, 13.225–7
    dyseidetic 13.227
    dysphonetic 13.227
    linguistic 13.227
    perceptual 13.227
specific genetic models of 13.101–7
  assortative mating 13.102–3

chromosomal abnormalities 13.103–4
genetic linkage 13.103–4
for reading, writing and dyslexia 13.105
spelling defects as distinct from reading
  deficits 13.104–5
and specific reading retardation 13.97–8
spelling 12.216–7
sub-types of 13.99, 13.121–8, 13.238–40
  with general language deficits 13.238–9
  with selective attentional deficits 13.238, 13.240
  validity of 13.125–8
  with visual–spatial deficits 13.238–41
surface 12.338
teaching reading and spelling in children with 13.196–202
  evaluation studies into 13.196–201
    basic attainments 13.196–8
    secondary reactions in 13.200
    syllabification sub-skills 13.198–200
    syllable skills 13.200
temporal vision in 13.73
types of 13.99, 13.115–8, 13.121–8, 13.238–40
visual 13.26–7, 13.116–8
visual anomalies in 13.48–51
and visual discomfort 13.169
and visual hemineglect 12.450
and visual processing 13.132–40
  clinical studies and observations 13.137–8
    cognitive factors and orthographic awareness 13.137
    in poor readers 13.137
    reauditorization, revisualization and modality 13.138
    visual and spatial deficits 13.137
  historical perspective 13.132–5
  methodology of 13.135–7
    in poor readers 13.135–6
    predictive and correlational studies 13.136
    stimulus complexity 13.136
    subtype labelling 13.135
visual search in 13.58–83
visuospatial performance tests in 13.182–5
  binocular stability 13.182, 13.185
  dot localization 13.182–5
  the Dunlop Test 13.182–3
  stereoacuity 13.182–3, 13.185
  vergence eye movement control 13.182–3
Dysmetria, saccadic 8.124–5, 8.236, 8.312–3
Dysmorphopsia 12.289, 12.412, 12.434, 12.465
Dysphasia 12.294
Dysplasia
  Dunlop Test 13.121–46, 13.182
  dysgenic cytoarchitectural 13.278
Dystrophy, fundus 7.117

E

EAA (excitatory amino acid) **11**.355–6, **11**.360
  in synaptic rearrangement **11**.260–1, **11**.265, **11**.271
Eagle dioptrics **2**.100, **2**.102–3
Ear, suppression in dichotic listening experiments **12**.349
Early receptor potential (ERP) **7**.60
Ebbinghaus's colour pyramid **6**.222
Eccentric photorefraction, *see* Photoretinoscopy
Eccentric vision **5**.117
Eccentricity
  in cat retina **3**.16
  dendritic **11**.162–5
  in foveal sampling **3**.20–2, **3**.24
  and ganglion cells **3**.50–1, **3**.56
  Glossary explanation of **4**.445
  and horizontal cells **3**.39–40
  in hyperacuity **10**.91
  and relationship with asphericity parameter **1**.3
  retinal **3**.4–6, **3**.13, **5**.163, **5**.188, **10**.93–4, **10**.110, **12**.317,
      12.322, **12**.325
    in peripheral vision **5**.47–8, **5**.52, **5**.54, **5**.57, **5**.60–1,
        5.65, **5**.68, **5**.70–3
    primate **3**.14–5
  and saccadic latency **8**.113
  and visual acuity **8**.6–9
Eccentrization **7**.118, **7**.131, **7**.163
  in Stargardt's disease **7**.141–3
ECDP, *see* Equivalent carbon dioxide pressure
Echidna **2**.442, **2**.467–70
Ecological optics **8**.5
ECT, *see* Emission computed tomography
Ectoderm **2**.35, **11**.393, **11**.401
  surface **2**.17, **2**.25–6, **2**.31, **2**.44, **11**.386–7, **11**.389,
      11.391–2, **11**.397
    and retinal development **3**.70–7, **3**.80, **3**.85, **3**.118
    and retinal expansion **3**.107
Ectostriatum **2**.432–3, **2**.435
Ectosylvian area **4**.360–2
Ectosylvian visual area (EVA), in visual cortex **3**.309–11
Edge, sharp *vs* blurred **5**.178
Edge colour **5**.248
Edge detection **2**.313, **5**.102–5, **5**.209, **14**.34–5, **14**.101
Edge detectors **14**.42
Edge illumination **5**.234
Edge intensity **14**.34–5, **14**.40, **14**.42
Edge labelling **14**.35
Edge map **14**.42
Edge orientation **12**.206
Edge polarity **2**.252–3, **2**.262
Edge recognition **12**.12
Edinburgh Inventory **12**.241
Edinger–Westphal nucleus **1**.233, **8**.184
EEG, *see* Electroencephalography
Eel **2**.69
Effective-disparity invariance principle **9**.79
Efferent copy **8**.209, **8**.214
  Glossary explanation of **4**.445
Efferent fibres, to vestibular organs **8**.26

Efferent motion perception, Glossary explanation of **4**.443
Efferent pathways **4**.239–40
  to the extrastriate cortex **4**.239–40
  to subcortical nuclei **4**.240
Efferent saccadic delay **8**.117
Efferents
  dendrites as **11**.148
  of visual thalamus **3**.215
Ego movement **12**.433–4
Ego space **12**.433
Egocentric absolute distance tasks **9**.79–81
Egocentric co-ordinates **12**.463
Egocentric directions **9**.180
Egocentric distance **9**.78
Eicosanoids **11**.200
Eigengrau **12**.158, **12**.162, **12**.466–8, **12**.472, **12**.476
Eigenlicht **12**.158
Eigenvectors **1**.311
Eikonometers
  alternating vision **1**.171
  simultaneous vision **1**.171–2
    fusional **1**.172
    the ophthalmo-eikonometer **1**.172
    standard **1**.172
  space **1**.173–5
    clinical uses of **1**.175
    design of **1**.173–5
    modifications of **1**.175
    'office model' of **1**.175
  stereoscopic **1**.172–3
    and the frontal plane horopter **1**.173
    and the leaf room **1**.172–3
    and tilting planes **1**.173
Eikonometry **1**.163, **1**.171–5, **1**.178
  alternating vision eikonometers **1**.171
  credibility of clinical **1**.179
  objective **1**.175
Eisenbahn-nystagmus **8**.46
Elasmobranchs **2**.67–8, **2**.400, **2**.406, **2**.410, **2**.412–4, **2**.477
  in evolution of retina **2**.137–9, **2**.141
Elasticity **3**.107
Elderly **12**.315
Electric fields **11**.182
Electrical activity **2**.382–3
  effects on growth cones **11**.281–2
  in neuronal cytoskeleton **11**.287–8
Electrical stimulation
  of posterior parietal cortex **4**.377
  in understanding brain function **4**.388
Electrocorticogram **12**.167
Electrodes
  intracerebral
    chronically implanted **12**.474
    location of **12**.474
Electroencephalogram (EEG)
  backward and forward averaging of signals **12**.242
  and flowers **12**.247
  migraine studies **12**.177
  and prosopagnosia **12**.275

recordings, bipolar **12**.242, **12**.252–3, **12**.255
recordings and computerised data evaluation **12**.241–2
responses
    to flowers **12**.248–50
    to photographs of faces and non-faces **12**.244–6
    to realistic drawings **12**.243–14
    to schematic faces **12**.242–3
visual evoked potentials (VEPs) **12**.240–58
Electroencephalography (EEG) **5**.179, **5**.183
Electromagnetic fields **15**.1, **15**.3
Electromagnetic radiation, from visual-display terminals **15**.1
Electromagnetic theory **2**.89
Electron **16**.35–9, **16**.49
    doublet **16**.32
    free **16**.50
    lucky **16**.50
    shells **16**.30–3
    sub-shells **16**.31–3
    valency **16**.32, **16**.34
Electron microscopy
    and microtubules **11**.136–7
    quantitative analysis **11**.271
Electro-oculogram (EOG) **7**.128–30
    during reading **12**.311
    in retinitis pigmentosa **7**.145, **7**.147
    in Stargardt's disease **7**.141
Electro-oculography **8**.95, **16**.70
Electro-ophthalmology **7**.139
Electrophysiology **5**.63, **7**.5, **7**.93
    of colour deficiencies **7**.64–71
    and colour mechanisms **5**.216–7
    and cone fundamentals **5**.192
    and evolution of eye **2**.6
    and flicker **5**.179–80
    and motion detectors **5**.156
    and non-human primates **7**.200–2, **7**.204, **7**.208–10, **7**.212
    and peripheral vision **5**.56–7, **5**.59–61, **5**.73, **5**.255
    quantitative, of visual cortex neurones **4**.173–222
    in retinotectal projection **11**.89
    and trichromacy **2**.310
Electroretinogram (ERG) **2**.73, **2**.376, **2**.382, **5**.179,
    10.185–6, **10**.251–2, **10**.254–5, **16**.110, **16**.112
    and developing visual system **16**.124–5
    and phototoxicity **16**.70
    X-ray-induced **12**.166
Electroretinography **2**.74–5, **7**.1, **7**.128
    b-wave **7**.126
    and colour deficiencies **7**.56–63
    in cone disease **7**.135–6, **7**.140
    flicker **7**.57–8
    measurements **7**.27
    in ophthalmic disease **7**.131–2, **7**.135, **7**.141, **7**.145,
        7.147–8, **7**.155
    recording **7**.56–7
    red–green deficiencies **7**.57–9
    and tritanopia **7**.98
Electrotechnical Commission, International (IEC) **16**.6
Ellipsoid **3**.9–12, **3**.16
Ellipsosomes **2**.66, **2**.73, **2**.78, **6**.115

Embryogenesis **11**.50
Embryonic fissure **11**.387–8, **11**.391, **11**.394, **11**.402
Embryonic organizer **11**.47
Emergent properties **2**.229
Emmetropia **1**.29, **1**.53, **1**.154, **2**.84, **2**.97–9, **2**.105, **2**.107,
    2.111, **2**.469, **13**.50
    explanation of **1**.400
    in young adults **1**.45
Emmetropization **1**.39–41, **2**.84, **5**.92, **10**.180
    active feedback mechanism in **1**.39
    animal studies into
        to address the link between visual experience and eye
            growth **1**.40–1
        deprivation of form vision **1**.41
        modification of accommodation **1**.41
Emotion
    content of facial expression **12**.226
    expression **12**.218, **12**.224, **12**.233–4, **12**.275, **12**.297
        asymmetry of **12**.229
    state **12**.219–20, **12**.471
    stressful situations **12**.301
Empedocles **12**.25–7
Empire, Pharaonic **12**.306
Encephalitis **12**.262, **12**.269, **12**.277
    diffuse brain **12**.199
    Herpes simplex **12**.269
Encephalization **2**.146–7, **2**.435–6
Encephalomyelitis, disseminated **7**.117
End inhibition, Glossary explanation of **4**.445
Endfree cells, of cat visual cortex **4**.175
Endocytosis **11**.175
Endoillumination, fibre-optic **16**.97
Endolymph flow **8**.14
Endoplasmic reticulum, and oriented growth in plants **8**.13
Endspectral, Glossary explanation of **4**.445
End-stopped cells, of cat visual cortex **4**.175
End-stopping **4**.298
    see also under End inhibition, Glossary explanation of
Energetic arousal **15**.94
Energy
    constant **5**.227
    diagram, Grotrian **16**.32, **16**.35
    radiant **16**.1–2, **16**.58
    transduction **16**.67
Engelking-Trendelenberg anomaloscope **7**.23, **7**.218, **7**.220
Engelking-Trendelenburg equation **7**.120, **7**.125–6, **7**.179
    in glaucoma **7**.153–4
Engelking-Trendelenburg matching range **7**.126–7, **7**.134
Engels, Johann Jacob **12**.218
English, word frequency **12**.314–5
Engram, sensorimotor **12**.334
Enhancement phenomenon, applied to parietal visual
    neurones **4**.381
Enhancement of visual responses **8**.153, **8**.248, **8**.281, **8**.283
Ensemble processing **2**.241, **2**.251, **2**.260
Ensor, James **12**.290
Entoptic phenomena **1**.345–56
    chromatic aberration **1**.352
    classification of **1**.345

Entoptic phenomena (*continued*)
  defects of focusing 1.350–2
    disability glare 1.351
      equivalent veiling luminance 1.351
      Stiles-Halladay formula 1.351
    halos 1.351–2
      causes of 1.351–2
      corneal 1.352
      glaucomatous 1.352
      lens 1.352
    irregular aberrations 1.350–1
      ciliary cornea 1.351
      effects of cataracts 1.351
      polyplopia 1.351
      star images 1.350–1
  definition of 1.345
  effects on retina of 1.352–6
    acquired scotomas 1.353
    after-images 1.353
    'aliasing' 1.355
    edge effects 1.353
    Mach bands 1.352–3
    migraines 1.355
    overaccommodation 1.354–5
    phosphenes 1.354–5
      cosmic rays 1.354
      effects of pressure 1.354
      electrical stimulation 1.354
    Purkinje's blue arcs 1.353–4
    retinal ischaemia 1.355
    television rasters 1.355
    Troxler fading 1.353
  and the optical function of the human eye 1.345
  recording of 1.345–6
    co-ordinate system and visual angles 1.345–6
    and ocular dimensions 1.346
  self-light of 1.355–6
  types of 1.346–9
    scotomas 1.349
      acquired 1.350, 1.353
      Amsler grid 1.350
      the blind spot 1.349
      low level central 1.350
      retinal haemorrhage 1.350
    shadows 1.346–9
      Haidinger's brushes 1.348–9
      Maxwell's spot 1.348
      ocular components casting 1.346–7
        blood in vitreous 1.347
        corneal corrugations 1.346–7
        entoptic worms 1.347
        'floaters' 1.347
        lens structure 1.347
        the lids and lashes 1.346
        mucus 1.347
        muscae 1.347
        the pupil 1.346
        the tear film 1.346
      parallax 1.348

      Purkinje's tree 1.347–8
        and parallax 1.347–8
      retinal blood corpuscles 1.349
    ultra-violet fluorescence 1.352
Entrance pupil 1.281, 5.83
Entropy 16.78
  signal 14.70
Enucleation
  bilateral 3.142
  monocular 3.136, 3.140–2, 3.180–1
  unilateral 3.141–3
Environment 14.91–2
  and ideal observer 14.87–8
Enzyme cascade 5.58
Enzyme stain technique 7.73–4
Enzymes
  proteolytic 11.282
  restriction 7.102–4, 7.106–7
EOG, *see* Electro-oculogram
EOP, *see* Equivalent oxygen percentage
Ependyma, ventricular 12.335
Epidemiological studies, of computers and displays in the
    workplace 15.56–8
  in relation to asthenopia 15.58
  in relation to musculoskeletal complaints 15.58
  in relation to pregnancy 15.57
  in relation to visual complaints 15.57–8
    asthenopia 15.57–8
    display quality 15.57
Epikeratophakia 1.147–55
  complete epithelialization after 1.150
  complications of 1.152
  histology of 1.152
  lens manufacture for 1.149
  patient selection in 1.147–9
    keratoconus 1.148
    for myopia 1.148
  results in 1.150–2
    in children 1.151
    and contrast sensitivity measurements 1.151
  see also Intraocular lens implants
  surgical techniques in 1.149–50
Epilepsy 12.262
  after-discharges 12.480
  discharges in temporal lobe 12.473–4
  dreamy states 12.480
  focal discharges 12.480
  and heautoscopy 12.298–300
  and hemialexia 12.350
  photosensitive 13.155, 13.162–4
  primary generalized 13.168
  seizures 12.477, 12.479
    intractable 12.347
  temporal lobe 12.299, 12.301–2, 12.475, 12.477, 12.479–80
  visual sensations 12.474
  zone 12.266
Epithelium
  ciliary 11.393
  lens 11.389–90

pigment 11.315–6, 11.326, 11.332, 11.388, 11.392–3, 11.402
EPSP (excitatory postsynaptic potential) 11.262
Equal innervation 9.2
Equilibrium colours 6.45
    and the four unitary hues 6.45
Equiluminance 2.306, 2.308–9, 2.312, 5.227, 5.234–48, 10.139–41, 15.19
    critical zone 5.234, 5.242
    and single neurones 10.153–5
Equivalent carbon dioxide pressure 1.92
Equivalent oxygen percentage 1.91–2
Equivalent veiling luminance (L_{eq}) 1.15, 1.351
Erasistratos 12.25, 12.27
ERG, *see* Electroretinography
Ergonomic objectives, in relation to work involving visual displays 15.55–6
Error
    disconjugate 8.126–7, 8.167, 8.310
    motor 8. 326, 8.97, 8.209, 8.211, 8.251, 8.262, 8.267
    retinal 8.123, 8.131
Erythrocebus patus (patus monkey) 2.77
Erythropsia 7.124, 7.132, 16.29
Eskimos and North American Indians, and the Barrow, Alaska near-work study 1.32–3
Esotropia 8.168
Estimation
    hue 6.51–2
    immediate 14.137
    magnitude 6.52, 14.130–2, 14.138
    numerosity 14.125–6, 14.128–31, 14.137–8
    of proportions 14.127
    ratio 14.131
    statistical 14.85
Estimators
    Bayesian 14.92
    MAP 14.85, 14.93
Ethnic origin and spectral sensitivity 5.207
Euclid 12.29
Eumelanin 16.39, 16.68
Evoked potential, *see* Visual evoked potential (VEP)
Evolution
    coevolution 2.12–3, 2.302, 2.313–4
    convergent 2.217, 2.273, 2.376, 2.450
    fish vision 2.398–417
    parallel 2.343, 2.348, 2.360, 2.450
    through duplication 2.356
Ewald's law 8.299
Excitation purity, CIE definition of 6.227
Excitatory burst neurones 8.206, 8.258–63
Excitatory postsynaptic potential (EPSP) 3.283, 12.131
Exemplars 14.108, 14.117
    concept 14.118
    encoding of variation 14.112
Exhaustion, somatic 12.480
Exit pupil of the eye 5.87
Exitance, radiant 16.3, 16.6–7, 16.20–1
Exner, Sigmund 12.48, 12.359
Exocytosis 11.227

Exons 6.92, 7.102, 7.105–7, 7.109
Expansion
    conformational 3.106
    minimal central 3.106
    retinal 3.103, 3.105–10, 3.116–7
        non-uniform 3.118
        patterns of 3.106
Expansion rate, angular 9.140
Expectation and eye-movement 8.77
Experience
    conscious 12.276
    and prosopagnosia 12.271
Exploration test, Poppelreuter's visual 12.454
Exposure duration in hyperacuity 5.227–9, 5.231
Express saccades 8.112, 8.114–5, 8.290
    and lesions of the striate cortex 8.279
    and superior colliculus 8.252–3
Extinction 4.413
    with double simultaneous stimulation 12.426
    effect, and visuo-spatial disorders 12.443
    Glossary explanation of 4.445
    and hemi-inattention 12.453
    phenomena 12.191
    and posterior parietal lobe 12.95
    and visual hemineglect 12.431
Extracellular matrix (ECM) 11.71–3
    in axon growth 11.108, 11.234
    in cell locomotion 11.171–3, 11.177–9
    and cell recognition 11.82, 11.84
    contacts (fibronexus) 11.173
    in neuronal cytoskeleton 11.279–80, 11.282, 11.297
    and optic nerve regeneration 11.211–2
Extracellular single unit recordings, of flicker 5.180
Extracellular space 3.12
Extraction, centroid 10.92–3
Extrafovea 2.168
Extrafoveal vision 5.268, 5.270
Extrageniculate thalamic nuclei, in visual cortex 11.338, 11.340
Extramission (interaction) theory 12.26–8, 12.31
Extraocular muscle, embryology of 8.177–8
Extraocular muscles 8.175–99
    accessory 8.177
    blood flow 8.182
    development and differentiation 8.177–8, 8.189–90
    effect of denervation 8.190–1
    embryology 8.177–8
    fibre statistics 8.182
    global layer 8.178–81
    histochemical profiles 8.178
    inferior oblique 8.175–6, 8.182
    inferior rectus 8.175–6, 8.182
    inter-and intraspecies differences 8.182–3
    intermediate zone 8.180–1
    kinematics 8.175
    lateral rectus 8.175–6, 8.178–9, 8.182, 8.185
    levator palpebrae superioris 8.175–6, 8.182–3
    medial rectus 8.175–6, 8.182
    microscopic anatomy 8.178–83

Extraocular muscles (*continued*)
  motor innervation 8.183–7
    junctional ultrastructure 8.186–7
  multiply and singly innervated fibres 8.179–81
  myosin ATPase 8.182, 8.189
  nerve endings 8.186
  oribital layers 8.178–80
  retractor bulbi 8.177, 8.183
  sensory innervation 8.187–9, 8.321
  superior oblique 8.175–6, 8.182, 8.184
  superior rectus 8.175–6, 8.182
  weakness 8.309–12
Extra-personal space 12.463–5
  bilateral visual inattention in 12.462
Extrapolation acuity 10.91, 10.101–2
Extraretinal distance signals 9.81
Extraretinal feedback
  in saccades 8.122, 8.131–2
  in smooth pursuit 8.149–51
Extrasplenial pathway, predeveloped alternative 12.350
Extrastriate cortex 8.245, 8.281–2, 8.284–5, 8.306
Extrastriate cortical areas 4.445
Extrastriate visual cortex
  apes 4.169
  cat 4.342–62
    areas 18 and 19 of 4.342–3
  comparisons of, between species 4.365–6
  congruent borders of 4.170
  2-deoxyglucose studies in 4.282
  in development and evolution 4.170
  functions of
    in non-primate species 4.339–70
    within-species analysis 4.365
  Glossary explanation of 4.445
  hierarchical system of interconnections in 4.371–2
  humans 4.169
  orientation columns in 4.282
  and the parietal visual system 4.371
  rabbit 4.363
    area V2 4.363
    temporal visual area 4.363–4
  rodent 4.362–3
  sheep 4.364
  tree shrew 4.364–5
Extrinsic eye muscles 4.389–90
Extrusion in cell locomotion 11.176–7
Eye
  accessory 2.374
  agnathan 2.402–3, 2.405
  amphibian 11.61
  aphakic 5.282–3, 16.42, 16.63
  apposition 2.351, 2.353
  aquatic lens 2.121–2
  arc 16.3
  binocular function 16.126
  and brain 2.237
  camera 2.4, 2.13, 2.119–21, 2.238
  camera-type 2.266
  cephalic 2.368, 2.371–83

  cephalopod 2.382, 2.384, 2.386
  chambered 2.47
  changes in length 2.109, 2.111
  Chrysopa 2.234
  compound 2.47
    apposition 2.4, 2.127, 2.132, 2.134
    arthropod 2.203–4, 2.213–4, 2.217–22, 2.341–60
    bee 2.265
    evolution 2.3–4, 2.13, 2.132, 2.222–4
    fish 2.417
    invertebrate 2.26, 2.28
    mollusc 2.364, 2.371
    ommatidia 2.57
    optics 2.118–20, 2.125–7, 2.130, 2.134
    origins 2.54–5, 2.59
    reflecting superposition 2.134
    refracting superposition 2.134
    superposition 2.4, 2.127, 2.132
    in visual processing 2.261
  contralateral, in retinal transplantation 11.319, 11.321, 11.328, 11.330
  Cubomedusa 2.238
  cyclopean 2.354
  dark-adapted 5.61
  day 2.232
  degenerate 2.142
  depth-of-focus 2.85, 2.104–12
  dermal 2.382
  design 2.119–20, 2.134, 2.351
  diffraction-limited 2.93, 2.99, 2.104–7
    aberration-free 5.89, 5.92
  dioptrics 5.92
  displacement 12.361, 12.364, 12.378
  dorsal 2.368–9
  dragonfly 2.233, 2.235
  'drifts' 12.369
  echidna 2.468
  electronic 2.55–6
  embryological theories of 11.395–403
  embryology of 2.467
  embryonic development of 2.403, 2.442, 11.386
  emmetropic 2.83
  evolution of 2.3–5, 2.118, 2.230–7
  evolutionary development of 11.394–403
  evolutionary origin of 11.386
  freely accommodating 5.216
  frontal 2.442–3, 2.446, 2.448, 2.459
    bird 2.429–30, 2.436
  frontalization 2.455
  genesis of vertebrate 11.386–403
  geometry 2.235, 2.237, 2.266
  geometry of exposure 16.23–9
  'gradations' 2.53
  human 2.119–20
    functional organization 12.52–63
    optical point-spread function 12.54
  immobilized 12.416
  injury by radiation 16.1–21
  intracellular 2.118

invertebrate
  chambered **2.21**
  origins **2.15–48**
ipsilateral, in retinal transplantation **11.328**
irradiated **16.71**
lateral **2.442–3, 2.448**
  bird **2.429–30, 2.436**
lens **2.3–4, 2.126, 2.375–83**
'lobster' **2.130**
mantis **2.231**
marsupial **2.470–1, 2.477**
medusae **2.237–8**
mirror **2.369–71**
monocular stimulation **12.325**
monotreme **2.467–9, 2.477**
multicellular **2.21**
multi-lensed **2.417**
muscles **2.187–9**
nauplius **2.222–3**
neural superposition **2.128**
'neurocrystalline' **2.222**
nocturnal **2.91, 2.232, 2.234, 2.477**
non-Caucasian **5.278**
non-cephalic **2.390**
optical performance of human **5.88–90**
optical quality **5.279**
optics **5.120, 5.124, 5.128, 5.230, 12.36**
origins of **2.52–9**
oxygenation of **2.414**
parabolic reflecting **2.125**
parabolic superposition **2.131**
parameter **2.237, 5.72–3**
parietal **2.31–5, 2.138**
patching **16.125–6, 16.128**
photochemical injury **16.26–7**
photoreceptor lattice **5.120**
physical constraints on design **2.86–92**
pineal **2.31–6, 2.406**
pinhole **2.3, 2.21, 2.23, 2.25, 2.54, 2.122**
  mollusc **2.364, 2.374–5**
placentalian **2.473, 2.476–8**
polarity **11.61**
position **12.100, 12.232**
  related to object **12.103**
  two-dimensional recordings **12.452–3**
pre-retinal defences **16.93**
prevertebrate **2.19**
protection **2.414**
proto compound **2.133**
real **2.105–7**
reduced **2.85, 2.91–2, 2.94–5, 2.105**
reflecting superposition **2.129–30**
reflector **2.4**
refracting superposition **2.129–30**
reverse suture **11.262**
scanning **2.52, 2.55–9, 2.122, 2.237**
  mollusc **2.364, 2.375–6**
schematic **2.82–6, 2.91**
sexual dimorphism in **2.123**
shape of **2.412–3**
simple **2.21–9, 2.39, 2.133**
  aggregate **2.21–2, 2.28**
  arthropod **2.218**
  composite **2.21–2, 2.28**
  compound **2.22, 2.24**
  evolution **2.220, 2.222–3**
  mirror **2.134**
  mollusc **2.372–4**
  origins **2.54–5, 2.59**
single-lens **2.4, 2.54**
spherical lens **2.134**
stalked **2.222, 2.382**
  mollusc **2.364–5, 2.376**
stationary **2.239**
superposition **2.351, 2.353**
sutured **11.258, 11.374**
thermal injury **16.26–7**
transmittance characteristics **2.86**
tremor **12.53**
tubular **2.91–2, 2.473**
unicellular **2.21**
vertebrate
  cerebral origin **2.17–8**
  origins of **2.15–48**
without brain **2.237**
worm **2.237–8**
Eye behaviour
  of developing readers **13.253–61**
    frequency distributions in **13.254–6**
    global eye movement parameters for **13.253–4**
      mean fixation duration **13.253–6**
      mean number of regressive saccades **13.253–4**
      saccade length **13.253–6**
      silent reading tasks **13.253**
Eye chart
  Landolt-C **16.110**
  Snellen **16.110**
Eye cup **2.3, 2.22, 2.54, 2.58, 2.123, 2.133–4**
Eye dominance **9.97**
Eye dominance test **9.11**
Eye field, frontal (FEF) **12.109, 12.463**
Eye fields
  frontal **3.313–4, 3.316, 3.331**
  supplementary **2.180, 2.187, 2.191**
Eye models
  and distribution of parameters in real eyes **1.7–8**
  and intraocular lenses **1.5**
  ocular ametropia **1.6–7**
  paraxial **1.5–6**
  and refractive error **1.5–8**
  wide angle **1.6**
    Gullstrand's 'No. 1' schematic **1.6**
Eye movements **9.100, 9.112, 9.121, 9.147, 10.184–5, 10.264–5, 16.108**
  abnormal reading **13.221–5, 13.248**
    in dyslexia **13.222, 13.238–41, 13.243–50**
    secondary to the linguistic problem **13.221–2**
      in dyslexic children **13.221**

Eye movements (*continued*)
 specific 13.222–5
  and Broca's Aphasia 13.222
  and Duane's Syndrome 13.222
  and left homonymous hemianopia 13.222
  leftward saccadic 13.222
  'reverse staircase' 13.222–5
 analytical examination of 13.257–60
  landing-site distributions 13.257–8, 13.261
   noise effect in 13.257
   range effect in 13.257
  refixating words during reading 13.258–9
  skipping words during reading 13.259
 binocular 2.186
 changes in spontaneous explorative 12.95
 children's
  average characteristics of 13.252–3
   average fixation durations 13.252
   frequency of regressions 13.252
   saccade length 13.253
  during reading 13.251–62
 compensatory 9.126
 compensatory slow 2.186
 conjugate 2.443, 2.446, 2.448, 2.459
 conjugate saccadic 2.186
 in contrast encoding 5.111
 and contrast sensitivity 5.294–5
 control of 2.187–8
  and the functional properties of the cortico-ponto-
   cerebellar pathway 13.8
  pursuit 13.8
 and deLange functions 5.178
 and developing visual system 16.120, 16.123–4
 developmental changes in 13.252–3
 differences in, between normal readers and
  dyslexics 13.247–8
 and dioptrics 2.92, 2.103
 disjunctive 2.279
 dual-mode control of 13.206–16
  calibration and adaptation in 13.216
  fixational 13.209
   microsaccades 13.209
  gaze 13.209
   with synchronous electromyographic signals 13.209–
    10
   and the vestibulo-ocular reflex 13.210
  latencies for 13.208, 13.212–3
  pulse target changes in 13.206–7, 13.212
  ramp stimuli in 13.207, 13.212
  ramp–step target jump in 13.207–8, 13.212
  spatial constancy in 13.214, 13.216
  step changes in 13.206, 13.212
  step–ramp stimuli in 13.208, 13.212
 during reading 12.316–20
 during saccades 12.53
 in dyslexia 13.222, 13.238–41, 13.243–50
  when reading standard text 13.246–7
  recording methods and analysis of 13.267–8
  target search tests in 13.244–6

 and equiluminance 5.236, 5.245
 erratic, studies of 13.264–9
 in eye evolution 2.415
 faulty, as a cause of dyslexia 13.240–1
 fixational 1.248, 13.209, 13.214, 13.217, 13.233–4, 13.248
 free 5.59
 goal-directed 12.96, 12.101
 horizontal quick 2.186
 illusion and hallucination 12.479
 indicative of neurological conditions 13.263
 involuntary 5.216, 12.168, 12.363, 12.370–1
  and visuo-spatial disorders 12.434–5
 and light hazards 16.97
 micro 13.263
 miniature 2.167
 mollusc 2.374–5, 2.377, 2.390
 monitoring 12.340
 multi-level control of 13.203–32
  dual mode 13.206–9
   fixational 13.209
   gaze 13.209–16
  kinematics of 13.203
   oblique saccades 13.203
  kinetics of 13.204–6
   saccades 13.204–7
    dynamic overshoot 13.205
    glissadic overshoot 13.205
    static overshoot 13.205
   vergence 13.204, 13.207
  synkinetic responses 13.204
 and the near vision 13.216–7
 in normal readers 13.243–50
  when reading standard text 13.246–7
  target search tests in 13.244–6
 normal reading 13.216–21
  attention shifts in
   disengaging 13.236
   moving through space 13.236
  basic characteristics of 13.233–4
  control of 13.236–8
   and fixation duration 13.237
   and saccade lengths 13.237
  fixation pauses 13.217
  patterns of, in Chinese compared with
   English 13.218–9, 13.223
  qualitative 13.218
  regressive 13.261
  saccadic 13.217–8, 13.222
  smooth pursuit in 13.218
  vergence adjustments 13.218
  vestibular system activation in 13.218
 observation of 12.452–3
 and optics 5.92
 and origins of eye 2.58–9
 passive 12.363–4
 pendular 12.363, 12.365, 12.370
 and the perceptual span 13.234–6
 in peripheral vision 5.44–5, 5.75, 5.262
 ϕ-pursuit 12.376

postpursuit (PPEM) 2.188, 2.191
predicting reading skill levels from 13.256–7
pursuit 12.174, 12.375
  and hemi-inattention 12.453
rapid 2.167, 2.186, 13.204
recording of 13.263
recordings 12.452
  electro-oculographic 12.376–7
regressive 13.233–4, 13.248, 13.251–2, 13.254
residual 5.67
saccadic 2.166, 2.172, 2.448, 3.204, 3.207, 4.388–442, 12.6,
    12.57, 12.309–11, 13.9, 13.217, 13.223, 13.233–4,
    13.263
  and multimodal convergence 11.370–1
  reading and script 12.318–9
  and visual hemineglect 12.432
  and visuo-spatial disorders 12.436
scanpath 13.216
  during visual imagery 13.216, 13.220–1
searching 13.216
see also Pursuit system; Saccadic eye movements
and senescence 5.281
shearing forces during 11.209
sigma-pursuit 12.367–70, 12.376
sinusoidal passive 2.188
in skilled readers, and implications for developmental
    dyslexia 13.233–42
skilled reading, continued practice requirements for
    13.219
smooth 2.179–80, 2.182
smooth disconjugate 2.180
smooth-pursuit 12.52, 12.363, 12.365, 12.368, 12.376–7,
    12.462
  and posterior parietal lobe 12.97
  and visuo-spatial disorders 12.436, 12.438
and spatial hemineglect 12.454, 12.463
spontaneous 2.185, 2.187, 2.443
spontaneous saccadic 2.186
stepwise 2.188
and velocity perception 5.160
vergence, control of 13.8
vertical 2.187
vertical rapid 2.186
and the vestibulo-ocular reflex 13.8
and visual acuity 13.234
and visual pathways 2.443, 2.455, 2.457
and visual perception 12.6–7
and visual processing 2.268
visually guided 3.207, 3.217
visually induced 2.179
visually induced saccadic 2.186
zero, *see* Zero eye movement reading

Eye muscles
  external 2.402
  extra-ocular 2.401, 2.404
Eye opening 11.289–91
  and axon growth 11.238, 11.243
  and differentiation 3.98, 3.100
  and fovea 3.115–6
  and neuronal death 3.96
  and retinal development 3.69, 3.80, 3.82, 3.85–6, 3.90, 3.94
  and retinal expansion 3.105, 3.107
  and retinofugal pathways 3.134
  in visual cortex neurogenesis 3.360, 3.368
Eye optics 10.180–1
Eye placement, consequences of, for optokinetic
    asymmetries 4.132–4
Eye spots 2.19–21, 2.24, 2.26, 2.35, 2.342–3, 2.369
Eye stalks 2.342
Eye torsion, effects of 9.27–8
Eye/head movements 5.160, 5.167
Eyeball
  binocular deformation 12.161
  deformation 12.160–2
  human 12.36
  immobilization 12.112, 12.217
  indentation 12.159, 12.176
  passive movement of 12.363–4
  and phosphenes 12.158–9
  spherical 2.473
Eye–hand co-ordination 9.158–60, 15.116–8
  judgements of time to contact and trajectory 9.158–60
  see also Sensory modalities
Eye–head co-ordination 8.13, 8.33–4, 8.38, 8.99, 8.106–9,
    8.264–7, 8.306
Eye-in-head position 12.432
Eyelid suture, binocular/monocular 11.346–7
Eyelids 16.116, 16.118, 16.126
  blinks 12.370
  and developing visual system 16.120–1
Eye-movement characteristics 15.25–8
Eye-movement voting (EMV) 16.107–8
Eye-opening 2.145
Eyes-free operation 15.122
Eye-strain
  and disorientation 13.162–3
  and fluorescent light 13.168
  and phosphorescence 13.168
  prevention of 13.164–7
    reading masks 13.164
      and the Cambridge Easy Reader 13.164–6
      and Prentice's Typoscope 13.164–5
  and reading 13.155, 13.162–3
Eye-voice span 12.317–8

F

Fabricius ab Aquapendente, Hieronymus **12.34–5**
Face
    bi-quantized images **14.108, 14.110**
    classification **14.114–7, 14.120–1**
    clock **12.455**
    common configuration **14.113**
    distinctiveness **14.110–1, 14.114–5, 14.117–23**
    identification **14.121–2**
    perception **16.158**
    prototype **14.114, 14.118–21**
Face cells **12.125**
Face and facial expression **12.274, 12.285**
    alienation **12.302–3**
    animal **12.219**
    childhood recognition development **12.238**
    computer-generated **12.230**
    configuration **12.276**
    covert recognition **12.271**
    deformed **12.224, 12.290**
    development of **12.237–9**
    discrimination **12.284–5**
        of facial material **12.263**
        of monkey **12.117**
        tests **12.272**
    disfiguration **12.220**
    double-left and double-right **12.226, 12.230**
    effect of orientation **12.236**
    encoding **12.276**
    familiar **12.122, 12.261, 12.276**
        and prosopagnosia **12.260, 12.262, 12.266, 12.279**
        and pure alexia **12.347**
    famous **12.224, 12.231, 12.234, 12.276–7**
        and prosopagnosia **12.262–3, 12.269, 12.279**
        and pure alexia **12.347, 12.352**
        and visual evoked potentials **12.241, 12.248–9**
    features **12.274**
    female superiority in recognition **12.231, 12.234–5, 12.239**
    half- **12.275**
    and heautoscopy **12.297**
    hemispheric specialization **12.230–5**
    hominid phylogenesis **12.220–1**
    human **12.385**
        illusion and hallucination **12.468, 12.470–3, 12.475**
    hypo-or paramimic patterns **12.220**
    identification **12.219, 12.281–2**
        delayed **12.285**
        and pure alexia **12.355**
    identity **12.279**
    inborn recognition mechanisms **12.235**
    inborn releasing mechanisms **12.237**
    individual **12.219, 12.221, 12.224**
    inversion **12.283**
    inversion effect **12.238**
    'jumbled up' **12.274**
    known **12.241, 12.248–9**
    left half of **12.275, 12.302**
    long-interval **12.235, 12.237**

    long-term recognition abilities **12.238–9**
    lost, *see* Prosopagnosia
    masks and portraits **12.221–4**
    matching **12.262–3, 12.272–4, 12.285**
    material **12.263**
    memory, *see* Memory, face
    mother–child interaction **12.238**
    neuronal activity **12.117**
    neuronal mechanisms **12.219, 12.221, 12.224, 12.226, 12.235**
        innate **12.237**
    neuronal schemata **12.235**
    neuronal templates **12.238**
    new **12.269**
    not sympathetic (not pleasing) response **12.282**
    optimum stimulus features **12.120–1**
    own **12.239**
    perception **12.272, 12.286**
        of human **12.467**
        illusionary **12.290**
        primitive **12.260**
        and recognition of **12.218–39**
    of personal relevance **12.276**
    photographs **12.224, 12.229, 12.231, 12.233–4, 12.238, 12.247, 12.275, 12.282, 12.285, 12.339**
        black and white **12.244–6, 12.257**
        in fragmentary mode **12.281**
    'pure' **12.275**
    reading and script **12.307**
    real **12.275**
    recognition **12.118, 12.144**
        animal **12.274**
        context-related **12.269**
        contextual cues **12.266**
        of facial material **12.263**
        familiar **12.270, 12.272–3**
        famous **12.274–5**
        generic **12.269**
        impairment in non-prosopagnosic patients **12.280–6**
        and prosopagnosia **12.261–2, 12.268, 12.283–6**
        and size **12.121**
        and spatial frequency **12.121**
        unfamiliar **12.272–3**
        unknown **12.274**
        upright **12.282, 12.284**
        upside down **12.284**
    responsive components **12.240–58**
    rotation **12.283**
    schematic **12.221, 12.224, 12.234, 12.237, 12.467**
        computer-generated **12.226**
        illusion and hallucination **12.479**
        and visual evoked potentials **12.244, 12.257**
    see also Schizophrenia
    semantic information **12.278**
    signals **12.224**
        dynamic **12.219**
        human **12.224**
        processing **12.231, 12.257**
    specificity of **12.271–2**

stylized drawings of **12**.274
superiority effects **12**.195
symmetry and left–right laterality **12**.226–30
sympathetic (aesthetically pleasing) response **12**.282
unfamiliar **12**.271, **12**.276–7
  and prosopagnosia **12**.263
unknown **12**.230, **12**.234, **12**.248–9
upright **12**.282
upside down **12**.121, **12**.235, **12**.237, **12**.282
visual category of human **12**.273
as visual stimuli **12**.224–6
Face identification, after cortical lesions **10**.274–5
Face perception, in infants **10**.201
Face recognition **5**.267–8, **5**.271, **14**.107–23
component information **14**.107–10
computational level theory **14**.111–8
and computational vision **14**.43
configural information **14**.107–10
information available **14**.107–11
models of concept learning **14**.118–22
structural descriptions **14**.113–4
Face recognition unit (FRU) **14**.122
Face representations **14**.112–4, **14**.118, **14**.123
Face-sensitive neurones **10**.262
Facial expressions **12**.124
Facial identity **12**.124
Facial signals, social **12**.124
Facilitation **10**.144
binocular **12**.74, **12**.76
semantic **12**.277
by words **12**.355
F-actin **11**.137, **11**.174
in critical period plasticity **11**.288–9
in neuronal cytoskeleton **11**.286
Falant and Holmes-Wright lantern **7**.229
Falciform process **2**.408
False positives **5**.8, **5**.16–8, **5**.57, **5**.60, **5**.64, **5**.203–4, **5**.281
Familiarity **12**.418
context-free **14**.121–2
environmental **12**.420–1, **12**.425–6
with extrapersonal space **12**.417
facial **12**.271
feeling of lost **12**.450
loss of **12**.270
pattern **14**.138
personal **12**.271
personal emotional **12**.273
recognition of **12**.261, **12**.271
route **12**.427
of surroundings **12**.420, **12**.423, **12**.428
topographical **12**.271, **12**.416, **12**.427–9
  loss of **12**.424–7
and visual hemineglect **12**.450
Far neurones **9**.187, **9**.227
Far point **1**.53
Farnsworth arrangement tests **7**.118
Farnsworth D15 test **7**.216, **7**.218, **7**.222–4, **7**.229–31
in Alezzandrini's syndrome **7**.147–8
in cerebral hemisphere lesions **7**.192–3

7.6, **7**.174–5, **7**.192–3, **7**.216, **7**.218, **7**.223–8, **7**.230–2, **12**.372, **12**.393, **12**.395–6, **12**.399–401, **12**.404–5, **16**.152
and achromatopsia **7**.100
acquired colour deficiency **7**.41
in AION **7**.157
and cerebral achromatopsia **7**.187
and cerebral blindness **7**.194
in cone dystrophy **7**.136–7
in CSNB **7**.148
in diabetes **7**.149
in glaucoma **7**.152–3
in hemiachromatopsia **7**.184–5
in ophthalmic disease **7**.119, **7**.125–6, **7**.128, **7**.130–1, **7**.134
in optic neuritis and MS **7**.158–9, **7**.179, **7**.181–3
in optic-nerve disease **7**.176
in optic-nerve and optic-tract conduction **7**.163
red–green heterozygotes **7**.20–1
in retinitis pigmentosa **7**.144–6
in Stargardt's disease **7**.143
in toxic optic neuropathy **7**.161
Fascicles **11**.107–8
age-related **11**.104–5, **11**.108
axon **11**.235
in cell locomotion **11**.180
microtubule **11**.133
tectal **11**.103–4
Fasciculation, axon **11**.71–3, **11**.80, **11**.232–4, **11**.236
Fast phase, of nystagmus **8**.46, **8**.65, **8**.98, **8**.111–2, **8**.325
Fatigue
of accommodation **8**.102
of saccades **8**.102
Feature catastrophes **14**.102, **14**.106
Feature detection **14**.102, **14**.106
Feature discrimination **2**.259
Feature extraction **14**.76, **14**.81, **14**.102
Feature identification **14**.100
Feature operator **14**.100–2
Features
first-level **14**.100–2
invariant **14**.76
and line images **14**.98
regular and singular classes **14**.101–4, **14**.106
space **14**.71, **14**.74, **14**.80
spatial relations **14**.107–8, **14**.113
translation invariant **14**.78–9
Fechner–Benham discs **12**.397
Fechner–Benham flicker colours **12**.399
Fechner's law **12**.4, **12**.8
Feedback
extraretinal
  in saccades **8**.122, **8**.131–2
  in smooth pursuit **8**.149–51
local (internal) **8**.97–8, **8**.119, **8**.123, **8**.209, **8**.215, **8**.257
negative **3**.40, **10**.2–3, **10**.256
  in optokinesis **8**.48–9, **8**.235
  in saccades **8**.96
  in smooth pursuit **8**.138–9, **8**.211, **8**.214, **8**.309
parametric **8**.35, **8**.125–6

Feedback (*continued*)
  in cone dystrophy 7.136–7
  in cone–rod dystrophy 7.141–2
  in CSNB 7.148
  in diabetes 7.150
  and digitalis poisoning 7.133–4
  in DIOA 7.155
  in ophthalmic disease 7.119, 7.128–9, 7.131
  in retinitis pigmentosa 7.144, 7.146
Farnsworth–Munsell 100-Hue (F-M 100-Hue) test 5.282–3,
  positive 8.152–4, 8.235, 10.3
  synapse 3.40
Feedback connections 3.336, 3.351
Feedback inhibition 4.332
Feedback path, Glossary explanation of 4.445
Feedback pathway from IPL to OPL 3.41–2
Felis domesticus (domestic cat) 2.74
Fernelius, Johann 12.34
Ferrier, David 12.48
Ferrier's Mistake 13.2
Ferry–Porter law 5.147
Fever, high 12.300
Fibre optics
  free-viewing systems 5.204–5
  retinal 2.100–2
  see also Retinal fibre optics
Fibre-optic effects 5.87
Fibres
  bundles 12.346
  callosal 12.334, 12.344
    extrasplenial 12.112, 12.337
  carrefour of tracts 12.334
  specific connections 12.346
  splenial 12.269
  tracts 12.346
Fibrescope, and transverse magnification 1.205
Fibroblasts
  in cell locomotion 11.173–81
  cultured 11.179
  locomotion 11.171–2
Fibronectin, in neuronal cytoskeleton 11.280
Fibronexus (extracellular matrix contacts) 11.173
Fick, Adolf Eugene, and the development of the afocal glass
    scleral contact lens 1.82
Field, visual 8.5–6
Field of view 2.412, 2.414
  in peripheral vision 5.46
Figure–ground discrimination 12.205
Figure–ground formation 12.192
Figure–ground relations 12.199
Figures
  ambiguous 12.192
  geometric 12.210
  geometrical 12.193
  hidden 12.192–3, 12.207, 12.209
  human 12.467–8, 12.470–3
  overlapping 12.209
  unstable 12.192–3

Filaments
  intermediate, neuronal cytoskeleton 11.276, 11.279, 11.284
  polar 11.137
  see also Actin filaments
Filling-in, blind spot 12.137–8, 12.142
Filling-in scotoma 12.146
Filopodia 11.172–3
  axon 11.235
  in cell locomotion 11.174–6, 11.178
  dendrite 11.150–2, 11.160–1
  and GAP-43 11.226
  in neuronal cytoskeleton 11.287
Filter instrument 7.229
Filtering 14.4, 14.40
  bandpass 5.227
  circular harmonic, and pattern recognition 14.25
  correlation 14.75
  Gabor 5.58
  Gaussian 3.27
  holistic matched 14.75
  linear, of flicker 5.186
  low-pass 5.92, 5.227, 5.246, 10.88–90
  in pattern discrimination 5.273–4
  in peripheral vision 5.45, 5.51–2
  postreceptoral 3.24
  predictive 5.58
  random 5.55
  spatial 3.30, 5.164–5, 5.262
    in hyperacuity 10.93–4, 10.97
    in psychophysical models 10.64, 10.81
  spatial frequency 10.141–2, 10.161–2, 10.165, 10.232–3
    and face recognition 14.108–10
  spatiotemporal 8.7, 10.95–6
  temporal 5.114–5
Filters 2.409, 14.14, 14.27
  anti-aliasing 3.8–9, 3.27, 3.57
  barrier 2.410
  blue light 16.66
  broad-band 7.220
  cut-off, in cone–rod dystrophy 7.140
  effects of 7.162
  Gabor 5.121–3, 5.128
  Gabor-like 5.67, 5.73
  Gaussian 5.60
  Glossary explanation of 4.445–6
  holistic matched 14.74
  infrared 16.66
  interference 7.220–1
  linear 5.154, 5.188
  linear spatial 10.123–4
  in localization modelling 14.16
  and location 14.10, 14.12
  low-pass 5.25, 5.66
  low-pass cortical 5.198
  'most active' 5.110
  neutral density 5.280
  optimal 5.67
  orientation-tuned spatial 5.110
  and preFilters 5.92

see also Coloured lenses; Coloured overlays; Irlen lenses
  spatial 5.224–5, 5.303
  spatiotemporal 5.166–9
  spectral 2.87
  temporal frequency 5.165, 5.302–4
  UVA 16.66
  UVA-blocking 16.89–90
  variable colour 5.246
  yellow 2.95
Fine lines 5.320
Fine-focus-control hypothesis 1.251
Finger, movements 12.95, 12.102–3
FINST index 14.65
First degree fusion 9.201
Fish
  colour vision 2.285–6, 2.290, 2.295–6, 2.298–300, 2.302
  deep-sea 2.68, 2.77, 2.88, 2.112
    colour vision 2.290
    dioptrics 2.91, 2.103
    visual pathways 2.442, 2.446
  dioptrics 2.84–5, 2.87, 2.89, 2.94–7, 2.103, 2.109–10
  evolution of retina in 2.138–9, 2.141–2
  eye embryology of 11.394
  feeding selectivity 2.157
  four-eyed 2.110, 2.112
  optics 2.122
  photoreceptor system 2.67–71, 2.78
  shape recognition 2.162–3
  visual cortex 2.152
Fixation 12.95, 12.191, 12.196, 12.204
  accuracy 2.172
  in arthropods 2.212
  binocular 3.110
  control of saccadic shifts of 13.50–1, 13.261
  eccentric 7.53
  inaccurate 12.355
  neurones of cerebral cortex 8.285
  oculomotor neurones during 8.203
  point 2.443
  in pursuit system 2.165–8, 2.172, 2.175, 2.178–85, 2.188, 2.191
  task 12.96–7, 12.99–100
  TR(S)Ns 8.248, 8.251, 8.253–4
  visual 3.204
  in visual processing 2.254–60, 2.262, 2.268
Fixation cells 4.381–2
Fixation disparities 9.125
  and tonic vergence 8.162
Fixation marks 9.121
Fixation period 12.7, 12.310–1
  duration of 12.316, 12.319–20
  lexic span 12.316
  reading and script 12.318
  short 12.309, 12.316
Fixation plane 9.132
Fixation regarded as smooth pursuit 8.303, 8.329
Fixation target, central 10.198
Fixational eye-movements
  control by position-correcting saccades 8.89

drift 8.72
measurement 8.71–3
micro-saccades 8.72
tremor 8.71–2
Flag salute 12.307
Flags, colours of 12.385
Flash tubes 16.21
Flashback 12.481
Flashes 10.265, 10.271–2
  coloured 12.166–7
  single, seen in space 12.166
Flechsig 3.324
Flechsig, Paul 12.50
Fletcher–Hamblin simplified test 7.230–1
Flicker 5.114, 5.291, 8.3, 8.74, 10.5, 10.241, 15.59–61
  achromatic 5.171, 5.199
  and agnosia 12.194
  bandpass 5.179
  channel 5.167
  chromatic 5.172, 5.176, 5.178, 5.198–9
  colour 12.397–8
    Fechner–Benham 12.399
  counterphase 5.240
  definition of 5.171
  detection 5.149–50, 5.208
    frequency 5.38, 5.173, 5.177, 5.182, 5.184
    fusion curves 5.176
    just-noticeable 5.177–8
    sensitivity 5.25, 5.147–9, 5.176, 5.188
    thresholds 5.149, 5.172–3, 5.175–7, 5.217
  elimination of 15.7–9
  and equiluminance 5.237, 5.245
  25Hz 5.207
  linear filtering 5.186
  low-pass 5.178–9
  luminance 5.171–2, 5.176, 5.178, 5.180, 5.182–3
  modelling 5.185–8
  modulation detection 5.10–1
  monochromatic 12.396
  and motion perception 5.150
  perception 12.8
    and phosphenes 12.164
  in peripheral vision 5.47, 5.50, 5.65, 5.74
  phosphene 12.169
  photopic 12.398
  physiological data 5.179–88
  psychophysical data 5.179, 5.182, 5.184–5, 5.188
  residual 5.173
  see also Critical flicker fusion frequency
  sine-wave 5.172
  and spectral sensitivity 5.205–6
  stimulation 12.74, 12.76, 12.172
  theory 5.186
  and velocity perception 5.160–1
Flicker frequency, critical (CFF) 7.5, 7.7, 7.18, 7.25, 7.181–2, 7.184
Flicker fusion 5.296–7
  and prosopagnosia 12.270
Flicker fusion frequency 7.50, 7.61

Flicker fusion frequency (*continued*)
    critical (CFF) **10**.45, **10**.241, **12**.4, **12**.6, **12**.8, **12**.53, **12**.63, **12**.398
        chromatic stimuli **12**.59
        and perimetry **12**.140
        photopic **12**.396–7
        of rod system **12**.58
        in visual fields **12**.142
        and visual movement agnosia **12**.370, **12**.372
Flicker modulation sensitivity (de Lange curves) **7**.52, **7**.54
Flicker photometry **7**.20, **7**.22, **7**.29, **7**.77, **7**.96, **7**.118
    and brightness matching **5**.173–4
    and equiluminance **5**.235
    heterochromatic **5**.171–4, **5**.184–6, **10**.157, **10**.173
        and chromatic patches **5**.215
        equal luminance **5**.211
        from ganglion cells **5**.180–2
        in psychophysical colour studies **5**.204
    and spectral sensitivity **5**.195–7, **5**.207
Flicker sensitivity **10**.50, **10**.250
    measurement of **15**.8
Flicker submodality **5**.295–7
Flicker thresholds, in specifically disabled readers and controls **13**.58, **13**.149, **13**.151
Flicker/motion threshold **10**.254
'Flight of colours test' in multiple sclerosis **7**.183
Flight simulators **12**.363, **12**.433, **12**.463
Floccular target neurones **8**.232
Flocculus **2**.180–4, **2**.187–8, **8**.37–8, **8**.153–4, **8**.226–33, **8**.238, **8**.302, **8**.328
Flow, transinformational **12**.115
Flow field, visual **12**.360
Fluorescein, and contact lens examination by slit-lamp biomicroscopy **1**.100
Fluorescence **5**.278, **5**.282, **6**.47, **16**.35–6
    and lenticular absorption **1**.9
    and phototoxicity **16**.67
    and radiation **16**.61
Fluorescent light
    and eye-strain **13**.168
    and spectacles **13**.169
Flux **5**.46, **5**.48, **5**.50, **16**.1–3
    light **2**.87
    luminous **10**.124, **10**.127
    photon **2**.89–92, **2**.103, **2**.410, **16**.60
    radiant **16**.6–7
Flux scaling **5**.258, **5**.269
Fly-back, in cathode-ray tubes **15**.7
Flying fox, and retinoscopy **1**.405
Flying performances, of pilots **9**.165
Fly's-eye array **1**.332–3
FMR, *see* Retinitis, foveomacular
F-number **2**.232, **2**.235–6, **2**.411, **16**.25
Focal adhesion contacts **11**.282
    in neuronal cytoskeleton **11**.280, **11**.297–300
Focal contacts **11**.172–3
Focal vision **3**.204, **3**.217
Focalization, axon **11**.237, **11**.240–1, **11**.248
Focimeter, and measurement of back vertex power of contact

lenses **1**.428
Focus **5**.236
Focus errors **5**.85
Focus of expansion **9**.163–4
Foetal subplate, Glossary explanation of **4**.445
Fonda's Rule **1**.200
Font, effect of, on search velocity and comfort **15**.32–4
Fontana's space **2**.474
Forced-choice paradigm **5**.266
Forced-choice preferential looking (FPL) **10**.37, **13**.44–5, **16**.107–8, **16**.112, **16**.124–5
Forced-choice procedure **10**.36
Forceps major **12**.344
    involvement of **12**.345
Forebrain **2**.436, **2**.444
    basal structures **12**.269
Form
    constancy **12**.192
    perception **12**.182, **12**.185–6, **12**.188
        simultaneous **12**.196
    processing **12**.188
    and prosopagnosia **12**.270
    recognition **12**.182, **12**.196, **12**.259, **12**.271
        amorphous **12**.185
    synthesis **12**.184
Form discrimination **2**.387–8, **2**.456
Form element **14**.80
Form perception **2**.456
    colour contrast in **6**.188, **6**.198–217
        and chromatic coding of two-dimensional form **6**.201–12
        and colour vision beyond the primal sketch **6**.212–4
Form vision **5**.235, **5**.248, **5**.268, **5**.274
Form/intensity crosstalk **14**.71
Forsius's colour circle **6**.219
Förster, Richard **12**.65
Fossil record **2**.350, **2**.450
Fossorial niche **2**.428
Foucault knife-edge technique **1**.13, **5**.88
Fourier analysis **4**.291–2, **5**.58, **5**.121, **10**.122, **10**.195
    and computational vision **14**.37
    decomposition of square wave grating **5**.102
    Glossary explanation of **4**.446
    series analyser **5**.184
    spectrum **5**.152–3
        2D **5**.53, **5**.108
    transforms **5**.88, **5**.155–7
        inverse **5**.155–7
Fourier descriptors **12**.113
Fourier methods, spatial **10**.18–9
Fourier power spectrum **10**.119
Fourier series **10**.15
Fourier transforms **2**.92–3, **3**.6–8, **3**.29, **4**.248–9, **4**.256, **4**.260, **12**.9
    forward **10**.5
    inverse **2**.94, **10**.4
    two-dimensional, in spatial-frequency measurement **13**.159
Fourier's theory
    and pattern recognition **14**.25

and theorem 1.252
Fourth power of contrast 5.97–9
Fourth power transform 5.28–9, 5.31, 5.33, 5.97–8, 5.100, 5.102
Fovea 2.168–9, 2.272–3, 3.113–7, 8.2, 8.7–8, 8.45
  and ageing 16.62
  and ageing macula 16.79–81, **16.89**
  amacrine cells in 3.44, 3.46
  binocular 2.273
  centre 12.317–9, 12.322
    and paralexia 12.330
    and word recognition 12.324
  cone density 3.17
  cone spacing 3.20
  cytoarchitecture 3.114
  dendritic fields at 3.103
  and developing visual system **16.110–1, 16.118–9, 16.123**
  development of human 3.15
  in evolution of retina 2.139, 2.144
  in evolution of vision 2.411
  in eye evolution 2.413
  and functional organization of retina 3.2, 3.4–6, 3.9, 3.11
  ganglion cells 3.52, 3.56
  Glossary explanation of 4.446
  Henle fibres of 1.282
  horizontal cells 3.39–40
  human 3.16, 3.24
  illusion and hallucination 12.466
  and ipsilateral projection 3.110, 3.112–3
  and light damage 16.64
  in mammals 2.476, 2.478
  Mantis 2.231
  mask 12.319–20
  monocular 2.273
  ontogeny 3.115
  in pattern discrimination 5.268–9
  primate 3.11–2, 3.14–6, 3.20, 3.33
  projection 12.320
  in pursuit system 2.166–72, 2.177, 2.180, 2.183, 2.191
  and retina 3.81–2, 3.118
  and retinofugal pathways 3.130
  sampling process 12.320
  and visual pathways 2.443, 2.453
  in visual processing 2.255–8, 2.266
  and visual thalamus 3.182, 3.200
Foveal pathways 5.45
Foveal photochromatic interval 7.43
Foveal pit 2.103–4, 2.139, 2.143, 2.443, 2.454
Foveal sensitivity, absolute 5.277
Foveal sparing 4.378
  Glossary explanation of 4.446
Foveal test spot 7.44–5
Foveal vision 5.67
Foveation 6.187
Foveation hypothesis 11.370
Foveolae opticae 11.386–7, 11.395–7, 11.402–3
FPL, *see* Forced-choice preferential looking
F-profiles, Glossary explanation of 4.445
Frames of reference

internal (retinal) 8.98, 8.132, 8.210, 8.327
  optokinetic 8.46, 8.66
  spatial 8.98, 8.132, 8.210
  vestibular 8.20–2, 8.216, 8.232
Framingham Eye Study (FES) 16.136–7, **16.139–43**
Framingham Heart Study 16.142
François-Verriest-Seki (FVS) test plates 7.229–30
Franz's theory of eye embryology 11.397, 11.400–1, 11.403
Fraser spiral 5.242
Free radicals 16.39–40, 16.42–4, 16.67–8
  and ageing macula 16.79–80
  and light damage 16.66
  and light hazards 16.93
  and phototoxicity 16.69–70
  and radiation 16.60–1
Freeze-fracture 2.377, 2.380
Fregoli syndrome 12.302
Frequency domain
  colour signals in 3.28
  in extrafoveal sampling 3.22–3
  and foveal sampling 3.17–9
  two-dimensional 3.17
Frequency doubling 5.150, 5.185
Frequency response
  of motion perception 8.150
  of semicircular canal 8.20, 8.24–9, 8.216
  of smooth pursuit 8.142–5, 8.148–51
  of vergence 8.163
  of visual sensitivity 8.3–5, 8.87–9
Frequency-of-seeing 5.8, 5.11, 5.57, 5.60, 5.64, 5.68
  see also Psychometric functions
Fresnel prisms
  for increasing peripheral field awareness 1.220–1
  'jump' in 1.221
Fresnel reflection losses 1.8
Fresnel spectacle lenses 1.213
Friedmann Visual Field Analyser 7.153
Fringe, interference 5.88, 5.90–2
Frisby test 9.211
Frog 2.71
  dioptrics 2.83–4, 2.95, 2.99
  prey tracking 2.161–2
  shape recognition 2.163
  visuomotor system 2.153–9
Frontal eye fields 2.174, 2.176, 2.178–9, 2.188, 2.191, 4.414–8, 8.67, 8.115, 8.213, 8.244–6, 8.255, 8.270, 8.277, 8.283, 8.286–8
  connectivity of 4.415
  effects of electrical stimulation of 4.414–5
  effects of lesions of 4.418
  physiological properties of 4.415–7
  relationship to superior colliculus 4.417–8
Frontal lobe
  Glossary explanation of 4.444
  supplementary motor area 12.463
Frontal-eyed animals, accessory optic system in 4.111–39
Fronto-parallel plane 9.204
Fruit 2.313, 2.316–7
  coloured 2.314

Function approximation theory 14.44
Functionalism 14.45, 14.91
Functionals 14.80
Functions
  principle of indifference 12.128
  principle of localized 12.128
  somatosensory 12.449
  tactile 12.449
Fundamental formalisms 14.70
Fundamentals
  cone 5.191–2, 5.196, 5.198
  in edge detection 5.102–3
  and flicker 5.184
  M/L, luminosity function 5.207
  and sine-wave gratings 5.103
Fundoscopy 12.191
Fundus and ageing retina 16.134–5
Fundus albipunctatus (Lauber) 7.126
Fundus cameras 1.376–8
  confocal laser scanning ophthalmoscope 1.378
  and holographic examination 1.378
  scanning laser ophthalmoscopes 1.377–8
  stereo photographs from 1.376–7
Fundus flavimaculatus 7.141–3
Fundus photographs 16.135
Fundus reflectometry 1.323

Funduscopy 16.106, 16.109–10, 16.128
Fused image, oculocentric direction of 9.133
Fusiform cells
  Glossary explanation of 4.448
  see also Cortical cells
Fusion 9.31–3
  binocular 8.9, 8.158, 8.168, 8.330, 9.224, 12.29, 12.39–40, 12.43
    suppression theory of 9.93
  characteristics of 9.30–3
  and diplopia, physiological basis of 9.30–1
  first degree 9.201
  neurophysiological correlates of 9.187
  of random-dot stereograms 9.128
  spatial limits of 9.33–4
  spatio-temporal interaction in 9.35–6
  suppression theory of 9.107
  temporal aspects of 9.34–5
Fusion horopter 9.33
Fusion hysteresis 9.212
Fusion range, reduction of 9.131
Fusion theory 9.13–5
Fusional area, *see* Panum's fusional area
Fusional mechanism 9.118
Fusional responses, human 9.111
Fuzzy relations 14.53, 14.55

G

GABA 3.278–9, 3.281–2, 4.45, 4.237, 4.271, 4.286, 4.298, 7.76, 8.237, 8.255, 8.314, 11.157–8, 11.260, 11.356–60, 11.363
  in amacrine cells 3.43, 3.46
  Glossary explanation of 4.446
  in horizontal cells 3.39, 3.41
  immunocytochemistry 3.192
  in interneurones 3.189
  in interplexiform cells 3.47
  in LGNv 3.204
  in neurones 3.190, 3.192
  see also $GABA_A$; $GABA_B$
  and shell nuclei 3.211
  in visual cortex neurogenesis 3.363, 3.369
  in visual thalamus 3.199, 3.201, 3.217
GABA agonists 4.407
  muscimol 4.399, 4.403
GABA antagonists 4.407
  bicuculline 4.399, 4.403
$GABA_A$ mediation 4.53
$GABA_A$ receptors, Glossary explanation of 4.446
$GABA_B$ inhibition, presynaptic, at bipolar cells 4.3–4
$GABA_B$ receptors 4.4, 4.6
GABAergic cells 4.237–8
GABAergic intrinsic neurones 4.237–8
Gabor filters 5.121–3, 5.128
  2D 4.249, 4.255
  Glossary explanation of 4.446
Gabor function hypothesis 4.259, 4.263
Gabor function models 4.264
Gabor functions 10.20–1, 10.69–70, 12.9, 12.113
  Glossary explanation of 4.446
  two-dimensional 4.247, 4.253–6, 4.260
Gabor patches and separation 14.12
Gabor signal, compound 12.210
G-actin 11.137, 11.174, 11.285–6, 11.289
GAD 3.189, 3.192, 3.197, 3.204, 3.279–81, 3.283, 3.288–9, 3.291–2, 4.237, 11.356–8
  Glossary explanation of 4.446
Gadus morrhua (cod) 2.68
Gain 3.35, 3.351
  constant 3.26
  contrast 3.49, 3.53
  Glossary explanation of 4.446
  of horizontal cell output synapse 3.39
  of optokinesis 8.48–51, 8.57–60, 8.65
  receptive field centre 3.32
  of saccades 8.117–27
  of smooth pursuit 8.138–9, 8.141–3, 8.148–51
  in synaptic complexity 2.359
  of vestibular afferents 8.18–20, 8.23–31
  of vestibulo-ocular reflex 8.32–40, 8.45, 8.79–81, 8.299, 8.314
  voltage 3.27, 3.34
Gain control 3.30, 3.58, 5.58–61
  adaptive 5.50, 5.59
  automatic 10.292

  contrast 10.145
  mechanisms of 3.25
  multiplicative 5.58, 5.112–4
  in peripheral vision 5.45–6, 5.55, 5.67, 5.69
  retinal 5.60
  subtractive contrast 5.114
Galactosaemia, as a possible cause of abrupt change in refraction 1.48
β-Galactosidase 11.32
Galago 2.456–7, 2.473, 7.203
  visual areas in 4.164
Galago crassicaudatus (bush baby) 2.75, 2.91
Gal-C (galactocerebroside) 11.30
Galenos, Claudius 12.27–9, 12.34, 12.39
Galiana's model of eye–head co-ordination 8.264–5
Galilean telescopes 1.61–2, 1.385
Gall, Franz Joseph 12.46–7, 12.61
Gamma-aminobutyric acid, *see* GABA
Ganglia, basal 12.463
Ganglion cell layer 2.137, 2.139, 2.145, 2.444–6, 3.48, 3.94, 3.96–8, 11.68
Ganglion cells 2.139–40
  and bipolar cells 3.36
  birth 3.80, 3.111, 3.113
    and death 3.132–5
  bistratified 3.44, 3.55
  broad band 6.174
  cat 4.10–40
    Glossary explanation of 4.446
  cat retinal
    and direction selectivity 4.20
    and orientation selectivity 4.19–20
    and retinal eccentricity 4.20
    sensitivity of various types of 4.14–5
    spatial organization and interactions of 4.15–9
      centre-surround 4.15–7
    various types of 4.12–26
      off 4.12–4
      on 4.12–4
      Q 4.14
      W 4.12–26
      Y 4.12–26
    and wavelength selectivity 4.20–1
  class specification 3.101
  classes of 3.191
  classification scheme 3.49–50
  death 3.106, 3.111, 3.117
    and retinofugal pathways 3.129, 3.139–42
  delta- 3.50–1, 3.55
  in dendrites 11.160–1
  dendritic fields 3.102–3
  dendritic structure 3.50
  density 2.454–5, 3.16, 3.102–3, 3.116–7, 5.252–6, 5.259
  density underestimation 5.255
  differentiation 3.98–100, 3.136–7
  directionally selective 3.44
  displaced (DGC) 2.427, 2.433, 2.449, 3.48
  distribution 3.56–8
  dominators 6.166

Ganglion cells (*continued*)
  electrical activity **11.**269
  and flicker **5.**179–84
  flicker responses **5.**180
  functional diversity **3.**48–9
  giant **2.**427
  heterochromatic flicker photometry from **5.**180–2
  and horizontal cells **3.**41, **3.**54
  importance of **4.**10
  injury **11.**316
  in inner plexiform layer **3.**48–58
  ipsilateral projection **3.**110–1
  M-49 **3.**52–4, **11.**33, **11.**388
  magnocellular pathway **5.**181
  in mammals **2.**470, **2.**476
  in mature retina **3.**129–32
  membrane resistance **3.**48
  midget **3.**52, **6.**141–3, **6.**170–1, **6.**187
  misprojecting **3.**111
  monkey **4.**10–40
  monkey retinal
    M **4.**29–36
    P **4.**29–36
    receptive fields of **4.**27–36
    S **4.**29–36
    sensitivity to luminance contrast **4.**29–30
    types and properties of **4.**27–36
  monoaminergic **3.**51
  morphological variation **3.**48
  and neurone death **3.**97
  OFF-centre **3.**42, **3.**44, **3.**49, **3.**55, **11.**154–6, **11.**162–3,
      11.259
  ON-centre **3.**42, **3.**44, **3.**49, **3.**202–3, **11.**154–6, **11.**162–3,
      11.259
  on–off **11.**154, **11.**157, **11.**162–4
  opponent **6.**165
  overproduction of **3.**139–40
  P- **3.**49, **3.**52–4
  Pα- **3.**52
  parasol **3.**52
  parvocellular pathway **5.**181
  Pβ- **3.**52
  perifoveal midget **3.**54
  phasic **5.**48, **5.**181–4, **5.**197, **6.**174
  in plexiform layer **3.**32–3, **3.**42, **3.**48–58
  population **3.**48, **3.**52, **3.**56
  positional disorder **3.**57
  as postreceptoral mechanisms **3.**30
  primate, Glossary explanation of **4.**446
  Q- **3.**51
  receptive field density **5.**262
  and retina **3.**1–2, **3.**4–6, **3.**73–7, **3.**85, **3.**91–2, **3.**94–6,
      3.118
  retinal **2.**141–7, **8.**4, **8.**7–8, **10.**46
    and binocular vision **2.**274–5, **2.**278
    in cat **5.**41–2
    classes **2.**143, **2.**145–7
    distribution **2.**143–5, **2.**147
    in evolution of retina **2.**136–7

  numbers **2.**142–3
  in peripheral vision **5.**47–8, **5.**50–2, **5.**56, **5.**58–9, **5.**63
  in pursuit system **2.**170–3
  responses **5.**39–40
  and visual pathways **2.**443, **2.**445, **2.**450, **2.**452, **2.**454
  and retinal expansion **3.**105–10
  in retinal maturation **3.**117
  in retinal transplantation **11.**323
  in retinofugal pathways **3.**138–9, **3.**141–2
  roles of the various types of, in vision **4.**21
  sampling interval **5.**256
  see also Midget cell system
  separation **5.**251
  spatial antagonism **6.**166
  and spectral sensitivity **5.**198
  spectrally non-opponent **5.**173, **5.**181–2
  spectrally opponent **5.**173, **5.**181–2
  sustained **5.**48
  and synaptic rearrangements **11.**257–8, **11.**264–6, **11.**269
  tonic **5.**181–3, **5.**185, **6.**175
  type A **3.**52, **3.**185
  type B **3.**52, **3.**185
  type C **3.**186
  type E **3.**186
  W1- **3.**52
  W2- **3.**52
  W-like **3.**197
  W-type **3.**202, **3.**210–1
  W(epsilon)- **3.**51–2, **3.**131–2, **3.**183
  W(γ)- **3.**49–53, **3.**55–6, **3.**131–2, **3.**136, **3.**183, **3.**185–6,
      3.189, **11.**154, **11.**156
  X-class **3.**152, **3.**154
  X-like **3.**196
  Xβ- **3.**49–51, **3.**55–8, **3.**131–2, **11.**154–7, **11.**161–4
    in retinofugal pathways **3.**136–7, **3.**142–3
    in visual thalamus **3.**183–4, **3.**186, **3.**189
  Y-class **3.**152
  Y-like **3.**197
  Y-type **3.**202, **3.**210
  Yα- **11.**154–7, **11.**161–4
  Yγ- **3.**44, **3.**49–51, **3.**55–8, **3.**130–2
    in retinofugal pathways **3.**142–3
    in visual thalamus **3.**183–6, **3.**189
Ganzfeld **5.**290, **9.**96
Gap junctions **2.**386, **3.**11, **3.**32
  amacrine cell **3.**42
  bipolar cell **3.**35
  conductance **3.**41
  horizontal cell **3.**38
Gap paradigm **8.**114
GAP-43 **11.**176, **11.**228–9
  in adult mammals **11.**221
  in axon growth **11.**219–21, **11.**223, **11.**225–9, **11.**243
  and calcium channels **11.**227
  and calmodulin **11.**226
  and dendrites **11.**149, **11.**152
  hypothesis **11.**223–5
  in nerve growth **11.**225–7
  in neuronal cytoskeleton **11.**279–80, **11.**293, **11.**297

and phospholipid metabolism 11.226–7
phosphorylation 11.220–1
properties 11.219–20
in regeneration 11.192, 11.194, 11.196
in synaptic plasticity 11.219, 11.221–3, 11.225–8
GAPs (growth associated proteins)
and axon growth 11.220, 11.243
and memory 11.291
in neuronal cytoskeleton 11.293
and optic nerve regeneration 11.223
in regeneration 11.192, 11.194, 11.196, 11.200
in superior colliculus 11.224
Gas 16.10
Gas-plasma visual displays 15.56, 15.59
Gastrulation 11.17–9
Gates–MacGinnitie Word Discrimination Test 13.177
Gaub, Hieronymous David 12.434
Gaussian bars 10.94
Gaussian contrast envelopes 10.94
Gaussian contrast profiles and separation 14.12
Gaussian curvature 14.5
Gaussian detector 5.68
Gaussian distributed point spread function 5.123
Gaussian distribution 5.137, 10.90
Gaussian envelope 5.58, 5.68
and separation 14.12
Gaussian filtering 3.27
Gaussian functions 5.58, 5.73, 5.143
and wavelet analysis 12.255–6
Gaussian luminance profiles and separation 14.12
Gaussian mechanisms 5.71
Gaussian noise 5.24–6, 5.39, 5.41–2, 5.100, 14.93
Gaussian profile 3.31, 3.48, 5.208–9
Gaussian pyramid 10.123
Gaussian receptive field centre 5.57
Gaussian sensitivity 5.58
Gaussian thick-lens theory 2.82
Gaussian time functions 12.242
Gauthier effect 13.216
Gaze 5.45, 8.1, 8.45, 8.84, 8.244, 12.475, 13.209–10
and area 7 neurones 12.101
asthenia 12.452
control defects 12.95
control hypothesis 8.266
control of spatially directed 12.464
direction, as stimulus parameter 12.122
direction of 12.123
eye–head co-ordination in control of 8.13, 8.71
and superior colliculus 8.34
field of 12.99, 12.103–6, 12.229, 12.232, 12.238, 12.274
fixation of 13.23, 13.27–8, 13.182
motor complex 12.78
motor error 8.267
movements 12.191, 12.341
control during reading 12.318
illusion and hallucination 12.472
and posterior parietal lobe 12.96–7
problems 12.357
saccadic 12.431

slow (pursuit) 12.431
and spatial hemineglect 12.452, 12.454, 12.463
and visual hemineglect 12.433
and visuo-spatial disorders 12.437
palsy 12.463–4
position 12.100, 12.103, 12.105
control 12.99–100
region of supplementary motor area 12.463
saccades 8.107–9, 8.265, 8.328
shifts in 12.464
social contact 12.219
of the social partner 12.123
and spatial layout 14.4–5
stability 8.71–84
during active head rotation 8.81–2
in freely moving subjects 8.79–84
role of saccadic and slow movements 8.75
role of velocity and position signals 8.77–8
role of visual and non-visual signals 8.75–9
technical considerations 8.82–4
with unrestrained head 8.80–1
upward paralysis 12.348
vertical paralysis 12.464
and vision 8.1–11, 8.71–92
Gaze direction 12.123
neuron activity related to 4.382–3
Gaze fixation, neuron activity related to 4.381–2
Gaze palsy, Glossary explanation of 4.446
Gaze position, of the social partner 12.123
Gaze stability 9.126
Gaze-evoked nystagmus 8.236, 8.301–2, 8.314
Gaze-holding 8.1–5, 8.34
after lesions 8.227, 8.297–303, 8.312
Gaze-paretic nystagmus 8.322
Gaze-shifting 8.1–3, 8.5–9
and acuity 8.6–9
disorders 8.304–8
and field of view 8.5–6
Gaze-velocity neurones 8.217, 8.230, 8.322, 8.328
G-binding proteins 4.4
Geborgenheit (safety) 12.417
Gecko 2.73, 2.111, 2.428
Gedächtnisfarben 12.386, 12.398
'*Gedankenexperimente*' 12.462–3
Gel electrophoresis 7.103, 7.105, 7.108
Gelbstoff 2.8
Gender, and face recognition 12.226, 12.231, 12.236–8
Gene photopigments 7.17
Generalization 14.70, 14.76, 14.79
of visual response 3.347–9
Generalized cylinders 14.39
Generalized point horopter 9.26–7
Genes
Abdominal A 11.12
Abdominal B 11.10, 11.12
activation 11.55–7, 11.65
Antennapedia (Antp) 11.3–8, 11.12, 11.20–1, 11.38, 11.40
Antennapedia (Antp)-like 11.6–7, 11.11
basic FGF 11.115–6

Genes (*continued*)
  bicoid **11.4**
  cdx **11.11**
  coding visual pigments **2.78**
  in colour vision **2.284, 2.316–7**
  Deformed **11.8, 11.12, 11.20**
  delta **11.116–7**
  domains of expression **11.23**
  dorsal **11.121–2**
  engrailed **11.3–4, 11.6, 11.21, 11.38, 11.61**
  expression **11.38–41, 11.59**
    in adult rat optic nerve **11.224**
    domains **11.11–7**
    of GAP-43 **11.228**
    in reGenesration **11.196, 11.200**
  faint little ball **11.116**
  function in embryos **11.123**
  function in vertebrates **11.123**
  Fushi tarazu **11.3, 11.5, 11.20, 11.23**
  homeotic **11.3–5, 11.7–9, 11.37–8, 11.40**
  Hox **11.40**
  Hox-1 **11.7–8**
  Hox-1.1 **11.22**
  Hox-1.2 **11.8, 11.11–2**
  Hox-1.3 **11.8, 11.11–2, 11.14–5, 11.19, 11.21**
  Hox-1.4 **11.11–2, 11.14, 11.19, 11.22–3**
  Hox-1.5 **11.17–8**
  Hox-1.6 **11.9**
  Hox-2 **11.7–8, 11.12–3, 11.41**
  Hox-2.1 **11.8, 11.12, 11.14–5, 11.19**
  Hox-2.2 **11.8, 11.12, 11.14**
  Hox-2.3 **11.12, 11.14**
  Hox-2.3/1.1 **11.14**
  Hox-2.4 **11.12, 11.14**
  Hox-2.5 **11.12, 11.15**
  Hox-2.6 **11.12, 11.14, 11.19**
  Hox-2.7 **11.12, 11.17**
  Hox-2.8 **11.12, 11.17**
  Hox-2.9 **11.12, 11.17**
  Hox-3 **11.7–8, 11.20**
  Hox-3.1 **11.11–2, 11.14, 11.17–8**
  Hox-3.3 **11.8, 11.11–2, 11.14, 11.17, 11.20**
  Hox-3.4 **11.8, 11.12, 11.14–5, 11.19–20**
  Hox-4 **11.7–8, 11.20**
  Hox-4.2 **11.19**
  Hox-4.4 **11.15, 11.20**
  Hox-4.5 **11.20**
  Hox-4.6 **11.20**
  Hox-4.7 **11.20**
  Hox-5.1 **11.14**
  Hox-7 **11.6**
  Hox-7.1 **11.7, 11.20**
  Hox-8 **11.6**
  hunchback **11.4**
  hybrid **2.314**
  intra-abdominal (iab) **11.8**
  irp **11.114**
  junB **11.120–1**
  Knirps **11.4**

  Krox-20 **11.40**
  Kruppel **11.4**
  Labial **11.8, 11.12**
  mix l **11.11, 11.19**
  mutations **11.116, 11.118–9, 11.121–3**
  notch **11.116–7**
  Oct 1 **11.21**
  Oct 2 **11.21**
  opsin **2.295**
    in photoreceptor system **2.67, 2.69, 2.71, 2.77**
  paired **11.20–1**
  photopigment **2.293, 2.297, 2.311**
  Pit-1 **11.6, 11.21**
  Probosipedia **11.8**
  rare mutant **2.316**
  regulation **11.120–1**
  segment polarity **11.38**
  sevenless **11.117**
  Sex combs reduced **11.8, 11.12**
  slit **11.116–7**
  torpedo **11.116**
  torso **11.119**
  in trichromacy **2.313–4**
  tumour suppressor **11.123**
  Ultrabithorax (Ubx) **11.3, 11.8, 11.10, 11.12, 11.20**
  Unc86 **11.21**
  visual pigment **2.26, 2.44**
  wingless **11.38**
  X-chromosome-linked deviations **12.386**
  XHox3 **11.19, 11.22**
  XHox-1-A **11.22**
  XlHbox1 **11.9, 11.20–1**
  XlHbox2 **11.21**
  XlHbox8 **11.11**
  Zerknult **11.3, 11.8, 11.12**
  ZFX **11.7**
  ZFY **11.7**
Genetics
  of inherited colour deficiencies **7.88–114**
    achromatopsias **7.98–101**
    blue **7.95–8**
    molecular biology **7.101–11**
    red–green **7.88–95**
    types of defect **7.88–101**
  Mendelian **7.88**
  and the right hemisphere and right-handedness **13.84–7**
Geneva lens measure **1.423**
  and the sag formula **1.416**
Geniculate wing **3.51–2, 3.210**
Geniculo-cortical afferents **4.298**
Geniculo-cortical fibres
  postsynaptic targets of **13.244–52**
    in carnivores **3.248–50**
    in primates **3.251–2**
    in rodents **3.248**
Geniculostriate pathway **5.252–3, 5.255, 5.272**
Geniculostriate system, location of neurotransmitters in **3.278–301**
Gennari, Francisco **12.47–9**

Gennari stria 3.255–6, 3.262–3
Gennari, stripe of 12.146
Geodome, cellular 11.279
Geometric horopter 9.28–9
Geometrical illusions 6.213–4
Geometry
    fractal 11.275, 11.304
    ocular exposure 16.23–9, 16.59
Geons 14.112–3
Geotaxic behaviour 8.13
Gerbil photoreceptor system 2.74
German 12.308
    prose texts 12.317
    shorthand 12.330
    texts 12.311–3
    word frequency 12.314–5
Gerstmann's syndrome 12.350, 12.404, 12.406–7, 12.419,
        12.462, 13.225
Geschwind's theory of cerebral lateralization 13.106–7
Gesichtserscheinungen phantastische (scenic visual
        illusions) 12.468–70, 12.477
Gestalt
    fusion frequency 12.59
    grouping principles 12.204, 12.206
    perception 12.8, 12.59, 12.71, 12.189
    theory 12.185–6, 12.188–9
    vision 12.184
Gestalt properties of pattern recognition 14.21, 14.27
Gestalt psychology and visual perception 14.19–20
Gestalt rules of organization 14.26, 14.91
    closure 14.6
    good continuation 14.6
    grouping by proximity 14.6
    similarity 14.6
Gestalt theories of perception 5.152, 14.90
Gesture 12.117, 12.219–20, 12.224, 12.254–5
    as communication 12.331–2
    and heautoscopy 12.297
    and prosopagnosia 12.280, 12.285
    reading and script 12.307
    ritualized 12.307
Ghost images 9.46–7
Gibbs distribution 14.93
Gibson invariants 14.19, 14.26, 14.91
Gibson's concepts of visual perception 14.19–28, 14.90–1
Gibson's flow field concept 5.258
Gibson's hypothesis of direct perception 14.84
Gierer's gradient theory 11.89, 11.92–4
Gigantocypris mulleri 2.125
Giles Archer lantern 7.229
Gilmore Oral Reading Test 13.192
Gisborn (New Zealand) Eye Study 16.138
Glare 5.39–40, 5.86, 5.280, 13.171–80, 15.59, 16.152–3,
        16.158
    dazzling 1.222
    disability 1.222–3
        and CPF tints 1.223
        and intra-ocular light scatter 1.223
        and yellow-tinted lenses 1.223

discomfort 1.222, 16.157
    effects of, on reading ability 13.171
    recovery 16.152–3
    resistance 16.152
Glass, as a material for contact lenses 1.128
Glassblowing 16.96
Glasses
    see also under Spectacles
    tinted, in cone dystrophy 7.138–9
Glaucoma 5.172, 7.152–5, 7.158, 7.163, 7.177, 7.220, 7.229
    open angle 1.297
Glia
    adhesion molecule on (AMOG) 11.71–2
    goldfish optic tract 11.198
    Müller 11.32, 11.43
    in vertebrate neurogenesis 11.30–4
Glial cells 11.68
    axon environment 11.243–7
    and axon growth 11.248–50
    and cellular organization 11.72–4
    in mammals 11.207–8
    in neuronal cytoskeleton 11.277, 11.282
    non-supportive 11.207
    and optic nerve injury 11.206–13
    reactive 11.207, 11.210
    in regeneration 11.192, 11.198, 11.201
Glial derived nexin (GDN) 11.179
Glial fibrillary acidic protein (GFAP) 11.30, 11.208–9,
        11.244–6
'Glial knot' 3.135
Glioblastoma 12.354
    left posterior 12.351
    occipito-temporal 12.351–2
    posterior 12.426
Gliogenesis and TOP molecules 11.75
Gliomas 3.83
Glissades 8.123, 8.125–7, 13.211
Global effect on saccadic amplitude 8.119–20
Global hysteresis, in cyclopean perception 9.65–6
Global layer of extraocular muscle 8.178–81
Global stereo acuity 9.208
Global stereo thresholds 9.208
Global stereopsis
    neuronal mechanisms of 4.215
    and random-dot stereograms 4.215
Glomerulus 3.195–8, 3.201, 3.211
Glucose, metabolism 12.267
Glutamate 3.34, 11.152, 11.200, 11.281, 11.287
    Glossary explanation of 4.446
    and horizontal cells 3.41
    in visual cortex 3.311, 3.368–9
    in visual thalamus 3.183–5, 3.192
Glutamic acid decarboxylase, *see* GAD
Glycine 3.33, 3.41–2
Glycolipids 11.199
Glycoproteins 11.199
Glycosylation 11.196, 11.201
Goals, operators, methods and selection rules models, *see*
        GOMS models

Goethe, Johann Wolfgang von **12.469**, **12.471**
Goethe's colour circle **6.220–1**
Gold particles **11.177**
Goldfish **2.69–70**
  colour vision **2.286–7**, **2.289–92**, **2.298**, **2.301**
  dioptrics **2.85**
Goldmann perimeter **12.137**, **12.393**
Goldstein, Eugen **12.147**
Golgi apparatus and dendrites **11.148**
Golgi complex and microtubules **11.134**
Golgi preparations **3.236**, **3.239**, **3.244–6**, **3.251**
Golgi stain **2.141–2**
  Glossary explanation of **4.446**
Golgi tendon organs **8.188**
GOMS models **15.103–4**, **15.106**
Gorillas **7.199**
G-proteins **2.63–4**, **2.380**, **4.4**, **6.69**, **6.100**, **6.103**
Graded density red filters **9.203**
Gradient index lens **5.81**
Gradient theory **11.88–9**, **11.92–4**
Gradient-based segmentation **5.121**
Gradients **11.50–2**
  directional guidance by **11.92**
  low-spatial-frequency **5.103–4**
  molecular **11.70**, **11.84**
  morphogenetic **11.47–8**, **11.51**, **11.55–6**, **11.58**, **11.65**
  of neurogenesis **3.363–5**
  orthogonal **11.77–8**, **11.84**
  simple light–dark **12.359**
  TOP **11.77–9**
  topographic **11.74**
Granular layers, Glossary explanation of **4.446**
Grapheme sequences **12.310**
Grapheme–phoneme correlation **12.306**, **12.308–9**
Graphics, complex analysis **12.356**
Graphics tablets **15.117–8**
Graphology **12.315**
Graphs and graphics **15.75–7**
  graphical *vs.* textual representation of information **15.75**
  graphics **15.76**
  graphs **15.76**
Grasping
  impairment of visually guided **12.95**
  manual **12.412**
  movements **12.451**
  oral **12.412**
  and posterior parietal lobe **12.94**
  range **12.417–8**
  space **12.430**
    Euclidean structure **12.415**
    extrapersonal **12.417**
    object position in **12.103**
    personal **12.417**
    and posterior parietal lobe **12.95–7**
    and spatial hemineglect **12.454**
    and topographagnosia **12.422**
    and topographical disorientation **12.411–4**
    and visual hemineglect **12.448**, **12.450–1**
    and visuo-spatial disorders **12.435–9**, **12.443**

Grasping movements, control of **12.464**
Grassmann's Laws **7.6**
  and colour matching **6.29**, **6.149**, **6.271**, **6.274–5**
Gratings
  acuity **5.90**, **5.258**, **10.224–9**
  chromatically defined **10.142**
  complex **1.252–4**
  compound **5.103**
    detection of **5.97–101**
    75% threshold value **5.98**
  counter-phased **5.149–50**
  and deLange functions **5.178**
  drifting light–dark **12.377**
  equiluminant **10.141–2**
  low-spatial-frequency sine-wave **5.103–4**
  luminance-defined **10.142**
  motion-defined **10.165**
  negative masking of **5.31**
  printed **10.27–33**
  sensitivity **5.35**
  simple **5.97–9**, **5.101**, **5.103**
  simple sinusoidal **1.250–2**
  sine-wave **5.33**, **5.97**, **5.110**, **5.113**, **5.149–54**, **10.19**, **10.87**, **10.96**
  square-wave **1.250–2**, **5.102–3**, **5.110**, **5.113**, **10.142**
  threshold **5.42**
  trapezoidal **5.103**
Gravito-inertial stimuli **8.13**
Grey matter **12.127–35**
  associative mechanisms of brain **12.127**
  brain lesions **12.127–35**
  nerve cell layers and columns **12.127**
Greyscale filtering **15.15–7**
Grotrian energy diagram **16.32**, **16.35**
Group, interaction **12.219**
Grouping
  and computational vision **14.31**
  figural **14.16**
  hierarchical **14.38**
  in numerosity **14.127**, **14.137**
  by proximity **14.6**
Growth associated proteins, *see* GAPs
Growth cones
  axonal **11.90–1**, **11.93**, **11.108–9**, **11.149**, **11.152**, **11.233**, **11.236**
    pathfinding **11.280**
  behaviour **11.80**, **11.280–1**
  calcium regulation of **11.280–1**
  in cell locomotion **11.171–82**
  and cell recognition **11.83**
  collapse **11.73–4**, **11.102**, **11.181**
  in critical period plasticity **11.289**
  dendritic **11.150–2**, **11.160–1**
  effects of neurotransmitters **11.281–2**
  fish **11.101**
  and GAP-43 **11.219**, **11.225–7**
  guidance **11.68**, **11.70**, **11.73**, **11.176**, **11.181**
  inhibition **11.73**
  and microfilaments **11.139**

migration **11.70, 11.72**
navigation **11.70**
neuritic **11.280–2**
in neuronal cytoskeleton **11.278, 11.284–7, 11.293, 11.297,
    11.300–1**
orientation **11.48, 11.62–3, 11.65**
pathfinding **11.70**
pioneer **11.180**
in regeneration **11.195–6**
regulators **11.282**
in retinofugal pathways **3.135**
Growth control mechanisms and proto-oncogenes **11.113**
Growth factors
    and axon growth **11.245, 11.248–9, 11.251**
    in optic nerve regeneration **11.211, 11.213**
    and proto-oncogenes **11.113–4, 11.116, 11.120**
Growth vigour **11.241, 11.250**
Growth-associated triggering factors **11.197**
Guanine **7.102**
Guanine crystals **2.126**
Guanylate cyclase **6.102**
Guessing
    and pure alexia **12.341, 12.358**
    reluctance **12.351**
    task **12.354**
Guidance, nature of visual **14.20**
Guillain–Barré syndrome **8.310**
Gullstrand's 'No. 1' schematic eye model **1.6**
Gullstrand's reflex-free ophthalmoscope **1.376**
Gunshot wounds **10.266, 10.271**
Guppy **2.12–3, 2.69–71, 2.73**
Guy's colour vision test **7.230**
Gyrus
    inferior temporal **12.404**
    mesial occipito-temporal, *see* Gyrus fusiformis
    superior temporal **12.264**
Gyrus angularis **12.264**
    and alexia **12.334**
    and colour agnosia **12.405–6**
    and colour anomia **12.407**
    and colour deficiencies **12.410**
    left **12.355**

and posterior parietal lobe **12.94**
and pure alexia **12.356–8**
and spatial hemineglect **12.462**
and visuo-spatial disorders **12.436**
Gyrus cinguli **12.278**
    ventral posterior **12.94**
Gyrus circumflexus
    and colour deficiencies **12.410**
    and posterior parietal lobe **12.94**
    and spatial hemineglect **12.462**
    and visuo-spatial disorders **12.436**
Gyrus fusiformis **7.71, 7.184–5, 7.188, 12.123, 12.390–1**
    adjacent **12.344**
    anterior infero–calcarine region **12.403**
    and colour agnosia **12.404**
    and hemiachromatopsia **12.401–3**
    and loss of topographical familiarity **12.425**
    and prosopagnosia **12.263, 12.266–7, 12.269–70**
    and pure alexia **12.342**
    and visual object recognition **12.108**
Gyrus hippocampalis **12.269, 12.287, 12.390, 12.393**
    formation **12.269, 12.347**
    and hemiachromatopsia **12.401**
    illusion and hallucination **12.470, 12.480**
    and pure alexia **12.344**
    and visual object recognition **12.108–9**
Gyrus lingualis **7.71, 7.184–5, 12.390–1**
    anterior **12.344–5**
    and hemiachromatopsia **12.402**
    left **12.344**
    and loss of topographical familiarity **12.425–7**
    posterior **12.344**
    and prosopagnosia **12.263, 12.266, 12.270**
    and pure alexia **12.342**
Gyrus parahippocampalis **12.347, 12.387, 12.465**
    and colour agnosia **12.404**
    illusion and hallucination **12.471**
    and loss of topographical familiarity **12.425–7**
    and posterior parietal lobe **12.94**
    and prosopagnosia **12.263, 12.266, 12.269, 12.274–5**
    and pure alexia **12.344**

H

H1 horizontal cells 7.75–6
H2 horizontal cells 7.75–6
H3 horizontal cells 7.75–6
H16 test 7.224
Habituation 10.184
Haemangiomas 1.45
Haematoma
   intracerebral 12.266, 12.276
   occipito-temporal 12.266
   subdural 12.343
Haematopoiesis 11.117, 11.208
Haematoporphyrin 16.71
   derivatives 16.69, 16.72
Haemoglobin 16.38, 16.45–6
Haemorrhage 12.262, 12.334, 12.343, 12.381, 16.48–9
Hagfish 2.31, 2.33, 2.401–2, 2.405, 2.416
Haidinger's brushes 1.312, 1.348–9, 5.88
   and the macula 1.319–23
Hair-cells 8.22–6
Half width at half height, Glossary explanation of 4.446
Half-image 5.229–30
Half-wave rectification, Glossary explanation of 4.446
Half-wave rectified output 5.100
Hallden test 9.194–5
Haller, Albrecht von 12.46
Hallucinations 2.268, 7.193, 12.3, 12.27, 12.31, 12.466–74
   afterimages 12.467–8
   auditory 12.288
   'autoscopique ou speculaire' 12.299
   caused by brain lesions 12.49
   coenaesthetic 12.289
   complex 12.148, 12.157, 12.466
   Doppelgänger 12.301
   drug-induced 12.299
   Eigengrau 12.466–7
   face-specific 12.275
   and heautoscopy 12.297–9, 12.302–3
   hypnagogic 12.301
   obscurations 12.472–3
   olfactory and gustatory 12.288
   palinopsia 12.473–5
   patterns and scenes from meaningless random
      stimuli 12.470–1
   'peduncular' 12.478
   simple-structured 12.474
   sterotype 12.479
   vestibular 12.288, 12.300
   visual 12.288, 12.426, 12.466
      complex 12.474, 12.477–2
      elementary 12.477–1
      hypnagogic ('falling asleep') 12.481
      hypnopomp ('waking up') 12.481
      multimodal scenic 12.466, 12.473–4
      and pseudohallucinations 12.154–7, 12.176, 12.476–4
      scenic 12.468–70, 12.479–81
Hallucinosis
   continuous 12.477
   'peduncular' 12.478
Halobacterium habolium 2.39
Haloperidol 10.251, 10.256
Halos
   causes of 1.351–2
      corneal 1.352
      glaucomatous 1.352
      lens 1.352
Halteres 8.13
Ham's data 16.63, 16.89
Hand, recognition 12.274
Hand movements
   control of spatially directed 12.464
   goal-directed 12.103
   intended 12.103
   visually guided 12.95
Handedness 11.60–1, 12.144
Hands-free operation 15.122
Handwriting
   familiar 12.356
      recognition of 12.270
   identification of 14.98, 14.103, 14.105
   individuality of 12.315–6, 12.356
   loss of ability to read 12.333
   new 12.356
Haplochromis burtoni (cichlid fish) 2.290
Haploscope 1.235
Haploscopic matching 6.50
Haploscopic tests
   with camouflaged form 9.210–1
      Frisby 9.210–1
      random-dot E 9.210–1
      random-dot stereo 9.210–1
      TNO stereo 9.210–1
Haptic lenses, *see* Contact lenses, scleral
Hardy–Rand–Rittler plates, *see* AO HRR plates
Harmonic sinusoidal components, fundamental of first
   1.252
Harmonics 5.102–4, 5.184, 5.270, 10.7
Hazards
   analysis 16.2
   assessment of ocular 16.3–4
   blue light 16.7, 16.42, 16.63, 16.65–6, 16.89
      and developing visual system 16.109
   burn 16.2
   functions, blue-light and burn 16.5, 16.7
   laser 16.5
   light 16.93–100
      clinical 16.97–100
      environmental 16.93–5
      occupational 16.94–7
      recreational 16.93–5
   non-laser 16.5
   optical
      ionization 16.30
      mechanical 16.30
      photochemical 16.30
      radiation 16.17
      thermal 16.30

Head
  closed injury **12**.268, **12**.277, **12**.281, **12**.343, **12**.393
  open injury **12**.343
  penetrating injury **12**.284
Head movements **8**.81–2
  combined linear and angular **8**.34–5
  co-ordinated with eye movements **8**.13, **8**.33–4, **8**.38, **8**.99,
    8.106–9, **8**.264–7, **8**.306
  effects of, in binocular vision **9**.126–9
  and gaze stability **8**.79–84, **8**.297–9
  illusion of **12**.433
  and spatial hemineglect **12**.452, **12**.463
  and visuo-spatial disorders **12**.435, **12**.438, **12**.442
Head nystagmus **8**.47
Head oscillations, voluntary **9**.127
Head position **12**.124
Head rotation **12**.98
Head turning
  forwards or backwards **12**.121
  to left or right **12**.121
Headache **12**.347, **16**.97
  frontal **12**.275, **12**.402
  right frontal **12**.275
Headaches
  prevention of **13**.164–7
    tinted glasses **13**.164–7
      and the Irlen Institute **13**.164, **13**.166
  and reading **13**.155
Head-centred co-ordinates **4**.383
Head-in-space position **12**.464
Head-on-trunk position **12**.432
Head-shaking nystagmus **8**.301
Heautoscopy **12**.297–303
  chronic **12**.301
  Doppelgänger **12**.297–300
  face alienation **12**.302–3
  illusionary **12**.298
  inner (a-type) **12**.297
  negative **12**.302
  neuropathology and pathophysiology **12**.300–2
  outer (b-type) **12**.298–300
  partial (d-type) **12**.298–9, **12**.301–2
  phenomena **12**.480
  and social partners **12**.297
  somaesthetic *Doppelgänger* (e-type) **12**.299
  and topographical disorientation **12**.411
  visual–vestibular (c-type) **12**.298–300
Hebbian synapse hypothesis **11**.240, **11**.258–63, **11**.268–9
Hebrew **12**.308, **12**.324
Hegel, Georg Wilhelm **12**.311, **12**.318
Heine, Heinrich **12**.299
Heinicke **12**.136
Helicopter flight, map of the earth **10**.172
Helix-turn-helix motif **11**.6, **11**.20
Helmholtz, Hermann von **12**.6, **12**.162, **12**.371
Helmholtz's theory of colour perception **6**.4, **6**.11–2
Helmholtz's theory of unconscious inference **14**.89
Hematoma, intracerebral right parieto–temporal **12**.429
Hemiachromatopsia **7**.183–5, **7**.188, **7**.190, **7**.192, **12**.388,

  12.390–2
  and achromatopsia **12**.401
  and alexia **12**.335–6
  and colour agnosia **12**.405–6
  and colour deficiencies **12**.409
  incomplete **12**.401
  and pure alexia **12**.337, **12**.343, **12**.357
  pure homonymous **12**.401–2
Hemiagnosia **12**.212, **12**.357
  left visual field **12**.348
Hemialexia
  after splenial lesions **12**.347–8
  and attention **12**.347
  auditory and tactile transfer **12**.349
  bilateral lexical decision paradigm **12**.350
  'deblocking' methods **12**.350
  hemisensory loss **12**.348
  hemispatial neglect **12**.348
  and hidden meaning **12**.350
  increased intracranial pressure **12**.347
  Kana **12**.357
  left **12**.348
  left visual field **12**.347–8
  lexical decision **12**.350
  mental status examination **12**.349
  position sense **12**.349
    loss of **12**.348
  tachistoscopic studies **12**.348–50
  for words **12**.349
Hemiamblyopia **7**.184–5
Hemianaesthesia **12**.449
Hemianopes **10**.270
Hemianopia **7**.183, **7**.185, **7**.188, **7**.191–3, **9**.199, **10**.266–8,
    12.27, **12**.40, **12**.47, **12**.49–50, **12**.136–57
  and achromatopsia **12**.395
  acute **12**.156
  and agnosia **12**.179, **12**.182, **12**.215
  bilateral **12**.146, **12**.148, **12**.180, **12**.391
    upper **12**.209
  by cerebral brain lesions **12**.136
  complete homonymous **12**.351
  cortical **12**.155–6
  heteronymous bitemporal **12**.144–5
  homonymous **1**.218, **12**.136, **12**.156–7, **12**.180, **12**.390–1
    and agnosia **12**.181, **12**.197, **12**.199, **12**.214, **12**.216
    and colour anomia **12**.408
    left **12**.259, **12**.342–3, **12**.426
      and hemiachromatopsia **12**.402
      and topographagnosia **12**.421–3
      and visual hemineglect **12**.445
    partial left **12**.446
    right **12**.146
      and alexia **12**.334, **12**.336
      and hemiachromatopsia **12**.401
      and hemialexia **12**.350–1
      and pure alexia **12**.347, **12**.354
      and topographagnosia **12**.420–1, **12**.423
  and spatial hemineglect **12**.452
  and visual movement agnosia **12**.379

Hemianopia (*continued*)
  and visuo-spatial disorders 12.443
  illusion and hallucination 12.473
  inferior horizontal 12.436
  left homonymous 13.222
  partial 12.335, 12.390
  patients, blindsight in 12.149–54
  and pure alexia 12.339, 12.357
  right-angled prisms for 1.220
  by unilateral brain lesions 12.136
Hemianopsia 8.279, 8.306
Hemiasomatognosia 12.449
Hemidecortication 10.270
Hemifield 5.109
  advantage 12.144
  blind 10.268, 12.152–3
    nasal and temporal 12.154
  contralateral 12.341
  left, in reading and script 12.321
  left and right 12.136
  lower quadrant 12.322
  and migraine phophenes 12.172
  and motion perception 12.86
  nasal 5.128, 12.142
    and temporal 12.153
  right, in reading and script 12.321
  tachistoscopic testing 12.349
  testing 12.357
  two binocular 12.357
  upper quadrant 12.322
  visual
    left and right 12.230–1, 12.234–5, 12.324–5
      advantage 12.233–4
      and alexia 12.335
      and letter recognition 12.322
      periphery 12.328
      and pure alexia 12.353, 12.356–7
      and semantic paralexia 12.329
      and shorthand 12.331
      superiority 12.322–5
        for Kanji signs 12.329–30
          semantic classification 12.330
          semantic congruency decisions 12.330
        in word recognition 12.325–8
      and visual hallucinations 12.477
    and spatial hemineglect 12.462
Hemifield dominance 5.271–2
Hemifield specialization 5.274
Hemifovea, left and right 12.309
Hemihypaesthesia 12.354
Hemi-inattention 12.341–2, 12.357, 12.453
  and brain lesions outside parietal lobe 12.462–4
  tests to evaluate symptoms 12.452–62
  and visual hemineglect 12.447, 12.450
Hemineglect
  concept for topographical relations 12.462
  conception of spatial relations 12.462
  diagnosis 12.448
  frontal 12.463

  local 12.447–8
  local object-related 12.455
  and loss of topographical familiarity 12.425
  and perception 12.462
  pulvinar 12.463
  spatial 12.341–2
    and brain lesions outside parietal lobe 12.462–4
    dissociation of 12.448–9
    tests to evaluate symptoms 12.452–62
    unilateral 12.452
  and topographical disorientation 12.418
  visual 12.302, 12.414, 12.431–65
    alterations caused by vestibular and optokinetic
      stimulation 12.464
    constancy of space perception 12.431–4
    history of spatial neglect 12.434–8
    illusory phenomena 12.450
    from left hemisphere lesions 12.447–52
    multimodal aspects of extrapersonal space 12.431–4
    and posterior parietal lobe 12.95
    space coordinates 12.431–4
    symptoms 12.438–47
  visuo-spatial 12.441
  and visuo-spatial disorders 12.443
Hemiparesis 12.275, 12.351
Hemiplegia
  illusory phenomena 12.450
  left, and visual hemineglect 12.445
  right 12.336, 12.408
  and visual hemineglect 12.447
  and visuo-spatial disorders 12.438, 12.441–3
Hemiretina 2.443
  nasal 3.131
  temporal 3.131
  upper and lower 12.142
Hemisphere 12.40, 12.49
  cerebral 12.259, 12.261
  covert knowledge 12.355
  homotopic regions of contralateral cortical 12.93
  language dominant 12.335, 12.342
    zones 12.346
  laterality 12.233–4
  lateralization 12.231–2
  left 12.47
    and alexia 12.334
    illusion and hallucination 12.480
    language-dominant 12.447
    and prosopagnosia 12.263–5, 12.267, 12.269, 12.271,
      12.274, 12.278–9
    in reading and script 12.320
    superiority 12.232
    and topographagnosia 12.419
    visual zones 12.346
  left dominant, diminished control by 12.351
  non-dominant 12.339
  and prosopagnosia 12.280
  right 12.47
    cerebral functions 12.287
    developmental organization 12.348

functions **12.356**
illusion and hallucination **12.480**
infero-medial temporo-occipital area **12.268**
intrahemispheric multimodal association areas of **12.346**
Kanji and Kana alexia **12.348**
occipital **12.267**
processing of emotional information in **12.327**
and prosopagnosia **12.263–5, 12.267, 12.269, 12.277–9**
in reading and script **12.310, 12.320**
superiority **12.232**
and topographagnosia **12.419, 12.423–5**
and topographical orientation **12.428**
and visuo-verbal operations **12.355**
and written signals **12.355**
specialization **12.276**
in human face perception **12.230–5**
speech-dominant **12.337**
left **12.309–10**
subcortical region **12.267**
wound in occipital pole of both **12.146**
Hemispherectomies **10.267**
in childhood **12.279**
right **12.266, 12.268, 12.279**
Hemispheric asymmetry, and dyslexia **13.181, 13.271**
Hemispheric specialization **13.37, 13.187**
Henle fibre layer **1.320**
Henle fibre-optic transmission **16.95**
Henle fibres, of the fovea **1.282**
Henschen, Salomon E. **12.49, 12.65**
Herculaneum **12.221**
Hering, Ewald **12.57, 12.63, 12.385–6, 12.397–8**
Hering opponency **5.199**
Hering–Bielchowsky after-image test **9.185, 9.193**
Hering–Hillebrand deviation **9.200**
Hering's law **8.157–8, 8.161–2, 8.310, 9.16, 9.119, 9.183,**
9.216, 12.8, 12.23, 13.203, 13.205
Hering's opponent theory of colour vision **4.332, 6.5–6, 6.34,**
6.222–4, 10.92
Hering's windowpane demonstration **9.12**
Hermissenda **2.372, 2.383–5**
Herniation **12.201**
Herophilos **12.25, 12.27**
Herpes simplex encephalitis **12.269**
Herschel, John, and the development of the contact lens **1.82**
Hess–Gullstrand theory **1.264**
Heterochromatic flicker photometry **6.48**
Heterochrony **2.145, 2.147**
Heterophoria **9.216**
correction of, in visual-display operators **15.65–6**
Heteropods **2.375–7, 2.383–4, 2.390**
Heterozygotes **7.20–1, 7.29**
Heterozygous advantage **2.316, 7.212**
HFP
see Flicker photometry, heterochromatic
see Heterochromatic flicker photometry
'Hidden units' **12.105–6**
Hierarchical processing **5.287**
Hilbert, David **14.50, 14.52**
Hilger–Chance refractometer **1.421**

Hillebrand hyperbola **9.2**
Hindbrain **11.39–41, 11.43, 11.59–60**
Hippocampus **11.288**
Hippocrates **12.25, 12.27**
Histamine **2.218, 2.360**
Histochemistry
of muscle fibres **8.178–9**
and neurotransmitters **11.353–5**
Histogenesis **11.28–30, 11.42–3**
Histogram, flicker peristimulus time **5.181, 5.184–5**
Histology **16.106–7, 16.109–11**
and developing visual system **16.124, 16.126**
fluorescent tracer **11.355**
'Hitting-the-head' cells **9.150**
Hoffmann, E. T. A. **12.299**
Holmes, Gordon M. **12.65**
Holmes syndrome **12.418–9**
Holmgren's test **7.174, 12.395, 12.400**
Holograms
colour **1.339**
volume **1.339**
Holographic examination, of the fundus **1.378**
Holography
basic theory and methodology of **1.335–9**
colour **1.339**
using the rainbow hologram method **1.339**
using the volume hologram method **1.339**
'in-line' **1.337**
off-axis arrangement for **1.338**
Holonomy **14.21**
Homeoboxes **11.3–23, 11.61**
conservation during evolution **11.7–19**
Drosophila **11.3–5**
gene structure **11.8–10**
vertebrate **11.6–7**
Homeoproteins **11.19–21**
Homeosis **11.37–8**
Homer **12.25**
Hominids
brain size **12.287**
phylogenesis **12.219–21, 12.297**
reading and script **12.304, 12.309**
Homo erectus **12.16, 12.52, 12.220**
Homo habilis **12.16, 12.52, 12.220, 12.287, 12.304, 12.309**
Homo praesapiens **12.16**
Homo sapiens sapiens **12.16**
Homograph **12.308, 12.311, 12.328**
Homologous, Glossary explanation of **4.446**
Homology
antigen **2.351**
apomorphic **2.136**
cell **2.357–8, 2.360**
of compound eye **2.342–3, 2.360**
dipteran ommatidium **2.346–8**
evolutionary **2.346**
ommatidia **2.345**
photoreceptors **2.348**
plesiomorphic **2.136, 2.138, 2.140–1, 2.145**
of visual system **2.342**

Homophone 12.307–8
Honeycomb, Glossary explanation of 4.446
Hooke, Robert 12.43–4
Horizontal cells 4.319–20, 6.134–43, 6.165–8, 10.256
Horizontal meridian 3.333, 3.345
Hormone status 12.232
Hormones, female sex 12.232
Horn
  left occipital 12.344
  roof, lower 12.345
Horner's Law of Inheritance 7.91
Horopter 9.19–37, 9.79, 12.36, 12.143
  in anomalous retinal correspondence 9.190–3
  and binocular fusion 9.19–37
  distorted 9.193
  fusion 9.33
  geometric, empirical deviations from 9.28–9
  Glossary explanation of 4.446
  identical visual directions 9.190
  and stereoperimetry 9.42–3
  types of 9.20
  vertical 9.213
    effects of inclination of 9.29–30
Horse dioptrics 2.83
Horseradish peroxidase 11.33
  axon staining 11.90–1
  in retrograde tracing 3.154–5, 3.161, 3.165–6
    intra-axonal and intracellular injections of 3.155–6,
      3.239, 3.243–4, 3.248, 3.255, 3.258, 3.260, 3.265,
      3.267, 3.279, 3.282, 3.289–90, 3.293–4
Hot spots 16.112
Hough transform 2.248, 2.256
Howard–Dolman two-rod test 9.210
HRP, *see* Horseradish peroxidase
Hue 6.43–6
  binary, CIE definition of 6.225
  CIE definition of 6.225
  estimation of 6.51–2
  invariant 6.45
  unique, CIE definition of 6.225
  unitary 6.45
    CIE definition of 6.225
Hue cancellation method 7.20
Hue cancellation paradigm 6.50–1
Hue discrimination 7.179
Hue discrimination studies 7.82–4
Hue discrimination tests, *see* Arrangement tests
Hue sensation, primary 7.8
28-Hue test 7.216
40-Hue test 7.216
28-Hue test 7.227
40-Hue test 7.227
Hughes's terrain hypothesis 2.143–4, 2.147
Human eye
  corneal contour of 1.2
  corneal transparency of 1.2
  general shape of 1.1–2
  as a gradient-index optical component of 1.4
  optical components of 1.1–5

aqueous humour, anterior chamber of 1.3
axis 1.5
cornea 1.2–3
lens 1.3–4
  and accommodation 1.4
  cortex of 1.3
  and lenticular birefringence 1.4
  new fibre growth of 1.3
  nucleus of 1.3
  and role of as aperture stop 1.3
  transmittance characteristics of 1.4
ocular asymmetries 1.5
pupil 1.3
retinal surface 1.5
  and hypermetropia 1.5
  and myopia 1.5
  and waveguide effects 1.5
vitreous body 1.4–5
optics of 1.1–26
reduction of spherical aberration in 1.4
tear film of 1.2
Human lens
  cortex of 1.3
  as a gradient-index optical component 1.4
  new fibre growth of 1.3
  and role of as aperture stop 1.3
Hung and Semmlow's model of the accommodation
  system 1.266
Hunting 12.309
Huntington's disease 4.401, 8.314
Hyaloid artery 11.391
Hyaloid circulation 11.391–3
Hyaloid membrane 11.393
Hyaloid system 16.118
Hybrid offspring 2.70
Hybrid population 2.71
Hybridization
  in situ 11.11, 11.17–8, 11.120, 11.359–60
    of proto-oncogenes 11.114, 11.117–8
  of visual pigments 2.71
Hybrids 2.71
Hydra 11.51–2
Hydrocephalus, *see* Apoplexy, cerebral
Hydrogel lenses 1.155–6
Hydrogels, in the manufacture of contact lenses 1.85
Hydroxyethyl methacrylate 1.85
3-Hydroxyretinal 6.62, 6.70, 6.266–7
4-Hydroxyretinal 6.62
3-Hydroxyretinal 2.348–50
Hyperacuity 2.239, 2.255, 2.454–5, 5.120, 5.130, 5.260–1,
    5.269–70, 5.274, 5.281, 5.320, 8.4, 8.72, 9.203, 10.192,
    10.223, 12.57–8, 14.9, 14.12, 14.15
  in amblyopia 10.224–9
  centroid analysis 10.89–91, 10.110
  classification 10.109–10
  cyclopean 10.108–9
  defined 10.87–9
  foveal 10.74
  interpolation 10.91–3

inventory 10.100–9
limiting factors 10.93–6
neural mechanisms 10.109
opponent-process theory 10.91–3
physical constraints 5.221–31
spatial interference 10.225
spatial primitives 10.96–100, 10.110
and stereoscopic depth 5.123–8
theories 10.110
thresholds 5.224, 5.228–31
Hyperbilirubinaemia 16.114, 16.124, 16.126
Hypercapnia, and contact lenses 1.93
Hypercolumn information capacity 5.73–4
Hypercolumns 4.301–3, 6.180–1, 12.465
  Glossary explanation of 4.446
Hypercomplex cells, Glossary explanation of 4.446
Hypercyclopean discrimination 10.161
Hypercyclopean object constancy 9.70
Hypercyclopean orientation specificity 9.68–9
Hypercyclopean perception 9.67–71
Hypercyclopean specificity
  for depth corrugation frequency 9.68
  for inclination in depth 9.69–70
Hyperexcitability 12.133, 12.177
Hypermedia 15.110
Hypermetria, Glossary explanation of 4.446
Hypermetric saccades 8.124, 8.310–2
Hypermetropia 2.111
  apparent 2.84
  in children 1.45
  following surgery 1.51
  genetics as a causative factor in 1.31
  and the retinal surface 1.5
Hyperopia 1.53, 13.49, 13.52–4, 16.143, 16.147
  and esotropic strabismus 8.168–9
  explanation of 1.400

latent 1.400
manifest 1.400
Hyperphagia 12.108
Hyperpolarization 2.27–8, 2.42–3, 3.38–40, 3.42
  in colour vision 2.298
  in cones 5.192
  in evolution of retina 2.140–1
  in photoreception 2.366, 2.369–71
  in visual processing 2.206, 2.217
Hypersexuality 12.108
Hyperstereoscopy 1.329
Hypertension 16.141–2
Hypnagog 12.299, 12.301
Hypnopomp 12.299, 12.301
Hypnosis 12.301
Hypoaesthesia, reduction of, and the wearing of contact
      lenses 1.105
Hypoemotionality 12.276
  selective 12.278
  visual 12.278
Hypoglycaemia 16.150
Hypometria, Glossary explanation of 4.446
Hypoperfusion 12.207
Hypothalamus 2.17, 2.31, 2.45, 12.60, 12.287
  and visual pathways 2.423, 2.425–8, 2.433
Hypoxia 12.261
  cerebral 12.300
  closed lid 1.93
  and corneal oxygen uptake 1.91
  general 12.337
  and wearing of contact lenses 1.91
Hysteresis 9.131, 10.5, 10.35
  in cyclopean perception 9.65–6
Hysteria 12.302
  phenomena 12.297

I

Ibotenic acid **8**.212
Iceland Eye Study **16**.137–8
I-cells **4**.92
Icons **15**.77–8, **15**.115, **15**.117, **15**.119–20
Ictal attack **12**.479
Ideal detector model **10**.110
Ideal observer **10**.79
Ideal observer calculations **5**.222
Identical visual directions **9**.6
Identical visual directions horopter **9**.190
Identification, absolute, in numerosity **14**.127–30, **14**.136
Identity **12**.276
   facial **12**.278
Ideogram **12**.306, **12**.355
   Chinese **12**.307
   Kanji **12**.348–9
   meaning of **12**.349
   shape of **12**.349
   and shorthand **12**.316
Illiteracy **12**.309
   global **12**.304
   and pure alexia **12**.339
   in societies **12**.306
Illuminance
   and ageing **16**.157–8
   ambient **16**.152
   and developing visual system **16**.105, **16**.108, **16**.114–6, **16**.124–6, **16**.128
   glare **16**.152
   and light measurement **16**.23
   mean **5**.36–7
   mesopic **5**.193
   photopic **5**.193
   retinal **2**.98–9, **5**.82, **5**.86, **5**.89–90
     in contrast sensitivity **5**.36, **5**.42
     in peripheral vision **5**.45–6, **5**.49–50, **5**.55–6, **5**.61, **5**.66–7
     and spectral sensitivity **5**.193, **5**.198
   scotopic **5**.56
   and spatial shape **14**.5
   time-integrated **5**.56, **5**.69
   transition **5**.13, **5**.37–8, **5**.41–2, **5**.63
Illuminant C **5**.202
Illumination
   and colour vision **12**.13
   intermittent **12**.6
   mutual **14**.36
   of receptive field **12**.473
   and shape perception **14**.35–6
   spectral **12**.385
   stroboscopic **12**.379
   surface **14**.83–4, **14**.90, **14**.93
   transplant **11**.320, **11**.326–30, **11**.332
Illusions **5**.242–4, **12**.466–74, **14**.41, **14**.132
   afterimages **12**.467–8
   auditory **12**.469, **12**.471
   colour **6**.158–9, **12**.389

Craik–Cornsweet **12**.5, **12**.398–9
Craik-Cornsweet **5**.25, **5**.38
Eigengrau **12**.466–7
face-and person-generating **12**.303
figures **5**.246
geometrical **5**.240, **5**.242–4, **6**.213–4
hallucination and pseudohallucination **12**.476–4
of head movement **12**.433
and heautoscopy **12**.302
horizontal/vertical **5**.242–4
motion (apparent motion) **12**.85
movement **12**.369, **12**.371
   with vestibular sensations **12**.467
Mueller–Lyer **12**.184, **12**.191
obscurations **12**.472–3
palinopsia **12**.473–5
patterns and scenes from meaningless random stimuli **12**.470–1
and prosopagnosia **12**.275
scenic visual **12**.468–70, **12**.477
of self-movement **12**.362
simple visual **12**.466
transient **12**.303
visual **2**.263, **2**.267, **12**.270, **12**.478
and visual movement agnosia **12**.362–3
waterfall **12**.366
Illusory borders, Glossary explanation of **4**.446–7
Image analysis **2**.377, **14**.98
Image array, toroidal **14**.70, **14**.73–6, **14**.79
Image blurring **14**.91
Image contrast **2**.126
Image degradation **2**.6, **2**.413, **3**.5
Image disambiguation **14**.89
Image formation **13**.1–7
Image formation process **14**.88–9
Image geometry **2**.127, **2**.239
Image intensifier **5**.68
Image motion **5**.125–7, **5**.151, **5**.167
   in hyperacuity **10**.95–6
Image motion processing **5**.160
Image operations **14**.3–4
Image partition, retinal **10**.135
Image pyramid **10**.123
Image quality **2**.5, **3**.4–6, **3**.14, **3**.16, **3**.24, **3**.56, **5**.88, **5**.120, **5**.124–5
   in dioptrics **2**.85–6, **2**.89, **2**.102
     limits on **2**.92–9
   and eye optics **2**.119–20
   near fovea **5**.89
   in periphery **5**.90
   and visual pathways **2**.448
Image rotation **14**.55–6
Image segmentation **2**.209, **14**.102
Image stabilization **5**.179, **5**.216
Image structure **2**.259
Image synthesis **14**.98
Images
   body **12**.416
   central representation of visual **12**.33

centre for optic **12**.335
centre for word **12**.350
chromatic **5**.234, **5**.237
descriptor functions of optic **12**.7–14
diffraction limited **3**.5
disturbance of object-related **12**.180
double **12**.36–7
eidetic **2**.261–3, **12**.392, **12**.470, **12**.476
equiluminous **5**.244–5
foveal **5**.88–9
isoluminant **5**.216
line (line-spread function) **5**.88, **14**.98–106
luminance-defined **5**.234
luminance-modulated **5**.216
man's mirror **12**.297, **12**.302
mental **12**.462
    description of **12**.457–8
    of extrapersonal space **12**.420
    illusion and hallucination **12**.470, **12**.475
    strange and unfamiliar **12**.259
    and topographagnosia **12**.418
    and topographical disorientation **12**.413–4
noise-free **14**.89
noisy **14**.93
off-axis **2**.85–6
one-dimensional **2**.243, **2**.245, **2**.255–8
patterns in **14**.2–3
plane **3**.1, **3**.16
point (point-spread function) **5**.88
processing **12**.16
retinal **2**.5, **3**.5, **5**. 120, **5**.88–90, **5**.160, **5**.268
retinal double **12**.475
sampling by retina **3**.4
somatosensory body **12**.297–8
spatial **2**.244
spatio-temporal **2**.246
spectral information from **3**.28–9
stabilized **5**.209
structured **12**.474
two-colour **5**.245–7
visual **12**.179, **12**.191, **12**.335
    letter **12**.335
    palinopsia **12**.475
X-ray **2**.130
Imaginal discs **11**.61
Imagination **12**.188, **12**.190–1
    mental **12**.418, **12**.420
        spatial **12**.457
            impairment of and loss of **12**.457–8
Imaging
    inner, of city topography **12**.342
    magnetic resonance, *see* Magnetic resonance imaging
        (MRI)
Immune system **3**.85
Immunocytochemistry **2**.67, **2**.146
    and actin filaments **11**.139
    in cell locomotion **11**.173
    and cytoskeletal proteins **11**.133
    light microscopic **11**.221

localization of spectrin **11**.278–9
in neuronal cytoskeleton **11**.277–8, **11**.280, **11**.293
and neurotransmitters **11**.359–60
and proto-oncogenes **11**.115
Immunofluorescence
    indirect **11**.75–6, **11**.82
    and MAPs **11**.135
Immunogenetic mismatch **11**.319
Immunohistochemistry
    and neuronal cytoskeleton **11**.276
    and neurotransmitters **11**.353–7, **11**.360, **11**.363
    and synaptic rearrangement **11**.262
Immunoperoxidase, and MAPs **11**.135
Immunosuppression **16**.70–1
Impact-resistant lenses, *see under* Spectacle lenses
Impedance cyclography **1**.236
Implants, as visual prosthesis **12**.169
Imprinting **11**.288
Impulse blockade
    of axons **11**.94–6
    retinal **11**.347
Impulse rates **14**.81
Inattention
    hemispatial, and visuo-spatial disorders **12**.437
    and spatial hemineglect **12**.462–3
Incandescence **16**.6–7, **16**.20
Increment detection **5**.10–3
    by chromatic mechanisms **5**.197–8
    in contrast sensitivity **5**.36, **5**.38, **5**.41
    as function of area **5**.104–5
    in negative masking **5**.31
    recommended experimental paradigm **5**.21
    by signal detection **5**.19–21
    simple estimation procedure **5**.20–1
    stimulus circumference **5**.104
    in visual processing **5**.23–4, **5**.33
Increment near-thresholds **5**.23
Increment thresholds **3**.25, **5**.12, **5**.63, **10**.157
Increments
    grating **5**.39
    luminance **5**.39
    transition illuminance **5**.42
Indexing **14**.52, **14**.65–6
Indicator responses **9**.75
Individuality, in prosopagnosia **12**.273
Indomethacin (indocid) toxic retinopathy **7**.128
Induction **11**.52
    by unspecific stimuli **11**.49
Induction model **11**.61
Infants
    full-term **16**.104, **16**.118–20, **16**.122–5
    preterm **16**.104, **16**.110, **16**.113, **16**.118–25, **16**.128
    strabismus in **9**.177
Infarction
    angular gyrus, left **12**.335
    below parieto-occipital junction **12**.334
    bilateral **12**.394
        cerebral **12**.271
        occipital **12**.337

Infarction (*continued*)
  at carrefour of fibre tracts 12.334
  cerebral 12.132–3, 12.262
    posterior 12.426
  cerebral artery, posterior, left and right 12.275, 12.335, 12.339
  cerebrovascular 12.390
  inferior medial, occipito-temporal 12.260
  internal capsule, posterior 12.463
  ischaemic 12.263, 12.343
  medial occipital, and loss of topographical familiarity 12.426
  and metamorphopsia 12.275
  occipital 12.335
    left 12.260
    right 12.475
  occipito-temporal 12.209, 12.354
    junction 12.335, 12.342
  and prosopagnosia 12.263–4, 12.267, 12.274, 12.276
  right posterior medial 12.264
  right-sided infero-medial temporo-occipital 12.264
  of splenium of corpus callosum 12.335, 12.408
  thalamic 12.343
  vascular 12.343
Infection 12.300
  bacterial 12.199
  viral 12.199
Inferior oblique 8.175–6, 8.182
Inferior olive 8.201–2, 8.214, 8.226, 8.228, 8.234–5, 8.248
Inferior parietal lobule 4.411–2
  connectivity of 4.412
  effects of electrical stimulation of 4.412
  effects of lesions of 4.413
    contralateral neglect 4.413
    extinction 4.413
  physiological properties of 4.413–4
Inferior rectus 8.175–6, 8.182
Inferotemporal cortex 2.456, 8.277, 8.285–6
Inferotemporal groups 4.164
Inferotemporal lobe 2.310
Inflow 8.76, 8.149
Information
  capacity of channels 3.30
  capacity of sampling array 3.25
  coding 3.48
  colour signal 3.28
  complex 12.346
  emotional colour 12.357
  pictorial-prelinguistic 12.306
  processing, hierarchical order of 3.326
  processing theories 12.338
  spectral 3.20, 3.28
    from natural images 3.49
  static 12.341
  theoretical analysis 12.114
  transfer 12.306
    interhemispheric 12.350
    limited information-carrying capacity of 12.346
  transfer channels 12.346
  verbal 12.306
  visual, cortical processing chain 12.346
  of visual display devices 14.2
  written, preserved access to 12.350–5
Information processing channels 9.155
Information theory 10.34
Infragranular layers of cortex, Glossary explanation of 4.447
Infra-red radiation *see* Radiation
Infra-red recording, objective 1.238
Ingling–Martinez mechanism 10.154–5
Inheritance
  autosomal dominant 7.98
  autosomal recessive 7.101
Inherited colour deficiencies, *see* Colour deficiencies, inherited
Inhibition
  binocular 2.277–8
  cortical 10.193
  cross-orientation 4.283
  feedback 3.189
  feedforward 3.189, 3.194
  interhemispheric 12.354
  intra-cortical 4.283
  lateral 10.195, 10.292, 12.369
  left hemispheric 12.350
  long-range 11.48–55, 11.63
  transcallosal 12.350
  vs. disinhibition 5.321–2
Inhibition mechanism, lateral 11.62–3, 11.65
Inhibitory burst neurones 8.258
Inhibitory display profiles, broad 4.200
Inhibitory neurones 9.187
Inhibitory postsynaptic potentials 3.283
Inhibitory sidebands, Glossary explanation of 4.447
Inhibitory transmitters, laminar variation in 4.237–9
Initial motor error 8.97
Initial segment of axon, Glossary explanation of 4.447
Injury
  anoxic 12.201
  closed head 12.268, 12.277, 12.281, 12.343, 12.393
  open head 12.343
  penetrating head 12.284
  reperfusion 16.67
Ink-blots 12.470–1
Inner plexiform layer of retina
  Glossary explanation of 4.447
  separation of response phases within 4.3
  vertebrate 4.1–9
    separate on and off pathways to 4.2–3
Innervation
  density of 11.300–2, 11.321–2, 11.327, 11.329
  equal 9.2
  vergence 9.2
  version 9.2
Insects
  colour vision in 2.294, 2.299, 2.302, 6.262–93
  eye evolution 2.341–3, 2.345–6, 2.348–51, 2.353–4, 2.358, 2.360
  pattern recognition 2.262

see also Colour vision, in insects
   stick 2.260
   visual processing 2.235, 2.238–42, 2.246, 2.251, 2.253–4,
     2.260
Inspection, industrial 15.83
Instability of vergence 9.124
Insula 12.300
Integration
   binocular 12.31
   in computational vision 14.41–2
   contrast 14.15
   temporal 10.152
     in localization judgments 14.13–5
Integrators 8.97, 8.153, 8.160, 8.208, 8.217, 8.302, 8.324–5
   cascaded 5.187
Integrins 11.172, 11.178, 11.212, 11.280
Intelligence, artificial 12.3, 12.190, 12.196
Intensity, radiant 16.1, 16.3
Intensity range of vision 5.48–54
Intensive care unit, neonatal *see* NICU
Interactions
   binocular 3.193
   fibre–fibre 3.135–6
   hand–mouth 12.412, 12.416–7
   hand–object 12.417
   proprioceptive 12.411
   social 12.385, 12.392
   somatosensory 12.411
   spatiotemporal 10.194
   vestibular 12.411
   visual 12.411
Interblob
   Glossary explanation of 4.447
   see also Cytochrome oxidase blobs
Interblob regions 12.68–9, 12.71
   and contour perception 12.81
Intercalary regeneration 11.57–9
Intercalated layers, *see* Interlaminar zones
Intercalation 11.65
Interference
   by semantic associates 12.355
   word-colour 12.355
Interference fringe techniques 5.88
Interference fringes 1.17, 3.20, 3.24
Interhemispheric processing 3.348
Interhemispheric transfer 5.272–4
   callosal V1-V2 in cat and monkey 5.273
Interlacing 15.7
Interlaminar connections 3.294
Interlaminar zones 2.177
   cell sparse 3.142
   koniocellular 3.193
   in visual thalamus 3.179–80, 3.186, 3.188, 3.190–3, 3.195
Interleukin-1 (IL-1) 11.211
Intermediate collicular lamina, organization of visual
    representations in 3.169
Intermetamorphosis 12.302
Intermodal interactions, limits of 11.380–1
Internal feedback 8.97–8, 8.119, 8.123, 8.209, 8.215, 8.257

Internal medullary laminar 4.407
Internal representation of target motion 8.143–6
Interneurones 3.187–92
   GABAergic 3.279–81
   inhibitory 3.189, 3.193
   intranuclear 2.187–8
   lateral geniculate nucleus 4.46
   LGNd 3.194–5
   LGNv 3.203–4
   plasticity of 11.243
   and shell nuclei 3.211
   in visual thalamus 3.196–8
Internuclear neurones 8.184, 8.205, 8.216, 8.219
Internuclear ophthalmoplegia 8.205, 8.310–1
Interocular co-ordination 11.201
Interocular transfer 5.267, 9.182
   functions of ocular dominance columns in 4.273
   and motion after-effects 9.182
   and tilt after-effects 9.182
Interpolation
   in hyperacuity 10.91–3
   spatiotemporal 5.157–8, 10.95
Interposition 14.4
Interpretation and line images 14.98–100
Intersection set 14.6
Interstitial nucleus
   of Cajal 8.200–1, 8.216, 8.248, 8.314
   of the medial longitudinal fasciculus 8.200, 8.314
   of the optic tract 8.201, 8.314
Intertectal commissure 10.270
Interval encoding 5.133–4
Interval of Sturm 1.400, 1.408
Intonation 15.124
Intoxication 12.150, 12.477
   carbon monoxide 12.201, 12.207, 12.300
   CS_2 12.300
   drug 12.303
   inorganic mercury vapour 12.201
   mercury 12.207
   with organic solvents 12.199
Intracellular recordings 3.350, 4.283
Intrageniculate nucleus 3.283–4
Intralaminar complex 3.194, 3.204–6, 3.217
Intralaminar nuclei 3.215
Intralaminar thalamic nuclei
   in visual function 4.407–9
     connectivity in 4.409
     and effects of lesions and electrical stimulation
       on 4.407–8
     physiological properties of 4.408–9
Intramembranous particles 3.41
Intraocular flare 2.89
Intraocular lens implants 1.120–37, 5.92, 5.278, 5.280, 5.282
   see also Lens implants, intraocular
Intraocular lenses, and eye models 1.5
Intraocular light-scatter 5.280
Intraocular pressure 1.317, 3.71, 3.85, 3.105, 3.107, 3.116–7,
   7.152–3
   and accommodation 1.38–9

Intraocular scatter 1.15–6
Intraoperative findings 12.266
Intrapariatal sulcus 13.15
Introns 6.92, 7.102, 7.105
Invariance 14.55–6
    feature-operator 14.101
    and pattern classification 14.69–81
Invariance problem 14.72
Invariant hues 6.45
Invariants, Gibson 14.19, 14.26, 14.91
Inverse cyclopean effects, and psychoanatomy 9.49
Inverses 14.54, 14.57
Inversion
    and face recognition 14.108, 14.110, 14.115, 14.117–20,
        14.122–3
    preorder 14.54
Invertebrates, colour vision in 2.288, 2.294–5, 2.297
Iodopsins 6.120
Ion equilibrium 2.42–4
Ion translocation 2.40, 2.42–4
Ion transport 2.16, 2.28, 2.39
Ionochromic shift 2.73
IOP, *see* Intraocular pressure
Iowa Tests of Basic Skills 13.256
IPL, *see* Plexiform layers, inner
Ipsilateral crescent 3.110–1
Iridotomy 16.49, 16.51
Iris 11.392–4
    ageing processes in 5.277
    blue/medium colour 16.143–4
    circular 2.414
    in evolution of vision 2.399, 2.404, 2.412
    in eye evolution 2.413–4
    in mammals 2.469, 2.471, 2.473–5
Irlen differential perceptual schedule, and the scotopic
        sensitivity syndrome 13.173–6, 13.178
Irlen photopic transmission lenses
    for the scotopic sensitivity syndrome 13.173–6
    studies on patients using 13.173–6
Iron Age 12.221
Irradiance 16.1–3
    and ageing 16.63
    and ageing macula 16.76, 16.87–9
    backlight 2.409
    calculations 16.24–6
    and developing visual system 16.105, 16.109, 16.112,
        16.116, 16.121, 16.123, 16.128
    effects on eye 16.55, 16.59
    and light damage 16.65
    and light interactions 16.41–3, 16.45, 16.48–50, 16.52

and light measurement 16.24, 16.27
and optical radiation 16.4–5, 16.11–3, 16.16–8, 16.21
and radiation 16.60–2
at retina 16.23
scotopic retinal 5.49
Irradiation, and illusions 5.242
Ischaemia 12.150
    acute cerebral attack 12.334
    diverse sensitivities to 12.409
    general 12.199
    local 12.132, 12.177
        cerebral 12.472–3
    retinal 1.355, 12.165, 12.472–3
        prolonged 12.158–9
    transient 12.199, 12.472, 12.475
Ishihara pseudo-isochromatic plates 2.306, 2.308–10, 7.191,
        7.216, 7.220–2, 7.230–1
    in cerebral hemisphere lesions 7.192
    in cone dystrophy 7.136, 7.138
    in ophthalmic disease 7.118
    in optic neuritis and MS 7.179, 7.181
    in toxic optic neuropathy 7.161
Iso-accommodative formula
    in calculation of magnification in low vision 1.190
    and the maximum possible magnification obtainable from a
        given magnifier 1.190
Isochromes 1.314
Isoclinics 1.314
Iso-cortex, Glossary explanation of 4.447
Isoeccentricity 14.11
Isolation 12.300
    prolonged 12.480
Isoluminance 5.177, 5.214–5, 6.205, 6.210–4
    interpretation of 6.212
Isoluminance tests 6.202–4
Isoluminant conditions, responses under 4.32
Isoluminant external stimulus 5.85
Isoluminant figural stereograms 6.214
Isomerization
    thermal 2.299, 3.25–6
        by body heat 5.57
    of visual pigment 5.48–9
Isomorphism 10.120, 14.13
Isomorphs 2.357
Isomorphy, cell 2.357, 2.360
Iso-second-order pair 10.118–9
IT neurones
    and expectation 12.126
    and familiarity 12.126

J

Jackson, Hughlings 12.418–9
Jackson crossed cylinder 1.411
Jaeger and Grützner classification 7.117–8
Jaeger tritanomaloscope 7.137, 7.153
Jaggies 15.15, 15.21
Jaundice 16.114, 16.116
Jessen, Johannes 12.36
Jitter 15.10–1, 15.59–61
  elimination of 15.7–8, 15.10–1
JND-steps, *see* Just noticeable difference steps
Joysticks 15.117–8
Judgement
  interfield 12.348

  intrafield-different 12.348
  intrafield-same 12.348
  intrahemispheric same 12.349
  tachistoscopic interfield same/different paradigm 12.348
  transfer capacity for same 12.349
'Julesz conjecture' 10.116
Julesz patterns 5.267
Julesz random-dot patterns 10.160–1, 10.282
Julesz random-dot stereogram technique 10.108
Julesz texture perception theory 10.117–9
Just-noticeable blurred border (JNBB) 5.75
Just-noticeable-difference (JND) 5.204, 5.213, 10.37
  in hyperacuity 10.90, 10.93, 10.106
Just-noticeable-difference (JND) level 6.300
Just-noticeable-difference (JND) steps 6.271–2

K

K-48, *see* Arrestin
Kabuki theatre 12.221
Kahlbaum–Capgras syndrome 12.289, 12.296, 12.302
Kainic acid, Glossary explanation of 4.447
Kalt, Eugène, and the development of the afocal glass scleral contact lens 1.82
Kanisza's triangle 14.38
Kanizsa's triangle 12.191–2
Kant, Immanuel 12.22
K-cells 4.224–5
Keeler A system, in prescribing magnification for near viewing 1.216
Keeler charts, 'A-series' scale of 1.215
Kelly surface 8.3–5
Kepler, Johannes 12.36–40, 12.43, 12.53
Keplerian array 9.43
Keplerian projection, and the pre-cyclopean aspects of the correspondence problem 9.43–5
Kepler's projection theory 9.12
Keratectomy 1.153
　radial 1.154
Keratin
　K8 11.209
　type-2 11.209
Keratitis
　infectious, and the wearing of contact lenses 1.105
　ulcerative, and the wearing of contact lenses 1.105
　welding arc 16.95
Keratoconjunctivitis, superior limbic 1.110–1
Keratoconus 1.45–6, 1.148, 1.150–1
　correction of, by contact lenses 1.114
Keratocytes, death of, and the wearing of contact lenses 1.107
Keratometers 1.378–81
　alternative designs of 1.380
　extending the range of 1.380
　surgical 1.144
　topographic 1.380
　utilization of Moiré fringes in 1.380
Keratometry 1.133
Keratomileusis 1.153–5
　homoplastic 1.153–4
　hyperopic 1.154
　myopic 1.153–4
　surgical techniques in 1.153
　　complications after 1.154
　　results of 1.153–4
　　use of the microkeratome 1.153
Keratopathy, Labrador 16.59
Keratophakia 1.154–5, 1.157
　complications of 1.155
Keratotomy
　post-radial, and soft contact lenses 1.115
　radial 1.138–43
　　complications of 1.142–3
　　　and aniseikonia 1.143

and contact-lens fitting 1.142
and multifocal rendering of the cornea 1.140
pre-operative assessment of 1.140–1
　and optic zone size determination 1.141
　and pachymetry 1.141
results of 1.141–2
　and the PERK study 1.141
surgical technique for 1.141–3
trapezoidal astigmatic 1.146
Kerner, Justinus 12.299, 12.471
Keyboard tapping task 12.457
Kielmeyer–Haeckel rule 12.19, 12.288
Kinase 11.135
　C (PKC) 11.143
　in dendrites 11.152
　GAP-43 11.219
　in regeneration 11.192–3, 11.195
　see also Protein kinase C
　serine 11.112–3, 11.118–9
　type-II cAMP 11.149
　tyrosine 11.112–3, 11.116–9
Kinematogram 5.239, 5.244
Kinesin 11.190
Kinetic depth effect 5.240, 9.137–8
　and 3D representation 14.44
Kinetic stereopsis 9.207
Kinetics, Michaelis–Menten 12.8
Kinetopsia 12.480–1
Kinocilia 8.23
Kleist, Heinrich 12.1–2, 12.77, 12.80, 12.299
Kleksographien (ink-blots) 12.470–1
Klüver–Bucy syndrome 11.374, 12.108
Knapp's law 1.62, 1.178, 9.215–6
Knowledge
　covert
　　and alexia 12.334, 12.352
　　in prosopagnosia 12.266, 12.276–9, 12.355
　　in pure alexia 12.334, 12.354–5, 12.357
　　paradoxical 12.277, 12.279
Köhler illumination system 1.385
Köllner classification 7.117
Köllner's rule 7.40, 7.117, 7.177, 7.230, 16.62
　and ageing macula 16.81, 16.89
　in colour perimetry 7.122
　confirmation and modification of 7.174–5
　exception 7.155
　and ophthalmic disease 7.158, 7.160, 7.163
Koniocellular layers, Glossary explanation of 4.447
Korsakoff psychosis 12.268, 12.303, 12.476–7
Krypton 16.12, 16.21
Kryptopterus bicirrhis (cat-fish) 2.290
K-streams, Glossary explanation of 4.452
Kubicki, Stanislaus 12.228
Kuffler's discovery 4.10–3
　the concentric, antagonistic centre-surround organization 4.11–2
Kundt and Munsterberg partition errors 9.192

L

Labidocera 2.121–3, 2.134
Labyrinthectomy, and optokinesis 8.56
Labyrinths 8.13–22
  caloric stimulation of 12.473
Ladd-Franklin, Mrs Christine 2.311, 2.313
Lambert's law 5.49
Lamella
  in cell locomotion 11.174–7
  in crawling 11.171–2
Lamellipodia 11.172, 11.174–5
LaMettrie, Julien Offray de 12.45, 12.330–1
Laminae 3.189, C 3.187
  A1 3.187, 3.192, 3.198
  A 3.187–9
    of LGNd 3.210
  in visual thalamus 3.183–4, 3.192–4, 3.196–201, 3.215
  arthropod 2.213, 2.216–9
  C, in visual thalamus 3.192–4, 3.196, 3.201, 3.215
  cartridges 2.344, 2.348, 2.353, 2.355–8
  cholinergic activity 2.218–9
  cortical 3.336
  in eye evolution 2.343–5, 2.347–8, 2.353–4, 2.356–8, 2.360
  eye-specific 11.237
  optic lobe 2.204–6, 2.208, 2.211–2, 2.220, 2.222–4
  synaptic connections in fly 2.217
Laminar distribution 3.331, 3.337
Laminar segregation
  in the lateral geniculate nucleus 4.46
  of pathways in the lateral geniculate nucleus 4.71
Laminar variation
  in cells of the striate cortex 4.231–2
  in cellular morphology 4.231–4
    in spinous cells 4.232
  in inhibitory transmitters 4.237–9
  in the morphology of smooth stellate cells 4.238–9
  in the response properties of spinous cells 4.234–7
Lamination 2.426, 2.443, 2.449–51, 2.476
  of LGNd complex 3.177–82
  of smooth stellate cells 4.237–9
Laminin 11.177–8
  in axon growth 11.234
  in neuronal cytoskeleton 11.280
  in optic nerve regeneration 11.210
  in regeneration 11.197–8
  in retinal transplantation 11.323–4
  UV-degraded 11.178
Lampreys 2.66–7, 2.477
  dioptrics 2.110
  in evolution of retina 2.137–8, 2.140
  evolution of vision 2.398, 2.401–2, 2.404–6
  eye embryology of 11.394–5, 11.399–401
  in eye evolution 2.415–7
  photoreceptor system 2.69
Lamps 16.1, 16.8–17, 16.20
  agricultural applications of 16.10
  electroluminescent 16.21
  flash 16.21

fluorescent 16.7, 16.10, 16.23, 16.25–7, 16.89
  compact 16.13–4
  gas discharge 16.11
  general lighting 16.13–4
  special applications 16.14–5
gas discharge 16.21
glow 16.21
high intensity discharge (HID) 16.15
high pressure
  mercury 16.10, 16.15–6
  sodium 16.10, 16.15
incandescent 16.6, 16.10–2, 16.23
industrial applications 16.9
lighting applications 16.9
low pressure 16.10
  gas discharge 16.12–3
  gas/vapour 16.7
  sodium 16.14, 16.17
medical, cosmetic and germicidal 16.10
metal halide 16.10, 16.15–7
pulsed xenon arc 16.21
slit 16.65–6, 16.99
solid state 16.21
tungsten halogen 16.6, 16.9–12
  incandescent 16.7
very high pressure (super)
  mercury 16.17
  mercury xenon 16.17
  xenon 16.17
Landmarks 2.263, 12.418, 12.421, 12.423, 12.430
  anatomical 12.344
  information 12.429
  local 12.420, 12.428–9
  orientation by 12.416
  'verbalizable' 12.422, 12.425, 12.429
Landolt rings 5.257, 10.25
  and pure alexia 12.339
Landolt-C acuity 5.258, 7.100, 14.14
Landolt-C eye chart 16.110
Land's 'Colour Mondrian' experiments 5.25
Land's retinex model of colour vision 6.57, 6.192–3, 6.282
Landscape, illusion and hallucination 12.471
Language
  acquired 12.338
    disorder 12.333
  American sign 12.331
  area 12.335
    traditional 12.345
  behaviour, human 12.288
  centres 12.346
    oral 12.349
  competence 12.304, 12.307–10
    learned 12.330
    and word recognition 12.328
  computer 12.307
  Far-East 12.338
  functions of 12.268
  human 12.331
  lateralization of 3.324

Language (*continued*)
  learning by training **12**.330–1
  lexicon **12**.311
  metaphoric use of **12**.444
  and motor co-ordination **13**.271
  native **12**.333
  sign **12**.307
  statistical structure **12**.324
  syntactic structure **12**.328
  Western **12**.311, **12**.313, **12**.338
  written **12**.333, **12**.335
    peripheral 'perceptual' form of **12**.337
  zones **12**.346
Lantern test **7**.232
Lanthony Desaturated D15 test **7**.119, **7**.179, **7**.216, **7**.224,
    7.232
  in Alezzandrini's syndrome **7**.147–8
  and AR-L 115 BS **7**.135
  in diabetes **7**.150
  and digitalis poisoning **7**.133–4
  in DIOA **7**.155
  in glaucoma **7**.154
  in ophthalmic disease **7**.129, **7**.131, **7**.161
  in retinitis pigmentosa **7**.144, **7**.146
Lanthony Tritan Album **7**.222
Laplace transforms **12**.251
Laplacian of Gaussian operator **14**.35
Large cell node **3**.110–1, **3**.117
Laser optometer **1**.235
Laser rangefinder **14**.40
Laser speckle optometry **1**.411–3
  see also Optometry, laser speckle
Laser speckle patterns **1**.340
Lasers **16**.1, **16**.7–8
  and ageing macula **16**.82, **16**.88
  applications and uses **16**.20
  argon **16**.20, **16**.66, **16**.89
  arrays **16**.19
  carbon dioxide **16**.19–20
  dye **16**.19–20
  emission characteristics and applications **16**.19
  excimer **1**.157–8, **16**.58, **16**.93
    for refractive correction
      as a knife for precise control of depth of cut **1**.157–8
      as a sculpting tool for changing refractive
        power **1**.157–8
  gas (and vapour) **16**.8
  helium–neon **16**.19–20
  injuries **16**.96
  krypton **16**.20
  and light damage **16**.62–3
  and light hazards **16**.98
  liquid **16**.8
  medical uses **16**.20
  military **16**.96
  neodymium **16**.19–20
  ocular hazards **16**.5
  and optical radiation **16**.1–2, **16**.19–20
  and phototoxicity **16**.69, **16**.73

  Q-switched **16**.50–1
  ruby **16**.19–20
  semi-conductor **16**.8, **16**.19–20
  solid state **16**.8
  standards **16**.6
  surgical **16**.98
L-aspartate (Asp) and neurotransmitters **11**.355–6
Late receptor potential (LRP) **5**.179–80
Latency **1**.241
  of optokinesis **8**.52–3
  of saccades **8**.96, **8**.112–7, **8**.121–2, **8**.305
  of vergence **8**.158–61, **8**.163
Late-onset myopia **1**.31
Lateral aniseikonia **9**.216
Lateral geniculate body (LGB) **12**.62
  in axon growth **11**.233–6, **11**.249
  dorsal and ventral **12**.60
  magnocellular layer of **1**.258
Lateral geniculate lamination **2**.278–9
Lateral geniculate nucleus **2**.16, **3**.316, **4**.124, **4**.146, **4**.175,
    4.178, **4**.224–7, **4**.229–30, **4**.234–7, **4**.240, **4**.252,
    4.260–1, **4**.282, **4**.285–7, **4**.290–1, **4**.297–9, **4**.321–2,
    6.170, **6**.174–6, **6**.180–1, **6**.184, **6**.186–7, **6**.213, **7**.69,
    7.209, **8**.2, **8**.245–6, **9**.104, **13**.48
  afferents of **4**.263
  axons of **4**.327
  and binocular vision **2**.274–5, **2**.277–8
  and blindsight **12**.149, **12**.154
  cells of **4**.191
  and changes in magnification from retina to cortex **4**.72–3
  chromatic properties of cells of **4**.68–9
  chromatic sensitive cells of **5**.205
  classification of cells of **4**.44–5
  and colour deficiencies **12**.409
  in colour vision **2**.316
  cone-opponent units in **6**.207
  contributions to vision of **4**.75–6
  cross-level comparisons of **4**.44–5
  and cross-modal connections **11**.379–80
  cross-species comparisons of **4**.44
  and flicker **5**.179
  flicker responses **5**.182–3
  functional organization **12**.52–63
  Glossary explanation of **4**.447
  illusion and hallucination **12**.468, **12**.480
  lagged cells generated at **4**.59
  laminar segregation in **4**.46
  laminar segregation of pathways in **4**.71
  of macaque monkey **4**.267–8
  magnocellular layers of **4**.321–2, **6**.174–5, **10**.154
  and neurotransmitters **11**.353, **11**.355–7
  non-retinal control in
    global neuromodulatory **4**.59
    of information flow through **4**.59–61
    retinotopic excitatory **4**.60–1
    specific neuromodulatory **4**.59–60
  non-retinal inputs to **4**.48–52
    brainstem **4**.51–2
    cortical **4**.49

mid-brain 4.49–51
off-centre cells of 4.52, 4.63–4
on–off channels in 4.63–4
on-centre cells of 4.52, 4.63–4
and optic nerve regeneration 11.206
output from 4.52
parallel pathways in 4.62–71
   and ocular dominance 4.63
parvocellular layers of 4.321–2, 6.174–5
in peripheral vision 5.44–5, 5.48, 5.72, 5.259
and phosphenes 12.155
physiology and function of 4.41–84
and pure alexia 12.356–7
in pursuit system 2.170–2, 2.174–5, 2.177, 2.188–9
rectifying on-and off-centre cells of 4.263–4
response latency of cells of 4.68–9
response transience of cells of 4.68
responses of cells of, to various stimuli 4.61–2
RLP terminals in 4.45–6
rodent 4.162
role of, in setting the stage for the cortex 4.74–5
shift effect of 4.70–1
signal detectability in 4.53–4
signal transfer in 12.61–4
signal transmission of cells of 4.52–62
as a spatial filter 4.56–8
and spectral sensitivity 5.192–3, 5.208
spillover from 4.271
structural organization of 4.45–52
as a temporal filter 4.58–9
in trichromacy 2.312–4
velocity sensitivity of cells of 4.68
in visual cortex 11.338–40, 11.345
and visual field defects 12.144–5
in visual function 4.405
visual information processing in 4.73–6
and visual pathways 2.423–30, 2.433, 2.435, 2.443–5,
   2.449–53, 2.459
Lateral inhibition 2.224, 9.91
  in visual processing 208, 2.206, 2.213, 2.245–7
Lateral interactions 5.45, 5.192, 9.134
  Glossary explanation of 4.447
Lateral interparietal area 4.412
Lateral intraparietal area 4.374
  neurones of 13.19
Lateral parietal cortex 12.465
Lateral pontine nucleus 8.213
Lateral posterior complex 3.214–5
Lateral posterior nucleus 3.209–11
Lateral posterior–pulvinar complex 3.207, 3.209–11,
   3.215–7, 4.141–7, 4.149–52
Lateral rectus 8.175, 8.182, 8.185
Lateral suprasylvian sulcus 3.186–7, 3.198, 3.203, 3.205,
   3.309
Lateral terminal nucleus 8.201, 8.213
  Glossary explanation of 4.443
  see also Accessory optic system
Laterality
  hemispheric 12.233–4

left–right, in human face recognition 12.226–30
Lateralization
  age-dependent 12.238
  different degrees of cerebral 12.144
  hemispheric 12.231–2
  of script 12.310
Latex rhodamine beads 3.138
Latimeria chalumnae 2.71
Lattice, hexagonal 3.18–9, 3.24, 3.38, 3.57
Lavater, Kaspar 12.218
Laws of binocular visual direction 9.7
Laws of monocular visual direction 9.6
Laws of oculocentric direction 9.6
Laws of visual direction 9.7, 9.77
L-cone channels 6.167–8, 6.170–6, 6.181–3
L-cones 4.317–8, 4.322, 4.332, 6.202–6, 6.208, 6.211–2,
   7.65–70
Learning
  differences in pure alexia 12.346
  interference in 12.277
  interhemispheric transfer of 3.324–5, 3.328, 3.348
  interocular transfer of 3.324
  and the neocortex 11.373
  in prosopagnosia 12.268
  verbal 12.347
Lebensohn's Rule 1.199–200
Leber, hereditary optic atrophy 7.47–8, 7.159, 7.175–6
Lectins 3.295
Left-handedness
  and atypical cerebral lateralization 13.96
  weaknesses of, and bias to right-handedness 13.86–8
Left-handers 12.304
  reading and script 12.310, 12.317
  and word recognition 12.324
Legibility, of text, on visual displays 15.7
  character size 15.17
  chromatic contrast 15.19–20
  greyscale filtering 15.15–7
    aliasing error elimination 15.15
    contrast energy difference metric 15.16
    jaggies elimination 15.15
  luminance contrast 15.18, 15.58–9
  and polarity 15.18–9
  resolution and addressability 15.14–5
  space modulation of display luminance 15.11–20
  spatial effects on 15.71
  typographic effects on 15.73
    acceptability of 15.74
  vs. readability 15.71
Lehmann illusion tests 5.242
Leibniz, Gottfried Wilhelm 12.321
Lemur catta (ring-tailed lemur) 2.75, 2.293, 7.203–4, 7.209
Lemur macaco (black lemur) 2.76
Lemurs 2.77, 2.476
  black 2.76
  colour vision 2.293
  ring-tailed 2.75
Length acuity 10.105–7
Length constants 3.26, 3.48

Length sensitivity
  of cells of cat visual cortex **4**.175–7
  Glossary explanation of **4**.447
Length summation
  of cells of cat visual cortex **4**.175–7
  Glossary explanation of **4**.447
Lens **3**.76, **11**.393–4
  absorption **5**.87–8, **5**.277–83
  as accommodative mechanism **2**.119
  achromatizing **5**.84, **5**.86, **5**.215–6, **5**.246
  ageing **5**.278–81, **16**.63–4, **16**.76, **16**.89
  aquatic **2**.121–2
  aspherical **2**.412
  camera **2**.123
  cellular **2**.44
  cephalopod **2**.377
  corneal **2**.119–21, **2**.132
  crystalline **5**.50, **5**.55–6, **5**.88, **5**.92, **5**.277–80, **7**.123, **7**.162
  cylinder **2**.130–3
  development **11**.389–91
  in dioptrics **2**.82, **2**.84–6, **2**.88–9, **2**.91, **2**.95–7, **2**.99, **2**.103,
      2.108–9
  embryology **11**.395–9
  epithelium **11**.389–90
  in evolution of eye **2**.3–4, **2**.6, **2**.17–8, **2**.21, **2**.24, **2**.26,
      2.47, **2**.417
  in evolution of vision **2**.399, **2**.403, **2**.405, **2**.409–12
  focus **5**.236
  gradient index **2**.96
  human
    and birefringence **1**.4, **1**.318–9
    cortex of **1**.3
    experimental data on **1**.318–9
    as a gradient-index optical component **1**.4
    hydration of, as a possible cause of abrupt change in
        refraction **1**.47
    and the lenticular cross **1**.318
    new fibre growth of **1**.3
    of patients with diabetes **1**.47–8
    of patients with galactosaemia **1**.47–8
    and role of, as aperture stop **1**.3
    structure and optical properties of **1**.318–9
  intraocular (IOL) **16**.42–3, **16**.51
    and ageing macula **16**.89–90
    and light damage **16**.63–4
    and light hazards **16**.94
    and radiation **16**.55, **16**.58
  light absorption in **7**.4–5
  and light damage **16**.64
  and light interactions **16**.43, **16**.50
  in mammals **2**.469, **2**.471, **2**.473–7
  Matthiessen **2**.122, **2**.128, **2**.130
  microlens **2**.89
  mirror **2**.417
  movement **2**.108–9, **2**.111
  multi-element **2**.122–3
  Noir **16**.71
  opacities **16**.142–3, **16**.145, **16**.147, **16**.151
  origin of **11**.400–3

  origin of vertebrate **2**.44–6
  and origins of eye **2**.55, **2**.57
  in photoreception **2**.369, **2**.372, **2**.374
  placode **11**.387, **11**.389, **11**.398, **11**.400
  quality **2**.411
  and radiation **16**.55–60
  refracting **2**.118
  resolution **2**.230–8
  see also under Lenses; Spectacle lenses
  senescence **11**.391
  senescent crystalline **16**.151
  sex difference in ageing **5**.277
  shape **2**.109–11
  simple **2**.131
  single **2**.128
  spectral transmittance **2**.88
  spherical **2**.4, **2**.97, **2**.121, **2**.134, **2**.410, **2**.412
  sutures **11**.390
  telephoto **2**.411, **2**.417
  transmissivity **5**.278
  triplet **2**.123
  two-element **5**.244
  vertebrate **2**.38–9
  vesicle **11**.386–7, **11**.389–90
  and vitreous **11**.392
  wide-angle **2**.411
  yellowing **2**.88, **5**.280, **5**.282
  zoom **2**.417
Lens absorbance **7**.154, **7**.162
Lens ageing **7**.118, **7**.156, **7**.218
Lens capsule, elastic forces of **1**.231
Lens ectoderm **3**.73
Lens implants
  intraocular **1**.120–37
    anterior chamber **1**.121
    complications of **1**.125–6
      capsular fibrosis **1**.126
      capsular opacification **1**.126
      capsulotomy **1**.126
      instability **1**.125
      lens-uvea interaction **1**.125–6
    design of **1**.129–32
      closed-loop anterior chamber **1**.130
      multifocal **1**.132
      open-loop anterior chamber **1**.130
      posterior chamber **1**.131–2
      pupil supported **1**.130–1
      solid/rigid anterior chamber **1**.129–30
    and extracapsular cataract extraction **1**.121–3
    history of **1**.121–3
      and Ridley's initiative **1**.121
    and intracapsular cataract extraction **1**.121
    iris-supported **1**.121
    materials for **1**.127–9
      future **1**.129
      polycarbonate **1**.129
      rigid **1**.127–9
        glass **1**.128
        nylon **1**.128

polymethylmethacrylate, and incorporation of ultra-
    violet-light blocking filters 1.128
  polypropylene 1.128–9
  soft 1.129
    HEMA 1.129
    polymethylmethacrylate 1.127–8
    silicone elastomers 1.129
  posterior chamber tripod 1.122
  and pseudophakodonesis 1.122
  selection of power of 1.132–4
    and anterior chamber depth 1.133–4
    and calculation formulae for 1.134
      multiple linear regression 1.134
      optical/mathematical 1.134
    of desired post-operative refraction 1.132–3
    empirical choice of 1.133
    keratometry 1.133
    ocular biometry 1.133
    ultrasonic biometry 1.133
  sterilization of 1.132
  surgical complications of
    early 1.124
    late 1.124–5
      corneal decompensation 1.124–5
      cystoid macular oedema 1.125
      retinal detachment 1.125
  surgical methods and results 1.123–6
    anaesthesia 1.123
    in extracapsular cataract extraction 1.124
    induced astigmatism 1.123–4
    in intracapsular cataract extraction 1.124–6
    and ultrasonic phakofragmentation 1.123
Lens pigment
  and acquired deficiency 7.41
  and threshold measurements 7.53–4
Lens vesicle 3.71, 3.80
Lens yellowing 7.116
Lenses
  bifocal, 'jump' in 1.58
  spectacle
    correction by 1.64–79
    see also under Spectacle lenses, correction by
Lenticular birefringence, of the human lens 1.4, 1.319
Lenticular lenses 1.70–1
  negative blended 1.71
Leonardo da Vinci 12.32–4, 12.39
  and the development of the contact lens 1.82
Lepidoptera optics 2.130
Lepomis macrochirus (bluegill fish) 2.69
Lesions
  aetiology 12.262, 12.337
    arteriovenous malformations 12.343
    non-ischaemic 12.343
  analysis of effects of 4.388
  area below calcarine fissure 12.425
  associated with foveal function 12.315
  asymmetric 12.277
  bilateral 12.261, 12.264
  frequency of 12.268

  infero-medial-occipito-temporal 12.278
  occipital 12.379
  parietal 12.359, 12.451
  parieto-occipital 12.359
  posterior 12.265, 12.271
    cerebral 12.266
  and prosopagnosia 12.269, 12.285
  and pure alexia 12.343
brain
  and achromatopsia 12.395
  acute 12.374
  bilateral 12.372–3, 12.378
    occipital 12.147
  frontal 12.395
  and hemi-inattention 12.453
  illusion and hallucination 12.475, 12.478, 12.480
  localized 12.477
  occipital 12.402, 12.475, 12.479–80
    lateral 12.344
  parietal 12.395
  outside parietal lobe 12.462–3
  planimetric estimation of 12.283
  posterior 12.262
  and prosopagnosia 12.260, 12.262
  reading and script 12.308
  right hemisphere 12.399
  and shorthand 12.316
  size 12.283
  temporo-occipital 12.108
  and topographagnosia 12.418
  and topographical disorientation 12.417
  unilateral 12.112
  and visual hemineglect 12.448
  and visual movement agnosia 12.359, 12.371
  and visual object recognition 12.117
  and visuo-spatial disorders 12.434, 12.436
brainstem 12.371
callosal 12.335
  posterior 12.348
cerebral
  aetiologies 12.342–3
  localization 12.263–4, 12.338, 12.342–3
  producing alexia 12.333
  and pure alexia 12.338
  see also Achromatopsia; Agnosia, colour; Anomia, colour;
      Aphasia, colour
  and visual movement agnosia 12.363
conditioning 11.193
cortical 3.56, 10.261
disciform 16.87
focal 12.198, 12.200, 12.269
  vascular 12.344
frontal 12.473
  eyefield 12.341
  lobe 12.462–3
global 12.198
of gyrus angularis 12.94
hemispheric 10.274–5
infero-medial occipito-temporal, left 12.335

Lesions (*continued*)
  left hemisphere 12.281–2, 12.284–5
    and alexia 12.335
    in prosopagnosia 12.267
    and semantic paralexia 12.328
    and spatial hemineglect 12.452, 12.462
    and visual hemineglect 12.447–8, 12.450
  localization of 12.337, 12.425
  location of 12.180
  outside medial occipito-temporal region 12.280–6
  mesial inferior occipito-temporal 12.418
  mesial infero-calcarine 12.418
  multi-focal disseminated 12.201
  neurophysiological mechanisms 12.338
  at non-typical sites 12.343
  occipito-parietal 12.462
  parietal lobe 12.341
    and extrapersonal visual space 12.92
    illusion and hallucination 12.473
    inferior 12.437, 12.462–3
    posterior 12.452, 12.463
    right, and visual hemineglect 12.450
    and spatial hemineglect 12.452–4
    and topographical disorientation 12.411–2, 12.418,
      12.430
    and topographical orientation, disorders 12.427–8
    and visual hemineglect 12.449
    and visuo-spatial disorders 12.435–6
  parieto-occipital regions 12.476
  posterio-lateral 12.264
  posterior cerebral 12.261, 12.430
    artery, left and right 12.342, 12.354
    right, and topographagnosia 12.422
  posterior medial hemispheric, posterior 12.425
  of the posterior parietal cortex 13.22–9
  prostrolandic 12.213
  pulvinar, left 12.463
  retinal 3.182
  retrochiasmatic 12.144
  right hemisphere 12.281–2, 12.285
    and achromatopsia 12.395
    anterior 12.281–2
    posterior 12.281–2, 12.284
    in prosopagnosia 12.278
    and spatial hemineglect 12.452, 12.462
    and visual hemineglect 12.450
  sites and symptoms 12.180
  size 12.338
    and semantic paralexia 12.328
  splenial 12.335, 12.346
    aetiology 12.335
    extent confirmed by operation 12.347
    extra-callosal damage 12.347
    location 12.335–6
    pre-and post-operative testing 12.347
    and pure alexia 12.357
    size 12.335
  suprageniculate 7.162
  surgical 12.262

  temporal lobe 12.473
  temporo-parieto-occipital, lateral 12.418
  unilateral 12.180, 12.213, 12.261, 12.266
    focal cerebral 12.280
    occipital, and topographagnosia 12.422–5
    parietal lobe 12.438, 12.443
    and prosopagnosia 12.285
    right posterior 12.271
Letter charts 5.279
  low-contrast 10.33–4, 10.244–5, 10.252
  Pelli–Robson Contrast Sensitivity 16.154
Letter(s)
  and alexia 12.334
  in alphabetical order 12.350
  capitalization of first 12.308
  configuration, specific 12.336
  cross-hatching 12.340
  discrimination 12.322
  frequency 12.325
  graphemic components 12.340
  graphically dissimilar 12.322
  graphically similar 12.322
  and hemialexia 12.350
  identity 12.321
  inverted 12.319
  lost, *see* Alexia
  lower-case 12.323, 12.328
  masking experiments 12.323
  matching 12.350
    tasks 12.321, 12.323
  meaning, and pure alexia 12.338
  motion-defined 10.170
  name identity 12.323
  non-letters 12.322
  orientation 12.321
  pairs 12.322, 12.324
    matching of 12.340
  perception
    angular size of stimulus 12.321
    orientation 12.321
    position in visual field 12.321
  physical identity 12.321, 12.323
  picture 12.307
  printed 12.315, 12.321, 12.350
  reading and script 12.309
  recognition 12.274, 12.317, 12.320–1
    frequency of correct 12.321
    probability 12.322
    and pure alexia 12.337
    of single 12.319, 12.322–3
  shadow 12.341
  single 12.317, 12.319, 12.322–3, 12.350
    and pure alexia 12.351–4
  size 12.317, 12.320, 12.322
  sorting 12.350
  spatial rotation by 90 degrees 12.342
  spelling 12.340
  strings 12.311, 12.315–7, 12.325, 12.327
    non-word 12.351

and shorthand 12.330
  tachistoscopic tests 12.331
tachistoscopic presentation 12.321
tachistoscopic projection 12.320–30
target 12.321–3
tracing 12.334, 12.338, 12.347
typography 12.322
upper-and lower-case 12.321, 12.323, 12.328
written on skin 12.357
Leucippos 12.27
Levator palpebrae superioris 8.175–6, 8.182–3
Lexicon
  internal 12.338
  of language 12.311
L-glutamate (Glu) 3.33
  and neurotransmitters 11.355–6
LGN, *see* Lateral geniculate nucleus
LGNd, *see* Dorsal lateral geniculate nucleus
LGNv, *see* Ventral lateral geniculate nucleus
Lids
  diseases of, tarsal cysts 1.45
  eye 11.393–4
Lie algebra 14.21
Lie group operators 14.22, 14.25
Lie group theory 14.21, 14.26–8
Lie transformation group (LTG/NP) 14.20, 14.26
Liebmann, S. 2.312
Liebmann effect 2.309, 2.312
Ligands, lipid-soluble 11.119
Light
  absorption of 16.62
  achromatic 2.293, 2.297–8
  blue 16.2–3, 16.5, 16.11, 16.14, 16.18–9
    and ageing 16.151
    and ageing macula 16.89–90
    effects on eye 16.54–66
    and light hazards 16.94–5, 16.97–100
    and light interactions 16.43
    and light measurement 16.24, 16.27–9
  dark 3.25–6
  detection function, dissociated recovery 12.402
  and developing visual system 16.104–29
    affected visual functions 16.109–13
    damage to 16.104–9
      measures of 16.106–8
      photochemical 16.105–6
      thermal 16.105–6
    infant populations 16.113–6
    infant visual apparatus 16.116–24
    visual dysfunction in infants and children 16.124–8
  diagnostic 16.99–100
  differential threshold 16.151
  discomforting reflections 12.270
  entopic stray 2.97
  increase in sensitivity to 12.390
  long-wavelength 2.288
  low 2.410–1, 2.417
  measurement of 16.23–9, 16.104–5
    photometric 16.116

monochromatic 2.289, 2.294, 2.297–8
narrow band monochromatic 16.62, 16.88
nature of 2.3, 2.5–7, 2.13, 5.48–9
neonatal exposure to 16.98–9
in ophthalmic practice 16.65–6
and photochemical damage 16.60
polarized 2.298, 2.382, 5.88
quantum, *see* Photon
and retinal ageing 16.61–4, 16.87–90
retinal stray 2.97
scattered 2.6, 2.8, 2.139, 2.265, 2.408, 2.410, 2.413
  and light measurement 16.26
see also Dark light
see also Hazard
sensations, diffuse 12.472
short-wavelength 2.6–7, 2.287–8
spectral composition of reflected 3.28
stray 2.97–8, 2.102
ultra-violet 2.6–7, 2.33, 2.35, 2.69–73, 5.282
  and ageing 16.63
  in colour vision 2.287–90, 2.292, 2.294–5, 2.298–9,
    2.302
ultra-violet blockers 16.64
visible 16.32, 16.39, 16.97
wavelength-modulated 10.151–2
'white' 2.289–90, 2.292, 2.294–5, 2.297–8
Light adaptation 3.9, 3.11, 3.40–1
Light air ions, produced by visual-display terminals 15.4–5
Light constancy 2.300
Light damage 16.24–5
  action spectra for 16.108–9, 16.112
  Class I 16.108–9, 16.112, 16.116
  Class II 16.108–9, 16.112
Light damage mechanisms 16.23, 16.62, 16.88
  mechanical 16.93, 16.96
  photochemical 16.63–4, 16.66, 16.89–90, 16.93–9, 16.107,
    16.109, 16.116
  thermal 16.93–4, 16.96–9, 16.109
Light flux 2.87
Light guides 2.230–2, 2.235
Light interactions 16.37–9
  with biological tissues 16.30–52
  mechanisms of 16.39–52
    ionization 16.39, 16.41, 16.49–52
    photochemical 16.39–44, 16.46, 16.52
      Type 1 damage 16.42–3
      Type 2 damage 16.42–3
    thermal 16.39, 16.41, 16.44–9, 16.52
    thermo-accoustic 16.49
  repair processes 16.49
    closed system 16.44
    open system 16.44
Light reflection by objects 14.88
Light reflex 3.217
  pupillary 3.194, 3.204
Light scattering 1.394–5, 3.1–2, 3.5–6, 3.20, 3.27
  backscatter 1.395
  measurement of 1.394–5
Light sensitivity 5.55, 5.57, 5.60–1, 5.63, 5.65, 5.68, 10.273

Light sensitivity (*continued*)
  and ageing **16.**150–8
  of cones 3.16
Light sources **16.**23, **16.**26
Light transmission
  by the eye media 1.8–9
    and absorption and scattering 1.8
    and fluorescence 1.9
    and Fresnel reflection losses 1.8
    and lenticular absorption 1.8
Light wavelength, and ageing macula **16.**78, **16.**89–90
Light-adapted vision 5.48
Lighting
  clinical **16.**62, **16.**65, **16.**87–8
  commercial **16.**62, **16.**87–8
  domestic **16.**62, **16.**88
  fluorescent **16.**62, **16.**88
  industrial **16.**87
  and lighting conditions **15.**41–54
  phototherapy **16.**123
  systems **16.**1, **16.**8–17
Lighting problems, associated with visual displays **15.**41–54, **15.**63–4
  alternative displays **15.**45
  balance between diffuse and specular **15.**45
  contrast polarity **15.**46, **15.**48–50
  direct lighting **15.**48, **15.**52–3
  discomfort ratings **15.**47
  distraction **15.**42
  dynamic luminance imbalance **15.**44–5
  high-luminance reflections **15.**45
    diffuse and specular **15.**46
  indirect lighting **15.**48, **15.**52–3
  and low-and high-character-density displays **15.**48–9
  luminaire luminance **15.**48, **15.**50
  luminance contrast reduction **15.**45–7
  reduction of luminance contrast **15.**42
  reductions in performance **15.**47
  screen reflection properties **15.**47
  static and dynamic luminance imbalance **15.**43–4
  static luminance imbalance **15.**43–4
Lighting regimes 5.49–50
Lightness, and the luminance factor 6.48–9
Lightness constancy 5.108
Lightness (of a related colour), CIE definition of 6.225
Lightpens **15.**117–8
Limb buds, homeobox expression in **11.**19–20
Limb field **11.**47, **11.**61
Limb movements, planning of **13.**35
Limbic cortex 2.430
Limbic structures **12.**387, **12.**393
  and colour deficiencies **12.**410
  illusion and hallucination **12.**470–1, **12.**480–1
  and posterior parietal lobe **12.**94, **12.**103
  and visual object recognition **12.**109, **12.**119
Limbic system **12.**269, **12.**278–9, **12.**387, **12.**393, **12.**400
  and posterior parietal lobe **12.**94
  and pure alexia **12.**356
  of right hemisphere **12.**405

and spatial hemineglect **12.**463
Limbs, vertebrate **11.**61
Limited bandwidth concept **10.**143
Limulus 2.132, 2.217–8, 2.342, 2.345–6
Lincoln, Abraham **12.**227
Line
  bisection task **12.**378, **12.**381, **12.**463
    and spatial hemineglect **12.**452–4, **12.**464
  contours **12.**205
  curved **12.**204–5
  discontinuation **12.**205
  straight **12.**204–5
Line drawings 5.241
  veridical **14.**114
Line element model **10.**68–9, **10.**72–4, **10.**93
Line images **14.**98–106
Line orientation, disorders of perception of **13.**26
Linear acceleration **12.**432
Linear discriminant analysis **10.**122
Linear discriminant function **14.**71
Linear filters
  and amplitude spectra 4.249
  Gabor 4.249
  neurones acting as 4.250
  of the striate cortex 4.247–9
  striate receptive fields as 4.246–65
Linear head movements 8.34–5
Linear and non-linear systems **10.**4–12
Linear perspective 1.249, 9.183
Linear reduction of dimensions **14.**79
Linear spatial summation 5.305
Linear summation hypothesis 8.108
Linear system dynamics 5.62
Linear systems 5.288
  convolution in 4.249
  of the striate cortex 4.247–9
Linear systems analysis 5.172
Linear systems theory 2.166
Linear vestibulo-ocular reflex 8.35
Linearity
  of vergence 8.159
  of vestibular transduction 8.25–6
Linearization **10.**8
Line-labelling 2.246, 2.248, 2.250, 2.267
Line-spread function 1.10–1, 1.16, 1.18, 3.5–6
Line-spread function (LSF) 2.99, 5.88–90, 5.288
Lineus 2.30, 2.35, 2.37
Linguistics, theories **12.**338
Linking feature 3.28
Lip reading **12.**219, **12.**307
Lipid flow theory **11.**177
Lipids **16.**84–5
  metabolism **16.**142
Lipofuscin **16.**82–3, **16.**85
Liquid-crystal visual displays **15.**56, **15.**59
Lissauer, Ernst **12.**180–4
Lissauer's case report **12.**260
Lissencephaly 3.363
Listing's law 8.66, 8.260, 8.262

Literacy
  and alexia **12**.333
  global **12**.304
  modern **12**.306
Lithium intoxication **8**.302
Lizard
  dioptrics of **2**.84–5, **2**.103
  visual pathways of **2**.422, **2**.427–9
L-neurones **8**.247, **8**.254
Lobectomy
  bilateral medial temporal **12**.269
  occipital **12**.268
Lobula
  arthropod **2**.216–7, **2**.219
  complex **2**.354–5
  in eye evolution **2**.353–5
  optic lobe **2**.204–6, **2**.210–1
Lobule, inferior parietal **12**.264, **12**.278
Local features **14**.65–6
Local feedback **8**.97–8, **8**.119, **8**.123, **8**.209, **8**.215, **8**.257
Local sign **14**.51–2
Localization **8**.8, **14**.51
  auditory **11**.374, **11**.376–7
  of brain spectrin **11**.286
  and equiluminance **5**.236
  judgments **14**.13–5
  Lotze's theory **14**.52
  problem **14**.65
  and spatial relations **14**.52–3
  test of spatial **12**.381
  visual **13**.1–280
Location **14**.127
  defined **14**.8–10
  and hyperacuity **5**.231
  relative, as basic visual function **14**.8–11
Location perception **10**.281
Locke, John **12**.17
Locomotion
  cell **11**.171–83
    chemotaxis **11**.181
    extrinsic factors **11**.177–82
    growth factors **11**.181
  contact inhibition of **11**.180–1
  crawling mechanism **11**.171–7
  oculomotor effects **8**.80–1, **8**.297–9
  visual effects **8**.13, **8**.88–9, **8**.297–9
Locus coeruleus **3**.166, **3**.169
Locust
  optic lobe **2**.222–4
  visual processing **2**.206, **2**.208–12
Logarithmic transformations **4**.283
Logistic distribution **5**.10
Logogram **12**.306–8
  associative **12**.307
  combined **12**.307
  diagrammatic **12**.307
  Kanji **12**.348
  phonetic transformation of **12**.307
  pictorial **12**.305

  primary **12**.307
  and shorthand **12**.316
Loligo opalescens (squid) **2**.383, **2**.385
Lolliguncula (squid) **2**.388
Long visual fibres (LVF) **2**.347–8, **2**.354, **2**.357, **2**.359
  photoreceptors **2**.204–5, **2**.208, **2**.214, **2**.217–8, **2**.221
Long-lead burst neurones **4**.391, **8**.206, **8**.208–10, **8**.258–60, **8**.262–3
Long-lead movement neurones **8**.249, **8**.252
Look-nystagmus **8**.47–50
Looming **2**.242
Looming detectors **9**.154
Lorenz matrices **12**.117, **12**.119, **12**.226
Lotze, Hermann **14**.52, **14**.65
Louis-Philippe, King **12**.222
Loupes, *see* Plus-lens magnifiers, hand held
Lovibond Colour Vision Analyser **7**.216, **7**.227
Low light **2**.410–1, **2**.417
Low vision
  aids for **1**.185
    closed-circuit television **1**.185
    different lighting arrangements **1**.185
    in mobility
      orientation and spatial awareness
        guide dog **1**.185
        long cane **1**.185
        remote sensing sonar **1**.185
    sensory substitution **1**.185
      Optacon **1**.185
      synthesized speech output **1**.185
      tactile Braille alphabet **1**.185
      tactile Moon alphabet **1**.185
    transverse magnification **1**.185
    the typoscope **1**.185
    utilizing optical methods **1**.185–6
  and blind registers **1**.183–4
  definition of **1**.183
  demographic prevalence of **1**.183
  future trends in **1**.184–5
  implications of **1**.185
    disability **1**.185
    disorder **1**.185
    handicap **1**.185
    impairment **1**.185
  magnification in **1**.186–218
  official UK statistics on **1**.184
    in relation to aetiology **1**.184
    in relation to prevalence **1**.184
  optical aids for **1**.183–228
    control of lighting **1**.221–3
      tints and filters **1**.222–3
        dazzling glare **1**.223
        disability glare **1**.223
        discomfort glare **1**.222
        photobia **1**.222
  and partially sighted registers **1**.183–4
  reading in patients with **13**.68–9
  registration criteria for **1**.183
  and the RNIB **1**.183

Low vision (*continued*)
   see also Low-level vision
   and visual impairment 1.183
Low-level vision 2.267–8
Low-vision aids, *see* Low vision, aids for
LP–pulvinar complex, *see* Lateral posterior–pulvinar complex
LSD (lysergic acid diethylamide) 12.471, 12.477
LSF, *see* Line-spread function
LTN, *see* Lateral terminal nucleus
LTP, *see* Potentiation, long-term
L-type calcium currents 4.3
Luciani 12.149
Luminance 3.30, 5.120, 5.286, 5.293–4, 10.173
   and ageing 16.152–4
   background 5.39–40
   and brightness 6.48–9
   channel 5.174, 5.196
   configurations 5.9–12, 5.23, 5.25, 5.30
   continuous background 5.38
   contours 5.234
   and contrast encoding 5.108–9
   contrast increment sensitivity 5.198
   dependence in amblyopia 10.219–21
   and developing visual system 16.105, 16.122–3
   effects on spatial processing 10.195–6
   equal 5.211–2
   and equiluminance 5.246–7
   equivalent veiling 2.97
   flicker 5.171–2
   and hyperacuity 5.222–3, 5.227–8, 5.231
   and illusions 5.242–4
   and light measurement 16.23–4, 16.27
   mean 10.44–5
   mechanisms 5.196–8
   mesopic 5.50, 5.60
   Palmer (equivalent) 5.50
   pathway 5.235–6, 5.244–8
   pedestal 5.32
   photopic 5.50
   pre-adaptation 5.278
   predictive coding effects 3.30
   profiles 5.224, 5.226
      mirror symmetric 5.270
   and psychometric functions 5.8
   and reading ability 13.172
   residual 5.245
   retinal 12.8
   scaling 5.7
   scotopic 5.49–51
   sensation 5.185
   signal transfer of 12.54–5, 12.58–9
   sinusoidal modulations 5.31, 5.33, 5.35
   space average 5.35
   subsystems 5.245
   suprathreshold 5.30
   texture and stereo depth 5.124–5
   uniform 5.35–6
Luminance adaptation (LA) 5.111–3
Luminance analysis 5.241
Luminance CFF 7.181–2
Luminance contrast 3.58, 6.201–3, 15.28–35
   definitions and formulae 15.18, 15.28–9, 15.46
   inner and outer 15.29, 15.59
   and visual-display terminals 15.18, 15.42, 15.58–9
Luminance and detection thresholds 7.50
Luminance equivalent background 7.25
Luminance factor
   CIE definition of 6.227
   and lightness 6.48–9
   and the V_λ curve 6.12–3
Luminance and ganglion cells 3.49
Luminance profiles, of displayed characters 15.11, 15.29, 15.59
Luminance reflections, and visual-display terminals 15.41–2
Luminance threshold 7.43
Luminescence in dioptrics 2.88
Luminosity, CIE definition of 6.225
Luminosity curve, photopic 12.393
Luminosity function 5.196–7, 5.205, 5.207
Luminous (perceived) colour, CIE definition of 6.225
Luneberg–Blank theory 9.82
LWS cone opsin 7.106–11
LWS cones 7.135, 7.144
LWS loss 7.117–8, 7.127
   in cone diseases 7.136, 7.140, 7.162
   in ophthalmic disease 7.128–31
   in spatial organization 7.162–3
   in Stargardt's disease 7.141–2
LWS-pigment (LP) gene 7.106–11
Lynx dioptrics 2.91
Lyonization 2.315, 2.317, 7.21, 7.29
Lyon's random inactivation 7.130
Lyrics, melodies and read aloud 12.358
Lysinated rhodamine dextran (LRD) 11.33
Lysippos 12.221

M

Macaca arctoides 5.256
Macaca fascicularis (crab-eating macaque) 2.168, 5.256, 7.199, 7.202
Macaca fuscata (Japanese macaque) 7.199–200
Macaca mulatta (rhesus macaque) 2.168, 5.256, 7.199–200
Macaca nemestrina (pig-tailed macaque) 2.168, 7.199, 7.202
Macaca speciosa 2.168
MacAdam ellipses 5.199, 5.214
Macaque monkeys 7.199–203, 7.205, 7.207, 7.212–3
  use of, in refraction development experiments 1.34–8
MacBeth Easel lamp 7.217
Mach, Ernst 12.3–6, 12.9
Mach bands 1.352–3, 12.4–5
Machine intelligence 15.124
Machine vision 14.30, 14.43
  computational primitives 14.40
Mach's border contrast 12.23–4, 12.397
Mach's organizing principles 14.90
Mackworth Clock Test 15.85
MacLeod's selective adaptation paradigm 1.298
Macroanatomy, autopsic 12.344
Macroglia 3.86
  genesis of 3.82
  and optic nerve regeneration 11.208
Macrophages
  and axon regeneration 11.207
  in optic nerve regeneration 11.197–8, 11.201, 11.206,
    11.210–1, 11.213
  and proto-oncogenes 11.117
Macropsia 12.412, 12.480–1
Macrosaccadic oscillations 8.310
Macula
  adult 16.79–80
  ageing 16.76–90
    pathology 16.85–7
  age-related disease 16.82
  degeneration 16.82
  disease 16.77
  embryology 16.79
  and Haidinger's brushes 1.319–23
  otolith organs 8.15–7, 8.22, 8.24
  in peripheral vision 5.50
  pigment molecules of, dichroic 1.319
  see also AMD (age-related macular degeneration); SMD
    (senile macular degeneration)
  testing the integrity of 1.323
Macular contrast sensitivity 5.291–2
Macular detachment in drusen 7.130–1
Macular pigments 2.89, 2.95, 5.56, 5.87–8, 5.247
  absorption by 1.9
  in achromatopsia 7.98–9
  in acquired deficiency 7.22–3, 7.41, 7.53
  and ageing 16.63
  in the ageing 16.79–80, 16.89
  and birefringence 1.9
  density 7.12, 7.15, 7.217
  and developing visual system 16.110, 16.118

  in DIOA 7.156
  light absorption in 7.4–5
  and longitudinal chromatic aberration 1.9
  in monochromacy 7.26
  in ophthalmic disease 7.124
  optical density of 1.320
  in pseudoisochromatic tests 7.220
  and threshold measurements 7.53
  variability and tritanomaly 7.120
Macular sparing 12.181
Maculo-macular test 9.193–4
Maculopathy 16.95
  age-related (ARM) 16.151
    and the Stiles–Crawford effect of the first kind 1.297
  bull's eye 16.70
Maddox 8.158
Maddox rod-cover test 9.195
Magendie, F. 12.47
Magic lines 9.5–6
Magnetencephalogram 12.177
Magnetic field recording 9.104
Magnetic resonance imaging (MRI) 10.54, 12.129, 12.177,
    12.260, 12.264
  and achromatopsia 12.393, 12.396
  and colour agnosia 12.403–4
  of cortical and subcortical structures 12.345
  and hemiachromatopsia 12.401
  and hemialexia 12.347
  and loss of topographical familiarity 12.425, 12.427
  and metamorphopsia 12.275
  and prosopagnosia 12.266–7, 12.274
  and pure alexia 12.342
  scans 12.207, 12.209
  in visualizing the eye 1.365–6
    and nucleus resonance frequency 1.366
    and spin-lattice relaxation time 1.366
    and spin-spin relaxation time 1.366
Magnetic-field sensor coil technique 8.80–3
Magnetophosphenes 12.166
Magnification
  cortical 5.251–6
    in pattern discrimination 5.269–70, 5.274
    in peripheral vision 5.259–62
  differential 5.244
  enhanced 5.254
  foveal 5.254
  in low vision 1.186–218
    alternative approach to universal formula and definition
      for 1.191–2
    and back vertex power 1.188
    calculations of
      in accordance with BS 5043 (1973) 1.190
      by the 'equivalent power' method 1.190
    conventional 1.189
    and equivalent power 1.188
    equivalent-power approach to 1.191
    and front vertex power 1.188
    iso-accommodative formula 1.190
    nominal 1.189

Magnification (*continued*)
  obtained by decreasing the viewing distance 1.187
    and resulting demands on accommodation 1.187
    using positive lenses 1.187
  obtained by increasing the object size 1.187
  plus-lens magnifiers in 1.189–91, 1.193–202
  real image 1.186
  relative 1.189
  relative distance 1.186
  and the standard viewing distance 1.188
  telescopic 1.186
  and thick lenses 1.188
  total 1.187
  transverse 1.186
  near isotropy 5.254
  and 'power factor' 1.60
  prescribing 1.214–8
    for distance viewing 1.214–6
      determination of that required 1.215
        and the Bailey-Lovie logMAR scale 1.215
        and the Keeler charts 'A-series' scale 1.215
      measuring monocular distance acuity 1.215
      modifications to 1.215
      monocular versus binocular correction 1.215
      optimizing refractive correction 1.214–5
      required acuity estimation 1.215
      task identification 1.215
      test performance 1.215
    for intermediate viewing 1.216–8
    for near viewing 1.218
      deciding on binocular versus monocular 1.217–8
      ensuring optimum distance correction 1.216
      estimation of that required 1.216
      Jaeger notation 1.216
      Keeler A system 1.216–7
      Kesterbaum's formula 1.217
      logarithmic scale 1.217
      measurement of near visual acuity 1.216
      N point system 1.217
      and patient instruction 1.218
      reduced Snellen notation 1.216
      Sloan M system 1.216
      task identification and acuity level estimation 1.216
      trying the predicted 1.217
  retinal 3.6, 3.16, 3.38, 3.57
  scaling 5.256–9, 5.262
  and 'shape factor' 1.60
  telescopic 1.206–14
  transverse 1.185
    and closed-circuit television 1.185–6, 1.192, 1.203–6
    and the compound microscope 1.206
    and the Fiberscope 1.205–6
    and the Viewscan system 1.205
Magnification discrimination 10.270
Magnification disparities 9.214–7
Magnification factor 3.333, 3.344
  collicular 3.151
  cortical 10.231
  Glossary explanation of 4.447

Magnification factor *M*, retino-cortical 12.65–7, 12.81, 12.170–1, 12.178
Magnification gradient 2.264
Magnifier-accommodation two-element system 1.191–2
Magnitude estimation 6.52, 14.130–2, 14.138
Magnitude production 14.127
Magnocellular axons, Glossary explanation of 4.447
Magnocellular cells 4.321–2
  Glossary explanation of 4.447
Magnocellular layers 7.69
  Glossary explanation of 4.447
  of lateral geniculate nucleus 10.154
  in MS 10.246
  in pursuit system 2.171, 2.175
  and visual pathways 2.444–5, 2.450–2, 2.458–9
  X type 10.174
  Y type 10.174
Magnocellular pathway 5.48, 5.135, 5.186, 5.197–9, 7.185, 10.52
  in peripheral vision 5.65, 5.68, 5.72–4
  and spectral sensitivity 5.192–5
Magnocellular system 5.259, 5.261, 6.175–6, 6.186–7, 6.205, 7.69–71
  and colour deficiencies 12.409
Magnus, Albertus 12.1, 12.26
Main sequence 8.100
Make-up 12.221, 12.224
Malacostraca 2.204, 2.214, 2.216, 2.219
  eye evolution 2.341, 2.351, 2.353, 2.355
  visual processing 2.221–3
Malformation
  arteriovenous 12.266
  vascular 12.150
Malpighi, Marcello 12.41
'Maltese' cross, and dichroism and birefringence 1.320
Mammals 2.467–78
  binocular vision 2.271, 2.274–6
  colour vision 2.288, 2.292–5, 2.299
  monotremes and marsupials 2.467–72
  photoreceptor system 2.73
  placentals 2.472–8
  visual pathways 2.424
Mandelbrot's law (canonic) 12.313
Mandibulata 2.213, 2.217
Mantis range measurement 2.265–6
Mantis visual processing 2.231, 2.261
Map reading 12.426
Mapping
  anatomical 11.94
  electrophysiological 11.94–6
  log-polar 14.73
  microelectrode experiments 3.311
  receptive field 3.327
Maps 12.307
  auditory 2.448, 11.370–1, 11.378, 11.381
  city location on geographic 12.462
  geniculocortical 11.236
  inverse projective 14.89
  mental 12.417, 12.433

misalignment **11.370–1**, **11.377**, **11.379**
motor **2.448**, **11.369–70**
 callosal connections **3.326–35**
 orientation with **12.342**
 projective **14.85–6**, **14.88**, **14.93**, **14.95**
 refinement and synaptic rearrangement **11.269**
 retinotectal **11.84**, **11.237**, **11.240**
 retinotopic **2.456**, **3.302**, **5.253**, **11.88**, **11.90–2**, **11.94**,
  11.103–8
  and axon growth **11.237**
  fish embryo **11.96**
  in superior colliculus **11.370**
  and synaptic rearrangement **11.269**
 route tracing on **12.428**
 sensory **11.369–70**
  callosal connections **3.326–35**
 somatosensory **2.448**, **11.370**, **11.381**
 spatio-temporal **2.245–6**, **2.248–9**, **2.254**, **2.256–8**
 and topographagnosia **12.420**
 topographic **2.240**, **2.456**, **11.69–70**, **11.84**, **11.267**
 topographic retinotectal **11.264–5**, **11.270**
 topologic **5.260**
 visual **2.448**, **11.370–1**, **11.377–9**
 visuotopic **3.342**
MAPs (microtubule-associated proteins) **11.133–6**
 estimator **14.85**, **14.93**
 in neuronal cytoskeleton **11.139**, **11.142–4**, **11.276–7**,
  11.282–4
 in regeneration **11.195**, **11.197**, **11.199**, **11.201**
 see also MAP2
MAP2
 in critical period plasticity **11.290**
 in dendrites **11.149–50**, **11.152**, **11.162**
 in neuronal cytoskeleton **11.277–8**, **11.283–4**, **11.287**,
  11.292
Marginal corneal degenerations **1.46**
Mariotte, Edme **12.137**
Markers, molecular **11.347–50**
Markov chain **12.311–2**, **12.315**, **12.317**, **12.319**, **12.325**
Markov random fields (MRFs) **14.42**
Marmosets **7.209–11**
 colour vision in **2.316**
 common (*C. jacchus jacchus*) **5.191**
 visual cortex of **3.314**
Marr, D. **12.12**, **12.14**
Marré and Marré classification **7.118**, **7.175–6**
Marr's primal sketch **6.200–12**
Marsupials **2.442**, **2.444–5**, **2.448**, **2.450–1**, **2.453–6**,
  2.467–72
 retinal development **3.69**, **3.72**, **3.74–5**, **3.80**, **3.82–3**, **3.85**
 visual cortex neurogenesis **3.360–1**, **3.370**
Martinotti cells **3.258–9**, **3.265**
Mask **12.221–4**, **12.237**
 foveal **12.319–20**
 public **12.229**
Masked threshold **15.119**
Masking **5.304**, **5.321**, **10.142–8**
 in contrast perception **5.115**
 contrast sensitivity function bandwidth **5.102**

dichoptic **5.33**
forward **5.112–3**
gratings **5.102**
interference (lateral) **12.323**
motion detection **5.157**, **5.167**
motion sensitivity **5.154–5**
mutual **12.317**
negative **5.27**, **5.30–2**, **5.38**
non-letters **12.323**
oblique **10.67**
and optics **5.86**
orientationally specific **5.34**
in psychophysical models **10.66**
and pure alexia **12.337**
by saturation **5.102**
and senescence **5.283**
specific properties of **5.305–6**
and spectral sensitivity **5.208–10**
transition from subthreshold summation to **5.307–9**
Masking experiments, letter **12.323**
Masking–adaptation paradigm **5.315–7**
Matches
 foveal, effects of bleaching on **7.14**
 large-field **7.14–5**, **7.21**
 under rod-free conditions **7.14**
 small-field **7.6–7**, **7.23**, **7.28**
Matching **5.66–7**, **5.91–2**, **5.106–8**
 conceptual **12.233**
 multi-resolution **14.33**
 see also Template
Mathematical models **10.2**, **10.4**, **10.9**
Matthiessen's ratio **2.97**, **2.121–2**, **2.376–7**, **2.411–2**
Maurice's specular microscope **1.390–1**
 and the corneal endothelium **1.390**
Maxwell colour matching **7.12–3**
Maxwellian-view system **5.175**, **5.204–5**
Maxwell's colour vision theory **6.4–5**, **6.10–2**, **6.221**
 colour box **6.10–1**
 colour top **6.11**
 colour triangle **6.221**
Maxwell's spot **1.348**
Mayer, Tobias **12.42–5**, **12.386**, **12.397**
Mayer's colour triangle **12.44–5**
McCollough effect (ME) **14.22–3**, **14.25**, **14.27**, **16.97**
M-cell pathways **7.178**, **7.181**
M-cells **4.32**, **4.34–6**, **4.65**, **4.224–5**, **4.322**, **6.205**, **10.52**
 function of, in monkey vision **4.35–6**
 phasic (transient) **10.154**
 in spectral sensitivity **5.192–9**
Mcmanus's genetic model **13.106**
M-cone channels **6.167–8**, **6.170–5**, **6.181–3**
M-cones **4.317–8**, **4.322**, **4.332**, **6.202–6**, **6.208**, **6.211–2**,
  7.65–70
MDB, *see* Minimally distinct border
Mean direction index **4.190**
Meaning
 phonetic **12.307**
 symbolic **12.305**
Medial interlaminar nucleus (MIN) **3.178**, **3.215**

in visual thalamus 3.183, 3.186–7, 3.192, 3.194, 3.198
Medial longitudinal fasciculus 8.184, 8.216–7
  rostral interstitial nucleus 8.200, 8.314
Medial rectus 8.175–6, 8.182
Medial superior temporal visual area 4.374, 4.412
Medial terminal nucleus 8.201
  Glossary explanation of 4.443
  see also Accessory optic system
Medial vestibular nucleus 8.153, 8.216, 8.302
Median interlaminar nucleus, Glossary explanation of
    4.447
Medicine, eighteenth-century literature 12.299
Medium-lead burst neurones 4.390–1, 8.206
Medulla 8.202, 8.248, 8.312
  arthropod 2.216–7, 2.219–20
  in eye evolution 2.347–8, 2.353–5, 2.357, 2.416
  optic lobe 2.204–6, 2.208–12, 2.222
Medullary reticular formation 4.390
Medusae 2.237–8
Megabats 2.451, 2.458
Megacolon 11.22–3
Melanin 3.85, 7.127–8, 16.42, 16.45–9
  and ageing retina 16.144
  and developing visual system 16.109
  and light interactions 16.39
  and phototoxicity 16.72
  and radiation 16.61
Melanogenesis 3.85
Melanoma
  choroidal 16.68, 16.72
  pigmented choroidal 16.72
Melatonin 2.33
Melton Mowbray Eye Study 16.137, 16.143
Membrane flow theory 11.175, 11.177
Membrane potential 12.466
Membrane proteins 11.175–7, 11.182, 11.279
Membrane of protrusions 11.175–6
Membranes
  Bowman's 2.470, 2.473
  dendritic 11.149
  Descemet's 2.470–1, 2.473–4
  neuronal 11.176
  nictitating 2.85, 2.470
  outer limiting 3.1–2, 3.9, 3.11–2, 3.16
  Verhoeff's 3.3
Memory
  and amygdala 11.374
  and computational vision 14.44–5
  contextual 12.270–1
  critical period plasticity 11.288
  face 12.184, 12.189, 12.219, 12.235–7, 12.268, 12.283–6
    famous 12.285
    ontogenetic development 12.238
    and prosopagnosia 12.269, 12.272
    unfamiliar 12.285
  for familiarity 12.270
  and gaze stability 8.76
  and intermodal interactions 11.381
  for localities 12.347

  long-term 11.291–2
    spatial 12.421
  multi-sensory 12.187
  and neocortex 11.373
  and neuronal cytoskeleton 11.279
  optic–agnosic disturbance 12.260
  for persons 12.268, 12.347
  and prosopagnosia 12.261
  and saccadic initiation 8.277
  semantic and episodic 12.269–71, 12.274
  short-term 10.280, 11.291, 12.235
    space-related 12.412
    visual 12.414, 12.462
  spatial 12.450
  topographical 12.436, 12.442–3
    loss of 12.271
  verbal 12.354
    and hemialexia 12.350
    impairment 12.339
  visual 12.179, 12.259
    and agnosia 12.181
    illusion and hallucination 12.470
    object 12.108
    processes 12.481
    short term 12.361
    TE neurone responses 12.116–7
  and visual processing 2.268
Memory areas, limbic 12.480
Memory centre of visual world 12.336
Memory centres 3.324–5
Memory decay 12.239
Memory deficit, topographical 12.428
Memory disturbance 12.180–1, 12.268–70
Memory fixation 11.291–2
Memory formation 11.281
Memory loss 12.200
  for persons, places, and images of word forms 12.179
Memory matching 6.50
Memory processes and pattern recognition 12.230
Memory recognition 14.110, 14.115, 14.121–2
Memory search processes 12.247
Memory-of-depth mechanisms 9.141
Mendelian genetics 7.88
Mendel's Laws 7.91
Meningioma 12.144
Meningoencephalitis 12.277, 12.300, 12.388
  cases of 12.477
Menstrual cycle 12.231–3
Mental fatigue 15.95
Mental rotation 14.56, 14.59, 14.66, 14.113
Mercury poisoning 12.199
Meridian, vertical, of V1 4.162
Meriones unguiculatus (gerbil) 2.74
Mescaline 12.471, 12.476–7
Mesencephalic reticular formation 4.390, 8.200–1, 8.208–9
Mesencephalon 8.200–1
Mesoderm 11.386, 11.392–3
Mesopic vision 5.49, 5.52
Mesopotamia 12.305–6

Messerschmidt, Franz Xaver **12**.290
Metabolism
  glucose **12**.266
  lipid **16**.142
  retinal **16**.151
Metacontrast masking **9**.96
  in specifically disabled readers and controls **13**.151
Metameric colours **6**.274
Metamerism **6**.16, **6**.55, **10**.121–2, **10**.127
Metamorphopsia **12**.198, **12**.260, **12**.274–5
  cerebral **12**.190
  facial **12**.274
  hemifacial **12**.275
  visual **12**.478
Metapigments **6**.267
Metarhodopsin II **6**.103, **6**.268
Metastasis, and pure alexia **12**.343
Metempsychosis **12**.25
Metre-angle **8**.160
Metric relations **14**.55, **14**.100
Metric space **14**.101
Metric tensor **8**.323
Mexican hat filters, in spatial-frequency
  measurement **13**.159, **13**.162
Meynert, Theodor **12**.50
Meynert cells **3**.255–7
Mice **15**.80, **15**.117–8
Michaelis–Menten equation **4**.29, **5**.59–60
Michaelis–Menten kinetics **12**.8
Michelson contrast **5**.106, **5**.109–10, **5**.180, **10**.19–20, **10**.290
Michelson–Morley contrast **5**.199
Microanatomy, autopsic **12**.344
Microbats **2**.451
Microcysts, and the wearing of contact lenses **1**.105
Microelectrode analysis **2**.385
Microelectrode recordings **12**.108
  multiple technique **12**.115
Microfilaments **11**.133, **11**.136–44
  in cell locomotion **11**.173–4, **11**.182
  in critical period plasticity **11**.289
  dendrite **11**.150
  development changes **11**.284–6
  in neuronal cytoskeleton **11**.276, **11**.278–9
Microglia **3**.90
  amoeboid **3**.85
  genesis of **3**.82, **3**.84–6
  in optic nerve regeneration **11**.211
  ramified **3**.85–6
  reactive **3**.86
Microinfarction **12**.265
Microkeratomes **1**.155
Microlens **2**.89
Microlesions **12**.198
Micropsia **12**.412, **12**.480–1
Microsaccades **8**.5, **8**.9, **8**.72, **8**.85, **13**.209, **13**.224
Microscopes **1**.384–5
  compound, and transverse magnification **1**.206
  numerical apertures of **1**.384
  operating **16**.65, **16**.97–8

scanning specular **1**.391
serial electron **3**.36
specular **1**.390–1
  Maurice's **1**.390–1
  Pocklington **1**.391
Microscopic lenses, *see* Plus-lens magnifiers, spectacle
  mounted
Microscopy
  confocal **11**.173
  electron **11**.175, **11**.223
  high voltage electron **11**.173
  interference reflection (IRM) **11**.172–4
  light **11**.278
  quick-freeze deep-etch electron **11**.279
  total internal reflection **11**.173
  ultrastructural **11**.278
  video enhanced **11**.175–7
Microspectrophotometry **2**.6, **4**.317, **5**.191–2, **7**.17, **7**.72–4,
  7.93
  and colour vision **2**.290–3, **2**.300, **2**.314, **2**.316
  and non-human primates **7**.200–3, **7**.206, **7**.209–10
  and photoreceptor system **2**.67, **2**.72, **2**.75–7
  and trichromacy **2**.310, **2**.312
Microspherometers **1**.427
  see also Sagometers
Microstimulation
  Glossary explanation of **4**.447
  intracortical **12**.169
Microtremor movements **13**.209
Microtubule organizing centres (MOCT) **11**.134
Microtubules **11**.133–7, **11**.139, **11**.143–4
  in cell locomotion **11**.175
  in critical period plasticity **11**.289–91
  dendrite **11**.133–6, **11**.148–52
  development changes **11**.282–3
  fast transport in **11**.190
  in neuronal cytoskeleton **11**.276–9, **11**.281, **11**.284–5,
    11.287, **11**.292, **11**.299
  polymerization **11**.134, **11**.201, **11**.281, **11**.288
  in regeneration **11**.190–2, **11**.194, **11**.196–7
  stability **11**.277
Microvilli
  in evolution of eye **2**.22, **2**.26–9, **2**.35, **2**.37, **2**.39–43
  photoreceptors **2**.365–8, **2**.370–3, **2**.376, **2**.378–80, **2**.383
Midbrain **2**.443, **8**.200–1, **8**.313–4
Midbrain parabrachial region **3**.194
Midbrain raphe region **3**.194
Middle and middle superior temporal cortex **8**.153, **8**.211,
  8.213, **8**.215, **8**.282–3
Middle temporal visual area **10**.172
  in galagos **4**.164
  Glossary explanation of **4**.447
  of the visual cortex **5**.135
Midget cell system **6**.141–3, **6**.170–4, **6**.181–2, **6**.187, **6**.190
Midline
  body **3**.326–8, **3**.330, **3**.340
  fusion principle **3**.325–6
  perceptual continuity across **3**.325, **3**.340, **3**.347, **3**.351
  of perceptual field **3**.326

Midline (*continued*)
  representations 3.330
  rule 3.340, 3.342, 3.347, 3.351
    vertical 3.342
Midline effect, selective 14.61
Midline vergence 8.158
Mid-match point 7.119
Midspectral, Glossary explanation of 4.447
Migraine attacks 12.176–8, 12.388, 12.475–6
Migraine fortification patterns 12.172–8
Migraine scintillations 12.172, 12.476
Migraine scotoma 5.254
Migraines 1.355
  and heautoscopy 12.301
  and hemiachromatopsia 12.401
  and movement of phosphene across visual field 12.177
  phosphenes 12.172–8, 12.393
    geometrical organization of area striata 12.178
    pathophysiology 12.176–8
    phenomenology 12.172–6
  and pure alexia 12.343
Migration, interkinetic 3.78–9, 3.82–3, 3.90
MII, *see* Metarhodopsin II
MIN, *see* Median interlaminar nucleus
Minimally distinct border technique 5.195, 5.197, 5.204,
    5.207, 6.211–2, 10.141
Minnow 2.285
Miosis
  accommodative 2.108
  senile 5.277–8, 5.280, 16.76, 16.155
MIRAGE model 10.97–8, 10.102
Miró, Joan 12.221
Mirror image
  man's 12.297, 12.302
  of words 12.326
Mirrors 2.128–31
  biological 2.126–7
  concave 2.123–6
  and eye optics 2.119
  and face recognition 12.239
  interference 2.127
  lens 2.417
  reflecting 2.118
Misadaptation to environment 14.89
Misalignment 2.279, 2.313, 2.317
Mislocalizations, spatial 10.227
Mislocation 12.412
Misrecognition 12.191
'Missing-the-head' neurones 9.150
Mistargeting 3.138
Mitochondria 3.12
Mitosis, reduction of, and the wearing of contact lenses 1.105
Mnemonics, devices 12.306
'Modality window' 5.46
Modelling, abnormal position acuity 10.232–5
Models
  adaptation, excitation-produces-fatigue 10.147–8
  adaptive gain control 5.59
  area-code 11.82
  autoassociative network 14.123

autocorrelation visual processing 2.251–3
balloon, of retinal expansion 3.107–10
Bayesian, for ideal observers 14.83
Bohr atomic 16.30
boundary contour system 5.237
Buckley and Gillman numerosity 14.133–4
Burgess and Barlow numerosity 14.134
Caelli's 5.121, 10.123, 10.129–32
canonical, of cortical microcircuitry 3.350
categorization 14.107, 14.118
cell locomotion 11.182
cell state 11.56–8
central signal-detection 5.27
cerebral space representation 12.103–6
chromatic flicker 5.188
classification of concept exemplars 14.118
compression 5.70–1
computational 14.27, 14.87, 14.107
  of motion detection 5.164–8
  of motion perception 5.160
  in texture perception 10.130
concept learning 14.118–23
cone opponency 5.195
connectivity graph 3.344
'conservative', of axonal growth 11.191
contrast constancy 5.116–7
contrast encoding 5.107–9, 5.116–7
contrast sensitivity impairment 5.59
correlation, of motion detection 5.165
cortical Gabor-like receptive fields 5.60
de Lange electrical analogue flicker 5.187
depth discrimination 5.137–40
difference-of-Gaussian (DOG) 5.121
discrimination 5.116
disparity discrimination 5.140, 5.143
disparity tuning curves 5.139–40
dynamic, of motion perception 5.158
effects of eccentricity 5.136
energy visual processing 2.252
exemplar-based, of face recognition 14.115, 14.119–21
of the eye 5.84
face recognition geometric 14.43
of flicker 5.185–8
of frames and buffers 5.158
functional
  development of ocular dominance columns in
    cats 11.287
  of ipsilateral visual projection in *Xenopus* 11.287
  refinement of regenerated visual projection in
    fish 11.287
Gabor-filter 5.121–3
gain control 5.112
gene activation 11.55
genetic 7.93–5, 7.108
global spectral sensitivity 5.199
growth cone guidance 11.181
growth cone orientation 11.62–4
Hallett's spatial 5.60
Harris ratio, of motion detection 5.165, 5.167–9
hierarchical, of agnosia 12.187

Models (*continued*)
Hinton's stereoacuity **5**.144
Hoffman's LTG/NP transformation **14**.20–3, **14**.25–8
human motion perception mechanisms **14**.41
ideal detector **10**.110
ideal observer **10**.79
identification **14**.107
impulse-response **5**.115
induction **11**.61
information processing, of face recognition **14**.119, **14**.122
inhibition growth **5**.71
of Ives ionic flicker diffusion **5**.186–7
Julesz dipole **5**.134
Julesz texture **5**.121–2
Kelly and van Norren's two-band **5**.176, **5**.178, **5**.186, **5**.188
Kelly's single channel flicker **5**.187
Le Grand eye **5**.83
linear neural network **14**.92–3
line-element **10**.68–9, **10**.72–4, **10**.93
line-element colour discrimination **5**.138–9
localization mechanisms **14**.15–7
loss **7**.101
Lotmar eye **5**.83
luminance adaptation **5**.147–9
Marr and Poggio **5**.134
Marr and Poggio disparity **5**.144–5
Marr and Ullman gradient, of motion detection **5**.164–5, **5**.168
Martinez–Uriegas chromatic flicker **5**.188
matching to **14**.6–7
mathematical
    of luminance adaptation (LA) **5**.112
    of ocular dominance column formation **11**.347
    of systems **10**.2, **10**.4, **10**.9
    thermal retinal injury **16**.47–8
mechano-pneumatic, of vision **12**.39
MIRAGE **10**.97–8, **10**.102
morphogenetic subfields **11**.60
multiplexed spectral sensitivity **5**.199
multiplicative, of luminance adaptation (LA) **5**.112
neural, of visual function **14**.30
neurolinguistic, of pure alexia **12**.338–9
neuronal recognition system **11**.83
neurone **14**.40, **14**.81
norm-based coding, of face recognition **14**.114–21, **14**.123
normalization **5**.109, **5**.117
numerosity **14**.133–6
object recognition **12**.213–4, **14**.118
opponent process **10**.81
parallel-distributed processing (PDP), of face recognition **14**.119, **14**.123
parametrized **14**.39
pattern formation **11**.47–8, **11**.50–1, **11**.54
peripheral vision **5**.251–2
    comprehensive **5**.254
    consensus **5**.254
    dichotomous **5**.259–60
    hierarchical **5**.259–60
        integrated **5**.261
        multichannel **5**.258–60
        quantitative **5**.261–2
        single channel **5**.257
peripheral visual pathways **5**.44–8
polar co-ordinate **11**.61
position judgments **14**.12
of possible neural substrates **5**.260
primate, of visual cognition **12**.15–7
probabilistic discrimination **5**.139, **5**.143
probability summation **5**.101–2
psychological, of visual function **14**.30
psychophysical, of hyperacuity **5**.224
psychophysical functions **7**.73
reading processing **12**.338
recognition of concept exemplars **14**.118
regularization **14**.93
Reichardt's correlation
    of direction selectivity **5**.156
    of motion detection **2**.240, **5**.164
relative position encoding **14**.16
replacement **7**.93–4, **7**.101
of retinal receptors **5**.87
'sandwich' **10**.9
see also under Computer-aided work
segmentation **11**.57–9
shape-based object recognition **14**.112
Shapley and Victor displacement hyperacuity **5**.137
$\Sigma\pi$, neurone **14**.81
signal detection **5**.16–21
signal/noise **5**.60, **5**.62–3
sinusoidal modulation detection **5**.28
spatial frequency channel localization **14**.16
spatial sampling by cone mosaic **3**.27
spectral sensitivity **5**.194
stereoacuity **5**.133–45
stereopsis **5**.145
subtractive, of luminance adaptation (LA) **5**.112
surface reflectance **14**.36
template visual processing **2**.243–51, **2**.266–7
theoretical
    of agnosia **12**.188
    of neural networks **14**.93
three-dimensional (3D), of objects **14**.30–1
three-dimensional (3D) object-centred **14**.45, **14**.112–3
TLU, neurone **14**.81
Vaitkevicius distributed representation **5**.134
Van Oeffelen and Vos numerosity **14**.134
van Santen and Sperling motion detection **5**.164
viewprint **10**.110
visual pattern recognition **5**.253
a visual processing stage **5**.24
visual recognition **14**.92, **14**.107
Voorhees and Poggio's texture **5**.121
Walraven flicker **5**.177–8
Watson's flicker **5**.188
wire world **14**.96
Zipser–Anderson **12**.105–6
zone **7**.8

Modification time **8**.128
Modular organization of superior colliculus **8**.247
Modulation **2**.235–7
  amplitude **10**.17
  detection **5**.10–2
  fourth power of the depth of **5**.23
  frequency **5**.11, **10**.17
  illuminance **5**.85
  sensitivity **5**.175
  signal **5**.70–1
  sinusoidal
    and compound gratings **5**.100
    of luminance **5**.31, **5**.33, **5**.35
    sensitivity to **5**.23, **5**.25
    and visual channels **5**.99
    in visual processing **5**.23–4, **5**.28
  temporal **5**.171
  threshold **5**.13
Modulation sensitivity function **5**.288–9
Modulation transfer function (MTF) **1**.10–2, **1**.19, **2**.92–3,
    2.99–100, **2**.102, **2**.104, **2**.106, **3**.5–6, **3**.16, **3**.27, **5**.65,
    5.85–6, **5**.88–91, **5**.124, **5**.172, **5**.199, **5**.288–9, **9**.140,
    10.23, **10**.96
  determination of **1**.323
  of dioptric apparatus **12**.53
  of human eye **12**.52, **12**.54
  see also System transfer function
Modulation transfer function (MTF) area **15**.59
Modules
  band-like **3**.317
  cortical **10**.225–7
  Glossary explanation of **4**.447
  processing **3**.317
  in visual cortex **3**.303, **3**.305, **3**.308, **3**.318–9
Moiré fringes, in keratometers **1**.380
Moiré interference techniques **5**.252
Moiré patterns **3**.19–20
Molecular genetics **2**.311, **2**.313
Molecular markers **2**.220
Molecules
  ageing **16**.78–9
  specific cell-surface **11**.347
Molluscs
  bivalve **2**.123, **2**.125
  classification **2**.364–5
  optics **2**.122
  photoreception **2**.364–91
Molyneux, William **12**.17
Molyneux's question **12**.17–8
Monads **2**.358
Mondino de Luzzi **12**.31–2, **12**.34
Mondrian patterns **12**.85, **12**.393
Monism **12**.23
Monitoring messages **15**.120
Monitoring tasks **15**.83–98
Monkey
  area 7 lesions **12**.95
  binocularly deprived **12**.21
  and face recognition **12**.220

perceptive visual systems **12**.346
Rhesus macaque **12**.95–7, **12**.102–4
  face expression **12**.119
  face-responsive neuronal activity **12**.117
  neurones **12**.121–2
  and visual object recognition **12**.115
squirrel
  and face recognition **12**.239
  face-responsive neuronal activity **12**.117
visual discrimination task **12**.108
see also under Monkeys, and specific names
Monkeys
  alert-behaving **9**.226
  awake-behaving, microelectrode recordings from single
      neurons in **4**.388
  binocular vision **2**.276–7
  cebus **2**.173
  colour vision **2**.287–8
  common marmoset (*Callithrix jacchus jacchus*) **5**.191
  galago **3**.328
    callosal pathways **3**.334–5, **3**.349
  macaque **2**.76, **2**.168, **2**.173, **2**.458, **3**.6, **5**.252–6, **5**.259–60,
      5.262
    callosal pathways **3**.325–9, **3**.331–2, **3**.336–7, **3**.342–3,
        3.345, **3**.347, **3**.349
    and developing visual system **16**.108–13, **16**.116,
        16.119–20, **16**.125–6, **16**.128
    foveal sampling in **3**.17
    interplexiform cells **3**.47
    photoreceptors **3**.14–5
    visual cortex neurogenesis **3**.360–1, **3**.363–6, **3**.368,
        3.370
  New World **3**.194
    callosal pathways **3**.328, **3**.331–2
    colour vision **2**.288, **2**.293, **2**.295–6, **2**.314–7
    interplexiform cells **3**.47
    LGNd **3**.179
    photoreceptor system **2**.76
    somatosensory cortex **3**.328
    visual cortex **3**.303, **3**.311–2, **3**.314, **3**.316, **3**.318
    visual pathways **2**.453, **2**.458
  Old World **3**.2, **5**.179–80, **5**.207, **5**.210
    callosal pathways **3**.328, **3**.331–2, **3**.335, **3**.349
    colour vision **2**.288, **2**.293, **2**.295–6, **2**.310, **2**.314,
        2.316–7
    LGNd **3**.178–81
    photoreceptor system **2**.73, **2**.76–8
    relay neurones **3**.192
    somatosensory cortex **3**.328
    visual cortex **3**.303, **3**.312, **3**.314–6
    visual pathways **2**.453, **2**.458
    visual thalamus **3**.193–4, **3**.197, **3**.204–5
  owl **2**.169, **5**.260
    callosal pathways **3**.328, **3**.331, **3**.334
    motor cortex **3**.331
    photoreceptors **3**.15–6
    somatosensory cortex **3**.328
    visual areas **3**.311–3
    visual cortex **3**.303, **3**.314

visual pathways 2.443, 2.451, 2.458
pigtail macaques, use of, in refraction development
    experiments 1.34–8
rhesus 2.173
squirrel (*S. sciureus*) 2.173, 2.293, 2.443, 3.314, 5.191
    visual pathways of 2.456–7
Monoamines 3.295
    antisera specific to 3.284
Monochromacy 7.24–8
    atypical 7.21–2, 7.24, 7.26
    blue-cone 7.98, 7.111
    blue-monocone 7.99–100
    classification 7.24
    congenital 12.390
    incomplete 7.26
    rod-'blue-cone' 7.26–7
    rod-'green-cone' 7.27–8
    rod-'red-cone' 7.28
    see also Achromatopsia
    typical 7.24–6
    unilateral 7.24
Monochromatic vision 6.24–7
    achromaticity of 6.25
    and the principle of univariance 6.24–5
    and the scotopic system 6.24
Monochromatism, *see* Monochromacy, typical
Monochromats 2.290, 2.300
    in achromatopsia tests 7.229–30
    blue-cone 7.26, 7.101, 7.110
    and F-M 100-Hue test 7.224
    and pseudoisochromatic tests 7.220
    rod 7.25–6, 7.31, 7.100–1
Monocular crescent 4.270
Monocular deprivation
    direction and velocity sensitivity in 4.125–6
    ocular dominance changes in 4.123–5
    studies of the effects of, in the abnormal accessory optic
        system 4.123–6
Monocular diplopia, *see* Diplopia
Monocular occlusion, in the treatment of binocular
    instability 13.144, 13.183
'Monocular takeover' 11.258–60
Monocular vision 2.276
    panoramic 2.271
Monocular visual direction, laws of 9.6
Monotremes 2.442, 2.444, 2.467–72
Mood, changes in, affect on accommodation 1.249
Moon alphabet 1.185
Moreland anomaloscope 7.121
Moreland equation (match) 7.98, 7.120, 7.220
    early detection of diabetic impairment 7.149
    early isolated widening 7.158
    in impaired optic-nerve conduction 7.160
    large-field 7.96
    in ophthalmic disease 7.123, 7.144–5, 7.150–1, 7.156,
        7.163
    small-field 7.96
Morgagni, Giovanni Battista 12.136
Morphogenetic fields 11.47–66

bipolar 11.52–3
Morphogenetic rule 11.90
Morphogenetic subfields, organizing regions for 11.60–1
Morphology
    axonal 11.90, 11.92
    of pursuit system 2.169–70, 2.174–5, 2.178–82, 2.184,
        2.187
Mosaicism 7.21, 7.29
Mosaics
    amacrine cell 3.44
    blue cone 3.22
    cone 3.27
    extrafoveal 3.23–4
    foveal cone 3.16–20, 3.22, 3.24
    horizontal cell 3.39–40
    photoreceptor 3.24
        in vertebrate retina 6.128–43
    of photoreceptor arrays 3.4
Mossy fibres 8.153, 8.224–5, 8.230
Motion 5.120
    apparent 5.152–3, 5.157–8, 5.274, 5.298, 10.270, 10.272
    apparent (ϕ-phenomenon) 12.85, 12.184, 12.195, 12.204,
        12.360–71
        and visual movement agnosia 12.377, 12.380
        visual object 12.379
    biological 12.204
    blindness, *see* Agnosia, visual movement
    'capture' 5.165–6
    coherent 12.12, 12.89–91, 12.204
        of random dots 12.379, 12.381–2
    colour blind 2.258–9
    compressive/expanding 10.172
    in computational vision 14.31, 14.33–5, 14.39, 14.41
    in depth 5.240
    detection of 2.212, 5.162, 5.166, 10.53
        see also Models
    in visual processing 2.237, 2.239, 2.241, 2.243, 2.252
    directional 2.210, 2.212–3, 2.458, 5.97, 5.161, 5.169, 5.240,
        5.267
    displacement-sensitive mechanism of 5.162
    and equiluminance 5.236, 5.239–40, 5.244–5, 5.247
    and flicker perception 5.150
    and illusions 5.244
    image 10.95–6
    incoherent 12.89
    lower threshold of (LTM) 5.161–3, 5.168
    measurement of visual 14.40–1
    non-Fourier 5.169
    null 5.240
    object 5.160
    parallax 10.135, 10.163–5, 12.12, 12.73, 12.91, 12.362
        and visual fields 12.143–4
        and visual hemineglect 12.431, 12.433
        and visual movement agnosia 12.360, 12.374, 12.378–80
        and visuo-spatial disorders 12.441
    real 5.157, 5.298–9
    referenced (relative) 5.258–9
    relative 2.161
    retinal image 5.67, 5.125–7

Motion (*continued*)
  sampled 5.152–3, 5.157
  self- 5.160
  shape from 12.381
  shearing 12.381
  shearing (S) 10.172
  smear 5.153, 5.157
  smear-free 5.157
  smooth 5.161
  'stopped' 5.163
  temporal frequency-constant mechanism 5.162
  unreferenced 5.258–9
  upper threshold of coherent (UTMc) 5.161–3, 5.167–8
  upper threshold UTMf and UTMp 5.161–3, 5.168
  velocity-constant mechanism 5.162
  velocity-sensitive mechanism 5.162
Motion acuity 5.221–2, 5.225–6, 5.229–30
Motion after-effect 5.162, 5.165, 5.239, 9.182
Motion in depth 8.165
Motion detection 7.178–9
Motion detectors 5.155–6
  insect 2.240
Motion mechanisms, in flicker detection 5.150
Motion parallax 2.160–1, 2.274, 2.281, 9.137, 9.166, 9.183,
    14.4–5, 14.89
  and absolute depth 9.140–1
  and absolute distance 9.140–1
  and relative depth 9.138–40
Motion perception 5.121, 5.151–2, 5.162–3, 5.169, 5.257,
    8.149–52, 8.211, 8.307, 10.53–4, 12.144
  and agnosia 12.204
  disorders of 13.27
  of in-depth 12.142
  mechanisms of 5.153–8
  neuronal networks 12.85–91
Motion processing, higher order 4.210–1
Motion sensitivity 2.160–1, 5.147, 5.149–58, 10.100, 12.70
  disparity coding of 9.144
Motion suppression, binocular 5.240
Motion theories 5.153
Motion thresholds 5.161–3, 5.240
Motion-in-depth 4.376, 4.379, 9.132, 9.137–69, 9.204–7,
    9.233–5
  and changing size 9.151–2
  discrimination between different directions of 9.148–50
  induced 9.133
  separate systems for 9.150
Motion-in-depth after-effects
  asymmetric 9.152
  and changing-size after-effects 9.153
Motion-in-depth channels 9.147
ϕ-Motion 10.269
Motor adaptation, prism adaptation test 9.195–6
Motor area, supplementary 3.331
Motor error 8.97, 8.209, 8.211, 8.251, 8.262, 8.267, 8.326
  Glossary explanation of 4.447
Motor error signalling, in the superior colliculus 4.401
Motor learning, cerebellar 8.327
Motor localization, visual direction sense in 13.35–6

Motor neurones 8.175–99, 8.202–5
  behaviour during saccades 8.205
  hysteresis 8.203
  position and velocity sensitivity 8.203
Motor outflow 9.183
Motor planning 13.32
Mouse
  homeoboxes 11.6–23
  Hox genes 11.40
  reeler 3.363, 11.35, 11.347, 11.349–50
    callosal afferents in 11.349–50
    thalamocortical axons 11.350
  transgenic 11.22–3, 11.123
  visual cortex 3.303–5, 3.308, 3.319
Mouse dioptrics 2.91, 2.95
Moutaineers, heautoscopy in 12.300–1
Movement
  goal-directed 12.416, 12.463
  handmotor 12.107
  locomotor 12.107
  photomechanical 3.9
  ritualized body 12.307
  self- 12.360, 12.362, 12.433
  visual
    after-effect of real 12.366
    after-effects 12.375, 12.396
    back-and-forth 12.360
    in depth 12.381
    detection 12.359, 12.367, 12.378
      and agnosia 12.360
      function, dissociated recovery 12.402
      task 12.374–5
    direction 12.88, 12.359–60, 12.375
    efferent 12.363
    global 12.85, 12.91, 12.359–61, 12.380–4
    illusion of 12.433
    induced 12.362
    local 12.85, 12.90–1, 12.359–61, 12.381–4
    movie test 12.382
    of object against stationary background 12.361
    parallax, *see* Motion, parallax
    perception 12.184, 12.359, 12.374–8
      3-D 12.381
      afferent 12.360–1, 12.371, 12.375
      and agnosia 12.191
      in depth 12.375
      efferent 12.360–1, 12.364, 12.371
      and form perception
        dissociation in recovery 12.379
        double dissociation in recovery 12.380
      four stages of 12.360
      impairment of 12.381
      impairment of: case report, Mrs L.M. 12.372–82
      recovered before shape perception 12.379
      and topographagnosia 12.418
      types of 12.359–62
      visual 12.437
    ϕ- 12.89–90, 12.144, 12.361–2, 12.366–8, 12.377,
      12.380–1

and prosopagnosia 12.270
  rotatory 12.360
  see also Motion
  selectivity 12.85–6, 12.88, 12.90
  sensitivity 12.85, 12.87, 12.89–90
  shape detection by 12.360
  sigma- 12.364, 12.366–7, 12.370–1, 12.377
  signal transfer of 12.54–5, 12.59, 12.61–3
  signals, afferent 12.380
  and space perception dissociation 12.379
  spiral 12.360
  thresholds 12.152
  and visual hemineglect 12.431–2
  as a visual cue 5.286
  visuo-motor 12.107
Movement cells, frontal eye fields 8.288
Movement detection
  Glossary explanation of 4.447
  by neural interactions at the vertebrate retina 4.1–9
Movement detection subunit 4.1–2
  Glossary explanation of 4.447
Movement field 8.209
  Glossary explanation of 4.447
Movement parallax, Glossary explanation of 4.447
Movie test 12.263, 12.284–5
  and schizophrenia 12.291–5
  and visual movement agnosia 12.382
MPTP-treated monkeys 10.250–7
MRI, *see* Magnetic resonance imaging
mRNA (messenger RNA) 7.102
MS, *see* Multiple sclerosis
M-scaling 12.66–7
MSP, *see* Microspectrophotometry
M-streams, Glossary explanation of 4.452
MT, *see* Middle temporal visual area
MTF, *see* Modulation transfer function; *see* Transfer
  function, modulation
MTFA, *see* Modulation transfer function area
MTN, *see* Medial terminal nucleus
Mueller matrix 1.311
Mueller matrix ellipsometry 1.316
Mueller–Lyer illusion 12.184, 12.191
Müller
  August, and the development of the first powered contact
    lens 1.83
  Johannes 12.155
Müller fibres 11.388, 11.392
Müller–Lyer illusions 5.242, 10.106
Multi-linear pattern decomposition and 'counting'
  (MDC) 14.75, 14.78–81
Multi-page text 15.74–5
  electronic 15.75
  printed 15.74
Multiple innervation, of extraocular muscle fibres 8.180–1,
  8.321
Multiple linear regression analysis 1.134
Multiple sclerosis 5.172, 5.208, 7.173, 7.176, 10.54–8,
  10.239–47, 12.199, 12.343
  abnormal eye movements in 13.263

colour disorders in 7.177–83
  contrast threshold abnormalities 10.239–45
Multiplexing, of colour and luminance signals 6.206
Multipoles 10.22
Multi-source tasks 15.84
Multi-unit receptive field (MURF) 11.269–70
Munch, Edvard 12.228
Munk, Hermann 12.47–8, 12.108, 12.147–9, 12.179
Munsell achromatic (grey) series 12.203
Munsell Book of Color 6.232–3
Munsell colour solid 5.202–3
Munsell Colour System 4.333–4, 6.46–7, 6.231–3, 6.246–54
Munsterberg illusions 5.242
Muscimol 8.255
Muscles
  ciliary 2.469, 2.471, 2.475
  extra-ocular 2.188–9, 2.470
  face 12.218, 12.220, 12.226
  vibration, neck 12.432–3, 12.464
Music 12.268
  sense of 12.335
Music behaviour, human 12.288
Music notes 12.307
Music scores 12.336
Mutations
  dorsal 11.121–2
  homeotic 11.3
  proto-oncogenes 11.116–9, 11.123
MW cones
  in acquired colour deficiency 7.38–40
  in colour perimetry 7.49
  and threshold methods 7.45–6
MWS cone opsin 7.106–11
MWS cones
  in ophthalmic disease 7.135
  in retinitis pigmentosa 7.144
MWS loss in glaucoma 7.152
MWS-pigment (MP) gene 7.106–11
  variable copy number 7.108
Myasthenia gravis 8.310
  accommodation anomalies in 1.271
Myelin, in visual cortex 3.308, 3.317–8
Myelin associated glycoproteins (MAG) 11.71–2
Myelination 3.311, 3.313, 3.315, 10.183, 11.199
Myelinization
  axonal, during postnatal brain development 12.288
  and axotomy 12.132
  degrees of, in white matter 12.127
Myeloarchitectonics 12.50
Myocloni, intermittent 12.201
Myoid 3.9–10, 3.12
Myopia 1.53, 2.84, 2.98, 2.110–1
  and ageing retina 16.143
  correction of
    by orthokeratology 1.115
    by post-radial keratotomy 1.115
  explanation of 1.400
  following surgery 1.50–1
  functional 1.270

N

N point system, in prescribing magnification for near viewing 1.217
Nagel, in optic-nerve disease 7.174, 7.179, 7.191–2
Nagel anomaloscope, *see* Anomaloscope
Naka–Rushton equation 10.296
Naming
  isolated defects 12.340
  visual 12.345
Naphthalocyanines 16.72
Narcolepsia 12.299, 12.481
Nasal hemiretinal suppession 9.199
Nasotemporal division 3.110–3, 3.117
National Health and Nutrition Examination Survey (NHANES-I) 16.46, 16.137–44
Natural colour system 6.233–5, 6.246–54
  basic concepts of 6.234
  elementary (unique) colours and elementary (unique) visual attributes of 6.234
  numerical notations of hue, blackness and chromaticness 6.234–5
Natural eye movements 8.80, 8.84, 8.87
Natural selection 2.356, 2.359
Natural vision copying 2.268
Nautilus 2.3–4, 2.54, 2.122, 2.374–5
Navigation 12.416
NBT-diformazan reaction 7.74, 7.80–1
N-cadherin in optic nerve regeneration 11.212
NCS, *see* Natural colour system
Neale's Analysis of Reading Ability Test 13.175–7, 13.197–8
Near centration distance 1.199
Near neurones 9.187, 9.227
Near triad 2.107
Near vision, triad of 13.216–7
Nearest neighbour 3.11
Nearest neighbour analysis 3.39, 3.58
Nearwork symptomatology 1.239
Neck, muscle vibration of 12.432–3, 12.464
Necker cube 5.240
Necropsy 12.264–6
Necrosis, cortical laminar 12.207
Negaprion brevirostris (lemon shark) 2.67
Negation, class concept of 12.331
Negative contrast 5.304
Negative feedback
  optokinesis 8.48–9, 8.235
  saccades 8.96
  smooth pursuit 8.138–9, 8.211, 8.214, 8.309
Neglect
  auditory left-sided spatial 12.442–3
  Glossary explanation of 4.447–8
  hemispatial visual, *see* Hemineglect
  spatial 12.418, 12.425
    auditory 12.438–9
    history of 12.434–8
    unilateral 12.448, 12.463
  unilateral 12.437, 12.450
  visual 12.339, 12.430

Neighbour and numerosity 14.139
Neitz anomaloscope 7.121, 7.216, 7.219
Nemertines 2.15, 2.17–8, 2.21, 2.25, 2.40–2
  and evolution of eye 2.34–5, 2.37
  and origin of lens 2.45–6, 2.48
  and vertebrates 2.29–32
Nemesios of Emesa 12.28
Neocortex 3.215, 3.328, 11.369, 11.381
  and callosal pathways 3.332, 3.339
  and cross-modal connections 11.380
  hamster, and axon growth 11.249
  layer IV cells 11.235
  learning and 11.371
  monkey 11.371–3
  and neurogenesis 3.363
  reading and script 12.304
  in visual cortex 3.302–5, 3.311, 3.314, 3.316, 3.319
  and visual pathways 2.424, 2.426, 2.430, 2.432, 2.435–6, 2.443, 2.445, 2.452–3, 2.457–9
Neographemes 12.340
Neologism 12.313
Neon 16.12
Neonates, and face recognition 12.237
Neoteny 2.222–3
Nerve growth factor (NGF) 11.73, 11.138, 11.181, 11.210–1, 11.227, 11.249
  in neuronal cytoskeleton 11.198, 11.293, 11.297–8
Nerve growth regulation 11.292–8
Nerve terminals, Glossary explanation of 4.451
Networks
  autoassociative 14.123
  classification 14.70, 14.72
  electrical 3.39
  horizontal cell 3.40
  linear classifier 14.76, 14.78–9
  neural 14.81, 14.83, 14.92–6, 14.101
  neuronal, face-specific 12.467
  $\Sigma\pi$ 14.78
Neural 'bottle-neck' 5.45, 5.72
Neural circuitry
  demultiplexing 6.181–4, 6.206–10
  insects 6.276–9
  retina 6.128–43, 6.163–77
  selectivity for colour 6.191–3
  visual cortex 6.180–5
Neural coding, of stereoscopic information 9.227–35
Neural integrators 8.97, 8.153, 8.160, 8.208, 8.217, 8.302, 8.324–5
Neural interactions, detection of movement by, at the vertebrate retina 4.1–9
Neural networks 2.167, 2.183, 2.189–91
  models of 9.85
Neural parallel capacitance 5.25
Neural processes, random arrangement of 5.24
Neural remapping 9.129
Neural responses, to random-dot stereograms 9.230–2
Neural substrates of peripheral vision 5.251–63
Neural subunits 4.6–8
  components of change-detecting circuitry of 4.6

components of change-sensitive subunits of **4.**6–8
implementing movement-gated functions with change-sensitive subunits **4.**7–8
incorporation of on–off signals into change-sensitive circuits of **4.**7
Neural tube **2.**45
  in eye evolution **2.**15–8, **2.**24, **2.**31, **2.**35, **2.**37–8, **2.**42, **2.**46
Neurites
  in cell locomotion **11.**171, **11.**173–82
  growth in neuronal cytoskeleton **11.**297–8
  in neuronal cytoskeleton **11.**278, **11.**285
  outgrowths **11.**207, **11.**275, **11.**280, **11.**287
    in axon growth **11.**249
    in neuronal cytoskeleton **11.**297
    in optic nerve regeneration **11.**212–3
  shaft **11.**173, **11.**177
  sprouting **11.**280, **11.**287, **11.**292
Neuritis
  optic **12.**162
  see also Optic neuritis
Neuroanatomy, progress in **12.**40–2
Neurobiology **2.**137, **11.**88
  comparative **2.**421, **2.**435
Neuroblasts **2.**354, **2.**403
Neurochemistry, of neurotransmitters **11.**353
Neurofibrillary tangles **11.**288
Neurofilaments **11.**133, **11.**136–7, **11.**139
  in critical period plasticity **11.**289–91
  dendrite **11.**144, **11.**148–9, **11.**152
  in neuronal cytoskeleton **11.**276–8, **11.**284–7, **11.**292
  in regeneration **11.**191–3, **11.**195, **11.**197, **11.**201
  subunits **11.**143–4
Neurogenesis
  and axon growth **11.**245
  dendrite **11.**160, **11.**163
  and neurotransmitters **11.**357–60
  of SRIF neurones **11.**359
  and TOP molecules **11.**75
  vertebrate **11.**28–43
Neurogliaform cells, *see* Clewed cells
Neuroimaging **12.**207
  and loss of topographical familiarity **12.**424–7
  and prosopagnosia **12.**266–7
  and pure alexia **12.**342–6
  see also Computer tomography (CT); Magnetic resonance imaging (MRI)
  techniques **12.**425, **12.**427
Neurolinguistics **12.**338–9
  experimental approach **12.**338
Neurological disease, *see* Disease, neurological
Neurology, behavioural **12.**212, **12.**261, **12.**336
Neuromeres **11.**39, **11.**41
Neuromodulin **11.**192
  'goldfish' **11.**194–6, **11.**198–9
  in regeneration **11.**200–1
Neuromuscular spindles **8.**188, **8.**321
Neuronal coding, of spatial positions **12.**464
Neuronal networks **8.**208, **8.**322, **8.**324

Neurone models **14.**40
Neurones
  antiphase conditionally direction selective **4.**208–10
  area 7 **12.**96, **12.**100–1, **12.**103
    bimodal responses **12.**101–3
    vestibular responses **12.**97–9
  area 7a **12.**97, **12.**99–102, **12.**104–6
    movement and direction-sensitive **12.**101
  area 17 of cat and monkey **5.**165
  area PG, visual properties of **4.**378
  associational–commissural **3.**338
  'attentional' **12.**96
  axotomized **11.**235
  back-propagating programmed network **12.**105
  basket cell, Glossary explanation of **4.**448
  binocular **2.**175, **2.**273–5, **2.**278–80, **2.**454, **3.**214, **3.**216
    disparity-selective **2.**276
    disparity-sensitive **2.**277
  bipolar **3.**190
  bipolar cell, Glossary explanation of **4.**448
  in blobs **3.**317
  burst **2.**185–6, **8.**97, **8.**206, **8.**208–11, **8.**256–63, **8.**325–6
    in superior colliculus **8.**249–54, **8.**257–65
  burst–tonic **2.**184, **2.**186–7, **8.**217
  Cajal–Retzius cell, Glossary explanation of **4.**448
  in cell locomotion **11.**173–4, **11.**176–8, **11.**180–2
  and cell recognition **11.**82–4
  and cellular organization **11.**68–9, **11.**71–4
  Chandeliere cell, Glossary explanation of **4.**448
  class 1 **3.**187–8
  class 2 **3.**187–8, **3.**190
  class 3 **3.**187
  class 4 **3.**187–9
  class A **3.**189–90
  class B **3.**190
  class V **3.**187–8
  clutch cell, Glossary explanation of **4.**448
  CNS **11.**228
  colour-opponent **2.**298, **2.**301
  and compartments **11.**42, **11.**133, **11.**144
  cortical **3.**341, **3.**362–3, **3.**366–7, **3.**369–70, **9.**227
    binocularly-activated **11.**257–8
    responses of, to static disparity and stereomotion **9.**150–1
    sensitive to changing size **9.**160–1
  cortical cell, Glossary explanation of **4.**448
  cortico-limbic circuits **12.**287
  cortico-thalamic circuits **12.**287
  in critical period plasticity **11.**289
  DCMD **2.**242–3
  death of **3.**85, **3.**94–8, **3.**116, **11.**212, **11.**358, **11.**360–1, **11.**363–4
  degeneration of **11.**212
  dendritic spread **3.**343
  directional **2.**241
  disparity-selective **9.**224
  doctrine **11.**306–7
  dorsal root ganglion **4.**4
  double bouquet cell, Glossary explanation of **4.**448

double-labelled 3.344, 3.346
DP area 12.103
excitatory burst 8.248, 8.256, 8.258–63
in extrastriate cortex 3.308
eye-position related 8.207–9
eye-velocity 2.185
face-responsive 12.118, 12.120–1
    activity 12.117–22
face-sensitive 5.268, 10.263
far 9.187, 9.227
fixation 8.285, 12.99–100, 13.17
    command function related to extrapersonal space 12.99
floccular target 8.232
function in primate visual system 5.262
fusiform cell, Glossary explanation of 4.448
GABA-immunoreactive 3.192
GABAergic intrinsic 4.237–8
and GAP-43 11.225, 11.227
gaze 12.105
    control 12.98–100
    motor 12.96
    movement 12.96–7
gaze-velocity 8.217, 8.230, 8.322, 8.328
geniculate 3.347
grating 2.241
in hyperacuity 5.224
immediate-phase 2.185
impulse rate 12.114
infragranular 11.36
inhibitory 3.195, 3.201
inhibitory burst 8.248, 8.258
internuclear 8.184, 8.205, 8.216, 8.219
intrinsic 11.353, 11.356
    of visual cortex 11.357–64
IT 12.111, 12.118
    contribution to object recognition 12.115
    responses 12.115–7
L- 8.247, 8.251, 8.254, 8.265
lagged 3.187, 3.189
layer V 11.235, 11.240
LGN 4.41–84, 4.226
LGNd 3.215–7
LGNv 3.202–3, 3.217
light-sensitive 2.178, 2.364, 2.366–7, 13.16–7
    and changes of sensitivity with changes in eye
        position 13.17
line-labelled 2.251
LIP area 12.103–4
locomotion 11.171
long-lead burst 4.391, 8.206, 8.208–10, 8.258–60, 8.262–3
long-lead movement 8.249, 8.252
of lower vertebrates 11.206
magnocellular 2.171, 5.259
magnocellular relay 5.48
medium-lead burst 4.390–1, 8.206
mid-temporal area (MT) 5.165–6
modification of responses by experience 12.122
monkey cortical, and spatial parameter coding 4.201–5
monkey visual cortex, and spatiotemporal

analyses 4.205–11
in morphogenetic fields 11.47, 11.62, 11.65
motor 8.175–99, 8.202–5
    behaviour during saccades 8.205
    hysteresis 8.203
    position and velocity sensitivity 8.203
movement-sensitive, phylogenetic development of 12.360
MT and MST, direction sensitivity of 4.375–7
multi-modal 2.184
multipolar 3.188, 3.190, 3.203, 3.211
near 9.187, 9.227
neuronal cytoskeleton 11.275–8
non-oriented 2.175
non-pyramidal 11.353
non-spiny (smooth) stellate cell, Glossary explanation
    of 4.448
normal 3.187, 3.189
object-detector 2.261
off-centre 4.276
omnipause 4.391, 8.206, 8.253–4, 8.256, 8.258, 8.262–3
on-centre 4.276
    segregation of
        into separate layers
            in cats 4.276–7
            in ferrets 4.276
            in minks 4.276
            in monkeys 4.276, 4.278
            in tree shrews 4.276
optic lobe 2.240, 2.246
optomotor 2.241, 2.243, 2.252
oriented 2.175
parietal cortical, visual response properties of 4.374–83
parietal cortical saccade 8.285
parietal visual 4.378
parvocellular 2.171
parvocellular relay 5.48
position-related 8.207, 8.217
position-vestibular-pause 8.217
post-receptoral 3.30
post-synaptic 11.258–9
preparatory set cell 4.420
pre-synaptic 11.258
in pulvinar complex 3.213–4, 4.141
Purkinje 11.135
pursuit 2.185–6
pursuit-related 2.179–80, 2.184, 2.189, 2.191
pyramidal cell 13.168
    Glossary explanation of 4.448
quasi-visual 8.249–53, 8.266
real-motion 2.175
reciprocal 9.87, 9.229–30
regenerating 11.190, 11.194, 11.196–7, 11.199, 11.201,
    11.206–7
    after CNS injury 11.242
relay 3.187–92, 3.194
    in LGNv 3.203
    and shell nuclei 3.211
    in visual thalamus 3.197–9, 3.201
retinal 12.160

Neurones (*continued*)
  saccade **2**.178
  saccade-related **2**.179–80, **12**.96, **12**.100
  saccade-related burst **8**.249–54, **8**.256–65
  short-axon **11**.250
  short-lead burst **8**.206, **8**.249–52
  $\Sigma\pi$-model **14**.81
  single **9**.104
  single visual cortex **12**.171–2
  spectrally non-opponent **5**.180
  spectrally opponent **5**.180
  spiny stellate cell, Glossary explanation of **4**.448
  sprouting after CNS injury **11**.242
  SRIF **11**.359
  star pyramid cell, Glossary explanation of **4**.448
  stereoscopic, operational properties of **9**.235–6
  striate cortical **4**.226
  structures, 'face-specific' **12**.471
  STS area **12**.120–4
  subcortical, sensitive to changing size **9**.160–1
  superior colliculus **4**.91, **4**.96
  supragranular **11**.36
  T- **8**.247–9, **8**.251–4
  target velocity **8**.214–5, **8**.234
  TE **12**.111, **12**.117, **12**.120
  TE area
    activity **12**.113
    in macaque **12**.116, **12**.118
    non-visual experimental conditions **12**.112–3
    optimum visual stimulus **12**.113–5
    receptive field properties **12**.112
    visual responses **12**.113–5
  tectogeniculate **3**.161–3
  tecto-reticular **8**.248, **8**.250–3, **8**.255–6, **8**.263, **8**.266–8
  TLU-model **14**.81
  tonic **4**.391, **8**.207
  tracking **8**.285
    type A **12**.97–8
    type B **12**.98
    type C **12**.98
  transient **11**.358
  transient subplate **11**.262–3
  triangular **3**.190
  tuned **9**.87, **9**.227–8
  tuned excitatory **9**.187
  tuned inhibitory **9**.187, **9**.228–9, **9**.231
    and correlation **9**.231
    and uncorrelation **9**.231
  type A **3**.190
  type B **3**.190
  type C **3**.190
  type II **3**.190
  type III **3**.190
  vergence velocity **8**.219
  in vertebrate neurogenesis **11**.30–4, **11**.39–40
  vestibular nucleus **4**.130, **8**.216–8, **8**.306
  vestibular-pause **8**.217
  vestibulo-ocular **8**.323, **8**.326
  VI

  of cat and monkey **5**.165
  and motion detection **5**.166
  visual **12**.96–7, **12**.100–1
    funtional properties of, using parameter-response
        curves **4**.173–4
    and neuroscience **14**.19
    primary coding function of **14**.21
  visual cortex **3**.308, **3**.318
    functional properties of **4**.173
    quantitative electrophysiology of **4**.173–222
    quantitative physiology of **4**.173–222
  visual fixation (VF) **2**.178, **8**.285
  visual movement **8**.249
  in visual pathways **2**.427, **2**.430–2, **2**.456–9
  visual tracking (VT) **2**.178–9, **8**.230–3, **8**.285
  visuo-motor **4**.377, **8**.249, **12**.96
  wide-field **2**.241, **2**.243, **2**.251
  X- **2**.42–3, **8**.247–9, **8**.251, **13**.59, **13**.185
    of cat **5**.259
  Y- **13**.59, **13**.185
    of cat **5**.259
Neurontropy, and the effects of binocular correlation **9**.66–7
Neuropathology **12**.264, **12**.391
  findings in prosopagnosic patient **12**.265
  of heautoscopy **12**.300–2
Neuropathy, optic **1**.297
Neuropeptide Y (NPY) **3**.279, **3**.294, **3**.363–4, **3**.369,
    11.360–1, **11**.363
Neuropeptides **3**.368, **11**.357–8
Neurophysiology **5**.113–4, **5**.259
  and pattern recognition **14**.27
  of pursuit system **2**.170–1, **2**.175–7, **2**.181–5, **2**.187–8
  and visual perception **14**.19–20
Neuropile **2**.343, **2**.347, **2**.353–5, **2**.360
Neuropile layers **2**.353
Neuropsychology **12**.212
  clinical **12**.261
  cognitive **12**.261, **12**.338
  Lie transformation group approach to (LTG/NP) **14**.20
Neuropsychology computations in pattern recognition **14**.28
Neuroptera **2**.234
Neuroscience **11**.248–50, **11**.275, **11**.304, **11**.307, **14**.19–21,
    14.40
Neurosurgery **12**.266–7
  and loss of topographical familiarity **12**.424–7
Neurotransmitters
  in cell locomotion **11**.182
  and cell recognition **11**.82, **11**.84
  and cellular organization **11**.70–1, **11**.73
  class specification **3**.101
  effects on axon growth **11**.251
  GABA **11**.281
  and GAP-43 **11**.225–7
  in growth cones **11**.152
  location of
    in cortical area 17 **3**.288–96
      contribution of GABAergic inhibition to cortical
          function **3**.295
      contribution of GABAergic neurones to interlaminar

projections 3.293–4
contribution of GABAergic neurones to lateral
projections 3.294
distribution of GABAergic cell bodies in 3.293
distribution of GABAergic terminals in 3.291–2
identification of subpopulations of GABAergic
neurones with miscellaneous markers 3.294–5
cholecystokinin 3.294–5
lectins 3.295
neuropeptide Y 3.294
somatostatin 3.294
substance P 3.294
morphology of GABAergic neurones and terminals
in 3.288–91
in the geniculostriate system 3.278–301
in mammalian visual system 11.353–64
neurochemistry of 11.353
in neuronal cytoskeleton 11.278–82, 11.287–8
and proto-oncogenes 11.118
release 11.227–8
and axon growth 11.248
in neuronal cytoskeleton 11.299, 11.301
and synaptic rearrangements 11.262
in vertebrate neurogenesis 11.35
in the visual cortex 3.311, 3.363, 3.368–70
in the visual thalamus 3.183–5, 3.189
Neurotrophic factor
brain-derived (BDNF) 11.73
ciliary (CNTF) 11.73
in regeneration 11.198, 11.201
Neutral bands 7.42–3
Neutral distance 8.117–8
Neutral point 2.293, 2.297, 7.12, 7.204–7, 7.210
determination of 7.109
Neutral zone 7.117–8, 7.158–60
in colour vision tests 7.215, 7.227
Neutral-filter test 7.136, 7.141, 7.159
Neutralstimmung, neutral or absolute 7.119
Neutron 16.30
New Colour Test 7.224, 7.232
Newton, Isaac 12.42–5, 12.47, 12.136
Newton's colour circle 6.23, 6.219
Newton's colour vision theory 6.2–3, 6.10, 6.219
Ng–CAM (neural–glia adhesion molecule) 11.282, 11.294
Nicotine 11.200
Nictitating membrane 2.85, 2.470
NICU (neonatal intensive care unit) 16.104, 16.113–6,
16.121–2, 16.124–5, 16.128
Night blindness 7.125–6, 7.144
congenital stationary (CSNB), X-linked 7.148
Night vision 5.72
after peripheral field loss 1.221
NILE (NGF-inducible large external
glycoprotein) 11.293–4
Nissl preparations 3.177–8, 3.180–1, 3.198, 3.207
Nissl stain 2.141, 2.143
Glossary explanation of 4.448
NMDA (*N*-methyl-D-aspartate) 3.368
in synaptic rearrangement 11.260–1, 11.263–71

NMDA (*N*-methyl-D-aspartate) receptors 11.199, 11.201,
11.240–1, 11.281
NMR, *see under* Magnetic resonance imaging
Nodes on a string 12.306
Noise 2.6, 5.20
additive 5.55, 14.72
broad band 3.24
broad-band photon 5.67
in computational vision 14.35, 14.41–2
dynamic background 12.173, 12.176
dynamic random 12.471
dynamic visual 12.173
environmental 2.7–8
in foveal sampling 3.18, 3.20
and human observer 14.89, 14.91
and hyperacuity 5.222, 5.224–5
and ideal observer 14.85–6
image 14.88, 14.93, 14.102
intrinsic 3.26, 3.33, 5.32
masking 5.107
multiplicative 5.55, 5.59–60, 5.70
neural 5.137, 10.173
in numerosity 14.134
in peripheral vision 5.44, 5.49–52, 5.63–4, 5.67
photon 5.55, 5.59–60, 5.65, 5.68, 5.70, 5.149
photoreceptor 5.57–8
photoreceptor coupling 3.25
physiological 2.8, 2.413
post-compression 5.70
power 5.28, 5.39
quantal 5.149
quantization 5.60, 5.62
quantum 5.55, 5.64, 5.70
see also Audible sound emissions
shot 2.7
signal 14.70, 14.72
spatial 3.22–3
statistics 14.69
stimuli, incoherent 12.381
synaptic 5.51
trial 5.17–8
visual 5.124, 12.471, 14.92
white 5.52, 5.108
Noise pattern (visual), Glossary explanation of 4.448
Noise-field campimetry 12.141–2, 12.173
Nomenclature 7.1
Non-Ionizing Radiation Committee, International
(INIRC) 16.4
Nonius horopter, in aniseikonia 1.169
Nonius lines 8.160, 9.145, 9.187
Non-letters, *see* Letter(s)
Non-linear analysis 10.8–9
of the changing-size channels 9.157–8
Non-linearities 5.49–50, 5.60, 5.62
compressive 10.122
essential and non-essential 10.5–8
of vergence 8.159
of vestibular transduction 8.25–6
Non-luminous (perceived) colour, CIE definition of 6.225

Non-neuronal systems **11**.47
Non-optical techniques for visualizing the eye **1**.359–70
   emission computed tomography **1**.366–8
   magnetic resonance imaging **1**.365–6
   positron emission tomography **1**.367–8
   single-photon emission computed tomography **1**.367
   ultrasonography **1**.359–62
   x-ray methods **1**.362–5
      measurement of axial length **1**.362–3
Non-primate eutherians retinal development **3**.69–71,
      3.74–6, **3**.78–80, **3**.82–7
Non-random cyclopean stereopsis **9**.52–4
Non-retinotopic areas **4**.163
Non-spiny (smooth) stellate cell neurones, Glossary
      explanation of **4**.448
Non-summation **5**.60
Non-topographic tectal input **4**.169
Non-words, *see* Word(s)
Noradrenaline **3**.194, **3**.368, **11**.247, **11**.260, **11**.353
   Glossary explanation of **4**.448
Noradrenergic fibres, to cerebellum **8**.228
Normal integral **5**.9–12
   detectability function **5**.27
   discriminability function **5**.32
   and pedestal effect **5**.32
   upper half, fourth power of contrast **5**.97–8
   in visual processing **5**.23, **5**.26–7
Normalization **14**.72
   holistic **14**.75
   and object recognition **14**.39
   pattern **14**.61
   pattern signal **14**.78
   problems **14**.76, **14**.80
   standard **14**.71, **14**.76–7, **14**.79
   viewpoint **14**.31, **14**.44
NOT, *see* Nucleus of the optic tract
Notation **7**.1
'Notch' **10**.243–4
NPY, *see* Neuropeptide Y
Nuclear layer **3**.101
   and fovea **3**.115–7
   inner (INL) **3**.2, **3**.42–4
      and amacrine cells **3**.48
      interplexiform cells **3**.47
      neurone death in **3**.96–7
   and ipsilateral projection **3**.112–3
   microglia in **3**.85
   outer (ONL) **3**.1–2
      neurone death in **3**.96–7
Nucleoli in regeneration **11**.193
Nucleosides **11**.200
Nucleotides, cyclic **11**.281
Nucleus
   accessory abducens **8**.185
   accessory oculomotor **8**.200
   caudate **8**.267, **8**.269–70, **8**.287, **8**.291, **8**.314
   central caudal **8**.184
   cuneate **8**.189
   deep cerebellar **8**.244, **8**.328
      dorsal terminal **8**.201, **8**.214
      dorsolateral pontine **8**.153, **8**.202, **8**.211–4
      Edinger–Westphal **8**.184
      interstitial
         of Cajal **8**.200, **8**.216, **8**.248, **8**.314
         of medial longitudinal fasciculus **8**.200, **8**.314
         of optic tract **8**.201, **8**.314
      lateral geniculate **8**.2, **8**.245–6
      lateral pontine **8**.213
      lateral terminal **8**.201, **8**.213
      medial terminal **8**.201
      medial vestibular **8**.153, **8**.216, **8**.302
      oculomotor **8**.2, **8**.184, **8**.201
      oculomotor accessory **8**.2, **8**.200
      trigeminal **8**.189
      trochlear **8**.184
      vestibular **8**.2, **8**.202, **8**.213–4, **8**.216–8, **8**.225, **8**.234,
         8.265, **8**.302, **8**.306
Nucleus abducens **8**.183, **8**.185, **8**.201, **8**.248
Nucleus centralis **3**.204–6, **3**.217
Nucleus of Darkschewitsch **8**.200–1, **8**.248
Nucleus isthmus **2**.158, **11**.200
Nucleus of the optic tract **8**.48, **8**.201, **8**.214, **8**.234, **8**.300
   Glossary explanation of **4**.448
   relationship with cat dorsal terminal nucleus **4**.119–20
Nucleus of the posterior commissure **8**.200
Nucleus praepositus hypoglossi **12**.60
Nucleus prepositus hypoglossi **8**.2, **8**.33, **8**.153, **8**.202, **8**.213,
      8.216, **8**.225, **8**.234, **8**.238, **8**.248, **8**.302
   and eye position encoding **4**.392
Nucleus raphe dorsalis **3**.167, **3**.169
Nucleus raphe interpositus **8**.202, **8**.207
Nucleus reticularis tegmenti pontis **4**.393–4, **8**.201–2,
      8.208–9, **8**.214, **8**.225, **8**.234–5, **8**.248, **8**.300, **12**.60–1
   connectivity in **4**.393
   physiological properties of **4**.393
Nucleus rostral interstitial of the medial longitudinal
      fasciculus **8**.200
Nucleus rotundus **2**.423–4, **2**.426–9, **2**.431–2
Null trial, *see* Catch trial
Nulling, *see* Contrast, matching
Number, concept of **14**.126–7
Number discriminations **14**.64
Number(s)
   copying **12**.340
   naming **12**.349
   reading **12**.335, **12**.392
   recognition **12**.337
   and script **12**.305, **12**.307, **12**.309
Numerical aperture **2**.91–2, **2**.96–7, **2**.100, **2**.102, **2**.104,
      2.110
Numerosity **14**.125–39
   absolute identification **14**.127–30
   cognitive penetrability **14**.137
   discrimination **14**.127, **14**.130, **14**.132–7
   estimation **14**.125–6, **14**.128–31, **14**.137–8
   illusions **14**.132
   internal measure **14**.127
   internal representation **14**.133–6

overestimation **14**.131, **14**.133
perceived **14**.125, **14**.129, **14**.132–3, **14**.135–6, **14**.138
psychometric functions **14**.132, **14**.135–6
psychophysical functions **14**.130–1
spatial factors **14**.128–9
strategies of judgment **14**.137
temporal factors **14**.129–30
terminology **14**.125–7
underestimation **14**.131, **14**.133, **14**.137–8
Nylon, as a material for contact lenses 1.128
Nyquist encoding limit 5.54, 5.66, 5.71–2, 5.90–2, 5.152
Nyquist limit 1.20, 2.102, 3.21, **10**.182, **15**.15–6
  and bipolar cells 3.38
  in extrafoveal sampling 3.22–3
  and foveal sampling 3.18–20
  and ganglion cells 3.57
  and postreceptoral mechanisms 3.31
  and retina 3.7–8
  see also Nyquist encoding limit
Nyquist sampling theorem 3.17, **10**.64, **10**.79, **10**.81
Nystagmus **12**.20, **12**.27, **12**.191
  abduction 8.310
  acquired 8.315–6
  and cone–rod dystrophy 7.140
  congenital 8.299, 8.302–3, 8.315–6, **12**.370
    accommodation anomalies in 1.270–1
  in CSNB 7.148
  divergence 8.302
  downbeat 8.301
  Eisenbahn- 8.46

fast phases 8.46, 8.65, 8.98, 8.111–2, 8.325
gaze-evoked 8.236, 8.301–2, 8.314
gaze-paretic 8.322
head 8.47
head-shaking 8.301
look- 8.47–50
optokinetic (OKN) 2.166, 2.169, 2.172–4, 2.178–80, 2.182,
    8.45–8, 8.75, 8.78–9, 8.138, 8.214, **12**.7, **12**.52, **12**.150
  horizontal **12**.142
  and posterior parietal lobe **12**.95
  sigma **12**.142–3, **12**.364, **12**.366–7, **12**.369
  and spatial hemineglect **12**.452
  vertical **12**.142
  and visual movement agnosia **12**.362–3
  and visual pathways 2.433, 2.455
and oscillopsia 8.314–6
pathological **12**.363, **12**.370–1
pendular 7.24, 7.28, 7.98–9
periodic alternating 8.234, 8.299–301, 8.312–3, 8.322
in photoreception 2.374, 2.386, 2.390
in pursuit system 2.180, 2.184
Schau (look) 2.166, **12**.143
stare, *see* Nystagmus, Stier (stare)
Stier (stare) 2.166, 8.47–8, 8.112, **12**.143
torsional 8.302
upbeat 8.301–2
vestibular 8.46, 8.301–2, **12**.363
from vestibular disorder 8.301
Nystagmus rivalry 9.104

O

Object
and 3D object-centred models **14**.45, **14**.112–3
3D representation of **14**.43–5
and alexia **12**.335
asymmetrical **12**.274
background separation **12**.385
borders **12**.403
classification **12**.14–5, **12**.217
colour correlation **12**.392
conceptualization **12**.400
contours **12**.403
depth **12**.5
familiar **12**.351–2
inner visualization of **12**.413
matching **12**.339
meaning **12**.199
in motion, recognition difficulties **12**.402
multiplication of visual **12**.475
names **12**.341
accessibility to **12**.339
association of visual impressions with **12**.410
naming **12**.217, **12**.340
in auditory modality **12**.339
and colour anomia **12**.406
difficulties **12**.345
and hemialexia **12**.350
in tactile modality **12**.339
and numerosity **14**.126–7, **14**.130
partial drawings **12**.340
personal, familiarity **12**.269–70
photographs of **12**.339, **12**.341
real **12**.339
in relative motion **12**.217
separation **12**.199
stationary **12**.217
stylized drawings of **12**.339–40
superiority effects **12**.195–6
surface **12**.405
symbolic component **12**.339
symmetrical **12**.274
texture **12**.403
typical views **12**.340
untypical views **12**.340
unusual views **12**.339
visual
localization **12**.427
recognition **12**.107–22
face-responsive neuronal activity **12**.117–22
historical review **12**.107–8
inferotemporal cortex
neuronal signal processing **12**.109–17
structure and connections **12**.109
postnatal development **12**.109
in wrong place **12**.476
Object decomposition **14**.39, **14**.112
Object detectors, insect **2**.255
Object discrimination **2**.262

Object recognition **2**.255–8, **12**.12, **12**.14, **12**.187, **12**.385, **14**.6, **14**.21, **14**.50, **14**.111–8
and agnosia **12**.179, **12**.181, **12**.193–7, **12**.199, **12**.202, **12**.206, **12**.208–9, **12**.213, **12**.217
alignment method **14**.112–4
and computational vision **14**.31, **14**.35–6, **14**.38–40, **14**.43–55
primate **12**.107
and prosopagnosia **12**.262
and pure alexia **12**.337
real **12**.186, **12**.194–5, **12**.208
through manipulation **12**.413
and visual movement agnosia **12**.359
Object understanding **14**.5–7
Objective angle of deviation **9**.180
Objective infra-red recording **1**.238
Obligate binocular cells, *see* Binocular only cells
Oblique
inferior **8**.176, **8**.182
superior **8**.176, **8**.182, **8**.184
Oblique astigmatism **1**.18
Oblique buffer, Glossary explanation of **4**.448
Oblique effect **14**.52, **14**.59
and orientation columns **4**.281
selective **14**.60–1
Oblique saccades **8**.103–12, **8**.118–9, **8**.210–1, **8**.258–60
Obscuration
cerebral **12**.271
transient **12**.472, **12**.475
of visual world **12**.472
Observation, monocular **12**.317
Observation window **5**.25, **5**.27, **5**.30, **5**.32
Observer
Bayesian ideal **14**.92
human **14**.88–92
ideal **14**.83–96
non-standard **14**.136
and numerosity **14**.125–7, **14**.134
standard **14**.137
static **14**.84
Obstacle avoidance and computational vision **14**.34
Occipital cortex **2**.174–6, **2**.178, **2**.443
Occipital extrastriate visual cortical areas **4**.411
V2 **4**.411
V3A **4**.411
V4 **4**.411
Occipital lobe
atrophy **12**.180
Glossary explanation of **4**.444
human **12**.171
inferior rostral, left **12**.345
injury **12**.184
lateral **12**.344
left **12**.335, **12**.342–3
surgical removal of **12**.343
penetrating wounds **12**.180
and prosopagnosia **12**.260, **12**.262
right **12**.343
and visual hemineglect **12**.450

Occipito-temporal junction 12.347
  mesial 12.344
Occipito-temporal lobe 12.263, 12.480
Occluders 16.113, 16.116, 16.125–6
Occlusion 5.241, 14.4, 14.6
  monocular 11.257
Occultism 12.299
Ocellus, *see* Eye, simple
Octave 10.35
Octopus 2.122
  photoreception 2.366, 2.374, 2.376–8, 2.382, 2.385–90
Ocular ageing 5.277
Ocular ametropia 1.6–7
Ocular apraxia 13.27–8
Ocular astigmatism 1.5
  and angle α 1.5
Ocular asymmetries, and the optical axis 1.5
Ocular biometry 1.133
Ocular dominance 2.436, 4.63, 4.192, 9.181, 11.260, 11.288
  in the accessory optic system of cat and primate 4.118–9
  during binocular rivalry 9.198
  in dyslexia 13.141
  Glossary explanation of 4.448
  in specifically disabled readers and controls 13.151
Ocular flutter 8.322
Ocular hypertension 5.172
Ocular media 2.94–5, 5.81, 5.87–8, 5.279, 7.31, 7.152, 7.217
  and developing visual system 16.108–9
  light absorption through 7.4–5, 7.12, 7.153–4
  and light measurement 16.24–5
  light transmission by 16.116–8, 16.128
  neural changes with age 16.155
  and optical radiation 16.5
  spectral absorption characteristics 16.3–4
  yellowing of 7.28
Ocular micro-tremor 5.281
Ocular muscle weakness 8.309–12
Ocular parameters
  optical methods for measurement of 1.371–98
    fundus cameras 1.376–8
    keratometers 1.378–81
    ophthalmophakometry 1.381–4
    ophthalmoscopes 1.371–8
    pachometry 1.388–90
    photokeratoscopes 1.381
    pupillometry 1.392
    refractometry 1.393–4
    scattering of light 1.394–5
    slit lamps 1.384–8
    specular microscope 1.390–1
Ocular radiometry, and retinal illumination 1.9–10
Ocular refraction 1.53
  definition of 1.399
  determination of 1.399–414
Ocular responses, to the wearing of contact lenses 1.104–11
Ocular transmittance 2.86–9
Ocular-dominance changes, effects of, in monocular deprivation 4.123–5
Ocular-dominance columns 3.235, 3.241, 3.252–5, 4.300,
  4.304, 6.180
  blobs in 6.181, 6.185
  in carnivores
    cat 4.272
    ferret 4.272–3
    mink 4.272–3
  comparative aspects of 4.271–3
  2-deoxyglucose method for demonstrating 3.252–4
  functions of 4.273–5
    binocular disparity 4.273
    binocular fusion 4.273
    binocular rivalry 4.273
    interocular transfer 4.273
    stereoscopy 4.273
  general features and layout of 4.267–71
  interblobs in 6.181
  investigation of
    by autoradiography using transneural transport 4.269, 4.271
    by simple reduced-silver fibre stain 4.269
    by tracer injections 4.267–9, 4.271
    by WGA-HRP 4.271
  in lagomorphs 4.273
  in monkeys 4.275
  in New World monkeys
    capuchin 4.272
    cytochrome oxidase methods in 4.272
    marmoset 4.272
    owl 4.272
    spider 4.272
    squirrel 4.272
  in prosimians 4.272
  reduced silver staining method for demonstrating 3.253
  in rhesus monkeys 4.267
  in rodents 4.273
  segregated 9.174
  in sheep 4.273
  in the tree shrew 4.272
Ocular-dominance plasticity 11.269
Ocular-dominance stripes 4.270–2
  in humans 4.272
  in macaque monkey species
    baboon 4.272
    chimpanzee 4.272
Ocular motor nuclei, *see* Oculomotor nuclei
Oculocentric direction
  of fused images 9.133
  laws of 9.6
Oculomotor accessory nuclei 8.2, 8.200
Oculomotor control 13.263
  as a significant factor in reading disability 13.141, 13.182, 13.266, 13.269
Oculomotor imperfection, effects of, on stereopsis 9.124–6
Oculomotor job description 8.9
Oculomotor maps 9.2
  Hillebrand hyperbola 9.2
  Vieth-Müller circle 9.2
Oculomotor maturation 8.299, 8.323
Oculomotor mechanisms, development of 13.50

Oculomotor nerve 1.233, 8.201
Oculomotor neurone discharges 8.202–5
Oculomotor nuclear complex 2.172, 2.179, 2.185–7
Oculomotor nuclei 2.173–4, 2.183, 2.187–9, 4.389–90, 8.2,
    8.184, 8.201
  connectivity of 4.390
  effects of electrical stimulation on 4.390
  effects of lesions on 4.390
  final common pathway of 4.389
  midbrain complex 1.233
  physiological properties of 4.389–90
Oculomotor plant 8.96, 8.139, 8.203–5
Oculomotor range 8.265–6, 8.324
Oculomotor subsystems 2.165–6, 2.169, 2.174, 2.191
Oculomotor system 2.165, 2.169–70, 2.174, 2.187–9, 2.191,
    2.424
  feedback signal from 12.152
  maturation of 8.299, 8.323
Odd-ball paradigm 12.277
Oedema
  cerebral 12.201, 12.277, 12.300
  collateral 12.150
  cystoid 16.68
    macular (CME) 16.59, 16.63–4, 16.89–90, 16.98
  and pure alexia 12.343
Off-cells 4.12–4
Off-centre bipolar system 7.58
Off-centre cells
  blue 7.77
  of the lateral geniculate nucleus 4.53–4
Off-centre channels 7.65–9
Off-centre ganglion cells 4.320–1
Off-centre receptive fields 4.226
Off-channels 6.163–5, 6.167–8, 6.189
  push–pull 6.33, 6.182
Off-response 7.58–60
Off-surround ganglion cells 4.320–1
Oil droplets 2.6, 3.9, 3.12, 6.84, 6.108–27, 6.129–31
  in colour vision 2.287, 2.289, 2.291–2, 2.296, 2.299
  coloured 3.29
  in dioptrics 2.89, 2.101
  in evolution of retina 2.138–9
  in evolution of vision 2.410
  in mammals 2.470, 2.472, 2.476–7
  in photoreceptor system 2.65–6, 2.71–3, 2.78
Oilbird 2.271, 2.280–1
OKN, *see* Optokinetic nystagmus
Okuma plates 7.230
Oligodendrocytes 11.30–1, 11.34
  and axon growth 11.244, 11.246–7, 11.249–51
  in optic nerve regeneration 11.206–11
  and proto-oncogenes 11.114
  in regeneration 11.197–8, 11.201
Olive inferior 8.201–2, 8.214, 8.226, 8.228, 8.234–5, 8.248
Ommatidia 2.132, 6.263–4, 6.266, 6.269, 6.271
  arthropod 2.214, 2.217, 2.342–4
    evolution 2.344–53
  developmental assembly of 2.346, 2.348
  in eye evolution 2.4, 2.24, 2.353, 2.359–60

fused-rhabdome 2.347–8, 2.355–6
mandibulate 2.345–8, 2.350
open-rhabdome 2.347–8, 2.355–6
optic lobe 2.224
and origins of eye 2.55, 2.57
in visual processing 2.238, 2.265
Omnipause neurones 4.391, 8.206, 8.253–4, 8.256, 8.258,
    8.262–3, 8.265
On and off responses, segregation of, in separate populations
  of bipolar cells 4.2–3
On–off cells 4.4–5
On–off centre cells 4.63–4
On–off centre streams 4.226
On–off channels, in the lateral geniculate nucleus 4.63–4
On–off columns, *see* Contrast columns
On–off cortical cells 4.64
On–off receptive-field centres 4.62
On–off responses, in direction-selective cells 4.345
On-cells 4.12–4
On-centre cells
  blue 7.77
  of the lateral geniculate nucleus 4.53–4
On-centre channels 7.65–9
On-centre ganglion cells 4.320–1
On-centre receptive fields 4.226
On-channels 6.163–5, 6.167–8, 6.189
  push–pull 6.33, 6.182
Onchidium 2.365–6, 2.368
Oncogenes, viral 11.112
Oncogenesis 11.112
One-dimensional vision 2.259–60, 2.262
On-surround ganglion cells 4.320–1
On-surrounds 4.54
Ontogenetic limitation 3.336
Opacification 7.116
Open-loop gain 1.241
Open-loop tasks 9.75
Operating characteristics 5.25
  asymmetric 5.19–21
  signal detection 5.17–9
Operations
  AND 14.71
  continuous-shift 14.55, 14.58–60, 14.62, 14.66
  independent of spatial relations 14.64–5
  internal 14.66
    compensatory 14.51
    pattern representation 14.63
    and spatial relations 14.51–2, 14.58–60
    spatially selective 14.51, 14.61–3
  local 14.81
  NAND 14.71
  sense-reversal 14.51, 14.54, 14.56–63, 14.66
    global 14.57–9
  seriation 14.126
  signal similarity evaluation 14.71
  spatial relations 14.50–66
Ophthalmic disease 7.115–72
  colour deficiency as symptoms 7.115–8
  colour vision evaluation tests 7.118–23

diagnosis 7.123–62
  conditions of inner retinal layers 7.148–52
  filter effects 7.123–4
  functional impairment of photoreceptors 7.132–5
  optic-nerve conditions 7.152–8
  optic-nerve conduction defects 7.158–62
  outer layer impairment 7.126–31
  photopigment metabolism defects 7.124–6
  photoreceptor diseases 7.135–48
  retinal ganglion cell damage 7.152–8
  of photoreceptors 7.135–48
Ophthalmic prescriptions 1.399
Ophthalmo-eikonometer 1.172
Ophthalmo-kinetograph, for early diagnosis of
  dyslexia 13.244
Ophthalmometer, *see* Keratometer
Ophthalmometry 1.381
  see also Keratometry
Ophthalmophakometry 1.234, 1.381–4
Ophthalmoplegia, internuclear 4.392, 8.205, 8.310–1
Ophthalmoscopes 1.371–6
  and developing visual system 16.106, 16.118, 16.124,
    16.128
  direct 1.372–4, 16.100
    corneal reflex with 1.373–4
    field of illumination 1.373
    field-of-view with 1.373
    magnification of 1.372–3
  double-pass 5.89–90
  fundus cameras 1.376–8
  Gullstrand's reflex-free 1.376
  handheld 16.99
  indirect 1.374–6, 16.65, 16.99, 16.109–10
    corneal reflex with 1.375–6
    and developing visual system 16.113, 16.125
    field-of-view with 1.374
    magnification with 1.374–5
  scanning laser 16.76
Ophthalmoscopy 7.130–1
  for refractive measurement
    advantages and disadvantages of the method of 1.401
    estimates of accuracy and precision of 1.401–2
    introduction and history of 1.401
    optical principles of the method of 1.40
    practical applications of 1.401
Opossum 2.467, 2.471, 2.477
  dioptrics 2.84, 2.91
  Virginian 3.328
Opponency
  chromatic 3.54, 3.58
  spectral 3.49
Opponency notch, red–green 7.44, 7.127, 7.130, 7.140
Opponent channel
  blue–yellow 7.8, 7.20
  red–green 7.8, 7.18, 7.20, 7.29
Opponent neurones, in toxic optic neuropathy 7.160
Opponent system 7.8
  blue–yellow 7.39, 7.44
  red–green 7.44, 7.46

Opponent vector organization 4.378
  Glossary explanation of 4.448
Opponent-colour mechanisms 7.176, 7.180
Opponent-colour response 7.77
Opponent-process model 10.81, 10.91–3
Opposed movement cells 9.235
Opsins 6.63–5, 6.72, 6.93–8, 6.108–9, 6.118, 7.103–5, 7.124
  in colour vision 2.284, 2.295–6, 2.315
  cone 7.93, 7.95, 7.105–11
  in evolution of eye 2.9–10, 2.39–40, 2.43–4
  in photoreceptor system 2.67–9, 2.71–4, 2.76–8
  primary structure of 6.63–8, 6.93–8
  in trichromacy 2.314
  and visual pigments 2.63–5
  in visual processing 2.229
Optacon 1.185
Optic arrays 9.163
  ambient 14.91
  and ideal observers 14.84
  and visual perception 14.19, 14.21
Optic ataxia 12.462
Optic atrophy 7.178–9
  dominant 7.40, 7.43, 7.47, 7.177
  dominant infantile (DIOA) 7.118, 7.155–7, 7.159–61,
    7.163
  dominantly inherited (DIJOA) 7.61, 7.98, 7.116
  Leber's hereditary 7.47–8, 7.159, 7.175–6
Optic axes 9.3
  of the cornea 1.313
Optic chiasm 2.48, 2.415, 3.130, 3.135–6, 3.176, 12.29, 12.31,
    12.33, 12.35–6, 12.42–3, 12.47
  mammalian 2.468
  and visual field defects 12.144
  and visual pathways 2.443, 2.446, 2.449
Optic cup 11.386–9, 11.393
  embryology 11.398–9, 11.401
  in the evolution of the eye 2.17–8, 2.42, 2.47
  and hyaloid circulation 11.391
  and retinal development 3.71, 3.73, 3.77, 3.85
  and vitreous 11.392
Optic discs 4.270, 4.303
  in the mature retina 3.130
Optic fissures
  and retinal development 3.71, 3.76–7, 3.80
  in vasogenesis 3.86
Optic flow 4.384, 8.47, 14.27, 14.88
  as a consequence of motion 14.85
Optic flow computation 14.34
Optic flow patterns 4.379
Optic flow-fields, Glossary explanation of 4.448
Optic lobe
  arthropod 2.203–24, 2.341–60
    evolution 2.212–24
    visual processing organization 2.204–12
  in eye evolution 2.353–60
  insect 2.240, 2.258
  pharmacology of 2.223
  in photoreception 2.376, 2.379, 2.385–6, 2.391
  retinotopic organization 2.204, 2.217, 2.222

Optic nerve 2.403, 3.180
  0-2A cells in 11.30–1
  acquired colour deficiencies 7.38–40, 7.173–83
    classification 7.173–7
  and agnosia 12.198, 12.201
  amphibian 11.208–10, 11.224, 11.269, 11.314
  axon growth in 11.235
  axons in neuronal cytoskeleton 11.299
  axotomy 12.129
  in binocular vision 2.273
  cell lineage in 11.43
  cellular organization 11.68–70, 11.72–3, 11.75
  compression of 7.116, 7.161–2
  conduction of, impaired 7.163
  disease of 7.39, 7.118, 7.173–83, 7.231, 12.199
  early development 11.208
  electrical stimulation of 12.167–8
  embryology 11.394–5
  ethambutol toxicity 7.116–7
  in evolution of eye 2.16, 2.35, 2.46–8, 2.415
  fish 11.206–13, 11.269, 11.314
  frog 11.228
  goldfish 11.190, 11.195, 11.197–8, 11.200–1, 11.293–4
  and hyaloid circulation 11.391
  infiltration of 7.161–2
  information channels of 3.30
  injury 11.206–13, 11.224, 11.228–9, 11.257, 11.269
  lesions of 7.230, 12.144
  mammalian 2.468, 11.209–10
  in mature retina 3.130
  and neurone death 3.96–7
  and origins of eye 2.55, 2.57
  pathology of 7.163
  in photoreception 2.383
  and proto-oncogenes 11.114
  rat 11.208, 11.210, 11.223–4, 11.228, 11.286–7, 11.328,
    11.330
  regenerating axons 11.91
  regeneration 2.154, 11.190, 11.193, 11.206–13, 11.248–9,
    11.314
    in *Bufo marinus* 11.219–20, 11.226–7
    in goldfish 11.221, 11.225, 11.293–7
    in mammals 11.225
    physiological activity 11.198–9
  and retinal development 3.76–7, 3.80
  in retinofugal pathways 3.133–6, 3.138–9
  TOP molecules 11.78
  and visual pathways 2.427, 2.433, 2.443–4, 2.446, 2.449,
    2.459
  and vitreous 11.392
  in *Xenopus* 11.224
Optic nerve head analyser 1.377
Optic neuritis 7.42, 7.116, 7.158–9, 7.173–4
  chronic 7.47
  disorders in 7.177–83
  and photophobia 13.171
  unilateral 7.179
Optic neuropathy 1.297
  anterior ischaemic (AION) 7.157, 7.163

  ethambutol 7.160–1
  tobacco 7.160
  toxic 7.160–1
Optic nuclei, accessory 2.416–7, 2.423–4
Optic pathways 10.266
Optic radiations 2.451–2, 2.455
  Glossary explanation of 4.448
Optic stalk 2.17, 11.323–4, 11.326, 11.386–8, 11.391, 11.399
  and retina development 3.71, 3.76–7, 3.85, 3.90
  in retinofugal pathways 3.132, 3.134–5
Optic sulcus, and retinal development 3.70–1
Optic system
  accessory 2.424–5, 2.427–9, 2.433
  accessory (AOS), nuclei of 12.60
Optic tectum 11.88–90
  and axon growth 11.232
  binocular neurones 2.274
  cell lineage in 11.42–3
  cellular organization 11.68–70
  in evolution of eye 2.15–6, 2.47, 2.415–7
  in evolution of retina 2.145–6
  in evolution of vision 2.402, 2.405
  fish 11.212–3
  fish embryo 11.97–8
  and GAP-43 11.224, 11.228
  Glossary explanation of 4.448
  goldfish 11.195, 11.198–201, 11.293–7
  multipotential precursor cells in 11.32, 11.34–5
  and optic nerve regeneration 11.206–7
  and regenerating axons 11.91–2, 11.94
  regeneration 11.190, 11.192–3
  retinotopically organized 2.427
  TOP molecules 11.74–8
  and visual cortex 2.152
  and visual pathways 2.421–2, 2.424, 2.426–8, 2.430–3,
    2.435–6, 2.443, 2.445, 2.452, 2.459
  and visuomotor systems 2.153–6
Optic tract 11.206, 11.323, 12.473
  accessory 2.172–3–3, 2.443, 2.448–9, 2.455
  and axon growth 11.232–9, 11.246, 11.248–50
  axons 12.60
  electrical stimulation of 12.167–8
  lesions 3.102–3
  and LGNv 3.204
  in mature retina 3.131–2
  nucleus (NOT) 8.48, 8.201, 8.234, 8.300, 12.60–1, 12.72
    and motion perception 12.91
    primate 12.86
    and visual data processing 12.78
  in pursuit system 2.172
  and retinofugal pathways 3.134, 3.136
  and signal processing 12.66
  and visual pathways 2.423, 2.426, 2.443, 2.451–2, 2.455–6,
    2.459
  and visual thalamus 3.177–8, 3.193–4, 3.207
Optic vesicle 2.44–5, 2.403, 3.71–7, 3.107, 11.386–9, 11.394
  embryology 11.399–400, 11.402
  in evolution of eye 2.15–8, 2.24, 2.31, 2.38, 2.42, 2.46
  and hyaloid circulation 11.391

Optical aberrations 5.81–6
Optical aids
  for binocular peripheral field loss 1.218
  for peripheral field loss 1.218–21
    field expanders, minification in 1.218–9
    full aperture refracting Fresnel prisms 1.221
    high minus lenses 1.219
    partial aperture refracting Fresnel prisms 1.220–1
    reduction of object size using a mirror
        arrangement 1.219–20
    spectacle reflecting systems 1.220
Optical anisotropy 1.311–2
Optical axis 2.272–3, 2.448, 8.5–6
  and ocular asymmetries 1.5
Optical blur 5.60, 5.68, 7.53
Optical colour stimuli, CIE definition of 6.226 7
Optical defects
  nomenclature of 1.400–1
    ametropia 1.400
    astigmatism
      against-the-rule 1.400
      and the interval of Sturm 1.400
      with-the-rule 1.400–1
    emmetropia 1.400
    hyperopia 1.400
    myopia 1.400
    presbyopia 1.401
Optical degradation 5.258–9, 5.261–2
Optical density (D) 1.312
Optical flow patterns 1.249
Optical mechanisms 2.351–3
Optical media 5.128
Optical modulation transfer 2.102–3
Optical monitoring 4.278–80
  techniques of 4.271
Optical neuritis 10.54–8
Optical resolving power 5.92
Optical Society of America uniform colour scales
      system 6.241–9, 6.254–6
  basic concepts and principles for spacing
    scaling and notation 6.242–6
      evaluation of colour-difference formulae for the
          regular rhombohedral selection of
          colours 6.244–5
      numerical OSA/UCS specifications of lightness,
          yellowness–blueness and
          greenness–redness 6.245–6
      regular rhombohedral lattice sampling of object colour
          space 6.242–4
Optical systems
  diffraction-limited 2.92
  duplicated 2.112
Optical technology 2.118–9
Optical transfer function (OTF) 1.10–1, 1.16, 1.18–9,
    2.92–4, 5.88–9, 10.23
Optical waveguides 5.86–7
Optics
  aberration-free 2.4
  of animals 2.118–34

apposition 2.127–8, 2.352
compound eye 2.214
ecological 8.5
of eye 5.124, 5.128, 5.230
geometrical 5.83
inhomogeneous 2.128
inverse 14.45
laws of 2.230–7
photoreceptor 1.280
reflecting superposition 2.351–3
refracting superposition 2.351–3
refractive 5.88
resolution limits 5.120
and retina 2.214
single-lens 2.353
superposition 2.128–33, 2.214
of vertebrate eyes 2.82–6
and visual performance 5.81–93
Optic-tract conduction, impaired 7.163
Optimal estimation methods 5.14
Optokinesis 8.4, 8.45–70, 8.214
  acceleration 8.56
  after labyrinthectomy 8.56
  asymmetries 8.51–2, 8.64
  attitude of subject 8.47–8
  binocular vs. monocular 8.52
  and brainstem 8.214
  build-up of velocity 8.53, 8.214
  cancellation 8.61–3, 8.148–9, 8.217–8
  and central scotomata 8.61–3
  and cerebellum 8.214, 8.234–6
  and climbing fibres 8.226
  contribution to gaze stability 8.78–9
  cyclorotatory 8.65–6
  direct and indirect components 8.56–8, 8.234, 8.329
  distinguished from smooth pursuit 8.78–9, 8.138, 8.329
  and dorsal terminal nucleus of the optic tract 8.214
  effect of alerting 8.56
  effect of instructions 8.47–50
  effect of labyrinthectomy 8.56, 8.58
  effect of lesions 8.214, 8.234
  gain 8.48–51, 8.57–60, 8.65
  latency 8.52–3
  learning effects 8.50
  and mossy fibres 8.235–6
  negative feedback in 8.48–9, 8.235
  neurophysiology 8.214
  open-loop 8.58–60
  torsional 8.65–6
  velocity-storage 8.54–6, 8.218, 8.299–300
  vertical 8.64–5
  and vestibular nuclei 8.32–3, 8.214–8
Optokinetic after-nystagmus 8.33, 8.51, 8.53–60, 8.65, 8.214,
    8.225, 8.234–5
Optokinetic asymmetries
  consequences of eye placement for 4.132–4
  consequences of translational motion for 4.132–4
Optokinetic co-ordinates 8.46, 8.66
Optokinetic nystagmus 4.132, 4.388, 5.236, 8.45–50, 8.75,

Optokinetic nystagmus (*continued*)
  8.78–9, 8.138, 8.214, 9.101, 10.189, 10.265–6, 13.50–1,
    13.208, 13.214
  Glossary explanation of 4.448
  horizontal 4.133–4, 12.462
  see also Nystagmus
  vertical 4.133–24, 12.462
Optokinetic response 8.4, 8.45–70, 8.78, 8.144, 8.214,
    8.234–6
Optokinetic system, visual input to 4.132
Optokinetic–vestibular synergy 8.32–3, 8.46, 8.53–6, 8.218
Optometers 1.405–6
  advantages and disadvantages of 1.406
  Badal 1.235–6
  coincidence 1.405–6
  dynamic 1.406
  and estimates of accuracy and precision 1.406
  laser speckle 1.411–3
    accuracy and precision of 1.412–3
    advantages and disadvantages of 1.412
    optical principles of the method of 1.411–2
    practical applications and utility of 1.412
  objective 5.83
  practical applications and utility of 1.406
  and provocation of proximal accommodation 1.405
  refractometers 1.405
  speckle, white-light 1.413
Optomotor reflexes 2.343
Optomotor responses 2.206, 2.210, 2.239, 2.241, 2.374, 2.390
  insect 5.164
Optotypes 5.320
Oral contraceptives 7.152
Orbital diseases, lesions 1.45
Orbital layer 8.178–81
Orbital mechanics 8.96, 8.139, 8.203–5
Orbitals 16.30–2, 16.35–7, 16.50
  atomic 16.40
  conjugated double 16.34
  electronic 16.32–3
  molecular 16.40
  polycentric 16.34
Ordering relations and numerosity 14.126
Ordering and spatial relations 14.51
Organelles
  cytoplasmic 11.133–4, 11.143
  differential distribution 11.279–80
  ultrastructure of synaptic 2.359
Organs of Hesse 2.24
Orientation 5.97, 5.221–2, 5.226–7, 5.272, 5.304
  colour vision coding for 6.180–4, 6.208–9
  Glossary explanation of 4.448, 4.450
  line 10.283
  by local landmarks 12.416
  pattern 14.65
  and perception in extrapersonal space 12.411–7
  single bar 12.152
  spatial
    and visual hemineglect 12.449
    and visual movement agnosia 12.359

and visuo-spatial disorders 12.437
symmetry-axis 14.63–4
topographical 12.419, 12.422–3, 12.426, 12.429–30
  difficulties finding way 12.428
  disorders and parietal lobe lesions 12.427–8
  environmental 12.428
tuning 12.70–2
  and colour perception 12.83
  and contour perception 12.81–3
visual, responses 12.448
visuo-spatial 12.415–6, 12.435, 12.437
Orientation acuity 10.94, 10.103–5, 10.110
Orientation columns 4.284
  biases of 4.280–1
  cat 4.294–5
  comparative aspects of 4.281–2
  discrete 4.280
  evidence for existence of
    in black gibbon 4.281
    in ferret 4.281
    in lagomorphs 4.281
    in mink 4.281
    in opossum 4.282
    in rodents 4.281
    in sheep 4.281
    in tree shrew 4.281
  in extrastriate cortex 4.282
  functions of 4.282–3
    inhibition 4.282
    perception 4.282
  layer extending of 4.279–80
  layout of 4.278–9
    around central singularities 4.278
    in cat 4.278–9
    in macaque monkey 4.278–9
  in monkey 4.303–4
  and the oblique effect 4.281
Orientation disparities 9.112, 9.119, 9.232–3
Orientation hypercolumns 4.278, 4.283
Orientation modules 4.279
Orientation perception 10.281
Orientation selectivity 4.323, 10.200
  of cells of cat visual cortex 4.177
Orientation sensitivity, and the oblique effect 10.199
Orientation singularities 4.284
Orientation specificity 10.199–200
  and the correspondence problem 9.44–5
Orientation TR(S)Ns 8.248
Orientation tuning 11.344
  in MS 10.241
Orientation tuning functions 10.144
Orientierungsstörungen (disorientation symptoms) 12.420
Ornithorhynchus (platypus) 2.467–71
Ortho-eikonization 1.170
Orthokeratology
  and hard contact lenses 1.115
  in refractive error 1.42
Orthoptic therapy 1.269–70
Orthostereoscopy 1.327

Ortsblindheit 12.428
OSA Uniform Color Space 6.46–7
Oscar Colour Vision test 7.216, 7.229
Oscillating disparities, adaptations to 9.146–7
Oscillations
  forced **10.9**
  in frequency range 35–80 Hz **12.73–4**
  non-linear 10.9–11
  relaxation 10.10–1
Oscillopsia 8.299, 8.314–6, **12.431, 12.464, 13.216**
Oscilloscope displays 5.223
Osteichthyes 2.406
Ostracods 2.125
Ostrich dioptrics 2.83
Ostwald, Wilhelm 12.45
Ostwald's colour system 6.230
OTF, *see* Optical transfer function
Otoconia 8.17
Otolith membrane 8.21
Otolith organs 8.14–7, 8.21–2, 8.24, 8.329
  neural responses 8.23–6, 8.29–31

striola of 8.24–6
Ototoxic aminoglycerides 8.23–4
Ouabain 7.134
Outer plexiform layers, Glossary explanation of 4.448
Outflow 8.76, 8.149
Over-accommodation 1.354–5, 2.108
Overcompleteness 8.324
Overestimation, numerosity **14.131, 14.133**
Overlap 1.249, 9.183
Overlap paradigm, for saccades 8.114
Overlapping-figures test 12.455
Overload, of the visual system 13.168
Over-sampling 2.411
Overshoot 8.24
Owl 2.91
  binocular vision 2.271, 2.273, 2.276–7, 2.280–1
  visual pathways 2.429–30, 2.436, 2.442, 2.446
Oxygen, singlet **16.67, 16.69–70, 16.72**
Oxygyrus (snail) 2.122
Ozone **16.3, 16.13, 16.18**

P

Pachometry 1.430
   measurement of anterior chamber depth 1.390
   measurement of apparent corneal thickness 1.389–90
   measurement of corneal thickness 1.388–90
      simultaneous observation of specular reflexes 1.389
      successive focusing upon anterior and posterior
         surfaces 1.388–9
Pachygyria 3.363
Pachymetry, *see* Pachometry
Paedomorphy 2.223
Painters, and visual hemineglect 12.444–7
Paintings
   form-colour 12.385
   recognition of familiar 12.270
Palaeoneurobiology 2.435
Pale stripes, *see* Cytochrome oxidase pale stripes
Palinopsia 12.198, 12.426, 12.473–5
Palisade endings 8.188, 8.321
Palmer, G. 12.389
Palmer (equivalent) luminances 5.50
Palmer transform 5.50
Palmer trolands 5.50
Palsy, third nerve 12.348
Pan paniscus (pygmy chimpanzee) 12.331–2
Panoramic vision 2.273, 2.448
Panoramogram 1.332
Pantomime 12.292, 12.307
Panum's fusional area 5.136, 5.258, 8.9, 9.19, 9.31–6,
      9.111–3, 9.116, 9.130, 9.135, 9.185–7, 13.141
   dynamic properties of 9.131
'Paper', clay tablet as 12.306
Papilio xuthus (swallowtail butterfly) 2.294
Papillitis 7.157
Papilloedema 7.177, 12.472
Papio papio (guinea baboon) 2.77, 7.203
Parabigeminal nucleus 3.162, 3.193
Parabrachial nucleus 3.200
Paracentral nuclei 4.407
Paraflocculus 2.180–2
Parafovea in pursuit system 2.166, 2.168–70
Paragraphia 12.407
Paralexia, semantic 12.328–9
Parallax 2.239, 2.242, 2.254–5, 2.257–61
   and equiluminance 5.240
   motion 10.163–5
Parallax motion, *see* Motion, parallax
Parallel circuits 2.267
Parallel hierarchies 5.288
Parallel pathways
   in the cortex 4.169
   in the lateral geniculate nucleus 4.62–71
   and visual information processing 4.74–6
   X-, Y- and W- 4.64–7
Parallel processing 5.287–8
   distributed 2.229, 2.239, 2.244, 2.246, 2.249, 2.251, 2.253,
      2.259
   of form and colour information 4.323

Parallelism 2.214, 5.47–8, 12.23, 12.206, 14.6, 14.38, 14.45,
      14.93, 14.112
Paralysis, luetic 12.300
Paramedian pontine reticular formation 4.390
Parameter-response curves 4.174
   choices for the establishment of 4.174
   Glossary explanation of 4.448
Parametric feedback 8.35, 8.125–6
Paramnesia, reduplicative 12.279
Paraphasia 12.294
   verbal 12.334, 12.407
Paraphernalia 12.263, 12.278, 12.280
   and prosopagnosia 12.261, 12.285
Paraphrenia, visual 12.451
Parapineal 2.404–6
Paraprosopia 12.289–90, 12.296
   and heautoscopy 12.303
Parapsychic phenomena 12.299
Parasympatholytic drugs, topically applied 1.265
Parasympathomimetic drugs, topically applied 1.265
Paravermis 2.182
Paraxial models 1.5–6
   reduced eye 1.6
   schematic eye 1.6
Paraxial optics 1.53–63
   effectivity 1.53–6
      and accommodation
         ocular 1.55–6
         principal plane 1.56
         spectacle plane 1.55
      back vertex power 1.54
      vertex correction and contact lenses 1.54–5
   magnification in 1.58–62
      in astigmatic corrections 1.61
      consequences of 1.58–62
      and Galilean telescopes 1.61–2
      and 'power factor' 1.60
      and 'shape factor' 1.60
      and 'size' lenses 1.61
      spectacle 1.59
   notation used in 1.62–3
   prismatic effects 1.56–8
Paraxial photorefraction, *see* Photoretinoscopy
Pareidolias 12.303, 12.470–1
Parietal cortex 2.174, 2.177–80, 2.191, 2.458, 8.40, 8.153–4,
      8.283–5
Parietal cortical neurones, visual response properties
      of 4.374–83
Parietal groups 4.164
Parietal lobe 4.372–4
   cerebral lesions of 12.465
   efferent connections to 13.7–8
      and basal ganglia 13.7
      and the cerebellum 13.7
      and cortico-cortical relays 13.7
      and the pontine nuclei 13.7–8
      and the superior colliculus 13.7
      use of horseradish peroxidase in determining 13.7–8
   functional homologies of posterior cortical regions 12.94

Glossary explanation of **4.444**
inferior
  posterior **12.448**
  structures **12.334**
  and visual hemineglect **12.434**
posterior
  anatomical subdivision and connections of primate area
    7 **12.92–4**
  and cerebral representation of extrapersonal
    space **12.92–106**
  functional deficits after inferior parietal lobule
    lesions **12.94–5**
  quantitative evaluations of area 7 neoronal
    responses **12.103–6**
  upper **12.449**
  visuospatial and visuomotor functions of **13.12–43**
  visuo-spatial and visuo-motor neuronal data processing
    in area 7 **12.96–103**
right **12.343**
see also Lesions
superior **12.343**
unilateral, impairment of **12.447–52**
visual cortical pathways to **4.372–4**
Parietal lobule
inferior **12.92, 12.96**
  functional deficits after lesions **12.94–5**
Parietal visual neurones **4.378**
and the enhancement phenomenon **4.381**
Parietal visual system **4.371–87**
functions of **4.383–4**
Parieto-temporal areas **1.233**
Parkinson's disease (PD) **4.402, 10.250–7, 12.220, 12.463**
abnormal eye movements in **13.263**
Parmenides **12.26**
Pars-pro-toto defect, visual **12.337**
Pars-pro-toto function **12.288, 12.309**
and colour deficiencies **12.410**
and pure alexia **12.358**
visual **12.357**
Pars-pro-toto perception **12.309**
Parvocellular, Glossary explanation of **4.448**
Parvocellular cells **4.321–2**
Parvocellular layers **7.69, 10.52**
Glossary explanation of **4.447**
of lateral geniculate nucleus (LGN) **10.154**
in MS **10.246**
in pursuit system **2.171–2, 2.175**
and visual pathways **2.444–5, 2.450–1, 2.453, 2.458–9**
Parvocellular pathway **5.48, 5.72–3, 5.192–5, 5.197–9, 7.185**
Parvocellular system **5.259, 5.261, 6.174–6, 6.181, 6.186–7,**
  7.69–71
broad band cells **6.175**
and colour deficiencies **12.409**
input to cortex **6.174–5**
multiplexing colour **6.181–3, 6.204–5**
narrow band cells **6.175**
off-centre **6.206**
on-centre **6.206**
output from cortex **6.174–5**

P-cells **6.205**
tonic cells **6.174**
Patches, in the superior colliculus **8.247**
Pathology
brain **12.390**
cerebral **12.344**
splenial **12.347**
Pathophysiology, of heautoscopy **12.300–2**
Pattern adaptation **5.306**
Pattern after-effects **14.4, 14.21–3, 14.25**
Pattern bindings, inner **14.80**
Pattern constancy **14.26**
Pattern decomposition, multilinear **14.78–9**
Pattern decomposition and 'counting' (PDC),
  polynomial **14.75–81**
Pattern detection **5.92, 5.295, 5.304**
of chromatic isoluminant **5.215**
Pattern direction **5.166–7**
Pattern direction selectivity **4.211**
Pattern discrimination **2.263, 2.456, 5.221**
limits of **5.266–74**
parallel process **5.274**
peripheral vision **5.268–70**
serial process **5.274**
Pattern disruption **2.261, 2.263**
Pattern electroretinogram (PERG) **10.254–5**
Pattern elements **14.75, 14.78**
Pattern familiarity **14.138**
Pattern formation **11.47–55, 11.60, 11.62–5, 11.68–84**
Pattern formation systems **11.52–4, 11.64–5**
Pattern goodness **14.129**
Pattern invariance and classification **14.69–81**
Pattern meaning **14.3**
Pattern normalization **14.61, 14.78**
Pattern orientation **11.50, 11.64, 14.65**
Pattern plaids **5.110**
Pattern processing **14.3–4**
levels of **9.49**
limits of **5.286**
relation of, to the site of fusion **9.49–50**
Pattern recognition **2.459, 5.267, 5.304, 10.280, 12.190,**
  12.210–1
and agnosia **12.196**
algorithms **14.26**
biological **14.70, 14.79, 14.81**
character **14.69**
computational **14.26**
conscious **12.206**
consequences of LTG/NP **14.21–5**
and Gibson's concepts **14.20**
invariant **14.26, 14.69–70**
invariant classification **14.73**
levels **14.99–100**
problems **14.99, 14.101**
process
  input to **14.1–4**
  output from **14.1**
role of transformation **14.21**
signal similarity **14.71**

Pattern recognition (*continued*)
   and spatial relations **14.50**
   statistical **14.69–70, 14.72**
   system **14.81**
   template matching **14.69**
   under transformation **14.25–6**
   and visual perception **14.1–7**
Pattern regeneration **11.48–9, 11.51, 11.64–5**
Pattern sensitivity **5.54, 5.64, 10.50**
Pattern signal **14.72–3, 14.75, 14.78–80**
   binary **14.79**
Pattern signal normalization **14.78**
Pattern size **5.216**
Pattern suprathreshold, perception of **10.200–2**
Pattern transfer of learning effects **5.273**
Pattern transfer of practice effects **5.268**
Pattern visual evoked potential (PVEP) **10.254–5**
Pattern-ERG (PERG) **16.107**
Patternless fields **5.178**
Patterns **5.291**
   achromatic **5.209–10, 5.216–7**
   chequerboard **12.209–10**
   chromatic **5.209–10, 5.215–6**
   complex **5.271, 12.195**
      visual **12.230**
   computer-generated coloured fractal **12.116–7**
   computer-generated multicoloured fractal **12.118–9**
   context facilitation **12.339**
   cortical organization of **5.266**
   and effects of practice **5.266–8**
   and equi-luminance **5.195, 5.239**
   face-responsive neuronal activity **12.118**
   fine **10.159**
   flickering **12.23**
   flickering plaid **5.150**
   fortification **12.175**
      flickering migraine **12.176**
      of migraine phosphenes **12.172–8**
   highly complex **12.210**
   and hyperacuity **5.231**
   hypo-or paramimic face **12.220**
   identical **14.51, 14.55–6, 14.59–61, 14.64, 14.66**
   in images **14.2–3**
   Julesz **5.267**
   Julesz random-dot **10.160–2, 10.282**
   laminar **3.316**
      feedback **3.308, 3.317**
      feedforward **3.308, 3.317**
   Moiré **3.19–20**
   Mondrian **12.85, 12.393**
   net-like **11.63–4**
   orthogonal **11.53–4, 11.64**
   periodic **11.54**
   peripheral **10.76**
   point-inverted **14.59–61, 14.66**
   polar **11.48–51, 11.60**
   random-dot **5.160, 5.267, 5.274, 14.55, 14.60–4**
   reflected **14.51, 14.58–61, 14.64, 14.66**
   rotated **14.51, 14.55–9, 14.62, 14.66**
   rotated random-dot **14.56–8**
   segmental **11.39–41**
   self-regulating **11.50**
   spatial relations **14.52**
   striped
      and duty cycles **13.155–6**
      effects of **13.155–7**
      measuring of **13.155–62**
         and ascenders of letters **13.155–7**
         contrast **13.156–7, 13.160**
         and descenders of letters **13.155–7**
         interletter spacing **13.159**
         interline spacing **13.156**
         letter cell area **13.159**
         page width **13.156, 13.159**
         reading distance **13.156, 13.159**
         spatial characteristics responsible for illusions and seizures **13.155**
         two–dimensional **13.158–9**
         typeface **13.158, 13.160, 13.162**
         x-height **13.156, 13.159, 13.162**
      and spatial frequency **13.155–6**
      text as **13.155**
      visual and clinical effects of
         in text **13.162–4**
            anomalous, rhomboid lattice **13.162**
            epileptic seizures **13.163–4**
            eye-strain **13.162–3**
   stripe-like **11.54**
   symmetrically positioned **14.59–61, 14.66**
   types of **14.2–3**
   vision and peripheral vision **5.54–6**
   visual
      from meaningless random stimuli **12.470–1**
      in palinopsia **12.475**
Paul, Jean **12.299**
Pauli exclusion principle **16.30, 16.33**
P-cell pathway **7.178, 7.181**
P-cells **4.29–36, 4.224–5, 4.234, 4.322, 5.192–5, 10.52**
   function of, in monkey vision **4.35–6**
   tonic (sustained) **10.154**
PD, *see* Parkinson's disease
PDC, *see* Polynomial pattern decomposition and counting
PDE, *see* Phosphodiesterase
PDGF, *see* Platelet derived growth factor
PDR, *see* Peak density region
PE cells, disparity selective **4.198**
Peabody Picture Vocabulary Test **13.89**
Peak density region **3.69, 3.80, 3.91**
   and cytogenesis **3.82**
   and dendritic field size **3.102–3**
   and differentiation **3.100**
   and neurone death **3.96**
   and retinal expansion **3.106–10**
   in retinal maturation **3.117–8**
Pecten (scallop) **2.40, 2.124–6, 2.417**
   eye **2.4, 2.26–8**
   photoreception **2.368–71**
Pectinate ligament **2.474**

Pedestal **5.32, 5.208**–10
Pedestal effect **5.27, 5.31**–2
Pedicle **3.11, 3.32, 3.93**–4
Peduncle, superior cerebellar **8.216**
Peep-hole viewers, door **1.218**
Pelli–Robson Contrast Sensitivity letter chart **16.154**
Pellucid marginal degeneration **1.46**
Penetration depth **16.45, 16.52, 16.58**
Pentachromacy **2.295**
Pentachromatic colour vision, in insects **6.269, 6.275**
Peptide histidine isoleucine (PHI) **11.361**
Perca falvescens (perch) **2.69**
Perca fluviatilis (perch) **2.290**
Perceived visual direction **9.19**–20, **9.77**
Percept
    illusionary **12.467**
    pareidolic visual **12.471**
    spatial **12.450**
    visual, delusionary/illusionary **12.466**
Perception
    and agnosia **12.179, 12.198**
    and brain activity **12.21**–4
    and cognition **12.209**
    and computational vision **14.30**
    darkening of visual **12.390**
    defect **12.320**
    defective categorization **12.201, 12.212**–5
    development **12.17**–21
    Gibson's concepts **14.19**
    historical observations **12.25**–51
        Ancient Greek thought on **12.25**–32
        creation of modern physiological optics **12.36**–40
        localization theories **12.46**–7
        Newton and Mayer **12.42**–5
        progress in neuroanatomy **12.40**–2
        Renaissance approach **12.32**–5
        visual cortex and agnosia **12.47**–51
    illusionary **12.470**–1
    information processing approach **14.89**–90
    integration of visual qualities **12.200**
    Marr's computational approach **14.90**
    mechanisms **12.321**
    modularization **14.90**–1
    motion **10.53**–4
    and orientation in extrapersonal space **12.411**–7
    pars-pro-toto **12.309**
    Praegnanz concept of **14.90**
    probabilistic approach **14.83**–6
    and prosopagnosia **12.261**
    of rotation **8.33, 8.40**
    simultaneous **12.216**
    spatial **12.428**
    subjective **12.467**
    of target motion **8.149**–52, **8.211, 8.307**
    top-down mechanisms **12.205**
    visual **12.466**
Perception theories, texture **10.114**–32
Perceptrons **14.76, 14.81, 14.101**
Perceptual analysis **10.116**

Perceptual blur threshold **1.241**
Perceptual continuity **5.273**
Perceptual correlates, of vestibular adaptation **8.39**–40
Perceptual delay **10.243**
Perceptual image quality **15.24**
    measures of **15.24**–6
Perceptual learning **5.266**–8, **5.272**
Perceptual organization **2.308**–9
Perceptual psychology **10.116**
Perceptual segregation **8.90**
Perceptual span **13.251**
    in reading **13.67, 13.251**
Perceptual vector analysis **9.152**
Perceptuo-motor tasks **12.269**
PERG, *see* Pattern electroretinogram
Perigeniculate nucleus **2.171**–2, **2.174**–6, **2.184, 3.200**–2,
        3.215, 3.217, 3.282–4
    Glossary explanation of **4.448**
Perikarya microtubules **11.133**–6
Perikarya neurofilaments **11.144**
Perimeter
    Goldmann **12.137, 12.393**
    Purkinje **12.136**–7
    Tübingen **12.137, 12.139, 12.141, 12.150, 12.194, 12.393,**
        12.396
Perimetry **12.136**–42
    and achromatopsia **12.393**
    and agnosia **12.202**
    automatized static light **12.194**–5
    binocular **12.141, 12.393**
    clinical **12.390**
    colour **12.138**–40, **12.339, 12.349, 12.390, 12.396, 12.399**
        and hemiachromatopsia **12.402**
    dynamic **12.140**–1, **12.203**
    flicker **12.140**
    form **12.339**
    isopter **12.139**–40
    kinetic **12.139**
    light **12.144, 12.339**
    monocular **12.393**
    profile **12.139**–40
    quantitative **12.139**
    quantitative dynamic **12.194**
    see also Colour perimetry
    shape **12.141**
    static **12.194, 12.203**
        light **12.139**
    structural **12.141**
    testing by **12.402**
    visual acuity **12.141**
Periodic alternating nystagmus **8.234, 8.299**–301, **8.312**–3,
        8.322
Periodic disparity modulation **9.59**–60
Peripheral nervous system (PNS) **11.35**
    amphibian, neurone regeneration **11.212**
    and GAP-43 **11.220, 11.224**
    mammal, neurone regeneration **11.206**–10
    regeneration **11.227**–8
    Schwann cell environment **11.248**

Peripheral vision 2.454, **10**.196–8
  and contrast encoding 5.116–7
  cortical magnification 5.255–7
  dark-adapted 5.54, 5.68, 5.73
  decline of sensitivity 5.251
  decline in visual acuity in 5.268
  limitations to human 5.44–76
    intensity range of vision 5.48–54
    light sensitivity 5.54–65
    model of peripheral visual pathways 5.44–8
    pattern sensitivity 5.65–76
  neural substrates 5.251–63
  psychophysical correlates 5.256–61
  threshold gradients 5.251–63
Peripheral-field loss, *see under* Optical aids, for peripheral
    field loss
Periphery (shift) effect 4.17
Peristimulus time histograms 4.174
Peritrigonal region 12.344
Perseveration, visual 12.190, 12.198, 12.275, 12.473–5
Person familiar 12.259
Person recognition, impairment in non-prosopagnosic
    patients 12.280–6
Perspective
  and agnosia 12.184
  central 12.456
  unusual 12.209, 12.212
  and visuo-spatial disorders 12.441
Perspective drawings 5.240–1
Perspective and vergence 8.166
PET, *see* Positron emission tomography
Petroglyph 12.309
Pfaff, J. Ch. 12.162
PGN, *see* Perigeniculate nucleus
Phagocytosis in optic nerve 11.210
Phakofragmentation, ultrasonic 1.123
Phakometry 1.382–4
  techniques of 1.383
Phantasy, artistic visual 12.471
Pharmacology 2.218
Phase 5.103, 5.156
  reversal, apparent (APR) 5.112
  shift 5.112, 5.173, 5.182
  spatial 5.272
Phase analysis 12.9
Phase lead 2.181–2, 2.185–8
  in vestibular afferents 8.29–32
Phase sensitivity 5.304
Phase transfer function 1.10–1, 1.16, 2.93, 5.88–9, 10.23
Phase transition 11.197
Phasic cells, monkey retinal 4.27–8
Phasic–tonic index 4.58
Phenomena, reduplicative 12.279
Phenothiazine 16.70
Phenothiazine derivatives 7.128–9
Pheomelanin 16.39, 16.68
PHI, *see* Peptide histidine isoleucine
Philipon, Charles 12.222
Philosophy, Greek 12.221

Phi-phenomenon, *see* Motion, apparent
Phoneme sequences, audible 12.310–1
Phoneme–grapheme system 12.304
Phonetics 12.304
Phonogram, Kana 12.348–9
Phoria 8.162, 8.313, 9.8, **9**.90
  distance/near 1.249
Phoropter 1.411
Phosphenes 1.354–5, 7.193, 12.133, 12.154–5, 12.158–78
  accommodation 12.162, 12.467
  binocular deformation 12.176
  binocular patterns 12.467
  coloured flash 12.167
  deformation (pressure) 12.25, 12.36, 12.158–62
  electrical 12.162–6
  electromagnetic 12.166
  evoked by electrical stimulation of afferent visual
    system 12.166–8
  evoked by electrical stimulation of primary visual
    cortex 12.168–72
  first symptom of pituitary adenoma 12.162
  fortification patterns 12.172–8
    flickering migraine 12.176
  in hemianopic field 12.169
  illusion and hallucination 12.472–4, 12.476–81
  migraine 12.27, 12.172–8, 12.393
    fortification patterns 12.178
  retinal 12.158–66
  saccadic 12.162, 12.166
  threshold 12.164
  x-ray 1.362–3
Phosphodiesterase (PDE) 7.135, 7.144
Phosphoinositol 11.200
Phospholipid cascade, inositol 11.281
Phospholipids 11.226–7, **16**.84
Phosphoproteins 11.118, 11.195, 11.201
Phosphor luminescence 15.8–10
Phosphorescence 16.35–6
Phosphorylation 11.133
  F1 11.222
  GAP 11.119
  GAP-43 11.220–1, 11.223, 11.225–8, 11.282, 11.297
  MAP2 11.290
  in neuronal cytoskeleton 11.277
  nucleotide 11.193
  protein 11.201, 11.287
  in regeneration 11.196–7
  serine 11.118
Photisms 12.133, 12.155–6
  illusion and hallucination 12.472–4, 12.476–1
Photoablation 16.52
  corneal 16.93
Photobia
  and dazzling glare 1.222
  and disability glare 1.222–3
  and discomfort glare 1.222
Photobleaching 16.41–2
Photochemical changes 2.103
Photochemical damage 2.95

Photochromatic interval 5.195
Photocoagulation
    argon laser 16.135
    krypton laser 16.135
Photocoagulation therapy 7.150–1
Photoconjunctivitis 16.59–60
Photoelastic stress patterns, analysis of, using polarized
        light 1.324
Photofrin II 16.72
Photographic negative, faces in 14.108–9
Photoisomerizations 2.64, 2.66, 5.48, 5.55–6, 12.466
    rod 5.46, 5.49–50, 5.61
Photokeratitis 16.3, 16.24, 16.41, 16.59–60, 16.93–5
Photokeratoconjunctivitis 16.27
Photokeratoscopes 1.381
Photometry 5.50, 5.196, 5.235, 16.105
    detection of minimal flicker in 5.297
    flicker 7.176
    heterochromatic flicker 6.48
    heterochromatic foveal 7.175
    see also Flicker photometry
Photon capture rates 5.191
Photon catch 5.50–1, 5.55–6
    in peripheral vision 5.52, 5.58–9, 5.62, 5.66–70, 5.73, 5.75
Photon count 2.5–6, 2.8
Photon counters 2.242–3, 2.248
Photon flux 2.89–92, 2.103, 2.410
Photon noise 2.237, 5.55, 5.59–60, 5.65, 5.68, 5.70, 5.149
Photons 3.12, 3.25–7, 5.49
    in dioptrics 2.86–7, 2.103
    in hyperacuity 10.88, 10.90–1
    nature of light 2.3, 2.5–7, 2.13
    in peripheral vision 5.50–2, 5.54–7, 5.59–60, 5.63, 5.65,
        5.67, 5.70–1
Photo-ophthalmia 16.60
Photo-oxidation 2.299
Photophobia 7.24, 7.28, 7.98–9, 7.140, 12.31, 12.270,
        12.274–5, 12.388, 12.390, 13.162, 13.177
    relief from 13.171
Photophores 2.367, 2.381, 2.408, 2.413
    in fish 6.112
        blue emitting 6.113
        red emitting 6.113
Photopic function 7.5–6, 16.105
Photopic luminosity (V_λ) curve 10.139, 10.157
Photopic system 2.168–70, 16.110, 16.120–1, 16.123
    and ageing 16.150
    and developing visual system 16.125–6, 16.128
Photopic vision 2.66–8, 2.74, 2.76, 2.78, 5.49, 5.52, 5.73–4,
        12.386, 12.393
    in infants 10.203
Photopigments 2.39, 3.1, 3.9, 3.25, 3.30, 12.386
    blue 7.84–5
    in colour vision 2.284, 2.287, 2.289–97, 2.299, 2.315–6
    cone 7.18, 7.72–4
    evolution of 6.62–7
    in evolution of retina 2.138–9
    in eye evolution 2.348–50
    in insects 6.266–7

ecology aand evolution of 6.285–8
    rhodopsin, with retinal chromophore 6.266–7
    xanthopsin, with 3-hydroxyretinal
        chromophore 6.266–7
    in photoreception 2.378, 2.380–3, 2.390
    in trichromacy 2.311–4
Photopsia 12.155–6
Photoreception 2.16, 2.18–9, 2.21, 2.26, 2.39
    basic concepts of 6.93, 6.108–10
        11-*cis* retinal 6.93–4, 6.109
        and opsins 6.93, 6.108
        photopigment molecules 6.93, 6.108–12
    cephalic eyes 2.371–83
    extra-ocular 2.364–8
    and genes and pigments in normal colour vision 6.93–8
    in molluscs 2.364–91
    non-cephalic eyes 2.368–71
    vertebrate 2.28
    visual processing 2.383–91
Photoreceptor metabolism 7.85
Photoreceptor mosaics, in vertebrate retina 6.128–33
Photoreceptor optics 1.280
Photoreceptor organs 2.19–29
Photoreceptor outer segment misalignment 7.126
Photoreceptor systems 2.19, 2.21, 2.26–9
Photoreceptors 4.316–8, 5.55, 6.108–27
    absorption of light by 2.383
    acceptance angle of 1.284
    action spectra of, in insects 6.264–7
    ageing 16.62–3
    and ageing macula 16.80–2, 16.85–90
    alignment of 1.280
    and amacrine cells 3.42
    ancestral 2.137–8
    and bipolar cells 3.33–6
    blue 7.72–3, 7.78, 7.84–5
    ciliated 2.27–8, 2.365–6, 2.368–72, 2.375–6
    classes of, spectral, spatial and temporal response
        properties 12.54–9
    as classical waveguides 1.280
    in colour vision 2.292, 2.294–7, 2.299–300
    cone
        birth of 3.82
        differentiation 3.100–1
        physiology of 6.146–62
        and retinal development 3.80
        see also Cone photoreceptors
    cone spectral sensitivity 5.210
    coupling between 3.11
    and developing visual system 16.106–11, 16.119, 16.126
    displaced 3.91, 3.96, 3.98
    distribution of 2.139, 3.14–6
    ectopic 3.97, 3.101
    in evolution of eye 2.3–11
        arthropod 2.343–4, 2.351, 2.353–4, 2.358–60, 2.413
        vertebrate and invertebrate 2.16–21, 2.24–7, 2.35–44,
            2.63–78
    in evolution of retina 2.136–40, 2.142–3
    in evolution of vision 2.405, 2.409–10

Photoreceptors (*continued*)
 extra-ocular 2.368, 2.390
 foveal 3.113
 and ganglion cells 3.48
 in hyperacuity 5.123–4, 5.224, 5.230
 and ipsilateral projection 3.112–3
 lattice of eye 5.120
 light absorption in 7.4–5
 and light damage 16.63–4, 16.66
 long visual fibres (LVF) 2.204–5, 2.208, 2.214, 2.217–8,
  2.221
 in molluscs 2.364–7
 noise 2.299
 optical properties 3.11–4
 output synapses 3.25–7, 3.39
 in pattern discrimination 5.268
 in peripheral vision 5.44–51, 5.57–9, 5.72
 as photon counters 2.242–3, 2.248
 in plexiform layer 3.90
 processes 3.32
 in pursuit system 2.170
 and radiation 16.57, 16.59, 16.61
 responses of 4.318
 and retina 3.1–2, 3.4–5, 3.9–30, 3.83, 3.118
 retinal 5.120, 12.386, 14.88
 rhabdomeric 2.344, 2.366, 2.370, 2.375, 2.378
 rod 7.73, 7.76
  class specification 3.101–2
  differentiation 3.100
  foveal 3.115
  in retinal development 3.80, 3.82, 3.84
  and retinal expansion 3.107
 and rods and cones 1.281–2
 see also Ophthalmic disease
 sensitivity 3.13
 short visual fibres (SVF) 2.204–7, 2.214, 2.217
 skin 2.402–3
 spacing 3.25
 spatial sampling by 3.16–24
 specializations 2.138–9
 spectral sampling by 3.27–30
 spectral sensitivity of, influence of waveguides on 6.268
 texture and stereo depth 5.125, 5.128
 and trichromacy 2.310–1
 types 2.204, 2.284, 2.287–9, 2.295, 2.297, 2.300
 in vertebrate retina
  connections between 6.133–7
  cones and horizontal cells 6.134–7
 in visual processing 2.210, 2.229–30, 2.232, 2.235, 2.237,
  2.242, 2.245, 2.265
 and waveguides 1.280–7
Photorefraction 1.407, 2.107
 advantages and disadvantages of 1.409
 dynamic 2.112
 eccentric, *see* Photoretinoscopy
 paraxial, *see* Photoretinoscopy
 pointspread techniques 1.407–8
  advantages and disadvantages of 1.409–10
  and the interval of Sturm 1.408

 isotropic 1.407–8
 orthogonal 1.407
  practical applications and utility of 1.410
 retinoscopic-like methods 1.408
Photoretinitis 16.24, 16.27, 16.60
 solar 16.59
Photoretinoscopy 1.408–9
 advantages and disadvantages of 1.410
 infra-red video 1.409
Photosensitive epilepsy 13.162
Photosensitive vesicles (PSVs) 2.366–7, 2.381
Photosensitivity 2.406
 and epilepsy 13.155
 extra-ocular 2.367
Photosensitization
 endogenous 16.68–9
 exogenous 16.68–9
Photosensitizers 16.61, 16.67, 16.72–3
 chemical characteristics 16.69
Photoskiascopy, *see* Photoretinoscopy
Photostress 5.278, 7.125–6, 7.132, 7.134, 16.25, 16.153
Photostress recovery time 5.278
Photostress test 7.116
Phototaxis 2.212, 2.374–5, 2.390
Phototherapy 16.112–6, 16.123–5
 and developing visual system 16.126, 16.128
Phototoxicity 16.67–73, 16.107, 16.114, 16.116
 defined 16.68
 and developing visual system 16.106, 16.123
 retinal 7.80, 7.82
 syndrome 16.128
 visual 16.104–5, 16.108
Phototransduction 2.380
Phototrauma 7.135
Phototropic mechanisms, and receptor alignment 1.301
Phototropic response 2.390
Phototropism 2.367
Phoxinus laevis (minnow) 2.285
Phrenology 12.47
Phthalocyanines 16.72
Phylogenesis, hominid, development 12.220–1
Phylogenetic tree 2.341–2, 2.344, 2.349
Phylogeny
 birds 2.421–3
 mammals 2.421–3
 molecular 2.341
 reptiles 2.421–3
Physiognomy
 human 12.218, 12.220
 and prosopagnosia 12.259–60
 quality of 12.296
Physiological recordings, in relation to saccadic eye
  movements 4.388
Physiology
 and 3D representation 14.44
 comparative sensory 2.285
 cortical 3.348
π (spectral response) mechanisms 5.85, 5.88, 5.196, 5.283,
  7.7–9, 7.12, 7.15–9, 7.23–4

Pi mechanisms, *see* π (spectral response) mechanisms
Piaget's theory of number **14**.126
Piccolomini, Archangelo **12**.34
Pickford–Lakowski match **7**.220
Pickford–Nicolson anomaloscope, *see* Anomaloscope
Pictograms **12**.305–7, **15**.79
Pieron's law **5**.50
Pig dioptrics **2**.103
Pig photoreceptor system **2**.74
Pigeon **2**.70
  colour vision **2**.286, **2**.288, **2**.291–2, **2**.298–9
  dioptrics **2**.86, **2**.97–8
Pigment epithelial cells **3**.9
Pigment epithelium **2**.40–2, **3**.136, **11**.388, **11**.392–3, **11**.402,
    12.56
  mammalian **2**.470–1, **2**.476
  melanin production **3**.74–5
  and neurone death **3**.97
  and retinal development **3**.69, **3**.71, **3**.73–6, **3**.79, **3**.84–5
  and retinal expansion **3**.105–6
  retinal (RPE)
    and ageing **16**.63–5
    and ageing macula **16**.82–90
    and ageing retina **16**.134, **16**.137, **16**.141
    blue/medium colour **16**.143–5
    and developing visual system **16**.106, **16**.108–10, **16**.112
  in transplantation **11**.315–6, **11**.326, **11**.332
Pigment pairs **6**.109–10
Pigment triangles **6**.81–3
Pigments
  ancestral **3**.28
  anomalous **2**.78
  chemistry of visual **3**.28
  cone **3**.28–9
  foveal **5**.281
  rod **2**.409, **3**.28
  visual **2**.6
Pineal **2**.401–6
Pineal stalk **2**.405
Pineal window **2**.405
Piracetam, effect of, on patients with reading
    disabilities **13**.178–9
Pituitary, adenoma **12**.144–5, **12**.162, **12**.166
Pituitary complex **2**.17, **2**.31
Pixel-point spread functions **15**.11
Pixels **14**.98–9, **14**.101
  binary **14**.102–3, **14**.105
  chain **14**.103, **14**.105–6
  chain of black **14**.102
  numerical **14**.102–4
PKC, *see* Protein kinase C
Place, recognition **12**.259, **12**.270
Placentals **2**.444, **2**.450, **2**.459, **2**.467–9, **2**.471–8
Placode theory of eye embryology **11**.397–8
Placoderms **2**.406
Plaid patterns, Glossary explanation of **4**.449
Planck's constant **5**.48
Planck's radiation law **16**.6–7, **16**.20
Plane waves

orientation estimates of **4**.255
  twist estimates of **4**.255
Plant, oculomotor **8**.96, **8**.139, **8**.203–5
Plants, in illusion and hallucination **12**.471
Planum temporale **12**.287
Plasma formation **16**.50–1
Plasma shielding **16**.50
Plasticity
  brain **11**.288
  changes in transcription **11**.289
  critical period for **3**.366, **3**.368–9, **11**.288–91
  functionally driven **11**.287–92
  horizontal cell **3**.40
  neuronal **11**.133
  in pattern discrimination **5**.274
  synaptic **11**.133–45, **11**.281
    role of GAP-43 **11**.219, **11**.221–3, **11**.225–8
  visual cortical **3**.368
Plasticity effects **5**.253
Plasticizers **16**.84–5
Plastics, hard, in the manufacture of contact lenses **1**.85
Plate
  cortical **3**.363–4, **11**.337–40
    and axon growth **11**.235
    and neurotransmitters **11**.357–60, **11**.363
    in synaptic rearrangement **11**.262–3
  subcortical **3**.370
Platelet derived growth factor **11**.30, **11**.113–4, **11**.118–9
  in optic nerve regeneration **11**.208, **11**.211
  see PDGF
Plato **12**.25–6
Platter, Felix **12**.36, **12**.38, **12**.53
Platypus **2**.442, **2**.467–71
Platyrrhine monkey **7**.210–2
Plexiform layers **2**.139–47
  and class specification **3**.101
  development **3**.90–4
  differentiation **3**.100
  and fovea **3**.115
  Glossary explanation of **4**.449
  inner (IPL) **2**.139–41, **2**.145–6, **3**.4, **3**.32, **3**.34–5, **3**.41–58
    amacrine cells **3**.41–8
    dendritic stratification in **3**.49
    ganglion cells **3**.48–58
    sublamina b **3**.33, **3**.36
  and ipsilateral projection **3**.112
  in mammals **2**.470, **2**.476
  microglia in **3**.85
  and neurone death **3**.97
  outer (OPL) **3**.4, **3**.11, **3**.32–42
    interplexiform cells **3**.47
  in retinal development **3**.88–9
  in retinal maturation **3**.117–8
Ploucquet, G. W. **12**.434
PLS, *see* Polarized-light sensitivity
Plus-lens magnifiers
  comparison with telescopes for near tasks **1**.214
  hand held
    advantages of **1**.200

Plus-lens magnifiers (*continued*)
    disadvantages of 1.200
    types available 1.200
  hand held and stand 1.196–7
  in low vision 1.189–91, 1.193–202
  practical considerations in the use of 1.193–202
    binocular versus monocular viewing 1.198–200
      contra-indications to 1.199
    depth-of-field 1.194–7
      and aberrations 1.194, 1.196–7
    field-of-view 1.197–8
      angular semi-field-of-view of 1.197
      and influence on reading speed 1.198–200
      linear dimension of 1.197
    focusing range 1.195–6
      and the near point 1.195
    real image or transverse magnification 1.202–4
    in relation to spectacle-mounted devices 1.193–4
    working distance 1.193–4
    working space 1.193–4
  spectacle mounted 1.196
    achromatic 1.196
    advantages of 1.200
    aplanatic 1.196
    and aspheric surfaces 1.196
    disadvantages of 1.201
    and distortion 1.196
    and field curvature 1.196
    hyperocular 1.196
    in lenticular form 1.196
    and oblique astigmatism 1.196
    reduction of chromatic aberration in 1.196
    and spherical aberration and coma 1.196
    and spherical surfaces 1.196
    Stigmagna range of 1.196
    types available 1.201
      clip-on aids 1.201
      head-band mounted 1.201
      spectacle aids 1.201
Plus-lenses, *see* Plus-lens magnifiers
PMMA, *see* Polymethylmethacrylate
PND, *see* Posterior nodal distance
Pneuma 12.25–9
PNS, *see* Peripheral nervous system
Pocklington specular microscope 1.391
Poe, Edgar Allan 12.299
Poecilia reticulata (guppy) 2.69–70
Poeppel's paradox 11.370
Poetry 12.299
  written 12.306
Poggendorf illusion 5.242–4
Poincaré sphere 1.311
Poincaré's problem 9.151–2
Point horopter 9.24–8
  fixation at infinity 9.24
  generalized 9.26–7
  and the Helmholtz vertical shear 9.24
  and the role of vertical disparities 9.21
  significance of 9.21
  with symmetrical fixation in the visual plane 9.24
  vector representation of 9.21–2
'Point images' 4.299
  Glossary explanation of 4.449
  in the macaque monkey striate cortex 4.299, 4.301
Point source 5.49
Pointers 15.79–80
Pointing devices 15.108, 15.117
Point-inversion 14.56, 14.58–61
  global 14.62–3
  non-uniform 14.62–3
  position 14.62–3
  subpattern 14.62–3
Point-process generator 5.26–7
Point-spread function 1.10, 2.92–3, 5.88–9, 5.155, 5.288
Poiseuille–Hagen formula, and semicircular canals 8.18
Poisson process 10.90
Poissonian statistics 2.89, 5.12, 5.25, 5.39, 5.41, 5.55, 5.99
Pokorny and Smith revised Verriest classification 7.176–7
Polarity
  edge 2.252–3, 2.262
  neuronal 11.279–80
Polarity sensitivity 5.304
Polarization 2.230
  anodal 12.163
  cathodal 12.163
  circular 1.310
  in dioptrics 2.87, 2.89, 2.100
  elliptical 1.310
  methods of 1.331
    printed vectographs 1.331
  plane 2.230, 2.265, 2.382–3, 2.388, 2.391
  see also Polarized light
  Stokes parameters for the state of 1.311
  theory of 1.310–1
Polarized light 1.310–25
  clinical applications of 1.323–4
    amblyopia 1.323
    analysis of photoelastic stress patterns 1.324
    biomicroscopy 1.323
    determination of the modulation transfer function 1.323
    fundus reflectometry 1.323
    retinoscopy 1.323
    testing the integrity of the macula 1.323
  see also Polarization
Polarized-light sensitivity (PLS) 2.378, 2.383, 2.390–1
Polarography, in contact-lens measurements 1.432
Pole
  occipital 12.275–6
  temporal 12.269
Pollachius pollachius (pollack fish) 2.69
Polycarbonate, as a material for contact lenses 1.129
Polymerization
  actin 11.137–8, 11.174, 11.176, 11.226
  of cytoskeletal proteins 11.226
  of cytoskeleton 11.191, 11.196
  microtubule 11.134, 11.201, 11.281, 11.288
  tubulin 11.152, 11.280, 11.284, 11.288
Polymethyl methacrylate

as a material for contact lenses **1**.84–5
as a material for intraocular lenses **1**.127–8
Polymorphism **2**.13, **2**.70–1, **2**.76, **7**.5, **7**.94
   colour vision **2**.288, **2**.314–7
   in non-human primates **7**.199, **7**.202, **7**.207–13
   photopigments **2**.293–4
Polynomial discriminant functions **14**.74
Polynomial pattern decomposition and counting
      (PDC) **14**.75–81
Polyopia **12**.475–6
   circular **12**.475
   porroptic **12**.475
Polypeptides, in optic nerve regeneration **11**.211
Polyplopia, effects on focusing of **1**.350
Polypropylene, as a material for contact lenses **1**.128–9
Polysensory integration, as a suggested function of the
      pulvinar **4**.149
Polysensory regions **11**.369
Polysulphone lenses **1**.155–6
Pompeii **12**.221
Pons **8**.201–2, **8**.283
   dorsolateral nucleus **8**.153, **8**.202, **8**.211–3, **8**.224
      speed tuning **8**.212
   lesions **8**.312
Pontella **2**.122–3
Pontine nuclei **2**.175–83, **2**.189
Pontine reticular formation **8**.202, **8**.206–9, **8**.217, **8**.224
   paramedian zone of **8**.202, **8**.225, **8**.248, **8**.312
Ponzo illusion **5**.242–4
Pool cells **10**. 171
Pop-out effect **12**.182, **12**.191–2
Poppelreuter's visual exploration test **12**.454
Population, ageing **16**.77
Population inversion **16**.8, **16**.19–20
Porphyropsins **6**.108–10, **6**.115–8, **6**.120
   in colour vision **2**.291, **2**.299
   in evolution of eye **2**.6, **2**.8–9
   in evolution of vision **2**.403–4, **2**.409
   in photoreceptor system **2**.65–72
Portia fimbriata (jumping spider) **2**.120
Portrait **12**.221–4
   computer-digitized **12**.228
   Gothic **12**.224, **12**.229
   paintings **12**.224, **12**.227, **12**.230, **12**.233
   photographs, averaging **12**.229
   Renaissance **12**.224, **12**.229
Position
   contribution to gaze stability **8**.77–8
   contribution to smooth pursuit **8**.146
   sensitivity of oculomotor neurones **8**.203
Position disparity
   of Area 17 complex cells **4**.198–9
   of Area 17 S-and B-cells **4**.194–8
   of Area 17 simple cells **4**.198
   of Areas 18 and 19 cells **4**.199
   and responses to correlation-uncorrelation sequences **4**.215
   studies in the paralysed and anaesthetized
         preparation **4**.215–6
Position disparity selectivity **9**.227–30

local stereoscopic mechanisms in the awake fixating
      monkey **4**.213–5
and monocular cells **4**.213
and near and far cells **4**.213
and tuned excitatory cells **4**.213
and tuned inhibitory cells **4**.213
Positional acuity **10**.223
Positional information **11**.47, **11**.51–2, **11**.61, **11**.65
   cell **11**.70
   and cell recognition **11**.83–4
   gradients **11**.48
   interpretation **11**.55–7
   system **11**.53
Positional uncertainty, in amblyopia **10**.229–31
Position-in-depth
   loss of sensitivity to **9**.151
   separate system for **9**.150
Position-in-depth perception, dynamics of **9**.141–3
Position-related neurones **8**.207, **8**.217
Position-vestibular-pause neurones **8**.217
Positive contrast **5**.304
Positive feedback **8**.152, **8**.235
Positron emission tomography **12**.427
Positron emission tomography scans **12**.266
Posterior capsule opacification **1**.131
Posterior commissure, nucleus of the **8**.200
Posterior nodal distance (PND) **5**.49
Posterior parietal cortex **13**.12–38
   anatomy of **13**.12–3
   electrical stimulation of **4**.377
   functions of **13**.29–38
      attention **13**.34
      direction constancy **13**.30–1, **13**.182
      and eye position **13**.31, **13**.182
      motor planning **13**.32
      perception of visual motion and smooth pursuit eye
            movements **13**.37
      planning of eye and limb movements **13**.35
      and right hemisphere specialization **13**.37–8, **13**.182
      space perception **13**.31
      space representation **13**.30
      spatial localization **13**.30–1, **13**.34–5, **13**.182
      visual direction sense in sensory and motor
            localization **13**.35–7
      visuomotor localization **13**.31–2, **13**.35–7, **13**.182
   inferior parietal lobule of **13**.12
   lesions of **13**.22–9
      to area MT **13**.27–8
      and constructional apraxia **13**.24
      and depth perception **13**.25–6, **13**.182
      and disorders of perception of motion **13**.27
         motion sensitivity **13**.27
         smooth pursuit **13**.27
      and eye vergence movements **13**.27, **13**.182
      and fixation of gaze and ocular apraxia **13**.27–8
      and optic ataxia **13**.28–9
      right parietal lobe, and visuospatial deficits **13**.22, **13**.182
      and simultaneous agnosia **13**.24
      and visual disorientation **13**.24–5

Posterior parietal cortex (*continued*)
　　and visual dyslexia 13.26–7
　　and visual extinction 13.23
　　and visual inattention 13.23–4
　　and visual neglect 13.23–4
　　and visuomotor ataxia 13.28–9
　microanatomy and connectivity of 13.13–5
　physiology of 13.15–22
　　area 7a 13.16–8
　　area 7b 13.18
　　area LIP 13.18
　　　and memory-related activity 13.18
　　　and motor error 13.18
　　　and saccade-related activity 13.18
　　　and saccadic eye movements 13.18–9
　　areas MT and MST 13.18–22
　　　and apparent motion 13.20
　　　and coherent motion 13.20
　　　and perception of motion 13.21
　　　and relative motion detection 13.21
　　　and sensitivity to smooth pursuit 13.21
　　　and visual tracking 13.22
　right hemisphere, special role of 13.25, 13.181
　superior parietal lobule of 13.12
　and the visual world 13.182
Posterior suprasylvian area (PS area) 3.309, 4.360
Posterior vermis 8.233–4, 8.237–8
Posterolateral lateral suprasylvian cortex 4.357–9
　motor properties of 4.359
　　lens accommodation and pupillary constriction 4.359
　　saccadic eye movements and optinokinetic
　　　nystagmus 4.359
　ocular dominance in 4.358
　receptive-field, size of 4.357–8
　receptive-field properties of 4.358–9
　　centre-surround organization 4.358
　　directional tuning and preferred directions 4.358
　　shape and orientation selectivity 4.358
　　spacial-frequency tuning 4.358–9
　　velocity sensitivity and temporal-frequency tuning 4.359
　visuotopic map of 4.357–8
Posteromedial lateral suprasylvanian cortex 4.343–56
　behavioural functions of 4.354–6
　　image motion 4.355–6
　　interocular transfer 4.355
　　the near response 4.356
　　optinokinetic nystagmus 4.356
　　orientation and attention to visual clues 4.355
　　saccadic eye movements 4.356
　　spatial, form and pattern vision 4.355
　centre-surround organization of receptive fields of 4.347–9
　　remote stimulation 4.348–9
　　selective effects of surround stimulation 4.347–8
　contrast sensitivity and gain of 4.350–1
　direction-selective cells of
　　properties of 4.344–7
　　　directional tuning 4.345–6
　　　mechanisms of direction selectivity 4.345
　　　preferred directions 4.346

　　　receptive-field structure 4.345
　　　selectivity for 3D motion 4.346–7
　　motor properties of 4.352–4
　　　lens accommodation 4.354
　　　optokinetic nystagmus 4.354
　　　pupillary constriction 4.354
　　　saccadic eye movements 4.353–4
　　ocular dominance of 4.343–4
　　receptive-field properties of 4.343–5
　　shape and orientation selectivity of 4.349–50
　　spatial and temporal linearity of 4.352
　　stimulus size and spatial-frequency tuning of 4.350
　　velocity sensitivity and temporal-frequency tuning
　　　of 4.351–2
　　visuotopic map of 4.343
Postnatal development, of extraocular muscle 8.189–90
Postnatal synaptogenesis 9.174
Postreceptoral mechanisms 3.20, 3.30–58
　inner plexiform layer 3.41–58
　outer plexiform layer 3.32–41
Postreceptoral processing 6.204–5
Postsaccadic cells 4.417
Postsaccadic drift 8.123, 8.125–7, 8.236, 8.320, 8.322
Postsynaptic density 11.139, 11.142, 11.277
Post-translation
　of GAP-43 11.223
　modifications 11.223, 11.225, 11.276, 11.284
　in regeneration 11.196–9, 11.201
Postural problems
　in relation to visual displays 15.58
　　correlation with asthenopia 15.58
Posture
　measurements of 12.378
　performance 12.378
　visual stabilization of 12.379
Potentiation
　long-term (LTP) 11.143, 11.192, 11.199, 11.221–2
　　and GAP-43 11.225, 11.227
　　and memory 11.291
Pötzl's syndrome 12.337
POU domain 11.21
Power factor 1.60
Power function 5.29, 5.33, 5.116, 5.184
　threshold corrected 5.111
Power law transform 5.10–1, 5.102
Praegnanz concept of perception 14.90
Pre-adaptation 5.283
Preattentive vision 5.44–8, 5.75
Precentral cortex 2.179–80, 2.189, 2.191
Precision
　of saccades 8.96, 8.117–22
　of vergence 8.160
Predators 2.448
Prediction
　and pattern 14.3
　in smooth pursuit 8.79, 8.143–6, 8.152, 8.154
Predictive coding 3.30, 3.40, 3.49
Preferential looking 5.107, 10.183–4, 13.51
　forced-choice (FPL) 10.37, 10.188

Preferential looking procedure **9**.170
Prefrontal cortex **4**.422, **8**.284, **8**.288–9
Pregeniculate nucleus **3**.180
   LGNv homologue **3**.202, **3**.204
   in visual function **4**.405
Pregeniculomesencephalic tract **2**.172
Pregnancy, adverse outcomes of, among visual-display
      terminal operators **15**.2–4, **15**.57
Prenatal development, of extraocular muscle **8**.189
Prentice's rule **1**.57, **9**.216
Prentice's Typoscope **13**.164–5
Pre-ocular media **7**.28
Preorder relations **14**.54
Preorders **14**.54
Preparatory set cells **4**.420
Prepositus hypoglossi **2**.184–7
   nucleus **8**.2, **8**.33, **8**.153, **8**.202, **8**.213, **8**.216, **8**.225, **8**.234,
      8.238, **8**.248, **8**.302
Presaccadic cells **4**.417
Presbyopia
   correction of
      by alternating-vision bifocal contact lenses **1**.112–3
      by diffractive bifocal contact lenses **1**.113
      by monovision **1**.112
      by pinhole contact lenses **1**.112
      by simultaneous-vision bifocal contact lenses **1**.113
      by spectacle over-correction **1**.112
      in visual-display terminal operators **16**.65–6
   definition of **1**.263
   Duane–Fincham theory of **1**.264
   explanation of **1**.401
   functional **1**.237
   Hess–Gullstrand theory of **1**.264
   and topically applied diagnostic ophthalmic drugs **1**.264–6
Prescriptions, ophthalmic **1**.399
Pressure
   intercranial **12**.201
   intracranial, increased **12**.472
   intraocular, increased **12**.472
   perfusion **12**.473
      retinal **12**.472
PRESTEL **15**.73
Prestriate cortex **2**.452, **4**.449, **8**.281–2
Presubiculum **12**.94
Pretectal nuclear complex **3**.194
Pretectum **2**.152–4, **8**.213–4, **8**.245, **12**.60
   and detour movements **2**.158–60
   in eye evolution **2**.416–7
   feeding selectivity by **2**.157
   in pursuit system **2**.173–4, **2**.183–4
   and visual pathways **2**.424–5, **2**.427–9, **2**.433, **2**.449, **2**.455,
      2.457
   and visual thalamus **3**.205, **3**.207, **3**.210
Prey, bioluminescent **2**.412
Prey selection **2**.157–8
Prey-catching **2**.154–5, **2**.161
Priestley, Joseph **12**.389
Primal sketch **6**.200–12
Primary visual cortex **12**.465

thalamic input to **3**.236–44
   in carnivores **3**.239–41
   non-geniculate afferents **3**.244
      in the hedgehog **3**.244
      Lorente terminology **3**.244
   in primates **3**.241–4
   in rodents **3**.236–9
Primate cones **7**.72–5
Primate physiology and achromatopsia **7**.189–90
Primate retina **7**.69, **7**.74–5
Primate vision, spectral sensitivity in **5**.191–200
Primate visual system **5**.235
Primates **2**.476, **3**.1, **3**.11, **3**.28
   anatomical subdivision and connections of area 7 **12**.92–4
   bipolar cells **3**.33–4
   commissural pathways **3**.326
   cone pigments in New and Old World **5**.191
   ecological needs **12**.387
   LGNd projections **3**.200
   New World **2**.13
   non-human
      variations in colour vision **7**.199–214
         genetics **7**.211–3
         New World **7**.204–11
         Old World **7**.199–204
   object recognition **12**.107
   Old World **3**.27–9
   photoreceptor distribution in **3**.14–5
   pulvinar complex **3**.211–4
   retinal development **3**.69, **3**.72, **3**.74–5, **3**.77–8, **3**.80, **3**.82,
      3.86
   visual cortex **3**.303, **3**.308, **3**.311–9
   visual pathways **2**.442, **2**.450–2, **2**.458–9
   visual pathways of **5**.192
Priming tasks **12**.277
Primitive/derived characters, Glossary explanation of **4**.449
Primitives
   computational **14**.40
   and face recognition **14**.112–4
Principal point refraction **1**.53
Principle of univariance **2**.284, **2**.311, **6**.148–9
   first validation of **6**.149
Print **12**.308, **12**.312
   and alexia **12**.334
   loss of ability to read **12**.333
   and pure alexia **12**.342–3
   size of **12**.315
Printed gratings **10**.27–33
Prism adaptation **12**.416–7
Prism adaptation test **9**.195–6
Prism displacement and cross-modal functions **11**.377–8
Prismatic effects
   convergence **1**.58
   and major reference points **1**.58
   and paraxial optics **1**.56–8
Prisms, reversing **12**.416
Probability and numerosity **14**.129
Probability summation **10**.47
Probability theory in computer vision **14**.41

Prodoma 12.473
Product units 14.78
Progressive myopia 1.30
Projections
  associational 3.338, 3.344, 3.347
  axonal 11.239–41
  binocular 2.404
    of *Xenopus* 11.267–9
  callosal 3.326–7, 3.330, 3.334, 3.337, 3.344, 3.346–7,
      11.249, 11.337–8, 11.342–3, 11.346–7, 11.349
    heterotopic 3.338
  colliculogeniculate 3.193
  cortical 3.345
  corticocortical 11.337–8, 11.345–6
  corticogeniculate 3.192–3, 3.216
  corticothalamic 3.193
  exuberant 3.129, 3.132, 3.138–9, 3.370, 11.235, 11.341
  feedback 3.217, 3.310–1, 3.319, 3.338–9, 3.345–7, 3.350
  feedforward 3.310–1, 3.316, 3.319, 3.336, 3.339, 3.345,
      3.347
  geniculocortical 3.198, 11.235, 11.340–1, 11.345, 11.349
  Glossary explanation of 4.449
  heterotopic 3.346
  homotopic 3.346
  ipsilateral 3.110–3
  isthmotectal 11.267–9
  overlapping 3.140
  retinal 3.131–3
    refinement of 3.139
  retinocollicular in cat 3.138
  retinofugal 3.141
  retinogeniculate 3.137, 3.182, 3.198, 3.215, 11.237
  retinotectal 11.70, 11.84, 11.99
    and axon competition 11.240
    and axon growth 11.237, 11.243
    in fish 11.89
    in ranid frogs 11.89–90
    reformation of 11.96
    regeneration in fish 11.269
    and synaptic rearrangement 11.263, 11.265, 11.268
  retinotopic 11.88, 11.103
    refinement 11.192, 11.199–201
    reformation of 11.97
    and synaptic rearrangement 11.269
  subcortical 3.371
  thalamocortical 11.262, 11.337
  topographic, and axon growth 11.237, 11.240
  topographically organized 11.88–109
  transient retinal 3.136
[³H]-Proline, Glossary explanation of 4.449
Promptness 8.112
Pronounciation 12.307
  oral 12.355
Pro–Pointer 15.117–8
Proportionality 10.141
Proprioceptive cues 15.118
Proprioceptive extraocular muscle afferents 8.76, 8.189,
    8.238
Proprioceptive feedback 15.115, 15.118

Prosimian monkeys 2.74–7, 2.451–2, 2.473–4, 2.476,
    7.203–4
  colour vision of 2.293
  visual pathways in 2.453, 2.456–7
Prosopagnosia 7.30, 7.185, 7.187–92, 10.274–5, 10.280–1,
    12.157, 12.179–80, 12.183, 12.194, 12.198, 12.208–9,
    12.211–2, 12.219, 12.226, 12.259–86, 12.392
  and achromatopsia 12.394, 12.401
  active denial 12.279
  aetiology 12.263
  anatomical location 12.261
  awareness in 12.271
  brain neuropathology 12.264–5
  cerebral localization 12.266, 12.277
    of lesions 12.263–4
  childhood 12.279
  clinical examination 12.261–2
  and colour agnosia 12.406
  contextual cues 12.269
  covert knowledge in 12.266, 12.276–9, 12.355
  developmental 12.279
  estranged percept 12.278
  frequency and aetiology 12.262
  and heautoscopy 12.302
  history and clinical signs 12.259–60
  illusion and hallucination 12.475
  interdisciplinary approach 12.261
  and loss of topographical familiarity 12.425–7
  memory disturbances 12.268–70
  mental status examination 12.275
  movie test 12.284
  neuroimaging and neurosurgical reports 12.266–7
  neurological examination 12.275
  non-prosopagnosic patients 12.280–6
  pathology 12.261, 12.264, 12.269
  process of identification 12.261
  prosopo-metamorphopsia 12.274–6
  pure 12.268, 12.270, 12.276, 12.280
  and pure alexia 12.342, 12.347
  reading and script 12.315
  recognition of faces and items 12.271–4
  research questions 12.260–1
  response latencies 12.277
  and schizophrenia 12.296
  and semantic knowledge 12.270
  sematic/episodic dichotomy 12.270
  specificity 12.268
  and specificity of faces 12.271
  symptoms and formal testing of patients 12.262–3
  time constraints 12.272, 12.284
  Token-test data 12.283
  and topographagnosia 12.420–2, 12.424
  topographical disorientation 12.275
  and topographical disorientation 12.429–30
  topographical disorientation 12.275
  and topographical disorientation 12.429–30
  and topographical orientation 12.428
  transient 12.267, 12.273
  unawareness of 12.279

Prosopagnosia (*continued*)
  unconscious access to knowledge 12.278
  visual disturbances 12.270–1
  and visual evoked potentials 12.240
  and visual hemineglect 12.445
  and visual object recognition 12.117–8
  and visuo-spatial disorders 12.440
Prosopamnesia 12.269
Prosopo-metamorphopsia 12.274–6
Prosthesis
  visual 12.170
    implants as 12.169
Protanomalous trichromacies 6.98
Protanomaly 7.9, 7.15–8, 7.20, 7.23, 7.88, 7.90, 7.92
  alleles 7.93–5
  extreme 7.88
  unilateral 7.28
Protanopes 2.314, 6.98, 7.9–12, 7.14–5, 7.18–20, 7.89, 7.91, 7.94, 7.215, 7.217, 7.220–1
Protanopia 7.9, 7.17, 7.26–7, 7.88, 7.90, 12.386, 12.389
  alleles 7.93–5, 7.101, 7.111
  carriers 7.93
  deuteranopic 7.101
  and ERG 7.57
  and non-human primates 7.207
  unilateral 7.28–9
Protease 11.178–9, 11.197
  in cell locomotion 11.174
  inhibitors 11.178–9, 11.282
Protein binding, to actin filament sides 11.138–9
Protein binding CRABP 11.19–20
Protein cell surface 11.75, 11.84
Protein cross-linking 11.138
Protein kinase C 3.34, 11.143
Protein kinases
  in dendrites 11.152
  GAP-43 11.219
  type-II cAMP 11.149
Protein phosphorylation 11.201
  of axonal 11.195
Protein synthesis 11.193–6, 11.198–201
  in axon growth 11.250
  GAP-43 11.220
  in neuronal cytoskeleton 11.279, 11.294–7
Proteins
  actin capping 11.138
  actin-associated 11.137–9, 11.143–4
  actin-binding 11.174, 11.278–80, 11.286
  bicoid 11.48
  cytoskeletal 11.133, 11.226
  end-blocking 11.138
  even-skipped 11.20–1
  F1 11.221–2
  G 11.118–9
  GTP-binding 11.119
  inhibitory, in axon growth 11.250
  MAT 11.20
  MAT α2 11.20
  membrane 11.175, 11.177, 11.182, 11.279

  nuclear 11.112–6
  ON/ON2/ON3 11.194–5
  polymerization inhibiting 11.138
  Sca 11.191, 11.193
  Scb 11.191, 11.193–4, 11.197
  secreted 11.112–6
  see also GAPs; MAPs
  synaptosomal 11.195
  tau 11.138, 11.144, 11.277
  zinc-finger 11.40
Proteolysis 11.195, 11.223, 11.282
Protochordates 2.15, 2.17, 2.24–5, 2.32
Proton 16.30
Proto-oncogenes
  biochemical function 11.112–3, 11.122–3
  c-abl 11.113, 11.116, 11.118, 11.122
  c-erb-A 11.113, 11.119
  c-erb-B 11.113, 11.116–7, 11.122
  c-fms 11.113, 11.116–7, 11.122
  c-fos 11.113, 11.119, 11.121–2
  c-jun 11.113, 11.119, 11.122
  c-kit 11.113, 11.116–7, 11.122
  c-mos 11.113, 11.118–9, 11.122
  c-myc 11.113, 11.119–20, 11.122
  c-neu 11.113, 11.116–7, 11.122
  as components of signal transduction 11.112–3, 11.122–3
  c-raf 11.113, 11.122
  c-ras 11.122
  c-rel 11.113, 11.120, 11.122
  c-ros 11.113, 11.122
  c-sis 11.113–4, 11.122
  c-src 11.113, 11.116–8, 11.122
  encoding cytoplasmic serine kinases 11.112–3, 11.118–9
  encoding GTP-binding proteins 11.112–3, 11.119
  encoding membrane receptors 11.112–3, 11.116–8
  encoding secreted proteins 11.112–6
  encoding tyrosine kinases 11.112–3, 11.116–9
  FGF-5 11.114
  Ha-*ras* 11.113, 11.119
  hst 11.114
  hst/kFGF 11.113
  identification 11.112
  int-1 11.113–5, 11.122–3
  int-2 11.113–6, 11.122
  Ki-*ras* 11.113, 11.119
  L-*myc* 11.113
  mas 11.113, 11.116, 11.122
  N-*myc* 11.113, 11.122
  N-*ras* 11.113, 11.119
  products, nuclear 11.112–3, 11.119–22
  in vertebrates 11.114, 11.117–9, 11.122
Prototype (norm) of face 14.114, 14.118–21
Protrusions
  in cell locomotion 11.174–7, 11.180–1
  in crawling 11.171–2
Proximal vergence 8.165–6
PSD, see Postsynaptic density
Pseudemys scripta elegans (turtle) 2.72, 2.286–7, 2.291–2, 2.299, 2.427

Pseudo-agnosia 12.185
Pseudoalexia 12.341–2
Pseudobranchs 2.414
Pseudohallucination 12.274–5
    eidetic 12.289
    and heautoscopy 12.303
    illusion and hallucination 12.478–81
    and pure alexia 12.343
    'realistic' 12.476
    visual 12.342
Pseudoisochromatic chart 7.119
Pseudoisochromatic Ishihara plates 5.234
Pseudoisochromatic plate tests 7.118, 7.215–8, 7.220–2,
    7.230–2
    see also Ishihara plates
Pseudoisochromatic plates 2.306–10, 2.312, 7.29, 7.98, 7.109,
    7.124, 7.174, 7.187, 12.388
    Ishihara 5.234, 12.203, 12.393, 12.399, 12.401, 12.405,
        12.407
        averbal 12.394–5
    Stilling 12.390, 12.394, 12.399, 12.406
Pseudomonas aeruginosa, infection of contact-lens wearers
    by 1.103
Pseudophakia 16.94
Pseudo-protanomaly 7.116–7, 7.219
    in cone dystrophy 7.136–7
    in CSNB 7.148
    in ophthalmic disease 7.125, 7.131, 7.134
    and oral contraceptives 7.152
    and perimetry 7.230
    in phototrauma 7.135
    in spatial organization 7.162–3
    in Stargardt's disease 7.141, 7.144
Pseudo-retinitis pigmentosa 7.145–8
Pseudoscopes 1.328
Pseudoscopic vision, in aniseikonia 1.170
Pseudosimultanagnosia 12.217
Pseudo-tritanomaly 7.149–51
PSF, *see* Point-spread function
Psoralens 16.69–71
PSRT, *see* Photostress recovery time
P-streams, Glossary explanation of 4.452
PSVs, *see* Photosensitive vesicles
Psychic phenomena 12.300
Psycholinguistics 12.338
Psychology 14.39
    cognitive 5.46, 12.338
        pattern and 14.2
    ecological 14.91
    Gestalt 14.91
    information processing 14.91
Psychometric functions
    and colour 5.203
    for colour detection and discrimination 5.204
    for detection and discrimination tasks 5.212
    and detection limits 5.8–9
    shapes of 5.12, 5.14, 5.25
    in signal detection, delta 5.21
    and signal detection theory 5.15–6

    in threshold determination 5.13
    and visual processing 5.23–4
Psychopharmaca 12.477
'Psychophysical dissection' 10.2
Psychophysical methods, *see* Colour deficiencies, acquired;
    Threshold methods
Psychophysical techniques 4.318
Psychophysics 2.168–9, 2.310, 5.10, 5.88, 5.137–8, 5.156,
    5.160, 7.1, 12.7, 13.58–65
    and 3D representation 14.43
    and agnosia 12.195–6
    classical 10.12–3, 10.36
    and cognitive descriptors 12.3
    of colour perception 12.85
    and colour vision 13.63
    and developing visual system 16.107–8
    and hyperacuity 10.105
    and object classification 12.14
    and prosopagnosia 12.261
    quantitative 12.13
    of reading 13.65–8
        effective visual field (perceptual scan) of 13.67
        geometrical considerations of 13.65–7
    and saccadic eye movements 13.63–4
    see also Colour deficiencies, inherited
    and spatial vision 13.58
    and spatio-temporal response channels 13.59–63
    and the Stiles–Crawford effect 1.295
    and temporal vision 13.58–9
    in texture perception 10.116–8, 10.129–30
    Thurstonian 14.134
    of vision 12.34, 12.43–5
    visual 15.11
    and visual search 13.64–5
Psychophysiology, testing by electrodermal responses
    12.276
Psychosis
    acute state 12.289
    degree of 12.291
    epileptic 12.302
    exogenic 12.299
    experiences 12.290
    Korsakoff 12.268, 12.303, 12.476–7
    manic 12.385
    organic 12.302
    schizo-affective 12.301, 12.385
    states 12.476
Pteromyzonids 2.402
Pterygia 16.60
PTF, *see* Phase transfer function
Ptolemy, C. 12.29
Pulfrich effect 1.340, 9.143–4
Pulfrich refractometer 1.421
Pulse train, short electrical 12.480
Pulse-slide-step 8.205
Pulse-step 8.96, 8.123, 8.236
Pulvinar 2.173–5, 4.287, 12.60–1
    and blindsight 12.148–9
    direct retinal input to 4.143

electrical stimulation of 12.167
functional differentiation of visual areas of 4.143–8
functional organization of, in behaving animals 4.148–9
illusion and hallucination 12.480
inferior, lateral and medial 12.93
in pursuit system 2.176–8
research into 4.140–3
suggested functions of 4.149–55
  higher integrative 4.154–5
  polysensory integration 4.149
  the relay hypothesis 4.149–52
  sensory-motor 4.154
  visual attention 4.152–4
in visual function 4.140–59
  connectivity of 4.405–6
  effects of lesions in 4.406
    and visual neglect 4.406
  effects of pharmacological manipulation on 4.407
  physiological properties of 4.406–7
and visual pathways 2.424, 2.426, 2.435, 2.456–7
Pulvinar complex 3.211–4
Pulvinar nucleus 3.183, 3.193–4
Pulvinar/lateral posterior complex 3.187
Punctum proximum, recession of 1.263
Punctum remotum, *see* Far point
Pupil 11.392–4
  active 2.100
  aperture 2.3–6
  control 2.21
  and developing visual system 16.121–3
  in dioptrics 2.85, 2.92–3, 2.96–8, 2.100, 2.105, 2.108, 2.110
  ellipticity in peripheral view 5.90
  entrance 2.85, 2.94, 2.98–9
  and evolution of vision 2.411–2
  exit 2.85, 2.100–2, 3.13
  in eye evolution 2.413–4
  light reflex 16.98, 16.121–3
  in mammals 2.469, 2.474, 2.477
  periphery 5.87
  photic stress 5.278
  reactions 12.191
  reflex 2.172, 11.327
  slit 2.93, 2.111
  slit-shaped 2.99
  stenopaic 2.111
Pupil reactivity, changes in 9.101
Pupil responses 10.185
Pupillary aperture 1.282
Pupillary light reflex 2.424, 2.433
Pupilloconstriction 11.328–30
Pupillometry
  direct observation 1.392
  electronic techniques 1.392
    measuring reflective light 1.392
    orthogonal linear arrays 1.392
    scanning infra-red beam 1.392
  photographic systems 1.392
  video-based systems 1.392
Pupillomotor control 12.60

Pupillomotor pathway 5.46
Purines 7.102–3
Purkinje, Jan Evangelista 1.233, 12.6, 12.46, 12.137–9, 12.162, 12.364, 12.366, 12.371, 12.388, 12.434–5
Purkinje cells 8.38, 8.224–39, 8.328, 13.8–9
  and adaptation of vestibulo-ocular reflex 8.37–8
  complex and simple spikes 8.224–6
  and gaze-velocity 8.230, 8.322, 8.328
  inputs 8.224–6
  and retinal slip signals 8.225, 8.234
  and smooth pursuit 8.230
  and target velocity 8.234
  and vergence 8.238–9
Purkinje images 1.5, 1.233, 1.378, 1.381, 1.383–4
Purkinje images of the first kind 1.378, 1.381, 1.383–4
Purkinje images of the second kind 1.381
Purkinje images of the third kind 1.381, 1.383–4
Purkinje images of the fourth kind 1.381, 1.383–4
Purkinje perimeter 12.136–7
Purkinje shift 2.73, 5.41, 5.49, 7.22, 7.24, 7.26
  in honey bees 6.268
Purkinje's blue arcs 1.353–4
Purkinje's tree, and parallax 1.347–8
Purkyne, *see* Purkinje, Jan Evangelista
Pursuit 8.78–9, 8.86–7, 8.90, 8.138–56, 8.232–4
  acceleration 8.139–40, 8.212, 8.215
  active vs. passive 8.147–8
  after-nystagmus 8.145
  against a background 8.148–9
  asymmetry 8.213, 8.306
  and attention 8.79, 8.86, 8.147–8
  and brainstem 8.153, 8.211–5
  and cerebellum 8.153–4, 8.232–4
  and cerebral cortex 8.215, 8.283, 8.285
  continuation 8.145
  distinguished from optokinesis 8.78–9, 8.138, 8.329
  extraretinal motion signals and 8.149–51
  frequency-response 8.142–5, 8.148–50
  gain 8.138–9, 8.141–3, 8.148–51
  Glossary explanation of 4.449
  interactions with saccades 8.110–2, 8.329
  lesions affecting 8.153, 8.213–4, 8.232, 8.306–8, 8.312, 8.314
  models 8.151–3
  negative feedback in 8.138–9, 8.211, 8.214, 8.309
  neurophysiology 8.153–4, 8.211–4
  oculomotor neurones discharge during 8.203
  onset 8.139–41, 8.212, 8.230
  open-loop studies 8.140, 8.142–3
  prediction in 8.79, 8.143–6, 8.152, 8.154
  and Purkinje cells 8.230
  steady-state 8.141–3
  stimuli for 8.146–7
  target position and 8.146
  twitch 8.140
  velocity 8.142
  visually guided 4.388
Pursuit deficits 2.178–80, 2.184
Pursuit eye movements (PEM), *see* Pursuit movements;

Q

Q-cells 4.14
Quadranopia
  homonymous
    left lower 12.342
    left upper 12.270
    right superior 12.344
  lower 12.420
  right upper 12.354
  upper 12.276
Quadrant
  left upper 12.270
  lower right 12.259
  upper 12.275
Quadrantanopia, bilateral upper 12.394
Quadrupedal position 12.124
Quality factor (Q) 10.35, 10.174
Quandrantanopia, upper 12.146
Quanta 6–8, 5.41, 5.125, 5.222, 16.32, 16.36–7
  of energy 5.48
  in peripheral vision 5.46, 5.55–8
Quantal absorptions 5.24, 5.26
Quantitative electrophysiology, of visual cortex
    neurones 4.173–222
Quantitative physiology, of visual cortex neurones 4.173–222
Quantities and units
  light-measurement 16.23–4
  photometric 16.23–4

  radiometric 16.1–3, 16.23–4
Quantization 14.70
Quantization jump 14.100
Quantum 14.102–3
  see also Quanta
Quantum 'bumps' 5.57
Quantum catch 2.284, 2.296, 2.300, 5.41–2, 5.176
Quantum efficiency 5.44, 5.55, 5.57–8, 5.63, 5.66, 5.68–9,
    5.71
Quantum fluctuations 5.50
Quantum limits 5.13, 5.44, 5.72
'Quantum manifesto' 5.55, 5.65
Quantum noise 5.55, 5.64, 5.70
Quantum per spike ratio (QSR) 5.50, 5.63, 5.66
Quantum physics 14.100
Quantum statistics 2.91
Quarter-wavelength multi-layers 2.126
Quasi-crystal growth 11.302
Quasi-cyclopean depth motion 9.55–6
Quasi-visual neurones 8.249–53, 8.266
Quasi-visual responsive units 4.397
Quaternary relations 14.53, 14.64
Quaternion theory 8.260–2, 8.324
Questions, cueing 12.350
Quick phase, of nystagmus 8.46, 8.65, 8.98, 8.111–2, 8.325
Quinidine 7.135
Quisqualate glutamate receptors 8.226, 8.328
QWERTY keyboards 15.116

R

Rabbit
  binocular vision 2.272–3, 2.275
  cerebellar responses 8.228–9
  dioptrics 2.83–5, 2.88, 2.97
  eye–head co-ordination 8.47
  vestibulo-ocular reflex 8.227–9
  visual system 8.2, 8.5–7
Race and face recognition 14.111, 14.117–8, 14.120–3
Räderscheidt, Anton 12.445–6
Radial keratotomy 1.138–43
Radiance 16.1, 16.3
  and developing visual system 16.105, 16.121
  and light measurement 16.24–7
  and optical radiation 16.5, 16.7, 16.12, 16.17
Radiation
  acoustic 15.1
  adaptive 2.136
  blackbody 2.86–7
  continuous wave (CW) laser 16.19
  damaging 16.67
  and dioptrics 2.88, 2.103
  electromagnetic 2.86, 2.289, 15.1, 16.30, 16.50, 16.78
  exposure 16.2–6, 16.58, 16.60–1
    environmental 16.54
    guidelines 16.4–5
    levels 16.4–6
    occupational 16.54
  frequency 16.1
  infrared (IRR) 2.86, 2.428, 16.1, 16.5–6, 16.10–2, 16.17, 16.24
    and light hazards 16.93, 16.96–100
    and light interactions 16.43–6
  laser 16.5–6
  non-laser 16.5–6
  and ocular transmittance 2.86–9
  optical 12.66, 12.344
    damage by 16.54–61
    exposure 16.59–60
    production of 16.6–8
    repair mechanisms 16.57–8
    sources 16.1–21
      incandescent 16.20–1
    transmission and absorption 16.54–5, 16.57
  protection 16.55, 16.58
    mechanisms 16.61–2
    standards 16.4–6
  pulsed laser 16.19
  quantities and units 16.1–3
  solar 16.1, 16.17–9, 16.21, 16.58
  ultraviolet (UVR) 2.18, 2.95, 2.299, 16.1–5, 16.11–3, 16.16–8, 16.32, 16.52
    and ageing macula 16.78
    effects on eye 16.54–66
    and light hazards 16.93–100
    and light interactions 16.36, 16.39, 16.42–3
    and light measurement 16.23–4, 16.27–9
    and phototoxicity 16.68

    solar 16.54, 16.59
  UVA
    and ageing macula 16.89
    effects on eye 16.60
    and light interactions 16.40–1
    and phototoxicity 16.70–1
  UVB, effects on eye 16.60
  UVC
    damage by 16.58
    damage thresholds 16.58–9
    effects on eye 16.60
    and light interactions 16.38
    repair mechanisms and processes 16.58
  visible 16.5–6, 16.20–1
  visual 12.144–5, 12.147, 12.357
    and blindsight 12.154
    illusion and hallucination 12.480
    impairment 12.199
    and phosphenes 12.155
  wavelength 16.1–4, 16.6–7, 16.13–4, 16.17–9, 16.21
    effects on eye 16.54–5, 16.57–8, 16.60
    IRA 16.3–4, 16.11, 16.55
    IRB 16.3, 16.7, 16.55
    IRC 16.3, 16.55
    light 16.3
    UVA 16.3, 16.5, 16.9–10, 16.12–6, 16.18, 16.55
    UVB 16.3, 16.5, 16.9–10, 16.13–5, 16.18, 16.55
    UVC 16.3, 16.9–10, 16.55
Radiation Protection Association, International (IRPA) 16.5
Radioimmunoassay of VIP 11.361
Radiometry 16.105
Radioscopes, Drysdale's 1.380
Radioscopy 1.430
Radiuscopes 1.426
Rainbow 12.386, 12.406
Raindrop test 12.457
Raja (skate) 2.67
RALBP, *see* Retinal-binding protein
Raleigh equation 12.393–5
Ramapithecus 12.52
Rana esculata (frog) 2.99
Rana pipiens (frog) 2.71
Random-dot E 9.211
Random-dot kinematograms 6.200
Random-dot stereo test 9.210
Random-dot stereogram technique 10.108
Random-dot stereograms 4.215, 6.200, 6.213, 8.9, 9.97, 9.134, 9.203
  and cyclopean perception 6.213
  dynamic 9.170, 9.230
  isoluminant 6.214
  neural responses to 9.230–2
  solid-figure 9.231
Random-texture patterns 4.179
Randot test 13.145, 13.183
Range measurement 2.242, 2.254–5, 2.261, 2.265–7
Raphe interpositus, nucleus 8.202, 8.207
Rapid eye movements 4.388–442, 13.204
  see also Saccadic eye movements

RAR, *see* Resolution-addressability ratio
Raster autostereoscopy 1.332
Rat 2.74
  and developing visual system 16.106, 16.108–12
  dioptrics 2.84–5, 2.95, 2.97
  lateral posterior nucleus 3.214–5, 3.217
  LGNd projections 3.199
  visual cortex 3.304–5, 3.308, 3.366–71
Rating-procedure, *see* Confidence-rating procedure
Rattus norvegicus (rat) 2.74
Raven's Coloured Progressive Matrices Test 13.89, 13.91,
  13.176, 13.192
Rayleigh contrast 10.290–1
Rayleigh equation (match) 7.6–7, 7.9, 7.89–90, 7.120–1
  in achromatopsia 7.99, 7.101
  bimodality 7.95
  bleaching in diabetes 7.150
  and colour vision tests 7.218–20, 7.229
  in cone diseases 7.136–7, 7.140, 7.162
  in glaucoma 7.153–4
  green-shifted 7.126
  large-field 7.94
  later stage detection of diabetic impairment 7.149
  LWS and MWS cone function 7.119
  in monochromacy 7.28
  in non-human primates 7.200, 7.202, 7.204–10
  in ophthalmic disease 7.116, 7.123, 7.125–31, 7.134, 7.145,
    7.158
  in optic-nerve disease 7.179
  in phototrauma 7.135
  pseudo-protanomalous, in diabetes 7.149
  red–green 7.13–5, 7.17, 7.19
  small-field 7.94
  in Stargardt's disease 7.142, 7.144
  widened matching range 7.162
Rayleigh scatter 2.8, 2.407
  and light measurement 16.28
Rayleigh's quarter-wave criterion 1.11, 2.92, 2.104–5,
  10.87–8
'Razione negra', Glossary explanation of 4.449
RDS, uncorrelated 9.66
Reaching tasks, visually guided 12.95
Reaction time 12.225, 12.233–5, 12.238, 15.26
  experiments 12.230
  in letter recognition 12.324
  psychomotor 12.322
  of saccades 8.96, 8.112–7, 8.121–2, 8.305
  in tachistoscopic reading 12.321
  and visual movement agnosia 12.378
Reactivation of cortical responses 8.281, 8.285
Reading 12.304, 12.309–10
  in absence of foveal function 12.319
  acquired disturbances 12.336
  aloud 12.307, 12.310, 12.316–8, 12.326, 12.340
    lyrics with monotonous intonation 12.358
    and pure alexia 12.348–9, 12.354
  and anomalous visual effects 13.155
  area, sensory 12.356
  area R 12.357

  auditory–verbal function 12.309
  capacity, right hemispheric 12.348
  centre, left hemispheric 12.350
  children first learning to 12.323
  children's eye movements during 13.251–62
  competence 12.316–20
  conscious verbal 12.352
  difficulty, and visual movement agnosia 12.373
  disabilities 12.388
  distance 12.317
  disturbances 12.338
    due to peripheral visual problems 12.339
    due to primary visual sensory disturbance 12.339
    functional nature of 12.338
  electro-oculogram during 12.311
  for emotional lexical information 12.354
  errors 12.328
  eye movements during 12.316–20, 13.68, 13.233–4, 13.236
  and eye-strain 13.155
  of figural symbols 12.358
  gaze movement control during 12.318
  and headaches 13.155
  impairment, dissociated deficits 12.348
  inability 12.334
  Kanji word 12.348
  letter-by-letter 12.334, 12.338, 12.340–1, 12.351–2, 12.357
  letters, and alexia 12.336
  limbic structures for 12.356
  lip 12.307
  mathematical symbols 12.336
  by motor tracing 12.336
  neurobiological mechanisms 12.308
  neuronal circuits 12.356–8
  numbers 12.335–6
  oral 12.338, 12.351
  own name 12.334
  in patients with low vision 13.68–9
  preserved 12.350–5
    unconscious 12.351
  process, 'alternative' 12.327
  and prosopagnosia 12.268, 12.277–8
  psychophysics of 13.65–8
  refixating words during 13.258–9
  right-hemisphere 12.328–9, 12.352
    comprehension 12.354
  rudimentary, with right hemisphere 12.328
  sampling strategies, visuo-motor 12.321
  see also Paralexia
  and seizures 13.155
  shorthand 12.310, 12.330
  silent 12.310, 12.318, 12.340
  single letters 12.341
  skills 12.316
  skipping words during 13.258–9
  spatial scanning strategy 12.326
  speed 12.311, 12.316–7, 12.319, 12.337, 12.345
  strategies 12.317
    in hemispheres 12.329
    visuo-motor 12.320

Reading (*continued*)
  systems, Japanese **12**.348
  tachistoscopic **12**.321
  target movements **12**.340
  track **12**.309, **12**.358
  training **12**.316
  two-route model of **13**.189–90
    direct lexical **13**.189–90
    phonological **13**.189–90
  and visual discomfort **13**.155–70
  and visual object recognition **12**.112
  without eye movements **12**.320–30
    Kanji signs and kana words **12**.329–30
    shorthand **12**.330
    single letter recognition **12**.322–3
    word recognition **12**.323–8
  and 'writing' in apes **12**.330–2
Reading ability
  evidence for environmental effects in **13**.107–8
    birth order **13**.107–8
    miscellaneous **13**.108
    parental age **13**.108
  prediction and measures of
    from eye movement data
      reading comprehension measures in **13**.256
      reading rate measures in **13**.256
      use of models in **13**.256
      word identification measures in **13**.256
Reading disorders, diagnosis of **13**.261
Reading eye camera **13**.253
Reading masks **13**.164
Reafference principle **12**.6, **12**.371–2
Recall **12**.347
Receiver operating characteristic (ROC) **10**.36
Receptive field complex **11**.344
Receptive field density **5**.255
Receptive field illumination **12**.473
Receptive field motion detection **5**.155–8
Receptive fields **3**.159–66, **4**.147, **5**.26, **5**.39, **5**.99, **5**.262,
    12.464
  amacrine cell **3**.46
  bandpass **5**.188
  bipolar cell **3**.33–4, **3**.40
  and callosal pathways **3**.332, **3**.351
  in cat retina, pharmacological aspects of **4**.24–6
  centre-surround **3**.49, **5**.41–2, **5**.99–100, **5**.188, **5**.234
  changes in, in the progression to the striate cortex **4**.226–8
  of collicular neurones **3**.166–9
  concept of **4**.10
  in contrast encoding **5**.108–10
  difference-of-Gaussians (DOG) **5**.52–3, **5**.66–70
  dimensions, ganglion cell **3**.48, **3**.54
  exploration of
    using condition-and-test paradigms **4**.260
    using models **4**.260–4
      modified push–pull **4**.262–3
      push only **4**.260–2
      push–pull **4**.261–3
      push–pull plus cortical lateral inhibition **4**.262

Gabor-like **5**.52–4, **5**.58, **5**.60, **5**.67, **5**.69
of ganglion cells **3**.33
  in the cat retina **4**.11–24
Glossary explanations of (two) **4**.449
hierarchy in **4**.164
horizontal cell **3**.38–9
large **5**.64–5
lateral geniculate nucleus **4**.261
low-pass **5**.188
multiunit (MURF) **11**.90–1, **11**.94, **11**.96
near fovea **5**.143
non-oriented **2**.453
off-centre **2**.450–1, **3**.179, **4**.226
on-centre **2**.450–1, **3**.179, **4**.226
organization of, models of **4**.260–4
overlapping **5**.224
in pattern discrimination **5**.271, **5**.273
in peripheral vision **5**.46–8, **5**.51–2, **5**.55–60, **5**.64–6, **5**.68,
    5.73, **5**.75
of postreceptoral neurones **3**.30
properties of **2**.275, **2**.280, **11**.346
  in accessory optic system of cat and primate **4**.113–5
  ganglion cell **3**.48–9
  maturation of **11**.344–5
  orientation-selective **11**.345
  and visual object recognition **12**.120
and retina **3**.8
simple **11**.344
size estimates of **4**.255
size and scatter **3**.333–4, **3**.340–1, **3**.346, **3**.348–9, **3**.351
sizes and shapes of **4**.54
space–time separable **4**.251–2
in striate cortex **4**.223–45
surround **3**.40–1
visual
  and area 7 **12**.103–4
  excitatory (ERF) **12**.100–1, **12**.104–6
and visual pathways **2**.426, **2**.431–2, **2**.436, **2**.449
Receptive-field centres **2**.444
  bipolar cell **3**.35
  and flicker **5**.180, **5**.182
  ganglion cell **3**.48, **3**.51–2, **3**.54, **3**.57
  Gaussian shape **3**.57
  horizontal cell **3**.40
  and postreceptoral mechanisms **3**.30–1
  push–pull mechanism **3**.55
Receptive-field organization **4**.173, **10**.150
  in cat retina, effects of adaptation on **4**.26–7
  of cortical neurones **4**.173
Receptive-field size, of the accessory optic system **4**.128
Receptive-field structure
  estimation of, in striate cortex **4**.250–7
  Glossary explanation of **4**.449
Receptive-field symmetry **4**.23
Receptor cells
  retinal **8**.7–8
  vestibular **8**.14–7, **8**.22–6, **8**.215–7, **8**.320
Receptor disorder **5**.92
Receptor models, of colour vision in insects, *see* Colour

vision, in insects, receptor models of
Receptor mosaic of retina **5.91–2**
Receptor types
  cones **6.110–1**
  rods **6.110–1**
Receptors
  acetylcholine (ACh) **11.198, 11.200, 11.298**
  benzodiazepine **3.48**
  CSF-1 **11.116–7**
  D1 **3.41**
  D1 and D2 **10.257**
  deep cutaneous **3.327**
  EGF **11.116–7**
  glutamate **3.34**
  integrin **11.178**
  membrane, and proto-oncogenes **11.112–3, 11.116–8**
  mosaic **2.102–3**
  NMDA **3.368–9, 11.199, 11.201, 11.240–1, 11.281**
  spectral, in insects **6.263–9**
  ultra violet **6.80–1**
Reciprocal neurones **9.87, 9.229–30**
Reciprocity
  and light interactions **16.41, 16.44**
  and light measurement **16.26–7**
Recognition
  and agnosia **12.179, 12.191**
  algorithm **14.26, 14.43**
  auditory **12.260**
  and computational vision **14.30–2, 14.44–5**
  extravisual **12.207**
  of items with personal emotional familiarity **12.273**
  nature of visual **14.20**
  see also Face; Object; Pattern
  of similar shape **12.273**
  of similarly looking visual items **12.273**
  three-dimensional (3D) objects **14.38–40**
  two-dimensional (2D) objects **14.38–9**
  visual-linguistic **12.335**
Recombination, intergenic **7.108, 7.110**
Recording, multiple microelectrode **12.73**
Recovery dissociation **12.409**
Recovery of visual function **10.261**
Rectification **5.121, 5.123**
  half-wave **5.25–7, 5.39, 5.41, 5.100**
Rectifiers **10.7–8**
  half-wave **5.25–7**
Rectus
  inferior **8.175–6, 8.182**
  lateral **8.175–6, 8.182, 8.185**
  medial **8.175–6, 8.182**
  superior **8.175–6, 8.182**
Red field **4.449**
Red-glass test **9.217**
Reference distance function **9.79**
Reference frame
  horizontal–vertical **14.51, 14.59–61**
  object-centred **14.112**
  retinal **14.53**
  and spatial relations **14.52–3**

Reference parallax function **9.79**
Reflectance **2.126–7, 2.306, 2.309, 10.292–3**
  of natural objects **3.28**
  spectral **2.300–1, 2.310, 12.385**
  surface **14.36, 14.83–4, 14.87, 14.89–90, 14.93**
Reflection
  aiming beam **16.98**
  and optical radiation **16.3**
Reflection properties
  of visual displays **15.48**
    circular polarizing filter **15.64**
    $\Gamma/4$ coating **15.64**
    micromesh filter **15.64**
Reflection-axis effect **14.60**
Reflex **12.40**
  galvanic skin **12.276**
  pupillary **11.327**
  see also Vestibulo-ocular reflex (VOR)
Refraction
  abrupt changes in
    possible causes of **1.45–52**
      accommodation **1.46–7**
      corneal diseases **1.45–6**
        keratoconus **1.45–6**
      drug therapy **1.51–2**
      lens **1.47–8**
        diabetes **1.47–8**
        galactosaemia **1.48**
        hydration of **1.47**
      lid and orbital diseases
        dacryoceles **1.45**
        haemangiomas **1.45**
        tarsal, adnexal tumours **1.45**
        tarsal cysts **1.45**
      marginal corneal degenerations **1.46**
      retinal diseases **1.48–9**
      surgery
        astigmatism **1.49–50**
        hypermetropia **1.51**
        myopia **1.50–1**
      systemic disease **1.49**
  clinical subjective
    accuracy and precision of **1.411**
    advantages and disadvantages of **1.411**
    an alternative procedure for **1.411**
    by lens substitution **1.410–111**
      fogging and testing for sphere **1.410**
      procedure of **1.410–111**
        refractor heads **1.410–111**
      refinement of cylinder **1.411**
      test for cylinder **1.410–1**
    practical applications and utility of **1.411**
  cycloplegic **1.399**
  development of **13.49–50**
  in dioptrics **2.103, 2.107, 2.109**
  error **5.81, 5.90, 5.124, 5.130**
  in evolution of vision **2.408**
  instruments **2.111**
  methods of **1.401–13**

comparison of objective and subjective 1.413
objective 1.401–10
  dynamic optometers and automated infrared
    refractometers 1.406–7
  ophthalmoscopy 1.401–2
  optometers 1.405–6
  photorefraction 1.407–10
  retinoscopy 1.402–3
subjective 1.410–3
  laser speckle optometry 1.411–3
  by lens substitution 1.410–1
ocular, determination of 1.399–414
and optical radiation 16.3
peripheral 5.83, 5.90
in photoreception 2.377
and senescence 5.278, 5.283
Refractive correction
 surgical techniques for 1.138–62
  corneal relaxing and tensioning 1.138–47
   radial keratotomy 1.138–43
  epikeratophakia 1.147–53
  keratomileusis 1.153–4
   homoplastic 1.153
  lamellar procedures
   corneal inlays 1.154–8
    keratophakia 1.154–5
    polysulphone 1.154–5
    synthetic 1.155–7
   excimer laser 1.157–8
Refractive error
 and against-the-rule astigmatism 1.31
 and astigmatism 1.31
 clinical implications of
  atropine 1.41
  Bates system of relaxation in 1.42
  bifocal lens prescriptions 1.41
  biofeedback in 1.41–2
  full correction in 1.42
  orthokeratology in 1.42
 comparative studies in monkeys and humans into
   1.34–8
 and emmetropization 1.39–40
 in eye development 1.29–44
 and eye models 1.5–8
 and late-onset myopia 1.31
 ocular components of 1.29–30
  correlation between 1.29–30
 owing to increasing age 1.30–1
 possible causative factors of 1.31–3
  genetics
   and 'component ametropia' 1.31
   and 'correlation ametropia' 1.31
   and correlation mechanisms 1.31
   and hypermetropia 1.31
   and myopia 1.31
   role of 1.31
  the role of congenital and acquired abnormalities 1.33
  the role of the environment in 1.31–3
   and the Alaska Study on Eskimos 1.32–3

influence of illumination 1.33
influence of posture 1.33
and progressive myopia 1.30
and the role of accommodation in myopia 1.38–9
and with-the-rule astigmatism 1.31
Refractive index 2.118, 2.126, 3.12–3, 5.87
 in basic optics 2.82, 2.84
 of the cornea 1.313
 and dioptrics 2.92, 2.94, 2.97, 2.100, 2.102–3,
  2.105
 in evolution of eye 2.4
 and evolution of vision 2.408, 2.411–2
 graded 2.55
 and photoreception 2.369
 in visual processing 2.232
Refractive index gradient 2.120–3, 2.377
 and dioptrics 2.85–6, 2.95–7
 in evolution of vision 2.412
 and optics 2.129–31
Refractive optics 5.88
Refractive state, explanation of 1.399
Refractometers
 Abbe 1.421
 automatic infra-red 1.406–7
  advantages and disadvantages of 1.407
 Hilger–Chance 1.421
 Pulfrich 1.421
Refractometry 1.393–4
 of the aqueous 1.393
 of the cornea 1.393
 of the crystalline lens 1.393–4
  optical quality of 1.394
 using the Abbe refractometer 1.393
 of the vitreous 1.393
Refresh rate 15.7–8, 15.59–61
Regan High and Intermediate Contrast chart 16.154
Regeneration, intercalary 11.57–9
Regression, linear 5.19–21
Regularities in line images 14.98–106
Regularization, standard 14.93
Regularization model 14.93
Regularization techniques 14.86, 14.89
Regularization theory 14.92
Reichardt's autocorrelation theory 2.251
Reichardt's motion perception model 2.240
Rejection, transplantation 11.319
Related (perceived) colour, CIE definition of 6.225
Relational label 14.114
Relations, conditional 12.331
Relative depth
 and motion parallax 9.138–40
 role of motion in the perception of 9.137–41
Relative depth effect 9.137–8
Relative direction selectivity 4.191
 Glossary explanation of 4.449
Relative disparities 9.145
Relative distance tasks 9.77–9
Relative size 9.183
Relaxation 14.20

Relaxation time, thermal **16.**47–8
Relay cells **3.**282, **3.**287
  lagged **3.**283
  X- **3.**283
Relay hypothesis, as a suggested function of the
    pulvinar **4.**149–52
Relearning process **12.**350
Release of function **12.**354
Release phenomena **12.**478–9
Releasing mechanisms, inborn **12.**218
Remembrance, covert **12.**276
Remyelination **10.**243
Repellent component, axon sensitivity to **11.**101–2
Repetitive strain injury **15.**58
Representation
  face **14.**112–4, **14.**118, **14.**123
  internal, of numerosity **14.**133–6
  levels **14.**98–9
  of a line **14.**102–3
  signal **14.**70–2
  three-dimensional (3D) objects **14.**43–5
Reprocessing time **8.**128–9
Reptiles **2.**72–3, **2.**78
  colour vision **2.**287–9, **2.**291–2, **2.**296, **2.**299, **2.**302
  dioptrics **2.**89
  eye embryology of **11.**394
  visual pathways **2.**421–36
Residual function **10.**265, **10.**272–3
Resolution
  bipolar array **3.**38
  chromatic **10.**89
  double-flash **10.**241
  double-pulse **10.**153
  in foveal sampling **3.**21
  in hyperacuity **10.**87–9, **10.**99
  least-motion **2.**231
  lens **2.**230–8
  limit **10.**87–8
  minimum visual angle of **12.**57–8
  and photoreceptor coupling **3.**27
  in primates **3.**14
  psychophysical **3.**58
  sampling **3.**30
  spatial **2.**231, **2.**236–8, **2.**240–3, **2.**257, **2.**259–60, **2.**266,
    2.454, **2.**459, **12.**57
    and colour signals **3.**29
    in foveal sampling **3.**20
    and ganglion cells **3.**49, **3.**53–4, **3.**57–8
    and horizontal cells **3.**40
    of photoreceptors **3.**25
    and postreceptoral mechanisms **3.**31
    and retina **3.**1, **3.**6
  spatial sampling **2.**235, **2.**237
  spatiochromatic **5.**75
  spurious **10.**24
  visual **3.**48
  and visual pathways **2.**456
  in visual processing **2.**230
  window **3.**18–9, **3.**22–3

Resolution acuity **5.**222–3, **5.**228–9, **10.**188–90
Resolution–addressability ratio **15.**14–5
Resonance, non-linear **10.**9–11
Resource demands **15.**92
Response amplitudes **5.**184
Response components, sustained and transient **5.**187
Response latencies **3.**339
  of cells of lateral geniculate nucleus **4.**68–9
Response ratios **2.**242
Response time (RT)
  for Kanji signs **12.**330
  psychomotor **12.**321
  in word recognition **12.**328
Response transience, of cells of lateral geniculate
    nucleus **4.**68–9
Responses
  human brain **10.**155–60
  motor **12.**463
  orienting **10.**185
  overlearned emotional **12.**358
  pupil **10.**185
  rapid behavioural **12.**358
  steady-state **10.**35
  template **2.**256–7, **2.**267
    ratios of **2.**260–3
  visual, dynamics of **10.**151–3
Restriction fragment length polymorphism **6.**93, **7.**103,
    7.106–10
  in deuteranopes **6.**95
  and green-cone opsin **6.**93
  and red-cone opsin **6.**93
Reticular formation
  mesencephalic **8.**201, **8.**208–9, **12.**463–4
  pontine **8.**2, **8.**201–2, **8.**206–9, **8.**216–7, **8.**225, **8.**248, **8.**312
  prepontine **12.**463–4
Reticularis tegmenti pontis, nucleus **8.**201–2, **8.**208–9, **8.**214,
    8.225, **8.**234–5, **8.**248, **8.**300
Reticulum, endoplasmic **12.**128
Retina
  accessory **2.**412
  activity in visual cortex **11.**347
  afferents **3.**191
  ageing **16.**76, **16.**87–90, **16.**134–47
  ageing processes in **5.**277–8
  anatomy **5.**192
  areas of **3.**107
  and axon growth **11.**233, **11.**235
  bifoveate **2.**272–3
  and binocular vision **2.**277–9
  blue absorption across **5.**244
  cat **3.**16
  cell lineage in **11.**42–3
  cell recognition **11.**81–4
  and cellular organization **11.**68–70, **11.**72–3
  cephalopod **2.**376
  complex **11.**395
  of compound eye **2.**204
  cone dominated **3.**38
  cone mosaic **5.**91–2

Retina (*continued*)
  and visual performance 5.81–93
  contralateral 3.139, 3.141, 3.198, 11.238
    and LGNv 3.204
    in visual thalamus 3.176–8, 3.181, 3.186
  corrugated 2.111
  cortical 12.391
  cup-shaped 2.371
  damage 3.82, 3.86
  deformation of 12.472
  degeneration of 12.199
  detachment of 1.125, 5.129, 12.199
  and developing visual system 16.118–20
  development of 2.137, 2.144–5, 2.147, 10.181–2
  development 'timetables' 3.118
  developmentally advanced region of 3.73–8, 3.80
  differentiation 11.388–9
  and dopamine 10.256
  double 2.369–70
  duplex 2.478, 3.27, 7.99
  ectopic 11.314
  embryology of 11.397–403
  embryonic 11.315, 11.321–3, 11.327, 11.329, 11.332
  in evolution of eye 2.16–8, 2.21–2, 2.24–6, 2.28, 2.40,
      2.42–4, 2.47, 2.412–4, 2.417
  in evolution of vertebrate neural 2.136–47
  in evolution of vision 2.402–4, 2.406, 2.408, 2.410
  functional organization of 3.1–59
    image quality 3.4–6
    photoreceptors 3.9–30
    postreceptoral mechanisms 3.30–58
    sampling 3.1, 3.6–9
  fundus 11.389
  histological analysis 12.142
  histological examination 7.24
  human
    and hypermetropia 1.5
    and myopia 1.5
    and waveguide effects 1.5
  and hyaloid circulation 11.391
  illuminance 2.98–9
  illusion and hallucination 12.472–3
  inhomogeneity 5.244, 5.247–8
  injury 11.332
  injury thresholds 16.26
  inversion 11.396, 11.398
  inverted 2.82
    in evolution of eye 2.23, 2.25, 2.35
    invertebrate 2.25–7
  ipsilateral 3.139, 3.198, 11.238
    and LGNv 3.204
    in visual thalamus 3.176–8, 3.181, 3.186
  irradiance 16.62
  ischaemia of 1.355
  laminar organization 3.1–4
  and light damage 16.63–5
  linear scanning 2.122
  location 5.109, 5.120, 5.203, 5.206–7, 5.245
  mammalian 2.471, 2.473, 2.476, 3.69–118.

  cytogenesis in ventricular zone 3.78–84
  embryonic development 3.71–8
  fovea 3.113–7
  ipsilateral projection 3.110–3
  maturation 3.117–8
  neuronal death 3.94–8
  neuronal differentiation 3.98–104
  non-neural cells 3.84–90
  non-uniform expansion 3.105–10
  plexiform layers 3.90–4
  mantis 2.231
  marsupial 2.471–2
  maturation 3.117–8
  mature 3.129–32
  monofoveate 2.272
  monotreme 2.469–70
  motion direction 5.160
  multipotential precursor cells in 11.32–4, 11.36
  nasal and temporal 3.135, 3.176, 3.198
  neurogenesis 3.80
  non-foveal 7.14
  and optic cup 11.386
  organization 3.129–30, 3.132, 5.41
  origin of 2.18, 11.400
  and origins of eye 2.57–8
  parafoveal, bleaching of 7.24
  peripheral 5.83, 5.92, 5.206
  in peripheral vision 5.44, 5.46
  photopigments 5.7
  in photoreception 2.377–9
  primate 7.69, 7.74–5
    bipolar cells in 3.32
  profunda 2.376, 2.385–6
  in pursuit system 2.167–71, 2.189–91
  and radiation 16.55, 16.57–61
  'ramp' 2.111
  reflection of, and preservation of polarization 1.322–3
  retardation of 1.321
  retinotopic organization 12.64
  ribbon 2.58, 2.375
  rod dominated mammalian 3.38
  scanning 2.390
  see also Transplantation
  signal processing of neuronal channels in 12.59–61
  spatial sampling at 6.71–2
  specialization 2.274
  in spectral sensitivity 5.191
  squid 2.383
  surface shape 2.98
  synaptology 11.154
  temporal specialization 2.272
  tiered 2.139
  TOP molecules 11.74–7, 11.79–81
  transplanted 3.71, 3.76, 3.136
  triggers 2.275
  TTX treatment of 11.258–9, 11.265, 11.269
  and velocity perception 5.160–1
  vertebrate
    anatomical basis for colour vision in 6.128–45

chromatic organization of photoreceptor mosaics
    in **6.**128–33
    in birds **6.**129–31
    in fish **6.**129, **6.**131
    in frogs **6.**129
    in groung squirrels **6.**132–3
    in humans **6.**131–3
    in primates **6.**132–3
    in reptiles **6.**129, **6.**131
    in turtles **6.**129–31
  physiology of **6.**163–7
in vertebrate neurogenesis **11.**37
and visual pathways **2.**421–2, **2.**424–5, **2.**427, **2.**430–1,
    2.443–7, **2.**449, **2.**452, **2.**454–6, **2.**459
and vitreous **11.**392
X-ray-induced responses **12.**166
Retinal **2.**63–5, **2.**69, **2.**349–50, **2.**381, **6.**108–9, **6.**266, **16.**41
  cis–trans isomerization of **6.**70
Retinal area **10.**180
Retinal axons, W- **3.**154
Retinal co-ordinates **8.**98, **8.**132, **8.**210, **8.**327
Retinal detachment **7.**124–5
  and the Stiles–Crawford effect of the first kind **1.**297
Retinal diseases, and the Stiles–Crawford effect of the first
    kind **1.**297
Retinal disparity **8.**9, **8.**158–60
Retinal eccentricity **1.**258–9, **4.**15, **4.**20, **12.**464, **15.**17–8
Retinal error **8.**123, **8.**131
  Glossary explanation of **4.**449
Retinal fibre optics **1.**280–309
  action of Henle fibres of the fovea as **1.**282
  numerical aperture of **1.**283
  refractive index in **1.**282
Retinal flow pattern, and self-motion **9.**162
Retinal ganglion cell damage **7.**155
Retinal ganglion cell drop-out **7.**152
Retinal ganglion cell impairment **7.**158, **7.**163
Retinal ganglion cells **4.**191, **8.**4, **8.**7–8, **10.**300–1
  Glossary explanation of **4.**449
  receptive-field structure of
    in cat **4.**10–40
    in monkey **4.**10–40
Retinal grating modulation **1.**260
Retinal illumination, and ocular radiometry **1.**9–10
Retinal image
  final quality of **1.**16–9
    calculation by ophthalmoscopic methods **1.**17–9
    calculation by the psychophysical methods **1.**17
    calculation from the wavefront aberration **1.**16–7
  quality of **1.**10–9
    and the line-spread function **1.**10
    and the modulation transfer function **1.**10
    and the optical transfer function **1.**10
    and the phase transfer function **1.**10
    and the point-spread function **1.**10
  stabilized **8.**87
Retinal image motion **8.**71, **8.**75, **8.**84, **8.**90, **9.**126
  and contrast sensitivity **8.**3–5, **8.**86–9
  natural **8.**73, **8.**84, **8.**87–9

velocity of **8.**1, **8.**85–7
visual consequences **8.**84–9
Retinal image velocity **1.**260
Retinal locus **1.**259
Retinal luminance gradient **1.**260
Retinal pigment epithelium **7.**126–8
Retinal projections, uncrossed **3.**157
Retinal receptors **6.**17, **8.**7–8
Retinal-binding protein (RALBP) **2.**381–2
11-*cis*-Retinal **6.**62, **6.**70
Retinex model of colour vision, Land's **6.**57, **6.**192–3, **6.**201
Retinex theory **4.**332, **6.**57–8, **12.**385
Retinitis
  foveomacular (FMR) **16.**95
  solar **16.**27–8, **16.**94–5
Retinitis pigmentosa **5.**172, **7.**118, **7.**120, **7.**124, **7.**135,
    7.143–4, **16.**81
  autosomal recessive carriers **7.**145
  pseudo- **7.**145–8
  and the Stiles–Crawford effect of the first kind **1.**297
  symptomatic **7.**145–8
  X-linked carriers **7.**145, **7.**147
Retinoblastoma **3.**84, **16.**72
Retinochrome **2.**366, **2.**378, **2.**381–2
Retinocollicular axons **3.**155
Retinocortical projections **5.**269
Retinofugal pathways **3.**129–43
  development **3.**132–43
    binocular interactions **3.**141–3
    early projections **3.**137–9
    exuberance and refinement of projections **3.**139–41
    ganglion cell birth and death **3.**132–4
    outgrowth of axons **3.**134–7
  mature retina **3.**129–32
  refinement **3.**140
  remodelling **3.**140
Retinogeniculate pathway **2.**456
Retinoic acid **11.**19–20, **11.**48
Retinomotor movements **2.**413
Retinopathy
  canthaxanthine **7.**126
  central serous (CSR) **7.**125
  chloroquine toxic **7.**126–8
  diabetic **1.**297, **7.**148–51, **7.**228
  hypersensitive **7.**151–2
  hypertensive **7.**151–2, **16.**134
  indomethacin (indocid) toxic **7.**128
  photic **16.**93–5
  of prematurity (ROP) **16.**99, **16.**112–4, **16.**124–6, **16.**128
  proliferative diabetic **7.**124
  retinoid **7.**126
  solar **16.**110
  thioridazine **7.**128–9
  toxic, due to phenothiazine derivatives **7.**128–9
Retinopia **6.**189
Retinorecipient nuclei
  in mature retina **3.**129–32
  in retinofugal pathways **3.**132, **3.**136–41
Retinoschisis, X-linked juvenile **7.**148

Retinoscopy 1.234, 1.402–5, 2.83–4, 5.83, 16.123
  accuracy and precision of 1.404
  the artefact of 1.405
  dynamic 1.236
  and the flying fox 1.405
  introduction and history of 1.402
  optical principles of the method of 1.402–3
  and polarized light 1.323
  practical applications and utility of 1.403
  and the spot retinoscope 1.403
    'against' movement reflexes 1.403
    and 'cut-off' 1.403
    'with' movement reflexes 1.403
  and the streak retinoscope 1.403
  techniques of 1.404
    chromo- 1.404
    'near' 1.404
    neutralizing lens 1.404
    point-spread 1.404
Retinotectal axons 3.155
Retinotectal connections and neuronal cytoskeleton 11.287
Retinotectal influences, development of, in the superior
    colliculus 4.99–100
Retinotectal pathways 2.446, 2.456
  in goldfish 11.102–8
Retinotectal projections 3.168
Retinotopic columns 4.293–4
Retinotopic co-ordinates 12.463–4
Retinotopic maps 4.299–301
  of superior colliculus 8.245–6
Retinotopic organization 4.378, 12.125
  of area V1 12.464–5
Retinotopic specificity 11.199
Retinotopic/non-retinotopic area, Glossary explanation
    of 4.449
Retinotopy
  in the superior colliculus 3.150–75
    traditional approaches to the study of 3.151–2
Retractor bulbi 8.177, 8.183
Retrobulbar neuritis 7.159, 7.175–6, 7.179–80, 7.228, 7.230
Retrograde tracing 3.153–5
  using Horseradish peroxidase 3.154–5
Retro-illumination, measurement of light scattering
    by 1.387–8
Retroviral vectors 11.31–2, 11.34
Retroviruses, acutely transforming 11.112
Reverse correlation, Glossary explanation of 4.449
Reverse correlation technique 4.250–2
'Reverse staircase' eye movements 13.222–5
Revised Difference of Gaussians model 4.23–4
Revolving field eye-movement monitor 8.80
Reynolds number, of semicircular canals 8.18
RFLP, *see* Restriction fragment length polymorphism
RGB colour-mixing curves, transformation of 6.14–6
RGD (Arg-Gly-Asp) 11.178
Rhabdom 2.344, 2.381
  fused 2.344, 2.347
  open 2.344, 2.347
  and optics 2.127–8, 2.132

  in photoreception 2.368, 2.372
  self-screening in 6.267–8
  in visual processing 2.230–4, 2.238
Rhabdomeres 2.128, 2.378
  in evolution of eye 2.4, 2.39, 2.347, 2.355–6
  fused 6.263
  long 6.267
  narrow 6.267–8
  open 6.263–4
  in visual processing 2.230, 2.234–5, 2.238
Rhodopsin 6.93–8, 6.108–10, 6.114, 6.117–8, 6.120–1, 6.166,
    6.266, 7.103–5
  bovine 6.63
  in coevolution 2.12
  in colour vision 2.290, 2.292, 2.294, 2.299
  and developing visual system 16.108–9, 16.111, 16.117–8,
    16.122
  in evolution of eye 2.6–10, 2.39–40, 2.413
  in evolution of vision 2.404, 2.409
  and exons 6.92–3
  and eye optics 2.118
  and introns 6.92
  and light interactions 16.38, 16.42
  and light measurement 16.23
  in photoreception 2.366, 2.379–82
  in photoreceptor system 2.64–72, 2.74, 2.77
  in trichromacy 2.311–2
  and visual pigments 6.94
  in visual processing 2.229
Rhomboid lattices, and stripes 13.162
Rhombomeres 11.17, 11.39–41
Rhyme 12.306
  finding 12.358
Rhythm 12.306
Ribbon, synaptic 3.32, 3.41
Ribonucleic acid 7.102–3
  homeobox gene 11.21–2
  ribosomal, in regeneration 11.193
Ribosomes, dendrite 11.148
Ricco's area of complete summation 5.60, 5.66
Ricco's law 5.41, 7.78, 10.44
Richards' hypothesis 9.236
Richards' perception by natural computation 14.91
Riddoch effect 10.58–60
Riddoch phenomenon 12.380
Right hemisphere
  and disadvantages of right-handedness 13.84–93
  of dyslexics 13.184–5
    abnormalities of 13.184
  specialization of 13.37–8
  visuospatial functions of 13.30–5, 13.181–2
  weaknesses of, and bias to right-handedness 13.86–8
Right shift theory 13.84–6, 13.89–90, 13.92
  and genotype distribution of the *rs* + locus 13.84–6
Right-handedness
  bias to, and causes of left hand and right hemisphere
    weakness 13.86–8
  evidence for differences in abilities in 13.88–91
    in English and arithmetic tests 13.90–1

in mathematicians 13.89
in sports 13.88–9
in veterinary surgeons 13.89
in vocabulary and matrices tests 13.89–90
implications for reading of 13.91–2
right hemisphere costs of 13.84–93
see also Right-handers
Right-handers 12.304
and Kanji alexia 12.348
and Kanji and Kana alexia 12.348–9
and paralexia 12.330
and pure alexia 12.342, 12.344, 12.354–5
reading and script 12.309–10, 12.317
see also Right-handedness
and semantic paralexia 12.329
and word recognition 12.324
'Rigid' versus 'rubbery' transformations 9.153–4
Rigidity 6.193
Rindenblindheit (cortical blindness) 12.147
Risley prisms 9.226
'*Rita*' (Old Norse word for inscribing) 12.304
Ritter, Johann 12.162
Rivalry
nystagmus 9.104
temporal course of 9.100–1
temporal pattern of 9.106
Rivalry alternation, stimulus determinants of 9.97–101
RLP terminals, in the lateral geniculate nucleus 4.45–6
RLPs, Glossary explanation of 4.449
RNA, *see* Ribonucleic acid
Roach 2.70–1
Robotics and pattern recognition 14.26
ROC, *see* Receiver operating characteristic
Rod 'colour blind' system 12.386
Rod contributions 7.14–5, 7.21–3
Rod intrusion, *see* Scotopization
Rod pathway 10.301–2
Rod vision 5.49, 12.398
absolute threshold 5.278
adapting field 5.278
dark-adapted 5.58
experiments 5.64
in peripheral vision 5.50–1, 5.55–7, 5.61, 5.69, 5.71
Rod/cone ratio in nocturnality 7.209
Rodenstock retinometer 5.279–80
Rodenstock's optic nerve head analyser 1.377
Rodieck's Difference of Gaussians (DOG) model 4.12
Rods 10.45
ageing 5.277, 16.62
and ageing macula 16.81, 16.85, 16.89
broad band light saturation 5.210
in colour vision 2.296
dark light 3.25
density 3.15–6, 3.38
and developing visual system 16.106–7, 16.110–1, 16.117,

16.119, 16.124, 16.126, 16.128
embryology 11.394–6, 11.398–400
in evolution of eye 2.5–8, 2.12, 2.15–6, 2.37, 2.39–44,
2.413
in evolution of retina 2.136–41, 2.143
in evolution of vision 2.404
in fish colour vision 2.290
foveal 3.113, 3.115
in foveal sampling 3.21
and horizontal cells 3.38–40
in mammals 2.472, 2.476–8
output synapse 3.26
in peripheral vision 5.44–9, 5.55–60, 5.66, 5.70
photoreceptors 3.9–12, 11.32–3
pigment 2.409
in pursuit system 2.168–70
and radiation 16.57, 16.61
recognition 11.81, 11.83
and retinal organization 5.41
spherules 11.158–9
Rods and ERG 7.57
Root mean square deviation 1.252
Rorschach test 12.470
tables (Z-test) 12.303
Rostral interstitial nucleus of the medial longitudinal
fasciculus 8.200, 8.314
Rotation 14.20, 14.53, 14.55
horizontal sinewave 12.363
hyperbolic 14.21
in line images recognition 14.101
mental 14.56, 14.59, 14.66, 14.113
pattern 14.51, 14.55–9, 14.62, 14.64, 14.66
perception of 8.33
and spatial relations 14.51, 14.65
Rotation tests, mental 12.462
Roth's 28-Hue test 7.119, 7.155, 7.157
Route
familiar 12.427
finding 12.417, 12.427, 12.429
verbal description of 12.422
Routines, visual 14.37–8
RPE, *see* Pigment epithelium, retinal
rRNA (ribosomal RNA) 7.102
rs^+ locus, genotype distribution of, and the right shift
theory 13.84–6
RSDs, Glossary explanation of 4.449
RT, *see* Response time
'Rubbery' transformations 9.152–4
Rubens, Peter Paul 12.36–7
Rudd 2.70–1
Ruiz procedure, *see* Trapezoidal astigmatic keratotomy
Runge, Phillip Otto 12.386
Runge's colour pyramid 6.219–20
Rutilus rutilus (roach) 2.70–1

S

S cones 7.65–6, 7.68–9
S-1 fragment 11.137
Saccade generation, model of 4.393
Saccade neurones, of the parietal cortex 8.285
Saccade rates 8.73, 8.75, 8.85
Saccade-related burst neurones 8.249–54, 8.256–65
Saccades 2.59, 8.325–7, 12.3, 12.7, 14.55, 14.125
  accuracy 8.96, 8.117–22
  active 12.174
  adaptive processes 8.123–7
  amplitude
    bistable pattern 8.120–1
    computation 8.95–6, 8.98, 8.117, 8.127–9
    and diazepam 8.119
    global effect 8.119–21
    transition function 8.128–9
  anti- 8.102–3, 8.113, 8.244, 8.270, 8.304–5
  anticipatory 8.112, 8.114
  and area 7 neurones 12.101
  and attention 8.114, 8.282, 8.284, 8.289, 8.304
  auditory 8.102, 8.250
  averaging responses 8.121
  backward 12.318–9
    and reading 12.316
    in reading and script 12.320
  and basal ganglia 8.267–71
  and blinks 8.304
  and the brainstem 8.206–9
  catch-up 8.140, 8.329
  centrifugal 8.101–2, 8.117
  centripetal 8.101, 8.118
  and cerebellum 8.236–8
  cognitively driven 8.250
  continuous error-processing in 8.131–2
  correctional 2.167
  corrective 8.9, 8.122–3
  and counting 8.85
  decision processes 8.116–7
  direction transition function 8.130
  disconjugate 8.167
  divergent 2.271
  double-step 8.115–7, 8.119–21, 8.127–32, 8.252
  duration of 8.95, 8.99
  during smooth pursuit 8.110–2, 8.329
  dynamics 8.99–112
    and attention 8.102–3
    and fatigue 8.102–3
    interacting with smooth movements 8.110–2
    oblique and vertical 8.103–5
    and orbital direction 8.101–2
    skewness of 8.101
    and visual field 8.102–3
  exploration 12.436, 12.452
  express 8.112, 8.114–5, 8.290
    and lesions of the striate cortex 8.279
    and superior colliculus 8.252–3
  extraretinal feedback and 8.122, 8.131–2

  and eye–head co-ordination 8.106–10
  fast gaze 12.176
  fatigue 8.102
  forward
    in reading and script 12.319–20
    size of 12.316, 12.318
  foveating 2.167, 2.172, 2.176
  frequency 12.432
  and frontal lobes 8.244, 8.270
  with gap paradigm 8.114
  gaze 8.107–9, 8.265, 8.328
  Glossary explanation of 4.449
  goal-directed 12.462
  goal-oriented 12.453
  human eye 12.52
  hypermetric 8.124, 8.310–2
  'hypometric' 12.452
  latencies 12.95
  latency 8.96, 8.112–7, 8.121–2, 8.305
    affecting accuracy 8.121–2
  lesions, cerebellum 8.236–7
  main sequence 8.100
  memory-guided 8.270, 8.277
  and multimodal convergence 11.369–71
  neutral distance 8.117
  non-visually guided 8.102–3
  oblique 8.103–12, 8.118–9, 8.210–1, 8.258–60
  with overlap paradigm 8.114
  overshoot 8.118
  peak acceleration 8.95
  and posterior parietal lobe 12.97
  in pursuit system 2.165–7, 2.172–3, 2.176, 2.179–82,
    2.184–6
  reaction times 8.96, 8.112–7, 8.121–2, 8.305
  reflex 12.452–3
  role in maintaining stability of gaze 8.74–5
  and signal transfer 12.58–9
  spontaneous 8.250, 8.270
  from stimulation of superior colliculus 8.255
  and substantia nigra 8.211, 8.267–80
  and the superior colliculus 8.252–3
  symmetrical 8.101
  undershoot 8.118
  velocity 8.95, 8.99–112
  vertical 8.97, 8.103–12, 8.118
  and visuo-spatial disorders 12.438, 12.442
  voluntary 12.363, 12.365, 12.368, 12.370–1
Saccadic dysmetria 8.124–5, 8.236, 8.312–3, 12.462, 13.216
Saccadic eye movements 4.377, 5.45–6, 5.57, 13.32–3,
    13.35–6, 13.63–4, 13.149–50, 13.204, 13.210, 13.214,
    13.246–8
  and area LIP 13.18–9
  in children 13.251
    fixation durations of 13.260–1
      and two-step attention shifts 13.260
    very short 13.260
  control of, physiology of 13.273–4
  experiments with multiple targets 13.274–6
    and the cross-inhibitory settling delay 13.276

Saccadic eye movements (*continued*)
    directional preferences 13.275
    relative onset, time of 13.275
    target brightness 13.275
    target eccentricity 13.275
  leftward regressive 13.218
  neural basis of, in primates 4.388–442
  overshoot in 13.204–5
    dynamic 13.205
    glissadic 13.205
    static 13.205
  in peripheral vision 5.48, 5.50, 5.56, 5.59
  in reading 13.68
Saccadic hypermetria 8.310
Saccadic oscillations 8.304
Saccadic pulse generator 8.96–7, 8.209–11
Saccadic pursuit 5.71
Saccadic suppression 4.407, 8.5, 8.9, 9.102, 13.209, 13.263
  Glossary explanation of 4.449
Saccadic vergence 8.167
Saccule 8.14
Sag gauges 1.416–8
Sag measurements 1.426–7
Sagometers 1.427
Saguinus 7.209, 7.212
Saguinus fuscicollis (saddle-backed tamarin) 2.76, 7.209–10
Saguinus oedipus (cotton-top tamarin) 7.211
Sahlgren's Saturation Test 7.216, 7.227–8
Saimiri 7.209
Saimiri sciureus (squirrel monkey) 2.76–7, 2.287–8, 2.293, 2.315–6, 7.204–12
Salamandra salamandra (tiger salamander) 2.285–7, 2.290, 2.295, 2.299
Salience 8.120
Salinity 2.21, 2.39–40, 2.42–5
  in evolution of eye 2.16–7, 2.31
Salmo trutta (brown trout) 2.69, 2.290
Salmonids 2.70–1
Salvelinus fontinalis (brook char) 2.71
Salvelinus namaycush (lake char) 2.71
Same discrimination 14.63
Same–different discrimination 14.51, 14.55–7, 14.60, 14.64
  performance 14.60–2, 14.65–6
Same-detection 14.51, 14.59
  performance 14.56, 14.58, 14.60–2
'Sameness' detection 12.322–4
Sampled data control systems 8.127
Sampling
  aperture 3.16–7, 3.27, 3.57
  colour signal 3.28–30
  extrafoveal 3.20–4
  foveal 3.17–20
  in hyperacuity 10.88–90, 10.110
  and optics 5.92
  oversampling 5.269
  photoreceptor 3.12–3
  in primate retina 3.14
  retinal 3.4, 3.6–9, 5.268
  spatial 3.4, 3.11, 5.48, 5.65, 5.75, 5.262, 6.71–4, 10.64,

    10.81, 10.233–5
  characteristics of bipolar array 3.36
  by cone mosaic 3.27
  ganglion cell 3.48
  by photoreceptor array 3.16–24
  of retina 3.1
  spatial domain 3.28
  spectral 3.27–30
  two-dimensional 3.31
  wavelength domain 3.28
Sampling array 2.240, 2.242
Sampling density 2.266, 5.65, 5.68, 5.71
  cortical 10.232
Sampling efficiency 5.58, 5.66, 5.68
Sampling elements 3.57
Sampling intervals 3.19, 5.255–6, 5.259–61
  colour signal 3.28–9
  distribution of 3.21
  and functional organization of retina 3.7–9
  and ganglion cells 3.57–8
  and postreceptoral mechanisms 3.31
Sampling points 5.45, 5.48, 5.74
Sampling strategies 3.56–7
Sampling theorem 5.262
Sampling theory 1.20, 2.73, 2.102–3, 2.237, 2.299, 5.91
  two-dimensional 5.73
Sampling thresholds 5.152
'Sandwich' model 10.9
SANE models 15.106–7, 15.110
S-antigen, *see* Arrestin
Sarcopterygii 2.400–1, 2.407
Saturation 5.102, 5.202–3, 6.43–5, 7.179, 7.182–3, 7.189, 7.231, 10.294–6, 12.395–6
  CIE definition of 6.226
Saturation discrimination, *see* Colour discrimination, purity
Sauropsida 2.423–4, 2.426, 2.468–70
SCa protein 11.191, 11.193
Scale
  grey-tone 12.397–9
  happy/sad 12.226
Scaling
  across-species 5.71
  additive 14.131
  F (flux) 5.258, 5.269
  grating thresholds 5.74–5
  luminance 5.7
  M (magnification) 5.256–9, 5.262
  magnitude 14.131
  multidimensional 10.122
  partition (category) 14.127, 14.131
  in peripheral vision 5.55, 5.60, 5.73–5
  Rovamo–Virsu 5.75
Scaling factor, Tolhurst and Ling's 5.255
Scallop 2.124–7, 2.130, 2.368–71, 2.390
Scanning 2.122, 4.409
  asymmetric 12.229
    attentional 12.325
  dynamic 2.103
Scanning laser ophthalmoscope 1.377–8

Scanning specular microscope 1.391
Scanpaths 13.216, 13.220–1
Scar, glial 11.207, 11.209–10
Scar reaction, to damage in transplantation 11.319
Scar tissue 11.206, 11.213, 11.249
Scardinius erythrophthalmus (rudd) 2.70–1
Scatter 2.87, 5.81
    and ageing 16.155
    in ageing lens 16.76
    intra-retinal 2.103
    intraocular 5.86–7
    lenticular 5.280
    light 2.88–9, 2.97–8, 2.100, 2.408–9, 16.94
    and light damage 16.63
    and light interactions 16.37, 16.45
    and light measurement 16.28
    Mie 16.93
    and optical radiation 16.3, 16.18
    Rayleigh 2.407
    retinal 5.88–9
SCb protein 11.191, 11.193–4, 11.197
SCE I function, *see under* Stiles–Crawford effect
SCE II, *see* Stiles–Crawford effect, of the second kind
S-cells 4.29–36, 4.226–8, 4.234–8, 4.240–1
    Glossary explanation of 4.450
    of monkey cortex 4.203
Scene
    analysis 14.100
    attributes 14.83–91, 14.93
    description 14.1
    understanding 14.4–5
    visual, from meaningless random stimuli 12.470–1
Scenery, complex visual 12.481
Schaunystagmus 8.47, 12.143
Scheimpflug's principle 1.385–7
Scheiner, Christoph 12.36, 12.38, 12.53
Scheiner double-pinhole 2.111
Scheiner's principle 1.234–5
Schiff's base, protonated 2.64–5
Schimkewitsch's theory of eye embryology 11.397, 11.401–2
Schizophrenia
    abnormal eye movements in 13.263
    acute paranoic-hallucinatory 12.296
    in children 12.288–9, 12.477
    defects 12.291
    and heautoscopy 12.301–3
    movie test 12.291–5
    perception and recognition of faces, facial expression and
        gestures 12.287–96
        neuropsychological investigations 12.290–5
        paraprosopia 12.289–90
        phylogenetic development of human brain 12.287–9
    psychological symptoms 12.288
    reading and script 12.313
    types 12.291
Schmidt's sign 7.20–1, 7.90
Schonell Graded Word Reading Test 13.91
Schreber, Daniel Paul 12.290
Schultze's duplicity theory of vision 2.137

Science, cognitive 14.45
Scintillation, fortification 12.172, 12.476
Sciuridae (squirrels) 2.74
Sciuromorpha 2.73
Sciurus carolinensis (grey tree squirrel) 2.74
Sclera 2.414
    mammalian 2.468, 2.470–1, 2.473
    and radiation 16.55, 16.57, 16.59
SCN, *see* Suprachiasmatic nuclei
S-cone channels 6.169–70, 6.172–3, 6.175, 6.181–2
S-cones 4.317–8, 4.322, 4.326, 4.332, 6.203–4, 6.208–9,
    6.212
Scotomas 1.218, 16.27
    absolute 12.150, 12.173
    acquired 1.350, 1.353
    Amsler grid 1.350
    binocular 12.144
    and the blind spot 1.349
    central 2.168–9
    local 12.468
    low level central 1.350
    migraine 12.142, 12.172
        completion of figures across 12.176
    monocular 12.144
    by occipital lesions 12.149–50
    and optokinetic nystagmus 8.61–3
    patchy 12.203
    and phototoxicity 16.70
    physiological 12.146
    quartermoon-shaped 12.173
    retinal haemorrhage 1.350
    and striate cortex 8.279
Scotomata 10.266, 10.270
Scotomata and threshold measurements 7.53
Scotopic function 7.5–6
Scotopic functions 16.105, 16.124–5
Scotopic optokinesis 8.63
Scotopic sensitivity function 16.118
Scotopic sensitivity syndrome 13.172–8
    and glare 13.172–3
        use of Irlen photopic transmission lenses for 13.173–6
    studies of
        using coloured overlays 13.176–8
        using Irlen photopic transmission lenses 13.173–6
        using non-Irlen colour lenses 13.176
    theoretical basis of 13.172–3
Scotopic system 16.110, 16.120–1
    and ageing 16.150
    and developing visual system 16.125–6, 16.128–9
Scotopic vision 2.66–8, 2.74, 2.78, 2.168–70, 2.407, 3.49,
    3.186, 5.48–9, 5.63, 5.68, 5.72, 5.74, 5.195, 6.24, 12.386,
    12.393, 12.398, 12.471
    in infants 10.203
Scotopic visual processing, development of 10.196–8
Scotopization 7.22
    in cone diseases 7.135–8, 7.140, 7.162
    defined 7.64
    in ophthalmic disease 7.116, 7.118
    rod 7.68

Scotopization (*continued*)
  in Stargardt's disease 7.142, 7.144
Screen, tangent 12.137
Screening pigment 2.351, 2.374, 2.377
Screening strategy, serial 12.182, 12.191
Script
  alphabetic 12.307–8, 12.310
  boustrophedon period 12.308
  Braille 12.309
  cuneiform 12.333
  Egyptian 12.305–7
  graphical similarity 12.311
  history of 12.304–8
  ideographic 12.308, 12.348
  Kana 12.348
  Kanji 12.307, 12.348, 12.357
  left–right linearity 12.308
  logographic (ideographic) system 12.308
  logographic–syllabic system 12.306
  mnemonic device 12.306
  modern 12.306
  normal 12.356
  phonological syllabic 12.348
  phylogenetic considerations 12.308–9
  pictorial 12.306–7
  precursors 12.308–9
  proto-cuneiform 12.305
  right–left direction 12.308
  sexagesimal system 12.305
  shorthand 12.342
  statistics 12.310–5
  stenographic 12.355
  Sumerian cuneiform 12.305–6
  syllabic 12.307–8, 12.310
  syllabic–alphabetic system 12.308
Scudder model, of saccade generation 8.258–9
Sculpture 12.221, 12.224
Scutigera 2.220, 2.342, 2.345–6
Search coil technique, electromagnetic 12.365, 12.367
Search strategies 12.195–7
Search velocity, as a measure of performance 15.25
Second stage of analysis
  of a compound grating 5.101
  of a near-threshold grating 5.100
Secondary discontinuities 4.162
Second-order relational information 14.108, 14.118
Second-order relational properties 14.108
Sedative 12.477
Seelenblindheit (psychic blindness) 12.107–8, 12.147, 12.187–8
  clinical case descriptions 12.179–80
Segmentation 11.39–41, 14.6
  gradient-based 5.121, 5.123
  texture 5.121–3
Segmentation models 11.57–9
Segmentation morphogenetic subfields 11.61
Segments 11.38–41
  inner
    cone 3.17, 3.21

and functional organization of retina 3.1–2, 3.11–4
  photoreceptor 3.9, 3.16–7
as morphogenetic fields 11.57–60
outer
  class specification 3.101
  cone 3.25
  differentiation 3.100–1
  and fovea 3.115
  and functional organization of retina 3.1–2, 3.4, 3.12–4
  photoreceptor 3.9
  in retinal development 3.88–9
Segregation 2.308–9, 2.312
  in colour vision 2.316–7
  eye-specific 3.141, 11.265–7, 11.269–70
  figure-ground 10.163–5
  laminar 3.303
  in mammals 2.476
  morphogenetic fields 11.65
  morphogenetic subfields 11.60
  and pattern formation 11.54–5
  in retinofugal pathways 3.132, 3.135–9, 3.141–2
  in visual cortex 3.317–8
  and visual pathways 2.450–1, 2.453, 2.458
  in visual thalamus 3.179, 3.187, 3.199, 3.215
Sehen, directes (direct vision) 12.137
Sehen, indirectes (indirect vision) 12.136
Sehsinnsubstanz (substance of visual sensation) 12.469
Seidel aberrations 1.10–1, 1.13, 10.137
Seizures
  activity 12.275
  epileptic 12.477, 12.479
  generalized 12.347
  intractable epileptic 12.347
  prevention of 13.164–7
  and reading 13.155, 13.162
  temporal lobe 12.300
  and visual cortex 13.155
Selective adaptation 9.150
Selective attention
  colour related 4.331
  and the enhancement phenomenon 4.381
Selectivity
  for direction in depth, and dynamic stereopsis 4.216–7
  Glossary explanation of 4.449
  orientation 10.200
Self, the 12.297–8
Self-absorption 2.230
Self-assembly 11.275
Self-identification 12.297
Self-inhibition 2.208
Self-motion 2.443, 2.459, 5.160
  and the retinal flow pattern 9.162
  visual guidance of 9.162
Self-movement 12.360
Self-organization 3.351, 11.303–7, 14.81
  global behaviour 11.302
  of networks 14.70
Self-screening pigments 6.267
Self-shadowing 14.36

Self-vision **12**.299, **12**.301
    see also Heautoscopy
Semantics
    rapid unaware access to lexical **12**.351
    rules **12**.317
    system **12**.338
Semaphore **12**.307
Sememes **12**.310
Semicircular canals **8**.14, **8**.24, **8**.46, **8**.175, **8**.215, **8**.320–1
    afferent fibres **8**.27–31, **8**.215–6, **8**.320
    allometry **8**.20
    frequency response of **8**.20, **8**.24–9, **8**.216
    mechanics **8**.17–20
    orientation **8**.20–1, **8**.320
    receptors **8**.215
    short time constant of **8**.18
    time constants of **8**.18–20
    vestibular stimulation of receptors **12**.432
Semivision **2**.229, **2**.253–60
    image recognition by **2**.260–3
    insect **2**.259
    mechanisms **2**.248–9, **2**.266
    templates **2**.268
Senescence, *see* Ageing
Senile miosis **5**.277–8
Sensation
    epileptic visual **12**.474
    visual **12**.198
Sensation magnitude estimation **10**.13
Sense-reversal operations **14**.51, **14**.54, **14**.56–63, **14**.66
    global **14**.57–9
Sensitivity
    of cones **3**.29
        to light **3**.16
    directional **7**.5, **7**.12
    flicker **10**.50
    flicker/motion **10**.242
    light **10**.273
    motion **10**.100
    orientation, oblique effect **10**.199
    pattern **10**.50
    phase **10**.202
    photoreceptor **3**.13
    of receptive field centre **3**.30
    of subject **10**.36
Sensitivity decrement **15**.90–5
    explanations of **15**.93–5
        and automatic processing **15**.93
        and controlled processing **15**.93
        and processing resources **15**.93
        secondary task method **15**.93
    and task characteristics **15**.90–3
Sensitizers **16**.40, **16**.42, **16**.44
    endogenous **16**.41
    exogenous **16**.41
Sensory coding **2**.18
Sensory fusion
    definition of **9**.19
    robustness of **9**.195

and dissociating red-glass test **9**.195
Sensory localization, visual direction sense in **13**.35–6
Sensory modalities **12**.269–70
    for controls **15**.114–8, **15**.120
        by hand
            joysticks **15**.115
            keys **15**.115
            levers **15**.115
            push-buttons **15**.115
            sliders **15**.115
            switches **15**.115
            touch-sensitive panels **15**.115
    and display–control relationships **15**.115–6
        fitting of population stereotypes **15**.115–6
        QWERTY layout **15**.116
        tactual and proprioceptive feedback in **15**.115, **15**.118
        use and limitations of word labelling in **15**.115
        use of pictograms/icons in **15**.77–9, **15**.115, **15**.117
    for displays **15**.111–7
    eye–hand co-ordination **15**.116–8
        comparison of direct and indirect pointing devices **15**.118
        cursor-control keys **15**.116
        direct control on the screen surface **15**.117
            lightpens **15**.117–8
            touchscreens **15**.117–8
        direct manipulation **15**.116–7
        direct pointing devices **15**.117
        indirect control away from the screen surface and cursor control **15**.117–8
            graphics tablets **15**.117–8
            joysticks **15**.118
            mice **15**.117–8
            Pro-Pointer **15**.117–8
            trackballs **15**.117–8
        indirect pointing devices **15**.117–8
        peripheral pointing devices **15**.116
    interaction of, in the man–machine interface **15**.114–26
Sensory-motor function, suggested involvement of the pulvinar in **4**.154
Sensus communis **12**.38, **12**.40
Sentence **12**.341
    logographic **12**.331
    pictographic **12**.331
    stereotyped **12**.356
    writing from dictation **12**.340
Separability, general concept of **4**.251
Separation **14**.58–9
    discrimination, in temporal integration **14**.9, **14**.13–6
    encoding **14**.12
    figure-ground **14**.35
Separation–discrimination task **14**.9
Separation–discrimination thresholds **14**.10–2, **14**.14, **14**.16
Sequential method (QUEST) **5**.14
Sequential strategies **12**.208
SER, *see* Smooth endoplasmic reticulum
Seriation operations **14**.126
Serine and proto-oncogenes **11**.112–3, **11**.118–9

orientation of 13.148–9
spatial frequency of 13.148–9
Singing 12.335
Single cells 9.225
Single opponency 6.176
Single vision 9.1
Single-opponent colour cells, Glossary explanation of 4.450
Single-opponent units
   'double duty' of 6.204–6
     and sampling 6.205
     and spatial integration 6.205–6
Single-source tasks 15.84
Single-unit recording 9.87
Singularity
   Glossary explanation of 4.450
   in line images 14.98–106
SIT resources, *see* Sustained information processing resources
Size 5.286
   anisotropy 2.276
   appreciation 12.204
   changes 12.199
   constancy 2.157, 2.263–5, 2.267
   detection 12.204
   discrimination 12.191
Size after-effects 5.237–8, 5.248
Size change, and vergence 8.165
Size discrimination 10.270
Size disparity 9.214
Size lenses 1.61
   cylindrical surface 'meridional' 1.164
   'overall' magnification of 1.164
   power factor in 1.164
   shape factor in 1.164
   sperical surface power of 1.164
Size–distance constancy 2.156, 2.163
Skeletonization 14.103
Sketch
   2.5D 12.11
   primal 12.11–2, 12.14
Skiascopy, *see* Retinoscopy
Skin
   dermal elastoic degeneration 16.144
   Galvanic reflex 12.276, 12.400
Skin problems, and visual-display terminals 15.2
Sleep 12.467, 12.469
   REM phases 12.480
Sleep disturbances 12.478
Slip velocity 2.167–8, 2.170, 2.180–4, 2.189, 2.191
Slit lamps 1.384–8
   illumination systems of 1.385
     Köhler 1.385
   measurement of the anterior segment using Scheimpflug's principle 1.385–7
   and the degree of lens fluorescence 1.387
   and the degree of light scattering 1.387
   measurement of light scattering by retro-illumination 1.387–8

microscopes 1.384–5
Slit-lamp biomicroscopy 1.330
Sloan achromatopsia test 7.229
Sloan M system, in prescribing magnification for near viewing 1.216
Slow control 8.78–9
SMD (senile macular degeneration) 16.59, 16.63–5, 16.86–7, 16.90, 16.137
Smoking 12.133
Smooth dendrites 3.289–91, 3.293–4
Smooth endoplasmic reticulum (SER) 11.148–50
Smooth pursuit 8.78–9, 8.86–7, 8.90, 8.138–56, 8.232–4
   acceleration 8.139–40, 8.212, 8.215
   active vs. passive 8.147–8
   after-nystagmus 8.145
   against a background 8.148–9, 8.233
   asymmetry 8.213, 8.306
   and attention 8.79, 8.86, 8.147–9
   and brainstem 8.153, 8.211–5
   and cerebellum 8.153–4, 8.232–4
   and cerebral cortex 8.215, 8.283, 8.285
   continuation 8.145
   distinguished from optokinesis 8.78–9, 8.138, 8.329
   extraretinal motion signals and 8.149–51
   frequency-response 8.142–5, 8.148–50
   gain 8.138–9, 8.141–3, 8.148–51
   Glossary explanation of 4.450
   interactions with saccades 8.110–2, 8.329
   lesions affecting 8.153, 8.213–4, 8.232, 8.306–8, 8.312, 8.314
   models 8.151–3
   negative feedback in 8.138–9, 8.211, 8.214, 8.309
   neurophysiology 8.153–4, 8.211–4
   oculomotor neurones discharge during 8.203
   onset 8.139–41, 8.212, 8.230
   open-loop studies 8.140, 8.142–3
   prediction in 8.79, 8.143–6, 8.152, 8.154
   and Purkinje cells 8.230
   steady-state 8.141–3
   stimuli for 8.146–7
   target position and 8.146
   twitch 8.140
   velocity 8.142
Smooth pursuit eye movements, control of 13.37, 13.51, 13.208, 13.218
Smooth stellate cells 6.187
Smooth surfaces, and the cyclopean disparity gradient limit 9.56–8
Smoothness 14.33–4, 14.41, 14.92
SN, *see* Signal-plus-noise
Snail 2.122
Snake 2.477
   cat-eyed 2.103
   dioptrics 2.84–7, 2.100, 2.102, 2.110
   garter 2.102–3, 2.428–9
   visual pathways 2.422, 2.427–9
Snellen eye charts 1.215, 10.25, 10.239, 16.110
Snellen letters, low-contrast 10.252
Snellen visual acuity 7.100, 7.179, 7.183, 7.188, 7.192,

10.169–70, 10.224–9
inherited colour deficiencies 7.24, 7.28, 7.30
Snellen visual acuity tests 5.279
Snell's window 2.408
Social facial signals 12.124
Social gaze contact 12.123
Social gaze perception 12.123
Sociobiology 11.306–7
Solar spectrum 2.87
Solid angle 16.3
Soluble substances and optic nerve regeneration
    11.211
Somatoparaphrenia 12.299, 12.450–1
Somatosensory cortex, cat's primary 4.266–7
Somatosensory system 12.96
Somatosensory-motor cortex 2.430
Somatostatin 3.279, 3.294, 11.359–63
    in visual cortex neurogenesis 3.363–4, 3.369
Somatotropin release inhibitory factor 11.359–63
Somite 11.59
Sound localization 2.448
Sound, as a display medium in the man–machine
        interface 15.118–20, 15.124
    alarms and warnings 15.119
    encoded messages 15.120
    and the masked threshold 15.119
    status and monitoring messages 15.120
        auditory displays 15.119
        auditory tones 15.120
        icons 15.120
        stereotypes 15.120
Sound-direction discrimination 10.89
South American monkeys 7.207–11
Southern blotting 7.103, 7.105, 7.108–10
SP, *see* Substance P
Space
    appreciation 12.181
    colour 12.386, 12.395, 12.400
        perceptual 12.386
        three-dimensional 12.397
    coordinates 12.431–4
    ego 12.411, 12.433
    egocentric 5.160
    exploration 12.262, 12.427
    extrapersonal 12.143, 12.146, 12.149, 12.156, 12.217,
        12.430, 12.465
        and allaesthesia 12.476
        cerebral representation of 12.92–106
        coordinates of 12.415–6
            and prism adaptation 12.416–7
        emotional aspects of 12.417
        far-distant 12.413, 12.422, 12.437, 12.441, 12.448
        'gaze field' 12.99
        illusion and hallucination 12.466–7, 12.472, 12.474,
            12.477
        instrumental experiences 12.413
        near-distant 12.422
        and optic ataxia 12.451
        perception 12.427–8

perception and orientation in 12.411–7
and spatial hemineglect 12.452–3, 12.462–4
and topographagnosia 12.418
and visual hemineglect 12.431–4, 12.447–9
and visual movement agnosia 12.360, 12.362, 12.364,
        12.371, 12.374, 12.378
and visual object recognition 12.107
and visuo-spatial disorders 12.438–9, 12.442–3
far-distant action 12.203, 12.411
    non-Euclidean structure 12.415
    and visuo-spatial disorders 12.443
feature 14.71, 14.74, 14.80
grasping, *see* Grasping, space
metric 14.101
movement and orientation in 12.278
multidimensional 14.118–9
near-distant action 12.203, 12.374, 12.378, 12.411, 12.430
    Euclidean structure 12.415
    and posterior parietal lobe 12.96
    and visual hemineglect 12.448, 12.450
    and visuo-spatial disorders 12.437–8, 12.443
orientation and action in 12.412
perception 12.199, 12.411, 12.433
    constancy of 12.431–3
    extrapersonal 12.436
    and topographical disorientation 12.417
    of visual 12.378
    and visuo-spatial disorders 12.435–6
peripersonal 12.448
personal 12.411, 12.416
    perceived by inner senses 12.411
sensor 12.386
signal 14.71–4
as symbol of social or political power 12.417
Space constancy, experiments in 13.211
Space eikonometer 9.217
Space perception, binocular 9.75–92
Spache Diagnostic Reading Scales 13.246
Span of apprehension 14.128–9
Spatial acuity 5.24, 5.47, 5.50, 5.149, 5.236
    see also Acuity, spatial
Spatial antagonism 6.165–9
    and amacrine cells 6.165
    and horizontal cells 6.165
Spatial bindings 14.70
Spatial channels 5.42, 5.63
    band-pass 6.207–8
    low-pass 6.207–8
Spatial coding 12.464
Spatial constancy 13.214, 13.216
Spatial contrast
    achromatic and chromatic 7.64, 7.67–8
    in monochromacy 7.26
Spatial contrast sensitivity 12.149
    achromatic and chromatic 7.181
Spatial contrast sensitivity functions 15.13
    M scaling 5.257
Spatial co-ordinates 8.98, 8.132, 8.210
Spatial crowding 9.206

Spatial discontinuities 5.124
Spatial discrimination 10.33
Spatial domain
  edge detection 5.104
  and foveal sampling 3.18
  and functional organization of retina 3.6, 3.8
  sampling 3.28
  signal analysis in 10.18–23
Spatial filtering
  lateral geniculate nucleus as a 4.56–8
  see also Filtering
Spatial frequency 1.250–4, 4.291–3, 4.322, 5.289, 9.140,
    9.212, 12.9, 12.227
  and apparent motion 5.153
  and bandwidth estimation 5.102
  in the cat 4.292
  channels and contrast matching 5.106–7
  and colour vision 5.204
  components 12.224–5
  compound gratings and narrow bands of 5.101
  content 12.224–5, 12.228–9, 12.257–8
  contrast adaptation 5.112–4
  contrast encoding 5.110, 5.116
  contrast sensitivity 5.35–8, 5.42
  cortical channels 5.63–4
  edge detection 5.103
  and equiluminance 5.235–6, 5.239, 5.245, 5.247
  estimates of 4.255–7
  in extrafoveal sampling 3.22
  of eye's optical apparatus 12.52–5
  and flicker 5.149
  and form information 5.286
  fourth root of 5.103
  and foveal sampling 3.17–8
  and functional organization of retina 3.5–6
  and ganglion cells 3.49
  Glossary explanations of (two) 4.450
  harmonic and subharmonic 5.102
  and illusions 5.242
  of image 3.40
  modulation threshold 5.13
  motion detection 5.166
  motion detectors 5.156
  motion sensitivity 5.150–2
  and optics 5.84–6, 5.88–9, 5.91–2
  in peripheral vision 5.47–8, 5.52–4, 5.58, 5.63, 5.65–8,
    5.71, 5.73–4
  and photoreceptors 3.25
  and postreceptoral mechanisms 3.32
  power spectra averages 12.258
  and pure alexia 12.339
  sampling 3.24
  and senescence 5.279–80
  sensitivity of receptive field 5.99
  and sine-wave gratings 4.205
  and spatial sampling 3.16
  specificity of masking 5.209
  spectrum 12.225
  and stripes 13.155–6

systematic mapping of 4.326
tuning 12.70
  and contour perception 12.81
  and velocity perception 5.160–1, 5.163
  and visual channels 5.97–8
  in visual processing 5.25, 5.29, 5.33
  of visual stimulus 12.240
Spatial frequency analysis 13.148
  sustained channels 13.61, 13.149–51
    and reading 13.149–50
  transient channels 13.61, 13.149–51
    and reading 13.149–50
  and transient–sustained channel interactions in specifically
      disabled readers 13.150–2
  use of sinc-wave gratings in 13.148–9
Spatial frequency channel localization models 14.16
Spatial frequency channels 5.113, 5.117, 5.167, 5.169, 5.272
  and pattern recognition 14.25
Spatial frequency discrimination, *see* Discrimination
Spatial frequency domain, signal analysis in 10.18–23
Spatial frequency and face recognition 14.108
Spatial frequency filtering, *see* Filtering
Spatial frequency filters 9.86
Spatial frequency function, chromatic contrast sensitivity
    as 5.214–7
Spatial frequency processing, in dyslexic and normal
    readers 13.148–54
Spatial frequency tuning functions 10.144
Spatial gain fields 4.382
Spatial grouping, of text 15.71
Spatial hemineglect, right-sided 12.462
Spatial impulse response 4.248
Spatial integration, of colour information 6.212
Spatial integration zone 5.128
Spatial interval acuity 5.221–2, 5.226–30
Spatial layout of scene 14.4–5
Spatial limits, of fusion 9.33–4
Spatial linearity, two-dimensional 4.255
Spatial localization 13.12–38, 13.181
Spatial location dedicated encoding mechanism 14.17
Spatial mechanism, blue-sensitive 7.24
Spatial metaphor of similarity 14.115, 14.118–9, 14.121
Spatial organization 7.155, 7.159, 7.162–3
Spatial orientation, and agnosia 12.189
Spatial parameter coding
  length and width selectivity in 4.205
  by monkey cortical neurones 4.201–5
Spatial phase 10.19–20, 12.144
Spatial planning, large-scale 12.16
Spatial position, relative 14.8, 14.13–4
Spatial position coding 12.464
Spatial primitives 10.96–100, 10.110
Spatial probability summation 10.66
Spatial properties 14.50
Spatial relations 12.199
  affine 14.55
  binary 14.53
  classification 14.53–5
  counting 14.56–7

Spatial relations (*continued*)
  encoding 14.8–17
    modelling of localization mechanisms 14.15–7
    relative location 14.8–11
    temporal integration 14.13–5
    visual mechanisms 14.12–3
  extrinsic 14.53–6, 14.65–6
  general 14.51, 14.53
  global-position 14.54–5, 14.58–63, 14.66
  inside 14.51, 14.53–5
  intrinsic 14.53–5, 14.57, 14.66
  matching 14.56–8
  metric 14.55, 14.100
  operations 14.50–66
  operations independent of 14.64–5
  preorder 14.54
  quaternary 14.53, 14.64
  topological 14.51, 14.55
Spatial resolution 5.286, 7.7
  of P and M ganglion cells 4.32–3
  of visual displays 15.14–5, 15.34–6
Spatial response profiles, two-dimensional 4.255, 4.260–1
Spatial sampling, *see* Sampling
Spatial scaling in peripheral vision 5.257–9, 5.261–2
Spatial selectivity 4.147, 5.153–5, 5.262
Spatial sensitivity 15.11, 15.13
Spatial spectrum 5.97, 5.103
Spatial summation 5.68, 7.116, 7.155, 7.160, 10.165–6
Spatial tuning curves 5.155
Spatial vision
  development 10.179–204
    structural 10.180–3
      of cortex 10.182–3
      of eye optics 10.180–1
      of retina 10.181–2
  and dyslexia 13.71–2, 13.181
  neural mechanisms 10.204
  neural pathways 10.204
  psychophysics of 13.58
  role of colour in 6.198–200
    and detection of targets in foliage 6.200
    and perceptual segregation and binocular
      correspondence 6.200
    psychophysical mechanisms of 6.207–10
      adaptation 6.209–10
      and band-pass or low-pass spatial channels 6.207–8
      and colour vision coding for orientation 6.207–8
      interactions in the processing of colour and luminance
        contrast 6.209
      masking studies 6.209–10
    and random-dot kinematograms 6.200
    and random-dot stereograms 6.200
    relative constancy of 6.198–9
    and shading and shadows 6.199–200
Spatial window of attention 5.44–6
Spatial-frequency channels, of the striate cortex 4.247
Spatial-frequency domain, Glossary explanation of 4.450
Spatial-frequency selectivity, of cells of cat visual
  cortex 4.177–9

Spatial-order relations 14.51, 14.58–62, 14.66
  extrinsic 14.57
  pattern representation 14.63
  two-dimensional 14.54
Spatio-chromatic inseparability 5.47
Spatio-temporal analyses
  direction of motion 4.180
  and direction tuning and direction selectivity 4.208–10
  light and dark bars in 4.206
  of retinal images
    by cat cortical cells 4.180–92
    by monkey visual cortex neurones 4.205–11
  speed of motion 4.180
  speed selectivity in 4.205–8
Spatio-temporal channels 5.297–9
Spatio-temporal filtering 8.7
Spatio-temporal interaction, in fusion 9.35–6
Spatio-temporal interpolation 5.157–8
Spatio-temporal limits, summary of 5.300
Spatio-temporal response channels
  and the lateral geniculate nucleus 13.59
  'off'-type 13.60
  'on'-type 13.60
  psychophysics of 13.59–63
  W-type 13.59–60
    and the superior colliculus 13.59
  X-type 13.59–60, 13.62–3, 13.76
  Y-type 13.59–60, 13.62, 13.76
Spatio-temporal response profiles
  three-dimensional 4.252
  two-dimensional 4.252–3
Spatio-temporal selectivity of motion detector 5.157
Spatio-temporal separability 4.21–2
Spatio-temporal transformation 8.244, 8.326
Spatiotopic co-ordinates 12.463–4
Spatiotopic map 12.465
Speaker-dependent recognizers 15.121–2
Speaker-independent recognizers 15.120–1
Special complex cells 4.296
  Glossary explanation of 4.450
Specific visual cognitive disability 13.128
Specifically disabled readers 13.148, 13.150–3
  low-level visual processing in 13.151–2
  reduced effect of spatial frequency in 13.151
Specificity, in prosopagnosia 12.268
SPECT, *see* Single-photon emission computed tomography
'Spectacle' 2.84–5, 2.110
Spectacle lenses
  adaptation to 8.231, 8.301
  correction by 1.64–79
    history of 1.64
  design of 1.66–74
    and aberration control
      curvature 1.66
      of distortion 1.66, 1.68
      of oblique astigmatism 1.66–8
      transverse chromatic 1.66
    adjustable 1.74–5
    aspheric 1.69–70

'best form' 1.66
bifocal 1.71
and chromatic aberration 1.68–9
corrected curve 1.66
deformable 1.74
diffractive optics 1.75–6
and distortion 1.68
gradient index 1.74
hard coatings for plastic 1.77–8
impact resistant 1.78
   chemically toughened 1.78
   laminated 1.78
   thermally toughened 1.78
lenticular 1.70–1
liquid crystal 1.75
multi-layer anti-reflection coatings 1.76–7
and oblique astigmatism 1.67–8
photochromic tints 1.76
single-layer anti-reflection coatings 1.76–7
tinted 1.76
   coated
      CR39 1.76
      glass 1.76
   laminated 1.76
   solid glass 1.76
trifocal 1.72–3
varifocal 1.72–3
materials used in 1.64–5
   acrylics 1.65
   comparison of 1.65–6
   CR39 1.65
   glass 1.64
   plastic of high refractive index 1.65
   polycarbonate 1.65, 1.78
see also under Spectacles
Spectacle magnification 1.59
Spectacles
assessment of varifocal lenses 1.423
bifocal, and visual-display operators 16.65
determination of asphericity of 1.422–3
   and the American Optical 'Ful-Vue' lens 1.422
   and the Geneva lens measure 1.423
   and the Rank Taylor Hobson 'Talysurf' lens 1.423
and fluorescent light 13.169
instrumentation of 1.415–22
   centration 1.420–1
   chromatic dispersion of 1.421
   focimeters 1.418–20
      electronic 1.419
   Geneva lens measure 1.416
      and the sag formula 1.416
   lens thickness 1.420
   light transmissibility 1.421–2
   refractive index determination of
      using the Abbe refractometer 1.421
      using the Hilger-Chance refractometer 1.421
      using the Pulfrich refractometer 1.421
   sag gauges 1.416–8
   surface and material quality 1.422

of fused bifocal lenses 1.422
of fused trifocal lenses 1.422
lens standards for 1.423–4
   centration 1.424
   cylinder axis 1.424
   lens power 1.423–4
   near addition 1.424
see also Coloured lenses; Filters; Spectacle lenses
tinted 7.124, 13.164, 13.166–7
   benefits of, in patients with phorias and learning
      difficulties 13.166
   effects of, on mediating reading disabilities 13.155,
      13.175
Spectra
absorption 16.37–8
   and light interactions 16.42, 16.45
action 16.2, 16.11, 16.24, 16.37, 16.60
   and developing visual system 16.107
   for light damage 16.63–4, 16.106–9
   and light hazards 16.99
   and light interactions 16.40, 16.42, 16.45
   and light measurement 16.26–7
   and radiation 16.58
electromagnetic 16.67–8
Spectra of New World primates 7.209
Spectral antagonism 6.165–9
Spectral bandwidth in peripheral vision 5.50
Spectral composition 6.12
Spectral distribution, of daylight 6.58
Spectral efficiency function 5.50
Spectral emissivity 16.7
Spectral frequency domain, colour signals in 3.28–9
Spectral information 3.20, 3.28
Spectral inputs, number of, in insects 6.269
Spectral mixture curves 6.14
Spectral opponency
   in insects 6.276–81
   and neurophysiology of visual neurones 6.276–9
Spectral range 2.284–5, 2.288–9, 2.295, 2.298–9, 2.301
Spectral reflectance 6.58–9
Spectral response (π) mechanisms 7.7–9, 7.12, 7.15–9,
   7.23–4
Spectral response profiles, 2D 4.254–5, 4.259–60
Spectral response profiles, twist phenomenon in 4.260
Spectral selectivity, of the surround mechanism 4.33–4
Spectral sensitivity 6.17, 7.8
achromatic 5.198, 5.205, 5.207–8
and ageing 5.205
central foveal 5.204
chromatic 5.198–9, 5.205–7
chromatically opponent channels 5.198
cone 5.210
and ERG 7.59–60
and flicker 5.181
foveal 7.5, 7.11, 7.22, 7.27–8
of human observer 5.195–7
increment 7.121–2, 7.130
increment threshold 7.79–82, 7.85, 7.202, 7.205
large-field increment 7.140

Spectral sensitivity (*continued*)
  of LW, MW and SW cones 7.38–9
  measurements 5.192, 5.195–8
  mechanisms 5.191
  mesopic 5.195
  in optic-nerve disease 7.175–6
  in peripheral vision 5.48–9
  photopic 5.195–6, 7.5
  of photopigments 12.386
  physiological data 5.191, 5.195–6, 5.199
  in primate vision 5.191–200
  in red–green deficiencies 7.11–2, 7.16–7
  red–green heterozygotes 7.20
  rod, in achromats 7.25
  scotopic 7.24, 7.26, 7.28
    by rods 5.195
  and senescence 5.283
  spectral absorption 5.191
  threshold methods 7.43–5
  and wavelength discrimination 5.214
Spectral sensitivity curves 5.198
  photopic 12.396–7
Spectral sensitivity functions 2.285, 2.287, 2.289–95, 2.299,
    5.47, 5.196, 5.205–10, 5.212–3, 7.22, 7.72, 7.80
  and flicker 5.173, 5.179, 5.183–4
  and opponent-colour mechanisms 7.176
  red–green deficiencies 7.11–2, 7.15
  scotopic, in monochromacy 7.25
Spectral sensitivity threshold 7.22, 7.43–8, 7.77–8
Spectral suppression, Glossary explanation of 4.450
Spectral 'window' 2.299
Spectrin 11.284
  brain 11.278–9, 11.286–7
Spectroscopy 16.30, 16.35
Spectrum
  electromagnetic 3.28
  solar 2.87
  visible 3.29
Specular microscopy, of the corneal endothelium 1.125
Speech
  action, subliminal motor 12.310
  area
    Broca's motor 12.287–8, 12.356
    sensory and motor 12.304
    temporal 12.264
    Wernicke's sensory 12.287, 12.356, 12.358
  'automatic' 12.326
  centres 12.349, 12.356
  fluent 12.347
  in the man–machine interface 15.120–4
    concatenated 15.120
    controls 15.120
    display 15.120
    recognition of 15.120–2, 15.124
      by speaker-dependent machine recognizers 15.121–2
      by speaker-independent machine recognizers 15.122
    synthesized 15.120
  propositional 12.326
  in relation to visual interaction 15.122–4

eyes-free operation 15.122
  hands-free operation 15.122
  intonation 15.124
  personality impressions and speech rate 15.123
  spontaneous 12.347
Speech output 15.120–1
  concatenated 15.120–1
  synthesized 15.120–1
Speech rate 15.123
Speech recognition 15.120–1, 15.124
Speed, *see* Velocity
Speed dependence of direction selectivity, Glossary
    explanation of 4.450
Speed selectivity 4.180–6
  average firing rate 4.181
  duration of motion 4.182
  maximum firing rate 4.181
  rise time 4.182
  and stroboscopic illumination 4.182
Spelling, rapid 12.340
Spelling behaviour 12.340
Spermophilus (Citellus) lateralis (ground squirrel) 2.74
Sperry, Roger 11.88, 11.103–4
Sperry's chemospecificity theory 11.88–9, 11.92
Sperry's interhemispheric transfer of learning 3.324–5
Sphenodon 2.427–8
Spherical aberration 1.11–2, 1.247
  of the cornea 1.3
  in the human eye 1.4
Spherules 3.10–1
  rod 3.26, 3.32
    and bipolar cells 3.34
    in retinal development 3.93–4
Spider cells, *see* Clewed cells
Spider monkey 7.208–9
Spider optics 2.120
Spiders
  jumping 2.120
  net-casting 2.120
Spillover, of radioactive tracers 4.271–2
Spin–spin relaxation time 1.366
Spindles 8.188, 8.321
Spines
  dendritic 11.136–44, 11.149, 11.151, 11.158, 11.160–1,
    11.163
    differentiation of 12.19
    in neuronal cytoskeleton 11.278, 11.285–6
  globular 11.151
  sessile 11.149, 11.151
Spin-lattice relaxation time 1.366
Spinous cells
  of lamina IV 4.232
  of laminae I, II and III 4.232
  of laminae IV and VI 4.232–4
  laminar variation in the response properties of 4.234–7
    across the cortex 4.237
    in lamina IV 4.234–5
    in laminae II and III 4.234–5
    in laminae V and VI 4.236–7

Spinoza, Baruch de 12.469
Spinules 3.40
Spiny stellate cells 3.248–52, 3.265, 3.267–9, 3.293–4, 6.187
    Glossary explanation of 4.450
Spiritus animalis 12.28–31, 12.34, 12.36, 12.38–40, 12.127
Splenial visual area 4.362
Splenium, transection 12.112
Split-brain patients 3.325
Split-chiasm, cat 3.340–2
Split-chiasm preparation 3.340, 3.342
Splitting, visuo-vestibular 12.298
Spontaneous activity
    Glossary explanation of 4.450
    of vestibular afferents 8.8.27–30, 8.320
S-potentials 4.53–5, 4.57–8, 4.319–20, 4.325
    in LGN, Glossary explanation of 4.450
    in retina, Glossary explanation of 4.450
Spotlight of attention 4.405
SPP2 plate test 7.118, 7.220–2, 7.232
SPP (Standard Pseudoisochromatic Plates) 1 and 2 7.216
Spreading depression 12.177–8
Sprouting 11.275
    axon 11.232, 11.241, 11.243, 11.245, 11.247–8
        after lesions 11.250–1
    axonal 12.19
    collateral 11.250
    compensatory 11.303
    dendrite 11.149, 11.283
    in muscle 11.300
    neurite 11.280, 11.287, 11.292
    in neuronal cytoskeleton 11.293, 11.295, 11.297–300
    neurone 11.242, 11.250
    preterminal and terminal 11.235
Spurious resolution 10.24
Spurzheim, Johann Caspar 12.46–7, 12.61
Square-law behaviour 5.33
Square-law stages in bandwidth estimation 5.102
Square-law transform 5.10, 5.23–8, 5.30–3, 5.98
Square-root law 5.37–8, 5.41–2, 5.60–3, 5.67, 10.297
Squarewave gratings 10.142
Squid optics 2.121–2
Squid photoreception 2.366–7, 2.374, 2.376–83, 2.385, 2.388, 2.390–1
Squint 5.129, 8.168–9, 11.346
Squirrel 2.74
    colour vision 2.286, 2.292
    diurnal 2.476
    photoreceptors in 3.16
    tree 2.446–8
    visual cortex of 3.303, 3.305–9, 3.319
    visual pathways 2.450, 2.457
Squirrel monkey 7.204–12
SRF, *see* Serum response factor
SRI Dual Purkinje Image Eyetracker 13.253
SRIF, *see* Somatotropin release inhibitory factor
SSBS, *see* Simultaneous, symmetric, bihemifield stimuli paradigm
Stabilized retinal images
    effect on vision 8.73–4, 8.84, 8.87

and optokinesis 8.62
suppressing oscillopsia 8.315–6
Staircase method 10.36
Stand magnifiers
    advantages of 1.201
    disadvantages of 1.201
    fixed-focus types 1.192–3
    optical principles of 1.192
    types available
        fixed focus 1.201
        variable focus 1.201–2
Standard Observer 5.203, 5.207
    CIE's, for large-field colour matching 6.16
Standard Pseudoisochromatic Plates (2nd Edition), *see* SPP2 plate test
Standard reference patch, and the Mondrian experiment 6.57–8
Stanford Achievement Test 13.126
Star images 1.350
Star pyramid cells
    Glossary explanation of 4.448
    see also Cortical cells
Stare nystagmus 8.47, 8.112
Stargardt's macular degeneration 7.116, 7.141–5
Staring, in infants 10.198
Starlight, retinal mechanisms for 5.51–2
Starr's theory, of the Stiles–Crawford effect of the second kind in dichromats 1.305
State
    antibonding 16.33–4, 16.36
    atomic energy 16.32
    bonding 16.33
    molecular energy 16.35–7
    rotational 16.35–6, 16.38
    singlet 16.35–6, 16.39–40, 16.61, 16.67
    triplet 16.35–6, 16.40, 16.67, 16.69
    vibrational 16.35–6, 16.38, 16.44
Static luminance imbalance 15.43–4
    and best performance 15.44
    and visual comfort 15.44
    and visual-display terminals 15.41–2
Static stereopsis 9.207
Statistical efficiency 5.14
    in numerosity 14.134
Statistical estimation theory 14.85
Statistical uncertainty, state of 5.18
Statocysts 8.13
Statuettes
    Neolithic 12.221
    Palaeolithic 12.221
Status messages 15.120
Steatornis caripensis (oilbird) 2.271, 2.280–1
Stefan–Boltzmann law 16.7
Steinbuch, Johann Georg 12.6
Stellate cells 3.248
    see also Spiny stellate cells
    smooth 6.187
        laminar variations in the morphology of 4.238–9
        lamination of 4.237–9

Stellate cells (*continued*)
  spiny **6**.187
Steno, Nicolaus **12**.40
Stenogram **12**.342
Stenography **12**.339, **12**.342–3, **12**.355–7
  ideographic **12**.356
  parliamentary **12**.355–6
  shorthand **12**.330–1
  Stolze–Schrey **12**.330, **12**.355–6
  syllabic system **12**.356
Step vernier acuity, *see* Acuity
Stereo anomalies **9**.203–9
Stereo microscopes, low power **1**.330
Stereo pairs **1**.330
Stereo perimetry **9**.208
Stereoacuity **2**.454, **5**.126, **5**.133–45, **5**.258, **5**.261, **9**.171,
    10.107, **10**.282, **12**.19–20, **16**.126
  and hyperacuity **5**.221, **5**.225–30, **10**.93, **10**.99–101, **10**.110
  limitation of, by the precision of oculomotor control **9**.121
  with a moving head **9**.121–36
  in pattern discrimination **5**.266, **5**.269
Stereoanomalous subjects **8**.158
Stereoblind subjects **9**.182
Stereoblindness **2**.281, **9**.207
Stereocilia **8**.23
Stereograms **1**.331–2, **8**.9
  figural **5**.238, **5**.247
  Glossary explanation of **4**.450
  Julesz **12**.191, **12**.203
  Julesz random-dot **2**.276
  lenticular sheet **1**.332–3
  random-dot **2**.271, **2**.276, **3**.351, **5**.124, **5**.135, **5**.238–9,
    5.244, **5**.246–8, **9**.134, **14**.32–3
Stereograting **10**.161
Stereomotion **5**.240, **9**.144–51, **9**.166, **9**.208
Stereomotion blindness **9**.147–8, **9**.150–1
Stereomotion channels **9**.146–7
Stereomotion fields **9**.147–8
Stereomotion scotoma **9**.147–8
Stereomotion supresion **9**.144–51
Stereoperimetry, and the horopter **9**.42–3
Stereopsis **2**.274, **2**.436, **2**.446, **2**.448, **2**.455, **2**.459, **3**.330,
    5.228, **5**.239, **5**.259, **5**.274, **8**.160, **9**.123–4, **9**.203–11,
    11.374, **12**.19, **12**.400, **14**.5
  binocular **12**.381, **14**.44
  clinical tests for **9**.209
    haploscopic tests with camouflaged form **9**.210–1
    real depth **9**.209
      Aviator series **9**.210
      diastereotest **9**.210
      Howard-Dolman two-rod **9**.210
      pencil pointing **9**.209
      Titmus-Wirt stereo test **9**.210
      Vernoeff stereopter **9**.210
  coarse **9**.207
  and computational vision **14**.31–3, **14**.39
  crossed **9**.171
  and developing visual system **16**.126, **16**.128
  development of **9**.170–8

  and dynamic changes in absolute disparities **9**.132–5
  in dyslexics **13**.145
  effects of oculomotor imperfection on **9**.124–6
  evolution of avian **2**.280–1
  factors which degrade **9**.209
  false matches **5**.142, **5**.145
  global **5**.253, **5**.267
  in hyperacuity **10**. 107, **10**.99–100
  with isoluminant figural stereograms **6**.214
  with isoluminant random-dot stereograms **6**.214
  kinetic **9**.207
  machine **2**.273, **2**.275–7
  with a moving head **9**.121–36
  of moving targets **9**.131–2
  patent **5**.136
  qualitative **5**.136
  and rivalry **9**.96–7
  static **9**.207
  in strabismics **13**.49
  suppression of normal **9**.198
  tests of global **9**.171
  tests of local **9**.171
  theories **5**.133
  uncrossed **9**.171
Stereoscopes, Wheatstone's mirror **1**.330
Stereoscopic acuity **1**.327–9
  clinical tests of **1**.327–8
  and the pseudoscope **1**.328
  and the telestereoscope **1**.328
Stereoscopic depth **5**.123–8, **10**.283
Stereoscopic function **10**.282
Stereoscopic instruments **1**.326–44
  and binocular vision **1**.326–44
Stereoscopic learning and vergence **9**.65–6
Stereoscopic mechanisms
  in monkey visual cortex **4**.211–3
  and position disparity **4**.213–5
Stereoscopic neurones, operational properties of **9**.227–36
Stereoscopic precision, and aniseikonia **1**.179
Stereoscopic rangefinders **1**.330
Stereoscopic recording
  alternating images **1**.331
  anaglyphs **1**.331
  integral photography **1**.331–3
    and the autostereogram **1**.333
    and the fly's-eye array **1**.332 -3
    and lenticular sheet stereograms **1**.332–3
    and raster autostereoscopy **1**.332
  parallax methods **1**.331–3
    the panoramogram **1**.332
    the stereogram **1**.331–2
  polarization methods **1**.331
    printed vectographs **1**.331
  stereo pairs **1**.330
  sterescopes **1**.330–1
    Wheatstone's mirror **1**.330
Stereoscopic vision **5**.120, **6**.213–4
  clinical tests for **1**.341
    projected depth **1**.341

acuity variation in 1.341
real depth
    diastereo distance test 1.341
    Frisby near stereotest 1.341
    Howard–Dolman 1.341
  investigation of geometry of, through binocular visual
      instruments 1.326–30
  physiological basis of 9.224–38
see also Stereopsis
Stereoscopy, role of ocular dominance columns in 4.273
Stereo-scotoma 9.208–9
Stereotypes 15.115–6, 15.120, 15.123
Stereovision, binocular 12.441
Sterilization, of intraocular lens implants 1.132
Sticks, message 12.306
Stiernystagmus 8.47, 12.143
Stigmatoscopy 1.235
Stiles effect 7.17
Stiles π mechanisms 5.85, 5.88, 5.196, 5.283, 7.191–2
Stiles–Crawford apodization 1.16
Stiles–Crawford effect 1.12, 1.17, 2.100–1, 3.13, 5.49, 5.86,
    5.283, 7.25, 7.27, 7.54, 7.100
  and the exit-pupil 1.296
  of the first kind 1.280, 1.287–305, 5.87
    additivity of, within the pupil 1.290–1
    difference between photopic and scotopic 1.292–4
    effect of accommodation and eye movements on 1.291
    effect of drugs on 1.291
    empirical description of data of 1.289–90
      shape factor 1.289
    and luminance dependence 1.292–4
    and outer retinal and chorioretinal diseases
      age-related maculopathy 1.297
      Best's disease 1.297
      central serous chorioretinopathy 1.297
      gyrate atrophy 1.297, 1.302
      retinal detachment 1.297
      retinitis pigmentosa 1.297
    retinal origin of 1.289
    and retinal receptor alignment, factors maintaining and
      influencing 1.299–303
    and role of the optical media 1.294–5
      pre-retinal medial absorption 1.294–5
      reflection at ocular surfaces 1.294
    techniques of measurement of 1.290
    theories of 1.303–5
      based on fibre-optics/waveguides 1.304–5
      based on geometrical optics 1.303
      based on physical optics 1.303–4
    variation with receptor alignment
      histological evidence for, via psychophysics 1.295
      psychophysical evidence for 1.295–9
    variation with receptor directionality, rho-value as an
      indicator of 1.295
    variation with retinal receptor orientation 1.295
    variation with time of 1.291–2
    wavelength dependence of 1.294
  of the second kind 1.287, 5.87, 7.5–6, 7.12
    Starr's theory of 1.305

wavelength-dependence 5.88
Stiles–Halladay formula 1.351
Stiles's radiometric units 6.16
Stilling pseudo-isochromatic plates 2.306–9
Stimulation
  caloric, of labyrinths 12.473
  competitive, and visual hemineglect 12.431
  Coriolis 12.432
  electrical 12.479
    cerebral disinhibitory effects 12.478
    experiments 12.478
    of inferior parietal cortex 12.95
  flicker 12.74, 12.76, 12.172
  intermittent 12.370
  simultaneous, extinction with double 12.426
  somatosensory 12.103
  stationary 10.193–4
  vestibular 12.370
    of area 7 neurones 12.97–9
    and visual hemineglect 12.432
  visual movement 12.433–4
Stimuli
  visual
    angular velocity of 12.362, 12.375
    background contrast 12.121
    categories of 12.270
    complex material 12.144
    face 12.224–6, 12.230, 12.235, 12.238, 12.250–4,
      12.257–8
      processing 12.234
      and prosopagnosia 12.260, 12.274
      and visual evoked potentials 12.243–6, 12.248
    flicker 12.172, 12.194
      monochromatic 12.396
    high-contrast small 12.453
    high-frequency optic nerve 12.167
    intermittent light 12.164–5, 12.172
    key 12.218, 12.237
    luminance 12.241
    meaningless random 12.470–1
    monochromatic 12.396
    non-face 12.240, 12.242–6, 12.248, 12.251–2, 12.257
    object 12.278
    orientation 12.236
    pattern 12.240–1, 12.245, 12.252, 12.254–5, 12.257
    percutaneous magnetic field 12.171
    person 12.250, 12.253–5, 12.258
      in depressed mood 12.250
      greeting 12.250
      neutral 12.250
      unknown 12.257
    pseudorandom order 12.354
    reading 12.278
    sinewave electrical 12.163–5
    spatial frequency of 12.240
    subliminal 12.351–2
    tachistoscopic 12.238, 12.401
    velocity 12.360, 12.365, 12.371
Stimulus length, Glossary explanation of 4.450

Stimulus parameters, Glossary explanation of 4.450
Stimulus properties 14.8
STM resources, *see* Short-term memory resources
Stochastic ensemble 14.84–6, 14.94–5
Stochastic transfer 5.24, 5.27, 5.33
Stokes parameters 1.311
Stokes vector (S) 1.311
Strabismic suppression 9.198, 9.208
 clinical characteristics of 9.199–201
 stimuli for 9.197
Strabismus 2.271, 8.168–9, 8.330, 9.151, 9.202, 11.257–9,
  11.261, 13.48–9, 13.54
 and aniseikonia 1.179
 association with stereoanomalies 9.209
 development of 13.49–50
 in infants 9.177
 prediction of 13.51–2
 unilateral 9.200
 utrocular vision in 9.183–4
Streak
 horizontal 3.14
 visual 3.15–6
  amacrine cell 3.44
  dendritic fields 3.103
  and differentiation 3.100
  and fovea 3.117
  ganglion cell 3.56
  and ipsilateral projection 3.111
  and retinal development 3.118
  and retinal expansion 3.105–9
Stress 12.300–1
Stretch activated channels 11.182
Stretch reflex 8.321
Stria of Gennari 3.255–6, 3.262–3
Striate cortex 4.223–45, 4.322–30, 6.179–81, 8.245, 8.247,
  8.278–81, 8.306
 afferent inputs to 4.223–45
 blobs of, dual-opponent neurones within 6.208
 colour tuning of colour cells of 4.322
 complex cells of 4.246–7, 4.253–4
 current views on the laminar pattern of 4.228–31
 different laminae of 4.223–45
 Glossary explanation of 4.450–1
 hidden mechanisms in 4.257–9
 infragranular layers, laminae V and VI 4.230–1
 lamina IV and the III/IV border 4.228–30
 layer 4 of 6.181, 6.207
 linear filters of 4.247
 morphological cell types of 4.223–45
 organization of 3.235–77
 primary pathways to 4.224–6
 in pursuit system 2.174, 2.179
 receptive fields of, in cat and monkey 4.228
 receptive-field changes in the progression to 4.226–8
 receptive-field properties of 4.223–45
 simple cells in 4.246–7, 4.253–5, 4.260–1
 spatial-frequency channels of 4.247
 supragranular layers, laminae I, II and III 4.230
 in visual function

 effects of electrical stimulation of 4.410
 effects of lesions of 4.410
 physiological properties of 4.410
 and visual pathways 2.426, 2.430, 2.435–6, 2.452–5
Striate cortical cells 4.226
Striate receptive fields
 estimation of structure of 4.250–7
 as linear filters 4.246–65
Striate visual cortex 9.173
Striated glass test 9.187
Striatum
 in visual function
  connectivity of 4.404–5
  and implication of caudate nucleus in 4.403
  physiological properties of 4.403–4
Striola 8.24
Stripes 11.53–4, 11.58, 11.64
 α- 12.361, 12.373–4
 eye-specific 11.265
 of Gennari 12.146
 ocular dominance 11.300–1, 12.72–3
 see also Patterns, striped
 in synaptic rearrangement 11.271
Stroke 12.199, 12.264
 and alexia 12.335
 with bilateral diencephaic involvement 12.268
 in course of syphilitic disease 12.343
 left posterior 12.350
 posterior cerebral artery 12.335
  left 12.267, 12.339, 12.343–6, 12.351, 12.354
  right 12.262, 12.267, 12.271, 12.273, 12.275, 12.343
 unilateral 12.267
  posterior cerebral artery 12.262–3
Strombus 2.374, 2.376–7
Structure from motion theory 14.44
Structures
 branched 11.63–4
 'dissipative' 11.303, 11.307
 geometrical 14.52
 geometrical–topological 14.51, 14.55
 net-like 11.48, 11.62–4
 periodic 11.58
 stripe-like 11.58
STS, *see* Superior temporal sulcus
Student's Perception of Ability Scale 13.175
Studnicka's theory of eye embryology 11.399–401
Style
 German 12.311
 properties 12.315
 prose 12.318
Subclasses 14.74, 14.80
Subcortical areas and visual thalamus 3.205–6
Subcortical neurones 9.160–1
Subcortical nuclei 4.450
Subcortical–cortical interactions, general significance
 of 4.127
Subharmonics 10.11
Subitization 14.64–5, 14.126, 14.128–30
Subjective contours 9.94

Sublamina a **3**.33–4, **3**.42–3, **3**.55
Sublamina b **3**.33–6
  and amacrine cells **3**.42–3
  ganglion cell dendrites **3**.55
Subpatterns **14**.51, **14**.62–3
Subplate
  cortical **11**.338–40, **11**.342
    and axon growth **11**.235
    and neurotransmitters **11**.357, **11**.360
    synaptic rearrangements in **11**.262–3
    and visual cortex neurogenesis **3**.363–4
Subsampling **5**.54
Substance P **3**.279, **3**.294, **11**.363
  in amacrine cells **3**.47–8
Substantia nigra **3**.169, **8**.2, **8**.200, **8**.254, **8**.267–71, **8**.287, **8**.314
  and relationship with superior colliculus **4**.403
  in visual function **4**.401–3
Substitution, principle of **12**.128
Substrates, neuropsychological **14**.21
Substratum attached molecules (SAMs) **11**.177–8
Subthreshold summation **5**.304–5, **9**.181, **10**.65–6
Subventricular zone **3**.82–6
Successive colour contrast **6**.184
Successive discrimination tasks **15**.90
Succus nervosus **12**.127
Sulphation in regeneration **11**.196
Sum of the squares of the contrasts in grating
    detectability **5**.101
Sumeria **12**.305
Summation
  complete spatial **5**.104
  in contrast sensitivity **5**.38
  limit, complete areal **5**.104
  linear model of cone **5**.195
  linear spatial **3**.49, **5**.195
  M and L cone **5**.198–9
  and motion detectors **5**.155–6
  photopic **5**.74
  probability **10**.47
    and contrast encoding **5**.108–9
    and contrast perception **5**.115
    and flicker **5**.188
    and motion detectors **5**.156
    and motion sensitivity **5**.150
    in peripheral vision **5**.64, **5**.68–70, **5**.74
    and spectral sensitivity **5**.199
    and stereoacuity **5**.138, **5**.140, **5**.142
  spatial **3**.25, **5**.68, **5**.258, **7**.116, **7**.155, **7**.160, **10**.273
  in peripheral vision **5**.44, **5**.55, **5**.57, **5**.64, **5**.73–4, **5**.259, **5**.261
  and spectral sensitivity **5**.206–7
  spatial probability **10**.66
  square-root **5**.27
  subthreshold **5**.155, **5**.304–5, **10**.65–6
  temporal **5**.55, **5**.64, **7**.182, **10**.166–7
  temporal energy **5**.227–8
  of threshold increment **5**.27
  and visual channels **5**.98

Summed similarity rule **14**.122
Sun compass **2**.391
Sunburst chart **1**.410
Superior cerebellar peduncle **8**.216
Superior colliculus **2**.145, **2**.152, **2**.415, **4**.127, **4**.233, **4**.394, **8**.244–76, **12**.60–1, **12**.63, **13**.47, **13**.51
  anatomy **8**.201, **8**.245–8
  auditory receptive fields **8**.251
  and blindsight **12**.148–9, **12**.151, **12**.154
  burst neurones **8**.249–54, **8**.257–65
  cat **4**.144, **4**.149
  cell discharges **8**.248–54, **8**.256–7, **8**.326
  coding of signals **8**.256–66
  commissural fibres **8**.253
  deep-layer electrical stimulation of **4**.95
  and development of receptive-field properties **4**.100–1
  and development of retinotectal and tectofugal
    influences **4**.99–100
  electrically evoked saccades **8**.255
  enhancement of responses **8**.248
  and express saccades **8**.252–3
  and eye–head co-ordination **8**.34, **8**.262–7
  foveal representation **8**.251
  foveation hypothesis **8**.252
  and frontal eye fields **4**.417–8, **8**.244, **8**.286–7
  functional organization of **4**.85–110
  functional topography **8**.252, **8**.256, **8**.263
  and gaze control **8**.34, **8**.262–7
  Glossary explanation of **4**.450
  laminar organization of **3**.150, **4**.86–7
    and changes on visuotopy with depth **3**.157–9
  laminated structure **8**.245
  lesions **8**.255–6, **8**.314
  and maturation of receptive-field properties of **4**.99
  models of function **8**.257–65, **8**.326
  modular organization **8**.247
  motor activity of **4**.96–7
  motor representation of **4**.92–6
  omnipause neurones **8**.53–4
  output channels of **3**.160–6
  population coding of saccade vectors **8**.256–7
  and posterior suprasylvian cortex **4**.101–4
  in pursuit system **2**.171–4, **2**.176–9, **2**.184, **2**.186–9
  quasi-visual neurones **8**.249–53, **8**.266
  receptive-field properties of **4**.97–101
    and converging afferents **4**.99
    direction selectivity **4**.97
  retinotopic representations in **3**.150–75
  rodent **4**.162
  and saccades **13**.32–3
  sensory organization of **4**.86–92
    deep laminae **4**.90–2
    superficial laminae **4**.87–90
  and signalling of initial motor error **4**.401
  and spatio-temporal transformation **8**.244
  and substantia nigra **8**.254
  T-neurones **8**.247–9, **8**.251, **8**.253
  TR(S)N neurones **8**.248, **8**.250–3, **8**.255–6, **8**.263, **8**.266–8
  in visual function

Superior colliculus (*continued*)
    and connectivity of deeper layers 4.398–9
    and connectivity of upper layers 4.396–401
    and effects of electrical stimulation 4.400
    and effects of lesions 4.399
    and effects of reversible inactivation 4.399–400
    and effects of sensorimotor transformation 4.400–1
    and physiological properties of deeper layers 4.397–8
    and physiological properties of upper layers 4.396–7
    and visual pathways 2.424, 2.426, 2.435–6, 2.443–8, 2.452, 2.454–7
    visually triggered movement neurones 8.249
    visual-motor neurones 8.249
    visuotopic representations in 3.150–75
    X-neurones 8.247–9, 8.251, 8.254, 8.265
Superior oblique 8.175–6, 8.182, 8.184
Superior rectus 8.175–6, 8.182
Superior temporal polysensory area 4.411
Superior temporal sulcus 2.176–7, 2.459, 4.374, 11.373, 12.278
    neurones of 12.123–4
Superoxide 16.39
Superposition 5.305
    neural 2.355–6
Supplementary eye fields 4.418–22, 8.289–90, 8.305
    area 6 4.418
    comparison with frontal eye fields 4.421–2
    connectivity of 4.419–20
    effects of electrical stimulation on 4.419
    effects of lesions on 4.419
    physiological properties of 4.420–1
    and the 'readiness' potential 4.419
    supplementary motor area 4.418–9
Suppression 9.196–201
    developmental consequences of 9.197
    and dominance shifts 9.93, 9.107
    non-dominant eye 3.197, 3.201
Suppression hemianopsia 9.199
Suppression states 9.96
Suppression tests 9.202–3
    depth of 9.202–3
    screening tests 9.202–3
        confrontation tests 9.202
        Worth four-dot tests 9.202
    in strabismus 9.202
Suppression theory 9.13–5, 9.107
Suprachiasmatic nuclei 2.425, 3.204, 3.217, 11.322
Suprageniculate nuclei, and visual thalamus 3.209–11, 3.215
Supragranular layers, Glossary explanation of 4.450
Suprathreshold contrast 10.221–2
Suprathreshold contrast sensation 5.322
Suprathreshold perception 5.287, 5.320
Suprathreshold vision 6.211–2
Surface colour 4.332
    CIE definition of 6.225
Surface estimation 12.191
Surface illumination 14.83–4, 14.90, 14.93
Surface properties 14.83
Surface reflectance 14.36, 14.83–4, 14.87, 14.89–90, 14.93

Surface shape 14.83–4, 14.89, 14.93
Surface transmittance 14.83, 14.87
Surfaces
    and pattern correlations 14.3
    and segmentation 14.6
    and spatial shape 14.5
Surrounds 5.234
    activity 5.180
    antagonism 5.60, 5.63, 5.71, 5.192
    antagonistic 3.33
    bipolar cell 3.40
    catch 5.52
    centre component 5.41
    components of receptive fields 5.24
    and flicker 5.182
    ganglion cell 3.40
    inhibition 5.61, 5.193
    in peripheral vision 5.54, 5.56, 5.58
    receptive field 5.26
    receptive field centre 5.41
    spectral selectivity 5.195
    steady and flickering 5.178
Sus scrofa (domestic pig) 2.74
Suspensory ligament 11.393–4
Sustained attention 15.83–98
Sustained information processing resources 15.94
Sutures, tensioning 1.138–9
SVCD, *see* Specific visual cognitive disability
SVF, *see* Short visual fibres
SW cones 7.38–9, 7.45
    in colour perimetry 7.49
SW mechanisms, vulnerability of 7.191–2
Swammerdam, Jan 12.40
SWS
    depressed 7.127
    in visual field disturbances 7.163
SWS cone opsin 7.105–7
SWS cone opsin gene 7.105–6
SWS cones
    function of, in ophthalmic disease 7.120–1, 7.124
    in ophthalmic disease 7.130
    in retinitis pigmentosa 7.144
SWS loss 7.118, 7.152–3, 7.155, 7.158, 7.162
SWS rods, in retinitis pigmentosa 7.144
SWS system, vulnerability of 7.158
Sylvian fissure 3.330
Symbiosis 11.304–6
Symbols
    for absent objects 12.332
    abstract 12.331
    and alexia 12.335
    as communication 12.331
    figural 12.358
    graphic 12.331
        non-iconic 12.332
    man-made 12.332
    mathematical 12.307
        copying 12.340
    and pure alexia 12.352–3

recognition 12.350
  for script 12.305–6, 12.308
  shorthand 12.316
  written 12.337
    accessing meaning from 12.350
    preserved access to 12.350–5
Symmetric difference set 14.7
Symmetric disparity, presentation of 9.115
Symmetrical fixation in the visual plane, and the point
  horopter 9.24
Symmetry
  axial 12.226
    completion 12.444, 12.455–6
    and visual evoked potentials 12.244
  axis 14.63–4, 14.66
  bilateral 14.51–2, 14.63–4
  detection 14.53, 14.63–4, 14.66
  double 14.63–4
  and face recognition 14.112
  in human face recognition 12.226–30
  near 14.63
  and numerosity 14.129, 14.139
  positional 14.58–9
  quadruple 14.63
  rotational 5.81–3, 14.63–4
  single 14.63
Sympathetic nervous system 11.35
Sympatholytic drugs, topically applied 1.266
Sympathomimetic drugs, topically applied 1.265–6
Symptom complex 12.180
Symptomatic retinitis pigmentosa 7.145–8
Synaesthesia 12.393
Synapses
  and axon competition 11.240–1
  and cell recognition 11.84
  contacts 11.275, 11.299
  conventional
    and neurone death 3.94, 3.96
    in retinal development 3.88–9, 3.91–2
  dendrite 11.149
  differentiation of, in the visual cortex 3.364–6
  elimination of 3.366
  feedback 3.40
  feedforward 3.40
  formation of 11.238
    axo-dendritic 12.19
    in neuronal cytoskeleton 11.278–80, 11.287, 11.298–300
  geniculocortical 11.260–1
  Hebbian hypothesis 11.240, 11.258–63, 11.268–9
  optic, and GAP-43 11.228
  optic axon 11.224
  organization of 2.358–60
  receptor 2.358
  redistribution of 11.261–2
  and retinal transplantation 11.316
  ribbon 2.140–1, 3.34
  in retinal development 3.88–9, 3.91–4
  rod-bipolar 3.34
  sign conserving 3.33
  stabilization of 11.260–2, 11.271
  in superior colliculus 11.225
  and TOP molecules 11.80 1
  weight changes of 11.261–2
Synapsing-pair specific molecules 11.81, 11.83
Synaptic depression 8.328
Synaptic function, spectrin in 11.279
Synaptic glomerulus 3.280–1
Synaptic modifications 14.81
Synaptic plasticity, *see* Plasticity
Synaptic rearrangements
  cellular mechanisms 11.259–62
  critical period 11.268–9, 11.271
  in lower vertebrates 11.263–71
  mammalian visual system 11.257–8
Synaptic target 11.198, 11.200–1
Synaptic weighting 3.48
Synaptogenesis 11.81
  axon 11.238
  and class specification 3.101
  dendrite 11.150–1, 11.161
  and GAP-43 11.221, 11.224, 11.227
  and microtubules 11.135
  in neuronal cytoskeleton 11.279, 11.286
  and neurone death 3.96
  and neurotransmitters 11.355
  in plexiform layer 3.90–4
  post-natal 9.174
  reactive 11.222, 11.225, 11.228
  in regeneration 11.192, 11.194–5, 11.199, 11.201
  in visual cortex neurogenesis 3.366
Synaptosomes, in neuronal cytoskeleton 11.277
Synchronization
  columnar 12.467
  of cortical neuronal activity 12.73–4
Syndrome, disconnection 12.128
Synkinesis, triadic 13.222
Synonym 12.322
Syntax, rules 12.317
Synthesized speech 15.120–1
Syntonics 13.172
System transfer function 4.248
Systematic variation in functionally homogeneous cell
  groups 3.49
Systems 10.1–3
  functional identification 10.2
  piecewise linear 10.5
  stationary 10.35
  time-variant 10.35
Systems analysis 10.1–13
  linear and non-linear systems 10.4–12
  non-linear analysis 10.8–9
  non-linearities 10.5–8

T

Tachistoscope **12**.208, **12**.272, **12**.340
  testing in human face perception **12**.230–5
  tests **12**.462
Tachyglossus (spiny ant-eater) **2**.467–70
Tachykinin **3**.164
Tactile modality **12**.345
Tactual cues **15**.118
Tagging **14**.65, **14**.125
Talbot–Plateau law **5**.147
Tamarin **7**.209–10
Tandem array, X-linked cone opsin genes **7**.108
Tangential connections
  columns and **4**.294–6
  and patchy projections **4**.294
Tanning, commercial facilities (CTF) **16**.93, **16**.95
Tapetum **2**.26, **2**.84, **2**.92, **3**.6
  cat **2**.4–5
  and dioptrics **2**.97
  in eye evolution **2**.413
  Glossary explanation of **4**.450–1
  in mammals **2**.470–1, **2**.473
  and optics **2**.127
Target length and hyperacuity **5**.230–1
Target luminance **1**.260
Target motion
  effects of various kinds of **9**.129–35
  perception **8**.149–52, **8**.211, **8**.307
Target movements
  ramp **2**.166
  step-ramp **2**.166
Target recognition **11**.70, **11**.83
Target search, dyslexic and normal readers' eye movements
    in **13**.244–6
Target velocity neurones **8**.214–5, **8**.234
Targets
  'inappropriate' **3**.136
  retinal **3**.131–2, **3**.136
Target-specific factors, in arborization **11**.237
Task-evoked pupillary response **15**.94
Tattooing **12**.16
Tau protein **11**.138, **11**.144, **11**.277
Taxonomy, Glossary explanation of **4**.451
Taylor, John **12**.136
T-cells **4**.92
Tears
  physiology of **1**.93
    pH **1**.93
    tonicity **1**.93
Tectal markers, stability of **11**.96
Tectofugal influences, development of, in the superior
    colliculus **4**.99–100
Tectofugal pathway **2**.427–33, **2**.435
Tectofugal/thalamofugal pathway, Glossary explanation
    of **4**.451
Tectogeniculate neurones **3**.161–3
Tectoparabigeminal neurones **3**.164
Tectopulvinar cells **3**.161, **3**.164

Tecto-reticular neurones **8**.248, **8**.250–3, **8**.255–6, **8**.263,
    8.266–8
Tectum **2**.402–4, **2**.416
Telencephalon **2**.423–7, **2**.429–30, **2**.432–4, **2**.436
Teleosts **2**.78, **2**.281
  colour vision **2**.290, **2**.295, **2**.300
  dioptrics **2**.85, **2**.103, **2**.109–10
  in evolution of retina **2**.138–9, **2**.141–4, **2**.146
  evolution of vision **2**.398, **2**.406–7, **2**.410, **2**.412
  in eye evolution **2**.412–7
  feeding selectivity **2**.157
  freshwater **2**.290
  and photoreceptor system **2**.65–71
  plesiomorphic **2**.415
  and shape recognition **2**.162–3
  and visual cortex **2**.152
Telescopes
  angular fields of view of **1**.208
  astronomical **1**.206–9
    binocular **1**.212
    erecting systems for **1**.207
    Galilean **1**.212–3
      of fixed focus for near **1**.213
      of fixed focus with reading caps **1**.213
      of limited variable focus **1**.212–3
    monocular **1**.212
    right-angled prisms for **1**.207–8
  bioptic **1**.213
  comparison with plus-lenses for near tasks **1**.214
  contact lens **1**.213
  entrance and exit pupils of **1**.208
  eyepieces and objective lenses of **1**.207
  focal **1**.209–12
    ametropic correction in **1**.209–12
    power factor of **1**.209
    and the relative angular magnification **1**.209
    shape factor of **1**.209
    and spectacle magnification **1**.209–10
    and the total angular magnification **1**.209
    for viewing objects closer than infinity **1**.211–2
  Galilean **1**.61–2, **1**.206–7, **1**.385
  linear fields of view of **1**.208
  Newtonian **2**.125
  stops, apertures and fields of view of **1**.208
  terrestrial **1**.206
  and the vergence amplification effect **1**.209
Telestereoscopes **1**.328–9
Teletext **15**.71
Television rasters **1**.355
Telodendria **3**.11, **3**.26
Temperature, body **10**.242–3
Template models
  and candidate physiological bases **9**.165–6
  of visual processing **2**.243–51, **2**.266–7
Template theory **2**.259, **2**.262–3
Templates **2**.240–1, **2**.254–7, **14**.70, **14**.79–80
  holistic **14**.74–7
  larger **2**.260–3
  line-labelled **2**.246, **2**.248–50

Templates (*continued*)
  matching 14.69, **14.77**, **14.79**, **14.98**
    complexity **14.101**
    and computational vision **14.33**, **14.38–9**, **14.43**
    holistic **14.72–4**
  motion-detection **2.235**
  one-dimensional **2.245**, **2.254**
  properties of **2.246**
  responses of **2.249–50**
  semivision **2.258–60**, **2.268**
  two-dimensional **2.253–4**
  whole-eye **2.263–7**
Temporal acuity **5.24**, **5.147**
Temporal boundaries **5.24**
Temporal channels **5.296**
Temporal characterization
  of visual displays **15.7–8**
    display characterization **15.7–8**
      flicker **15.7–8**
      interlacing **15.7–8**
      jitter **15.7–8**
    flicker elimination **15.9–10**
    human spatial sensitivity, characterization of **15.8–9**
    jitter elimination **15.10–1**
    temporal modulation of display luminance of **15.7–11**
Temporal contrast sensitivity functions **15.8**
  M scaling **5.257**
Temporal cortex **2.174–6**
Temporal crowding **9.206**
Temporal discontinuities **5.24**
Temporal disparity **9.233**
Temporal filters **5.302–4**
  lateral geniculate nucleus as **4.58–9**
Temporal frequency **5.289**
  and apparent motion **5.152–3**
  and colour vision **5.204**
  in contrast encoding **5.116**
  and contrast perception **5.114–5**
  and equiluminance **5.236**, **5.240**, **5.245**
  and flicker **5.147–9**, **5.173**, **5.175**
  Glossary explanation of **4.451**
  and motion detection **5.166–7**
  and motion sensitivity **5.150–1**
  in peripheral vision **5.58**, **5.63**
  and spectral sensitivity **5.198**
  and velocity perception **5.160–1**, **5.163**
Temporal frequency channels **5.115**, **5.117**, **5.167**, **5.169**
Temporal frequency characteristics, chromatic flicker **10.152**
Temporal frequency discrimination **10.47–9**
Temporal frequency domain **10.152**
  signal analysis in **10.15–8**
Temporal frequency-constant mechanism **5.162**
Temporal lobe
  epileptic discharges in **12.473**
  functions and visual object recognition **12.107–22**
  inferior (IT) **12.107**, **12.109–10**, **12.269**
    bilateral ablation of **12.108**
    function **12.107–8**
  parastriate belt **12.107**

  peristriate belt **12.107**, **12.112–3**
  and pure alexia **12.342**
  uncus of **12.479**
  and visual signal recognition **12.125–6**
Temporal modulation **9.98–9**
  in monochromacy **7.26**
Temporal resolution **5.296–7**
Temporal selectivity **5.153–5**
Temporal sensitivity **15.8–9**
Temporal summation **7.182**, **10.166–7**
Temporal transients **5.103**
Temporal tuning curves **5.155**
Temporal vision **5.234**
  and dyslexia **13.73**
  psychophysics of **13.58**
Temporal window of attention **5.50**
Tension in cell locomotion **11.175–7**
TEPR, *see* Task-evoked pupillary response
Terminal contacts **11.299–300**
Terminals
  axon **3.39**
  D **3.202**
  F1 **3.211**
  F2 **3.201**, **3.211**
  F **3.202**
  F (flattened) **3.195–7**
  FD1 **3.201**
  FD2 **3.201**
  formation and axon growth **11.248**
  FP **3.201**
  horizontal cell axon **3.40**
  L **3.202**
  nerve, Glossary explanation of **4.451**
  presynaptic **11.281**, **11.292**, **11.299**
  RLD **3.201**
  RLP (round, large, pale) **3.195–6**
  RMD (round, medium, dark) **3.195**
  RSD (round, small, dark) **3.196**
  space **11.291**
    competition for **11.275**, **11.293**, **11.299–300**
  synaptic **11.281**
Ternary relations **14.53**
Terrain hypothesis **2.143–4**, **2.147**
Test of Early Written Language **13.137**
Tetrachromacy **2.295**
Tetrachromatic colour vision, in insects **6.269**, **6.274–5**
Tetrachromatic pigment space **6.83–4**
Tetrachromats **2.295**
Tetrads **2.358**
Text
  analysis **12.315**
  artificial **12.311–2**
  Braille **12.309**
  comprehension **12.318**
  difficulties in reading **12.319**
  difficulty **12.316**, **12.318**
  handwritten **12.317**
  improving patterns of **13.167–8**
    and the cost of printing **13.167**

Text (*continued*)
  judgements of clarity in 13.167–8
  meaning 12.310
  mirror 12.319
  mirror-image 12.319
  newspaper 12.314–5
  printed 12.317, 12.355
  processing 12.357
    visual 12.310
  semantic content 12.315
  semantic difficulties 12.317
  sequentially sampled 12.316
  stenographic 12.356
  structural processor 12.356–7
  structure 12.315, 12.318
  syntax 12.317
  understanding 12.311
    lag 12.316
Textons 5.121, 10.119, 10.131–2, 14.37
Texture 12.340
  computational models of 10.122–9
  and computational vision 14.37, 14.41–2
  discrimination 12.206
    immediate 12.182
  and equiluminance 5.234, 5.236–7, 5.240
  experimental techniques 10.116–7
  historical origins of 10.116
  and ideal observer 14.89–90
  and illusions 5.244
  mapping discontinuities 5.121
  and numerosity 14.139
  operator 14.101
  phase-altered 12.195
  and shape 10.129–30
  and spatial shape 14.5
  theory development of 10.117–21
  as a visual cue 5.286
Texture analyses 4.179, 10.116
Texture channels 9.158
Texture detection 10.116, 14.102
Texture discrimination 10.115–8
Texture elements 10.131–2
Texture gradients 1.249, 9.139–40, 9.183–4
Texture motion, in modulation of cortical cells 4.191–2
Texture perception 5.120–3, 5.130
Texture perception theories 10.114–32
Texture segregation 10.114–20, 10.131–2
Texture stimuli 10.115–7, 10.131
TH, *see* Tyrosine hydroxylase
Thalamic nuclei 3.177
Thalamic reticular nucleus 3.193, 3.198, 3.200–2, 3.282–3
  and LGNv 3.204
  and visual thalamus 3.211, 3.213–5, 3.217
Thalamocortical fibres 3.239
Thalamofugal pathway 2.426–9, 2.433, 2.435–6
Thalamotomy, right-sided 12.463
Thalamus 2.402, 5.161, 8.2, 8.286
  central 2.173–6, 2.178–9, 2.184
  in evolution of eye 2.16, 2.415–7

intrathalamic nuclei 12.463
non-specific intralaminar nuclei 12.76
nucleus reticularis 12.463
paramedian 12.478
posterior 12.478
in pursuit system 2.171, 2.189
ventro-lateral 12.463
visual 3.176–217
  cortical afferents to LGNd 3.192–3
  intralaminar thalamic nuclei 3.204–7
  lateral posterior and pulvinar nuclei 3.207–15
  LGNd complex 3.177–82
  LGNd relay cells and interneurones 3.187–92
  medial interlaminar nucleus 3.186–7
  projections from LGNd 3.198–200
  reticular nuclei 3.200–2
  retinal projections to LGNd 3.183–6
  retinofugal projection 3.176–7
  subcortical projections to LGNd 3.193–4
  ultrastructure of LGNd complex 3.195–8
  ventral lateral geniculate nucleus (LGNv) 3.202–4
  and visual pathways 2.423–30, 2.456–8
Thamnophis sirtalis (garter snake) 2.428–9
Theophrastus of Eresos 12.25, 12.27
Theory of Signal Detectability, *see* Signal detection theory
Therapy, photodynamic 16.69, 16.71–2
Thiamine deficiency 8.302
Thick and thin stripes, *see* Cytochrome oxidase thick and thin stripes
Thickness gauge 1.429–30
Thick/thin/interstripes, Glossary explanation of 4.451
Thinking, inverted 12.179
Thioridazine 16.70
Thioridazine retinopathy 7.128–9
Three-dimensional displays and images 1.326–44
  miscellaneous methods of producing
    artificial disparity 1.340–1
    chromostereopsis 1.340–1
    laser speckle patterns 1.340
    longitudinal chromatic aberration 1.340
    the Pulfrich effect 1.340
    the varifocal mirror 1.340
Three-dimensional television 1.333–5
  and the alternating-image technique 1.334–5
    using goggles with electronically switched shutters 1.334–5
    using liquid-crystal shutters 1.335
  and duplicated displays 1.333–4
Three-dimensional vection 12.462–3
Three-dimensional visual stimulation 12.463
Three-dimensionality 12.437, 12.450
Threshold detection 5.32–3, 10.184
Threshold discrimination 5.15
Threshold estimate 5.15
Threshold function
  retinally stabilized 10.44
  Riddoch effect 10.58–60
Threshold gradients of peripheral vision 5.251–63
Threshold grating detection 5.90

Threshold gratings **5.42**
  in visual processing **5.33**
Threshold increment experiments **5.61–4**
Threshold increments **5.33, 5.38, 10.157**
Threshold logic unit **14.73–4, 14.76, 14.78–9**
Threshold logic unit-model neurone **14.81**
Threshold measurements **7.7–8, 7.11, 7.40–1, 7.52–4**
  and visual fields **5.278**
Threshold methods
  chromatic **7.41–3**
  complicating factors in measurements **7.52–4**
  detection **7.41, 7.43–52**
    effects of adaptation and of spatial and temporal
      factors **7.48–50**
    relation to other threshold tests **7.50–2**
    test target colour **7.43–8**
  evaluation of ophthalmic disease **7.121–3**
Threshold ratio
  in bandwidth estimation **5.101–2**
  and visual channels **5.98**
Threshold sensitivity, in optic-nerve disease **7.175–6**
Threshold summation **5.38**
Threshold surface, spatiotemporal **10.150**
Threshold values **5.15–6**
Threshold variation, with age **5.278**
Threshold vision **6.211**
Threshold-duration functions **7.50**
Thresholds **5.8–9**
  absolute
    for large fields **5.64–5**
    for light **5.54**
    in negative masking **5.30–1**
    for pattern **5.54, 5.70**
    and pedestal effect **5.32**
    in peripheral vision **5.55, 5.57, 5.63, 5.69, 5.71, 5.73–4**
    of rod vision **5.51**
  and ageing **5.277–9**
  behaviour **5.41**
  characteristics of **5.12–3**
  classical idea of **5.15–6**
  contrast **5.35–8, 5.42, 5.67, 5.88, 10.193**
  difference **5.30, 5.32**
  experimental methods **5.13–4**
  flicker/motion **10.254**
  foveal **5.283**
  lower difference **5.15**
  perimetric, M scaling **5.257**
  saccadic **5.57**
  sensation (absolute threshold) **5.15**
  spatial relations **14.8**
  square-wave **5.102**
  subtense **5.262**
  upper difference **5.15**
  upper and lower **5.35**
Thurstone's law of categorical judgement **15.36–7**
Thymidine, triticated, *see* [³H]-Thymidine
[³H]-Thymidine **3.81–4, 3.96, 3.102, 3.115, 3.132, 11.32–3,**
  11.36
  autoradiography **11.262, 11.357–8, 11.361**

Glossary explanation of **4.451**
Thymine **7.102**
Thyroid hormone (T3) **11.120**
Tiering **3.9–10**
Tilt after-effects **5.237–8, 5.248, 9.182**
Tilt suppression, of the vestibulo-ocular reflex **8.301**
Time domain **10.152**
  signal analysis in **10.15–8**
Time intervals **5.204**
Time invariance **10.4**
Time-lapse cinemicroscopy in cell locomotion **11.172**
Timetable, technical railway **12.307**
TIMP (tissue inhibitor of metalloproteinases) **11.179**
Tinted lenses, *see under* Spectacle lenses
Tissue, ageing **16.57–8**
Tissue disturbance in peripheral vision **5.253–4**
Titmus–Wirt stereo test **9.210**
Titration method **10.140, 10.151–2**
TLU, *see* Threshold logic unit
T-neurones **8.247–9, 8.251–4**
TNO stereo test **9.210–1**
TNO test **7.216, 7.229**
Toad dioptrics **2.100, 2.103, 2.110**
Todarodes (squid) **2.382**
Tokens, as words **12.331**
Tolerance, of measurement **1.415**
Tolhurst and Ling's scaling factor **5.255**
Tolstoy, Leon **14.2**
Toluidene blue **16.40**
Tonic accommodation **8.164**
  and accommodative hysteresis **1.237–40**
    and apparent distance **1.239**
    and ciliary muscle input **1.239**
    and nearwork symptomatology **1.239**
    and parasympathetic and sympathetic components of the
      autonomic system **1.238–9**
    and space perception **1.239**
    task and cognitive demand in **1.238**
    time constants in **1.238**
Tonic cells, monkey retinal **4.27–8**
Tonic neurones **4.391, 8.207**
Tonic vergence **9.90**
Tool-making **12.16**
Top-down control **5.44–5**
Topographagnosia **12.180, 12.183, 12.198–9, 12.208, 12.262,**
  12.271, 12.343, 12.411, 12.428
  and achromatopsia **12.394, 12.401**
  aetiology **12.424–5**
  apperceptive **12.418–9, 12.428**
  associative **12.418, 12.420–2, 12.424–5, 12.427–8**
  caused by unilateral occipital lesions **12.422–5**
  cerebral localization **12.423–5**
  cognitive–emotional **12.418, 12.420–4, 12.428, 12.430**
  and colour anomia **12.408**
  compensating strategies **12.418, 12.420, 12.425, 12.429–30**
  detour strategies **12.418, 12.430**
  inner spatial transformations **12.422**
  neuropsychological test **12.421**
  perceptive **12.418–9, 12.427–8**

Topographagnosia (*continued*)
   spatial and constructional tests **12**.421
   and visuo-spatial disorders **12**.437
Topographic position **11**.68
   and cell recognition **11**.82–4
Topographic tectofugal pathways **4**.169
Topographically graded (TOP) expression **11**.77–9
Topographically graded (TOP) molecules **11**.74–8, **11**.84
Topography
   amacrine cell **3**.42
   blue cone **3**.15
   callosal input **3**.334
   convergence **3**.344
   cortical connectivity **3**.326
   ganglion cell **3**.56
   horizontal cell **3**.39
   inner imaging of city **12**.342
   interplexiform cell **3**.47
   optic nerve **3**.134–5
   optic tract **3**.134, **3**.136
   photoreceptor **3**.15–6
   retinal **3**.1, **3**.4, **3**.16, **3**.341–2
   retinal projections **3**.132, **3**.138–9
   rod **3**.15
Torsional disparity **9**.114–5
Torsional nystagmus **8**.302
Torsional optokinesis **8**.65–6
Torsional vergence **8**.167–8, **8**.330
Torsional vestibulo-ocular reflex **8**.308
Total internal reflection **3**.12–3
Touchscreens **15**.117–8
Tourette's syndrome **10**.255
'Towing' experiments **11**.176–7
Toxic compounds **7**.129
Toxoplasmaencephalitis, associated with AIDS **12**.343
Tracer substances **12**.128
Tracers **3**.139
   DiI **3**.138
   fluorescent **3**.138, **3**.140
Tracing
   with finger **12**.334
   letters **12**.334, **12**.338, **12**.347
   motor **12**.334, **12**.357
   speed **12**.336
   strategies **12**.206
Trackballs **15**.80, **15**.117–8
Tracking **12**.309
   visuo-motor **12**.339
Tracking eye movements **9**.145
Tracking method **10**.36
Tracking neurones, of the parietal cortex **8**.285
Tracking performance **14**.52, **14**.65
Traction in crawling **11**.171, **11**.173–4
Training
   effects on blindsight **10**.272
   principle of **12**.128
Transactionalism **14**.89–90
Transcription factor TFIIIA **11**.7
Transcription and GAP-43 regulation **11**.227–8

Transcription in regeneration **11**.196
Transducer function **10**.145, **10**.147
Transducins **2**.63–4, **2**.66, **2**.380, **6**.103–6
   and arrestin **6**.105
   α-subunit of **6**.103–4
   β-subunit of **6**.104
   and the cGMP phosphodiesterase **6**.104–5
   γ-subunit of **6**.104
   see also G-proteins
Transduction **6**.100–5
   basic concepts of **6**.100–5
     and cGMP phosphodiesterase **6**.102
   and G-proteins **6**.100
Transfer function
   exact **5**.27–8
   experimental measurement **5**.29
   modulation (MTF) **10**.23, **10**.96
   optical **10**.23
   phase **10**.23
   in systems analysis **10**.13, **10**.34
Transfer ratio
   of cells of the lateral geniculate nucleus **4**.52–3
   Glossary explanation of **4**.451
Transform
   fourth power **5**.28–9, **5**.31, **5**.33
   non-linear **5**.24, **5**.30, **5**.39, **5**.62
   normal deviate **5**.19–20, **5**.29
   power law **5**.10–1, **5**.102
   square-law **5**.10, **5**.23–8, **5**.30–3, **5**.98
Transform detectors **14**.26
Transformation
   affine **14**.51, **14**.53, **14**.55, **14**.73
   and computational vision **14**.45
   dilation **14**.20–1, **14**.25
   equivalent signals **14**.73
   feature-operator invariance to **14**.101
   geometric **14**.33–4, **14**.79–80
   Gibson **14**.19–28
   of global-position relations **14**.59
   Lie transformation group (LTG/NP) **14**.20
   low-level vision **14**.32
   motion **14**.34
   and object recognition **14**.113–4
   pattern recognition under **14**.25–6
   rotation **14**.20–1, **14**.25
   and spatial relations **14**.51, **14**.53, **14**.62, **14**.65
   translation **14**.20–1
Transgenics **11**.22–3
Transients **2**.246, **2**.259, **2**.267
   accoustic **16**.48–9, **16**.51
Transillumination **2**.86
Transinformational flow **12**.115
Transitivity **10**.141
Translation **14**.20–1, **14**.53, **14**.55, **14**.65
   invariant classification **14**.74–5, **14**.77–9
   invariant feature **14**.81
   invariant pattern classes **14**.74
   in line images recognition **14**.101
   and spatial relations **14**.51

Translational motion, consequences of, for optokinetic
    asymmetries **4**.132–4
Transmission
    Henle fibre-optic **16**.95
    interhemispheric **5**.261
    linear **5**.23, **5**.27–8, **5**.33
    lines, nonlinearity **5**.97
    non-linear **5**.40
    synaptic **11**.200
        variability of **5**.24
Transmittance
    ocular **2**.86–9
    of ocular media **5**.87–8
    surface **14**.83, **14**.87
    water **2**.87
Transmitter histochemistry **3**.363
Transmutation **2**.73
    of rods **6**.71–2
Transneural transport **4**.271
Transplantation
    dopamine cell **11**.314
    immunogenetic mismatch **11**.319
    organization **11**.315–6
    rejection **11**.319
    retinal **11**.314–32
        as clinical therapy **11**.315
        connectivity **11**.320–3
        development of projection **11**.323–6
        functional integration **11**.326–32
        immunological implications **11**.319–20
        rodent **11**.315–6, **11**.319
        survival **11**.316, **11**.319
        technical considerations **11**.315–9
        vasacular supply **11**.320
Transport
    anteretrograde **11**.190–1
    axonal **11**.144, **11**.175–6, **11**.190–201
        of GAP-43 **11**.219–21
        in neuronal cytoskeleton **11**.277–9, **11**.284, **11**.286–7,
            11.293, **11**.298–9, **11**.303
        orthograde **11**.292
    axoplasmic **11**.136, **11**.243
    cytoplasmic **11**.133, **11**.278
    fast **11**.190–2, **11**.194–5
        and dendrites **11**.151
        of GAP-43 **11**.219–21
        in neuronal cytoskeleton **11**.278, **11**.298
    intra-axonal **12**.128
    mechanisms and microtubules **11**.136
    particle **12**.128
    retrograde **11**.190–1, **11**.197
        as scavenger function **12**.128
    slow **11**.190–1, **11**.193–4, **11**.196–7
Trans-synaptic latency, Glossary explanation of **4**.451
Tremor **8**.71–2
Tretjakoff's theory of eye embryology **11**.401–3
Triads **2**.358, **3**.88–9, **3**.93–4, **3**.196–7
Trichromacy **2**.77, **2**.294, **2**.310–4
    anomalous **2**.78, **7**.31, **7**.53, **7**.89–90, **7**.95, **12**.386, **12**.388,

12.403
    carriers **7**.93
    interpretations **7**.16
    monochromat **7**.28
    photopigments **7**.17
    red–green **7**.21, **7**.30–1
    congenital **7**.40
    in non-human primates **7**.206, **7**.208–12
    normal, and non-human primates **7**.202–6, **7**.211
    in Old World primates **3**.54
    protanomalous **6**.98
    tritanomalous, diagnosis of **7**.218
Trichromatic colour vision, in insects **6**.269
Trichromatic theory **4**.317, **5**.134
Trichromatic vision **6**.40–1
Trichromaticity, and reading ability **13**.171–2
Trichromats **2**.290, **2**.293, **2**.295, **2**.300, **2**.312, **2**.315–7
    anomalous **6**.101, **7**.94, **7**.109–10, **7**.224
    chromaticity in **6**.40–1
    deuteranomalous **7**.89–91, **7**.94, **7**.110
    protanomalous **6**.98, **7**.89–90, **7**.110
    red–green **7**.9–10, **7**.12–20
Tridacna (giant clam) **2**.369, **2**.390
Trifocal lenses **1**.72–3
Trigeminal nucleus **8**.189
Trigone
    latero-basal area **12**.347
    left **12**.347
    ventricular **12**.343
Trigram, Hebrew **12**.324
Trilobites **2**.341–2
Triple-autocorrelation **14**.79
Tristimulus colorimeters **6**.19
Tristimulus space **6**.269, **6**.271
Tristimulus values **6**.298–9, **7**.31
Tritan acquired defect **7**.219
Tritan congenital defect **7**.95–6, **7**.98, **7**.120, **7**.215, **7**.217–8,
    7.220, **7**.228–9
Tritan defect **7**.126, **7**.130, **7**.135, **7**.152, **7**.154–5
    inheritance pattern **7**.21–2
Tritan deficit **7**.125, **7**.144, **7**.150
Tritan-like defect **7**.119–20, **7**.124, **7**.152–3, **7**.157–8, **7**.162–3
Tritan-like deficit **7**.144, **7**.146, **7**.152
Tritanomaloscope, Jaeger **7**.137, **7**.153
Tritanomaloscopy **7**.118, **7**.156–7
Tritanomaly **7**.88, **7**.95–6, **7**.98
    blue–green **7**.21–3
    monochromat **7**.28
Tritanopes **2**.309, **2**.312, **6**.39–41, **6**.31, **7**.96–8, **16**.111–2,
    16.128
    blue–green **7**.21–4
    cone absorption space cluster of **6**.35–6
    and other types of dichromats **6**.39–40
    red–green **7**.14
Tritanopia **7**.61, **7**.95–7, **7**.174, **12**.386, **16**.126
    acquired **7**.21, **7**.191
    'blue–yellow' blindness **7**.95–6
    complete **7**.88, **7**.96
    congenital **7**.21, **7**.72, **7**.82–3, **7**.155, **7**.220

Tritanopia (*continued*)
  and deuteranopia 6.39–41
  diagnosis of 7.218
  foveal 7.176
  genetics 7.110
  incomplete 7.88, 7.95–6, 7.98
  induced 7.83–5
  inheritance 7.98
  monochromat 7.27
  transient 7.78, 7.122, 7.130–1, 7.135, 7.152
  unilateral 7.21, 7.28
Tritanopic confusion line 5.181, 5.199, 5.215
Tritanopic pairs 5.181, 5.185
tRNA (transfer RNA) 7.102
Trochlear nucleus 8.184
Troland (Td) 16.23
Troxler effect 12.136, 12.151
Troxler fading 1.353
Troxler's effect 5.67, 5.253, 7.6, 9.94, 9.97
Truncation 10.16
Tscherning, M. H. E. 1.234
Tscherning's ellipses 1.67
Tuberculosis 7.161
Tübingen perimeter 12.137, 12.139, 12.141, 12.150, 12.194,
    12.393, 12.396
Tubulin 11.134–5
  acetylated 11.135
  in critical period plasticity 11.288–90
  in dendrites 11.150, 11.152
  development changes 11.282–3
  heterogeneity 11.284
  in neuronal cytoskeleton 11.276–7, 11.279–80
  polymerization 11.152, 11.280, 11.284, 11.288
  in regeneration 11.190–1, 11.193–4, 11.196, 11.200
  soluble 11.299
  synthesis
    after eye opening 11.282–3
    in neuronal cytoskeleton 11.293–5
  tyrosinated 11.135
α-Tubulin 11.135, 11.194–5
Tukey test 13.88
Tumour formation 11.112–4
Tumour necrosis 16.72
Tumours 11.114, 11.123
  amelanotic 16.72
  brain 12.199, 12.301, 12.336, 12.343
  and hemialexia 12.350
  left-sided occipito-temporal 12.354
  mesial temporal 12.347
  metastases 12.300
  and phototoxicity 16.69, 16.71, 16.73
  pineal 12.348
  pituitary 12.301
  and prosopagnosia 12.262, 12.264, 12.266
Tuned inhibitory neurones 9.228–9, 9.231
Tunica vasculosa lentis 16.118
Tuning, orientation, in MS 10.241
Tuning bandwidths, spatial frequency 10.145

Tuning curve, Glossary explanation of 4.451
Tuning functions 10.144
Tunnel vision 1.218, 12.196, 12.420, 12.423
Tupaia, *see* Shrew, tree
Turtle 2.68, 2.72–3
  colour vision 2.286–7, 2.291–2, 2.295, 2.298–9
  dioptrics 2.101
  visual pathways 2.422, 2.426–7
Tweed–Vilis model, of saccade generation 8.260–2, 8.324
Twilight, retinal mechanisms for 5.51–2
Twitch, in pursuit 8.140
Two corticotectal systems, concept of 4.101–4
Two visual systems, concept of 4.86
Two-dimensional vision 2.253–4, 2.260
Two-alternative forced-choice (2AFC)
  detection of simple grating 5.97
  difference discrimination 5.10
  experimental paradigm 5.29
  flicker detection 5.11
  identification task 5.32
  paradigm 5.8–9
  procedure 5.38, 5.161, 5.204
    for detection and discrimination tasks 5.212
    with immediate knowledge of results 5.13, 5.21
    as standard experimental practice 5.15
  task 5.13–4, 5.21, 5.138
Tyndall phenomenon, psychic 12.148
Type I acquired deficiency 7.118
  in Alezzandrini's syndrome 7.147
  and anomaloscopes 7.219–20
  in chiasmal compression 7.161–2
  in cone diseases 7.136, 7.140, 7.162
  juvenile retinoschisis 7.148
  in optic-nerve disease 7.175, 7.177
  and perimetry 7.231
  in spatial organization 7.162–3
  in Stargardt's disease 7.141
Type II acquired deficiency 7.118
  and anomaloscopes 7.219–20
  and colour vision tests 7.228
  in optic-nerve disease 7.175–7, 7.179
  in optic-nerve and optic-tract conduction 7.163
  and perimetry 7.231
  in toxic optic neuropathy 7.160
Type III acquired deficiency 7.118
  and anomaloscopes 7.219–20
  and colour vision tests 7.221, 7.228–9, 7.232
  in cone–rod dystrophy 7.140
  and crystalline lens 7.162
  in diabetes 7.149
  in optic-nerve disease 7.175–7, 7.179
  in perimetry 7.230–1
  and rod disease 7.162
Typewriter, Braille 12.309
Typoscope 1.185
Tyrosine hydroxylase 3.288, 11.35
Tysosine kinase 11.112–3, 11.116–9

U

Uhthoff's phenomenon 7.116
Uhthoff's syndrome 10.243
Ullman's alignment method in face representation 14.118
Ultrasonic biometry 1.133
Ultrasonic phakofragmentation 1.123
Ultrasonography 1.359–60, 1.430
  A-scan 1.359–60
  B-scan 1.360–2
  C-scan 1.361
  and Doppler methods 1.361
  D-scan 1.361
  M-mode 1.361–2
  practical applications of 1.362
Ultrasound, high-resolution A-scan 1.234
Ultrasound emissions, from visual-display terminals 15.5
Ultra-violet, *see* Light
Ultra-violet fluorescence 1.352
Ultra-violet light, *see* Light, ultra-violet
Ultra-violet radiation *see* Radiation
Ultra-violet vision 2.69
Ultra-violet-light blocking filters 1.128
Ultra-violet-sensitivity
  in cyprinids and salmonids 6.116–7
    possible polymorphism in 6.117
  in guppies 6.115
Umazume–Ohta test 7.231
Umstimmung, tuned or relative 7.119
Uncertainty
  position 10.76, 10.78
  spatial 10.76, 10.81
Uncertainty relations 14.100
Uncrossed disparities 9.144
Under-accommodation 2.108, 5.84
Under-estimation, numerosity 14.131, 14.133, 14.137–8

Under-sampling 2.102–3, 2.411, 3.8, 3.58, 5.91
  foveal 3.20, 3.24
  in hyperacuity 10.94
  spatial 10.76, 10.78
Under-shoot 8.118
Understanding, symbolic 12.182–3
Unencapsulated nerve endings, in extraocular muscle 8.188
Unfamiliarity, feeling of 12.418, 12.421
Uniform Color Space (OSA) 6.46
Unilateral strabismus 9.200
Union set 14.6
Unique hue, CIE definition of 6.225
Uniqueness 14.33
Unit area
  of achromatic space 6.176
  of chromatic space 6.176
Unitary hue 6.45
  CIE definition of 6.225
Univariance, principle of 6.24–5, 6.148–9
Universals 12.107, 12.126, 12.387
  in human communication 12.16
Unrelated (perceived) colour, CIE definition of 6.225
Unresponsiveness, visuo-motor 12.435
Up–down method 10.36
Upbeat nystagmus 8.301–2
Uracil 7.102
Urine sugar tests 7.151
Uruk, city of 12.305
Utricle 8.14–7, 8.24
Utrocular vision 9.180–4
  with either eye 9.180–4
  neurophysiological correlates of 9.181
  psychophysical correlates of 9.181–3
  role of eye movement in 9.183
  in strabismus 9.183–4
Utterances, combinatorial 12.332

V

V1
  binocular portion of 4.161–2
  Glossary explanation of 4.451
  human visual 4.167
  vertical meridian representation of 4.162
V2
  and area DM 4.164
  of galagos 4.164
  Glossary explanation of 4.451
  human visual 4.167
V3, differences in, between macaque monkey and owl
    monkey 4.167
V_λ curve
  for colour measurement 6.12–3
  and luminance factors when using 6.12–3
V_λ function 5.194, 5.207
$V_{\lambda'}$ function 7.100
V_λ photopic luminosity function 5.196–8
V_λ sensitivity 5.194
Variable-acuity displays 15.18
Variable-resolution displays 15.18
Variance, intrinsic, in numerosity 14.134
Variation, diurnal 16.113
Varicosities 3.44
Varifocal lenses 1.72–3
  assessment of 1.423
  and visual-display-terminal operators 16.65–6
Varifocal mirror 1.340
Vascularization 11.319
Vase
  inversion 12.283
  recognition 12.282–4
  rotation 12.283
Vasoactive intestinal polypeptide 3.279, 11.361, 11.363
  in visual cortex neurogenesis 3.363, 3.369–70
Vasogenesis 3.86–7
Vater, A. 12.136
VDTs, *see* Visual-display terminals
Vection
  circular 12.362, 12.364, 12.434, 12.464
  Glossary explanation of 4.451
  induced by visual movement stimulation 12.433–4
  linear 12.434
Vectographs, printed 1.331
Vector analysis, of the retinal flow pattern 9.160
Vector coding 8.209, 12.464
Vector summation models 4.399
Vectorfields
  and pattern recognition 14.22–3, 14.25, 14.27–8
  in visual organization 14.20–1
Velhagen plates 7.216, 7.222, 7.230
Velhagen–Broschmann plates 7.118, 7.134, 7.149–50, 7.154
Velocity
  acuity 5.152
  angular 2.239, 2.242, 2.246
    and perceived velocity relationship of a small moving
      object 12.361

apparent 5.161, 5.163
  Glossary explanations of (two) 4.450–1
  minimum angular 12.360
  and motion 5.151–3, 5.155
  and motion detectors 5.157
  and motion smear 5.153
  object 5.160
  perceived 5.163, 5.166
  perception limits 5.160–9
  perception in periphery 5.163
  physiological data 5.168
  psychophysical data 5.168–9
  saccadic 8.95, 8.99–112
  stimulus 12.360, 12.362, 12.365, 12.371, 12.375
  true 5.166, 5.168–9
  tuning curves 12.87
Velocity constancy 5.162
Velocity control, in optokinesis 8.45
Velocity fields, Glossary explanation of 4.451
Velocity overshoot 8.79
Velocity selectivity
  in accessory optic system of cat and primate 4.117
  and analysis by visual motion 4.128–30
  and correlation between direction selectivity in the lateral
    terminal nucleus 4.117–8
  monocular deprivation in 4.125–6
Velocity sensitivity
  of cells of lateral geniculate nucleus 4.68
  of oculomotor neurones 8.203–5
Velocity storage 8.54–6, 8.218, 8.299–301
Velocity-response curves, Glossary explanation of 4.451
Ventral intraparietal sulcus 4.373–4
Ventral lateral geniculate nucleus 3.162, 3.215
  in visual function 4.405
  and visual thalamus 3.200, 3.217
Ventral lateral suprasylvanian cortex 4.357
Ventral pathway 10.246
Ventricle, lateral, occipital horn of 12.334
Ventricular zone 3.82, 3.85
  cytogenesis in 3.78–84
Ventriculography 12.347
VEP, *see* Visual evoked potentials
Vergence 5.71, 5.142, 8.9, 8.157–72, 8.205, 9.2–3, 9.172,
    10.186–7
  AC/A ratio 8.158, 8.162, 8.164–5, 8.169, 8.239
  and accommodation 8.158, 8.162–5
  accommodative 8.60–2, 8.168
  and brainstem 8.218–9
  CA/C ratio 8.163–5
  and cerebellum 8.238–9
  combined with version 8.166–7
  comparative aspects 8.169
  control of 9.121, 9.174, 13.216
  cyclofusional 8.167–8, 8.330
  frequency response 8.163
  fusional 8.158
  Glossary explanation of 4.451
  and Hering's law 8.157–8
  midline 8.158

non-linearity 8.159
and perspective 8.166
proximal 8.165–6
and Purkinje cells 8.238–9
saccadic 8.167
and size-change 8.165
tonic 8.162, 8.165
torsional 8.167–8, 8.330
vertical 8.167–8
Vergence accuracy 8.160, 9.211–2
Vergence adaptation 9.90
Vergence angle, definition of 9.19
Vergence control systems 9.121, 9.174, 13.216
Vergence development 8.168–9
Vergence disparity 8.158–60
Vergence eye movements 9.166, 9.208, 13.204
and dyslexia 13.146
Vergence fluctuations 9.125
Vergence innervation 9.2
Vergence instability 9.124
Vergence precision 8.160, 9.125
Vergence velocity neurones 8.219
Verhoeff's membrane 3.3
Verification
of contact lens parameters 1.415–35
reliability in 1.415
of spectacle lens parameters 1.415–35
validity in 1.415
Vermis 2.182–3, 2.188–9
Vernier acuity 2.408, 2.411, 6.210–1, 8.4, 8.8
colour 6.210
and location 14.8–10, 14.12–3
luminance 6.210
see also Acuity
sex differences in 9.172
in temporal integration 14.14–5
Vernoeff stereopter 9.210
Vernon Graded Word Spelling 13.197
Verriest classification 7.118, 7.176–7
see also Type I, II and III acquired deficiencies
Version 9.2–3
Version innervation 9.2
Vertebrate retina, inner plexiform layer of 4.1–9
Vertical excitatory burst units 8.259–61
Vertical fusion 8.167–8
Vertical horopter 9.213
inclination of 9.29–30
and ecological significance 9.29–30
Vertical meridian 3.151–2, 4.162, 10.262
and callosal pathways 3.330, 3.332, 3.340, 3.346–7
representation of 3.333–5
in callosal pathways 3.341–2, 3.344–5, 3.348–9
Vertical meridians, shear of 9.22–4
Vertical optokinesis 8.64–5
Vertical saccades 8.97, 8.103–12, 8.118
Vertical smooth pursuit 8.314
Vertical vergence 8.167–8
Vertical vestibulo-ocular reflex 8.314, 8.323
Vertical/horizontal meridian, Glossary explanation of 4.451

Vertigo 9.215, **12.27**, **12**.180, **12**.184
galvanic **12**.435
height **12**.435
and hemiachromatopsia **12**.402
movement **12**.435
and pure alexia **12**.354
and visual hemineglect **12**.432
and visual movement agnosia **12**.371–2
and visuo-spatial disorders **12**.434–5
Vertrautheit (familiarity) **12**.417
Vesalius, Andreas **12**.34
Vestibular afferent fibres 8.18–20, 8.23, 8.27–32, 8.320
Vestibular co-ordinates 8.20–2, 8.216, 8.323
Vestibular cortex **13**.15
Vestibular efferent fibres 8.26
Vestibular nuclear complex 2.174, 2.182–4, 2.187, 2.424
Vestibular nuclei 8.2, 8.202, 8.213–4, 8.216–8, 8.225, 8.234,
8.265, 8.302, 8.306
Vestibular nucleus neurones 4.130
Vestibular nystagmus 8.46, 8.301–2
Vestibular and optokinetic signals, synergy of 8.32–3, 8.46,
8.53–6, 8.218
Vestibular receptors 8.14–7, 8.22–6, 8.215–6, 8.320
cilia 8.22–4
Vestibular stimulation, influence on accommodation 1.249
Vestibular system 2.424
central, in transformation of space coordinates **12**.434
Vestibular units 2.181
Vestibulo-collic reflex 8.324
Vestibulo-ocular reflex 2.165, 2.174, 2.181–2, 2.184–8, 4.132,
4.388, 4.451, 8.4, 8.31, 8.33–8, 8.45–6, 8.52–8, 8.60, 8.64,
8.108–11, 8.215–6, 8.218–9, 8.226–32, 8.238–9, 8.264–5,
8.306, 8.308–9, 8.320, 8.322–4, 8.327–30, **12**.6, **12**.176,
12.462, **13**.210
abnormalities 8.297–301
adaptive plasticity 8.35–40, 8.81
cerebellar 8.37, 8.226–32, 8.238, 8.312
single-unit recordings 8.228–32
cognitive and perceptual correlates 8.38–40
site of 8.229
volitional control of 8.39
and ascending tract of Deiters 8.216
asymmetry 8.299
bilateral model of 8.265
and brainstem 8.216–8
cancellation 8.108–10, 8.217–8, 8.308
and cerebellum 8.216, 8.226–32, 8.237–8, 8.327
development 8.299
disconnection of 8.109–10
effect of lesions
cerebellum 8.228
inferior olive 8.228
interstitial nucleus of Cajal 8.314
midbrain 8.314
pons 8.312
and the flocculus 8.231–3
gain 8.32–40, 8.45, 8.79–81, 8.299, 8.314
Glossary explanation of 4.451
and interstitial nucleus of Cajal 8.216, 8.248

Vestibulo-ocular reflex (*continued*)
  linear 8.35
  and the medial longitudinal fasciculus 8.216
  modifiability of, and saccadic calibration 13.9
  and the nucleus prepositus hypoglossi 8.216
  and oscillopsia 8.314–6
  and posterior parietal lobe 12.95, 12.97–9
  and the superior cerebellar peduncle 8.216
  tilt suppression of 8.301
  torsional 8.308
  and velocity storage 8.54
  vertical 8.314, 8.323
  and visuo-spatial disorders 12.435, 12.438
  volitional control of 8.39
Vestibulo-ocular response 9.126
Vestibulo-saccadic reflex 8.99
V-gauges 1.428–9
Video display terminal (VDT) 16.96–7
Videomicroscopy 11.89, 11.101, 11.172
Vieth–Muller circle 9.2, 9.27, 9.79, 9.191
  in the visual plane 9.28–9
Vieussens, Raymond 12.40–1
Viewpoint and computational vision 14.43–5
Viewpoint normalization 14.31
Viewprint model 10.110
Viewscan system, and transverse magnification 1.205
Vigilance 15.83–98
  criterion shifts in 15.87–90
    and β 15.88
    and correct rejection 15.90
    and detection 15.90
    and event rates 15.89–90
    and false alarms 15.88–90
    and hits 15.88
    and misses 15.90
    and probability matching 15.88–9
    and signal probability 15.89–90
    and signal rate 15.88
  reductions in
    due to suggestions of accumulated inhibition 15.85
    due to suggestions of increased distraction 15.85
    due to suggestions of lowered cortical arousal 15.85
    due to suggestions of lowered expectancy 15.85
  research into
    the Mackworth Clock Test 15.85
    the main listening task 15.85
    origins of 15.84–6
    synthetic radar task 15.85
  and the sensitivity decrement 15.90–5
  and signal detection theory 15.86–7
  and temporal uncertainty 15.86
Vigilance decrements 15.83, 15.95
Vigilance tasks
  and attentional demands 15.91
  cognitive 15.91
  simultaneous discrimination 15.90–2
  successive discrimination 15.90–2
  taxonomic analysis of 15.91
Vimentin 11.244–6

and retinal development 3.77, 3.81
Vinculin 11.172–3
VIP, *see* Vasoactive intestinal polypeptide
Vipera 2.428
Visibility
  and equiluminance 5.236
  and illusions 5.242
  threshold 5.237
Visible persistence 13.150–1
  in specifically disabled readers and controls 13.151
Visible spectra 4.326
Vision
  anthropocentric 2.229
  basis of 2.239
  biological and ecological constraints 14.19–28
  competence theory 14.45
  computer 12.5, 12.7, 12.11, 12.14, 12.17
  cone of 12.26, 12.34
  dedicated mechanisms 14.8, 14.12–5
  dimness of 12.402
  and display 15.55–69
    ergonomic objectives of 15.55–6
  distortions 12.473
  double 12.476
  evolution of 2.237–9
  form 12.401
  foveal 12.475
  free 12.335, 12.340
  global organizing properties 14.19–20
  Greek theories 12.386
  high-level 14.31–2, 14.40, 14.43, 14.45
  indirect 12.136
  light–dark 12.390–1, 12.401–2
  low-level 14.31–7
  machine 14.30, 14.40, 14.43
  man-specific cognitive abilities 12.1
  mental 12.259
  middle 14.31–2, 14.37–40
  residual 12.152
  see also Colour vision; Computational vision; Photopic
    vision; Scotopic vision
  stereoscopic binocular 12.400
  theory of direct 14.19
  tunnel 12.196, 12.420, 12.423
Vision modules, parallel organization of 6.193–5
Visual acuity 12.464
  and binocular vision 2.272–3
  and depth-of-focus/field 1.261
  and digitalis poisoning 7.132–3
  in dyslexia 13.145
  and evolution of vision 2.407–8, 2.411
  in eye evolution 2.413, 2.417
  and fovea 3.113, 3.115
  and functional organization of retina 3.1
  and nature of light 2.5
  and photoreception 2.377
  and pursuit system 2.168
  and retinal development 3.118
  and retinal eccentricity 8.6–9

Visual acuity (*continued*)
  and retinal expansion 3.110
  and retinal image velocity 8.3–5, 8.86–9, 8.314
  see also under Acuity
  and spontaneous nystagmus 8.315
  and tremor 8.71–2
  and visual pathways 2.443, 2.453–4, 2.456
  and visual-display terminals 16.65
    effect of ageing 15.61–3
    software magnifying facilities 15.65
    varifocal and bifocal lenses 15.65–6
Visual adaptation 6.54
Visual ageing 5.277
Visual areas 12.469
  7 of primate 12.92–4
    7a 12.92–8, 12.100–3, 12.465
    7b 12.92–6, 12.98, 12.101–3
    7ip 12.92–4, 12.96, 12.100–1
    7m 12.92, 12.94, 12.96
    FST 12.93–4, 12.465
    LIP 12.92–3, 12.96
    local and global (wide-field) visual movement
      responses 12.101
    MST 12.93–4, 12.97, 12.101, 12.465
    MT 12.93–4, 12.97, 12.101
    PIVC 12.93–4, 12.98
    PO 12.93–4
    quantitative evaluations of neuronal responses 12.103–6
    V1 12.94
    V2 12.94
    V3 12.94
    V4 12.94
    VIP 12.92–3
    visuo-spatial and visuo-motor neuronal data processing
      in 12.96–103
  7/8 2.173, 2.178–80, 2.184, 2.189–91
  7a of primate, V1 12.465
  8 lesions 12.448
  17 2.173–6, 2.452, 2.456, 2.458, 3.302, 3.341–2, 3.344–5,
    3.347, 3.349–50
    neurogenesis in 3.360–1, 3.363
    and visual cortex neurogenesis 3.366, 3.371
  18 2.173–4, 2.177, 2.456, 2.458, 3.341–2, 3.345, 3.347,
    3.350
  18 and 19 of Brodmann 12.168
  18
    neurogenesis in 3.363
    and visual cortex neurogenesis 3.371
  19 2.173–4, 2.176–7, 2.458, 3.341–2, 3.345
    neurogenesis in 3.363
  association (integration) 12.77–81, 12.84, 12.89, 12.134
    and prosopagnosia 12.278
    and pure alexia 12.345
  AST (anterior superior temporal) 12.87, 12.91
  connections 12.89
  DI (dorsointermediate) 3.313–4
  DL (dorsolateral) 3.312, 3.314, 3.316, 3.318–9
  DM (dorsomedial) 3.312–7, 3.319
  DP, and visual object recognition 12.109

  ectosylvian 2.444
  electrical stimulation 12.168
  extrastriate 2.456–9, 3.311, 3.316
  frontal 3.314
  FST (fundal area of superior temporal sulcus) 3.313,
    3.316, 12.87, 12.90–1, 12.465, 12.480
  hierarchical prominence of 3.336–7
  hierarchy of 3.305, 4.161
  high order 3.347
  intact primary sensory 12.346
  middle temporal (MT) 2.173, 2.175–7, 2.179, 2.191,
    2.458–9, 3.311–9, 3.334, 3.336–9, 3.347, 3.349, 12.78,
    12.80, 12.378, 12.381, 12.480
    motion perception in 12.86–91
  MST (middle superior temporal) 3.313–4, 3.316, 3.319,
    12.78, 12.80, 12.87, 12.90–1, 12.465, 12.480
  occipital movements association 12.480
  in owl monkeys 3.311–3, 3.316–7
  parietal 12.300
  parieto-temporal 12.345
  PIVC 12.78, 12.80, 12.91
  prestriate 12.154
  primary 3.302
  in primates 3.317–9
  processing hierarchies 3.316
  and pure alexia 12.343
  retinotopic organization 12.77, 12.84, 12.86
  retroinsular 12.300
  secondary 3.302
  ST (superior temporal) 3.313
  stimulation of 12.472
  STP 12.111
  STS 3.334, 12.109, 12.112, 12.118–9
  subcortical 11.353–7
  suprasylvian 3.341–2
  TE 12.108–9, 12.111–2, 12.118–9
    connections 12.111
  TEO 12.108–9, 12.111–2
  V1 2.171, 2.173–7, 2.189–91, 3.336–8, 3.347–9, 4.410,
    6.179–81, 6.184–91, 6.194–5, 9.224, 12.65, 12.68,
    12.77, 12.386, 12.396, 12.464–5
    and agnosia 12.197, 12.199–200
    and blindsight 12.153–4
    and colour agnosia 12.403, 12.405
    and colour deficiencies 12.409
    colour perception in 12.83–4
    columnar organization 12.69
    contour perception in 12.81–2
    and cortical blindness 12.148
    illusion and hallucination 12.466, 12.468, 12.472–4
    inactivation 3.339
    motion perception in 12.86–90
    nerve cells 12.66, 12.70, 12.72–6
    neurogenesis in 3.360–1, 3.363
    and phosphenes 12.155, 12.162, 12.170–1
    projections to higher visual centres 12.78–81
    and pure alexia 12.356–7
    signal transfer to 12.75–6
    and visual cortex neurogenesis 3.366

Visual areas (*continued*)
and visual object recognition **12.**109
V2 **2.**171, **2.**173, **2.**176–7, **2.**179, **2.**191, **2.**443, **2.**458,
   3.336–9, **3.**347, **3.**349, **6.**180, **6.**186–91, **6.**195, **12.**77–8
and colour deficiencies **12.**409
colour perception in **12.**83–4
contour perception in **12.**81–3
illusion and hallucination **12.**475, **12.**480
motion perception in **12.**86–7, **12.**90
and phosphenes **12.**155
and pure alexia **12.**356
and visual object recognition **12.**109, **12.**111–3
V2–V5 **9.**224
V3 **3.**332–4, **3.**336–9, **6.**180, **6.**190, **12.**480
and visual object recognition **12.**109, **12.**112
V3A **6.**180
V3d **12.**87
V4 356, **2.**177–8, **2.**458, **3.**332–4, **3.**336–7, **6.**180, **6.**186,
   6.189–90, **6.**192, **6.**194, **12.**77, **12.**386–7, **12.**393,
   12.480
and colour agnosia **12.**406
and colour deficiencies **12.**409
colour perception in **12.**83–5
and hemiachromatopsia **12.**402
input connections of non-visual origin **12.**80
and visual object recognition **12.**109, **12.**111–3, **12.**115
V4A **6.**180, **12.**85
V5 **6.**180, **6.**186–7, **6.**189, **6.**195
V-I **3.**302–4, **3.**331–2, **3.**334–5
V-II **3.**302–4, **3.**331–4
'visual area of the past' **12.**479
in visual cortex organization **3.**308–9
and visual pathways **2.**423, **2.**433
Visual association system **12.**278
Visual attention **3.**217
as a suggested function of the pulvinar **4.**152–4
Visual axis **2.**264, **2.**272–3, **2.**427, **2.**448
Visual capture **9.**183
Visual centre **12.**180
primary **12.**60–1, **12.**179, **12.**405
Visual channels **5.**97–105
development of selective **13.**44–7
and acuity and contrast sensitivity **13.**44–5
and binocularity **13.**47
and colour **13.**45–6
and discrimination of spatial relationship **13.**46–7
and orientation **13.**46
integration across **13.**50
Visual comfort and performance **15.**24–40
constancy of visual performance **15.**56
role of sharpness in **15.**34–6, **15.**58–9
scaled **15.**36–7
Visual cortex **2.**152–3, **2.**159–60, **3.**235, **6.**208, **9.**173–4
afferents **11.**346
area 17 **3.**312, **3.**315–6, **3.**318
area 18 **3.**309–10, **3.**315
area V1
binocular interaction of **6.**180–1
columns **6.**180–6

orientation selectivity of **6.**179–80
area V2 **7.**189
area V4 **7.**189–90
awake fixating macaque, stereoscopic mechanisms in **4.**212
in binocular vision **2.**274–5, **2.**277, **2.**279–81
callosal connections **3.**331–5
in carnivores **4.**162–4
cat **11.**288, **11.**290
broadband cells of **4.**182
curvature sensitivity of cells of **4.**179
length sensitivity of cells of **4.**175–7
orientation selectivity of cells of **4.**177
spatial parameters in **4.**174–80
curvature **4.**174, **4.**179
length **4.**174–7
orientation **4.**174–7
shape and texture **4.**174, **4.**179–80
spatial frequency **4.**174–9
time **4.**174
width **4.**174
spatial-frequency selectivity of cells of **4.**177
velocity high-pass cells of **4.**182
velocity low-pass cells of **4.**182
velocity tuning of cells of **4.**182, **4.**184
and discriminations of speed **4.**184
and response to slow movement **4.**186
and upper cut-off velocity **4.**185
cat primary **4.**267
cholinergic and monoaminergic innervation of **3.**295–6
pattern termination in **3.**295–6
acetylcholine **3.**296
monoamines **3.**295–6
sources of **3.**295
chronic drug treatments of **11.**259
columnar nature of **4.**294
columnar organization of **3.**252, **4.**266–315
columnar/modular organization of **3.**303
connections to **3.**370–1
critical period plasticity **11.**288–9
dendritic differentiation of **3.**366–8
in different mammalian groups **4.**161–7
effects of mutations on **11.**346
evolution of areas of **4.**167–70
extrastriate **2.**424, **2.**426, **2.**443, **3.**302–19
connections to **3.**267–9
modular organization in primates **3.**317–9
in non-primate species **3.**309–11, **4.**339–70
in owl monkeys **3.**311–3
in primates **3.**313–6
processing hierarchies **3.**316–7
simple brains **3.**304–9
hamster **11.**237
hierarchy of **3.**311
horizontal interactions in **3.**255–8
inhibitory neurones in **3.**258–65
interlaminar connectivities **3.**265–7
juxta-striate area 18 **3.**325
in lagomorphs **4.**162
large-scale processing units of **4.**299–306

hypercolumns **4**.301–3
modules **4**.303–7
layers of **6**.180–2
lesions **3**.198
magnocellular layer of **1**.258
mammalian **2**.423
   areas of **4**.160–72
   definition of **4**.160
moderately expanded **3**.305–9
monkey
   orientation of
     and MT **4**.204–5
     and V1 **4**.202, **4**.204–5
     and V2 **4**.202, **4**.204–5
     and V3 **4**.204–5
     and V3A **4**.205
     and V4 **4**.204–5
     and V5 **4**.205
     and VP **4**.204
   S-cells of **4**.203
   see also Visual cortex, in primates
   stereoscopic mechanisms in **4**.211–3
   variability of orientation of **4**.204
neurogenesis of **3**.360–4, **11**.28–9
and neurotransmitters **3**.368–70, **11**.356
ocular dominance bands **3**.252–5
organization **11**.337–8
in other animals **4**.167–70
primary **2**.455, **3**.305, **3**.309, **3**.311, **7**.185, **7**.189
   and callosal pathways **3**.340, **3**.344, **3**.347
   columnar organization of **3**.348
   and forebrain commissures **3**.325
   neurogenesis of **3**.360
in primates **4**.164–7
   humans **4**.167–8
   New World monkeys **4**.162, **4**.164–6
   Old World monkeys **4**.162, **4**.167
   prosimians **4**.164
in pursuit system **2**.172–4, **2**.188
rat **11**.235, **11**.282–3, **11**.286, **11**.289, **11**.291
reptile **2**.423
in rodents **4**.161–2
   cavies **4**.161–2
   murines **4**.161, **4**.167
   sciurumorphs **4**.161–2
secondary, and callosal pathways **3**.340
see also Cortex, visual; Extrastriate visual cortex
and seizures **13**.155
and shape recognition **2**.162–3
sheep's **4**.275
striate **9**.173
synaptic differentiation of **3**.364–6
tertiary, and callosal pathways **3**.340
and tracking **2**.161–2
treatment with TTX **11**.258–9
V1 neurones of **6**.207
V-I **3**.305–12, **3**.314–9
V-II **3**.305–12, **3**.314–9
and visual pathways **2**.427, **2**.444, **2**.448, **2**.453, **2**.455,

   2.459
Visual cortex neurones
   quantitative electrophysiology of **4**.173–222
   quantitative physiology of **4**.173–222
Visual cortical area, Glossary explanation of **4**.451
Visual cortical function, integration of **13**.47–8
Visual cortical pathways, to parietal lobe **4**.372–4
Visual crowding **10**.225, **13**.51–5
   effects of, in dyslexics **13**.54
   measurement of **13**.51–5
Visual deprivation **11**.340, **11**.381
   binocular **11**.290, **11**.345–6
   and cross-modal functions **11**.378–9
   effects on development of **11**.374–6
   monocular **11**.240, **11**.258, **11**.288, **11**.290, **11**.345–7
     in synaptic rearrangement **11**.259–62
   studies of the effects of, in the abnormal accessory optic
     system **4**.120–1
Visual development **10**.82
Visual direction **9**.1–18
   Cyclopean eye as a direction for **9**.8–12
   identical **9**.6
   laws of **9**.77
Visual discomfort **13**.168
   and flicker **13**.155
   and geometric patterns **13**.155
   and photosensitivity in epilepsy **13**.155
   and reading **13**.155–70
     eye-strain **13**.155
     headaches **13**.155
     seizures **13**.155
   and striped patterns **13**.155–7
Visual disorientation **13**.24–5
Visual displays **15**.56
   comparison of quality measures for **15**.28–32
   decay times of **15**.8
   epidemiological studies of **15**.56–8
   gas plasma **15**.56
   health-related aspects of **15**.1–6, **15**.56–8
     among operators **15**.2–4, **15**.57
     effects of stress **15**.4
     epidemiological studies into **15**.3–4
     serious malformations **15**.3–4, **15**.57
     spontaneous abortions **15**.3–4, **15**.57
     Swedish, Canadian and American experimental studies
       into **15**.3–4
   liquid crystal **15**.56
   multi-colour screens **15**.56
   quality of
     and visual functions **15**.58–63
       accommodation and distance **15**.61–3
       adaptation **15**.61
       colour **15**.63
       flicker and jitter **15**.56–61
       guidance of the eyes **15**.63
       sharpness of vision and contrast **15**.58–9
   using cathode-ray tubes **15**.56
   see also Visual-display terminals
Visual dyslexia **13**.26–7, **13**.116–8

Visual environment, aquatic 2.407–17
Visual ergonomics, of visual-display terminals 15.70–82
Visual error signal 8.131
Visual evoked potentials 4.140, 5.179, 5.183–5, 5.216–7,
    5.272–3, 5.278, 9.101, 9.150, 9.170, 10.137, 10.155–9,
    10.186, 12.125, 12.167, 13.45, 13.151, 16.107, 16.112,
    16.117–8
  and agnosia 12.195
  amplitudes of negative and positive peaks 12.245
  category-dependent subtraction curves 12.252
  category-related 12.241
    components 12.246–7
    difference curves 12.255–7
    differences 12.242–4, 12.251–2, 12.255
    subtraction curves 12.253–4
  category-specific subtraction curves 12.245–6
  to chequerboards 12.396
  computed category-specific difference curves 12.252
  and cortical lesions 10.266, 10.269
  development of 10.189
  and dopamine 10.250
  face-responsive components 12.240–58
  gender-related differences 12.242, 12.245
  grand averages 12.242–6, 12.248–58
  to isoluminant colour gratings 12.396
  in MS 10.247
  P300 component 12.277
  in Parkinson's disease 10.251
  pattern (PVEP) 10.254–5
  pattern-reversal 12.177
  and prosopagnosia 12.266
  response
    to flowers 12.251–4, 12.256, 12.258
    to known and unknown faces 12.247–8
  second harmonic of 12.397
  in specifically disabled readers and controls 13.151
  stimulus-category-related differences 12.244
Visual experience 11.346–7, 11.378
Visual extinction 13.23–4
Visual fields 2.246, 8.5–6, 10.244, 10.262
  anisotropy of 14.52–3
  asymmetries in face processing 12.231
  binocular 3.176–7, 12.141
  colour 12.347
  for colour detection 12.139
  and colour vision 2.300
  defects in 12.2, 12.136–57
    and agnosia 12.180, 12.199
    and alexia 12.334
    bizarre 12.146
    blindsight 12.148–54
    central 12.152
    concentric 12.203
    congruence of 12.391
    cortical blindness 12.147–8
      spontaneous visual sensations 12.154–7
    functional differences in different parts 12.142–4
    general 12.400–1
    historical background 12.136–8

  homonymous 12.151
  incongruent 12.146
  partial 12.194
  perimetry 12.138–42
  peripheral 12.197
  and prosopagnosia 12.262, 12.264, 12.270, 12.276
  rare ring-shaped 12.146–7
  right, and pure alexia 12.343
  topical diagnostic values 12.144–5
  upper quadrant 12.275, 12.400–1
  variability of homonymous 12.145–7
  in dioptrics 2.86, 2.91, 2.95, 2.97–100
  and evolutionary loss and gain 4.169
  full, awareness of 12.346
  Glossary explanation of 4.451
  growth of 10.197
  half of 12.473
  hemianopic 12.452
  left advantage (LVFA) 12.144
  left and right 12.136, 12.144, 12.345
  and loss of topographical familiarity 12.425
  midline 3.325
  movement of migraine phosphene across 12.177
  nasal 3.199, 3.202
  nasal and temporal 12.136, 12.143–4, 12.146
  and numerosity 14.127
  overlap 3.176
  peripheral 10.132
  periphery 12.137, 12.320, 12.322
  and pure alexia 12.341
  recovery from a completely blind 12.148
  representation of 2.279
  residual movement perception in blind 12.149
  right advantage (RVFA) 12.144
  and signal processing 12.65–7, 12.69, 12.72
  and signal transfer 12.74–5
  and spatial relations 14.52–4, 14.58, 14.66
  superiority 12.231
  temporal 3.199, 3.202
  and topographagnosia 12.420, 12.423–4
  and topographical disorientation 12.429
  and topographical orientation 12.428
  upper and lower 12.136, 12.142–3
  and visual thalamus 3.177–8, 3.180, 3.182, 3.200
Visual fixation neurones 8.285
Visual flow fields, analysis of 4.127–8
Visual functions 12.288
  conceptual limitations to the assessment of 5.286–328
  man-specific averbal 12.296
Visual guidance, of self-motion 9.162
Visual hemifields 3.182, 3.186–7, 3.198
  in pulvinar complex 3.212–3
  in visual cortex 3.309–10, 3.312
  in visual cortex organization 3.305
  and visual thalamus 3.209–10
Visual imagery 13.221
  affect on accommodation 1.249
Visual impairment
  and low vision 1.183

see also Low vision
    WHO's definition of 1.183
Visual inattention 13.23–4
Visual information flow, regulation of 4.74
Visual information processing
    and parallel pathways 4.74–6
    part played by the lateral geniculate nucleus in 4.73–6
Visual localization
    constancy of 9.183–4
    in dyslexia 13.12–38, 13.142–3, 13.181–2
Visual mapping 3.150–2
Visual masking 6.209–10, 9.102
Visual modality 12.345
    letter and colour learning by 12.337
Visual motion
    analysis of
        by the accessory optic system 4.128–30
        by direction and velocity selectivity 4.128–30
    perception of 13.37
Visual neglect 13.23–4, 13.181
    due to lesions in the pulvinar 4.406
Visual neurones, in insects, neurophysiology of 6.276–9
Visual pathway receptors 5.191–5
Visual pathways
    afferent 12.144–5, 12.148
        illusion and hallucination 12.466
        in reading and script 12.320
    anatomy of, in Old World primates 5.191–2
    cell death of 5.277
    central, lesions of 7.30
    columnar organization of 5.48
    cone signals of 5.191
    dorsal visuo-limbic 12.278
    extrageniculate afferent 12.149
    hierarchical organization of 5.44–5
    mammalian 2.442–59
    medial occipito-temporal 12.278
    primary 2.442–4
    retino-pulvinar-prestriate 12.154
    retino-tectal 12.153
    retino-tectal-pulvinar-cortical 12.153–4
    retino-vestibular 12.154
    spectral characteristics of cells of 5.191
    ventral visual-limbic 12.278–9
Visual perception, *see* Perception
Visual performance and ageing 16.150–8
Visual pigments 2.88, 2.120, 6.72–3, 6.75–6, 6.94, 6.100,
        6.108–27
    in amphibians 6.118–9
        and similarity with green rods 6.119
    chromophores of 6.62–4
    and colour vision 2.290–3, 2.299–300, 6.111–2
    in evolution of eye 2.8–13, 2.26, 2.39–40, 2.44, 2.417
    evolution of 6.62–89
    evolution of vertebrate 2.63–78
    in evolution of vision 2.404, 2.409
    in fish 6.112–8
        crepuscular predators 6.118
        deep sea 6.112–3

dichromatic 6.113–4
        freshwater 6.115
        inhabiting tropical freshwater environments 6.114, 6.118
        inhabiting tropical marine/coral environments 6.114
        mesopelargic 6.112
        photophores in 6.112
        polymorphic 6.115
        and red bio-illuminescence 6.112
        seasonal changes in dominance of 6.117–8
        teleost 6.113
            cone mosaic in 6.113
        tropical surface living, ellipsosomes in 6.115
        ultra-violet-sensitive, in guppies 6.115
    in mammals 6.122–5
        dichromacy in 6.123
        polymorphism in 6.124–5
    multiple 6.75–6
    multiple cone 6.84–6
    in paleognathous birds 6.122
    in photoreception 2.366, 2.378, 2.380–1, 2.390
    phylogeny and chromophores of 6.67–8
    phylogeny and photoreceptor organelles of 6.68
    in reptiles and birds 6.119–22
        oil droplets in 6.119–21
        sensitive in the near ultraviolet 6.120
    and the spectral distribution of λ_{max} 6.68–71
    of vertebrates and invertebrates, similarity between 6.62–7
    in visual processing 2.229–30, 2.234
Visual plane 9.24–5
    effect of asymmetrical fixation within 9.25–6
    symmetrical fixation in 9.24–5
    and the Vieth–Muller circle 9.28–9
Visual processes, primary 12.468
Visual processing 2.433
    in arthropods 2.203
    autocorrelation model 2.251–3
    and dyslexia 13.132–40
    evolution of 2.229–68
        evolution of vision 2.237–9
        larger templates 2.260–3
        laws of optics 2.230–7
        semivision 2.254–60
        template model 2.243–51
        whole-eye templates 2.263–7
    fundamentals of 5.322–3
    higher-level
        in specifically disabled readers and controls 13.152
            metacontrast masking 13.152
    low-level 2.212
        in specifically disabled readers and controls 13.151–2
            comparison of sustained system processing in 13.152
            flicker thresholds 13.151
            minimum contrast in 13.151
            reduced effect of spatial frequency in 13.151
            and visually evoked potentials 13.151
    mechanisms 2.212–3, 2.238–9, 2.242, 2.252, 2.254, 2.261,
        2.267, 2.436
    mollusc photoreception 2.383–91
    organization 2.204–12

Visual processing (*continued*)
  'top-down' effects 2.268
Visual proprioceptive nuclei 8.2, 8.48, 8.201, 8.213, 8.234
Visual psychophysics 15.11
Visual pyramid 12.34, 12.136
Visual qualities, primary 12.270
Visual resolution, two-point 5.222
Visual response, enhancement of 4.397
Visual scene, spatio-temporal 2.243, 2.247
Visual search
  in dyslexia 13.58–83
  psychophysics of 13.64–5
Visual signal recognition, and the temporal lobe 12.125–6
Visual signals 5.300–2
  central integration of 8.32–3
Visual space
  binocular
    geometry of 9.81–2
    models of 9.83
  detection of 6.193
  remapping of 6.189–90
Visual streak 2.86, 2.94, 2.97, 2.102, 2.445
  and evolution of retina 2.143–4
  horizontal 2.443–4
  and visual pathways 2.454
Visual streams, Glossary explanations of 4.452
Visual structures, amorphic 12.471
Visual systems
  achromatic 6.22–42
  afferent 2.168–9, 2.171, 2.184, 2.191, 12.357
    illusion and hallucination 12.478, 12.481
    and reading 12.323
  and alexia 12.335
  anatomical organization 12.190
  central, illusion and hallucination 12.475, 12.478–9
  chromatic 6.22–42
  concept of two 12.107
  evolution in reptiles and birds 2.421–36
  goldfish 11.190–201
  lamprey 2.402–5
  mammalian 2.435
  medio-basal posterior region 12.264
  non-mammalian 2.435
  overload of 13.168
  perceptive 12.346
  plasticity 2.430
  prenatal development of primate 12.19
  retino-geniculate cortical 12.453
  retino-tectal 12.453
  retinotopic organization 12.65–6
  right hemisphere 12.344, 12.349, 12.355
  sensitive periods 12.19
Visual tracking, activation of MST neurones during 4.376
Visual tracking Purkinje cells 8.230–3
Visual vestibular interactions 4.130–2
Visual work environment 15.70
Visual wulst 2.423, 2.426, 2.429–34, 2.436
Visual zones 12.346
Visual–auditory overlap 4.162

Visual-display terminals 15.1–6, 15.21
  and electromagnetic and magnetic fields 15.1–4
  and electromagnetic radiation 15.1
  and electronic text quality 15.80
  and flicker 15.50, 15.59–60
  graphs and graphics in 15.75–7, 15.108
    graphical versus textual representation of
      information 15.75–6
    visual languages 15.76
  health-related aspects of 15.1–6, 15.56–8
  and high luminance reflections 15.45–50
  and integration of text and figures 15.80
  legibility of texts on 15.70–5
    colour effects on 15.73
      coding 15.73
      conspicuity 15.73
      PRESTEL 15.73
      grouping 15.73
    multipage 15.74–5
      electronic, paging and scrolling 15.75
      printed 15.74–5
    spacial effects on 15.71–2
      and Teletext 15.71
    typographic effects on 15.73–4
      acceptability 15.74
      conflicting factors between 15.74
      identifiability 15.74
      individuality 15.74
  light-air ions produced by 15.4–5
  lighting criteria for 15.43–50
    subjective performance 15.43
    task performance 15.43
  lighting problems associated with 15.41–2, 15.63–4
    dynamic luminance imbalance 15.41–2
    high-luminance reflections 15.41–2
      and accommodation 15.42
      and attention switching 15.42
    luminance contrast
      distraction caused by 15.42
      reduction of 15.42
    recommendations for avoiding visual discomfort
      of the CIBSE 15.50, 15.52
      of the CIE 15.50
      of DIN 15.50
      limiting the luminance of luminaires 15.50
      reflectances 15.50
    solutions in practice for 15.51–3
      appearance of the room 15.53
      both direct and indirect 15.51–3
      direct lighting 15.51–3
      indirect lighting 15.51–3
    solutions in principle for
      polarity of contrast 15.50
      production of a uniform low-luminance interior 15.51
      reflection properties of the screen 15.50
      screen treatment 15.50
    static luminance imbalance 15.41–2
  personal aspects of 15.65–6
    heterophoria 15.65

presbyopia **15.65–6**
and visual acuity **15.65**
and work content **15.65**
and radiation-induced cataracts **15.2**
readability of texts on **15.71**
and skin problems **15.2**
ultrasound and high-frequency audible sound emissions
from **15.5**
visual ergonomics of **15.70–82**
windowing systems in **15.77–80**, **15.108**
and the desktop metaphor **15.79**
pictograms **15.79**
and icons and workstation screens **15.77–8**
and the pointer, cursor and caret **15.79–80**
and work design **15.64–5**
Visual-field defects
bilateral losses of **7.30**
bitemporal **7.155**, **7.157**, **7.161**
Bjerrum banana shape **7.152**
and digitalis poisoning **7.133**
in glaucoma **7.153**
homonymous **7.162**
and tests **7.215**
unilateral nerve-fibre-bundle **7.157**
Visual-field representation **4.160**
Visualization, metabolic **3.182**
Visually triggered movement neurones **8.249**
'Visuogram' **10.214**
Visuomotor functions **2.152**, **2.154**
Visuomotor integration **3.217**
Visuomotor localization **13.31–3**, **13.181**
Visuomotor mechanisms **2.159–60**

Visuomotor neurones **4.377**
Visuomotor response properties, in area POa **4.377**
Visuomotor systems **2.153–7**, **2.162**
Visuomovement cells **4.417**
Visuospatial deficits **13.22**
Visuotopic maps, Glossary explanation of **4.452**
Visuotopography **3.347**
Visuotopy
in the superior colliculus **3.150–75**
changes in, with depth **3.157–9**
traditional approaches to the study of **3.151–2**
Vitamin A **2.16**, **2.26**, **2.39**, **2.42**, **16.38**
deficiency of **7.124–5**, **16.150**
retinoid competition with **7.126**
Vitelliform macular degeneration (Best's disease) **7.129–30**
Vitiligo **7.146**, **7.148**
Vitreous **2.83–4**
primary/secondary/tertiary **11.391–4**
and radiation **16.56**, **16.58**
Vitreous body, human **1.4–5**
V_λ curve **5.197**
VMC, *see* Vieth–Muller circle
Vogt, Cecile and Oskar **12.50**
Vogt-Koyanagi's disease **7.147**
Voice, recognition of familiar **12.270**
Voice identification **12.268**
Voice personality **15.123**
Volitional control, of vestibulo-ocular reflex **8.39**
von Helmholtz, Hermann **1.231**
VOR, *see* Vestibulo-ocular reflex
Vowels **12.355**

W

W.D.W. system **7**.12, **7**.31
Waaler's model **7**.95
Wald technique **7**.191
Wald–Marré classification **7**.177
Wald–Marré method **5**.210
Wald–Marré technique **7**.45, **7**.118, **7**.121, **7**.130, **7**.135, **7**.137
Wallenberg syndrome **8**.313
Wallpaper phenomenon, global effects in **9**.48
Walls, Gordon **2**.136–8, **2**.142, **6**.76–8
Walsh functions **12**.114
Warning foreperiod and saccadic latency **8**.113–4
Warnings **15**.119
Watasenia scintillans (firefly squid) **2**.381, **2**.390
Watchkeeping tasks **15**.83–98
Water transmittance **2**.87
Waveforms, transient **10**.15–6
Wavefront aberrations **1**.10
  and final retinal image quality **1**.16–7
Waveguide effects, and retinal transmission and absorption **1**.5
Waveguide modes **2**.132
Waveguide parameter *V* **1**.286
Waveguides **2**.100, **2**.102, **2**.112
  modal properties and patterns of **1**.284–7
  optical **3**.1, **3**.12
  photoreceptor **3**.13
  and photoreceptors **1**.280–7
Waveguiding **3**.16
Wavelength **5**.213–4, **5**.227
  colour vision **2**.284
  discrimination **2**.11, **2**.285–9, **2**.292–4, **2**.298, **2**.300–1
  information-carrying **2**.7–8
  light **2**.399, **2**.402, **2**.406, **2**.408–10, **2**.412, **2**.433
  nature of light **2**.5–6
  noise **2**.407
  in photoreception **2**.388, **2**.390
  see also Radiation
  selectivity **2**.445, **2**.450
  short **2**.8–9
Wavelength discrimination **5**.211–4, **5**.227, **5**.287, **7**.6, **7**.9, **7**.176, **10**.68–9
  acquired colour deficiency **7**.42
  blue system **7**.82–4
  blue–green defects **7**.22
  'blue-cone' monochromacy **7**.27
  cerebral blindness and **7**.193–4
  in deficit evaluation **7**.122
  in glaucoma **7**.152
  in insects **6**.269
  and Köllner's rule **7**.174–5
  in lesions of cerebral hemispheres **7**.192–3
  in non-human primates **7**.203–5, **7**.207–8, **7**.210
  in optic neuritis and MS **7**.183
  in primates **7**.189–90
  red–green deficiencies **7**.17
  rod-'red-cone' monochromats **7**.28

  unilateral deficiencies **7**.29
Wavelength domain **3**.6
  colour signals in **3**.29–30
  and ganglion cells **3**.49
  and horizontal cells **3**.40
  and postreceptoral mechanisms **3**.30
Wavelength selectivity **4**.34
Wavelength swing **5**.177–8
Wavelength-selective behaviour, in insects **6**.282–4
Wavelet analysis **12**.255–7
Wavelet diagram (W-diagram) **12**.256
Wavelet function **12**.256–7
Waves, evanescent **3**.13
W-cells **4**.12–4, **4**.65–7, **4**.89–91, **4**.163, **4**.224–5, **4**.342–3
  in the cat **4**.62
  Glossary explanation of **4**.452
  and variation of properties across X-and Y-cells **4**.67–71
W-class ganglion cells **3**.157, **3**.164, **3**.281–2
Weakened wall hypothesis **3**.116–7
Weber contrast **10**.290–1
Weber fractions **5**.13, **5**.36, **5**.320–2, **6**.151, **7**.78, **12**.360
  and cone contrast **5**.199
  and contrast sensitivity **5**.37, **5**.42
  and hyperacuity **5**.225
  and numerosity **14**.132
  in peripheral vision **5**.61
  and velocity discrimination **5**.163
Weber function and spatial relations **14**.11
Weber–Fechner Law **6**.151–2
Weber–Fechner ratio **6**.281
Weber's law **3**.25, **5**.12–3, **10**.45, **10**.75–6, **10**.93–4, **10**.290
  and contrast sensitivity **5**.36–42
  and hyperacuity **5**.222, **5**.224–5
  in localization modelling **14**.15–6
  in negative masking **5**.30
  in peripheral vision **5**.55, **5**.61, **5**.63, **5**.67, **5**.69
  and spatial relations **14**.10–1
  in visual processing **5**.25
Wechsler Intelligence Scale for Children **13**.133–4, **13**.137
Wechsler Verbal and Performance Subscales **13**.243
Weibull distribution **5**.11
Weighting functions in hyperacuity **5**.224
Weightlessness, adaptation to **12**.411
Welding
  arc **16**.1, **16**.3, **16**.17, **16**.20, **16**.27, **16**.60, **16**.95
  gas **16**.1, **16**.17
  and light hazards **16**.93
Wells's experiments **9**.4–6
Wells's propositions **9**.4, **9**.7–9
Wernicke's sensory speech area **12**.287, **12**.356, **12**.358
Wheat-germ agglutinin-horseradish peroxidase **4**.271–2
Wheatstone's experiment **9**.15
Wheatstone's mirror stereoscope **1**.330
White matter **11**.34, **11**.43, **11**.235, **11**.263–4, **11**.269, **12**.127–35
  and alexia **12**.334
  brain lesions **12**.127–35
    acute **12**.129
  degrees of myelinization **12**.127

occipital paraventricular **12**.344
and prosopagnosia **12**.267, **12**.269
and pure alexia **12**.342
White noise **4**.250
in foveal sampling **3**.21
and functional organization of retina **3**.8
White noise method **10**.9
Wichterle, O., and the development of the first soft contact
lens **1**.83
Width acuity **10**.105–7
Wiener bodies **1**.319
Wiener kernels **10**.8
Wiener's sampling theorem **10**.88
Wien's displacement law **16**.7
Wigan, A. L. **12**.47
Wilbrand, Hermann **12**.65
Wilcoxon test, running **12**.242, **12**.245, **12**.252–5
Willis, Thomas **12**.40–1, **12**.136
Willmer, E. N. **2**.15–8, **2**.29–31, **2**.33–5, **2**.37–42, **2**.44–5,
2.48
Wilson's disease, accommodation anomalies in **1**.272
'Window function' **10**.16
Window operations **5**.44–7
Window of resolution **3**.18–9, **3**.22–3
Window of visibility **15**.20
see also Window of resolution
Windowing systems **15**.77–80, **15**.108
Wire world **14**.92–6
Wiring diagram **12**.357
for colour perception **12**.403
Wolff, Christian **12**.43–4
Wolffberg's test **7**.174
Woodcock Reading Mastery Tests **13**.253, **13**.256
Word(s) **12**.310
abstract **12**.322, **12**.325, **12**.329
emotional **12**.326
non-emotional **12**.326–7
abstract-concrete scale **12**.324
categories, hierarchical/identical/non-identical **12**.322
categorization **12**.352
correct **12**.353
forced-choice task **12**.351
semantic **12**.351, **12**.355
classes **12**.340–1
semantic **12**.341
colour interference **12**.354–5
concrete **12**.322, **12**.325–9, **12**.358
concreteness **12**.341
degrees of **12**.340
content, semantic **12**.313, **12**.325
cross-hatching **12**.341
cues, semantic **12**.355
degrees of complexity **12**.341
degrees of familiarity **12**.351
detection **12**.327
disambiguating **12**.328
discrimination **12**.322
emotional **12**.326–8, **12**.357–8
category **12**.354

connotation **12**.340
familiar **12**.351
negative (unpleasant) **12**.352–4
positive (pleasant) **12**.352–4
emotionality **12**.341
facilitation **12**.355
finding **12**.346–7
four-letter **12**.324–6
frequency **12**.313, **12**.317, **12**.324–5, **12**.328, **12**.341
in German and English **12**.314–5
function **12**.340–1
graphical classification **12**.357
graphical similarity **12**.349
guessing abilities/chances **12**.324–5
Hebrew **12**.325
high-frequency **12**.323–5, **12**.351
identification in multiple-choice set-up **12**.350
ideographic Kanji **12**.348
imageability **12**.341
interference **12**.355
Kana **12**.329–30
Kanji ideogram **12**.348
knowledge, semantic **12**.352, **12**.354
length **12**.313–5, **12**.318, **12**.322, **12**.325
and pure alexia **12**.338, **12**.340–1, **12**.351
lexical decisions **12**.324, **12**.330, **12**.341
'go-no-go' **12**.327
tachistoscopic paradigm **12**.351
low-frequency **12**.323, **12**.351
matching **12**.341
meaning **12**.334
access to, without awareness **12**.351
emotional **12**.354
and hemialexia **12**.350–1
and pure alexia **12**.336, **12**.338, **12**.342, **12**.357
metaphoric use of **12**.306
mirror images **12**.326
mismatching **12**.352
name identity **12**.322
naming, oral **12**.350
with narrow semantic distance **12**.330
neutral **12**.355
non-emotional **12**.327–8
nonsense **12**.321, **12**.324, **12**.327, **12**.340, **12**.351
pronounceability of **12**.322
non-words **12**.310, **12**.322, **12**.327, **12**.357
homophonic **12**.324
non-homophonic **12**.324
and shorthand **12**.330
noun-pairs **12**.329
poetic connotations **12**.329
semantic difference **12**.329
tachistoscopic presentation **12**.329
nouns
abstract **12**.326–7, **12**.352
emotional **12**.327, **12**.349
non-emotional **12**.327, **12**.349–50
categorization **12**.352–3
concrete **12**.352–3

Word(s) (*continued*)
    short 12.349
   four-letter 12.329
   high emotional content 12.352
  object matching 12.351–2
  overlearned 12.334
  overtrained 12.358
  pairs 12.330
   categorically related 12.327–8
   semantically related 12.327
   and shorthand 12.331
   syntactically related 12.328
   unrelated 12.327
   words and non-words 12.327, 12.331
  perception 12.345
  personal familiarity 12.341
  physical identity 12.322
  in pictorial form 12.350
  picture matching 12.349, 12.352
  position 12.328
  printed 12.316, 12.324, 12.331, 12.334
  pseudo- 12.319
  real 12.351
  recognition 12.314, 12.317, 12.320, 12.323–30
   fast 12.351
   of four-letter nouns 12.329
   lexical decisions 12.331
   of lists 12.325
   own name 12.350
   and pure alexia 12.337
   semantic priming effects 12.327
   shorthand 12.330
   speed of 12.334
   tachistoscopic tests 12.325–6
  semantic distance 12.329
   wide 12.330
  semantic processing of, unconscious 12.328
  semantically ambiguous (homograph) 12.328

  sequence orders 12.308
  and shorthand 12.330
  spatial organization of letter sequence 12.322
  spelling 12.340
  structure 12.317
  subliminal 12.324
   stimulus conditions 12.328
  tachistoscopic projection 12.320–30
   emotional factors 12.326
   food/water relevance 12.326
   thresholds 12.326
  tachistoscopic tests 12.330
  tokens as 12.331
  unrelated 12.328
  written 12.307
  Yiddish 12.325
Work design 15.64–5
Working memory load 15.92
World Health Organization (WHO) 16.5
Worm detectors 12.126
Worms 2.122, 2.237–8
Wortblindheit, reine, see Alexia, pure
Worth four-dot tests 9.195, 9.202
Wound, stab 12.349
W-retinal axons 3.154
W-2-retinal axons 3.157
'Write' 12.304
Writing 12.347
  cursive 12.356
  ideographic system 12.355–6
  neurobiological mechanisms 12.308
  and reading in apes 12.330–2
  shadow 12.340
  shorthand, Western 12.339
  system, ideographic 12.339
W-streams, Glossary explanation of 4.452
Wundt's colour sphere 6.222

X

X-, Y- and W-pathways **4.64–7**
X chromosome inactivation **7.92**
X and Y pathways **5.161, 5.259**
Xanthophyll **16.39**
  macular **16.93**
Xanthopsia **7.132**
Xanthropsin **2.349–50, 6.267**
X-cells **4.12–4, 4.29–36, 4.46, 4.61–2, 4.65–7, 4.89–90, 4.92, 4.163, 4.224–5, 4.229, 4.237, 4.240, 4.342–3, 10.8, 10.51, 10.246**
  Glossary explanation of **4.452**
  and variation of properties across W-and Y-cells **4.67–71**
X-chromosomes **2.313, 2.315–6**
  inactivation of **2.76**
X-class ganglion cells **3.152, 3.154, 3.241, 3.281–3**
Xenopus
  binocular projection **11.267–9**
  compartments **11.38–9**

homeoboxes **11.6, 11.9, 11.21–2**
  and proto-oncogenes **11.115, 11.119, 11.121**
  and synaptic rearrangements **11.264–5**
  in vertebrate neurogenesis **11.33, 11.37**
X-linked colour vision locus **7.91–5**
X-linked recessives
  achromatopsia **7.98**
  blue-cone monochromacy **7.101**
  red–green defects **7.90–2, 7.101**
X-linked retinitis pigmentosa **7.145, 7.147**
X-neurones **8.247–9, 8.251, 8.254, 8.265, 13.59, 13.185**
X-ray image **2.130**
X-ray methods
  for visualizing the eye **1.362–5**
    computed tomography **1.363–5**
    measurement of axial length **1.362–3**
X-ray phosphenes **1.362–3**
X-streams **4.228–30**
X-system axons **12.139–40**
XYZ colour-matching functions **6.14**

Y

Y-cells 4.12–4, 4.46, 4.65–7, 4.89–91, 4.163, 4.224–5, 4.229,
    4.237, 4.240, 4.342–3, **10**.8, **10**.51, **10**.246
  Glossary explanation of 4.452
  receptive fields of, sub-unit model of 4.17–9
  and variation of properties across W-and X-cells 67–71
Y-class ganglion cells 3.152, 3.157, 3.241, 3.281–3, 3.289
Yellow substance 2.8
Yellowing, lenticular 5.280, 5.282

Y-neurones **13**.59, **13**.185
Yoked versional acuity 9.183
Young, Thomas 1.231
  and the development of the contact lens 1.82
Young–Helmholtz theory 4.317, 4.332
Young–Helmholtz trichromatic colour theory **12**.386
Young–Helmholtz–Maxwell theory 6.12
Y-retinal axons 3.156–7
Y-streams 4.228–30
  Glossary explanation of 4.452

Z

Zaglossus (spiny ant-eater) 2.467–8, 2.470
Zero crossing 12.11, 12.13
Zero eye-movement reading 13.220–1, 13.224
Zero vertical meridian
    in amacrine cells 3.44
    in visual cortex 3.309
    in visual cortex organization 3.305
    in visual thalamus 3.176, 3.178, 3.182, 3.186, 3.199,
        3.209–10
Zero-crossings
    in hyperacuity 10.96–8, 10.110

and location 14.8–10
Zinc-finger motif 11.4, 11.7
Zinc-finger protein 11.40
Zinn, annulus of 8.176
Zipf's harmonic law 12.311, 12.313–4
Zollner illusion 5.242–4
Zona incerta 3.203–5
Zonule 11.393–4
Zoom effects 12.175
Zoom-FFT analysis 10.9
Z-test 12.303
Zuber effect 13.217, 13.225